Perspectives on the Economics of Aging

**A National Bureau
of Economic Research
Conference Report**

Perspectives on the Economics of Aging

Edited by   **David A. Wise**

The University of Chicago Press

Chicago and London

DAVID A. WISE is the John F. Stambaugh Professor of Political Economy at the John F. Kennedy School of Government, Harvard University, and director of the NBER Program on Aging. Among the many titles he has edited in this area are the recent *Themes in the Economics of Aging* and *Advances in the Economics of Aging.*

The University of Chicago Press, Chicago 60637
The University of Chicago Press, Ltd., London
© 2004 by the National Bureau of Economic Research
All rights reserved. Published 2004
Printed in the United States of America
13 12 11 10 09 08 07 06 05 04   1 2 3 4 5
ISBN: 0-226-90305-2 (cloth)
Chapter 11 is reprinted from *Journal of Econometrics,* vol. 112, Adams et al., "Healthy, Wealthy, and Wise? Tests for Direct Causal Paths between Health and Socioeconomic Status," pp. 3–56, 2003, with permission from Elsevier.

Library of Congress Cataloging-in-Publication Data

Perspectives on the economics of aging / edited by David A. Wise.
        p. cm.—(A National Bureau of Economic Research Conference report)
    Includes bibliographical references and index.
    ISBN 0-226-90305-2 (cloth : alk. paper)
    1. Aged—United States—Economic conditions. 2. Retirement—Economic aspects—United States. 3. Retirement income—United States. 4. 401(k) plans—United States. 5. Individual retirement accounts—United States. I. Wise, David A. II. Series

HQ1064.U5P467 2004
332.024′0084′60973—dc22

                                                                    2004041253

⊗ The paper used in this publication meets the minimum requirements of the American National Standard for Information Sciences—Permanence of Paper for Printed Library Materials, ANSI Z39.48-1992.

Relation of the Directors to the Work and Publications of the National Bureau of Economic Research

1. The object of the NBER is to ascertain and present to the economics profession, and to the public more generally, important economic facts and their interpretation in a scientific manner without policy recommendations. The Board of Directors is charged with the responsibility of ensuring that the work of the NBER is carried on in strict conformity with this object.

2. The President shall establish an internal review process to ensure that book manuscripts proposed for publication DO NOT contain policy recommendations. This shall apply both to the proceedings of conferences and to manuscripts by a single author or by one or more co-authors but shall not apply to authors of comments at NBER conferences who are not NBER affiliates.

3. No book manuscript reporting research shall be published by the NBER until the President has sent to each member of the Board a notice that a manuscript is recommended for publication and that in the President's opinion it is suitable for publication in accordance with the above principles of the NBER. Such notification will include a table of contents and an abstract or summary of the manuscript's content, a list of contributors if applicable, and a response form for use by Directors who desire a copy of the manuscript for review. Each manuscript shall contain a summary drawing attention to the nature and treatment of the problem studied and the main conclusions reached.

4. No volume shall be published until forty-five days have elapsed from the above notification of intention to publish it. During this period a copy shall be sent to any Director requesting it, and if any Director objects to publication on the grounds that the manuscript contains policy recommendations, the objection will be presented to the author(s) or editor(s). In case of dispute, all members of the Board shall be notified, and the President shall appoint an ad hoc committee of the Board to decide the matter; thirty days additional shall be granted for this purpose.

5. The President shall present annually to the Board a report describing the internal manuscript review process, any objections made by Directors before publication or by anyone after publication, any disputes about such matters, and how they were handled.

6. Publications of the NBER issued for informational purposes concerning the work of the Bureau, or issued to inform the public of the activities at the Bureau, including but not limited to the NBER Digest and Reporter, shall be consistent with the object stated in paragraph 1. They shall contain a specific disclaimer noting that they have not passed through the review procedures required in this resolution. The Executive Committee of the Board is charged with the review of all such publications from time to time.

7. NBER working papers and manuscripts distributed on the Bureau's web site are not deemed to be publications for the purpose of this resolution, but they shall be consistent with the object stated in paragraph 1. Working papers shall contain a specific disclaimer noting that they have not passed through the review procedures required in this resolution. The NBER's web site shall contain a similar disclaimer. The President shall establish an internal review process to ensure that the working papers and the web site do not contain policy recommendations, and shall report annually to the Board on this process and any concerns raised in connection with it.

8. Unless otherwise determined by the Board or exempted by the terms of paragraphs 6 and 7, a copy of this resolution shall be printed in each NBER publication as described in paragraph 2 above.

Contents

Preface ix

Introduction 1
David A. Wise

1. **The Transition to Personal Accounts and Increasing Retirement Wealth: Macro- and Microevidence** 17
James M. Poterba, Steven F. Venti, and David A. Wise
Comment: Sylvester J. Schieber

2. **For Better or for Worse: Default Effects and 401(k) Savings Behavior** 81
James J. Choi, David Laibson, Brigitte C. Madrian, and Andrew Metrick
Comment: James M. Poterba

3. **Aging and Housing Equity: Another Look** 127
Steven F. Venti and David A. Wise
Comment: Jonathan Skinner

4. **Intergenerational Transfers and Savings Behavior** 181
Jeffrey R. Brown and Scott J. Weisbenner
Comment: Alan J. Auerbach

5. **Wealth Portfolios in the United Kingdom and the United States** 205
James Banks, Richard Blundell, and James P. Smith
Comment: John B. Shoven

6.   **Mortality, Income, and Income Inequality over**
      Time in Britain and the United States   247
      Angus Deaton and Christina Paxson
      Comment: James Banks

7.   **Does Money Protect Health Status?**
      Evidence from South African Pensions   287
      Anne Case
      Comment: Robert T. Jensen

8.   **Socioeconomic Status, Nutrition, and Health**
      among the Elderly   313
      Robert T. Jensen
      Comment: David M. Cutler

9.   **Changes in the Age Distribution of Mortality**
      over the Twentieth Century   333
      David M. Cutler and Ellen Meara

10.   **Area Differences in Utilization of Medical Care**
      and Mortality among U.S. Elderly   367
      Victor R. Fuchs, Mark McClellan, and
      Jonathan Skinner
      Comment: Joseph P. Newhouse

11.   **Healthy, Wealthy, and Wise? Tests for**
      Direct Causal Paths between Health and
      Socioeconomic Status   415
      Peter Adams, Michael D. Hurd,
      Daniel McFadden, Angela Merrill, and
      Tiago Ribeiro
      Comment: James M. Poterba

      Contributors   527
      Author Index   531
      Subject Index   535

Preface

This volume consists of papers presented at a conference held at Carefree, Arizona in May 2001. Most of the research was conducted as part of the Program on the Economics of Aging at the National Bureau of Economic Research. The majority of the work was sponsored by the U.S. Department of Health and Human Services, through National Institute on Aging grants P01-AG05842 and P30-AG12810 to the National Bureau of Economic Research. Any other funding sources are noted in individual papers.

Any opinions expressed in this volume are those of the respective authors and do not necessarily reflect the views of the National Bureau of Economic Research or the sponsoring organizations.

Introduction

David A. Wise

This is the ninth in a series of volumes on the economics of aging. The previous ones were *The Economics of Aging, Issues in the Economics of Aging, Topics in the Economics of Aging, Studies in the Economics of Aging, Advances in the Economics of Aging, Inquiries in the Economics of Aging, Frontiers in the Economics of Aging,* and *Themes in the Economics of Aging.*

Most of the papers in this volume pursue areas of research begun in earlier volumes. For example, the work in this volume emphasizes the spread of personal retirement accounts and macrodata on the implications of the diffusion of these accounts. Prior work emphasized the net saving effects of personal retirement accounts based on microdata. Work in this volume also revisits the implications of housing wealth for the financing of general consumption as households age. The current work confirms previous findings that households typically do not withdraw equity from housing to finance general consumption, but such withdrawal is more likely when a spouse dies or enters a nursing home. In addition to discussion of the personal retirement plans and home equity, the first five papers in this volume consider other aspects of wealth accumulation and compare asset accumulation in the United States and the United Kingdom.

Trying to understand the explanation for the very strong relationship between health and wealth is one of the most challenging research issues in the economics of aging. Perhaps the most vexing issue that arises in this analysis is the direction of causality. Is it from health to wealth or from wealth to health, or perhaps both? There have been several papers on this

David A. Wise is the John F. Stambaugh Professor of Political Economy at the John F. Kennedy School of Government, Harvard University, and the director for Health and Retirement Programs at the National Bureau of Economic Research.

issue in past volumes. The next six papers in this volume continue analysis of several aspects of the relationship between health and wealth, with the general aim of advancing our understanding of the reasons for the relationship. The analyses include consideration of the decline in mortality in the United States and the United Kingdom and the relationship between medical care and mortality. The relationship between pension income and health in South Africa also contributes to our understanding of the health–wealth relationship. This volume also includes more formal discussion of econometric methodology to determine the direction of causality. This introduction provides a summary of the papers and draws heavily on the authors' own language.

Personal Retirement Plans

Implications of the Transition to Personal Accounts

Retirement saving in the United States has changed dramatically over the last two decades. There has been a shift from employer-managed defined benefit pensions to defined contribution retirement saving plans that are largely controlled by employees. In 1980, 92 percent of private retirement saving contributions were to employer-based plans, and 64 percent of these contributions were to defined benefit plans. Today, about 85 percent of private contributions are to plans in which individuals decide how much to contribute to the plan, how to invest plan assets, and how and when to withdraw money from the plan. In "The Transition to Personal Accounts and Increasing Retirement Wealth: Macro- and Microevidence," James M. Poterba, Steven F. Venti, and I use both macro- and microdata to describe the change in retirement assets and in retirement saving. We give particular attention to the possible substitution of pension assets in one plan for assets in another plan, such as the substitution of 401(k) assets for defined benefit plan assets.

Aggregate data show that between 1975 and 1999 assets to support retirement increased about fivefold relative to wage and salary income. This increase suggests large increases in the wealth of future retirees. The enormous increase in defined contribution plan assets dwarfed any potential displacement of defined benefit plan assets. In addition, in recent years the annual *retirement plan contribution rate,* defined as retirement plan contributions as a percentage of National Income and Product Accounts (NIPA) personal income, has been over 5 percent. This is much higher than the NIPA total personal saving rate, which has been close to zero.

Retirement saving as a share of personal income today would likely be at least one percentage point greater had it not been for legislation in the 1980s that limited employer contributions to defined benefit pension plans and the reduction in defined benefit plan contributions associated with the rising stock market of the 1990s. It is also likely that the retirement plan contribution rate would be much higher today if it were not for the 1986 retrenchment of the Individual Retirement Account (IRA) program.

Rising retirement plan contributions, as well as favorable rates of return on retirement plan assets in the 1990s, explain the large increase in these assets relative to income. Employee retirement saving under a defined contribution plan is easily measured and quite transparent to the employee. On the other hand, annual employee saving under a defined benefit plan is more difficult to measure. It is also less likely to be clearly understood by employees. The average annual saving rate under a typical 401(k) plan is roughly twice as high as the average saving rate under a typical defined benefit plan, when properly measured. In addition, the early retirement incentives inherent in the provisions of most defined benefit plans will tend to reduce the aggregate accumulation of defined benefit retirement assets relative to defined contribution assets because defined contribution participants are likely to work longer and contribute for more years.

The microdata show no evidence that the accumulation of 401(k) assets has been offset by a reduction in defined benefit assets. Because annual saving is much greater under 401(k) than under defined benefit plans, assets at retirement after lifetime employment under a 401(k) plan typically would be much higher than under a defined benefit plan. In addition, a large fraction of new 401(k) enrollees retained defined benefit coverage, which probably further increased their retirement saving.

The Importance of Plan Features

In the last several years, dozens of employers have automatically enrolled new employees in the company 401(k) plan. Employees can opt out of the 401(k), but few choose to do so. In "For Better or for Worse: Default Effects and 401(k) Savings Behavior," James J. Choi, David Laibson, Brigitte C. Madrian and Andrew Metrick analyze three years of 401(k) data from two firms that have experimented with automatic enrollment. They find that automatic enrollment has a dramatic impact on retirement savings behavior.

Under automatic enrollment (also called *negative election*), employees are automatically enrolled in their company's 401(k) plan unless the employee elects to opt out of plan participation. This contrasts with the usual arrangement in which employees actively elect to participate in their employer's 401(k) plan.

The institution of automatic enrollment manipulates the way the savings decision is framed. In theory, the existence of automatic enrollment should not influence the employee's decision; automatic enrollment doesn't change the economic fundamentals of the planning problem. But automatic enrollment nonetheless increases participation in 401(k) plans. Opting out requires workers to actively make a decision and then act on that decision. It is easier to follow the path of least resistance and passively accept the default.

Choi, Laibson, Madrian, and Metrick find that automatic enrollment has a dramatic impact on participation rates. Under automatic enrollment, 401(k) participation rates exceed 85 percent regardless of the tenure of the employee. In the absence of automatic enrollment, employees exhibit participation rates of only 25 percent after six months of tenure and 60 percent after three years at the firm.

They also find that automatic enrollment has a dramatic impact on savings rates and asset allocation choices. Under automatic enrollment, approximately 80 percent of plan participants save at the default saving rate and invest exclusively in the default fund. This percentage declines slowly over time, falling to 50 percent after two or three years of tenure.

Automatic enrollment encourages participation, but it anchors participants at a low savings rate and in a conservative investment vehicle. Higher participation raises average wealth accumulation, but low savings rates and conservative investments undercut accumulation. In the sample, the two effects are roughly offsetting. Controlling for income and tenure, they compare total 401(k) balances for employees who joined the firm before automatic enrollment and employees who joined the firm after automatic enrollment. They find that automatic enrollment has a positive impact on long-run wealth accumulation in one of the firms and no impact on long-run wealth accumulation in the other firm.

Although automatic enrollment does not have a dramatic impact on the mean level of balances, it does have a large impact on the distribution of balances. The high participation rate associated with automatic enrollment drastically reduces the fraction of employees with zero balances, thereby thinning out the bottom tail of the distribution of employee balances. In addition, anchoring on low savings rates and conservative investments sometimes shrinks the upper tail of the distribution of balances. Hence, automatic enrollment reduces the variance of wealth accumulation across all employees.

The Financial Implications of Housing Equity as People Age

Home equity is the principle asset of a large fraction of elderly Americans and can have important implications for the well-being of elderly households. In "Aging and Housing Equity: Another Look," Steven F. Venti and I have used Health and Retirement Study (HRS) and Asset and Health Dynamics Among the Oldest Old (AHEAD) panel data, as well as Survey of Income and Program Participation (SIPP) data, to understand the change in the home equity of households as they age. We give particular attention to the relationship between changes in home equity and changes in household structure.

There are two ways for households to change home equity: by discontinuing home ownership or by selling and moving to another home. We find that, overall, households are unlikely to discontinue home ownership. Ownership terminations are most likely to occur following the death of a spouse or the entry of a family member into a nursing home. But, even in these circumstances, selling the home is the exception and not the rule. In the absence of a precipitating shock, it is much more likely that a family will sell and buy a new home than discontinue ownership. And households that sell and buy again tend to increase rather than reduce home equity. That is, assets are transferred to housing.

Overall—combining the effects of discontinuing ownership and moving to another home—we find that housing equity of HRS households increases with age, and the equity of AHEAD households declines somewhat. The overall decline in the housing equity of the older AHEAD households is about 1.76 percent per year, which is accounted for primarily by a 7.84 percent decline among households experiencing precipitating shocks to family status. Families that remain intact reduce housing equity very little, only 0.11 percent per year for two-person households and 1.15 percent per year for one-person households.

We use two approaches to determine whether households wish to reduce home equity as they age. One approach is to compare the change in the home equity of movers with the change for stayers. If households withdraw equity when they sell and move to a new home, the reduction in the equity of the movers typically will be greater than the change for stayers. These comparisons, however, are confounded by the tendency of the self-assessed home values to exceed actual values, as measured by selling prices. A comparison of the selling prices of homes with the prior self-assessment of home values shows that home values reported prior to a sale far exceed realized sales prices. Comparing the change in the home equity of movers and stayers, but accounting for this bias, we conclude that families who sell and buy a new home increase home equity on average.

The second approach is based on the comparison of the selling price of the old home (minus the mortgage on the home) with the reported equity value in the newly purchased home. We believe that these are the most reliable data on the change in home equity when families move from one home to another. Based on these sale price data, we find that *on average* households increase home equity when they move to a new house. We also find, however, that equity-rich and income-poor families tend to reduce home values when they sell and buy a new house, whereas equity-poor and income-rich families tend to increase home equity. For continuing two-person HRS households, for example, we estimate that the between-wave reduction for those at the 80th equity quantile and at the 20th income quantile is –\$15,422. On the other hand, we estimate that households at the 20th equity quantile and the 80th income quantile increase equity by +\$54,778.

These results suggest that in considering whether families have saved enough to maintain their preretirement standard of living after retirement, housing equity should not, in general, be counted on to support nonhousing consumption. Families apparently do not intend to finance general retirement consumption by saving through investment in housing, as they might through a 401(k) plan or through some other financial form of saving. Rather, we believe the findings here, as well as our earlier findings, suggest that families purchase homes to provide an environment in which to live, even as they age through retirement years. In this case, the typical aging household is unlikely to seek a reverse annuity mortgage to withdraw assets from home equity. It may be appropriate, however, to think of housing as a reserve or buffer that can be used in catastrophic circumstances that result in a change in household structure. In this case, having used the home equity along the way—through a reverse mortgage, for example— would defeat the purpose of saving home equity for a rainy day.

Although these results are based largely on new HRS and AHEAD data files and are based on different methods of analysis, the findings correspond closely to the conclusions we reached in our earlier papers, based on different data sources. These conclusions also correspond closely to the findings of a recent survey of older households sponsored by the American Association of Retired Persons (AARP), showing that the preponderance of older families agree with the statement: What I'd really like to do is stay in my current residence as long as possible. Like our findings, the results of the AARP survey also imply that most households do not intend to liquidate housing equity to support general nonhousing retirement consumption as they age.

How Is Wealth Accumulated?

Economists generally agree that there are two possible sources of household wealth: households can engage in life-cycle saving by not consuming all of their income, or they can receive bequests or inter vivos transfers from individuals outside of their household. For at least two decades, however, there has been an ongoing debate about the relative magnitude of these two sources of wealth.

In "Intergenerational Transfers and Savings Behavior," Jeffrey R. Brown and Scott J. Weisbenner present further evidence of the importance of these two routes to wealth accumulation.

The source of household wealth is important for many reasons. The behavioral effects of many government programs, such as Social Security, the taxation of savings, and targeted savings programs, likely depend upon the source of wealth. Debates about the fairness of the wealth distribution in the United States, and the extent to which there is intergenerational mobility across this distribution, depend on whether wealth is primarily earned or inherited.

Brown and Weisbenner reach three conclusions. First, using the 1998 Survey of Consumer Finances, they provide evidence suggesting that transfer wealth accounts for approximately 20–25 percent of current household net worth, suggesting a large role for life-cycle savings.

Second, the authors examine the variation in the size of transfers received and expected. They find that while in aggregate, transfer wealth does not appear to be as large as some prior estimates suggest; it is important for a small subset of the population. They find that approximately one-fifth of households report receiving a transfer, and one-eighth expect a substantial transfer in the future. For those households that have received transfers, transfer wealth accounts for, on average, half of current net worth. For lower-wealth households (those with less than $75,000), transfer wealth on average exceeds current wealth.

Third, Brown and Weisbenner examine whether past transfers and expected future transfers cause people to save less from their labor income to reduce life-cycle saving. They find evidence that the receipt of transfers reduces life-cycle saving, with point estimates suggesting slightly less than dollar-for-dollar crowd-out. But expected future transfers do not reduce life-cycle saving, perhaps suggesting that a bird in hand is indeed worth more than a bird in the bush.

Wealth at Retirement in the United States and the United Kingdom

The accumulation of personal wealth differs substantially across countries. So does the distribution of wealth among assets. In "Wealth Portfolios in the United Kingdom and the United States," James Banks, Richard Blundell, and James P. Smith discuss a "housing equity puzzle": why do younger households in the U.K. accumulate so much of their wealth in housing equity compared to their U.S. counterparts?

In trying to address this puzzle the authors have built up a detailed picture of housing choices and wealth accumulation in both countries. Using microdata sources, they document how the difference in housing equity has evolved for different age groups, for different demographic groups, and for different education groups in both countries. They show that young adults in the United Kingdom leave their parental home later than in the United States, and when they do leave they are much more likely to accumulate wealth in housing equity rather than in other investment instruments.

Why? Is it just the differential tax treatment of mortgages or the different institutional structures of the housing and stock markets in the two countries? The authors argue that these differences explain some of the difference in housing equity, but the higher volatility of house prices in the United Kingdom is the key reason. They derive a modeling framework that explains the higher price volatility in the United Kingdom and use the model to explain the differences in housing equity and stock holdings across the countries.

The inefficient rental market, the authors say, places many more U.K. households in the owner-occupier sector at an earlier age than in the United States. The higher volatility of house prices in the United Kingdom adds to this incentive because, for those expecting to move up the house-size ladder, housing equity is an efficient insurance vehicle for house-price uncertainty. The only way to invest in housing equity is to become an owner. Once an owner, this insurance mechanism increases the incentive to hold a higher proportion of wealth in housing equity rather than in some other asset. Where house prices are less volatile, as in the United States, this incentive is much reduced. Consequently, as households age and wish to accumulate wealth, they will do this more through housing equity in the United Kingdom than in the United States.

Health and Wealth

A striking empirical regularity is the strong, positive relationship between wealth and health. Several papers discuss different aspects of this relationship and use different methods to understand the relationship. The last chapter in the volume presents formal methods to test for causal links between socioeconomic status and health.

Mortality, Income, and Income Inequality

In both the United States and Britain, for both men and women and for most age groups, there has been a very substantial decline in mortality rates since 1950. In "Mortality, Income, and Income Inequality over Time in Britain and the United States," Angus Deaton and Christina Paxson use cohort data from the two countries to understand the relationship between income and the decline in mortality.

The comparison between the two countries is interesting in part because of the different systems of health care—one country with universal coverage and the other with private provision until Medicare coverage at age sixty-five. Comparative analysis is also useful because there are both similarities and differences in patterns of income in the two countries. Although changes in income inequality are similar in Britain and the United States, patterns of income growth are not. According to purchasing power parity estimates, incomes are higher in the United States than in Britain, but, in recent years, real incomes have been growing more rapidly in Britain. Both countries experienced historically large increases in income inequality in the 1980s.

In both Britain and the United States, for men and for women and for most age groups, there has been a very substantial decline in mortality rates since 1950. The authors' examination of these rates, by sex and age group and in relation to the evolution of incomes and income inequality, does not suggest any simple relationship between income growth and the decline in mortality, or between income inequality and mortality rates. In the United States, the period of slowest income growth saw substantial accelerations in the rate of mortality decline, particularly among middle-aged and older men and women. In both the United States and Britain, the increase in income inequality took place at the same time as a deceleration in mortality decline at the younger ages, including infant mortality. But there are previously slow rates of decline when nothing was happening to income inequality, and the later rise in income inequality was associated with the acceleration in mortality decline among middle-aged and older adults in both countries. Deaton and Paxson conclude that a more plausible account of the data is that, over time, declines in mortality are driven by technological advances or by the emergence of new infectious diseases, such as AIDS. These advances and retreats are associated with specific conditions and specific treatments, and so affect men and women differently and different age groups differently. They also happen first in the United States, with the British experience following with a lag of several years. The authors say that this hypothesis needs a great deal more investigation, for example, by looking at more countries.

Deaton and Paxson then compare these results with their prior analysis, suggesting that if changes in mortality over time are driven by technology and not by income, there must be some doubt as to whether their previous analysis came to the correct conclusions about the role of cohort incomes in the decline of cohort mortality. Their prior results cannot be replicated on the British data. They suspect—but have not been able to demonstrate decisively—that the cohort analysis is flawed by the necessity to make the almost certainly invalid assumption that age effects in mortality are constant through time. This is contradicted, for example, by the spread of AIDS, which has almost certainly raised the early life relative to later life mortality rates among recently born men and women compared with their seniors. If this is a serious problem, the cohort method may not be useful in this context, or it will at least require substantial modifications in order to give sound results.

The authors conclude that this comparative international work is a productive direction for future research. Even so, they say, there remains a major puzzle about the role of income. Income growth seems to play little role in decline of mortality at the national level. At the cohort level the same is possibly true as they argue in this paper. Yet in the individual-level data from the National Longitudinal Mortality Study, as from many other data sets, income is protective against mortality, even when education and other socioeconomic variables are controlled. Why there should be such a contrast between the individual and national effects of income is a topic that requires a good deal of further thought and analysis, the authors conclude.

Money and Health in South Africa

In "Does Money Protect Health Status? Evidence from South African Pensions," Anne Case approaches the relationship between health and wealth by considering the effect on health status of an exogenous increase in income.

Case quantifies the impact on health status of the large increase in income associated with the South African state old age pension. Elderly black and colored men and women who did not anticipate receiving large pensions in their lifetimes, and who did pay into a pension system, are currently receiving more than twice median black income per capita. These elderly men and women generally live in large (three, four, or five generation) households, and this paper documents the effect of the pension on the pensioners, on other adult members of their households, and on the children who live with them. She finds, in households that pool income, that the pension protects the health of all household members, working in part to protect the nutritional status of household members, in part of improve living conditions, and in part to reduce the stress under which the adult household members negotiate day-to-day life. The health effects of delivering cash provide a benchmark against which other health-related interventions can be evaluated, Case concludes.

Socioeconomic Status, Nutrition, and Health

Robert Jensen explores the relationship between "Socioeconomic Status, Nutrition, and Health among the Elderly."

In his paper, Jensen uses data from a nationally representative household-level survey to explore the relationship between health and socioeconomic status (SES) for the elderly in Russia.

Jensen has two main objectives: first, to explore the basic relationship, which is valuable because there has been little evidence on the health-SES relationship for transition economies; and second, to present evidence from a variety of measures of health status, including measurements of blood pressure, weight and height conducted by trained enumerators, as well as nutrient intake, derived from twenty-four- and forty-eight-hour food intake diaries. Jensen uses these data to show that the relationship between health and SES in Russia can't be adequately described by simple statements, such as the poor are less healthy than the rich; although on net the rich are healthier than the poor in some overall sense, there are important ways in which the rich face greater health risks.

In the study of the relationship between health and income, the biggest challenge, Jensen says, is to decompose the health differentials into the root causes. There are numerous channels through which the two could be linked.

Jensen narrows the focus to one particular mechanism—nutrition—through which SES may affect health. The role of nutrition as a factor in the differential health status between rich and poor is often overlooked when examining middle- and upper-income countries, because widespread hunger and starvation, even among the poorest, have largely been eliminated and, in fact, widespread obesity is considered a greater public health concern. However, nutrition must be viewed as more complex than hunger or simply sufficient caloric intake. In particular, there are important micronutrients beyond calories that are important for good health, especially for the elderly. And the intake of these nutrients may be sensitive to income, as the lowest cost staple foods in most countries (for example, bread or rice) may yield sufficient 'bulk' or calories, but (unless fortified) may have low levels of vitamins, minerals, and protein. On the other hand, these foods tend to be low in fat, cholesterol, and sodium, compared with foods that may be more expensive and eaten in larger quantities by the rich, for example, meat. Therefore, Jensen concludes, it is quite possible that nutrition plays a role in the relationship between health and SES, even in countries where calorie malnutrition is scarce and obesity is widespread.

Jensen uses data on food intake to provide a detailed analysis of nutrient intake for the elderly, how it varies with income, the consequences of nutritional intake for health, and the relationship between health and SES. He does this by exploring differences in the diets of the rich and poor, how differences in diet translate into differences in nutrient intake, and the impact of nutrient intake on health.

Mortality

Mortality and Changes over the Twentieth Century

Mortality rates declined extremely rapidly in the United States over the twentieth century, as they did in all developed countries. In 1900, 1 in 42 Americans died annually. On an age-adjusted basis, the share in 1998 was 1 in 125 people, for a cumulative decline of 67 percent. Given such a substantial improvement in mortality, it is natural to ask how we achieved such gains in health and which innovations or policies contributed most to these gains. David M. Cutler and Ellen Meara do this in "Changes in the Age Distribution of Mortality over the Twentieth Century."

Cutler and Meara start by considering major trends in mortality over the century, noting how mortality declines differ by age and cause of death. By providing detailed information on which demographic groups experienced the largest mortality improvements and for what causes of death, these analyses motivate hypotheses to explain the overall improvement in mortality in the twentieth century.

The mortality decline is approximately linear over the time period. Mortality decreased at a relatively constant rate of 1 percent per year between 1900 and 1940. There was then a period of rapid decline from 1940 to 1955 in which mortality declined 2 percent per year, followed by essentially flat mortality rates until 1965. Since 1965, mortality rates have fallen at roughly 1 to 1.5 percent per year. This relative constancy of mortality decline suggests that perhaps a single factor can explain the trend in longer life.

But the aggregate trends mask as much as they reveal. While mortality declines have been relatively continuous over the twentieth century, the age distribution of mortality decline has not. Cutler and Meara start by highlighting a basic fact about mortality declines in the past century: mortality reduction used to be concentrated at younger ages but is increasingly concentrated among the aged. In the first four decades of the century, 80 percent of life expectancy improvements resulted from reduced mortality for those below age forty-five, with the bulk of this for infants and children. In the next two decades, life expectancy improvements were split relatively evenly by age. In the latter four decades, about two-thirds of life expectancy improvements resulted from mortality reductions for those over age forty-five; only one-third was from the younger population.

This change has been accompanied by several important epidemiological trends. Throughout the first half of the twentieth century, infectious diseases were the leading cause of death. Changes in the ability to avoid and withstand infection were the prime factors in reduced mortality in the first part of the century. This disease-fighting ability was not predominantly medical. Nutrition and public health measures were vastly more important in reduced mortality over this time period than were medical interventions, as substantial research documents. Nutrition and public health were particularly important for the young, and so mortality reduction was concentrated at younger ages.

Between 1940 and 1960, infectious diseases continued to decline, but was due more to medical factors. Antibiotics, including penicillin and sulfa drugs, became important contributors to mortality reduction in this era. Antibiotics help the elderly as well as the young, and so mortality reductions became more widespread across the age distribution.

Since 1960, mortality reductions have been associated with two new factors: the conquest of cardiovascular disease in the elderly and the prevention of death due to low birth weight infants. While it is not entirely clear what factors account for the reduction in cardiovascular disease mortality, the traditional roles of nutrition, public health, and antibiotics are certainly less important, the authors conclude. Taking their place are factors related to individual behaviors, such as smoking, diet, and high-tech medical treatment. Cutler and Meara term this change the *medicalization* of death: Increasingly, mortality reductions are attributed to medical care and not social or environmental improvements.

The medicalization of death does not imply that medicine is the only factor influencing mortality. For several important causes of death, income improvements and social programs have had and continue to have a large impact on mortality. For example, Medicare likely has a direct impact on mortality by increasing elderly access to medical care, but it also may have important income effects since it reduced out of pocket spending by the elderly for medical care. Social security and civil rights programs may also be important in better health. The authors do not quantify the role of medicine, income, social programs, and other factors in improved mortality in the last half-century, but they do show examples where each is important as a first step in their ongoing research.

Mortality and Age Differences in Medical Care

Perhaps the two most important, most enduring questions in health economics are "What are the determinants of expenditures?" and "What are the determinants of health?" Extensive research over the last thirty-five years has produced a variety of answers to these questions, depending in large part on the specific context within which the questions are posed. One crucial distinction is between explaining changes over time and explaining cross-sectional differences at a given time. With regard to secular changes in the United States in recent decades, most health economists now believe that advances in medical technology provide the major explanation for both increases in expenditures and improvements in health. With regard to cross-sectional differences, there is less agreement. Victor R. Fuchs, Mark McClellan, and Jonathan Skinner consider cross-sectional differences in "Area Differences in Utilization of Medical Care and Mortality among U.S. Elderly." By exploiting a rich body of data from the Centers for Medicare and Medicaid Services [formerly the Health Care Financing Administration (HCFA)], the U.S. Census of Population, and other sources, the authors hope to narrow that disagreement, at least with respect to area differences in utilization of care and mortality of the elderly.

Their focus on the elderly is motivated in part by the fact that the elderly account for a disproportionate share of national health care expenditures and an even greater share of government health care expenditures. Moreover, the elderly experience the bulk of the major health problems of the population. Approximately one-half of all deaths occur between ages sixty-five to eighty-four, and another one-fourth occur at ages eighty-five and above. These shares are based on the current age distribution of the U.S. population. For a stationary population experiencing current age-specific mortality rates, deaths at ages sixty-five to eighty-four would still account for almost one-half the total; the share at age eighty-five and above would rise to one-third. The focus on the elderly is facilitated by the fact that the Medicare program generates a large, detailed body of data on utilization and mortality.

One reason for focusing on area differences is that the large number of metropolitan and nonmetropolitan areas in the United States provides a convenient framework for aggregating individual data in the search for variables that may be related to utilization and mortality. Moreover, many health policy analysts believe that an understanding of area differences may suggest opportunities to limit expenditures and/or improve health.

The paper has two main sections: utilization and mortality. In most markets an interest in expenditures would require attention to prices as well as quantities, but given universal insurance coverage through Medicare and administrative price setting by HCFA, utilization is a natural subject for study. Mortality is only one of many possible measures of health, but there are several reasons to concentrate on it. First, mortality is by far the most objective measure. Secondly, it is, for most people, the most important health outcome. Thirdly, it is probably significantly correlated with morbidity since most deaths are preceded by illness.

In this paper, Fuchs, McClellan, and Skinner focus on whites ages sixty-five to eighty-four, or more specifically, those not identified as African American. They exclude blacks because at those ages both utilization and mortality of blacks are higher than for whites, and the percentage of blacks in an area is correlated with other variables of interest. Moreover, other research suggests that the relationship between those other variables and utilization and mortality may be significantly different for blacks than for whites. They exclude anyone aged eighty-five and over because it is more difficult to obtain accurate measures for self-reported variables, such as education and income. About one-half of the population aged eighty-five and over suffer from some form of dementia and about one-fifth are in nursing homes where measurement of income is particularly problematic. Moreover, most nursing home utilization is not covered by Medicare, the source of the data on utilization.

The authors find wide variation in the utilization of health services across regions. It is not simply that some regions are higher along all dimensions of care, but that in some regions there is much more diagnostic testing, even while per capita inpatient services are comparable to the national average. In general, utilization is strongly positively associated with mortality across areas—in other words, areas with more sick elderly use more health care, other things being equal. There remains, however, substantial variation in utilization after controlling for factors such as education, income, and mortality.

Cross-area variations in mortality rates among this elderly group are not as large as variations in utilization, but they are still substantial. The 10 percent of metropolitan statistical areas (MSAs) with the highest mortality (age-sex adjusted) have an average death rate 38 percent greater than the 10 percent of MSAs with the lowest mortality. The comparable differential between the high and low utilization areas is 49 percent.

Education, real income, cigarettes, obesity, air pollution, and the percentage of blacks account for more than half of the variation in mortality across areas, but there are still substantial differences across regions unexplained by these variables. Florida, in particular, has death rates significantly below the national average; the differential is particularly large for areas in the southern portion of the state. The final section of the paper explores two puzzles—why Florida is so different from the rest of the country with respect to utilization and mortality, and why the presence of more blacks in an area should be associated with higher mortality among elderly whites. The authors consider several possible solutions to these puzzles, including differential migration patterns of the elderly, but ultimately they arrive at conjectures rather than robust explanations.

Health and Wealth—Econometric Analysis of Causal Links

In their paper "Healthy, Wealthy, and Wise? Tests for Direct Causal Paths between Health and Socioeconomic Status." Peter Adams, Michael D. Hurd, Daniel McFadden, Angela Merrill, and Tiago Ribeiro test for the absence of causal links from socioeconomic status to health and mortality, and from health to wealth.

This paper is in large part a technical discussion of how econometrics test for causal links. The authors use innovations in health conditions and in wealth in the AHEAD panel to carry out tests for causality from SES to health, and from health conditions to wealth. By advancing beyond the detection of association to a framework in which there is some possibility of detecting the absence of causal links, this paper is an advance on much of the literature on this subject.

The authors conclude that for mortality and for accidents, the hypothesis of *no* causal link from SES is accepted, and for incidence of mental problems the hypothesis is rejected. The results for chronic and degenerative diseases are not definitive, but using the preferred test procedure, the hypothesis is marginally rejected in both cases. The hypothesis appears to be accepted for acute conditions, but the necessary invariance property fails, so the possibility that this is an artifact is not ruled out. The pattern of results suggests that incidence of acute, sudden onset health conditions does not exhibit a significant SES gradient, whereas incidence of chronic, mental, and degenerative conditions appears to have an association to SES due to some combination of direct causal links and common unobserved behavioral or genetic factors. Specifically, there may be an SES gradient in seeking treatment for the second class of conditions that may influence detection, or for maintaining preventative regimens that may maintain some conditions below the reporting thresholds. Adams, Hurd, McFadden, Merrill and Ribeiro's findings are not inconsistent with the possibility that for mental and chronic illnesses where the acute care procedures covered by Medicare are often inapplicable, ability to pay may be a causal factor in seeking and receiving treatment.

The technique put forth in this chapter has been applied to the Whitehall data in the United Kingdom with results very similar to the results found using U.S. AHEAD data. This chapter includes not only the technical paper but comments from many experts in econometric analysis as well. The authors are pursuing their line of investigation based on alternative models and using subsequent waves of AHEAD.

1

The Transition to Personal Accounts and Increasing Retirement Wealth
Macro- and Microevidence

James M. Poterba, Steven F. Venti, and David A. Wise

The transition from employer managed defined benefit pensions to retirement saving plans that are largely managed and controlled by employees has been the most striking change in retirement saving over the last two decades. Individual managed and controlled retirement accounts, particularly 401(k) plans but also 403(b) plans for nonprofit organizations, 457 plans for state and local employees, the Thrift Savings Plan for federal employees, Keogh plans for self-employed workers, and Individual Retirement Accounts (IRAs), have grown enormously. Employer-provided defined benefit (DB) pension plans have declined in importance. In 1980, 92 percent of private retirement saving contributions were to employer-based plans; 64 percent of these contributions were to DB plans. In 1999, about 85 percent of private contributions were to accounts in which individuals

James M. Poterba is the Mitsui Professor of Economics and associate head of the economics department at the Massachusetts Institute of Technology, and the director of the Public Economics Research Program at the National Bureau of Economic Research. Steven F. Venti is the DeWalt Ankeny Professor of Economic Policy at Dartmouth College and a research associate at the National Bureau of Economic Research. David A. Wise is the John F. Stambaugh Professor of Political Economy at the John F. Kennedy School of Government, Harvard University, and the director for Health and Retirement Programs at the National Bureau of Economic Research.

This paper was written while Poterba was a visiting fellow at the Hoover Institution. We are grateful to the National Institute on Aging, the Hoover Institution, and the National Science Foundation for financial support, and to Gary Engelhardt, Bill Gale, Al Gustman, Syl Scheiber, Jon Skinner, Tom Steinmeier and participants in the Berkeley Department Seminar, the Stanford Public Economics workshop, and two NBER meetings for helpful comments. We also thank Dan Beller at the Pension and Welfare Benefits Administration of the United States Department of Labor for generous help in understanding the Form 5500 data.

controlled how much to contribute to the plan, how to invest plan assets, and how and when to withdraw money from the plans.

We consider the changes in the magnitude and the composition of saving for retirement over the last two decades. We begin with an analysis of aggregate data on retirement plan contributions. We then turn to microdata, describe patterns in these data, and try to reconcile these patterns with the aggregate data. We document the changes in aggregate retirement saving over the past twenty-five years and describe how these changes are related to the shift from employer-sponsored defined benefit plans to individual-controlled retirement saving. We then investigate whether the shift toward individual retirement saving, and the accumulation of retirement assets in these accounts, has been offset by a reduction in the assets in other retirement saving plans.

In a series of earlier papers, summarized in Poterba, Venti, and Wise (hereafter PVW, 1996, 1998b), we found large net saving effects of IRAs and 401(k)s. We emphasized the potential offsets between saving in self-directed retirement accounts, other forms of financial asset saving, and the accumulation of home equity. On balance we found little, if any, offset in these cases. More recently, Benjamin (2003) and Pence (2001) have also found little or no offset between 401(k) contributions and non-401(k) financial asset saving, although the latter study also found little evidence that 401(k)s increased total wealth. Recent work by Engen and Gale (2000) finds little offset among low earners, but more substantial offsets among high earners.

Much less attention has been directed to the possible offset of personal retirement assets by a reduction in the assets in DB pension plans. Engen, Gale, and Scholz (1994) found a negative relationship between participation in DB pension plans and 401(k) plan assets in the 1987 and 1991 Surveys of Income and Program Participation (SIPP). Papke (1999) concluded that between 1985 and 1992 about one-fifth of ongoing sponsors of DB plans terminated their plans and adopted or retained a conventional defined contribution (DC) or a 401(k) plan. It is not clear from her analysis, however, whether the growth in 401(k) plans displaced DB plans. Papke, Petersen, and Poterba (1996) surveyed firms with 401(k)s and found that very few had terminated a preexisting DB plan when they instituted their 401(k) plan. Their sample, however, may not have been representative of the broader population of firms.

More recently, Ippolito and Thompson (2000) combined Form 5500 data with information from the Pension Benefit Guarantee Corporation (PBGC) to study within-firm changes in plans over time. They found little firm-level displacement of DB plans by 401(k) plans, and concluded that the replacement of a DB plan by a 401(k) is rare. Engelhardt (2000), basing his findings on data from the Health and Retirement Study (HRS), concludes that households eligible for a 401(k) have higher non-DB assets than households not eligible for a 401(k), but have the same level of assets when DB wealth is included. He interprets this as evidence of firm-level substitution of 401(k)s for DB pensions. However, as we explain later, the HRS does not allow accurate categorization of individuals into 401(k) eligible and noneligible status.

Most recently, LeBlanc (2001) has estimated the reduction in contributions to the Registered Retirement Saving Program (RRSP) in Canada when persons are newly covered by an employer-provided DB plan. Based on a longitudinal panel of individual tax data, and using a difference-in-difference estimation procedure, he finds that for a dollar of DB plan saving, RRSP contributions are reduced by only about $0.15.

Our analysis of these issues is divided into six sections. In section 1.1 we consider aggregate data on the total stock of retirement wealth. The very large increase in total retirement assets relative to income over the past twenty-five years strongly suggests that the enormous growth in individual retirement assets has more than offset any displacement of asset growth in traditional DB pension plans.

In section 1.2 we show that the "retirement plan contribution rate" is much greater than the personal saving rate reported in the National Income and Product Accounts (NIPA) in recent years. Our retirement plan contribution rate is determined by the retirement saving of current employees. The NIPA saving rate, in contrast, depends on the saving and consumption patterns of retirees as well as those who are currently working. We document the substantial growth over time in contributions to self-directed retirement saving programs, such as 401(k) plans. We also suggest that the retirement plan contribution rate was reduced by legislation restricting contributions to DB pension plans, as well as by the strong stock market performance of the late 1980s and 1990s and the associated reduction in required DB plan contributions.

In section 1.3, we distinguish between retirement saving from the standpoint of an employee, and employer contributions to retirement saving plans. We argue that from the perspective of the employee, 401(k) retirement saving is likely to be much greater than traditional DB plan saving at most ages. We use data on accruing DB plan liabilities to compare 401(k) and DB plan saving rates, and conclude that the saving rate under a typical 401(k) plan is about twice that under a typical DB plan.

In section 1.4 we begin to explore the possible substitution between different types of retirement plans. We use data from both the Department of Labor Form 5500 filings, and from the SIPP. We find no evidence of strong substitution patterns between 401(k) participation and other retirement plans. Section 1.5 shows that further analysis of substitution, using data from the HRS, supports the results in section 1.4.

A brief conclusion summarizes our findings.

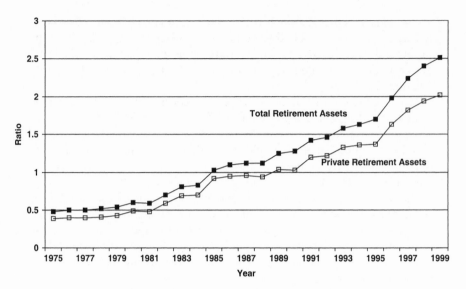

Fig. 1.1   Ratio of private and total retirement assets to wage and salary earnings

1.1   Aggregate Data on Assets in Retirement Saving Plans

1.1.1   Retirement Account Assets

While it is not possible to link particular assets with particular motives for saving, for many households assets in retirement saving accounts are the best single indicator of the amount that they have saved for retirement. A number of factors are likely to contribute to variation in retirement assets. For example, one would expect that households with higher earnings would have more retirement assets. For a given level of aggregate earnings, a larger share of the working population near retirement age is likely to be associated with greater retirement assets. Variation in life expectancy and in the typical retirement age can also affect the stock of retirement assets. The "adequacy" of any given level of assets depends on the years of support the assets are expected to provide.

Our analysis begins with measures of aggregate retirement assets that are not adjusted for demographic trends. We then explain the likely effect of adjustment for demographic changes. Figure 1.1 shows the ratio of assets in all private retirement accounts—including DB plans, 401(k), other DC plans, IRAs, 403(b) plans, and Keogh plans—to private wage and salary earnings.[1] This ratio increased more than fivefold between 1975 and 1998, from 0.39 to 2.02. The figure shows modest growth in the ratio of re-

---

1. Appendix A describes all of our data sources.

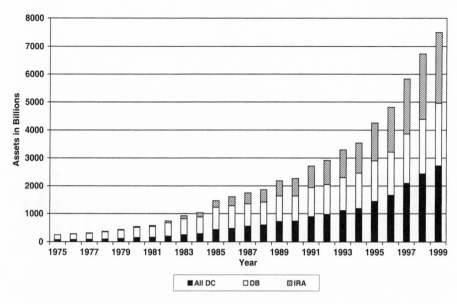

Fig. 1.2   Private retirement assets

tirement assets to earnings through 1981; more rapid growth between 1982 and 1994, after the introduction of IRAs and 401(k) plans and during a period of positive stock market returns; and rapidly accelerated growth beginning in 1995, corresponding to large increases in equity market returns. Figure 1.1 also shows the ratio of assets in all retirement plans, the private plans as well as public sector plans, to wages and salaries. The trend is very similar to that for private plan assets alone.

Figure 1.2 shows private retirement assets disaggregated into several components. It shows that assets in DB plans continued to grow after the introduction of 401(k) and IRA plans, but that the bulk of the gain was in individual accounts. In this figure, 401(k) assets are included with other DC plans. There is no evidence of a decline in the assets in conventional employer-provided plans during the time period when assets in individual accounts were growing most rapidly.

The foregoing data alone cannot rule out the possibility of substitution, because we do not have data on the time path that other retirement plan assets would have followed in the absence of the growth in DC assets. To place the growth in DC assets into perspective, however, we note that if *all* contributions to personal retirement accounts between 1985 and 1998 had come at the expense of DB contributions, DB assets would have grown by a factor of 8.4 instead of 2.7.

The private retirement assets in figure 1.2 exclude assets in federal, state,

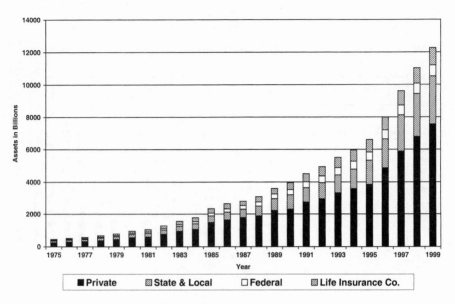

Fig. 1.3   Public and private retirement assets

and local retirement plans, and assets held by life insurance companies in retirement plans that are also part of the retirement asset pool.[2] Figure 1.3 shows the assets in private plans as well as the assets in these other plans. In 1999, about 40 percent of all retirement assets were in federal, state, and local and insurance plan funds.

Retirement account assets support current retirees as well as future retirees. Although we are unable to distinguish the assets held by current retirees from those held by the working-age population, we suspect that the increase in these assets represents a large upward trend in the assets of future retirees.

1.1.2   Housing and Other Nonretirement Assets

Aside from promised Social Security benefits, housing equity is the most important asset of a large fraction of Americans. Unlike the increase in retirement account assets, however, there has been no increase in housing equity relative to income over the past two and one-half decades. Figure 1.4 shows housing equity as a fraction of disposable income from 1975 to 1998. The ratio increased about 25 percent between 1975 and 1989, but by 1999 it was essentially at the same level as in 1975. The figure also shows non-

2. The Flow of Funds Accounts (FFA) defines the latter series as including "assets of private pension plans held at life insurance companies, such as guaranteed investment contracts and variable annuity plans, that are managed for the benefit of individuals who are not separately identified to the insurance companies."

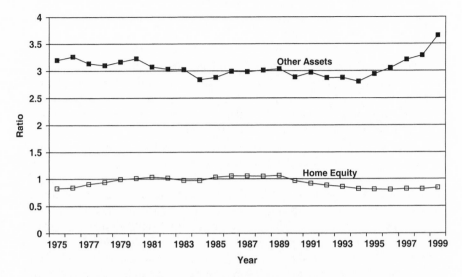

Fig. 1.4   Ratio of home equity and other assets to disposable income

retirement, nonhome equity net worth as a share of disposable income. This ratio decreased and then increased between 1985 and 1999. The increase between 1975 and 1999, 27 percent, was not nearly as great as the increase in retirement assets over this period.

1.1.3   Retirement Assets and Demographic Trends

The growth of retirement assets relative to income may be explained by a number of changes. These include the advent of new retirement saving vehicles as well as other factors, such as demographic change. Changes in three features of the population—demographic composition, mortality rates, and labor force participation—have likely contributed to the rise in retirement assets relative to income. We describe each of these changes, although we do not attempt a formal adjustment of retirement wealth to correct for these changes.

The increase in life expectancy at retirement age is the first substantial change that may have contributed to rising retirement assets. In 1975, life expectancy for a U.S. man at age sixty-two was 15.5 years, while that for a woman was 20.3 years. By 1997, male life expectancy at age sixty-two had increased to 17.6 years, while female life expectancy had risen to 21.4 years. For men, this implies a 13.5 percent increase in the number of years that need to be supported with retirement resources, beginning at age sixty-two. For women, the change was 5.4 percent. These proportional changes provide a crude measure—crude, because they do not reflect the potential role of risk and the prospect of drawing down resources too quickly—of the increase in retirement resources that would be needed to offset improved longevity. These changes might account for an increase in resources of roughly 10 percent, much less than the actual growth of retirement assets relative to income.

The second important demographic change that might have contributed to rising retirement assets was the aging of the labor force. Translating information on the age structure of the population into predictions about the wealth-income ratio requires detailed information on saving by age, yet there is no agreement on the relative importance of life-cycle, precautionary, and other factors in saving decisions. In 1975, the average age of those over the age of twenty in the U.S. population was 44.6 years. For men, the average age was 43.9 years. Between 1975 and 1985, the average age of those over twenty actually declined to 44.3 years for the entire population and 43.5 years for the male population. This reflected the entry of the "baby boom" cohorts into the 20-plus age group. By 1998, the working age population had grown older, the average age of all 20-plus persons was 45.5 years, and that of 20-plus men was 44.8 years. Thus between 1985 and 1998, the average age of the adult population rose by just over one year. Similarly, the average age of those in the labor force in 1985 was 38.5 years, whereas in 1998, it was 40.3 years.

These data on the population and labor force age structure suggest that by the late 1990s, those who were in their earning years were older and had fewer remaining years of work to accumulate assets for retirement than those in the working population in the 1970s and early 1980s. This also may have induced a rise in retirement assets.

The final change that may have affected retirement assets is the shifting age of retirement in the U.S. population. During the 1980s and 1990s, these changes were modest by comparison to earlier decades. Burtless and Quinn (2000) present detailed information on age-specific labor force participation rates for U.S. men in 1970, 1984–85, and 1998–89. Their data show a sharp decline in labor force participation rates between 1970 and 1984–85, but relatively little decline subsequently. The participation rates for 1998–99 were virtually identical to those in 1984–85. At ages above sixty-five, the labor force participation rate in the late 1990s was greater than that in the mid-1980s. There is no systematic difference in labor force participation rates at younger ages. Labor force participation rates for women in their early sixties increased between the mid-1980s and the late 1990s as cohorts of women with greater labor force participation rates when they were younger entered the retirement-age cohort.

Changes in retirement ages are therefore not likely to account for substantial changes in retirement wealth relative to income during the last two decades. Demographic factors—shifting age structure and lengthening life expectancy—seem likely to account for modest increases in retirement assets, but are unlikely to account for more than a small fraction of the large changes we observe.

1.2 Plan Contributions and the Retirement Plan Contribution Rate

The accumulation of retirement assets depends on the inflow of contributions, the payout of benefits, and the return on invested assets. Panel A of figure 1.5 shows private pension plan contributions, which increased almost sixfold between 1975 and 1999, while panel B of figure 1.5 shows con-

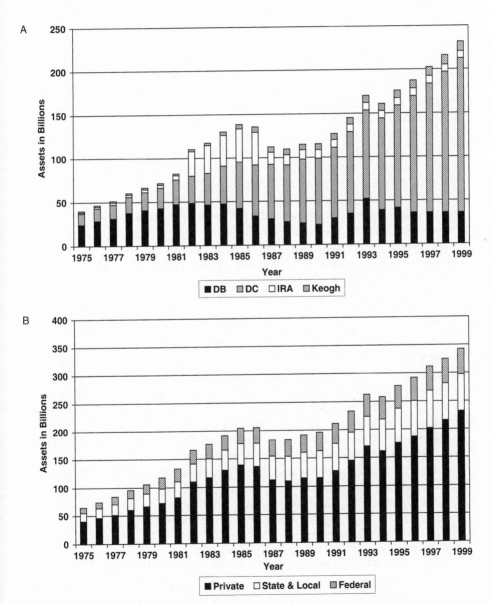

Fig. 1.5 *A*, Private pension contributions; *B*, all pension contributions

tributions to all retirement plans. Neither of the series includes contributions to privately held pension plans administered by insurance companies, which hold about 9 percent of the assets in all pension plans. Private plans include self-directed plans such as 401(k) plans and IRAs. IRA contributions exclude rollovers, while IRA assets include assets rolled in to these accounts.

The pronounced "hump" in retirement plan contributions between 1982 and 1986 corresponds to the beginning and subsequent retrenchment of the IRA program. The pattern strongly suggests that IRA contributions during this period were not offset by a reduction in other forms of retirement saving. Indeed, the rate of increase of non-IRA retirement saving was the same in the 1982–85 period as in prior years. This pattern suggests that the total pool of assets in retirement plans likely would be much greater today if the IRA program had not been limited in 1986.

Panel A of figure 1.6 shows both private and total retirement plan contributions scaled by disposable income. Panel B of figure 1.6 shows plan contributions over wage and salary earnings. In both figures, private contributions are scaled by private earnings, while all contributions are scaled by all wage and salary earnings. We define these ratios as *retirement plan contribution rates.* They measure the proportion of current earnings that is saved in retirement accounts by current employees. The contribution rates do not account for retirement plan earnings on existing assets, or for withdrawals from these plans. In the following, we compare retirement plan contribution rates to NIPA national saving rates.

Panels A and B of figure 1.6 show that retirement plan contribution rates are remarkably stable over most of the period. Scaled by personal disposable income, the private plan contribution rate was about 3.5 percent in 1975 and in 1999, and the contribution rate for all plans varied between 5 and 6 percent for most of the period. When scaled by private and by all wage and salary earnings, the contribution rates are also stable, although they are greater than the rates scaled by personal disposable income. The retirement plan contribution rate for all plans, including those in the federal and state and local government sector, is near 8 percent for most of the period, or about 2 percentage points higher than the rate for the private sector alone.

The relative stability in the retirement plan contribution rates was broken only by the large increase in the plan contribution rate when the IRA program was initiated, and the decrease when the program was curtailed in 1986. For example, relative to earnings, both the private and the all plan rates are about 2 percentage points higher during the IRA period—over 8 and 10 percent, respectively.

1.2.1   Time Series Changes in the Retirement Plan Contribution Rate

The relative stability of the retirement plan contribution rate conceals fluctuations in some of the factors that affect this rate. Contributions to private DC type plans increased sharply over the 1975–99 period, while DB

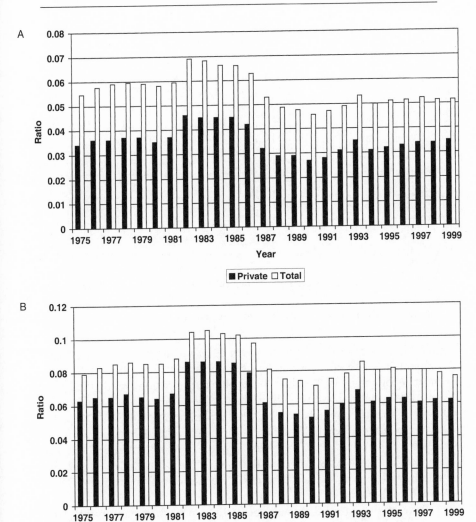

Fig. 1.6 *A,* **Ratio of private and total pension contributions to disposable income;** *B,* **ratio of private and total pension contributions to wage and salary earnings**

contributions varied widely. At the end of this period, DB plan contributions were only slightly higher than at the beginning.

Retirement plan contributions are the product of the number of participants and the average contribution per participant. Figure 1.7 shows the sum of the number of active participants in all DB and DC plans.[3] It illus-

3. These data, from Form 5500 filings and IRS tabulations of tax returns, show the number of persons participating in each type of retirement saving plan. Many persons participate in

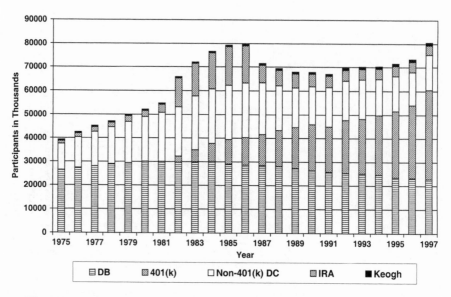

Fig. 1.7   Active participants in private pension plans (with double counting)

trates in particular the rapid growth of 401(k) plans. The number of participants in these plans, which first became available in 1982, grew to almost 38 million by 1997. While 401(k) plan participation grew in the 1980s and 1990s, participation in DB plans declined from about 30 million in 1984 to about 23 million by 1997. Participation in non-401(k) DC plans increased until about 1986 and then declined, ending the period about 30 percent higher than at the beginning. There is a clear "IRA effect" on plan participants, as well as plan contributions, in the early 1980s. In total, the number of plan participants increased from about 39 million in 1975 to over 80 million in 1997.

Panel A of figure 1.8 shows contributions per participant in DB, DC, and 401(k) plans. Panel B of figure 1.8 shows IRA and 401(k) contributions, while panel C of figure 1.8 shows contributions to Keogh plans. DB contributions per participant fluctuated substantially during the last two decades, and they were about 40 percent higher at the end of the period than at the beginning. Non-401(k) DC contributions per participant increased about twofold over the period, and on average were higher than DB contributions. Over the past fifteen years contributions per participant to 401(k) plans were, on average, twice as large as contributions per participant to DB plans. Contributions to 401(k)s increased almost 50 percent

---

more than one plan, so the total number of participants overstates the number of persons who participate in at least one plan. For 401(k) plans, participants include all persons eligible to contribute, regardless of actual contributions.

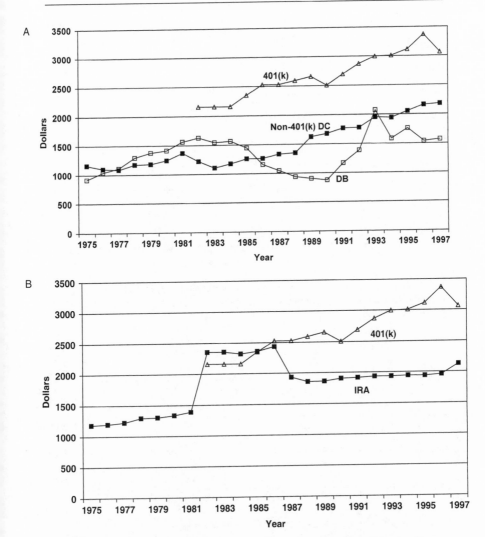

Fig. 1.8   *A,* **Contributions per active participant DB, DC, and 401(k);** *B,* **contributions per active participant IRA and 401(k);** *C,* **contributions per active participant Keogh**

between 1982 and 1996 alone.[4] During the "unrestricted" IRA period, 1982–86, IRA contributions on average were greater than 401(k) contributions.

4. 401(k) contributions are calculated by dividing total contributions to 401(k) plans by the total number of employees *eligible* to contribute, *not the number that actually make contributions.* There is much less change during this period in the participation rate of 401(k) eligibles, conditional on eligibility, than in the eligibility rate. Most of the change in the number of contributors is therefore due to changes in eligibility.

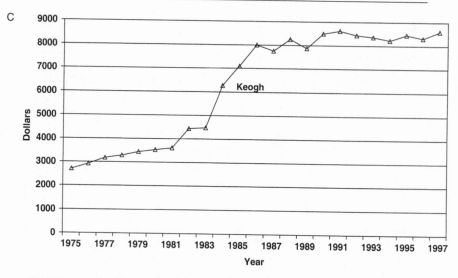

Fig. 1.8   (cont.) *A,* Contributions per active participant DB, DC, and 401(k); *B,* contributions per active participant IRA and 401(k); *C,* contributions per active participant Keogh

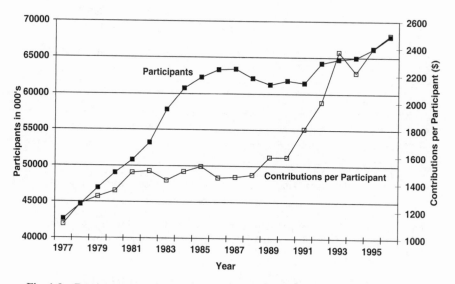

Fig. 1.9   Participants and contributions per participant for all plans

Keogh contributions, although a small proportion of total retirement saving, increased enormously between the early 1980s and late 1990s. There is a rise of more than 200 percent between 1981 and 1986, when the Economic Recovery Tax Act of 1981 raised Keogh contribution limits from $7,500 to $15,000.

Figure 1.9 shows the trend in the number of participants in all plans

combined and the trend in average contributions per participant. These two trends together yield the increase in total contributions previously shown. The participation numbers reflect substantial double counting, because many individuals participate in more than one plan. The increase in average contributions per unique covered employee would be substantially higher than the increase shown in figure 1.9.

1.2.2 Defined Benefit Contributions and the Retirement Plan Contribution Rate

Figure 1.10 shows an index of DB plan contributions per participant. It also shows an index for the number of participants and the flow of contributions to these plans. There are at least three reasons for the erratic variation in contributions to DB plans. The first is the slight rise and then steady decline in the number of active participants (current employees) in DB plans over the 1975–98 period. The number of total participants, including retirees, rose throughout the period.

A second is the link between returns on DB plan assets and current funding decisions. Benefits promised by DB plans are prescribed by a formula, which is typically based on years of service and final salary. The promised benefits are a liability of the firm, and the firm must insure that assets held in the plan are sufficient to cover this liability. Other things being equal, a rise in investment returns increases DB asset balances relative to obligations, thereby reducing the need for additional contributions. Bernheim and Shoven (1988) discuss this feature of DB funding.

A third reason for the fluctuation in DB contributions is the series of legislative changes that limited the level of benefits that could be funded un-

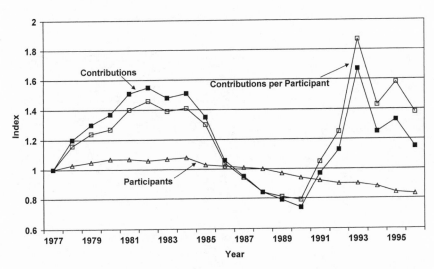

Fig. 1.10   DB contributions, participants, and contributions per participant (index: 1977 = 1)

der DB plans and discouraged firms from overfunding their pension plans. Prior to 1986, firms could fund their DB plans to a level greater than their legal liability. A series of laws beginning with a 10 percent reversion tax, which was part of the Tax Reform Act of 1986, put stricter limits on funding. Ippolito (2001) estimates that in the absence of various funding restrictions, DB pension assets in 1995 would have been 28 percent higher. Schieber and Shoven (1997) report that when the limits on contributions to overfunded plans that were part of the Omnibus Budget Reconciliation Act of 1987 took effect, 48 percent of a sample of large pension plans were precluded from making further contributions.

Our analysis of DB contributions, relative to contributions to other plans, is directed at understanding how fluctuations in DB contributions affect the retirement plan contribution rate. Although developing a precise estimate is an unrealistic target, we try to place a lower bound on the effect of movements in DB plan contributions on the retirement plan contribution rate.

Total DB contributions are the product of the number of DB plan participants and the average contribution per participant. Fluctuations are due largely to movements in the contribution per participant. Figure 1.11 provides information on DB, DC, and Keogh contributions per participant over the 1975–97 period. It shows that the wages of wage and salary workers increased 150 percent over this period. The DC plan contributions per participant increased about 150 percent as well, as one would expect if contributions were a proportion of wage earnings. On the other hand, DB contributions per participant fluctuated substantially and on average fell relative to wages.

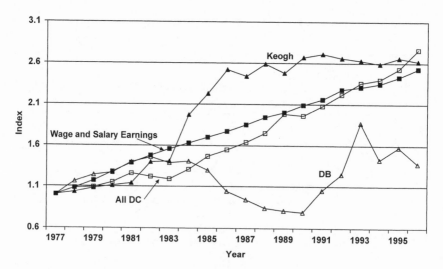

Fig. 1.11   Contributions per participant (index: 1977 = 1)

Suppose that there had been no legislation limiting contributions to DB plans, that market returns had not affected DB contributions, that life expectancy at retirement had been constant, and that there were no changes in the demographic structure of the workforce covered by DB plans. If the returns on DB plan assets were in line with expectations, one might have expected DB contributions per participant, relative to wages, to remain roughly constant. Given rising life expectancy and an aging workforce, one might have expected contributions per employee to increase relative to wages.

To explore the effects of legislative and return-induced downward pressures on DB plan contributions, we construct a "what if" scenario. Considering the *private sector only,* suppose that DB contributions per employee had increased at the same rate as wages in every year after 1977. Figure 1.12 shows the private retirement plan contribution rate under this counterfactual, together with the actual rate. The saving rate under this counterfactual assumption was 1 percentage point higher than the actual rate at the end of the period. In the years when the DB contribution rate was at its lowest, the counterfactual saving rate was close to 2 percentage points higher than the actual rate. This counterfactual suggests that legislative changes like those in 1986, and unexpectedly favorable returns on DB plan assets, probably reduced the private retirement plan contribution rate by a substantial amount.

The aggregate data also suggest that the retirement plan contribution rate would have been substantially higher were it not for the curtailment of the IRA program. Between 1982 and 1985, IRA saving added approxi-

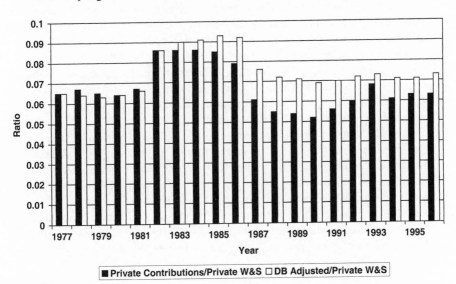

Fig. 1.12   Ratio of private and DB adjusted pension contributions to wage and salary earnings

mately 2.3 percentage points to the retirement plan contribution rate. Now it accounts for only 0.3 percentage points.

In summary, aggregate retirement assets increased dramatically over the past two decades. All else being equal, this reduces the likelihood that the rise of assets in DC retirement plans was offset by a reduction of assets in DB plans. This conclusion is consistent with the findings in previous studies using household data, which show increases in individual financial assets with the advent of 401(k) and IRA plans, and with the evidence that we present later. The decline in DB plans was probably due to many factors other than the growth of DC plans. Gustman and Steinmeier (1992), for example, find that at least half of the trend in DB plans from 1977 to 1985 "is due to a shift in employment mix towards firms with industry, size, and union status that have historically been associated with lower defined benefit rates." Ippolito (1995) concludes that "about half of the shift is attributable to a loss of employment in large unionized firms where DB plans are used intensively."

1.2.3   NIPA Saving and the Retirement Plan Contribution Rate

Contributions to retirement plans as a proportion of either wages and salaries or personal disposable income have substantially exceeded the NIPA personal saving rate in recent years. In the NIPA, saving equals disposable income, less consumption. This definition implies that increases in *measured income* increase saving, and increases in *measured consumption* decrease saving. Contributions to pension plans are treated as income in the NIPAs, so these contributions increase saving. Interest and dividends received by pension plans are also imputed as a component of income, and pension plan management fees are charged as a consumption outlay.

Neither capital gains on pension assets, nor distributions from pension plans, are included in NIPA income. If distributions from pension plans are partly consumed, however, the net effect of pension distributions will be to raise consumption and therefore, without any corresponding increase in income, to reduce NIPA saving.

The NIPA treatment of pensions can be illustrated with an example. Consider an employee who contributed to a 401(k) plan in 1982. Assuming that the contribution was made from income earned in that year, and reduced the contributor's consumption in 1982, the act of contributing would have raised personal saving in 1982. If the 401(k) assets were invested in non-dividend paying stocks, the internal buildup in their value would not have contributed anything to NIPA income in any year after 1982, until the date of distribution.[5] Assume that the assets were distrib-

---

5. The U.S. Department of Labor (1999) reports that in 1996, interest and dividends on 401(k) assets totaled $20.7 billion, while contributions were $104 billion and capital gains were $129.3 billion.

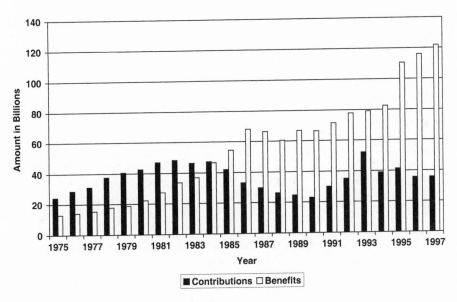

Fig. 1.13   DB contributions and benefits

uted from the 401(k) plan in 2001. At that point, there would be no increase in NIPA income. If the beneficiary of the distributions raised consumption as a result of these distributions, the net effect would be higher consumer spending and, therefore, lower saving. With large capital gains between 1982 and 2001, the distribution is likely to be very large relative to the initial contribution in 1982. Lusardi, Skinner, and Venti (2001) estimate that in 1999, the NIPA accounting of DB pension transactions alone *reduced* NIPA personal saving by almost $55 billion. Figures 1.13 and 1.14 show that in recent years, distributions from DB plans and IRAs have far exceeded contributions to these plans.[6]

The growth in retirement plan assets during the last decade highlights the limitations of the current NIPA treatment of pension saving. Gale and Sabelhaus (1999) and Reinsdorf and Perozek (2002) discuss limitations of the current definition of personal saving other than those associated with pensions. The distortions in the NIPA personal saving rate that result from the treatment of pension income will only become worse in the future. PVW (2001), for example, project that average 401(k) balances for the co-

---

6. Until 2000, the treatment of public pensions in NIPA was almost the reverse of the treatment of private pensions. Employee contributions to the federal civilian retirement plan, state and local pension plans, and Social Security were not included in income, while benefits from these plans were counted as income. Employee contributions thus reduced saving. If benefits were fully spent, the resulting increase in consumption would precisely offset the increase in income associated with the benefits and saving would not be affected. Since 2000, public and private pensions are treated the same in the NIPA.

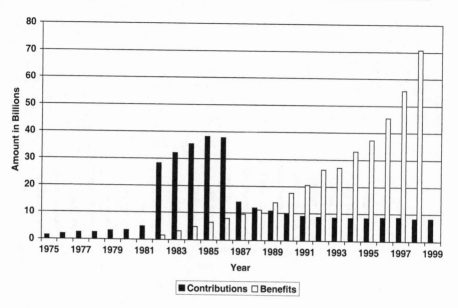

Fig. 1.14   IRA contributions and benefits

hort retiring in 2025 will be roughly ten times greater than the balances for those who retired in the mid-1990s.

1.3   Retirement Plan Contributions versus Employee Saving

In this section we compare lifetime saving under an illustrative DB plan to that under a DC plan. We show that the pattern of retirement asset accumulation under the two plans is very different, and we note that an employee's perception of retirement saving under the two plans is likely to be very different as well. In addition, the early retirement incentives inherent in many DB plans suggest that DB plan participants will retire earlier than DC participants, and thereby will accumulate less in retirement assets. We then discuss implications of these findings for the comparison of individual assets in DB and DC plans, as well as the aggregate accumulation of pension assets, and consider empirical evidence on asset accrual in DB plans.

1.3.1   Contributions versus Saving: A Conceptual Framework

Contributions to traditional non-401(k) DC plans are typically a constant percentage of employee earnings and are primarily funded by employer contributions. Contributions to 401(k) programs are also proportional to earnings, but the precise relationship between earnings and contributions depends on each firm's match rate and contribution limit, as well as on the saving choices of participants. About one-third of all 401(k) contributions are made by employers and two-thirds by participants.

In both 401(k) plans and other types of DC plans, contributions by employers and employees are easily observed by participants, making it unlikely that there are any differences between contributions to these plans and the amounts individuals perceive as "saved." This is not true for saving through DB plans. The annual DB saving that can be ascribed to a given plan participant may be very different from the employer contribution per participant. The amount a DB plan participant *perceives* to be saved on his or her behalf may be very different from the actual saving, as well as from the employer contribution to the plan.

Similarly, a participant's DB pension wealth is not easily observed and is difficult to determine. It is the discounted value of promised future benefits accrued to date. The annual *personal* DB saving rate is the change in promised benefits associated with working another year under the DB plan.[7] Because most DB plans are "backloaded," this annual benefit accrual is typically very small for young workers and much larger for older workers, particularly as they approach the plan's early retirement age.

Unless the specific features of a DB plan are known, it is not possible to calculate saving rates at different ages under the plan. This makes it difficult to compare personal saving—from the perspective of the participant—under DB and DC plans. We present a simple framework to fix these ideas and to compare DC and DB saving rates.

For a person covered by a DB plan, saving is defined in terms of promised future retirement benefits. The increment to future retirement wealth is the change in accrued future benefits associated with working another year at the firm. Current saving is the present value of this accrual. Defined benefit saving is defined by a formula that determines benefits in the future, whereas DC saving is defined by the current contribution. In a DC plan, the increment to future retirement wealth is determined by the future value of the current contribution, which depends on the intervening rate of return on the plan assets.

In a simplified case, DB benefits are given by $B_t = \lambda W_t s$, where λ is a parameter of the plan, typically between 0.01 and 0.02, and W_t denotes earnings at age t, and s is the number of years of service that the employee has at age t. After s years of employment, this is the accrued benefit promised at the normal retirement age, say sixty-five. If the employee leaves the firm after s years, future benefits at retirement are given by this formula. The change in B with another year of employment is given by

---

7. The measure of accrued DB pension wealth that we use corresponds to the firm's current, or terminal, liability. Firms also compute projected liabilities, which use a forecast of future wage growth to value the future cost of years of service accrued to date.

$$\Delta B_t = \lambda \left[W_t + s\left(\frac{dW}{dt}\right)\right] = (ws + 1)W_t \cdot \lambda,$$

where w is the annual rate of increase in earnings. The change in future pension wealth is given by this change in benefits, multiplied by the annuity value of a dollar at the retirement age of sixty-five, $A(65)$. Thus in the DB case, the increase in future retirement wealth associated with working another year is $\Delta\text{DBPW} = (ws + 1) \cdot W_t \cdot \lambda \cdot A(65)$. Saving at age t under the DB plan, which can be compared to DC saving at age t, is this amount discounted back to age t. This accrual is an increase in the DB plan obligation that must be funded by the employer.

The ratio of the change in future retirement wealth associated with working another year under the DC plan to the change in wealth from working another year under the DB plan is given by

$$\frac{\Delta\text{DCPW}(t)}{\Delta\text{DBPW}(t)} = \frac{kW_t(1 + r)^{65-t}}{(ws + 1)W_t\lambda \cdot A(65)} = \frac{(1 + r)^{65-t}}{(1 + ws)} \cdot \frac{k}{\lambda \cdot A(65)}.$$

Note that ΔDCPW depends on the market rate of return but not on the rate of increase in the wage rate, which affects ΔDBPW. The market rate of return may affect ΔDBPW through the $A(65)$ term. Suppose that $\lambda = .015$, that $k = .10$, and that $A(65) = 8$. Suppose also that people work from age twenty-five to age sixty-five. Then the ratio $\Delta\text{DCPW}/\Delta\text{DBPW}$ is $[(1 + r)^{65-t}/(1 + ws)] \cdot [.10/.12]$. Suppose further that $r = 0.09$ and $w = 0.05$. At one year of employment the ratio is 20.04, at twenty years it is 2.05, and at forty years it is 0.24. Defined contribution wealth accrues early in the working life and DB wealth accrues late—it is backloaded.

Most actual DB plans are not as simple as the one previously considered. Actual accruals depend on the specific provisions of the DB plan. An employee is usually not vested in the plan before working some minimum number of years.[8] Defined benefit saving is zero prior to vesting. In addition, most DB plans have an early retirement age (often fifty-five), which is an important determinant of the accrual pattern. After the early retirement age, benefit accrual typically declines (often becoming negative), creating an incentive to retire early. The more complicated accrual patterns under these circumstances, and the associated incentives to retire, are described in detail in Kotlikoff and Wise (1987, 1988, 1989a, 1989b). Lazear (1985) proposed that firms use these incentives to induce older workers—paid more than their marginal product—to retire. In the following illustration we use a typical plan, similar to a plan described in Kotlikoff and Wise (1989b), that incorporates a substantial incentive to retire after the early retirement age.

8. This is also true for some 401(k) plans in which the employer matching contribution is subject to a short vesting requirement.

Table 1.1   **Illustration of Saving under DB and 401(k) Plans**

Age (1)	Wage (2)	Saving/Wage DB (3)	Saving/Wage 401(k) (4)	Saving in Dollars DB (5)	Saving in Dollars 401(k) (6)	Saving as Increment to Wealth at Retirement DB (7)	401(k) to 65 (8)	401(k) to 55 (9)	401(k) to 60 (10)
25	9,229	0	0.09	0	831	0	26,089	11,020	16,956
29	11,991	0.053	0.09	636	1,079	5,973	24,012	10,143	15,606
30	12,754	0.016	0.09	207	1,148	1,640	23,433	9,898	15,230
35	16,983	0.029	0.09	494	1,528	2,539	20,279	8,566	13,180
40	21,784	0.049	0.09	1,063	1,961	3,552	16,906	7,141	10,988
45	26,908	0.078	0.09	2,097	2,422	4,554	13,572	5,733	8,821
50	31,998	0.119	0.09	3,809	2,880	5,376	10,490	4,431	6,818
54	35,757	0.162	0.09	5,782	3,218	5,782	8,304	3,508	5,397
55	36,623	−0.046	0.09	−1,672	3,296	−1,672	7,803	3,296	5,071
60	40,330	−0.118	0.09	−4,765	3,630	−4,765	5,585	—	3,630
64	42,363	−0.189	0.09	−8,016	3,813	−8,016	4,156	—	—
Average									
25–64		0.017	0.09	111	2,425	—	14,768	—	—
25–54		0.062	0.09	1,730	2,025	3,549	—	7,535	—
Total pension wealth if retire at age:									
55						102,911	—	221,182	
60						142,139	—	—	362,205
65						181,458	575,970	—	—

Source: Authors' calculations.

Suppose the DB plan has vesting after five years of service, early retirement at age fifty-five, normal retirement at age sixty-five, and an early retirement discount factor of 3 percent per year. The factor λ is set at 0.013. Table 1.1 shows saving at selected ages under this DB plan and under a 401(k) plan with a 9 percent contribution rate. In this example, the nominal rate of growth of earnings declines from 7 percent per year at age twenty-five to 1 percent at age sixty-five. These earnings should be thought of as the historical earnings of persons now approaching retirement. The associated saving should be thought of as the saving of workers covered under the DB or the 401(k) plan over a working lifetime.[9] The table shows three measures of saving: saving as a proportion of earnings at age t (columns 3 and 4), saving in dollars at age t (columns 5 and 6), and the associated increment to wealth at age sixty-five (columns 7 through 10).

Table 1.1, column (4) shows 401(k) plan saving as a percent of earnings. At age twenty-five, for example, 9 percent of earnings is contributed to a

9. Workers now approaching retirement could only have been covered by a 401(k) plan for about two decades.

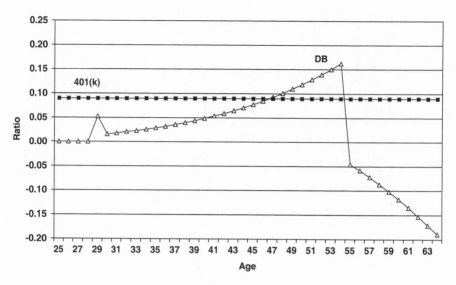

Fig. 1.15   Ratio of DB and 401(k) saving to earnings

DC account. The dollar amount, $831, is shown in column (6). At a 9 percent market rate of return, the $831 would grow to $26,089 by age sixty-five, as shown in column (8). At age forty-five, 9 percent of earnings is $2,422, and this amount grows to $13,572 by age sixty-five. The total accumulation of assets under the DC plan will be $575,970 by age sixty-five, if the employee continues to work and to make contributions until that age. This value is shown in the last row of column (8). Columns (9) and (10) show the increment to assets at retirement if the employee works until ages fifty-five and sixty, respectively. The total accumulation of assets at these ages is $221,182 and $362,205, respectively.

The calculation of saving under the DB plan is more complicated. There is no saving in the DB plan until the employee is vested, which occurs at age thirty. Much more important are the provisions that determine pension accrual at later ages. Like the typical DB plan, the provisions of the DB plan used in this illustration discourage work past the early retirement age of fifty-five,[10] while providing a strong incentive to stay at the firm until the early retirement age. Indeed, the accrual of pension benefits is negative after age fifty-five. Figure 1.15 shows this accrual pattern (saving) and the related incentive effects.

In this plan, the value of future DB pension benefits is maximized if receipt of benefits begins at age fifty-five. Consider, for example, saving at age

10. The HRS data show that 29.8 percent of all workers qualify for early retirement before age fifty-five, another 44.7 percent are eligible at exactly age fifty-five, and only 14.8 percent qualify for early retirement after age sixty. The average early retirement age is 54.2 and the average age of normal retirement is 61.3. See Gustman and Steinmeier (2000a).

forty-five. The increment to promised future pension wealth, shown in column (7), is $4,554, *if receipt of benefits begins at age fifty-five*. After age fifty-five, the 3 percent increment in benefits for each year that benefit receipt is delayed is not enough to offset the receipt of benefits for one fewer year. For each year benefit receipt is delayed after age fifty-five, the present value of retirement benefits declines. This is the common feature of DB plans that encourages retirement after the early retirement age.

The dollar saving shown in column (5) at age forty-five is $2,097. This is the increment to assets at age fifty-five, discounted back to age forty-five at 9 percent.[11] As a proportion of the wage, DB saving, shown in column (3), is 7.8 percent at age forty-five. If the DB employee remained in the firm until age fifty-five and then started to receive benefits, the value of lifetime benefits would be $102,911.

Notice that at age forty-five, for example, DB saving is only moderately less than DC saving—$2,097 versus $2,422. Yet the increment to total wealth at retirement is $4,554 under the DB plan, while it is $13,572 under the 401(k) plan, assuming that the employee works until age sixty-five. The difference in the increment to wealth at retirement is simply due to the difference in the assumed age of receipt of benefits. This is taken to be age fifty-five under the DB plan, because that is the age that maximizes benefits under the DB plan. The increment to DC wealth at age fifty-five (from saving at forty-five) is $5,733, as shown in column (9).

Over a working life, the maximum present discounted value of future DB benefits is achieved if the receipt of benefits begins at age fifty-five. At that age, the present value of future benefits is $102,911. Total accumulation in the 401(k) plan at that age is $221,182. Accumulation of assets in DB and DC plans, assuming retirement at age fifty-five under both plans, is shown in figure 1.16. But if the DC employee continues to work until age sixty-five, the accumulation in the DC plan increases to $575,970. The DC employee continues to make contributions at 9 percent of earnings, and assets accumulated at age fifty-five continue to grow at 9 percent.

For the DB employee, however, benefits grow much more slowly after the early retirement age. In our example, the nominal annual DB benefit continues to increase because of earnings growth and additional years of service. In addition, benefits are higher because they will be received for fewer

---

11. We realize that in principle the discount rate applied to future DB benefits need not be the same as the market return earned on DC contributions. However, there is no clear way to measure the risk under each type of plan, and thus no obvious way to make a risk adjustment to the discount rates. Employees covered by DC plans face investment risk, but in DB plans most of this investment risk is borne by employers. Conversely, as a consequence of job change or job loss, employees covered by DB plans face the risk of losing a large fraction of the benefits they would accrue without job change. The erosion of benefits that results from job change is much less severe under DC plans. The average discount rate used by DB plans in Form 5500 reports was 7.77 percent in 1997. For simplicity in this illustration we let the discount rate equal the assumed rate of return.

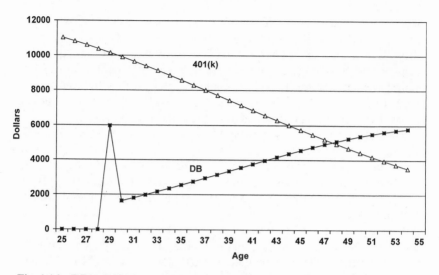

Fig. 1.16   DB and 401(k) saving increment to wealth (retirement at age 55)

years, but the increase is not enough to offset the fewer years of benefit receipt. This is reflected in the reduction in DB saving beginning at age fifty-five, shown in columns (3), (5), and (7) of table 1.1. The benefit at age fifty-five is determined by the promised benefit at age sixty-five discounted at 3 percent. That is, the adjustment for taking benefits before age sixty-five—and thus receiving benefits for more years—is only 3 percent per year. Thus when the receipt of benefits is delayed, say until age sixty-five, the benefit is increased by only 3 percent for each one-year reduction in the number of years benefits will be received. By age sixty-five, pension wealth in age sixty-five dollars is $181,458. The increase between ages fifty-five and sixty-five is not enough to offset the reduction in the number of years benefits will be received.

Figure 1.17 shows the accumulations of assets under DB and DC plans, assuming retirement at age sixty-five. In current dollars, DB pension wealth grows by a factor of 1.76 between ages fifty-five and sixty-five, while DC wealth grows by a factor of 2.64. At age fifty-five, DC assets are 2.12 times as much as DB assets. If employees work to age sixty-five, DC assets are 3.17 times as much as DB assets.

The assumption underlying figure 1.17, that DB plan participants work until age sixty-five, will tend to understate the difference between DB and 401(k) accumulation profiles. Given DB incentives to retire early, few employees covered by DB plans work until age sixty-five. Stock and Wise (1990a, 1990b), Lumsdaine, Stock, and Wise (1990, 1992, 1994), Gustman and Steinmeier (1989, 2000a), and Samwick (1998) present estimates of the effect of such incentives. Evidence on the early retirement effect of such in-

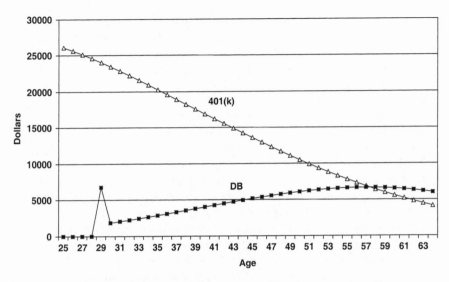

Fig. 1.17   DB and 401(k) saving increment to wealth (retirement at age 65)

centives in public social security programs around the world is presented in Gruber and Wise (1998, 1999), Coile and Gruber (2000) present recent estimates of such incentives in the U.S. Social Security program. Friedberg and Webb (2000) suggest that compared to a DB plan, a DC plan would increase the retirement age by two years. Samwick and Wise (2003) find that the average annual labor force departure rate for HRS respondents between ages fifty-five and sixty is 1.8 percent for persons without a pension plan, 3 percent for those with a DC plan only, 11.5 percent for persons with a DB plan only, and 12.1 percent for those with both a DB and a DC plan.

One other factor may lead our calculations to overstate the actual pension wealth of DB participants. Many employees do not remain under the same DB plan until the early retirement age, and thus do not accumulate the working life assets shown in the preceding illustration. The DB wealth at retirement would be much less if a person were to change jobs several times.

1.3.2   Implications for Analyzing Pension Assets and Retirement Saving

The previous illustration highlights the difference in the age profile of asset accrual under DB and 401(k) plans, and the fact that 401(k) participants are likely to work longer than DB participants, thereby accumulating more pension assets. Thus as larger and larger numbers of employees accumulate more years of employment under DC plans, retirement plan assets relative to current earnings are likely to rise.

To link our hypothetical DB-401(k) comparison with the earlier discussion of aggregate pension assets in DB and DC plans, consider a setting in which the potential "working life" is forty years, from ages twenty-five to sixty-five. Assume also that DC participants work the entire forty years, but DB employees work only thirty years, until age fifty-five. They are retired for ten of the forty working years. Suppose that the annual DC contribution per participant is C, and that the contribution per participant (employee) to the DB plan is $C/2$. Then over the working ages twenty-five to sixty-five, contributions to the DC account will be $C \cdot 40$. But contributions per participant to the DB plan will be only $(C/2) \cdot 30$, or only 3/8 of DC contributions. If the DB employees work thirty-five years, until age sixty, DB contributions will be 43.75 percent of DC contributions. Thus, for any given cohort of workers, the accumulation of assets will depend on not only the contribution per active (working) participant to DC and to DB plans, but also the number of years over which participants work.[12]

The DB-401(k) illustration can also help to inform the micro comparison of the accumulation of individual pension assets under DB and 401(k) plans, as discussed later. At age sixty-three, for example, individual (annuity) assets of DB participants are likely to be decreasing, while the assets of individual DC participants are likely still rising, as long as they are still in the labor force. Indeed, survey-based estimates of DB pension wealth are often calculated by capitalizing the survey respondent's reported annuity from a DB plan. Consider, for example, the pension assets of two persons at age sixty-five, one covered by a DB plan the other by a DC plan. Suppose the DC person just retired, while the DB person retired at age fifty-five. Working longer will increase the assets of the DC participant. Because relatively few employees now near retirement have worked for a long period of time under a DC plan, this effect may have only a modest influence on current comparisons, like those discussed later. The effect will become quantitatively more important with the spread of 401(k) plans. Although we do not have a quantitative estimate of the magnitude of this effect, the direction seems clear.

1.3.3 Empirical Evidence on Defined Benefit Accruals versus Contributions

To determine whether averaged over all ages the increase in retirement support from DC plan saving is greater than that from DB plan saving, we can consider external data. Kotlikoff and Wise (1989) estimate that contributions to DB plans average 4 to 6 percent of the wage earnings of DB enrollees. The average 401(k) contribution is about 9 percent of earnings. The Form 5500 data on contributions per active (working) participant discussed previously show 401(k) contributions per participant about twice as

12. Workers who retire earlier also get more leisure. Our focus, however, is on the accumulation of retirement assets, not on the comparison of utility of persons covered by DB and DC plans.

large as DB contributions per participant, and we noted previously that contributions to DC plans are likely to continue over more years than contributions to DB plans. Assuming that investment returns in the two plans are similar, the 401(k) plan should provide much greater benefits at ages such as sixty-five for persons with similar earnings histories.

We noted previously that DB plan contributions disproportionately benefit persons who are covered by the same plan over an entire working life. Employees who change jobs often will accumulate much less in DB pension assets, as documented by Kotlikoff and Wise (1989). This conclusion is consistent with the findings of Samwick and Skinner (1998). They compare DB and DC plans by running a broad range of earnings histories through plan provisions from the Pension Provider Supplements to the 1983 and 1995 Survey of Consumer Finances. They find that DC plans provide substantially higher retirement benefits than DB plans.

Form 5500 filings also provide data that matches closely the DC and DB annual saving rates (or accruals), as described algebraically above. For an individual DB plan participant, annual pension saving is the increase in promised future benefits due to working an additional year under the plan, not the contribution per participant that the firm makes to the plan. The annual accrual of promised DB benefits is reported in Form 5500 data for all plan employees combined.[13] This summary statistic combines employees of all ages, and thus may be very different from the accrual for any individual employee. Averaged over all DB plans, this accrual can be compared to the average contribution per participant in 401(k) plans.

Table 1.2 shows the DB change in accrued liability per active employee for 1990 through 1997, together with 401(k) contributions per participant. These data suggest that over these years the annual 401(k) saving rate per active (working) participant was more than twice the annual average DB saving rate. While the values reported in the Form 5500 data are imperfect—they depend on interest rate and mortality assumptions, and the response rate is low—the accrual values per employee correspond rather closely to contributions per employee in all years but 1993, when the DB contribution per employee was unusually large ($2,074). Thus contributions per employee, average accrued liability per employee, and the estimates of total DB versus 401(k) contributions as a percent of wages all seem quite consistent.

The annual accrual under DB plans is the increase in promised future benefits that the plan sponsor must fund. If the plan cannot be over- or underfunded, and there are no changes in the plan that might affect obligations to retirees, then the annual accrual puts a limit on the potential in-

13. These data are from Schedule B of the Form 5500. Each DB plan is asked for the "expected increase in current liability due to benefits accruing in the plan year." About 25 percent of all DB plans did not file or have missing data for Schedule B. The tabulations reported here are based on completed responses.

Table 1.2   Change in DB Plan Annual Accrued Liability per Active Employee, and
                     401(k) Plan Contribution per Participant

Year	DB Change in Accrued Liability per Active Employee	401(k) Contribution per Participant	Ratio 401(k) to DB Saving
1990	961	2,507	2.61
1991	976	2,694	2.76
1992	1,110	2,872	2.59
1993	1,252	2,996	2.39
1994	1,315	3,010	2.29
1995	1,359	3,115	2.29
1996	—	3,371	—
1997	1,784	3,065	1.72

Source: DB data are authors' calculations from Form 5500 data.

Note: To eliminate apparent data entry errors, plans with change in accrued liability greater than $10,000 per employee have been deleted. Essentially the same results are obtained if plans with a change greater than $20,000 per employee are eliminated.

crease in plan assets. Plan contributions would fluctuate depending on the accrual and on the market return on assets held in DB plans. In contrast, there are no limits on the accumulation of assets in DC plans, although there are limits on contributions. During periods of favorable asset returns, such as the 1990s, assets of DC plans are likely to rise much more rapidly than assets in DB plans.

1.4   Household-Level Data on Retirement Plan Asset Substitution

We now turn to direct analysis of substitution between defined contribution pension assets and DB pension assets, using household data. One of the implicit assumptions in many discussions of potential substitution between DB and DC plan assets is that workers have one pension arrangement or the other. Yet in many cases, workers have *both* plans; we call this *dual coverage.* Understanding dual coverage is essential for analyzing the potential for displacement of DB assets by 401(k) assets. We therefore begin our analysis of substitution by analyzing dual coverage, as well as other aspects of pension coverage, using the U.S. Department of Labor's Form 5500 filings.

After discussion of new findings based on the Form 5500 data, we consider the potential substitution between 401(k) assets and DB plan assets. There are several ways substitution may occur, including direct replacement of existing DB plans by 401(k) plans, shrinking or capping DB plans when 401(k) plans are introduced to firms with existing DB plans, and perhaps decisions not to introduce DB plans at firms that choose to introduce 401(k) plans instead. Engen, Gale, and Scholz (1994), Papke (1999), Engelhardt (2000), and Pence (2001) discuss the different channels of substitution. We consider several ways to evaluate the possible displacement of DB plan assets by DC assets, and 401(k) assets in particular.

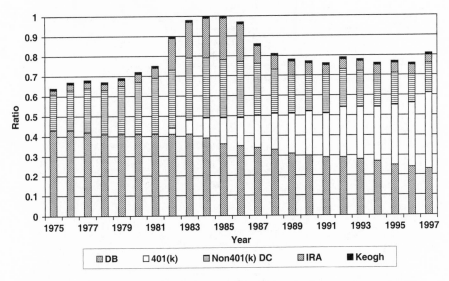

Fig. 1.18   Ratio of plan participants to private wage and salary employment, with double counting

In considering possible displacement of plan assets, it is useful to note the trend in the number of plan participants. Figure 1.18 shows the proportion of wage and salary workers who are pension plan participants, *including persons counted in more than one plan.* The total increased from 64 to 81 percent between 1975 and 1997. Note that in 1985 and 1986, about 20 percent of the labor force participated in the IRA program. This proportion fell to about 4 percent by the mid-1990s.

1.4.1   Dual Coverage and 401(k) Plans

Information on employer-provided pension plans, including 401(k) plans, is reported each year in firm Form 5500 filings, which provide data on funding and other financial features of pension plans. We have used these data as the basis for a number of calculations. The top panel of table 1.3 shows the fraction of 401(k) participants that also have a DB plan for the years 1984 to 1997. Three columns of data are presented. The first column pertains to all 401(k) plans. For the years 1988 to 1997, the second and third columns present results for preexisting 401(k) plans and new 401(k) plans in each year. The proportion of 401(k) participants with a DB plan declined substantially over the period—from 82.4 percent to 42.4 percent. The proportion of DB participants in new 401(k) plans was substantially smaller than the proportion in existing plans in all years. On average, the proportion in new plans was about 26 percent. There is notable year-to-year fluctuation, which we suspect is due to small sample sizes.

The second panel of table 1.3 shows the 401(k) participation rate, given

Table 1.3   401(k) Plans: Percentage with DB Plan and Participation Rate

Year	All 401(k) Plans	Pre-existing Plans	Plans in First Year of Coverage
	Percent of 401(k) Participants with a DB Plan		
1984	82.4		
1985	78.0		
1986	75.3		
1987	69.7		
1988	67.8	69.3	47.5
1989	65.3	66.8	46.0
1990	61.8	63.5	32.8
1991	58.2	60.2	26.1
1992	55.7	58.3	19.0
1993	52.9	54.4	22.9
1994	51.0	51.6	32.9
1995	46.9	47.6	28.0
1996	45.8	46.0	39.4
1997	42.4	43.2	22.5
	401(k) Participation Rate Given Eligibility (Percent)		
1990	83.4	83.7	77.3
1991	81.5	82.2	70.4
1992	81.4	82.0	72.8
1993	80.0	80.6	68.7
1994	79.9	80.4	63.0
1995	77.5	78.3	54.4
1996	77.0	77.1	63.6
1997	75.8	76.0	71.4
	Percent of All Plans (Participants)		
1988	100.0	86.3 (93.0)	13.7 (7.0)
1989	100.0	85.9 (92.7)	14.1 (7.3)
1990	100.0	87.7 (94.5)	12.3 (5.5)
1991	100.0	89.8 (94.1)	10.2 (5.9)
1992	100.0	89.6 (93.4)	10.4 (6.6)
1993	100.0	89.3 (95.2)	10.7 (4.8)
1994	100.0	94.6 (97.0)	5.4 (3.0)
1995	100.0	95.2 (96.7)	4.8 (3.3)
1996	100.0	95.9 (97.4)	4.1 (2.6)
1997	100.0	95.7 (96.4)	4.3 (3.7)

Source: Authors' calculations from Form 5500 filings.

eligibility, for the years 1990 to 1997.[14] These rates are in excess of 75 percent in all years. For preexisting plans, the rate is around 80 percent, declining from about 83 to 76 percent between 1990 and 1997. The participation rate for new plans is about 65 percent on average, with no clear

14. These data are not available prior to 1990. The participation rate is the ratio of participants with positive account balances to total participants. All other panels in this table are based on data for active (nonretired) participants.

Table 1.4   **401(k) Contribution and Participation Rate, by DB Coverage**

Year	All 401(k) Plans	With a DB Plan	Without a DB Plan
	Contributions per Active Participant		
1990	2,394	2,586	2,082
1991	2,433	2,700	2,061
1992	2,594	2,916	2,188
1993	2,718	3,075	2,310
1994	2,744	3,154	2,315
1995	2,896	3,417	2,435
1996	3,001	3,429	2,638
1997	3,056	3,615	2,645
	Participation Rate Given Eligible		
1990	83.4	83.4	83.3
1991	81.5	83.3	79.0
1992	81.4	83.9	78.2
1993	80.0	82.4	77.3
1994	79.9	82.3	77.3
1995	77.5	80.4	74.9
1996	77.0	80.5	74.1
1997	75.8	78.4	74.0

Source: Authors' calculations from Form 5500 filings.

trend over time. Although not shown in the table, in 1988, 86.3 percent of all plans were preexisting, and 93 percent of all participants were in preexisting plans. These proportions changed over time so that by 1997, 95.7 percent of all plans were preexisting and 96.4 percent of participants were in these plans. Very little of the decline in DB dual coverage is accounted for by 401(k) participants with dual coverage who subsequently lost their DB plan.

Table 1.4 shows 401(k) contribution and participation rates by dual DB coverage status. The average contribution per participant increased substantially over time, as shown previously. The information in table 1.4 shows that the average contribution is 25 to 40 percent higher for those with than for those without a DB plan. Perhaps firms with DB plans pay higher salaries than firms without DB plans. This may make both employer and employee 401(k) contributions higher in firms offering DB plans. It is also possible, as Katona (1965) suggested, that participation in one pension plan increases workers' awareness of saving-related issues and thereby encourages other saving. Participation rates in 401(k) plans are somewhat higher for persons who have a DB plan than for those who do not. Persons with a DB plan may also be older, and PVW (1998a) show that 401(k) participation rates tend to increase with age.

1.4.2   Loss of Dual Coverage

The data underlying table 1.3, in particular the proportion of new- and continuing-plan 401(k) participants with a DB plan, are shown in the first panel of table 1B.1. From these data, it is possible to determine the rate at which 401(k) participants with dual coverage lose DB coverage. We find that the loss rate is 1.0 percent for 1996–97, 4.6 percent (1995–96), 1.7 percent (1994–95), 0.7 percent (1993–94), –1.1 percent (1992–93), 6.1 percent (1991–92), and –5.1 percent (1990–91). A negative sign indicates that the number of 401(k) participants with DB plans *increased* from one year to the next. On average the year to year loss rate was 1.1 percent.

These data show that very few persons with dual coverage lost their DB coverage over this time period. The data also show that the decline in the number of persons covered by DB plans over this period cannot be accounted for by the loss of the DB plans of 401(k) participants; we have no reason to believe that the experience in earlier years was any different. These data suggest that the decline in the proportion of 401(k) participants with DB plans is largely accounted for by the entry of new 401(k) participants with low dual coverage rates. This is consistent with diffusion of 401(k) plans to smaller firms without prior DB plans.

1.4.3 Hypothetical Growth of Defined Benefit Assets Without 401(k) Plans

We now consider two simple scenarios of how DB assets might have evolved in the absence of 401(k) plans. The scenarios make extreme assumptions concerning the replacement of DB plans by 401(k) plans. The results can be interpreted as providing bounds on the extent of substitution between 401(k) plans and DB plans. The simulations are based on three data series for the period 1984 to 1997: (1) the number of participants in 401(k) plans and DB plans, (2) contributions per participant to 401(k) plans and to DB plans, and (3) the percent of 401(k) plan participants that also have a DB plan. We obtain the sum of plan contributions—both to 401(k) plans and to DB plans—by persons with a 401(k) plan. We then compare this sum to contributions that would have been made to DB plans in the absence of the 401(k) program. Table 1.5 shows the data and calculated values.

The number of DB and 401(k) plan participants is shown in columns (2) and (3) of table 1.5. The percent of 401(k) enrollees also enrolled in a DB plan is shown in column (4). The average contribution per participant in these plans is shown in columns (5) to (8). For persons with both a DB and a 401(k), total pension saving is necessarily greater than saving under a stand-alone DB plan.[15] In 1984, about 82 percent of 401(k) participants also had a DB plan. The percent of workers with dual enrollment declined rather consistently to about 42 percent in 1997. In the first years after they

15. DB plans generally preceded supplemental 401(k) plans. Because DB plans are formula based, it is difficult to scale back DB benefits when 401(k)s are introduced. Indeed, the data in table 1.5 show that DB contributions are higher in firms where DB plans are supplemented by a 401(k) plan.

Table 1.5   Contributions of Current 401(k) Participants With and Without a 401(k) Program

| | DB | 401(k) | | DB Contribution | | 401(k) Contribution | |
| | Participants | Participants | % with DB Plan | Without 401(k) | With 401(k) | Without DB | With DB |
Year (1)	(2)	(3)	(4)	(5)	(6)	(7)	(8)
1984	30,172	7,579	0.824	1,332	1,640	2,202	2,411
1985	29,024	10,352	0.78	1,350	1,350	1,866	2,605
1986	28,670	11,573	0.753	1,516	1,382	2,194	2,841
1987	28,432	13,163	0.697	1,287	1,250	2,312	2,796
1988	28,081	15,424	0.678	1,481	1,279	2,148	2,775
1989	27,304	18,449	0.653	1,385	1,067	2,176	2,728
1990	26,344	20,366	0.618	1,143	695	2,082	2,586
1991	25,747	21,130	0.582	1,270	1,018	2,061	2,700
1992	25,362	24,064	0.557	1,355	1,338	2,188	2,916
1993	25,127	25,576	0.529	1,538	2,333	2,310	3,075
1994	24,615	27,242	0.51	1,576	1,540	2,315	3,154
1995	23,531	30,803	0.469	1,809	2,094	2,435	3,417
1996	23,262	33,854	0.458	1,886	1,484	2,638	3,429
1997	22,866	37,716	0.424	1,979	2,247	2,645	3,615

(continued)

Table 1.5 (continued)

| | Persons with a 401(k) | | | | If all 401(k) Participants Had a DB Plan Instead (13) | DB Displacement = Decline in DB Plans | |
| | With a DB Plan | | Without a DB Plan (11) | Total (12) | | DB Participants Displaced (14) | Lost DB Contributions (15) |
	DB (9)	401(k) (10)					
1984	10,242	15,057	2,937	28,236	10,095	0	0
1985	10,901	21,034	4,250	36,185	13,975	1,148	1,550
1986	12,043	24,758	6,272	43,073	17,545	1,502	2,277
1987	11,468	25,652	9,221	46,341	16,941	1,740	2,239
1988	13,375	29,019	10,668	53,062	22,843	2,091	3,097
1989	12,854	32,865	13,930	59,649	25,552	2,868	3,972
1990	8,747	32,548	16,198	57,493	23,278	3,828	4,375
1991	12,519	33,204	18,203	63,926	26,835	4,425	5,620
1992	17,934	39,085	23,325	80,344	32,607	4,810	6,518
1993	31,565	41,604	27,827	100,996	39,336	5,045	7,759
1994	21,396	43,820	30,902	96,118	42,933	5,557	8,758
1995	30,251	49,364	39,828	119,443	55,723	6,641	12,014
1996	23,010	53,167	48,404	124,581	63,849	6,910	13,032
1997	35,933	57,810	57,461	151,204	74,640	7,306	14,459
Total	252,238	498,987	309,426	1,060,651	466,152	53,871	85,669

Source: Authors' calculations from Form 5500 filings.

became available, most 401(k) plans were initiated in large firms with an already existing DB plan. Subsequently, the diffusion of 401(k) plans included larger numbers of smaller firms that were less likely to have preexisting DB plans. To the extent that the expansion in 401(k) plans has been increasing through plans in smaller firms without prior DB plans, 401(k) contributions are not substituting for contributions to preexisting DB plans. Whether such firms would have adopted another plan if it were not for the 401(k) option is an open question; we address this in the following alternative scenarios.

On average, per enrollee contributions to 401(k) plans are greater than per participant contributions to DB plans. In addition, the average DB contribution is greater for those who also have a 401(k) plan, and the 401(k) contribution is greater for those who also have a DB plan.

Contributions to the plans of employees with a 401(k) are shown in columns (9) to (12). We separately report DB contributions in firms with and without 401(k) plans, as well as contributions to 401(k) plans in firms with and without DB plans. The nominal sum of pension contributions on behalf of employees covered by a 401(k) plan over the years 1984–97 is $1,061 billion. About $252 billion was contributed to the DB plans of 401(k) enrollees with dual coverage, about $499 billion to the plans of those with dual coverage, and about $309 billion to the plans of those enrolled only in a 401(k) plan.

How much higher might DB plan contributions have been in the absence of 401(k) plans? We consider two alternative scenarios that put an upper bound on the displacement of DB contributions by 401(k) contributions. First, we assume that all persons who have stand-alone 401(k) plans would otherwise have had stand-alone DB plans in the absence of the 401(k) program. (We also assume that DB contributions for persons with both 401(k) plans and DB plans are unchanged.) As a practical matter it is unlikely that most firms that now offer only 401(k)s—especially small firms—would ever offer DB plans in the absence of 401(k) plans, so this assumption should produce an upper bound on the amount of substitution.

Under this scenario, contributions to all DB plans would have totaled about $466 billion from 1984 to 1997. This is shown in column (13), which is the product of columns (3) and (7). This $466 billion is composed of $252 billion of actual contributions to DB plans by persons with dual coverage and $214 billion in additional DB contributions that would result if all stand-alone 401(k) plans were converted to DB plans, and if these converted plans then exhibited the average contribution rate for stand-alone DB plans. This additional $214 billion of DB contributions represents only 26 percent of the $1,061 billion of the total contributions to the plans of 401(k) participants.

The low estimate is the consequence of two factors. First, stand-alone 401(k) plans are a relatively recent phenomenon. Much of the growth of

401(k) participation, particularly in the early years, is among persons who retained DB coverage. For these persons there is little or no displacement. Second, average contribution rates to DB plans are substantially lower than contribution rates to 401(k) plans. Replacing a stand-alone DB plan by a stand-alone 401(k) plan will, on average, increase contributions per participant.

A less extreme scenario, but one that is still likely to overstate substitution, is that the entire reduction in DB plan participation between 1984 and 1997 can be attributed to displacement caused by the introduction of the 401(k) program. The number of DB participants displaced in each year under this scenario is shown in column (14). "Lost" contributions to DB plans under this scenario are shown in column (15), and they total about $86 billion. This is only 11 percent of all 401(k) contributions.

The absence of large-scale displacement is the consequence of several factors. First, much of the growth of 401(k) plans, particularly in the early years, is among persons who retain their DB coverage. Second, 401(k) contributions as a share of salary are about twice as great as DB plan contributions as a share of salary, so even in the most extreme case, 401(k) assets could not have been fully offset by a reduction in what otherwise would have been the DB assets of the 401(k) enrollees. Indeed, the earlier discussion suggests that accumulation of retirement assets resulting from 401(k) contributions is likely to be substantially greater than the accumulation from contributions to DB plans. Finally, the decline in the number of persons covered by DB plans but not by 401(k) plans is too small to account for much of the 401(k) growth.

1.4.4   Projections of 401(k) Assets

The foregoing calculations compare aggregate 401(k) plan assets with aggregate DB plan assets in two hypothetical scenarios. We can also make comparisons between 401(k) plan assets and DB plan assets using household-level data. Data from the HRS suggest that in 1992, the mean value of assets in DB plans was $54,800 for persons aged 51 to 61. The average for employees of all ages would be much less. In PVW (1998a), we estimated how much the 1992 HRS respondents would have accumulated in their 401(k) accounts if they had been eligible for 401(k) plans over their entire working lives. Based on our projections of the participation rates of future cohorts, we made forward-looking projections, one for the cohort reaching age sixty-five in 2025, and the other for those reaching age sixty-five in 2035. We compared our projected 401(k) assets to Social Security assets, assuming that the Social Security program remained unchanged.

We can also compare projected 401(k) assets to DB pension assets. While Social Security assets of HRS respondents averaged $103,392, DB pension assets average only $54,500. PVW (2001) suggest that projected 401(k) assets would be 136 to 451 percent of DB pension plan assets (depending on how contributions are invested), assuming no reduction in DB assets. Even if DB pension assets were set to zero for this cohort, which is tantamount to assuming that 401(k) plans crowded out all DB plans, there would still be substantial incremental 401(k) wealth. Data on 401(k) participation rates and contributions that have become available since we made our projections lead us to believe that, if anything, these 401(k) asset projections may underestimate future 401(k) assets.

The "cohort approach" used to obtain the projections described above has the advantage of combining all survey respondents. It is therefore not contaminated by saver heterogeneity. It is also unaffected by differences in the lifetime accumulation profiles of DB and DC assets, because the comparison is between the realized assets of persons at, or approaching, retirement. These comparisons reflect the realized assets, after a lifetime of pension saving, that are available to support retirement consumption.

1.4.5 The "Eligibility Experiment" Applied to Defined Benefit Plan Assets

In PVW (1998a), we used data from the SIPP to compare the financial assets and home equity of families eligible for a 401(k) plan with the assets of families who were not eligible. We found little difference in the assets of eligible and noneligible families in 1984—near the introduction of the 401(k) program. By 1991, however, the assets of the eligible group were substantially greater than those of the ineligible group. We concluded that there was essentially no substitution of 401(k) assets for other financial assets or for home equity. This comparison is the basis for our comparison of the pension assets of HRS respondents.

Following the same idea, we considered whether the apparent increase in the financial assets of the 401(k) eligible groups could have been offset by a reduction in their DB assets. For this to have happened, the DB coverage of persons who became eligible for a 401(k) plan would have had to decline. The results, however, are difficult to interpret. We now explain why and offer our interpretation of the data patterns.

In 1984, there was little difference in the non-IRA-401(k) financial assets or the home equity assets of the eligible and ineligible groups. But, the eligible group was much more likely to have a DB plan, especially at the lower income levels, than it was in later years. By 1991, there was still little difference in the non-IRA-401(k) financial assets or the home equity assets of the two groups. But the net total financial assets of the eligible group were much greater than the financial assets of the ineligible group. There is no measure of DB plan assets for either year in the SIPP. Could the DB plan assets of the eligible group, relative to those of the ineligible group, have fallen enough to offset the increase in financial assets of the eligibles? To judge the likelihood of this, we considered the change in the DB coverage of the two groups.

The key DB numbers are the percent change between 1984 and 1991 in DB coverage of eligible and ineligible families. The percent decline in DB coverage was much greater for the ineligible group than for the eligible group. One might judge from this fact that there was not a disproportionate fall in the DB assets of the eligible group. But interpretation of the data is confounded by two trends. One is the general decline over time in the proportion of employees covered by a DB plan, which would affect both the eligible and the ineligible groups. The other trend is the increase in 401(k) eligibility. As 401(k) eligibility increases, families who were ineligible become eligible. The effect of this movement from ineligible to eligible status on the percent of eligibles covered by a DB plan depends on the premove DB coverage of the new 401(k) eligibles.

Suppose we rely on Ippolito and Thompson's (2000) result that existing DB plans are very rarely terminated when 401(k) plans are started, and we accept our previous result that once dual DB-401(k) coverage is established, subsequent loss in DB coverage is very unlikely. The HRS data alone do not enable us to disentangle the various determinants of DB coverage. But our attempts to match the shift in the DB coverage of the 401(k) eligible and ineligible groups suggest that during this period, most of those who moved from ineligible to eligible status had a DB plan before becoming eligible—reducing the proportion of the ineligible group with a DB plan and increasing the proportion of the eligible group with a DB plan.

1.4.6   Cohort Analysis of Defined Benefit versus 401(k) Substitution

We emphasized before that if the increase in 401(k) assets is to be offset by a reduction in DB assets, the reductions must come for the most part through a reduction in DB participation. We showed that the reduction over time in the DB coverage of 401(k) participants with dual 401(k) and DB coverage was very small, and concluded that shifting composition of the 401(k) eligible pool was the most likely explanation for changing DB participation rates of eligibles and ineligibles. Another way to evaluate the extent of the reduction in DB participation with the increase in 401(k) plans is to consider cohort data. Figure 1.19 shows the relationship between 401(k) eligibility and participation in DB plans for three cohorts, using data from the SIPP for 1984, 1987, 1991, 1993, and 1995. These data span the first thirteen years of the 401(k) program. Each cohort is identified by its age in 1984. For example, the C(44) cohort is followed from ages forty-four to fifty-five.

Within each cohort, there were enormous increases in 401(k) eligibility. But the within-cohort increases in 401(k) eligibility are not nearly offset by corresponding within-cohort reductions in DB participation. Indeed, for the two younger cohorts, both DB participation and 401(k) eligibility increase with age. There is no evidence of DB-for-401(k) offset, with rising 401(k) participation associated with declining DB plan coverage. These data pertain to all employed persons, and are not confounded by the "mix-

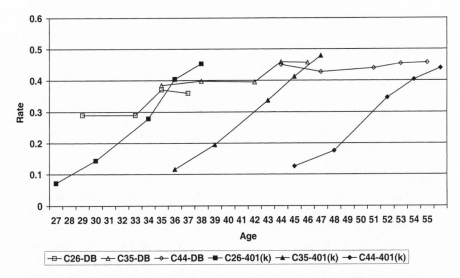

Fig. 1.19   DB participation and 401(k) eligibility: Data for three cohorts

ture" problem that makes the results of the eligibility experiment difficult to evaluate.

The evidence in figure 1.19 does not necessarily imply that 401(k) plans did not displace any DB plans. Perhaps DB participation would have risen more rapidly were it not for the spread of 401(k) plans, or firms would have offered more generous defined benefit plans if 401(k) plans had not expanded. But it seems to us extremely unlikely that DB plan participation would have increased, other things being equal, as quickly as 401(k) plans spread. For example, for a cohort like the C(44) group, it is likely that DB participation would have changed little with age, as figure 1.19 shows, even if 401(k) participation had not increased.

In addition, the 401(k) data show very large cohort effects. At any age, successively younger cohorts are much more likely to be eligible for a 401(k) plan. There are also DB cohort effects, with successively younger cohorts less likely, on average, to be covered by a DB plan. The data for the few cohorts shown in figure 1.19, however, do not reveal this trend. (The cohort data are only shown through age fifty-five. The SIPP data do not allow correction for the more rapid retirement of persons covered by DB plans after the plan early retirement age, which is often at age fifty-five. Thus at older ages it is not possible to use these data to make accurate comparisons of 401(k) and DB plan participation rates.)

1.5   Retirement Plan Substitution among Older Workers: HRS Evidence

The HRS provides the most comprehensive information available on persons approaching retirement. The heads of households for HRS families were ages fifty-one to sixty-one in 1992. Some of these persons could have participated in a 401(k) plan for up to ten years by 1992. In principle the HRS data should allow estimation of the contribution of the 401(k) program to the saving of persons in this age group during the early years of the program. Such estimates might be obtained through a comparison of 401(k) eligibles and ineligibles, as described in the previous section and in PVW (1995). Unfortunately, because the HRS asks respondents whether they *contribute* to a 401(k) plan, not whether they are *eligible* to contribute, it is not possible to directly estimate the 401(k) eligibility effect.

In this section, we explain the problems of inferring 401(k) eligibility status in the HRS. We then discuss estimates of 401(k) eligibility based on adjustments that at least partially address these problems. Finally, we use these estimates to analyze the relationship between 401(k) eligibility and pension plan assets. Consistent with the results reported previously, we find no evidence that the increase in 401(k) assets was offset by a reduction in DB assets. We believe, however, that comprehensive determination of 401(k) eligibility status in the HRS is not possible and that our HRS results are likely to underestimate the net gain in pension retirement assets from the 401(k) program.

The relationship between 401(k) plans and DB retirement assets in the 1992 HRS is also the focus of a recent study by Engelhardt (2000). He concludes that DB assets are higher among households ineligible for a 401(k) than among those eligible for a 401(k), suggesting substitution of 401(k) for DB pension assets. The findings presented previously suggest that employees covered by 401(k) programs should have more retirement assets than employees not covered by a 401(k) plan. We find that a key reason for the difference between Engelhardt's conclusions and ours is the assignment of eligibility status, which is critical to determining pension wealth.

1.5.1 Data Limitations in the HRS

Our aim is to provide estimates of the pension and other assets of HRS respondents who were and were not eligible for a 401(k) plan. To begin, we compare DB coverage rates, for persons eligible and ineligible for a 401(k) plan, in the HRS and in other surveys. The other surveys explicitly inquire about 401(k) eligibility, whereas the HRS does not. This comparison is presented in table 1.6 and pertains to pension status on the employees' current job.[16] The HRS rates are based on the assignment of eligibility used by En-

---

16. The HRS provides some information on pension status on prior jobs as well. We restrict attention to the current job since it is difficult to determine 401(k) eligibility on prior jobs. Many employees have rolled prior 401(k) balances into IRAs, and thus we are likely to underestimate 401(k) eligibility on prior jobs. The HRS percentages in the table pertain to respondents who indicated that they had a DB or 401(k) plan. We have made no attempt here to allocate other responses such as "both," "don't know," and "DC-type unknown." We have also dropped self-employed persons.

Table 1.6   Percent of 401(k) Eligibles and Ineligibles with a DB Pension, by Survey

Survey and Year	Eligibles	Ineligibles	Ratio
1992 HRS	40.8	43.6	0.94
Form 5500	55.7	—	
1993 CPS	53.9	25.4	2.12
1991 SIPP	69.5	28.4	2.45
1995 SCF	38.3	17.2	2.23

Source: Authors' calculations from the surveys listed in the first column of the table.

gelhardt (2000). All entries in the table are weighted and all entries except those derived from the Form 5500 data pertain to persons in the age range covered by the HRS.

The 1992 HRS stands out as the only survey in which DB coverage is higher among 401(k) ineligibles than among eligibles.[17] In the other surveys, the DB coverage rate for eligibles is more than *twice* as great as the DB coverage rate for ineligibles. The particular method used to assign eligibility is one reason for the large disparity between the HRS and other surveys. We also show later that even under alternative, and we believe more reasonable, conventions for assigning eligibility, there remains a wide gap between DB coverage rates reported in the HRS and the rates reported in other surveys.

The HRS does not inquire about eligibility for a 401(k) plan, although it asks about 401(k) contributions.[18] Consider the 1992 HRS data on 401(k) contributor status and DB coverage, shown in table 1.7. The HRS respondents report whether they contribute to a 401(k) plan and whether they are covered by a DB plan. These data are shown in the left panel of table 1.8. They pertain only to persons who indicate they are included in their employer's plan. (They differ from the HRS data in table 1.6, which were weighted and also include additional persons assumed to be eligible for a 401(k).) The unweighted percent of 401(k) contributors with a DB plan is somewhat greater than the percent of noncontributors with a DB plan—46 versus 41.7 percent. But compared to the DB coverage of 401(k) eligibles versus noneligibles reported in other surveys (table 1.6), these data for

17. Using households rather than persons, Engelhardt (2000) finds that 51 percent of the eligibles and 48 percent of the ineligibles have a DB plan. A household is classified as eligible if either member is eligible for a 401(k) plan. The data in table 1.6 are also consistent with the results of Engen, Gale, and Scholz (1994) who find the ratio of eligibles with DB coverage to ineligibles with DB coverage in the SIPP to be 1.65 in 1984, 1.77 in 1987, and 2.27 in 1991.

18. These are self-reported pension data. For persons who self-report having a pension, the HRS collected pension data from the employer. Thus persons who incorrectly self-report no pension coverage will be missing employer-reported data as well. In addition, the need to match every respondent to a pension combined with an employer response rate of only 65 percent means that fewer than half of the households have complete employer-reported pensions. Both Engelhardt (2000) and Gustman and Steinmeier (2000b) show an enormous degree of conflict between self-reported and firm-reported pension status.

Table 1.7	HRS 1992 Reported 401(k) Contributor Data and Illustrative Inferred 401(k) Eligibility

	Reported in the HRS 401(k) Contributor			Inferred from External Sources 401(k) Eligible		
DB Coverage	Yes	No	All	Yes	No	All
Number						
DB	622	1,699	2,321	919	1,402	2,321
No DB	729	2,376	3,105	729	2,376	3,105
All	1,351	4,075	5,426	1,648	3,778	5,426
Percent						
DB	46.0	41.7	42.8	55.8	37.1	42.8
No DB	54.0	58.3	57.2	44.2	62.9	57.2
All	100.0	100.0	100.0	100.0	100.0	100.0

Source: Authors' calculations from the HRS.

Table 1.8	HRS Conditional Median Assets by 401(k) Eligibility Status (with eligibility determined by our random assignment method)

	Income Interval ($)					
Asset Category and Eligibility Status	<20,000	20,000–30,000	30,000–40,000	40,000–50,000	50,000–75,000	>75,000
Net Non-Retirement Financial Assets						
Eligible	3,069	3,862	5,614	8,983	14,672	33,155
Ineligible	2,897	3,069	6,310	6,250	13,966	23,690
Difference	172	793	−697	2,733	707	9,466**
Retirement Assets Other Than 401(k)						
Eligible	18,634	24,539	40,746	46,996	83,533	180,000
Ineligible	15,326	22,738	37,827	50,338	73,270	146,859
Difference	3,308	1,801	2,919	−3,342	10,263**	33,141**
Total Retirement Assets						
Eligible	20,701	34,170	50,492	60,263	101,524	240,902
Ineligible	14,580	22,909	37,862	50,748	73,814	145,626
Difference	6,120	11,261**	12,631**	9,515	27,709**	95,276**
Net Housing Equity						
Eligible	35,135	37,248	45,641	42,496	59,043	83,409
Ineligible	21,596	32,854	45,233	48,861	55,350	79,517
Difference	13,539**	4,393	409	−6,365	3,693	3,891
DB Coverage						
Eligible	0.29	0.42	0.5	0.53	0.66	0.74
Ineligible	0.2	0.35	0.53	0.54	0.63	0.61

Source: Authors' calculations from the HRS.
**Statistically significant at the 5 percent level.

contributors versus noncontributors show a very low rate of DB coverage. Given that the HRS does not provide eligibility, we want to convert 401(k) contributor status data to 401(k) eligibility status data. In particular, to make the conversion we must identify persons among the 401(k) noncontributors who are eligible to contribute to a 401(k) plan.

There are two separate determinations to be made. The empirically more important case involves noncontributing 401(k) eligibles who are covered by another pension. These persons would be among the 1,699 persons in table 1.7 who do not contribute to a 401(k) plan, but have a DB plan. The sequence of questions in the first three waves of the HRS provides no way for a noncontributing 401(k) eligible, also covered by a DB plan, to self-identify as eligible for a 401(k) plan; such information will be available in the 2000 wave of the HRS. Since a large portion of 401(k) eligibles are covered by a DB plan, it is likely that a large fraction of the noncontributors with a DB plan are in fact eligible for a 401(k) plan. Engelhardt (2000) assumes that all of these are ineligibles without a DB plan, thus likely misclassifying a large fraction of persons with a DB plan.

Here, we simply want to illustrate what the unknown eligibility numbers could be. Suppose we convert the contributor data to eligibility data as follows. We know from the Form 5500 data that about 82 percent of eligibles contributed to their 401(k) plan in 1992. Thus there would be $1,351/.82 = 1,648$ persons eligible for a 401(k) – 297 more than contributed to a 401(k). Using an extreme example, suppose that all of the 297 had a DB plan but did not contribute. Then there would be $919 = 622 + 297$ eligibles with a DB plan, and 1,402 ineligibles with a DB plan. This estimate is shown in the right panel of table 1.7. The key point is that even with this assumption, only 55.8 percent of the eligible group would have a DB plan compared to 37.1 percent for the ineligible group, a ratio of 1.5. This ratio is still much lower than the ratios from any of the other surveys. Thus it would appear that if the data reported in the HRS are used to determine eligibility, the implied proportions of 401(k) eligibles and ineligibles with a DB plan are far from the values in other surveys that explicitly inquire about eligibility.

There is in fact an additional problem in the HRS data, and a second determination to be made, which is not addressed in the table 1.7 illustration. Respondents are asked whether they are "included" in a pension plan. Respondents who say no (and presumably do not have a DB plan), are asked whether they are eligible for a pension plan offered by their employer. About 175 respondents say yes. But we don't know what kind of pension is offered. In particular, is it a DB, 401(k), or a non-401(k) DC, or some other plan? Engelhardt (2000) assumes that all of these persons are 401(k) eligibles without a DB plan.[19] Thus this assumption adds respondents with no

---

19. Evidence from other surveys suggests that not all of these persons are eligible for a 401(k) plan. The 1995 Survey of Consumer Finances (SCF) asked a similar question but fol-

DB coverage to the pool of 401(k) eligibles. Recall that the first—and more serious—misclassification adds eligibles with DB coverage to the pool of 401(k) ineligibles. These two misclassifications bias upward the DB assets of 401(k) ineligibles, and bias downward the DB assets of 401(k) eligibles. The combined effect of these two forms of misclassification may be substantial.

1.5.2   HRS Results Based on Eligibility

There is no easy way to determine with certainty the 401(k) eligibility status of HRS respondents. The convention used by Engelhardt (2000), as explained previously, biases downward the proportion of 401(k) eligibles with a DB plan and biases upward the proportion of 401(k) ineligibles with a DB plan. We adopt assumptions that we believe are more neutral with respect to DB coverage by 401(k) eligibility status.

We need to determine the eligibility of each 401(k) respondent. All 401(k) contributors are clearly eligible. Among 401(k) noncontributors, some are eligible and some are not. Our approach is to determine the proportion of 401(k) noncontributors that is actually eligible to contribute to a 401(k) plan. We do this based on proportions of noncontributing eligibles that have a DB, as is evident in the Form 5500 data. In 1992, 82 percent of 401(k) eligibles in the Form 5500 data were 401(k) contributors. Let E_E be the total number of eligibles, E_C be the number of observed contributors (all eligible), and E_N be the number of noncontributors that should be eligible. Then the number of eligibles is $E_E = E_C + E_N$. From the Form 5500 data, the ratio of contributors to eligibles is $E_C/E_E = 0.82$. The number of additional eligibles among the HRS noncontributors is then $E_N = E_C(1/.82 - 1)$. Thus, the proportion of noncontributors that should be eligible is $P = (1/0.82 - 1)(E_C/N_N)$, where N_N is the total number of noncontributors.

These calculations suggest that the percentage of noncontributors predicted to be eligible to contribute to a 401(k) plan in the HRS is equal to P percent of all observed noncontributors. Of this P percent, the Form 5500 data indicate that 55.7 percent have a DB plan on their current job, and 44.3 percent do not. Thus we randomly reassign $.557 \times P$ percent of 401(k) noncontributors with a DB plan in the HRS to be noncontributing eligibles. We also randomly reassign $.443 \times P$ percent of 401(k) noncontributors without a DB plan to be noncontributing eligibles. This approach as-

---

lowed it up by asking what type of plan the respondent was eligible to be included in. Eighty percent of the weighted responses from persons aged fifty-one to sixty-one indicated a 401(k) plan for their first job, and 36 percent for their second job (62.2 percent overall). The 1993 Current Population Survey (CPS) asks for the reason why a respondent is eligible, but not included. Only one-quarter of the respondents indicated that they chose not to contribute, which would suggest nonparticipation in a 401(k) plan. Instead, part-time status and lack of tenure with the employer were the most frequently cited reasons for exclusion from an employer's pension plan. These other surveys suggest that some of cases assumed to be 401(k) eligibles in the HRS are instead persons not covered by their employer's DB plan.

sures that the DB coverage rate of the respondents added to the eligibility pool is the same as the DB coverage rate of the respondents already in the pool.

Unfortunately, the Form 5500 benchmark data is not available by age or by income. The 55.7 percent dual coverage rate that we use is undoubtedly a low estimate for the HRS respondents (aged fifty-one to sixty-one in 1992) because it applies to all ages, and we know from the previous cohort data that older persons are more likely to have a DB plan. The other surveys also show that the percent with a DB plan increases with age.

We have adopted a similar assignment convention for missing and ambiguous responses to pension questions in the HRS. If a respondent is "included" in a pension, then the respondent is asked for the plan type—DB or DC. The respondent is asked to indicate the type of pension for up to three pensions. The available choices include: "DB," "DC," or "both." A significant number of respondents did not provide a response. We use the following conventions. First, respondents answering "DB" were coded as having a DB plan. Second, respondents answering "DC" were then asked about the type of DC plan. The choices "thrift or saving" or "401K/403B/ SRA" or any combination involving these two choices were coded as 401(k) plans. The other choices offered pertain to non-401(k)-DC plans. For respondents indicating that they have a DC plan, but not providing the type of DC plan, we randomly assign the plan as 401(k) or not 401(k) in proportion to the number of valid responses indicating that they had 401(k) and non-401(k)-DC plans. Third, persons indicating "both" as the type of pension were coded as having a DB plan *and* a DC plan. For these respondents the DC plan is randomly assigned to be a 401(k) plan based on the ratio of 401(k) plans to all DC plans among completed responses. Fourth, a significant number of respondents who indicated they were included in a pension plan did not provide the type. These persons were randomly assigned as having a DB plan or a 401(k) plan in the same proportions as completed responses.

All of the previous calculations are done at the level of the respondent. After these assignments are made, we combine the individual data to obtain assignments on a family basis. The asset data is reported on a family basis. A family is a 401(k) contributor, or 401(k) eligible, if either partner is a contributor or is eligible.

Table 1.8 presents results comparing the assets of persons eligible and ineligible for a 401(k) plan.[20] The key results are in the panel labeled "total retirement assets." Total retirement assets are substantially higher (and the difference is statistically significant for all but the lowest income interval)

20. These are the results of weighted median regressions for 4,895 households. Each household had to have at least one member working and not self-employed. Covariates include marital status and the age and education of the head of household. Conditional median asset balances are evaluated at the sample means of the covariates.

for the 401(k) eligible group. The panel just above shows that retirement assets other than 401(k) assets do not differ much by eligibility status, except for the two highest income intervals. In these top intervals, the assets of eligibles are higher than the assets of ineligibles. Thus these estimates suggest that the accumulation of 401(k) assets was not offset by a reduction in the DB assets of the HRS respondents. Nonretirement financial assets do not differ much by eligibility status. Some of the cells show zeros because fewer than half of the observations have nonzero values, and thus the median is zero.

As previously explained, the HRS data—even after our assignment assumptions—are likely to exaggerate the proportion of 401(k) ineligibles with a DB plan, relative to the proportion of eligibles with a DB plan. After assignment of eligibility, the proportion of 401(k)-eligible households with DB plans is 59.3 percent and the proportion of ineligibles is 47 percent. The ratio is 1.26, which is still much lower than the ratio reported in other surveys. The coverage percent by income interval is reported in the bottom panel of table 1.8. The SIPP-based ratios reported in table 1.6 exceed 2, when averaged over all income groups. Thus we believe that the calculations in table 1.8 underestimate the addition to pension wealth of families eligible for a 401(k) plan.

1.6   Conclusions

The way Americans save for retirement has changed dramatically in the last two decades. In 1980, 92 percent of private retirement saving contributions were to employer-based plans and 64 percent of these contributions, or 59 percent of all contributions, were to DB plans. In 1999, about 85 percent of private contributions went to accounts directed largely by individuals. In this paper we have analyzed a broad range of aggregate and household data to understand the implications of this change.

The aggregate data show that assets in retirement plans have increased fivefold, relative to wage and salary earnings, over the past two decades. The increase in these assets to support retirement will likely mean very large increases in the assets of future retirees. The increase in DC assets has been so large that it is unlikely that a significant fraction of the growth in DC assets occurred at the expense of reduced DB assets.

In addition, over the past two decades, the annual retirement plan contribution rate has been over 5 percent, as a proportion of NIPA personal income, and over 8 percent relative to NIPA wage and salary earnings. Both are much higher than the NIPA personal saving rate, which is now close to zero. The treatment of retirement plan contributions and payouts in the NIPAs contributes to the very low measured personal saving rate.

Retirement saving today would likely be substantially greater if Congress had not enacted legislation in the late 1980s to limit firm contributions to DB pension plans. In the absence of this legislation, and the favorable asset market returns during the 1990s that reduced the need for employers to contribute to their DB plans, the retirement plan contribution rate would have been at least 1 percentage point higher in the late 1990s than it actually was. It is also likely that the retirement plan contribution rate would be much higher today if it were not for the retrenchment of the IRA program after 1986.

On average, the contribution per active participant to 401(k) plans has been about twice as large as contributions to DB plans, suggesting much higher wealth accumulation under 401(k) than under DB plans. In addition, differences in the pattern of saving by age can have an important effect on retirement asset accumulation under the two plans. From the employee perspective, retirement saving through a DB or DC plan each year can be thought of as the increase in the financial support that each plan will provide in retirement. Employee retirement saving under a DC plan is quite transparent to the employee, while annual employee saving under a DB plan is quite opaque and unlikely to be clearly understood. The pattern of saving by age is much different under DB and 401(k) plans, as we show using a hypothetical DB plan. The pattern of pension wealth accrual in the DB plan typically provides a large incentive to retire early. As a consequence, DB employees will typically accumulate assets over fewer years than DC employees. Taken together, the higher contribution rate under DC plans and the greater number of years over which assets accumulate are likely to increase very substantially the asset accumulation in DC plans relative to DB plans.

Our analysis of household-level data on retirement saving yields a number of findings that complement the conclusions from the aggregate analysis. Dual coverage under both 401(k) and DB plans is common, but it has declined over time as more employees without a prior DB plan have been offered 401(k)s. Over 80 percent of 401(k) eligibles had a DB plan in 1984, and about 43 percent had one in 1997. Few 401(k) participants covered by a DB plan—only about 1 percent each year—subsequently lose DB coverage. Our estimates suggest that between 1984 and 1997, total contributions to all pension plans of persons with a 401(k) plan were three times as great as what contributions to DB plans would have been in the absence of the 401(k) program. The displacement of DB plan contributions was probably less than 11 percent of the total plan contributions of 401(k) participants.

Based on our prior independent projections, the mean 401(k) balances of persons who will reach retirement age in 2035 will be 1.4 to 4.5 times as great, depending on asset market returns, as mean DB balances, assuming no decline in DB coverage. Cohort analysis shows a decline in DB coverage for successively younger cohorts, but no within-cohort reduction in DB coverage as 401(k) coverage increased.

The HRS data suggest that accumulation of 401(k) assets substantially increased the total retirement assets of persons approaching retirement in 1992. We find no evidence of substitution of 401(k) assets for DB assets for persons in the HRS age group.

Appendix A
Data Sources

Figure 1.1: Private retirement assets are the sum of DB, DC pension reserves from the Flow of Funds Accounts (FFA), and IRA assets from Sabelhaus (2000). Total retirement assets also include state, local, and federal pension reserves from the FFA. Wage and salary disbursements are from table 2.1 of the NIPA. Pension assets held by life insurance companies are excluded.

Figure 1.2: The DB and DC assets for 1985–99 are from the FFA. For the years 1975–84, estimates are obtained by applying the ratio of DB to DC assets from Form 5500 filings to total assets from the FFA. The IRA assets are from Sabelhaus (2000). The figure excludes private pension assets held by life insurance companies.

Figure 1.3: All series are from the FFA.

Figure 1.4: Housing equity is from the FFA. Other assets are total net worth (from the FFA), less housing equity, less private retirement assets as defined in note to figure 1.1. Personal disposable income is from table 2.1 of the NIPA.

Figure 1.5, panel A: The DB and DC contributions are from Form 5500 reports. The data for 1998 and 1999 are authors' estimates. The IRA and Keogh contributions are from the Internal Revenue Service (IRS) Statistics of Income. The IRA contributions pertain to tax-deductible contributions only.

Figure 1.5, panel B: Private pension contributions are the sum of the components described in panel A. State and local and federal contributions are from the NIPA.

Figure 1.6, panel A: Private pension contributions are the sum of the components described in figure 1.5, panel A. Total pension contributions are the sum of the components described in figure 1.5, panel B. Personal disposable income is from the NIPA.

Figure 1.6, panel B: Private pension contributions are the sum of the components described in figure 1.5, panel A. Total pension contributions are the sum of the components described in figure 1.5, panel B. Wage and salary earnings (disbursements) are from the NIPA.

Figure 1.7 and figure 1.8, panel A: All series except IRA and Keogh participants are from the Form 5500. The IRA and Keogh participants are from (SOI). 401(k) data for 1982 and 1983 are authors' estimates.

Figure 1.8, panel B: The 401(k) series is from the Form 5500. 401(k) data for 1982 and 1983 are authors' estimates. The IRA data are from the IRS Statistics of Income.

Figure 1.8, panel C: The Keogh data are from the IRS Statistics of Income.

Figures 1.9, 1.10, and 1.11: All DB and DC plan data are from the Form 5500, whereas Keogh data are from the IRS Statistics of Income.

Figure 1.12: Actual pension contributions are the same as in Figure 1.6, panel b. The DB adjusted series is as described in the text. Data to calculate this series are not available after 1996. Wage and salary earnings (disbursements) are from the NIPA.

Figure 1.13: All data are from the Form 5500.

Figure 1.14: IRA contributions are from the IRS Statistics of Income. The IRA contributions pertain to tax-deductible contributions only. IRA benefits are from Sabelhaus (2000).

Figures 1.15, 1.16, and 1.17: Authors' calculations as described in the text.

Figure 1.18: DB, DC, and 401(k) participants are from the Form 5500. IRA and Keogh participants are from the IRS Statistics of Income. Wage and Salary employment from the DOL web page.

Figure 1.19: Authors' calculations from the SIPP.

Appendix B
The DB Loss Ratio from Dual Coverage Participants

The top panel of table 1B.1 shows the raw data, calculated from Form 5500 filings, that we use to estimate the DB loss ratio. The lower panel (third column) determines the additions to existing plans. The number of additional participants to existing plans from years t to $t + 1$ is simply the increase in total participants, less the participants in plans just started that year. The identity governing its evolution is:

number in 401(k) with a DB in year $t + 1$
    = number in 401(k) with a DB in year t
        + number in *new* 401(k) with a DB in year $t + 1$
        − [(number in 401(k) with DB in t)
        + (DB coverage additions to existing 401(k)s)] · (DB loss rate)

The DB loss rate is the proportion of persons with a DB who drop (or lose) the DB plan. Positive values of the loss rate indicate that some 401(k) participants with DB coverage are moving to situations without such coverage. We assume that among the additional participants in existing 401(k) plans, the percent with a DB plan is the same as the percent with a DB in existing plans in the prior year. The components of the loss ratio calculations are shown in the last section of the table. DB denotes the number of workers

Table 1B.1   Calculation DB Plan Loss Ratio

Year	All Plans		Plans in 1st Year		Pre-existing Plans		Participant Increase in All Plans $[T(t+1)-T(t)]$	Additions to Existing Plans		Loss Ratio (l)	Participants Losing DB Plans
	Active Participants (T)	% with DB Plan (t)	Active Participants (n)	% with DB Plan (p)	Active Participants (N)	% with DB Plan (P)		Participants from New Plans	Additions to Existing Plans $[T(t)-n(t+1)-T(t+1)]$		
1990	20,365,592	61.8	1,113,387	32.8	19,252,205	63.5	763,965	1,237,212	−473,247	0.051	612,973
1991	21,129,557	58.2	1,237,212	26.1	19,892,345	60.2	2,934,691	1,587,113	1,347,578	−0.061	−837,105
1992	24,064,248	55.7	1,587,113	19.0	22,477,135	58.3	1,512,070	1,232,422	279,648	0.011	156,999
1993	25,576,318	52.9	1,232,422	22.9	24,343,896	54.4	1,665,475	817,009	848,466	−0.007	−105,307
1994	27,241,793	51.0	817,009	32.9	26,424,784	51.6	3,561,227	1,028,994	2,532,233	−0.017	−281,570
1995	30,803,020	46.9	1,028,994	28.0	29,774,026	47.6	3,051,407	873,167	2,178,240	−0.046	−769,228
1996	33,854,427	45.8	873,167	39.4	32,981,260	46.0	3,861,941	1,377,491	2,484,450	−0.010	−182,672
1997	37,716,368	42.4	1,377,491	22.5	36,338,877	43.2					
Total							17,350,776	8,153,408	9,197,368		−1,405,910

Determination of Loss Ratio

Year	Existing Plans with DB (NP)	New Plans with DB (np)	Additions $[A(t+1)]$ $(NP+np)$	$[DB(t+1)]$	Additions with DB $[A(t+1)P(t)]$
1990	12,229,001	365,080	12,594,080	12,295,289	−300,606
1991	11,973,202	322,912	12,296,115	13,401,380	811,107
1992	13,099,674	301,075	13,400,750	13,527,315	162,979
1993	13,245,514	282,225	13,527,738	13,898,763	461,650
1994	13,629,904	268,551	13,898,454	14,446,616	1,306,126
1995	14,160,527	287,604	14,448,131	15,508,713	1,035,971
1996	15,164,783	344,202	15,508,986	15,987,968	1,142,350
1997	15,680,225	309,935	15,990,161		
Total					4,619,577

Source: Authors' calculations from Form 5500 filings.

with DB plans, N denotes the number in existing plans, P the proportion in existing 401(k) plans with a DB plan (which equals the proportion of workers added to existing 401(k) plans who have a DB plan), n the number of workers in new plans, p the proportion in new plans with a DB plan, A the number of additions to participants in existing plans, l the proportion of those with a DB who drop the plan, and t the year. The formula for the loss ratio is then:

$$DB_{t+1} = (N_t P_t + n_t p_t + n_{t+1} p_{t+1}) - (N_t P_t + n_t p_t + A_{t+1} P_t)l$$

$$l = \frac{(N_t P_t + n_t p_t + n_{t+1} p_{t+1}) - DB_{t+1}}{(N_t P_t + n_t p_t + A_{t+1} P_t)}$$

References

Benjamin, Daniel J. 2003. Does 401(k) eligibility increase saving? Evidence from propensity score subclassification. *Journal of Public Economics* 87 (May): 1259–90.

Bernheim, B. Douglas, and John Shoven. 1988. Pension funding and saving. In *Pensions in the U.S. economy,* ed. Zvi Bodie, John Shoven, and David A. Wise, 85–111. Chicago: University of Chicago Press.

Burtless, Gary, and Joseph F. Quinn. 2000. Retirement trends and policies to encourage work among older Americans. Boston College. Mimeograph.

Coile, Courtney, and Jonathan Gruber. 2000. Social Security and retirement. NBER Working Paper no. 7830. Cambridge, Mass.: National Bureau of Economic Research, August.

Engelhardt, Gary. 2000. Have 401(k)s raised household saving? Evidence from the Health and Retirement Survey. Syracuse University. Mimeograph.

Engen, Eric, and William Gale. 2000. The effects of 401(k) plans on household wealth: Differences across earnings groups. NBER Working Paper no. 8032. Cambridge, Mass.: National Bureau of Economic Research, December.

Engen, Eric, William Gale, and John Karl Scholz. 1994. Do saving incentives work? *Brookings Papers on Economic Activity,* Issue no. 1:85–179. Washington, D.C.: Brookings Institution.

Friedberg, Leora, and Anthony Webb. 2000. The impact of 401(k) plans on retirement. Discussion Paper no. 2000-30. San Diego: University of California.

Gale, William, and John Sabelhaus. 1999. Perspectives on the household saving rate. *Brookings Papers on Economic Activity,* Issue no. 1:181–224. Washington, D.C.: Brookings Institution.

Gruber, Jonathan, and David A. Wise. 1998. Social Security and retirement: An international perspective. *American Economic Review, Papers and Proceedings* 88 (2): 158–63.

———. 1999. *Social security and retirement around the world.* Chicago: University of Chicago Press.

Gustman, Alan, and Thomas Steinmeier. 1989. An analysis of pension benefit formulas, pension wealth, and incentives from pensions. *Research in Labor Economics* 10:53–106.

———. 1992. The stampede towards defined contribution plans: Fact or fiction? *Industrial Relations* 31 (2): 361–69.

———. 2000a. Employer provided pension data in the NLS Mature Women's Survey and in the Health and Retirement Study. In *Worker well-being,* ed. Solomon Polachek, 215–52. New York: Elsevier Science.

———. 2000b. What people don't know about their pensions and Social Security: An analysis using linked data from the Health and Retirement Study. Dartmouth College. Mimeograph.

Ippolito, Richard A. 1995. Toward explaining the growth of defined contribution plans. *Industrial Relations* 34 (1): 1–19.

———. 2001. Reversion taxes, contingent benefits, and the decline in pension funding. *Journal of Law and Economics* 44 (1): 199–232.

Ippolito, Richard A., and John Thompson. 2000. The survival rate of defined benefit pension plans, 1987–1995. *Industrial Relations* 39 (2): 228–45.

Kotlikoff, Laurence J., and David A. Wise. 1987. The incentive effect of private pension plans. In *Issues in Pension Economics,* ed. Zvi Bodie, John Shoven, and David A. Wise, 283–336. Chicago: University of Chicago Press.

———. 1988. Pension backloading, wage taxes, and work disincentives. In *Tax policy and the economy,* Vol. 2, ed. L. Summers, 161–96. Cambridge, Mass.: MIT Press.

———. 1989. *The wage carrot and the pension stick.* Kalamazoo, Mich.: W. E. Upjohn Institute for Employment Research.

Katona, George. 1965. *Private pensions and individual saving.* Ann Arbor: Institute for Social Research, University of Michigan.

Lazear, Edward. 1985. Incentive effects of pensions. In *Pensions, labor, and individual choice,* ed. David A. Wise, 253–82. Chicago: University of Chicago Press.

LeBlanc, Pierre. 2002. *Essays on tax-deferred saving in Canada.* Ph.D. Diss. Harvard University, Cambridge, Mass.

Lumsdaine, Robin L., James H. Stock, and David A. Wise. 1990. Efficient windows and labor force reduction. *Journal of Public Economics* 43:131–59.

———. 1992. Three models of retirement: Computational complexity versus predictive validity. In *Topics in the economics of aging,* ed. David A. Wise, 19–57. Chicago: University of Chicago Press.

———. 1994. Pension plan provisions and retirement: Men & women, Medicare, and models. In *Studies in the Economics of Aging,* ed. David A. Wise, 183–220. Chicago: University of Chicago Press.

Lusardi, Annamarie, Jonathan Skinner, and Steven F. Venti. 2001. Saving puzzles and saving policies in the United States. *Oxford Review of Economic Policy* 17 (1): 95–115.

Papke, Leslie. 1999. Are 401(k) plans replacing other employer-provided pensions? Evidence from panel data. *Journal of Human Resources* 34:346–68.

Papke, Leslie, Mitchell Petersen, and James Poterba. 1996. Do 401(k) plans replace other employer provided pensions? In *Advances in the economics of aging,* ed. David A. Wise, 219–36. Chicago: University of Chicago Press.

Pence, Karen. 2001. 401(k)s and household saving: New evidence from the Survey of Consumer Finances. Federal Reserve Board of Governors. Mimeograph.

Poterba, James M., Steven F. Venti, and David A. Wise. 1995. Do 401(k) contributions crowd out other private saving? *Journal of Public Economics* 58:1–32.

———. 1996. How retirement saving programs increase saving. *Journal of Economic Perspectives,* 10 (4): 91–112.

———. 1998a. Implications of rising personal retirement saving. In *Frontiers in the economics of aging,* ed. David A. Wise, 125–67. Chicago: University of Chicago Press.

———. 1998b. Personal retirement savings programs and asset accumulation: Reconciling the evidence. In *Frontiers in the economics of aging,* ed. David A. Wise, 23–106. Chicago: University of Chicago Press.

————. 2001. Pre-retirement cashouts and foregone retirement saving: Implications for 401(k) asset accumulation. In *Themes in the economics of aging,* ed. David A. Wise, 23–56. Chicago: University of Chicago Press.

Reinsdorf, Marshall, and Maria Perozek. 2002. Alternative measures of personal saving and measures of change in personal wealth. *Survey of Current Business* 82 (April): 13–24.

Sabelhaus, John. 2000. Modeling IRA accumulation and withdrawals. *National Tax Journal* 53 (4): 865–76.

Samwick, Andrew. 1998. New evidence on pensions, Social Security, and the timing of retirement. *Journal of Public Economics* 70 (November): 207–36.

Samwick, Andrew, and Jonathan Skinner. 1998. How will defined contribution pension plans affect retirement income? NBER Working Paper no. 6645. Cambridge, Mass.: National Bureau of Economic Research, July.

Samwick, Andrew, and David A. Wise. 2003. Option value estimation with Health and Retirement Study data. In *Labor markets and firm benefit policies in Japan and the United States,* ed. S. Ogura, T. Tachibanaki, and D. A. Wise, 205–28. Chicago: University of Chicago Press.

Scheiber, Sylvester, and John Shoven. 1997. The consequences of population aging on private pension fund saving and asset markets. In *The economic effects of aging in the United States and Japan,* ed. Michael Hurd and Naohiro Yashiro, 111–30. Chicago: University of Chicago Press.

Stock, James H., and David A. Wise. 1990a. Pensions, the option value of work, and retirement. *Econometrica* 58 (5): 1151–80.

————. 1990b. The pension inducement to retire: An option value analysis. In *Issues in the economics of aging,* ed. David A. Wise. Chicago: University of Chicago Press.

U.S. Department of Labor, Pension and Welfare Benefits Administration. 1999–2000. *Private pension plan bulletin: Abstract of 1996 form 5500 annual reports.* Washington, D.C.: GPO.

Comment   Sylvester J. Schieber

This paper by Poterba, Venti, and Wise (hereafter PVW) documents the substantial shift toward defined contribution plans in the employer-based segment of the U.S. retirement system in recent years. It suggests that saving through this element of the retirement system has increased as a result of the shift toward defined contribution pensions. It helps to explain what has been a puzzle to many people regarding the decline in personal saving rates recorded in recent years during a time that more and more people have been saving through their defined contribution plans.

This is an important paper because of the deliberations that are now underway regarding potential changes in the structure of the U.S. Social Security program. It is important because it indicates the direction the market-based segment of our retirement system has taken over the past twenty years or so and gives us some clues as to how people might react un-

Sylvester J. Schieber is vice president of Watson Wyatt Worldwide.

der some Social Security reform options now being discussed. It may also show the way to reform Social Security so that workers will voluntarily put more money into retirement savings, a potentially positive outcome given underfunding of retirement programs today and the demographic demands that they face.

My comments on this paper are limited to three points. First, I agree with the authors' general conclusion that the transition to personal accounts has broadened the retirement security of many American workers; however, I will argue the effect has been skewed toward the more highly paid. The evidence presented here and elsewhere suggests that this has occurred more because of restrictions in plan coverage than because of workers', even those at lower wages, unwillingness to participate in contemporary defined contribution plans when offered the opportunity. Second, I will challenge the conclusion in the paper that the growth in reliance on defined contribution plans does not appear to have shrunk the level of defined benefit provision in absolute terms. Finally, I will attempt to apply the very positive results documented in this analysis to the contemporary debate about how to reform Social Security.

The spectacular shift in the employer-sponsored retirement system since the passage of the Employee Retirement Income Security Act (ERISA) in 1975 is probably as succinctly summarized by the relative shift in contributions to plans as in any other way. Poterba, Venti, and Wise note that contributions to private defined benefit plans varied widely between 1975 and 1999 but were essentially equivalent at the beginning and end of the period. During this same time period, contributions to private defined contribution plans increased fourteenfold. At the end of the period, average contributions per worker eligible to participate in 401(k) plans were much greater than those being made to either defined benefit or defined contribution plans solely dependent on employer contributions.

Despite all of the good news in this paper, there is reason to be cautious about the results presented in it. The major problem with our employer-based segment of the retirement system is the relatively limited coverage that it provides to certain segments of the workforce. For example, it is frequently observed that only about half the U.S. workforce at any point in time is participating in an employer-sponsored retirement plan. Figure 1C.1 shows that workers at lower earnings levels have been much less likely to participate in a plan than workers at higher earnings levels. The implications of the skewed participation in employer-sponsored plans are reflected in table 6 of the PVW paper, where they show the results of simulations of the potential retirement benefits that will be available to people retiring in 2035 by lifetime earnings.

I believe that PVW's conclusion that the private defined benefit system is "on its own track," largely unaffected by the shift toward defined contribution plans, deserves further scrutiny. The reason I believe this is that I am

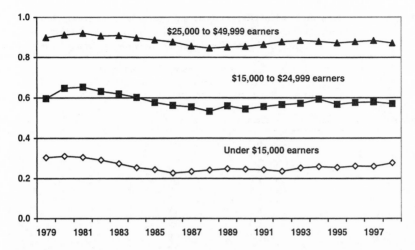

Fig. 1C.1   Pension participation rates for workers with earnings under $50,000 per year relative to those earning over $50,000 per year for selected years (amounts are in 1998 dollars): Ratio of pension coverage rate to coverage rate of those earning $50,000 or more

Source: Author's calculations from supplement of the March *Current Population Survey,* various years.

convinced the modification of existing defined benefit plans in response to the growth in supplementary defined contribution plans has been greatly delayed but is now underway. The 401(k) plans that most larger employers sponsor today evolved from thrift-saving plans that they sponsored as supplements to their defined benefit plans prior to the adoption of section 401(k) of the tax code. Employee contributions to these plans included no tax incentives and participation in them was relatively low. In addition, most of the plans had highly restricted investment options, often limiting the investment of assets to money market or Guaranteed Investment Contract (GIC) vehicles. The large employers that sponsored these plans had traditionally structured their defined benefit plans around Social Security and workers' saving behavior with specific retirement income targets in mind. The retirement income targets were set so workers could roughly maintain their preretirement standards of living after they quit working. Given the benefits provided by Social Security and the employer's defined benefit plan, the estimated saving rates required on the part of various sorts of workers could be determined. For example, one such set of estimated saving rate requirements is shown in table 1C.1.

The estimated savings rates in this case were developed for workers covered by four different defined benefit plans. These plans were selected from a sample of some 560 plans on which Watson Wyatt had benefit formulas that allowed estimation of pension benefits. From the whole set of plans,

Table 1C.1   Alternative Levels of DB Plan Generosity and the Estimated Savings Rates
                    Required to Maintain Preretirement Standards of Living from All Retirement
                    Income Sources for Workers Retiring at Age Sixty-five with Thirty Years of Service

	Required Personal Savings Rate Associated with the Pension Plan at the:			
Salary when Pension Coverage and Saving Begins	15th Percentile	40th Percentile	65th Percentile	90th Percentile
12,500	0.0	0.0	0.0	0.0
15,000	2.1	0.9	0.0	0.0
20,000	4.8	3.5	2.3	0.0
25,000	6.1	4.8	3.6	1.3
30,000	6.9	5.6	4.5	2.2
40,000	8.2	6.8	5.8	3.6
50,000	9.5	8.1	7.1	4.9
60,000	10.4	8.9	7.8	5.7
70,000	11.5	9.8	8.8	6.7
80,000	12.6	10.9	9.8	7.8

Source: McGill et al. (1996, 417).

Note: Sources of retirement income include Social Security, the employer defined benefit pension, and income financed through personal saving.

the four pension plans in the table were chosen from various points in the array of generosity of benefits provided. Someone covered by a very generous pension will not have to save as much in order to maintain preretirement living standards after retirement as a worker in a more limited plan. In the full analysis presented in McGill et al. (1996, chapters 18 and 19), target saving rates were developed for workers starting at various ages under their pension plans, retiring at various ages, and under a range of wage growth and interest rate assumptions. The set of projections shown in table 1C.1 was developed under the assumption that workers would receive a real return on their savings of 2 percent per year. The projections suggest that workers at low wage levels under most pension plans sponsored by large employers have faced relatively moderate saving requirements if they worked until normal retirement age and received even a relatively conservative return on their savings. Higher-wage workers would have to save more, primarily because of the redistributive nature of Social Security. Workers who wished to retire earlier would need to save at higher rates as well. But the rates of saving that would be required outside of Social Security and many of the pension plans that larger employers in the United States have sponsored in the past are well within the range of saving that goes on in most defined contribution plans today.

Poterba, Venti, and Wise document that workers' participation and contribution rates in 401(k) plans are relatively high where plans are offered. In addition, in virtually all plans that exist today, workers get to choose where to invest their money from a broad range of investment options. Much of the money in these plans is invested in financial assets that have paid much higher rates of return over time than was anticipated when 401(k) plans were first established (see Clark et al. 2000; Clark and Schieber 1998). The net result has been that the retirement portfolios offered by many employers have proven to be more generous than anticipated by both workers and their retirement plans sponsors. Until recently this was a fortuitous outcome to which plan sponsors paid little attention, but now there are a combination of forces that I believe are motivating employers to reconsider their retirement plan offerings. I believe the outcome of this process is that the defined benefit side of the retirement portfolio will shrink relative to the defined contribution plans that are so widely prevalent.

Poterba, Venti, and Wise have documented the slowdown in funding of defined benefit plans that arose because of various legislative actions taken after the beginning of the 1980s. Schieber and Shoven (1997) have argued that the aging of the workforce driven by the demographic composition of the U.S. population will lead to increased funding requirements for defined benefit plans as baby boom era workers approach retirement age. The front edge of the baby boom generation is now turning fifty-five, the age of early retirement eligibility in many large defined benefit plans. Throughout the latter part of the 1990s, the rapid escalation in pension asset values hid the implications of the baby boomers' aging, but recent financial markets performance is going to expose the resulting obligations that pension plan sponsors face because of the funding slowdown that PVW identify. If employers do not curtail accruals in their defined benefit plans, many of them are going to face much higher pension costs and funding requirements than they are accustomed to.

Compounding the effects of population aging on defined benefit pensions are the same demographics implications for retiree health benefits. In addition, where employers can fund at least some of their pension obligations as they accrue, they have been much more limited by the law in their ability to fund retiree health obligations. Retiree health benefit costs and obligations are expected to rise even more rapidly than those for defined benefit pensions. As a result, many employers have begun to significantly curtail or completely eliminate their retiree health benefit plans. As part of that process, many are reassessing the complete portfolio of retirement benefits that they provide. In an era where management has become very concerned about economic performance and limiting unexpected obligations, there is a natural tendency to shift away from the risks associated with promises of future benefits that cannot be fully funded as accrued.

The other major factor that has come into play in recent years is a very tight labor market compared to what managers have traditionally faced. Many employers that introduced early-retirement incentives into their defined benefit plans did so in the 1970s or 1980s when the baby boomers were rapidly expanding the available labor supply. The U.S. labor force growth rate in the 1990s was the lowest it had been since the 1950s (Lofgren, Nyce, and Schieber 2001). Indeed, very few managers still at work in the latter half of the 1990s would have remembered such a tight labor market in their working lives. By the end of the 1990s, the surplus labor phenomenon that had led to the creation of early retirement incentives had disappeared, and employers were beginning to consider ways to encourage workers to extend their working lives. At least in part, this change in attitude about keeping workers in the workforce until later in life helps to explain the shift to cash balance pensions or other types of hybrid pension plans (see Brown et al. 1999; Clark and Schieber 2004). Virtually every defined benefit plan that has been shifted to a new hybrid structure thus far has included the elimination of the early retirement incentives that were in the prior plan.

Although there have been several motivations for changing the structure of defined benefit plans, the thing that has facilitated most employers doing it has been the unexpectedly strong performance of their defined contribution plans. In that regard, the reaction of the defined benefit system to the growing dependence on individual account plans has been greatly delayed. There was a slowdown in the conversion of traditional defined benefit plans during 2000, but that was due largely to the strong negative reactions to earlier plan conversions that garnered both press and political attention. The underlying motivations for changing plans, however, have not gone away. The size of the defined contribution system today and the robust participation in it by workers will continue to give employers an opportunity to adjust their defined benefit plans to accommodate their needs to attract workers and control costs.

The final element of my comment on the PVW paper pertains to what we might learn from our 401(k) experience that would enlighten the discussion about Social Security reform. Ideally, our experience with individual account plans might help us to devise a way of reforming the system that would at once resolve the Social Security funding shortfalls and enhance retirement security for today's workers. President George W. Bush has suggested that we should reform Social Security by diverting a portion of the current payroll taxes into individual accounts. He has set down as principles that the new program not reduce benefits for people currently retired or close to retirement and that the existing commitment to disability insurance be maintained. He has said that participation in the revised plan will be voluntary and that it is not to be financed by new taxes.

The reason that Social Security is underfunded in the future is that current tax rates supporting the system cannot sustain the program if current retirement patterns persist into the future. Although virtually no one who has studied the program quibbles with this conclusion, there seems to be a tremendous reluctance on the part of policymakers to raise payroll tax rates to resolve the financing shortfall, and there is little support for raising retirement ages or implementing other universal benefit cuts. Despite the popular belief in some circles that setting up and funding individual accounts will solve the problem without having to invoke other tax increases or benefit reductions, the effects of funding will not occur rapidly enough or be sufficient to offset the projected underfunding in the system. Unless we are willing to cut benefits or raise taxes, it would seem that the laws of arithmetic dictate that we will have to put more money into the system from some other sources. That is where the 401(k) experience documented by PVW is instructive.

Consider for the sake of discussion a modified version of the plan that was put forward by Schieber and Shoven (1999) that they labeled *PSA2000*. Their original plan called for the creation of mandatory Personal Security Accounts (PSAs) as part of Social Security reform. This modified version of the PSA2000 proposal would allow workers to make a voluntary contribution of up to 2.5 percent of their pay to their PSA. For each dollar that the worker contributed to the account, Social Security would match it dollar for dollar. This would essentially replicate the way many employers sponsor and structure their 401(k) plans.

We know how people behave under 401(k) plans and might expect that they would behave somewhat similarly under this version of a PSA plan. In a prior paper to the one under review here, PVW (1998, 181) used *Current Population Survey* data to estimate that 71 percent of eligible workers during 1993 participated in a 401(k) or similar plan. Clark et al. (2000, 100) used administrative data on a sample of eighty-seven 401(k) plans to show that 79 percent of workers eligible to participate in them did so during 1995. Where the participation rates fall off in a way that would be of concern in considering a voluntary PSA proposal is at lower earnings levels, especially among younger workers. Getting workers with relatively low earnings to participate at nearly universal levels in voluntary retirement savings plans, especially very young ones, would likely take more than just a direct match of their contributions.

Once workers are motivated to participate in 401(k) plans, their contribution rates are significant as shown in table 1.2. Poterba, Venti, and Wise (1998, 181) found that in 1993, contributions by families participating in 401(k) plans averaged 8.7 percent of salary, with employee contributions accounting for roughly two-thirds of the total, and employer matching making up the rest. They also found little variation in contribution rates across the earnings spectrum. Clark et al. (2000, 104), using plan administration data, found that the average employee contribution in the eighty-seven plans they studied was 6.9 percent of the worker's wages. The lowest contribution rates reported in this latter study were 4.4 percent of pay for workers in their twenties earning under $25,000 in 1995. Even workers at the lowest earnings levels and at the youngest ages tend to contribute at rates significantly above the 2.5 percent level that would be allowed in the national voluntary PSA plan posited here for discussion purposes.

Poterba, Venti, and Wise's work and other independent research leads to the conclusion that a voluntary saving program that allowed workers to contribute up to 2.5 percent of pay to an individual account where Social Security matched it on a dollar-for-dollar basis would entice a large majority of workers to participate in the plan. These studies also suggest that if a 100 percent match on contributions was proffered, those who entered on their own would likely take advantage of the whole match offered to them. One way to address the natural tendency of workers at low earnings levels to forego participation in voluntary retirement saving plans is to provide them with a tax credit to help them participate in a national voluntary PSA plan of the type outlined here. For example, it might be desirable to give a full credit for any worker whose annual covered earnings were less than or equal to full-time employment at the national minimum wage. To limit its costs, the tax credit could be phased out on a sliding scale up to an annual earnings level at twice that amount. Such a tax credit clearly would make the plan redistributional toward lower-wage workers consistent with the current structure of Social Security. This should result in virtually universal participation by workers with earnings up to $20,000 per year. If we estimate that 90 percent of the workers above that would buy in on their own, which is consistent with Clark et al. (2000), a plan of this sort could end up with 95 percent or more of all workers participating on a voluntary basis. It would all be voluntary but would potentially be bringing a great deal of new savings into the system. Creation of a program of this sort on a national basis would not only offer the potential of bringing additional resources to bear on solving the Social Security financing problem, it would also greatly expand the availability of a 401(k) type vehicle to workers who have traditionally been left out of this powerful retirement saving opportunity.

References

Brown, Kyle N., Gordon P. Goodfellow, Tomeka Hill, Richard Joss, Richard Luss, Lex Miller, and Sylvester J. Schieber. 1999. *The unfolding of a predictable surprise.* Washington, D.C.: Watson Wyatt Worldwide.

Clark, Robert L., Gordon P. Goodfellow, Sylvester J. Schieber, and Drew A. Warwick. 2000. Making the most of 401(k) plans, who is choosing what and why. In *Forecasting retirement needs and retirement wealth,* ed. Olivia S. Mitchell, P. Brett Hammond, and Anna M. Rappaport, 95–138. Philadelphia: University of Pennsylvania Press.

Clark, Robert L., and Sylvester J. Schieber. 1998. Factors affecting participation rates and contribution levels in 401(k) plans. In *Living with defined contribution plans,* ed. Olivia S. Mitchell and Sylvester J. Schieber, 69–97. Philadelphia: University of Pennsylvania Press.

———. 2004. An empirical analysis of the transition to hybrid pension plans in the

United States. In *Public Policies and Private Pensions,* ed. William Gale, John Shoven, and Mark Warshawsky. Washington, D.C.: Brookings Institution, forthcoming.

Lofgren, Eric, Steven A. Nyce, and Sylvester J. Schieber. 2001. Designing total reward programs for tight labor markets. Paper presented at a Pension Research Council Symposium, Philadelphia.

McGill, Dan M., Kyle N. Brown, John J. Haley, and Sylvester J. Schieber. 1996. *Fundamentals of private pensions.* 7th ed. Philadelphia: University of Pennsylvania Press.

Poterba, James M., Steven F. Venti, and David A. Wise. 1998. Informing retirement-security reform, 401(k) plans and future patterns of retirement saving. *The American Economic Review* 88 (2): 179–84.

Schieber, Sylvester J., and John B. Shoven. 1997. The consequences of population aging on private pension fund savings and asset markets. In *Public policy toward pensions,* ed. Sylvester J. Schieber and John B. Shoven, 219–46. Cambridge: MIT Press.

———. 1999. *The real deal: The history and future of Social Security.* New Haven, Conn.: Yale University Press.

For Better or for Worse
Default Effects and 401(k)
Savings Behavior

James J. Choi, David Laibson, Brigitte C. Madrian, and
Andrew Metrick

2.1 Introduction

Seemingly minor changes in the way a choice is framed to a decision maker can generate dramatic changes in behavior. Automatic enrollment provides a clear example of such effects. Under automatic enrollment (also called negative election), employees are automatically enrolled in their company's 401(k) plan unless the employees elect to opt out of the plan. This contrasts with the usual arrangement in which employees must actively choose to participate in their employer's 401(k).

Standard economic theory predicts that automatic enrollment should not influence the employee's saving decision, because automatic enrollment does not change the economic fundamentals of the planning problem. But several studies and anecdotal accounts suggest that automatic enrollment has succeeded in dramatically increasing 401(k) participa-

James J. Choi is a Ph.D. candidate in economics at Harvard University. David Laibson is professor of economics at Harvard University and a research associate of the National Bureau of Economic Research. Brigitte C. Madrian is associate professor of business and public policy at the Wharton School, University of Pennsylvania, and a research associate of the National Bureau of Economic Research. Andrew Metrick is associate professor of finance at the Wharton School, University of Pennsylvania, and a faculty research fellow of the National Bureau of Economic Research.

We thank Hewitt Associates for their help in providing the data. We are particularly grateful to Lori Lucas and Jim McGhee, two of our many contacts at Hewitt. We are also grateful for the comments of James Poterba and other participants at the NBER Economics of Aging Conference held at the Boulders in Carefree, Arizona. Choi acknowledges financial support from a National Science Foundation Graduate Research Fellowship. Laibson and Madrian acknowledge financial support from the National Institute on Aging (R01-AG-16605 and R29-AG-013020, respectively). Laibson also acknowledges financial support from the Mac-Arthur Foundation.

tion.[1] For example, Madrian and Shea (2001) document a 48 percentage point increase in 401(k) participation among newly hired employees and an 11 percentage point increase in participation overall at one large U.S. company fifteen months after the adoption of automatic enrollment. Madrian and Shea (2001) also note that automatic enrollment has been particularly successful at increasing 401(k) participation among those employees least likely to participate in standard retirement savings plans: young, lower-paid, and black and Hispanic employees.

The U.S. Treasury Department has noted the potential positive impact of automatic enrollment on 401(k) participation rates. The first Treasury Department opinion on this subject, issued in 1998, sanctioned the use of automatic enrollment for newly hired employees.[2] A second ruling, issued in 2000, further validated the use of automatic enrollment for previously hired employees not yet participating in their employer's 401(k) plan.[3] In addition, during his tenure as Treasury Secretary, Lawrence H. Summers publicly advocated employer adoption of automatic enrollment.[4]

While automatic enrollment has, by all accounts, increased 401(k) participation, this "success" has come at some cost. The employer must choose a default contribution rate and a default fund in which to invest employee contributions. Madrian and Shea (2001) show that, at least in the short term, only a small fraction of automatically enrolled 401(k) participants elect a contribution rate or asset allocation that differs from the company-specified default. Therefore, low default savings rates and conservative default funds may *lower* employee wealth accumulation in the long run. A recent Profit Sharing/401(k) Council of America (2001) survey reports that 76 percent of automatic enrollment companies have either a 2 percent or 3 percent default savings rate and that 66 percent of automatic enrollment companies have a stable value or money market default fund. These findings are echoed in a report on Vanguard client experiences with automatic enrollment: 73 percent have a default contribution rate of 3 percent or less, and 53 percent have a stable value or money market default fund (Vanguard 2001). If employees stick to such defaults in the long run, they may not accumulate as much retirement wealth as employees in companies *without* automatic enrollment.

In this paper we evaluate the impact of automatic enrollment over a horizon of up to four years in three different companies. We use data from the

---

1. In addition to Madrian and Shea (2001), see Profit Sharing/401(k) Council of America (2001), Fidelity Institutional Retirement Services Company (2001), and Vanguard (2001).
2. See Internal Revenue Service (IRS) Revenue Ruling 98-30 (Internal Revenue Service 1998).
3. See IRS Revenue Ruling 2000-8 (Internal Revenue Service 2000a). See also Revenue Rulings 2000-33 and 2000-35 (both Internal Revenue Service 2000b).
4. See "Remarks of Treasury Secretary Lawrence H. Summers at the Department of Labor Retirement Savings Education Campaign Fifth Anniversary Event" at http://www.ustreas .gov/press/releases/ps785.htm and accompanying supporting documents.

company analyzed by Madrian and Shea (2001) and extend their analysis to twenty-seven months after the implementation of automatic enrollment. In addition, we analyze data extending to four years after the adoption of automatic enrollment in a second company, and to three years after the adoption of automatic enrollment in a third company.

Based on the Vanguard report and the Profit Sharing/401(k) Council of America survey data summarized previously, the three companies that we study have typical automatic enrollment programs. One of our companies has a default contribution rate of 2 percent and a stable value default fund, the second has a default contribution rate of 3 percent and a stable value default fund, and the third has a default contribution rate of 3 percent and a money market default fund.

We find that automatic enrollment has a dramatic impact on participation rates. Under automatic enrollment, 401(k) participation rates exceed 85 percent in all three companies regardless of the tenure of the employee. Prior to automatic enrollment, 401(k) participation rates ranged from 26 to 43 percent after six months of tenure at these three firms, and from 57 to 69 percent after three years of tenure.

We also find that automatic enrollment has a large impact on contribution rates and asset allocation choices. Under automatic enrollment, 65–87 percent of new plan participants save at the default contribution rate and invest exclusively in the default fund. This percentage declines slowly over time, falling to 40–54 percent after two years of tenure, and to about 45 percent after three years of tenure (in the two companies for which data extends this far).

Thus, while automatic enrollment encourages 401(k) participation, it at least temporarily anchors participants at a low savings rate and in a conservative investment vehicle. Higher participation rates raise average wealth accumulation, but a low default savings rate and a conservative default investment undercut accumulation.

In our sample, these effects are roughly offsetting. Controlling for income and tenure, we compare total 401(k) balances for employees who joined the firm before automatic enrollment with employees who joined the firm after automatic enrollment. We find that automatic enrollment has little impact on average long-run wealth accumulation. However, this analysis is biased by the fact that the employees hired before the adoption of automatic enrollment had the benefit of a spectacular bull market, whereas those hired after automatic enrollment experienced a period of relatively flat equity performance.

To eliminate these equity-market effects we compare the average 401(k) contribution rates of the cohorts hired before automatic enrollment with the average contribution rates of the cohorts hired after automatic enrollment. These average contribution rates include participants and nonparticipants (who have a zero contribution rate). For our companies we find that automatic enrollment has a modest positive effect on average contribution rates.

Although automatic enrollment does not have a dramatic impact on *average* 401(k) balances or contribution rates, automatic enrollment does have a large impact on the distribution of balances. The high participation rate resulting from automatic enrollment drastically reduces the fraction of employees with zero balances, thereby thinning out the bottom tail of the distribution of employee balances. In addition, the effect of automatic enrollment in anchoring employees at low savings rates and in conservative investments shrinks the upper tail of the distribution of balances. Hence, automatic enrollment reduces the variance of wealth accumulation across all employees.

The rest of this paper substantiates these claims and discusses their policy implications. In section 2.2 we provide background information on the three firms that we study. In section 2.3 we discuss the impact of automatic enrollment on 401(k) participation rates. In section 2.4 we analyze the impact on contribution rates and asset allocation. In section 2.5 we discuss the impact on balance accumulation. We conclude in section 2.6 by discussing ways that automatic enrollment can be used to promote both higher participation rates and higher rates of asset accumulation. In the conclusion we also acknowledge the important normative question raised by this research—whether employees are necessarily made better off when they are coaxed into saving more through automatic enrollment.

2.2   401(k) Automatic Enrollment in Three Large Companies

We consider the experience of automatic enrollment in three large U.S. corporations. Table 2.1 compares these companies. Company A is an office equipment company with approximately 32,000 employees; Company B is the health services firm analyzed in Madrian and Shea (2001) and has approximately 30,000 employees; and Company C is a food products company that has approximately 18,000 employees in the United States. In all three companies, the 401(k) plan is the only retirement savings plan available to employees. At Company C, however, there are three different 401(k) plans that apply to different groups of employees. We consider only the largest plan that is available to about 13,000 employees.

In Company A, automatic enrollment was implemented on January 1, 1997 for all new hires. As noted previously, the default contribution rate at Company A is 2 percent, and the default investment fund is a stable value fund. No other changes to the 401(k) plan at Company A were made concurrent with the adoption of automatic enrollment.

In Company B, automatic enrollment was implemented on April 1, 1998 for all new hires. The default contribution rate at this company is 3 percent, and the default investment fund is a money market fund. Concurrent with

Table 2.1   Automatic Enrollment in Three Companies

	Company A	Company B	Company C
Industry	Office equipment	Health services	Food products
Employment	32,000	30,000	18,000
Date automatic enrollment implemented	January 1, 1997	April 1, 1998	January 1, 1998[a] November 1, 1999[a]
Employees affected by automatic enrollment	Hired on or after January 1, 1997	Hired on or after April 1, 1998	Eligible on or after January 1, 1998[a] Eligible before January 1, 1998 and not participating on November 1, 1999[a]
Length of opt-out period	60 days	30 days	30 days
Default contribution rate	2%	3%	3%
Default investment fund	Stable value	Money market	Stable value
Matching provisions	$0.67/$1 up to 6% of pay put into company stock	$0.50/$1 up to 6% of pay after 1 year of employment	$0.50/$1 up to 6% of pay
Other changes in 401(k) plan over study period	Three new funds in 1999 One fund closed in 1999	1 year length-of-service requirement eliminated on April 1, 1998	1 year length-of-service requirement for employees under age 40 eliminated on January 1, 1998

Source: Summary plan descriptions and conversations with company officials.

[a]In Company C, the first round of automatic enrollment affected employees eligible on or after January 1, 1998. This includes all employees hired on or after January 1, 1998 as well as any employees hired during 1997 who were under the age of forty on December 31, 1997. The second round of automatic enrollment in Company C affected all employees not subject to automatic enrollment during the first round: those hired prior to 1997 and employees hired during 1997 who had reached the age of forty by December 31, 1997.

the switch to automatic enrollment, Company B also eliminated a one-year length-of-service requirement. All employees at Company B who had not satisfied this length-of-service requirement on April 1, 1998 became immediately eligible to participate in the 401(k) plan, although they were not subject to automatic enrollment. Our analysis of Company B accounts for this change in eligibility by only analyzing the behavior of employees who are eligible for the 401(k) plan at the time of observation.[5]

Company C first implemented automatic enrollment on January 1, 1998 for all new hires. As with Company B, Company C also eliminated a one-year length-of-service requirement that applied to employees under the age of forty.[6] Employees under the age of forty who had not satisfied the length-of-service requirement on January 1, 1998 became immediately eligible to participate in the 401(k) plan, but in contrast to Company B, these employees *were* subject to automatic enrollment along with the new hires at Company C. In addition, on November 1, 1999, Company C applied automatic enrollment to all employees hired before January 1, 1998 who were eligible to participate in the 401(k) plan at that time but who had not yet participated as of November 1, 1999.[7] The default contribution rate at Company C is 3 percent, and the default investment is a stable value fund. Because of the eligibility changes for employees under the age of forty that occurred at Company C concurrent with the adoption of automatic enrollment, we restrict our analysis at Company C to employees who were aged forty and above at the time of hire and who thus were immediately eligible to participate in the 401(k) plan both before and after the initial implementation of automatic enrollment.

In our empirical analysis, we distinguish between "employees hired before automatic enrollment" and "employees hired after automatic enrollment." In Companies A and B "employees hired before automatic enrollment" were *never* subject to automatic enrollment, because automatic enrollment only affected new hires. By contrast, in Company C, "employees hired before automatic enrollment" who failed to join the 401(k) plan *were* eventually subject to automatic enrollment.[8] For this reason, we make an additional distinction for the employees of Company C. We distinguish between "employees hired before automatic enrollment and observed before automatic enrollment" and "employees hired before automatic enroll-

5. Madrian and Shea analyze the effects of the eligibility changes on participation in Company B. They find that eligibility rules do not substantively affect participation rates (outside of the noneligibility period).

6. Prior to January 1, 1998, employees in Company C became eligible for the 401(k) plan after one year of employment or on their fortieth birthday, whichever came first.

7. The group of employees subject to this second round of automatic enrollment at Company C included all those hired through the end of 1996 and employees hired during 1997 who were forty years old or more on December 31, 1997.

8. Specifically, employees hired before January 1, 1998 who were forty years old or older on December 31, 1997 were subject to automatic enrollment on November 1, 1999.

ment and observed after automatic enrollment." Note that the same employee can appear in the former category and later can also be observed in the latter category.

For Company A, we have administrative data on all active employees from three year-end cross-sectional snapshots for 1998, 1999 and 2000. In Company C we also have administrative data from three year-end cross-sectional snapshots, although the 1998 and 1999 data only include employees who are active 401(k) participants, while the 2000 data include all active employees, both participants and nonparticipants. For both Companies A and C the data contain basic administrative items such as hire date, birth date, gender, and pay. The data also include variables that capture several important aspects of 401(k) participation, such as the date of initial participation, current participation status, and an individual's current contribution rate and investment allocation. In addition, we have information on former employees who continue to hold positive account balances with their former employer.

For Company B we have ten cross-sectional snapshots: June 1, 1997, and month-end data for December 1997; June and December of 1998; March, June, September, and December of 1999; and March and June of 2000. The data elements include substantively all of the same elements available for Company A, with the exception that we do not have the date of initial 401(k) participation, only 401(k) participation at the time of each cross section.

Note that for Companies A and C, all of the data were collected subsequent to the adoption of automatic enrollment. We can, however, observe the historical participation behavior of employees hired prior to automatic enrollment using the date of original plan participation. In Company B, although we do not have information on the initial date of 401(k) participation, we do have two cross sections that were collected before the implementation of automatic enrollment. We can thus examine the impact of automatic enrollment on 401(k) participation and savings behavior by comparing the outcomes for employees in these two pre-automatic enrollment cross sections with the outcomes for employees hired after automatic enrollment in the later cross sections.

In all three companies, we place some restrictions on the employees actually used in the analysis. In Company A, we exclude all employees hired before October 1995. This restriction is motivated by the consolidation in October 1995 of three different retirement savings plans into one. In Companies B and C, we exclude all employees hired before 1995 from the sample simply to keep the composition of employees in these three companies roughly comparable. In Company B, we also exclude all individuals who became employees by virtue of several large and small acquisitions undertaken by the company between 1995 and the last round of data collection. And, as previously noted, in Company C we exclude all employees under the age of forty at the time of hire.

2.3   The Effect of Automatic Enrollment on 401(k) Participation

In this section we examine the effects of automatic enrollment on 401(k) participation. We begin in figure 2.1 by plotting the relationship between tenure and 401(k) participation. Note that because of differences in the type of data available on 401(k) participation in the three companies, the measure of 401(k) participation differs across these companies. For Companies A and C, panels A and C of figure 2.1 show the relationship between tenure and ever having participated in the 401(k) plan. For Company B, panel B of figure 2.1 shows actual point-in-time participation rates.[9] The black bars show the tenure-participation profile of employees hired prior to automatic enrollment, while the gray bars show that of employees hired subsequent to automatic enrollment.

We first look at Company A. For employees hired prior to automatic enrollment, 401(k) participation starts out low, increases quite rapidly during the first few months of employment, and continues to increase at a slower pace after that. At forty-eight months of employment, the participation rate reaches about 70 percent. 401(k) participation also starts out low for employees hired under automatic enrollment and then increases very rapidly during the third and fourth months of employment. The jump in Company A arises because there is a sixty-day opt-out period between the hire date and the automatic enrollment date. Moreover, in practice it appears to take somewhat longer than sixty days for newly hired employees who do not opt out to be automatically enrolled. After the participation jumps in months three and four, the participation rate levels off at around 92 percent in month five. Between the fifth and thirty-sixth months of employment, there is a further increase from 92 percent to almost 98 percent of employees having ever participated. This increase is driven by two factors. First, some employees who initially opted out of 401(k) participation eventually elect to participate. Second, employees who opt out of 401(k) participation have a slightly higher turnover rate than those enrolled in the plan so that, as tenure increases, the sample of employees used to calculate the participation rate is increasingly composed of individuals who did not choose to opt out.

The effect of automatic enrollment on having ever participated in the 401(k) plan is the difference between the two sets of bars in panel A of figure 2.1. This difference is plotted in panel A of figure 2.2. Note that during the first two months of employment, automatic enrollment actually

9. The participation profiles in panel B of figure 2.1 exhibit more variability than those in panel A of figure 2.1 because the profiles for Company B are primarily identified off of cross-sectional variation in the participation rate of individuals with different amounts of tenure. In contrast, the profiles in panel A of figure 2.1 reflect longitudinal data on individual employees since we know the date at which each employee of Company A first enrolled in the 401(k) plan.

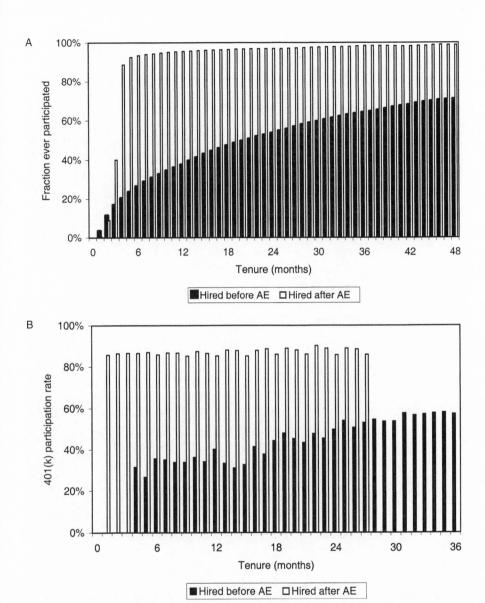

Fig. 2.1 *A,* 401(k) participation by tenure: Company A; *B,* 401(k) participation by tenure: Company B; *C,* 401(k) participation by tenure for employees aged forty-plus at hire: Company C; *D,* 401(k) participation by tenure for employees aged forty-plus at hire: Company C

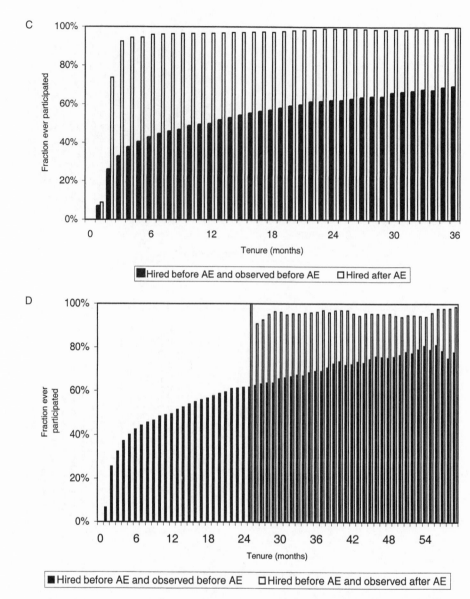

Fig. 2.1   (cont.) *A*, 401(k) participation by tenure: Company A; *B*, 401(k) participation by tenure: Company B; *C*, 401(k) participation by tenure for employees aged
forty-plus at hire: Company C; *D*, 401(k) participation by tenure for employees aged
forty-plus at hire: Company C

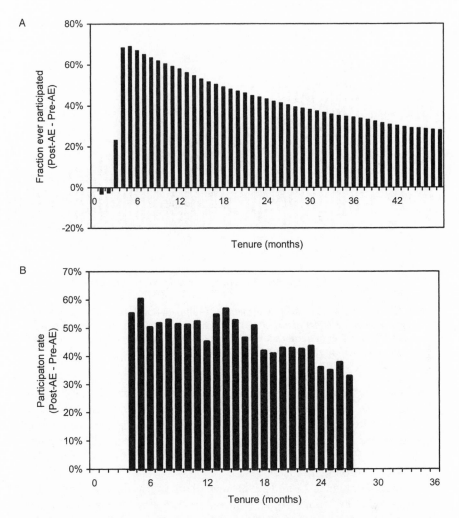

Fig. 2.2 *A,* **The effect of automatic enrollment on 401(k) participation: Company A;** *B,* **the effect of automatic enrollment on 401(k) participation: Company B;** *C,* **the effect of automatic enrollment on 401(k) participation for employees aged forty-plus at hire: Company C**

reduces the 401(k) participation rate by 2–3 percentage points. We attribute this to individuals deciding not to proactively enroll during the first two months of employment because they know that they will be automatically enrolled in the near future anyway. The effect of automatic enrollment on 401(k) participation peaks around five months of employment at almost 70 percentage points. After five months of employment, the participation rate of employees hired under automatic enrollment increases at only a very small rate each month, while that of employees hired before automatic en-

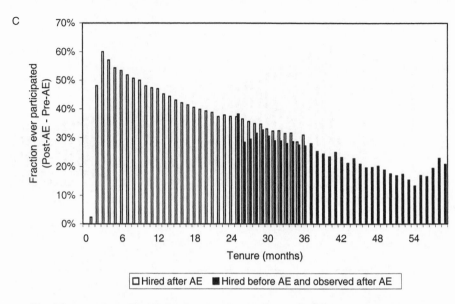

C

Fig. 2.2   (cont.) *A,* The effect of automatic enrollment on 401(k) participation: Company A; *B,* the effect of automatic enrollment on 401(k) participation: Company B; *C,* the effect of automatic enrollment on 401(k) participation for employees aged forty-plus at hire: Company C

rollment increases more rapidly. As a result, the effect of automatic enrollment on the 401(k) participation rate slowly decreases after month five. Even so, after forty-eight months, the fraction of employees having ever participated in the 401(k) plan is still 28 percentage points higher for employees hired after automatic enrollment than for employees hired before automatic enrollment.

Panels B of figures 2.1 and 2.2 show similar patterns for Company B. For the analysis of Company B, we control for Company B's change in 401(k) eligibility rules by only using observations from employees who are eligible at the time of observation. This restriction eliminates variation in participation due to variation in eligibility rules. As in Company A, the 401(k) participation rate of employees hired before automatic enrollment starts out low and increases steadily until it reaches 58 percent at thirty-six months of tenure.[10] In contrast, for employees hired under automatic enrollment, the 401(k) participation rate starts out high, at about 86 percent, and remains high, increasing only slightly, up to about 88 percent after two years. The higher initial participation rates in Company B relative to Com-

10. For this company, the 401(k) participation rate of employees hired before automatic enrollment is not observed until the fourth month of employment (taken from the June 1998 cross section). Earlier cross sections only contain information about employees who were not eligible to participate during their first year of employment.

pany A result from a shorter automatic enrollment delay period (sixty days in Company A versus thirty days in Company B), and from quicker enrollment of individuals once the opt-out period has ended. As in Company A, the effect of automatic enrollment on 401(k) participation is highest during the fifth month of employment, when it reaches 60 percentage points. By the twenty-seventh month of employment, the effect has fallen quite substantially, but remains sizeable at 33 percentage points (panel B of figure 2.2). Because the last Company B cross section is in June 2000 and automatic enrollment was introduced in April 1998, we have no postautomatic enrollment data beyond twenty-seven months for this company.

In Company C, we look at the effect of automatic enrollment on employees "hired after automatic enrollment," as in Companies A and B, and on employees who became subject to automatic enrollment during their tenure at the company, those "hired before automatic enrollment and observed after automatic enrollment." This second group can only be observed at Company C because this is the only company that applied automatic enrollment to previously hired employees. Panel C of figure 2.1, which we turn to next, profiles the effect of automatic enrollment on the participation rates of employees who were hired under the automatic enrollment regime. Panel D of figure 2.1 documents the effect of automatic enrollment on employees who were hired *before* automatic enrollment was put in place, but who subsequently became subject to automatic enrollment. Note that by the time automatic enrollment was applied to this latter group of employees, they all had at least twenty-three months of tenure at the company.

In panel C of figure 2.1, the black bars plot the 401(k) participation rates for employees "hired before automatic enrollment and observed before automatic enrollment" (i.e., observed prior to the point in time when they became subject to automatic enrollment, if not already participating).[11] These preautomatic enrollment participation rates start out low and increase with tenure. This pattern roughly matches the patterns observed in Companies A and B. At thirty-six months of tenure, the 401(k) participation rate for these preautomatic enrollment employees is about 69 percent. Panel C of figure 2.1 compares this profile with the participation profile of employees who were subject to automatic enrollment upon hire. Their 401(k) participation rate increases quite dramatically in the first two months of employment, and reaches 92 percent at three months of tenure, increasing only slightly thereafter.

In panel D of figure 2.1 the black bars are the same as those in panel C of figure 2.1 (plotting the participation rate for employees "hired before

11. Specifically, these employees include those hired during or before 1997 for tenures that take these employees up to November 1999, when automatic enrollment was applied to these employees.

automatic enrollment and observed before automatic enrollment"). The white bars represent employees who were hired *before* automatic enrollment was adopted, but use data for these employees at tenure levels *after* they became subject to automatic enrollment: those "hired before automatic enrollment and observed after automatic enrollment."[12] Panel D of figure 2.1 shows that automatic enrollment has a dramatic effect on the participation rate of these employees as well. At thirty-six months of employment, the participation rate for this group is 96 percent.

Panel C of figure 2.2 shows the impact of automatic enrollment on the 401(k) participation rates by tenure for both groups of employees subject to automatic enrollment in Company C: those "hired after automatic enrollment" and those "hired before automatic enrollment and observed after automatic enrollment."[13] As in Companies A and B, the effect of automatic enrollment on 401(k) participation is large initially and declines over time. In panel C of figure 2.2 we also see that automatic enrollment is slightly more effective at increasing 401(k) participation for new hires (i.e., those "hired after automatic enrollment") than for old hires (i.e., those "hired before automatic enrollment and observed after automatic enrollment"). One explanation for the slightly higher participation rates under automatic enrollment for new versus old hires is that old hires may have become accustomed to a certain level of take-home pay and are thus more likely to opt out of 401(k) participation in order to avoid a decrease in their level of consumption.

2.4   The Effect of Automatic Enrollment on
Contribution Rates and Asset Allocation

We now turn to the effect of automatic enrollment on the savings behavior of 401(k) participants. In their study of automatic enrollment, Madrian and Shea (2001) show that in the short run, 401(k) participants hired under automatic enrollment are very likely to passively accept the default contribution rate and fund allocation. In this section of the paper, we document the persistence of this type of default savings behavior over longer periods of time. We first document the effects of automatic enrollment on 401(k) contribution rates. Panels A, B, and C of figure 2.3 compare the distribution of contribution rates for 401(k) participants who are subject to automatic enrollment with participants who are not subject to

12. Specifically, the white bars include employees hired during or before 1997 for tenures beginning in December 1999, when automatic enrollment became effective for these employees.

13. The bars in this graph are formed by differencing the bars within panel C of figure 2.1—this generates the gray "hired after automatic enrollment" effect—and differencing the bars within panel D of figure 2.1—this generates the black "hired before automatic enrollment and observed after automatic enrollment" effect.

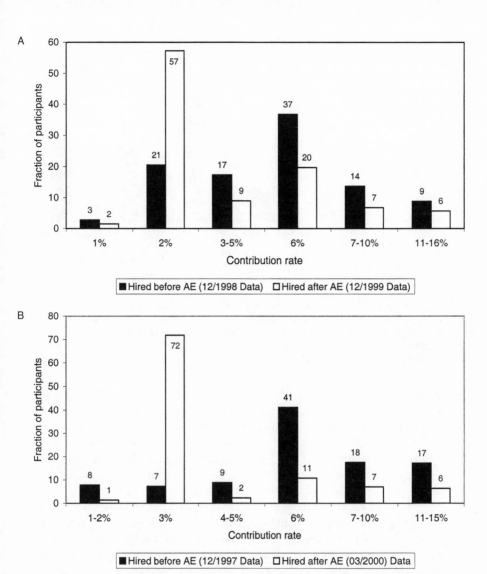

Fig. 2.3 *A,* The distribution of 401(k) contribution rates: Company A (twenty-four to thirty-five months tenure); *B,* the distribution of 401(k) contribution rates: Company B (zero to twenty-three months tenure); *C,* the distribution of 401(k) contribution rates for employees aged forty-plus at hire: Company C (twelve to thirty-five months tenure)

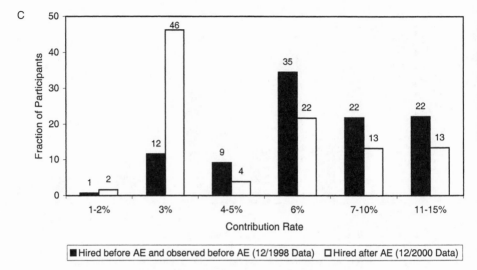

Fig. 2.3   (cont.) *A,* The distribution of 401(k) contribution rates: Company A (twenty-four to thirty-five months tenure); *B,* the distribution of 401(k) contribution rates: Company B (zero to twenty-three months tenure); *C,* the distribution of 401(k) contribution rates for employees aged forty-plus at hire: Company C (twelve to thirty-five months tenure)

automatic enrollment. For all three companies, employees are classified as participants if they have a nonzero contribution rate at the time of the data collection. Within each company we compare employees with similar months of on-the-job tenure to eliminate the possibility that differences in tenure drive our automatic enrollment effects. Because of differences in our underlying data sources and in the timing of automatic enrollment adoption, the tenure controls vary for each company.

Panel A of figure 2.3 plots the distribution of 401(k) contribution rates for participating employees in Company A with twenty-four to thirty-five months of tenure since their hire date. It compares the employees who were "hired before automatic enrollment" with the employees who were "hired after automatic enrollment." (Recall that in Companies A and B, automatic enrollment was only applied to new employees.) Panel B of figure 2.3 plots the distribution of 401(k) contribution rates for participating employees in Company B with zero to twenty-three months of tenure since their hire date. Like panel A of figure 2.3, panel B of figure 2.3 also compares the employees who were "hired before automatic enrollment" to the employees who were "hired after automatic enrollment." Panel C of figure 2.3 plots the distribution of 401(k) contribution rates for participating employees in Company C with twelve to thirty-five months of tenure since their hire date. It compares the employees who were "hired before automatic enrollment and observed before automatic enrollment" (the control group for Company C) with employees who were "hired after automatic enrollment."

These histograms show a striking difference between the contribution rates of 401(k) participants who were subject to automatic enrollment and those who were not. The modal contribution rate of participants hired before automatic enrollment in all three companies is 6 percent, the point after which employer matching contributions cease (see table 2.1). In contrast, for employees hired under automatic enrollment, the modal contribution rate is the automatic enrollment default: 2 percent in Company A and 3 percent in Companies B and C. For all three of our companies, the fraction of participants at the default contribution rate increases at least 30 percentage points as a result of automatic enrollment. In Company A, the fraction of participants at the default contribution rate increases from 21 percent to 57 percent. In Company B, the fraction of participants at the default contribution rate increases from 7 percent to 72 percent. In Company C, the fraction of participants at the default contribution rate increases from 12 percent to 46 percent.

Madrian and Shea (2001) show that for low-tenure employees, this shift in the modal contribution rate to the automatic enrollment default for employees hired subsequent to automatic enrollment is driven both by a movement from a 0 percent contribution rate (nonparticipation) to the default contribution rate and by a movement from higher contribution rates to the default. In table 2.2, we examine the effect of automatic enrollment on the distribution of contribution rates in Companies A and B by tenure to determine whether passive acceptance of the default savings rate persists over time.[14] To evaluate the extent to which the pronounced mass of participants at the default contribution rate is driven by the induced participation of would-be nonparticipants, we also include nonparticipation as one of the contribution rate categories. The nonzero contribution rates are aggregated into three broad categories: the automatic enrollment default contribution rate, contribution rates less than the default (<Default), and contribution rates greater than the default (>Default).

In Company A, we can combine multiple cross sections to obtain the distribution of contribution rates for employees hired both before and after automatic enrollment for employees with two to four years of tenure. In addition, we can calculate the distribution of contribution rates for employees hired after automatic enrollment with lower levels of tenure. Looking first at employees hired under automatic enrollment, we see that after six months of employment, the fraction of employees who are nonparticipants is fairly constant at about 8 percent. The fraction of employees with

---

14. We are precluded from including Company C in this analysis and the analysis in table 2.3 because we have only one cross-sectional dataset for this company that includes both 401(k) participants and nonparticipants.

Table 2.2   The Distribution of 401(k) Contribution Rates by Tenure for Employees Hired Before and After Automatic Enrollment (%)

Tenure (months)	Hired Before Automatic Enrollment				Hired After Automatic Enrollment			
	Non-Participant	<Default	Default	>Default	Non-Participant	<Default	Default	>Default
Company A								
6–11	—	—	—	—	8.4	1.3	63.4	26.9
12–17	—	—	—	—	8.5	1.4	61.0	29.1
18–23	—	—	—	—	8.8	1.4	56.5	33.4
24–29	46.9	1.7	12.0	39.4	9.0	1.7	53.3	36.1
30–35	40.8	1.4	10.9	46.9	8.4	1.6	50.3	39.7
36–41	40.2	1.7	12.7	45.5	6.8	1.3	48.5	43.4
42–47	35.3	0.9	10.7	53.2	8.3	1.6	45.8	44.3
48–53	31.5	1.9	13.4	53.3	—	—	—	—
Company B								
3–5	68.9	3.0	3.6	24.5	13.5	1.2	71.8	13.6
6–11	64.0	3.0	4.4	28.6	13.7	1.3	66.2	18.9
12–17	64.2	2.7	3.4	29.8	12.7	1.6	54.9	30.8
18–23	53.4	3.4	4.5	38.8	12.0	1.5	47.5	39.0
24–26	47.3	3.9	5.3	43.6	12.1	1.4	41.4	45.0

Source: Authors' calculations.

Note: Dashes indicate that lack of data for a given time period precludes obtaining a number for that particular cell.

a contribution rate in excess of the default, however, increases quite steadily with tenure, while the fraction of employees contributing at the default declines. For employees with twenty-four to twenty-nine months of tenure, the fraction of employees hired under automatic enrollment with a contribution rate exceeding the default is 36 percent, compared with 39 percent for employees hired before automatic enrollment. At forty-two to forty-seven months of tenure, the fraction of employees with a contribution rate exceeding the default is 44 percent for those hired under automatic enrollment and 53 percent for those hired before automatic enrollment. That the fraction of employees contributing at a rate higher than the default is larger for those hired before automatic enrollment than for those hired after suggests that, even after four years, some of the participants who contribute at the default rate would have chosen a higher contribution rate had they not been subject to automatic enrollment.

For Company B we have overlapping tenure data for employees hired before and after automatic enrollment with three or more months of tenure. As with Company A, the fraction of nonparticipants among those hired after automatic enrollment is fairly constant at about 12–13 percent for all tenure levels. And, similar to Company A, the fraction of employees hired under automatic enrollment with a contribution rate exceeding the default increases with tenure, while the fraction contributing at the default declines. In Company B, however, similar fractions of employees hired both before and after automatic enrollment have contribution rates exceeding the default after twelve months of tenure. Thus, after one year, the substantial mass of participants at the automatic enrollment default contribution rate in Company B appears to result largely from a conversion of nonparticipants into participants at the default rate.

We next consider how the automatic enrollment default affects investment allocations. We begin with table 2.3, which is similar in spirit to table 2.2 but shows the fraction of employees who are nonparticipants, participants invested wholly in the default fund, participants with some other investment allocation, and participants with no balances. This last category is omitted for Company B because in the Company B data there are only a handful of individuals in each tenure category who are participants with no balances. At all tenure levels in both companies, the fraction of employees wholly invested in the automatic enrollment default fund is very large for employees hired after automatic enrollment and much smaller for employees hired before automatic enrollment. In both companies we also see that the fraction of employees hired under automatic enrollment with a 100 percent default fund asset allocation decreases with tenure. For employees hired prior to automatic enrollment, there is no discernable tenure-based trend in the fraction of employees at the automatic enrollment default. When we compare employees hired before and after automatic enrollment with similar levels of tenure, the fraction with a nondefault as-

Table 2.3   The Distribution of 401(k) Fund Allocations by Tenure for Employees Hired Before and After Automatic Enrollment (%)

	Hired Before Automatic Enrollment				Hired After Automatic Enrollment			
Tenure (months)	Non-Participant	Zero Balances	100% Default Fund	Other Allocation	Non-Participant	Zero Balances	100% Default Fund	Other Allocation
Company A								
6–11	—	—	—	—	8.4	4.6	58.7	28.4
12–17	—	—	—	—	8.5	4.4	57.2	30.0
18–23	—	—	—	—	8.8	2.3	54.7	34.3
24–29	46.9	2.3	8.9	42.0	9.0	2.1	52.7	36.3
30–35	40.8	1.9	6.2	51.1	8.4	1.4	49.8	40.4
36–41	40.2	1.5	8.8	49.4	6.8	1.3	49.1	42.8
42–47	35.3	0.8	6.7	57.2	8.3	1.2	47.2	43.2
48–53	31.5	0.9	8.8	58.8	—	—	—	—
Company B								
3–5	68.9	—	0.7	30.4	13.6	—	76.7	9.7
6–11	64.0	—	0.9	35.1	13.5	—	71.2	15.3
12–17	64.2	—	2.9	32.9	13.7	—	64.0	22.3
18–23	53.4	—	2.2	44.4	12.0	—	50.0	38.0
24–26	47.3	—	2.3	50.4	12.1	—	43.6	44.3

Source: Authors' calculations.

set allocation is higher for those hired before automatic enrollment at all levels of tenure in both companies. Thus, under automatic enrollment, the group of employees who are wholly invested in the default fund is comprised both of employees who would have been nonparticipants in the absence of automatic enrollment and of employees who would have participated but with a different allocation of funds.

Figure 2.4 plots the relationship between tenure and three different measures of default savings behavior: (1) the fraction of participants contributing at the default contribution rate and investing exclusively in the default fund (the black lines); (2) the fraction of participants contributing at the default contribution rate and investing with a nondefault investment allocation (the dashed lines); and (3) the fraction of participants contributing at a nondefault contribution rate and investing exclusively in the default fund (the gray lines). We calculate these percentages for 401(k) participants who were and were not subject to automatic enrollment. The thin lines represent the fraction of participants hired prior to automatic enrollment (and, in the case of Company C, include only periods in which these employees were not yet subject to automatic enrollment). The thick lines represent the fraction of employees hired after automatic enrollment.

In Company A, all three measures of default savings behavior increase rapidly over the first three months of employment. This increase reflects the fact that it takes five months for automatic enrollment to fully take

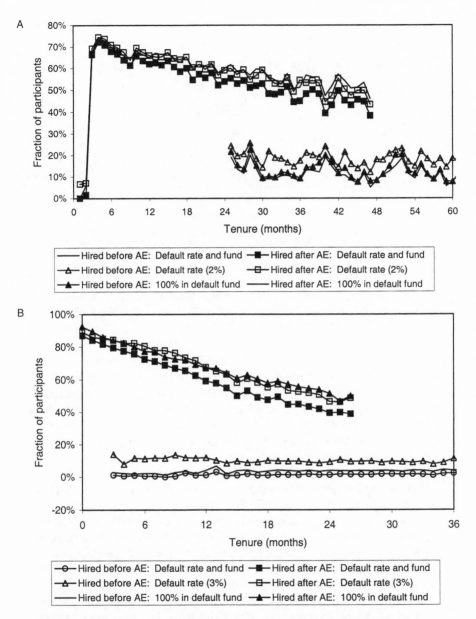

Fig. 2.4 *A*, Default savings behavior and tenure: Company A; *B*, default savings behavior and tenure: Company B; *C*, default savings behavior and tenure of employees aged forty-plus at hire: Company C

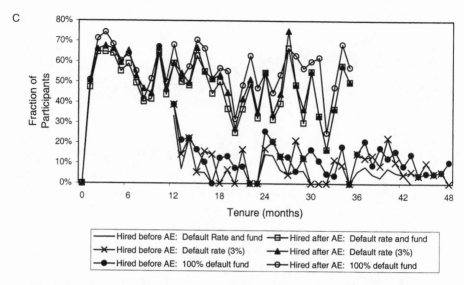

Fig. 2.4   (cont.) *A,* Default savings behavior and tenure: Company A; *B,* default savings behavior and tenure: Company B; *C,* default savings behavior and tenure of employees aged forty-plus at hire: Company C

effect in Company A. Individuals hired after automatic enrollment who show up in the data as participants in their first three months of employment are primarily comprised of individuals who initiated 401(k) participation before the end of the automatic enrollment opt-out period. Not having been automatically enrolled, these individuals are also not very likely to have either the automatic enrollment default contribution rate or the automatic enrollment default asset allocation. The fraction of participants who are at the default for each of these measures peaks in the fifth month of employment, as does the effect of automatic enrollment on participation in panel A of figure 2.2. For Company C the initial increase in the fraction of employees at the various default measures is much less pronounced than in Company A, because the opt-out period in this company is shorter. For Company B there is no initial increase in the fraction of employees at the various measures of the default because by the time individuals are observed in this company's data, the opt-out period has already ended. In all three companies, the fraction of employees at any of these default measures declines substantially with tenure. However, even at high levels of tenure, a large fraction of employees remain at the automatic enrollment default. In Company A, 38 percent of participants hired under automatic enrollment are at both the default rate and wholly invested in the default fund after four years. In Company B, this fraction is 39 percent after twenty-seven months, and in Company C it is 50 percent after three years. (Note, however, that in Company C there is much more variability in the fraction of employees at the various defaults with respect to tenure than at the other two companies as a result of the much smaller sample sizes underlying the analysis in Company C.)

Madrian and Shea (2001) also show that in a cross section of employees hired under automatic enrollment in Company B, there are significant differences across demographic groups in the fraction of employees who passively accept both the default contribution rate and the default investment fund. To examine whether demographic characteristics affect the persistence of default savings behavior over time as well, we estimate linear probability regressions for the likelihood that 401(k) participants exhibit these three different types of default savings behavior as a function of tenure (in months), gender, age, compensation, and an interaction between tenure and these three other factors.[15] In all three companies, the sample of employees used in these regressions is comprised of 401(k) participants hired after automatic enrollment. These samples are constructed from the pooled cross-sectional data.[16] For Company C, we also include separate regression results for participants who were hired *before* the adoption of automatic enrollment but who did not join the 401(k) plan until *after* they became subject to automatic enrollment: those "hired before automatic enrollment but first participated after automatic enrollment." The identification in these regressions comes both from variation by tenure within a cross section in the fraction of participants exhibiting default savings behavior and from variation over time as individuals in multiple cross sections accumulate more tenure. The coefficients from these regressions are reported in tables 2.4 and 2.5. The standard errors, reported in parentheses, are corrected for the potential of having more than one observation on the same individual at different points in time.

Consistent with the findings in Madrian and Shea (2001), the initial fraction of participants at the default varies quite significantly with demographic characteristics. Women are slightly (2–4 percent) more likely to be at the default than are men in many of the regressions for Companies A and B, but there is little significant effect of being female for either group of participants in Company C.

Relative to employees in the top third of the pay distribution, employees in the bottom and middle of the pay distribution are much more likely to be at the default.[17] For Company A, employees in the bottom third of the

15. We report linear probability regressions because the coefficients are readily interpretable. The qualitative nature of the results is very similar under a probit specification.

16. In Company A, we further restrict the sample to participants with four or more months of tenure. This restriction coincides with Company A's automatic enrollment implementation delay (see panel A of figure 2.1).

17. The position in the pay distribution for each individual is calculated relative to other employees hired in the same month. This pay category is calculated in the first month of employment and does not vary over time for individuals who appear in more than one cross section.

Table 2.4   Default Savings Behavior of 401(k) Participants Under Automatic Enrollment

	Company A (hired after automatic enrollment)			Company B (hired after automatic enrollment)		
	Default Rate and Fund	Default Rate	Default Fund	Default Rate and Fund	Default Rate	Default Fund
Constant	0.4654***	0.5221***	0.4828***	0.6691***	0.7439***	0.7304***
	(0.0148)	(0.0144)	(0.0147)	(0.0136)	(0.0132)	(0.0125)
Tenure	−0.0061***	−0.0069***	−0.0047***	−0.0265***	−0.0256***	−0.0226***
	(0.0008)	(0.0008)	(0.0008)	(0.0014)	(0.0015)	(0.0015)
Female	0.0178	0.0241***	0.0182**	0.0388***	0.0180	0.0446***
	(0.0093)	(0.0088)	(0.0091)	(0.0101)	(0.0097)	(0.0093)
Low pay	0.3263***	0.2999***	0.3172***	0.2366***	0.1977***	0.1853***
	(0.0113)	(0.0108)	(0.0111)	(0.0098)	(0.0094)	(0.0088)
Middle pay	0.1660***	0.1609***	0.1707***	0.1975***	0.1739***	0.1632***
	(0.0117)	(0.0113)	(0.0117)	(0.0100)	(0.0095)	(0.0090)
Age <30	0.1260***	0.1102***	0.1196***	0.0390***	0.0406***	0.0312***
	(0.0150)	(0.0142)	(0.0146)	(0.0120)	(0.0114)	(0.0108)
Age 30–44	0.0577***	0.0519***	0.0600***	0.0087	0.0100	0.0100
	(0.0152)	(0.0146)	(0.0150)	(0.0120)	(0.0114)	(0.0108)
Tenure · Female	−0.0006	−0.0007	0.0001	0.0033***	0.0041***	0.0029**
	(0.0005)	(0.0005)	(0.0005)	(0.0011)	(0.0012)	(0.0011)
Tenure · Low pay	0.0019***	0.0027***	0.0024***	0.0076***	0.0078***	0.0105***
	(0.0006)	(0.0006)	(0.0006)	(0.0012)	(0.0012)	(0.0012)
Tenure · Middle pay	0.0019***	0.0023***	0.0022***	0.0033***	0.0042***	0.0057***
	(0.0006)	(0.0006)	(0.0006)	(0.0012)	(0.0012)	(0.0012)
Tenure · Age <30	−0.0019**	−0.0010	−0.0023***	0.0004	0.0020	−0.0015
	(0.0018)	(0.0008)	(0.0008)	(0.0014)	(0.0014)	(0.0014)
Tenure · Age 30–44	−0.0013	−0.0003	−0.0019**	0.0027**	0.0035***	0.0000
	(0.0008)	(0.0008)	(0.0008)	(0.0013)	(0.0014)	(0.0014)
Sample size	37,365	38,992	37,365	51,157	51,157	51,157
R^2	0.1249	0.1215	0.1211	0.1728	0.1561	0.1569

Source: Authors' calculations.

Notes: Coefficients estimated from a linear probability regression of the dependent variable (column head) on the independent variables listed. The sample in Companies A and B includes all 401(k) participants hired after automatic enrollment. In Company A, the sample is further restricted to employees with four or more months of tenure (see text). Robust standard errors in parentheses.

***Significance at the 1 percent level.

**Significance at the 5 percent level.

distribution are 30–33 percent more likely to be at the default, while those in the middle third are about 16–17 percent more likely to be at the default. In Company B, the lowest-paid employees are 19–24 percent more likely to be at the default, while middle-paid employees are 16–20 percent more likely to be at the default. In Company C, the effect of compensation on being at the automatic enrollment defaults differs for employees "hired after automatic enrollment" relative to employees "hired before automatic enrollment but [who] first participated after automatic enrollment." For the

Table 2.5   **Default Savings Behavior of 401(k) Participants Under Automatic Enrollment**

	Company C (hired after automatic enrollment)			Company C (hired before but first participated after automatic enrollment)		
	Default Rate and Fund	Default Rate	Default Fund	Default Rate and Fund	Default Rate	Default Fund
Constant	0.2836***	0.3424***	0.3039***	0.9761***	0.9905***	0.9852***
	(0.0373)	(0.0382)	(0.0375)	(0.0163)	(0.0119)	(0.0131)
Tenure	−0.0089***	−0.0097***	−0.0051**	−0.0015	−0.0031	−0.0011
	(0.0019)	(0.0020)	(0.0022)	(0.0048)	(0.0047)	(0.0049)
Female	−0.0560	−0.0638**	−0.0128	0.0771	0.0343	0.0560
	(0.0324)	(0.0322)	(0.0299)	(0.0505)	(0.0417)	(0.0399)
Low pay	0.5421***	0.5032***	0.5487***	−0.1132**	−0.0628**	−0.0730
	(0.0378)	(0.0384)	(0.0397)	(0.0462)	(0.0314)	(0.0384)
Middle pay	0.2176***	0.2158***	0.2032***	−0.0668	−0.0612	−0.0357
	(0.0502)	(0.0509)	(0.0512)	(0.0547)	(0.0537)	(0.0399)
Age <30	—	—	—	—	—	—
Age 30–44	0.0602	0.0665**	0.0647**	0.0894**	0.0550**	0.0581**
	(0.0327)	(0.0325)	(0.0306)	(0.0348)	(0.0265)	(0.0276)
Tenure · Female	0.0071***	0.0073***	0.0028	−0.0136**	−0.0106	−0.0145**
	(0.0020)	(0.0020)	(0.0019)	(0.0064)	(0.0056)	(0.0060)
Tenure · Low pay	−0.0005	−0.0000	0.0009	0.0075	0.0033	0.0086
	(0.0023)	(0.0023)	(0.0023)	(0.0072)	(0.0065)	(0.0070)
Tenure · Middle pay	−0.0037	−0.0038	0.0010	−0.0128	−0.0080	−0.0067
	(0.0027)	(0.0028)	(0.0030)	(0.0091)	(0.0085)	(0.0084)
Tenure · Age <30	—	—	—	—	—	—
Tenure · Age 30–44	0.0008	0.0014	−0.0006	−0.0084	−0.0017	−0.0107
	(0.0021)	(0.0021)	(0.0021)	(0.0075)	(0.0071)	(0.0077)
Sample size	2,034	2,049	2,034	210	210	210
R^2	0.2528	0.2290	0.2558	0.1101	0.0881	0.1034

Source: Authors' calculations.

Notes: Coefficients estimated from a linear probability regression of the dependent variable (column head) on the independent variables listed. The sample in the first three columns includes all 401(k) participants aged forty-plus at the time of hire who were hired after automatic enrollment. The sample in the last three columns includes 401(k) participants aged forty-plus at the time of hire who were hired before automatic enrollment but who were not 401(k) participants when automatic enrollment became effective for employees of their hire cohort. Robust standard errors in parentheses.

***Significance at the 1 percent level.

**Significance at the 5 percent level.

first group, the lowest-paid employees are 50–55 percent more likely to be at the default, while middle-paid employees are 20–22 percent more likely to be at the default. The effects of compensation for employees "hired before automatic enrollment but [who] first participated after automatic enrollment" stand in marked contrast to those for newly hired employees at all three companies: There is no statistically significant difference between being at the automatic enrollment defaults for the middle- and highest-paid employees, whereas the lowest-paid employees are actually slightly *less* likely to be at the automatic enrollment defaults.

As with the effects of compensation on being at the default for employees hired after automatic enrollment, age is also negatively related to the initial likelihood of being at the default. Relative to employees over the age of forty-five, those under the age of thirty are 11–13 percent more likely to be at the default in Company A and 3–4 percent more likely to be at the default in Company B. Those aged thirty to forty-four are 5–6 percent more likely to be at the default in Company A, 6–9 percent more likely to be at the default in Company C (for both groups of employees),[18] while there is no differential effect for this age group in Company B.

In all three companies, tenure is negatively related to the fraction of participants at the defaults. Looking across the three default measures, the tenure effect is much smaller on being invested wholly in the default fund than on being at the default contribution rate. This suggests that there is more persistence in the default fund allocation than in the default contribution rate. The magnitudes of the tenure coefficients are much larger at Company B than at Companies A and C, implying that there is more persistence in the automatic enrollment defaults at Company A and C than at Company B. In Company B, the fraction of participants hired after automatic enrollment at the combined default (column [4]) falls by 2.7 percentage points with each additional month of tenure. In Companies A and C, on the other hand, the fraction of participants at the combined default (column [1] of tables 2.4 and 2.5, respectively) falls by only 0.6 (Company A) and 0.9 (Company C) percentage points with each additional month of tenure. Looking at the two groups of participants in Company C, there is less sensitivity to tenure in the automatic enrollment defaults for employees "hired before automatic enrollment but [who] first participated after automatic enrollment" than for employees hired after automatic enrollment. As just noted, the fraction of participants at the combined default falls by 0.9 percentage points with each additional month of tenure for employees hired after automatic enrollment at Company C, and by a much smaller 0.2 percentage points with each month of tenure for employees "hired before automatic enrollment but [who] first participated after automatic enrollment."

Overall, it appears that compensation and tenure (and to a lesser extent, age) are the key determinants of the fraction of employees at the default. More lowly paid participants are much more likely to be at the default than are more highly paid participants, and the fraction of participants at the default is more persistent for the more lowly paid. These patterns are con-

---

18. Note that because the sample in Company C is restricted to those aged forty-plus, this group is actually comprised only of those aged forty to forty-four.

sistent with a number of stories. To the extent that pay proxies for human capital, more highly paid employees may be better able to make informed savings decisions, and thus move away from the defaults more quickly. The cost of having the "wrong" contribution rate and asset allocation is also likely to be greater for the more highly paid, who face higher marginal tax rates and hence stronger incentives to take advantage of tax-deferred investment opportunities. In addition, high-income employees may have lower rates of time preference, raising their incentives to adopt high savings rates. However, high-income employees also have steeper income profiles, lowering their saving incentives when young.

2.5   Automatic Enrollment and Asset Accumulation

We now turn to the effect of automatic enrollment on overall asset accumulation, which is ultimately the measure that we care most about. The effects of automatic enrollment on asset accumulation are ambiguous. To the extent that automatic enrollment leads to increased or earlier 401(k) participation, automatic enrollment will tend to increase asset accumulation. However, to the extent that default elections under automatic enrollment result in a lower contribution rate or a more conservative asset allocation than individuals would have otherwise chosen, automatic enrollment will tend to decrease asset accumulation. The negative effect of conservative portfolio choices would have been particularly important during the last decade when stock returns were high.

To examine the effect of automatic enrollment on asset accumulation, we look at the 401(k) balance-to-pay ratio in Companies A and B.[19] The numerator of this ratio is simply the total 401(k) balances of an individual at a point in time. The numerator includes employer matching contributions and also incorporates the negative effects of employee 401(k) borrowing. In Company A, we exclude the value of balances rolled into the plan (presumably from a previous employer). In practice, very few employees have such balances, but they can be quite large for the employees who have them and greatly increase the variability in average measures of the balance-to-pay ratio. In Company B, the data do not include a separate measure of balances rolled into the plan, so the measure of total balances includes all balances regardless of their source. The denominator of the balance-to-pay ratio is annualized total compensation. For nonparticipants, the balance-to-pay ratio will generally be zero, with the exception of current nonparticipants who participated at some point in the past and have consequently accumulated some 401(k) balances. Because we are interested in total

19. We are precluded from including Company C in this analysis because we have only one cross-sectional dataset for this company that includes both 401(k) participants and nonparticipants.

401(k) asset accumulation and not just asset accumulation conditional on participation, we include nonparticipants in our analysis of asset accumulation.

Figure 2.5 shows the relationship between tenure since eligibility and the average 401(k) balance-to-pay ratio calculated across all employees, including nonparticipants. For employees hired after automatic enrollment

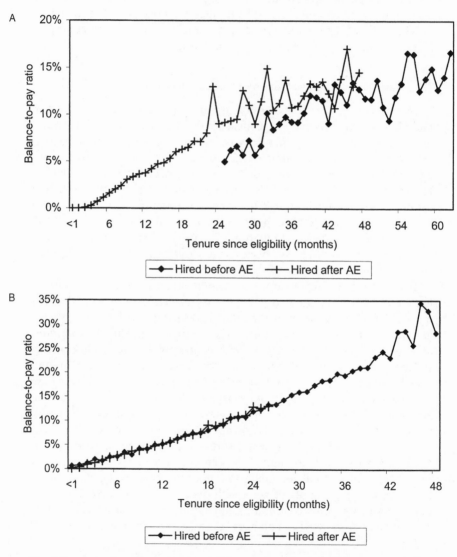

Fig. 2.5   *A,* Average 401(k) balance-to-pay ratio by tenure (including nonparticipants): Company A; *B,* average 401(k) balance-to-pay ratio by tenure (including nonparticipants): Company B

in Company B (and for all employees in Company A), months since eligibility and total months of tenure are the same. For employees hired before automatic enrollment, these two measures are different. This is because Company B eliminated a one-year length-of-service requirement concurrent with the adoption of automatic enrollment. Asset accumulation is clearly only a relevant measure over the period for which individuals are eligible to contribute to the 401(k) plan. Hence, the measure of time that we use for this analysis is the months since 401(k) eligibility. The data used in constructing figure 2.5 are the pooled cross-sectional data from each company. The identification in these graphs thus comes from both variation by tenure within a cross section and from variation over time as individuals in multiple cross sections accumulate more tenure.

In both companies, the average balance-to-pay ratio starts out close to zero and increases steadily over time. The increase in the balance-to-pay ratio with tenure appears to be fairly linear in both companies, as would be expected when balances are low and most of the increase in value comes from additional savings contributions. In Company A, the balance-to-pay ratio for employees hired after automatic enrollment is above that for employees hired prior to automatic enrollment for tenures up to about forty-two months, at which point the curves start to intersect each other. In contrast, in Company B, the balance-to-pay ratio is virtually identical for employees hired before and after automatic enrollment with the same length of eligibility.

These average balance-to-pay ratios mask considerable heterogeneity, however, in the distributional effects of automatic enrollment on asset accumulation. In figure 2.6, we plot the balance-to-pay ratio for employees at the 25th, 50th, 75th, and 90th percentiles of the balance-to-pay distribution both before and after automatic enrollment. In both companies, the very low 401(k) participation rates prior to automatic enrollment are reflected in the zero balance-to-pay ratios of employees in the 25th percentile of the balance-to-pay distribution. For these employees, automatic enrollment clearly increases asset accumulation because it turns nonparticipants into participants.

As suggested in tables 2.2 and 2.3, among those hired after automatic enrollment, the individuals at the 25th percentile of the balance-to-pay distribution are primarily contributing at their respective company's default contribution rates and have their money invested almost entirely in the conservative default funds. For example, an employee who was automatically enrolled during her fourth month of tenure in Company A would accumulate 2 percent of her paycheck in a stable value fund each month. If we assume that the return on her stable value account is roughly equal to the rate of growth in her nominal earnings, this worker would have a balance-to-pay ratio of (2 percent) $(9/12 + 11/12)(1.67) = 5.6$ percent at the beginning of her twenty-fourth month at Company A. The factor of 1.67

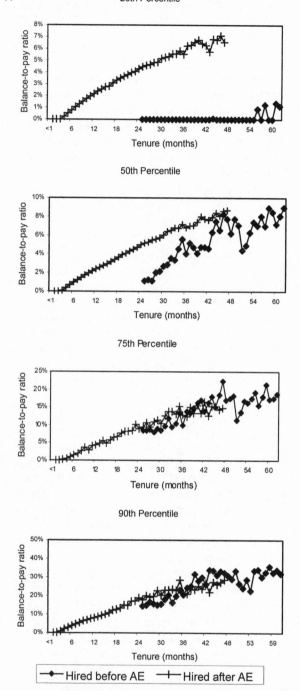

Fig. 2.6 *A*, The distribution of the 401(k) balance-to-pay ratio by tenure: Company A; *B*, the distribution of the 401(k) balance-to-pay ratio by tenure: Company B

B

25th Percentile

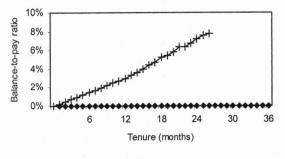

50th Percentile

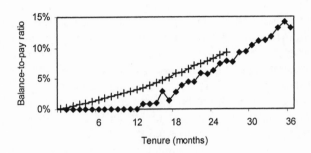

75th Percentile

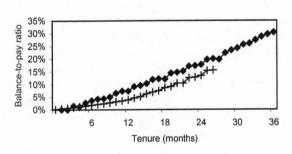

90th Percentile

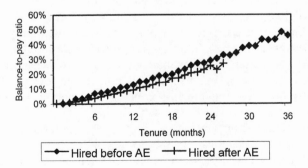

Fig. 2.6 (cont.)

reflects the employer matching rate of 67 percent at Company A (on the first 6 percent of pay). The predicted accumulation level of 5.6 percent of earnings is close to the empirical accumulation level of 4.3 percent (at the 25th percentile of the balance-to-pay distribution). The slight discrepancy may reflect a gap between the rate of nominal wage growth and the rate of return on the stable value fund since wages are in the denominator of the balance-to-pay ratio. Likewise, an employee who was automatically enrolled during her first month of tenure in Company B would accumulate 3 percent of her paycheck in a money market fund each month. If we assume that the return on her money market fund was roughly equal to the rate of growth in her nominal earnings, this worker would have a balance-to-pay ratio of (3 percent)(12/12 + 11/12)(1.5) = 8.6 percent at the beginning of her twenty-fourth month at Company B. This predicted accumulation level is comparable to the empirical accumulation level of 7.3 percent (at the 25th percentile of the balance-to-pay distribution).

In the 50th percentile of the distribution, we see nonzero balance accumulations for employees hired before and after automatic enrollment in both companies. Over the tenure ranges plotted in figure 2.6, employees at the 50th percentile of the balance-to-pay distribution hired after automatic enrollment have greater asset accumulation than do employees hired prior to automatic enrollment in Company B. This is also true in Company A for tenures of less than four years. This is due largely to the fact that before automatic enrollment, the typical employee does not join the 401(k) plan until he or she has worked for one to two years (see figure 2.1).

At the 75th and 90th percentiles of the balance-to-pay ratio, the asset accumulation profiles look fairly similar for employees hired before and after automatic enrollment. For Company A, the profiles are nearly indistinguishable. For Company B, employees hired after automatic enrollment at all tenure levels have slightly lower levels of asset accumulation at both the 75th and 90th percentile, although the differences between the two groups are small.

In summary, figures 2.5 and 2.6 tell a mixed story about the impact of automatic enrollment on asset accumulation. Automatic enrollment increases participation, raising wealth accumulation. But the typical automatic enrollment plan anchors participants at a low contribution rate and in a conservative asset class, lowering wealth accumulation. On average, these effects appear to be approximately offsetting. However, automatic enrollment *does* increase wealth accumulation in the lower tail of the wealth distribution by dramatically reducing the fraction of employees that do not participate in the 401(k) plan.

It is also useful to augment our study by analyzing a complementary measure of wealth accumulation: the average 401(k) contribution rate. This wealth accumulation measure is *not* distorted by the variability in market returns that potentially biases our analysis of balance-to-pay ratios. Recall that our data covers the latter half of the 1990s and that in all three companies automatic enrollment was implemented in 1997 or 1998. Thus, employees hired before the adoption of automatic enrollment had the benefit of a spectacular bull market, whereas those hired after automatic enrollment were more likely to experience a period of relatively flat equity performance. Such bull market effects will influence balance-to-pay ratios but may have only a small impact on average contribution rates.

Panels A and B of figure 2.7 plot the average contribution rates with respect to tenure of employees from Company A and Company B. Each figure plots an average contribution rate profile for employees hired before automatic enrollment and a profile for employees hired after automatic enrollment. The average contribution rate in these profiles includes *all* employees in the relevant tenure groups, including those who elect *not* to participate in the plan. We find that automatic enrollment weakly raises the average contribution rate. This effect is strongest for Company B, where the effect is a little less than 1 percentage point.[20]

This contribution rate analysis abstracts away from asset allocation issues. However, asset allocation decisions cannot be ignored, and they will probably continue to have important effects in the future. One way to gauge the long-run impact of the conservative investment default is to ask whether the default still has an effect after participants make at least one active decision in their 401(k) plan. Table 2.6 addresses this question by comparing participants hired before automatic enrollment to all participants hired after automatic enrollment, as well as the subset of participants hired after automatic enrollment who have elected at some point to change their 401(k) savings elections away from either the default contribution rate, the default investment fund, or both.

Participants hired before automatic enrollment (column [1] of table 2.6) are much less likely than participants hired after automatic enrollment (column [2]) to have any balances in the default fund and to have all their balances in the default fund. In addition, participants hired before automatic enrollment have a lower fraction of balances in the default fund.[21] Of greater interest is the comparison of participants hired before automatic enrollment (column [1]) to the subset of the participants hired after auto-

---

20. Note that the slope of the average contribution rate profile is driven mostly by increases in the 401(k) participation rate for employees hired prior to automatic enrollment, and mostly by movements away from the default contribution rate for employees hired after automatic enrollment.

21. For Company A, the fraction of balances in the default fund is calculated excluding company matching contributions, which are made in company stock, from the denominator. We make this exclusion because participants cannot elect to reallocate these matching contributions out of company stock until reaching the age of fifty-five. Thus, they do not represent balances over which the individuals have any control. Because participants can reallocate their matching contributions out of company stock upon reaching age fifty-five, we also restrict the sample for Company A in table 2.6 to individuals under the age of fifty-five.

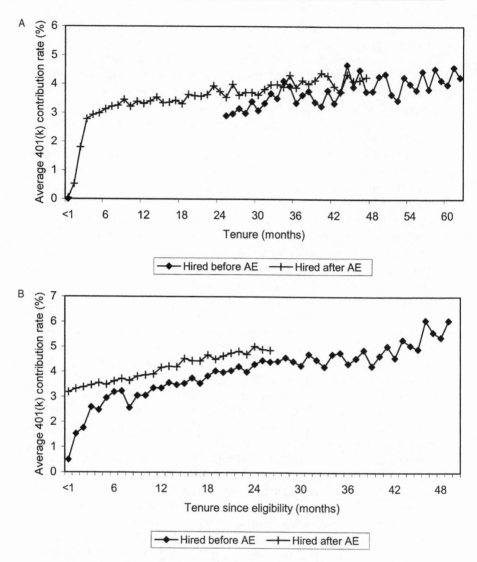

Fig. 2.7   *A,* Average 401(k) contribution rate by tenure (including nonparticipants): Company A; *B,* average 401(k) contribution rate by tenure (including nonparticipants): Company B

matic enrollment who have changed some aspect of their 401(k) savings
away from at least one of the defaults (column [3]). In all three companies,
participants hired before automatic enrollment are less likely to have any
balances in the default fund and have a lower fraction of balances in the default fund than do participants hired under automatic enrollment who
have made at least one active savings election. In Companies B and C, par-

Table 2.6   **Retention of the Default Fund Among Non-Default Participants Subject to Automatic Enrollment (%)**

	Hired Before Automatic Enrollment (1)	Hired After Automatic Enrollment	
		All (2)	Made Change (3)
Company A (tenure 24–35 months)			
Any balances in the default fund	35.5	71.7	41.5
All balances in the default fund	13.8	58.1	12.6
Fraction of balances in the default fund	19.1	62.5	21.9
Company B (tenure 0–23 months)			
Any balances in the default fund	14.8	86.0	60.6
All balances in the default fund	18.2	71.1	18.4
Fraction of balances in the default fund	6.8	76.0	32.4
Company C (tenure 12–35 months)			
Any balances in the default fund	27.5	59.8	33.9
All balances in the default fund	13.0	54.3	20.1
Fraction of balances in the default fund	16.9	55.7	23.8

Source: Authors' calculations.

Notes: The statistics in column (1) come from 12/1998 for Companies A and C and 12/1997 for Company B. The statistics in columns (2) and (3) come from 12/1999 for Company A, 03/2000 for Company B, and 12/2000 for Company C. The fraction of balances in the default fund in Company A excludes matching contributions made in company stock. The sample for Company A is 401(k) participants under the age of fifty-five. The sample for Company B is all 401(k) participants. The sample for Company C is 401(k) participants aged forty-plus at the time of hire. For Company C, the data in column (1) comes from before nonparticipants in the observed hire cohort became subject to automatic enrollment.

ticipants hired before automatic enrollment are also less likely to be wholly invested in the default fund than are participants hired under automatic enrollment who have made some change to the parameters of their 401(k) participation. Hence, it appears that the conservative investment defaults act as an anchor, even for participants who actively make changes to their 401(k) plan.

We conclude our analysis by asking what happens to 401(k) balances when a job separation occurs. Several recent papers suggest that a substantial fraction of individuals who change jobs take their 401(k) balances from a previous employer as cash distributions, and that this is particularly likely to be true for employees with low account balances.[22] Unfortunately, we do not have the data that would reveal whether automatic enrollment

22. See, for example, Poterba, Venti, and Wise (1998) and McCarthy and McWhirter (2000).

simply results in short-term deferred consumption for terminated employees or whether these employees actually continue to hold higher levels of retirement savings even after termination. For Companies A and C, however, we do have some information that is potentially informative. Our data for these two companies include terminated employees who had some account activity during the previous calendar year, along with their date of termination, whether a final distribution of the 401(k) balances was made from the account, and whether this final distribution was rolled directly over into another qualified plan or taken as a cash distribution. Because we have administrative data, we do not know whether cash distributions were subsequently rolled into a qualified plan by the participant receiving the distribution. However, from previous research on 401(k) distributions, we know that the likelihood of a cash distribution being used for consumption is high for low account balances,[23] and we can look to see whether employees hired under automatic enrollment are more likely to have a cash distribution than are employees hired prior to automatic enrollment.

To do this, we take the subset of all employees in Companies A and C who were active plan participants on December 31, 1998 or 1999 but whose employment terminated sometime in 1999 or 2000. These employees appear in the 1999 and 2000 data as terminated employees and have either a positive account balance if they have not taken a distribution, or a zero account balance and some positive value for final distributions if they have taken a cash distribution or a rollover. The average fraction of terminated employees who received a cash distribution is 67 percent in Company A and 64 percent in Company C. Using the entire group of terminated plan participants, we estimate a linear probability regression for the likelihood of having a cash distribution as a function of gender, age, pay, the month of termination, and whether the employee was hired under automatic enrollment. All of these variables, except the month of termination, are computed on December 31 of the year prior to termination.

Columns [1] and [3] of table 2.7 show the coefficients from this regression for Companies A and C, respectively. We do not report the month of termination coefficients, which are all highly significant but economically uninteresting (the likelihood of a distribution increases with the length of time since the job ended). Younger employees are slightly more likely to take a distribution in Company A, as are lower-paid individuals in both Companies A and C. Employees with greater levels of tenure, however, are less likely to take a cash distribution. Our key variable of interest, however, is whether an individual was hired under automatic enrollment. For Company C we are also able to analyze the effect of becoming subject to automatic

23. Poterba, Venti, and Wise (1998) report that the probability that a cash distribution is rolled over into an individual retirement account (IRA) or another employer's plan is only 5 to 16 percent for distributions of less than $5000. The probability that a cash distribution is rolled over into an IRA or another employer's plan or invested in some other savings vehicle is slightly higher at 14 to 33 percent.

Table 2.7   **Automatic Enrollment and the Distribution of 401(k) Account Balances**

	Company A		Company C	
	Exclude Balances	Include Balances	Exclude Balances	Include Balances
Constant	−0.1773***	−0.7513***	−0.1296	−0.0468**
	(0.0315)	(0.0365)	(0.0175)	(0.1832)
Automatic enrollment				
Hired after AE	0.0960***	0.1001***	0.0528	−0.1514
	(0.0162)	(0.0158)	(0.0794)	(0.1194)
Hired before AE but first participated after AE	—	—	0.1802	−0.0241
			(0.0991)	(0.0781)
Balances				
$0	—	0.6647***	—	—
		(0.0244)		
$1–$100	—	0.6920***	—	0.5119***
		(0.0247)		(0.1159)
$101–$500	—	0.6730***	—	0.4899***
		(0.0216)		(0.1004)
$501–$1,000	—	0.6205***	—	0.3878***
		(0.0206)		(0.0121)
$1,001–$2,000	—	0.5353***	—	0.3965***
		(0.0202)		(0.0925)
$2,001–$5,000	—	0.3387***	—	0.1830**
		(0.0200)		(0.0833)
$5,001–$10,000	—	0.0457	—	0.0965
		(0.0230)		(0.0865)
>$10,000 (omitted)	—	—	—	—
Female	−0.0042	−0.0122	−0.0738	−0.1050**
	(0.0075)	(0.0070)	(0.0435)	(0.0428)
Compensation				
Low pay	0.2069***	0.0177	0.4200***	0.2488***
	(0.0100)	(0.0111)	(0.0567)	(0.0634)
Middle pay	0.1681***	0.0050	0.3086***	0.1901***
	(0.0092)	(0.0100)	(0.0627)	(0.0650)
High pay (omitted)	—	—	—	—
Age				
<30	0.0649***	0.0281**	—	—
	(0.0124)	(0.0117)		
30–44	0.0522***	0.0374***	0.0246	0.0178
	(0.0126)	(0.0118)	(0.0465)	(0.0451)
45+ (omitted)	—	—		
Tenure	−0.0024***	0.0056***	−0.0057**	−0.0010
	(0.0004)	(0.0005)	(0.0027)	(0.0027)
Sample Size	11,590	11,590	429	429
R^2	0.3013	0.3910	0.3121	0.3681

Source: Authors' calculations.

Notes: Coefficients estimated from a linear probability regression of having taken a non-rollover 401(k) distribution on the independent variables listed and dummy variables for the month/year of termination. The sample includes active 401(k) participants under age sixty-five in 1998 and 1999 whose employment terminated in 1999 and 2000. The sample in Company C is further restricted to employees aged forty-plus at the time of hire. AE = automatic enrollment. Standard errors in parentheses.

***Significance at the 1 percent level.

**Significance at the 5 percent level.

enrollment as a nonparticipant who was hired before automatic enroll-ment.[24] In Company A, being subject to automatic enrollment as a new hire increases the probability of a distribution by 10 percentage points. In Company C, in contrast, automatic enrollment appears to have little im-pact on taking a cash distribution for those hired under automatic enroll-ment. Individuals subject to automatic enrollment as nonparticipants in Company C, however, are 18 percentage points more likely to take a distri-bution than are individuals not subject to automatic enrollment, although this effect is only significant at the 10 percent level.

The positive effect of automatic enrollment on taking a distribution in Company A (and on those who were hired before but first participated af-ter automatic enrollment in Company C) could be driven by the "coerced" participation of individuals subject to automatic enrollment who, not re-ally having wanted to save in the first place, use a job termination to access their 401(k) balances in order to consume them. Alternatively, these results could be driven by the fact that participants who were subject to automatic enrollment tend to have low 401(k) account balances. The induced partic-ipants under automatic enrollment have a low contribution rate, corre-spondingly lower employer matching contributions, and lower returns from the conservative default fund. In general, low-balance accounts tend to be distributed at a higher rate than high-balance accounts because em-ployers may compel a cash distribution of low account balances (<$5,000) for terminated employees if the employee does not elect a rollover into an-other qualified plan.

We can gauge the extent to which lower account balances are driving the positive automatic enrollment coefficients in columns [1] and [3] by includ-ing measures of balance size (see columns [2] and [4] of table 2.7). When we do so, the magnitude of the automatic enrollment effect is virtually un-changed in Company A. In Company C, in contrast, the automatic enroll-ment coefficients decline quite significantly in magnitude (and in fact, be-come negative) and are not statistically significant. Thus, the effect of automatic enrollment on the likelihood of taking a cash distribution ap-pears to vary quite substantially across these two companies.

It is also interesting to analyze the balance coefficients themselves. All but one of the balance measures are large and significant for both compa-nies. Employees with balances of less than $5,000 are 34–69 (18–51) per-centage points more likely to receive a cash distribution than are employ-ees with balances in excess of $10,000 in Company A (Company C). Employees with balances between $5,000 and $10,000, however, are no more likely to receive a cash distribution than are their counterparts with higher balances. In both companies, these coefficients imply that there is a

---

24. Note that this particular regression coefficient confounds both treatment and selection effects.

rather significant drop in the probability of a cash distribution once balances reach a threshold of $5,000. Interestingly, $5,000 corresponds to the legal threshold below which employers can compel a cash distribution for terminated employees.[25,26]

These results suggest that the effectiveness of automatic enrollment at increasing overall retirement savings accumulation will depend on the fraction of employees whose tenure ends before they reach the $5,000 balance threshold at which employers can compel cash distributions. Note that the law gives employers the *option* to compel a cash distribution for terminated employees with low account balances. Employers could choose to retain these balances unless the employee requests a distribution or a rollover. Alternatively, the employer could automatically roll over the account balances into an IRA unless the employee requests some other type of distribution.[27] Our evidence on the importance of defaults suggests that either of these actions would increase the impact of automatic enrollment on long-term retirement savings.

Going forward, the problem of automatic cash distributions for terminated employees with low account balances will be substantially lessened as recently enacted provisions of the Economic Growth and Tax Relief Reconciliation Act of 2001 take effect. This law changes the default treatment of $1,000 to $5,000 account balances for terminated employees. Under the new law, employers will no longer be able to compel a cash distribution if a former employee does not elect a rollover; rather, employers will be required to establish an IRA on behalf of participants if they choose not to maintain these accounts. Although this provision of the law will not take effect until regulations are issued by the Department of Labor (which must be done by June 2004), it will make automatic enrollment a more effective retirement savings tool when finally implemented.

25. Given this threshold, one might expect that all employees with balances of less than $5,000 would receive a cash distribution. There are two reasons why we do not observe this in our data. First, employees with balances of less than $5,000 may elect a direct rollover to another qualified plan before the compelled distribution would occur. Second, our measure of balances is that on December 31 of the year prior to termination, and is thus an imperfect measure of actual balances at the date of termination (in particular, it is likely to understate balances at the date of termination). Some employees with year-end balances of less than $5,000 will have balances in excess of $5,000 upon termination and thus will not be subject to an automatic cash distribution. This is more likely to be true for employees with higher year-end balances, which is consistent with the pattern of balance coefficients reported in table 2.7. See Choi et al. (2001) for a more detailed analysis of automatic cash distributions for individuals with balances below $5,000 at these two companies.

26. We should note that although employers can compel a cash distribution for terminated employees with an account balance of less than $5,000, the employee can take this distribution and roll it over into an IRA or another employer's retirement savings plan with no negative tax consequences. As noted earlier, however, the previous literature on this subject suggests that most of these small distributions are in fact consumed.

27. This type of automatic rollover was sanctioned in IRS Revenue Ruling 2000-36 (Internal Revenue Service 2000b).

2.6   Conclusions

Automatic enrollment dramatically changes 401(k) savings behavior. Most employees passively accept the automatic enrollment defaults, including the default savings rate and the default fund. This default behavior has an ambiguous impact on total savings. High 401(k) participation rates increase wealth accumulation, but low default savings rates and conservative default investment funds undercut wealth accumulation. We have traced out these effects over a two to four year horizon in three different companies.

For the two companies in which we can evaluate asset accumulation, automatic enrollment probably had a modest positive impact on employee balances, controlling for tenure. For Company A, automatic enrollment raised the average balance-to-pay ratio. For Company B, automatic enrollment did not affect the average balance-to-pay ratio. However, our analysis implicitly disadvantages automatic enrollment, because employees hired before automatic enrollment enjoyed a period of abnormally high equity returns. Had equity returns in the mid-1990s been typical instead of extraordinary, the employees hired before automatic enrollment would have had lower 401(k) balances, and hence would have achieved less wealth accumulation than the employees hired after automatic enrollment.

We also look at average contribution rates both before and after automatic enrollment. Averaging over all employees, including those with zero contribution rates, we find that automatic enrollment in our companies raises the average contribution rate by roughly half a percentage point.

Whether automatic enrollment had a positive impact on wealth accumulation, our analysis demonstrates that defaults make an enormous difference. For the companies in our study, automatic enrollment dramatically changes the distribution of wealth accumulation across employees. Automatic enrollment effectively cuts off the lower tail of the distribution (the employees who were not contributing), raising the participation rate to around 90 percent.

For the firms in our sample, automatic enrollment failed to dramatically raise wealth accumulation because of the conservative nature of the automatic enrollment defaults. Default savings rates of 2 to 3 percent of income and default investments in money market accounts undermine long-term wealth accumulation. Firms seeking to increase employee savings should adopt automatic enrollment with more aggressive defaults, including defaults that slowly raise the employee's contribution rate over time (e.g., Benartzi and Thaler 2001). Such firms may also want to consider either maintaining the small (<$5,000) account balances of terminated employees or automatically rolling them over into an IRA.

Of course, some firms may not wish to increase the aggressiveness of their defaults. High default savings rates may lead employees to "over-save," although there is a growing body of evidence that workers over-whelmingly perceive themselves as saving too little and welcome mechanisms that help them save more.[28] High default savings rates may increase firm matching costs.[29] Aggressive default investment funds, including equity exposure, may leave the firm vulnerable to employee lawsuits when volatile asset classes suffer capital losses. We do not know what a firm should optimally do. But we can confidently conclude that firms have the power to dramatically change patterns of retirement saving by simply changing the defaults that their employees face.

References

Benartzi, Shlomo, and Richard Thaler. 2001. Save more tomorrow: Using behavioral economics to increase employee saving. *Journal of Political Economy,* forthcoming.

Choi, James J., David Laibson, Brigitte C. Madrian, and Andrew Metrick. 2002. Defined contribution pensions: Plan rules, participant decisions, and the path of least resistance. In *Tax policy and the economy.* Vol. 16, ed. James M. Poterba, 67–113. Cambridge, Mass.: MIT Press.

Fidelity Investments. 2001. *Building futures: A report on corporate defined contribution plans.* Vol. 2. Boston: Fidelity Investments.

Internal Revenue Service. 1998. *Internal revenue bulletin 98–25* (June 22): 8. http://ftp.fedworld.gov/pub/irs-irbs/irb98-25.pdf.

———. 2000a. *Internal revenue bulletin 2000-7* (February 14): 617. http://ftp.fedworld.gov/pub/irs-irbs/irb00-7.pdf.

———. 2000b. *Internal revenue bulletin 2000-31* (July 31): 138–42. http://ftp.fedworld.gov/pub/irs-irbs/irb00-31.pdf.

Madrian, Brigitte C., and Dennis F. Shea. 2001. The power of suggestion: Inertia in 401(k) participation and savings behavior. *Quarterly Journal of Economics* 116:1149–87.

McCarthy, Mike, and Liz McWhirter. 2000. Are employees missing the big picture? Study shows need for ongoing financial education. *Benefits Quarterly* 16:25–31.

Poterba, James M., Steven F. Venti, and David A. Wise. 1998. Lump sum distributions from retirement savings plans: Receipt and utilization. In *Inquiries in the economics of aging,* ed. David A. Wise, 85–105. Chicago: University of Chicago Press.

Profit Sharing/401(k) Council of America. 2001. Automatic enrollment 2001: A study of automatic enrollment practices in 401(k) plans. http://www.pcsa.org/data/autoenroll2001.asp (accessed April 19, 2001).

Vanguard Center for Retirement Research. 2001. Automatic enrollment: Vanguard client experience. http://institutional.vanguard.com/pdf/automatic_enrollment_clientexp.pdf (accessed September 6, 2001).

28. See Choi et al. (2001) and Benartzi and Thaler (2001).

29. In equilibrium these increased matching costs should be offset with reduced rates of wage growth. However, employees and their unions may not be willing to make wage concessions in light of higher effective match rates. Hence, some firms may see highly successful retirement plans as a source of higher labor costs.

Comments   James M. Poterba

This paper offers provocative and compelling new evidence on how the structure of 401(k) plans can affect the saving decisions of workers who are eligible for these plans. The paper focuses on two firms that adopted "default-in" 401(k) plans in the late 1990s. The authors demonstrate that 401(k) participation rose markedly after the adoption of these plans. This confirms the earlier findings of Madrian and Shea (2001). The novelty of this paper is the analysis of how default asset allocation options affect the behavior of 401(k) contributors, in particular the mix of bonds and stocks in their accounts. The paper makes the important point that when employees are reluctant to change their asset allocation choices, the default chosen by a plan sponsor can have substantial and long-lasting effects. It appears that relatively conservative default allocations lead some 401(k) participants who might otherwise have chosen riskier asset allocations to adopt a more conservative investment posture. The evidence for this finding is that the fraction of workers choosing conservative asset allocation mixes *after* the firm adopts a conservative default mix is greater than the fraction choosing conservative mixes before the switch. Workers who select more conservative asset allocations after the institution of the default policy may experience reduced long-run 401(k) accumulations as a result of this difference in asset allocation.

The findings in this paper are important for several reasons. First, they suggest that participation in and asset allocation in retirement saving programs can be directly affected by employer decisions about plan defaults. This is encouraging evidence for public policy makers who seek to find policy instruments that can affect retirement saving. It may also be worrying evidence for corporate executives with responsibility for 401(k)-type retirement plans. If the defaults that the firm chooses for its saving plan have significant consequences for worker wealth accumulation, then firms may face future court challenges if workers reach retirement with inadequate resources and their resource shortfall can plausibly be traced to the firm's default policies. The evidence in this paper suggests that the 401(k) plan design that employers choose may have important long-term consequences. It should lead to careful analysis of how such defaults are chosen.

Second, the results provide interesting new evidence on the role of "status quo bias" in individual decision making. Even with respect to decisions as important as the amount one saves for retirement, it seems that many individuals do not make an effort to compare the costs and benefits of alter-

James M. Poterba is the Mitsui Professor of Economics and associate head of the economics department at the Massachusetts Institute of Technology, and the director of the Public Economics Research Program at the National Bureau of Economic Research.

native policies, and that they follow paths of least resistance in choosing their saving rates. The findings in this study are broadly consistent with other evidence on behavior of participants in retirement plans. For example, Samuelson and Zeckhauser (1988) report that only 2.5 percent of Teachers Insurance and Annuity Association College Retirement Equities Fund (TIAA-CREF) participants change their asset allocations in a typical year, and that roughly three-quarters of TIAA-CREF participants have *never* changed their asset allocation. These statistics are based on data from the 1980s, and the recent advent of on-line account access in retirement plans may have increased the frequency of portfolio changes. Nevertheless, the probability of account changes is likely to remain small. Benartzi and Thaler (2001) show that policies that commit individuals who join a 401(k) plan to increase the fraction of their salary devoted to the plan in future years tend to increase the employee saving rate in such plans.

The empirical findings in this paper are quite convincing. The authors have tried to address a range of factors that might confound their findings. There is a lingering worry, however, that firms that alter the default policies in their 401(k) plans also change other aspects of their retirement saving programs. If firms that switch from "default-out" to "default-in" policies also adopt policies to communicate the benefits of retirement saving to their workers, this could increase participation in the retirement program for reasons *not* related to the default policy. It is difficult to know how one can control for this possibility, except by contacting the sample firms and carefully evaluating each company's retirement policy.

A distinct concern about these findings involves their power to generalize to the setting in which default-in 401(k) plans have been in operation for many years. One finding that emerges in earlier studies of 401(k) participant behavior with respect to decisions such as the use of lump sum distributions (e.g., Poterba, Venti, and Wise 2001) is that participant behavior varies with the *size* of the 401(k) balance. In the lump sum distribution case, individuals with small 401(k) balances are much more likely than those with substantial balances to withdraw their assets from the retirement saving system. It is possible that similar behaviors might arise with respect to asset allocation within the 401(k) plan. When individuals have relatively small balances in their accounts, they might not pay much attention to their asset allocation. When the balances grow larger, however, they might take an active interest in the account, and the importance of the default allocation may diminish. As firm experience with 401(k) plans cumulates, it should be possible to explore these issues.

The findings on the salience of default policies raise a challenge to neoclassical analysis of saving behavior. One is led to ask whether it is possible to explain the findings without resorting to the argument of status quo bias. There are a number of possibilities. One is that there are decision-making costs associated with trying to decide how much to save, and how to allocate that saving across different investment options. In the presence of such costs, individuals may be prepared to simply follow the default option offered by their employer. A second possibility is that individuals assume that the default options offered by the employer are based on a careful analysis of what is "right" for the typical employee. This suggests that individuals confronting the default options may decide that they are receiving some financial advice when they are told about the default. In this setting, the plan participants—perhaps incorrectly—assume that they need substantial information that differentiates their situation from that of other workers before they alter their allocations relative to the default. This might be heightened by a concern that managers will know, and somehow disapprove, if they choose a saving policy other than the company's default policy. Yet a third possibility is that the importance of the default simply reflects procrastination on the part of plan participants. If individuals think that they will evaluate the information on investment options at some point after they enroll in the plan, but then never find time to do so, this could explain the patterns we observe. Procrastination and status quo bias may be closely related.

The findings in this paper raise a number of issues for further analysis. The first concerns the impact of changes in 401(k) plan default provisions on economic welfare. Evaluating this question is likely to prove difficult, because the finding that default policies matter casts some doubt on standard neoclassical models of saving behavior. Building nonstandard models of saving behavior, and then using them to evaluate the welfare impact of changes in default provisions, is a substantial research challenge. A second issue for further study involves determining whether individuals are in fact roughly indifferent to the fraction of their income that they allocate to saving. The apparent importance of default options with regard to the amount that individuals contribute to their retirement plans suggests that a substantial group of workers do not have strong views about the appropriate fraction of their salary to save. Direct sample survey questions about this issue might reveal useful information about the structure of household saving preferences.

A final question, which is more tractable than the others, is determining how the default contribution level affects participation decisions. Previous work has established that defaulting in to the retirement saving plan increases plan participation. The next question is whether defaulting in at 2 percent of salary, 4 percent of salary, or 6 percent of salary has a differential effect on the rate of participation. Measuring the shape of this response function should provide some evidence on whether these decisions in fact reflect some degree of optimization. If workers face liquidity constraints or other considerations that lead them to assign a cost to making 401(k) contributions, then defaults that require greater contributions are likely to result in lower participation rates than defaults with low contribution rates.

The evidence on the importance of default options raises another issue about the current trend toward 401(k) plans that offer more and more options to their participants. It is possible that a substantial group of 401(k) participants does not wish to have a broad menu of choices, if these choices require them to collect information on different investment options and make decisions about how to allocate their retirement assets. Such participants may value default plans or stratified choice structures that permit them to select among only a few options, rather than to consider a broad menu. If such workers account for a substantial share of 401(k) participants, however, the results in this paper suggest that designing the default structure is extremely important.

References

Benartzi, Shlomo, and Richard Thaler. 2001. Naïve diversification strategies in defined contribution saving plans. *American Economic Review* 91:79–98.

Madrian, Brigitte, and Dennis Shea. 2001. The power of suggestion: Inertia in 401(k) participation and savings behavior. *Quarterly Journal of Economics* 66 (4): 1149–88.

Poterba, James M., Steven F. Venti, and David A. Wise. 2001. Preretirement cashouts and foregone retirement saving: Implications for 401(k) asset accumulation. In *Themes in the economics of aging,* ed. David A. Wise, 23–56. Chicago: University of Chicago Press.

Samuelson, William, and Richard Zeckhauser. 1988. Status quo bias in decision-making. *Journal of Risk and Uncertainty* 1:7–59.

3

Aging and Housing Equity
Another Look

Steven F. Venti and David A. Wise

Except for Social Security and, for some, employer-provided pension assets, housing equity is the most important asset of a large fraction of older Americans. In principle, these assets might be used to support consumption after retirement. In this paper we take another look at the change in the home equity of older families as they age, beginning at ages just before retirement. We use data from the Health and Retirement Study (HRS), the Asset and Health Dynamics Among the Oldest Old (AHEAD) survey, as well as the Survey of Income and Program Participation (SIPP). We distinguish changes in housing equity that might be thought of as part of a financial plan to use housing equity as a means of general support in retirement from changes in housing equity that are precipitated by family shocks—death or severe illness.

This paper extends the analysis in Venti and Wise (2001), in which we found that in the absence of changes in household structure, most elderly families are unlikely to move.[1] We also found that even among movers, those families that continue to own typically do not reduce home equity. However, precipitating shocks, like the death of a spouse or entry into a nursing home, sometimes lead to liquidation of home equity. Home equity

Steven F. Venti is the DeWalt Ankeny Professor of Economic Policy at Dartmouth College and a research associate of the National Bureau of Economic Research. David A. Wise is the John F. Stambaugh Professor of Political Economy at the John F. Kennedy School of Government, Harvard University, and the director for Health and Retirement Programs at the National Bureau of Economic Research.

We thank the National Institute on Aging and the Hoover Institution for financial support.

1. The AHEAD initially surveyed persons aged seventy and over in 1993 and resurveyed them in 1995 as part of the second wave of AHEAD and resurveyed them again in 1998 as part of the fourth wave of the HRS. For convenience we refer to these surveys as the first three waves of AHEAD.

is typically not liquidated to support *general* nonhousing consumption needs. The analysis in the current paper is also based on both the HRS and AHEAD data, as well as data from eight panels of the SIPP. Again, the key question is whether housing wealth is typically used to support the general consumption of older persons as they age, although the analysis is based on more extensive data. The present analysis also presents a more formal accounting for the change in home equity when ownership is discontinued and the change in home equity when moving to another owned unit ("up-sizing" or "downsizing"). In addition, we give brief consideration to parallel changes in nonhousing assets as persons age.

The change in housing equity as persons age has been considered in several earlier papers, using data that covered an earlier time period or data for persons at younger ages. In Venti and Wise (1989, 1990), we concluded that households don't want to reduce housing equity as they age. We found that large reductions in home equity were typically associated with the death of a spouse, retirement, or with other precipitating shocks. These analyses were based on the Retirement History Survey (RHS) and covered persons in the fifty-eight to seventy-three age range. Merrill (1984), basing her findings on the Retirement History Survey (RHS), found that unless there was a change in family status there was little if any reduction in housing equity as families aged. Feinstein and McFadden (1989), basing their findings on the Panel Survey of Income Dynamics (PSID), including households with heads over age seventy-five, also concluded that in the absence of change in family status housing equity was typically not reduced. Megbolugbe, Sa-Aadu, and Shilling (1997) also used the PSID and found that the change in housing equity varied by age. The oldest households (age seventy-five-plus) were as likely to trade up as to trade down when they moved. Sheiner and Weil (1993) found some decline in home equity at older ages, but these declines were primarily associated with shocks to family status and health. Hurd (1999), in a general analysis of wealth change based on the first two waves of the AHEAD, concluded that there was a modest decline in housing wealth and rates of home ownership for two-person households that survived the two-year period intact, but larger declines for two-person households that lost a member between the waves. He also found that total wealth increased between the waves for all types of households and at all ages.

Whether the elderly perceive home equity as a source of funds for general consumption as they grow older is an important issue for at least two reasons. A concern of some is that older households have substantial wealth locked in illiquid housing and would like to release it. A proposed solution to this perceived problem is a reverse annuity mortgage that allows the household to draw down home equity while remaining in the home. To date, there has been little apparent interest in reverse mortgages. It is not clear whether the failure is due to unfavorable financial terms of reverse mortgages or simply to a lack of demand for a product that is intended to exhaust housing equity over the life of the occupant. Several studies, including Venti and Wise (1991), Mayer and Simons (1994), and Merrill, Finkel, and Kutty (1994), have shown that a significant segment of the population appears to be "income-poor and house-rich" and might benefit from a reverse mortgage. We concluded in our earlier analyses, however, that the equity choices of older persons were inconsistent with substantial interest in such products. Nonetheless, knowing whether older households wish to withdraw assets from housing equity helps to evaluate the extent of the potential market for reverse mortgages, and we judge it important to revisit the issue.

A second reason to consider whether the elderly plan to, or will, use home equity to support general consumption is to understand the adequacy of saving for retirement. If housing equity is used just like financial assets to support consumption after retirement, then it might also be considered as a substitute for financial wealth and perhaps treated interchangeably with financial wealth in considering the well-being of the elderly. On the other hand, if households do not plan to draw down home equity as they age, it may be more realistic to assume that general consumption expenditures will come largely from accumulated financial wealth, including Social Security and other annuities. Analysts considering how well households are prepared for retirement have treated housing equity in various ways. Moore and Mitchell (2000) include housing wealth in the set of assets that can be used to finance retirement. The Congressional Budget Office (1993) also includes housing wealth with other wealth. On the other hand, in "Is the Baby Boom Generation Preparing Adequately for Retirement," Bernheim (1992) excluded housing wealth in making a determination. Engen, Gale, and Uccello (1999) include zero percent, 50 percent, and 100 percent of housing equity. Gustman and Steinmeier (1999) conduct analyses using zero and 100 percent of home equity.

In this paper we first consider the relationship between age and housing equity over the life cycle, based on data from the SIPP. This analysis is drawn largely from Venti and Wise (2001). The results are based on cohort analysis and are presented graphically. Next, we present more detailed cohort analysis for older households, based on the HRS and the AHEAD data.

We then focus on within-household changes in housing equity, giving particular attention to the effect of precipitating shocks. We find that on average there is no reduction in housing equity among persons who continue to own homes, even as they age through their eighties and even into their nineties. Indeed, persons who sell one house and buy another tend to increase housing equity, on average. Large reductions in housing equity are typically associated only with selling and discontinuing home ownership. Giving up ownership is most often associated with the death of a spouse or entry into a nursing home. In these cases, home equity may be used to pay medical expenses or indeed to support more general consumption of a surviving spouse, although we have not attempted here to document such expenditures. In general, however, we find that home equity is not systematically converted to liquid assets to support nonhousing consumption.

Finally, our analysis draws attention to two limiting features of the HRS and AHEAD data. The first feature concerns the use of imputations in analysis of panel data. Our earlier analysis of the AHEAD data was based on preliminary releases of AHEAD wave 2 and HRS wave 4 (the third wave of AHEAD). In the current paper we use more recent releases of the second wave of AHEAD and the fourth wave of the HRS that include asset imputations—including home equity—provided by the HRS staff.[2] Tabulations from the new data sources are similar to tabulations presented in Venti and Wise (2001) that did not use these imputations. We find, however, that in many instances the imputations appear to increase the randomness in the data. This is perhaps not surprising, given that imputed values are "hot-decked," based on contemporaneous cross-section data. In panel applications, the imputed values should be based on both family-specific longitudinal data, as well as cross-section data. In this paper, all analyses using the "selling price" data (section 2.5 forward) drop imputed observations.

A second, related concern is the large number of inconsistent responses in the *reported* data, particularly when comparing "move" and "stay" transitions to "own" and "rent" housing tenures. For example, many households are reported to own in one wave then rent in the next, and then return to ownership in the third wave, without reporting a move between either the first and second waves, or between the second and third waves. Many of these households begin and end with the same (or similar) home equity. Most of these anomalies are apparently reporting errors. Each such error results in two changes in housing equity that are of equal magnitude but opposite sign and thus may have a large effect on calculated changes in home equity. In some of our analyses we have dropped observations that reported a change in tenure but did not report a move. We also find many unrealistically large wave-to-wave swings in home equity among households that *stay* in the same home. These apparent errors are comparable in magnitude to the changes in home equity reported by movers.[3]

Much of the analysis in this paper is based on recent selling prices and on the reported equity in newly purchased homes. We believe these data are likely to be the most reliable data on home equity. We also have given considerable attention to evaluating the extent of bias in self-assessed home values. Thus, on balance, while we believe that more attention can be given to improving the data, we are comfortable with our principal conclusions.

2. The newer data also use additional information on death and nursing home entry that has recently become available.

3. The HRS is currently using "callback" procedures to resolve these issues.

3.1   Cohort Description

3.1.1   SIPP Data on Home Ownership and Equity over the Life Course

The SIPP provides housing equity (obtained from home value and mortgage debt) data for seven years—1984, 1985, 1987, 1988, 1991, 1993, and 1995. The survey panels and waves that provide the data are as follows:

Panel	Wave	Dates in Field
1984	4	Sept.–Dec. 1984
	7	Sept.–Dec. 1985
1985	3	Sept.–Dec. 1985
	7	Jan.–Apr. 1987
1986	4	Jan.–Apr. 1987
	7	Jan.–Apr. 1988
1987	4	Feb.–May 1988
1990	4	Feb.–May 1991
1991	7	Feb.–May 1993
1992	4	Feb.–May 1993
1993	7	Feb.–May 1995

From the random sample of cross-section data in each of these years we have created cohort data. For example, to trace the home equity of persons who were aged twenty-six in 1984, we begin with the average home equity of persons aged twenty-six, based on the random sample of persons aged twenty-six in 1984 survey. Next we obtain the average equity of persons aged twenty-seven from the 1985 survey, aged twenty-nine in the 1987 survey, and so forth. We identify cohorts by their age in the 1984 survey. We do this for seventeen cohorts defined by the age of the cohort in the first year of the data. In fact, to obtain more precise estimates of housing equity, the data for a cohort, like age twenty-six, is the average of data for a three-year age interval—twenty-five, twenty-six, and twenty-seven. We do this for cohorts age twenty-six, twenty-nine, . . . to age seventy-one, seventy-four. All cohorts are followed until age eighty in the SIPP.[4]

Figure 3.1 shows the percent of two-person households who own a home, by cohort. These data can be affected by differential mortality. For example, suppose that home owners were less likely to die at any age than renters. In this case, the ownership rate would be increased with age simply because the owners lived and the renters died. To account for this possibility, we made a mortality correction to the data, which is explained in the appendix. The mortality-corrected data for two-person households is shown in figure 3.1. To make the figure easier to read, only selected cohorts are shown. The key message of the figure is that home ownership does not

---

4. Data for households over age eighty are not used because age is top coded at eighty.

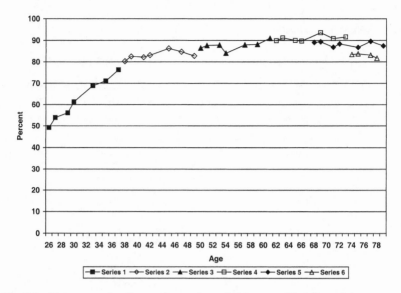

Fig. 3.1   Percent owning for two-person households, mortality adjusted data from SIPP

Source: Authors' calculations, SIPP data.

decline with age, through age seventy-nine. In addition, there appear to be no important cohort effects until about age seventy. That is, there are no large jumps when the data for one cohort ends and the data for another cohort begins. At older ages, however, there do appear to be noticeable cohort effects. Home ownership is lower for the last two cohorts. But like the trends for the other cohorts, there is no evident decline in ownership as these cohorts age.

Home ownership data for one-person households are shown in figure 3.2. Again there is no apparent decline in ownership with age, through age seventy-nine. Indeed, the data seem to show some increase in ownership at the oldest ages.

Cohort home equity data for two-person families are shown in figure 3.3. These data are in 1995 dollars and are corrected for mortality. The within-cohort data show no decline in home equity as the cohort ages. The data may even show some increase in equity within cohorts for ages sixty-five to seventy-nine. There do appear to be some cohort effects in equity, as evidenced by the jumps when the data for one cohort ends and the data for another cohort begins.

In estimates reported in Venti and Wise (2001), we show rather systematic cohort effects. The estimates show that both older cohorts—those over age seventy in 1984, and younger cohorts—those younger than thirty-six in 1984, have lower home equity than the average, while the middle-aged

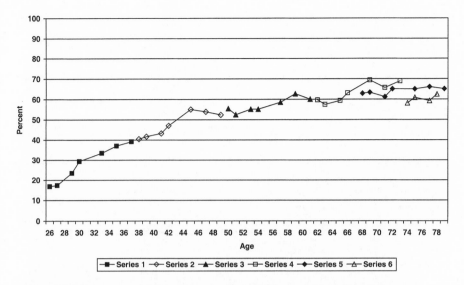

Fig. 3.2   Percent owning for one-person households, mortality adjusted data from SIPP

Source: Authors' calculations, SIPP data.

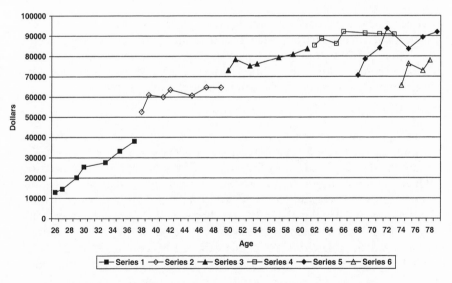

Fig. 3.3   Home equity for two-person households, mortality and CPI adjusted data from SIPP

Source: Authors' calculations, SIPP data.

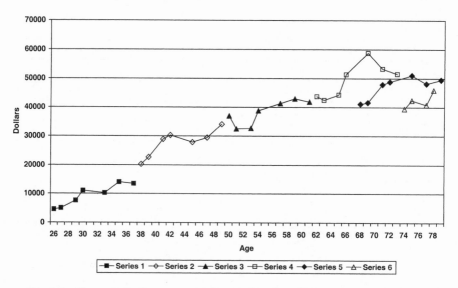

Fig. 3.4   Home equity for one-person households, mortality and CPI adjusted data from SIPP

Source: Authors' calculations, SIPP data.

cohorts have higher equity than the average. The cohort effects are likely determined in large part by differences in housing price changes over time.[5]

Figure 3.4 shows the cohort equity data for one-person households, corrected for mortality and inflation. As with the two-person households, there seems to be no decline in equity through age seventy-nine.

3.1.2   At Older Ages: HRS and AHEAD

To understand trends in home equity at older ages, we use the AHEAD as well as the HRS. Both are panel studies. The HRS follows persons in households with heads aged fifty-one to sixty-one in 1992. Members of these households were interviewed in 1992 and again in 1994, 1996, and 1998. In 1998, the heads were aged fifty-seven to sixty-seven. Thus this age range is included within the SIPP ages. The AHEAD study follows persons in households with heads aged seventy and older in 1993. These households were interviewed in 1993 and again in 1995 and in 1998 (as part of the fourth wave of the HRS).[6] The AHEAD age range overlaps the older

5. For example, assume that homes are bought at age thirty-five on average, and consider the cohort that was aged fifty in 1984 compared to the cohort that was aged thirty-eight in 1984. The older cohort bought homes in 1969, on average, and would have gained from large home price increases in the 1970s. On the other hand, the younger cohort would have bought homes in 1981, on average, and would have seen much lower increases in home equity during the 1980s and 1990s.

6. Juster and Suzman (1995) provide details of the survey design.

SIPP ages. Thus both HRS and AHEAD allow comparison with components of the longer life-cycle SIPP data. Details of the survey design are presented in Juster and Suzman (1995).

In this analysis, we follow households in both the AHEAD and HRS files. One complication is tracking households over time. A household may split through divorce or separation, members may die, or a family member may enter a nursing home. For the purposes of this analysis, we have adopted these conventions: In the first wave of each survey households are identified as either one-person or two-person households (institutionalized persons are excluded from the original sample). In subsequent survey waves we classify each household—according to the change since the prior wave—into one of the following six "states":

1 = continuing one-person household
2 = continuing two-person household
D = one of the original members has died
T = both of the original members have died
N = one or more members has entered a nursing home
S = household composition has changed for some other reason (most often a split through divorce or separation or the addition of a new adult member)
0 = household refused the interview or is missing for other reasons

The sequences observed in the HRS and AHEAD are presented in table 3.1. These sequences are used to distinguish households included in the following analyses. In cohort analysis in the next section we restrict attention to continuing two-person or one-person households identified as "2222" or "1111" for the HRS and "222" or "111" for the AHEAD. In the following section we consider changes in housing equity and other assets between waves. For this analysis we use each two-period sequence (creating an interval), and we focus in particular on the within-household relationship between home ownership and home equity on the one hand and change in household composition on the other hand. We consider cohort data on home ownership first. Then we consider cohort data on home equity, as well as nonhousing net assets.

Home Ownership

To obtain cohort data comparable to the SIPP cohort data, we construct cohorts from the HRS and AHEAD data by grouping households in two-year age intervals. These constructed cohorts are the basis for the cohort data shown in the following.

The home ownership cohort data for two-person families are shown in figure 3.5, which covers ages from fifty to ninety-three. To make the individual cohort data easier to view, only selected—largely nonoverlapping—cohorts are shown. The first three cohorts plotted in the figure are from the

Table 3.1   Household Status Sequences in the HRS and in the AHEAD/HRS

		HRS				AHEAD/HRS	
Sequence	N	All (%)	Group (%)	Sequence	N	All (%)	Group (%)
2222	3,311	43.75	68.39	222	1,203	19.93	55.75
2220	225	2.97	4.65	22D	293	4.86	13.58
222D	156	2.06	3.22	220	133	2.2	6.16
222S	42	0.55	0.87	22N	33	0.55	1.53
222N	10	0.13	0.21	22T	27	0.45	1.25
2200	307	4.06	6.34	2DD	234	3.88	10.84
22DD	131	1.73	2.71	200	112	1.86	5.19
22SS	47	0.62	0.97	2DT	47	0.78	2.18
22D0	10	0.13	0.21	2ND	26	0.43	1.20
2000	377	4.98	7.79	2TT	20	0.33	0.93
2DDD	116	1.53	2.40	2D0	19	0.31	0.88
2SSS	94	1.24	1.94	2NN	11	0.18	0.51
2D00	15	0.2	0.31	Subtotal	2,158		100.00
Subtotal	4,841		100.00	111	2,217	36.74	57.70
1111	1,832	24.21	68.61	11D	405	6.71	10.54
1110	119	1.57	4.46	11N	186	3.08	4.84
111D	52	0.69	1.95	110	142	2.35	3.70
111S	12	0.16	0.45	1DD	462	7.66	12.02
111N	10	0.13	0.37	100	266	4.41	6.92
1100	179	2.37	6.70	1ND	98	1.62	2.55
11DD	69	0.91	2.58	1NN	66	1.09	1.72
11SS	10	0.13	0.37	Subtotal	3,842		100.00
1000	323	4.27	12.10	Other	35	0.6	
1DDD	64	0.85	2.40	All	6,035	100.02	
Subtotal	2,670		100.00				
Other	57	0.74					
All	7,568	99.98					

Note: N = number of observations. See text for explanation of sequences.

HRS; the last five are from the AHEAD. Overall, the within-cohort data show an increase in home ownership through age seventy. Thereafter the cohort data suggest a small decline in ownership. A more detailed analysis of these data, presented in the following, shows that for the AHEAD sample the within-cohort decline in ownership for continuing two-person households is about 0.66 percent per year for cohorts aged seventy to seventy-eight in the initial year and 0.34 percent for cohorts aged eighty or more in the initial year. A comparison of these data with the SIPP data in figure 3.1 shows that for persons aged fifty to seventy-nine the SIPP and the HRS-AHEAD data are very similar. Both data sources show ownership rates of about 90 percent for families over age sixty. The within-cohort SIPP data, however, show no decline in ownership through age seventy-nine.

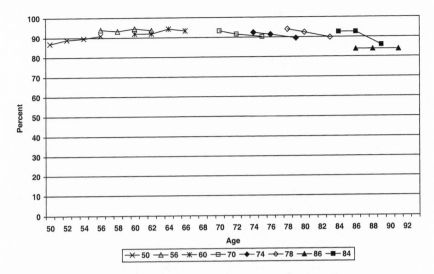

Fig. 3.5   Percent owning for two-person households, data from HRS and AHEAD
Source: Authors' calculations, HRS and AHEAD data.

The pattern of home ownership for continuing one-person households, shown in figure 3.6, is quite different. Again, there are some cohort effects. The within-cohort data for one-person households show a distinct rise in ownership between ages fifty and seventy-five and a decline in ownership at older ages. For AHEAD households—aged seventy and older—the within-cohort decline for the continuing one-person AHEAD households is a little over 1 percent per year. (The data used to produce figures 3.5 and 3.6 differ in some respects from the data used in similar calculations presented in subsequent sections of the paper. First, the figures are based on persons who were continuing one- or two-person households over all of the survey waves. Some of the subsequent calculations are based on continuing one- or two-person households between two consecutive survey waves. Second, the figures account for both own-to-rent (or other) and rent-to-own transitions. Rent-to-own transitions offset to some extent own-to-rent transitions. Some subsequent calculations are based only on the transitions of initial homeowners. Third, a noticeable number of reported changes in tenure are not associated with a move. We believe that most of these changes in tenure are reporting or coding errors, as discussed in section 3.2.1. For example, considering the AHEAD portion of figure 3.6, the within-cohort decline in ownership for continuing one-person households is 1.29 percent per year, using the data as reported. If households that report changes in tenure without a move are not included in the calculations, the decline is only about 0.98 percent per year. Using the latter data, home ownership of continuing one-person households is 74.7 percent at age sev-

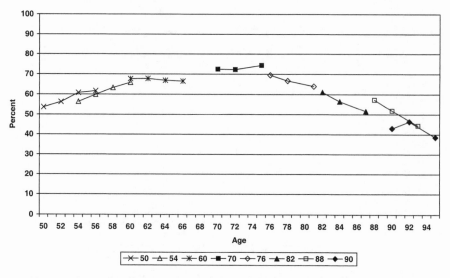

Fig. 3.6   Percent owning for one-person households, data from HRS and AHEAD
Source: Authors' calculations, HRS and AHEAD data.

enty. At an annual decline of 0.98 percent per year, 61.28 percent of these one-person households would still be owners at age ninety.)

Home Equity

Mean home equity cohort data for two-person households are shown in figure 3.7.[7] These within-cohort data show an increase in home equity through about age seventy or seventy-five. At older ages, the randomness within cohorts makes it hard to see clear trends, although there appears to be a within-cohort decline in equity. In fact, data presented below show that the average mean decline is about $2,100 per year, which is largely accounted for by the reported decline in the same-home equity of continuing owners.

The home equity cohort data for one-person households are shown in figure 3.8. As with the two-person households, there is a clear within-cohort increase in home equity through age seventy or seventy-five. At older ages a consistent within-cohort trend is not apparent. Data presented in the following show that the average decline is about $3,000 per year, again, largely accounted for by the reported decline in the same-home equity of continuing owners. There appear to be substantial differences in

7. All dollar amounts for the SIPP and AHEAD have been converted to 1998 dollars using the consumer price index (CPI).

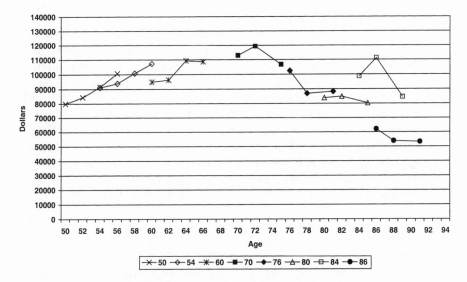

Fig. 3.7   Mean home equity for two-person households, data from HRS and AHEAD

Source: Authors' calculations, HRS and AHEAD data.

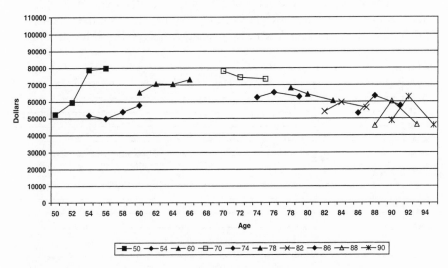

Fig. 3.8   Mean home equity for one-person households, data from HRS and AHEAD

Source: Authors' calculations, HRS and AHEAD data.

home equity by cohort, although the randomness in the data makes it hard to distinguish cohort effects from within-cohort changes in home equity.

Median cohort data for two- and one-person households are shown in figures 3.9 and 3.10, respectively. There is less randomness in the median data than in the mean data, and thus within-cohort trends are easier to discern in these figures. For example, for older two-person households the medians suggest modest within-cohort decline in home equity beginning at about age seventy-five, but cohort effects are not apparent. On the other hand, the median cohort data for older one-person households show little within-cohort decline in home equity but rather substantial cohort effects. Older cohorts seem to have successively less home equity. In the following, we present quantitative estimates of the within-cohort changes in home equity.

Nonhome Equity

In considering the equity value of housing as these cohorts aged, it is informative to compare the value of housing with other assets. Cohort data on nonhousing assets are shown in figures 3.11, 3.12, 3.13, and 3.14. Like the home equity data, mean and median cohort data are shown for two- and one-person households, and separate figures are shown for the older AHEAD households. As with the home equity data, the trend in the nonhome equity data for the HRS households is quite clear. But the extent of randomness in the data makes the cohort data for the AHEAD households

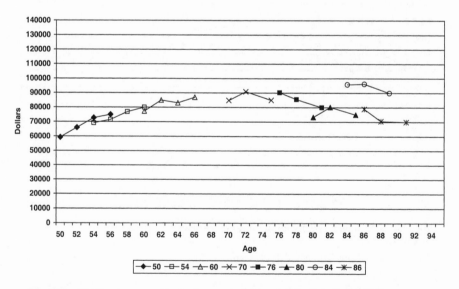

Fig. 3.9   Median home equity for two-person households, data from HRS and AHEAD

Source: Authors' calculations, HRS and AHEAD data.

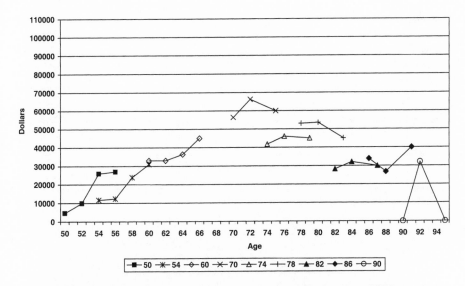

Fig. 3.10   Median home equity for one-person households, data from HRS and AHEAD

Source: Authors' calculations, HRS and AHEAD data.

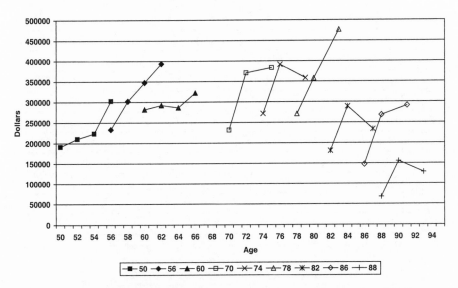

Fig. 3.11   Mean nonhousing equity for two-person households, data from HRS and AHEAD

Source: Authors' calculations, HRS and AHEAD data.

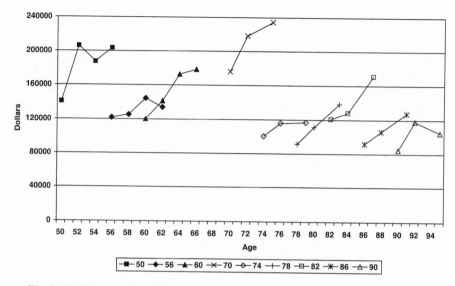

Fig. 3.12 Mean nonhousing equity for one-person households, data from HRS and AHEAD

Source: Authors' calculations, HRS and AHEAD data.

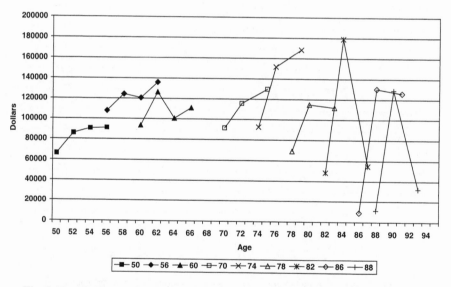

Fig. 3.13 Median nonhousing equity for two-person households, data from HRS and AHEAD

Source: Authors' calculations, HRS and AHEAD data.

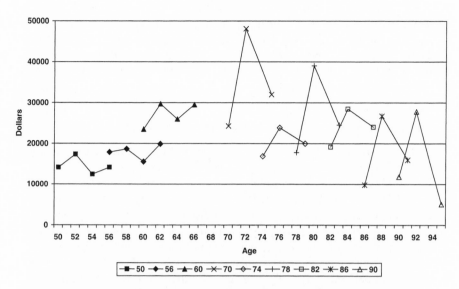

Fig. 3.14   Median nonhousing equity for one-person households, data from HRS and AHEAD

Source: Authors' calculations, HRS and AHEAD data.

much harder to interpret. Nonetheless, some trends are clear from the cohort data. (In the following we show quantitative within-cohort changes in nonhome assets, as well as home equity.)

First, it is clear for the HRS households that both home equity and housing increased with age, but the nonhousing assets increased much more. For example, from figure 3.7 it can be seen that the mean home equity of continuing two-person households increased from about $80,000 at age fifty to about $120,000 for households in their early seventies. There seem to be no apparent cohort effects. In figure 3.11, it can be seen that nonhousing assets of the HRS households increased from about $200,000 at age fifty to close to $400,000 at age seventy-four, about five times as much as the increase in home equity. Again, cohort effects are not apparent in this age range. In future analysis we will try to determine which components of nonequity assets account for the large increase.

Second, for the older HRS households there are also large within-cohort increases in nonequity assets. For the older households, however, there are also large cohort effects, with successively older cohorts having lower nonhousing assets. And, for the older cohorts there is some within-cohort decline in home equity.

It may be that there are in fact very large wave to wave changes in both home equity and nonhousing assets. We believe, however, that the data is likely to reflect substantial reporting or recording errors. Thus further verification and "cleaning" of the data—including callbacks to correct retrospective information—might result in more consistent cohort patterns. These steps would have to be based on joint evaluation of all assets over all waves of the HRS and AHEAD surveys—looking perhaps at a $X \times Y$ matrix of data for each household.

3.2   Family Status and Home Equity: HRS and AHEAD

We now turn to the relationship between changes in home equity and changes in family structure. Again we consider two- and one-person households separately and provide separate estimates for the HRS and the AHEAD families. Before considering within-cohort household transitions, cross-section summary data on household tenure (own, or rent, or other combined) are shown by age and household structure (one-person or two-person) in table 3.2. Home ownership of two-person families exceeds 90 percent between ages fifty-four and seventy-four and then declines to around 80 percent at ages eighty-five and older. For one-person families, home ownership increases to about 68 percent for households aged seventy to seventy-four and then declines to about 50 percent for households aged eighty-five and older. The home ownership rate for one-person households peaks in the seventy to seventy-four age range, declines modestly over the next decade, then falls sharply after age eighty-four.

3.2.1   Within-Household Transitions

We focus on the events that precipitate changes in home ownership and the changes in home equity that are associated with the ownership changes. Table 3.3 shows ownership transitions between consecutive survey waves (an "interval"). The first two panels of the table pertain to households that owned a home at the beginning of the interval. The third and fourth panels pertains to households that did not own a home at the beginning of the interval. The table entries show the percent of households who make a

Table 3.2   Percent Own, Rent, and Other, by Age (from wave 1 of the HRS and wave 1 of the AHEAD)

	One-Person Households			Two-Person Households		
Age	Own	Rent	Other	Own	Rent	Other
51–53	58.3	34.0	7.7	87.7	10.8	1.5
54–56	54.5	37.0	8.4	90.9	7.7	1.4
57–61	62.5	29.5	8.0	90.5	7.1	2.4
70–74	67.5	22.8	9.8	91.1	7.0	1.9
75–79	64.0	25.6	10.3	87.8	8.6	3.7
80–84	60.3	25.3	14.4	81.1	12.8	6.0
85+	48.4	31.8	19.9	78.7	15.1	6.2

Table 3.3   **Tenure Transitions, by Initial Tenure and by Change in Household Status (for HRS and AHEAD households, in percent)**

Change in Household Status	Tenure	Subsequent Period Status (%)	% Move	N
		Initial Homeowners in the HRS		
22	Own	98.3	7.1	9,173
	Rent or other	1.7	65.7	165
2D	Own	95.6	8.4	316
	Rent or other	4.4	55.6	13
2N	Own	88.6	18.9	12
	Rent or other	11.4	0	1
11	Own	95.2	6.1	3,150
	Rent or other	4.8	54.5	169
1N	Own	100	0	3
	Rent or other	0		0
		Initial Homeowners in the AHEAD		
22	Own	96.9	3.9	2,332
	Rent or other	3.1	38.5	75
2D	Own	88.8	9.4	358
	Rent or other	11.2	76.1	51
2N	Own	75	6.4	35
	Rent or other	25	79.9	14
11	Own	91.3	4.5	2,841
	Rent or other	8.7	47.2	269
1N	Own	39.9	0	57
	Rent or other	60.1	92.6	79
		Initial Renters in the HRS		
22	Own	22.3	51.3	220
	Rent or other	77.7	21.1	822
2D	Own	12.4	46.8	8
	Rent or other	87.6	40.2	64
2N	Own	0		0
	Rent or other	100	47.5	5
11	Own	11.4	46.5	239
	Rent or other	88.6	22.2	2,002
1N	Own	0		0
	Rent or other	100	43.6	3
		Initial Renters in the AHEAD		
22	Own	11.9	8.8	31
	Rent or other	88.1	10.4	253
2D	Own	14.5	49.5	11
	Rent or other	85.5	22.1	77
2N	Own	5	0	1
	Rent or other	95	34.3	17
11	Own	7.4	12.6	128
	Rent or other	92.6	14.4	1,744
1N	Own	3.4	0	7
	Rent or other	96.6	89.1	204

Source: Based on authors' estimates from the HRS and AHEAD.

Notes: All percentages are based on weighted samples. However, the sample sizes presented in the table are unweighted. Initial renters in the last two panels include households with "other" living arrangements. See text for explanations of household status abbreviations.

transition between adjacent waves of each survey. For example, the transition labeled "22" identifies a two-person household at the beginning of the interval (the first of the two waves) and at the end of the interval (in the subsequent wave). The HRS yields as many as three transitions (wave 1 to wave 2, wave 2 to wave 3, and wave 3 to wave 4), and each represents a two-year interval. The AHEAD yields two transitions. The first interval is two years, and the second is three years. All intervals in the HRS are combined to obtain the HRS results, and all intervals in the AHEAD are combined to obtain the AHEAD results.

Consider first the top panel of the table which pertains to the HRS households who were homeowners at the beginning of an interval. The first column shows the percent of households that own and the percent that rent (or have some other living arrangement) at the end of the interval. Of continuing two-person households, 98.3 percent still owned at the end of the interval; 1.7 percent no longer owned. The ownership of initial owners declined about 0.85 percent per year. Now consider continuing two-person HRS households who were nonowners at the beginning of the period shown in the third panel of table 3.3. Of these households 22.3 percent became owners during the interval, about 11.1 percent per year. On balance the number of homeowners increased: some initial owners became nonowners, but a larger number of initial nonowners became owners. This net addition to the homeowner group is shown graphically for the younger—HRS—cohorts in figure 3.5. The figure, however, pertains to households who continued as two-person families through all four waves of the HRS. The data for continuing two-person households in the table, however, is based on all households that continued as two-person families during any two adjacent survey waves.

Other rows of the first panel of table 3.3 show that if a spouse dies (2D), the ownership rate remains high, at 95.6 percent. If a spouse enters a nursing home (2N), the ownership rate declines more, to 88.6 percent, although the sample of nursing home entrants is quite small for the younger HRS households. For continuing one-person HRS households, the ownership rate also remains high, at 95.2 percent. (There are only three single-person households in which the person entered a nursing home during the interval.)

The percent moving between adjacent waves is shown in the next column of table 3.3. Of two-person HRS households that own in both waves, 7.1 percent moved over the two-year interval. For two-person households that change from "own" to "rent or other," the move rate is an unexpectedly low 65.7 percent. It is possible that ownership is transferred from parents to children, so the parents do not move, but also no longer own. However, this low move rate is more likely a reflection of reporting error. Inspection of some of these cases shows households owning a house of roughly constant value for three of the four waves. This evidence, combined with the absence of a move (which is verified by survey-takers), suggests errors in reporting or coding for one of the waves. Because there are a relatively small number of these households, a few errors can have a substantial effect on the move rate.

Similar results for the AHEAD sample are presented in the second and fourth panels. Initial homeowners in AHEAD were also likely to remain owners unless there was a change in family status. For example, 96.9 percent of continuing two-person households continued to own. But if one of the members died, the ownership rate dropped to 88.8 percent. If one of the members entered a nursing home, the rate dropped to 75 percent. For continuing one-person households, 91.3 percent remain owners. But if the single person enters a nursing home, the ownership rate drops to 39.9 percent. Thus, as with the younger HRS households, in the absence of precipitating shock, most AHEAD homeowners continue to own. But in the event of a shock, the decline in ownership is greater for older than for younger households. In addition, the decline is greater for one-person than for two-person households.

The move rate for the older AHEAD households that own in both waves is quite low, about 3.9 percent for two-person households and 4.5 percent for one-person households. Because the interval between waves is about 2.5 years for the AHEAD, the annual move rates are 1.6 percent and 1.8 percent, respectively. Again, the low move rates among households that report changing tenure suggest that some changes in tenure in the AHEAD may be incorrectly reported.

Overall, table 3.3 suggests that homeowner households in the HRS age group are very likely to remain owners. And even if one of the household members dies or enters a nursing home, the rate of ownership remains high. Homeowners in the AHEAD age group are also likely to continue to own unless there is a change in family status, especially continuing two-person households. When a member of this older household dies or enters a nursing home, the decline in ownership is greater than for younger households. The greatest decline in ownership is for single-person AHEAD households who enter a nursing home. Even among this group almost 40 percent continue to own.

3.2.2   Change in Home Equity

We next consider changes in home equity that parallel the transitions shown in table 3.3. Home equity changes are presented in two formats. The first format shows changes for all households—initial owners and initial renters-others. It shows changes for households who switch from owning to renting, as well as those switching from renting to owning. And it shows the net change in home equity for both groups combined. The second format is directed to the primary focus of our analysis, the change in home equity for initial homeowners. In this format we give particular attention to the change in the equity of movers who continue to own compared to stayers—those who remain in the same house. Although we discuss changes based on changes in self-assessed home values here, we show below that the exaggeration of self-assessed home value imparts large bias to the implied changes in home equity. Then we consider changes based on home selling prices compared to reported equity in newly purchased homes. We believe these latter data are the most reliable, as discussed in the following.

In addition, the mover–stayer comparison is complicated by the data inconsistencies discussed in the previous section. Some households report a change in tenure without moving. While such changes are possible, we believe most such cases reflect reporting or coding errors. The information on whether a household moved since the previous wave is likely to be accurate because the prior address is incorporated in the survey question on moving.[8] In all calculations reported in the following, we delete all observations with apparent transitions involving a change in tenure without a reported move. Following this procedure, 1.1 percent of the HRS households and 3.4 percent of the AHEAD households are deleted.[9]

Change in home equity using the first format is presented in table 3.4. The family status designations are the same as those used in table 3.3. There are four tenure designations: OO, OR, RO, and RR, where "O" indicates own and "R" indicates rent or other living arrangement. Large reductions in home equity are typically associated only with a home sale and subsequent rental. Those who move from renting to owning, of course, increase home equity. No matter what the change in family status, there is an increase in the average equity of HRS households (with the exception of the few 1N families). On the other hand, there is a decrease in the mean home equity of AHEAD families, no matter what the change in family status. The greatest decrease occurred when a family member entered a nursing home. For all continuing two-person households, the mean increase in housing equity was $6,192 in the HRS and –$5,241 in the AHEAD. The median increase was close to zero for households in each of the surveys. In general, the median changes are smaller in absolute value than the mean changes, but the relative patterns by family status and change in tenure are similar.

Change in home equity of initial owners using the second format is

8. For example, in wave 4 of the HRS (also wave 3 of the AHEAD) noninstitutionalized respondents were asked "Are you still living, all of the year or part of the year, in the same apartment/house in <previous wave address and city>?" Respondents in nursing homes were asked "Do you still have the same apartment/house in <previous wave address and city>?" If respondents in nursing homes answered affirmatively, they may still be homeowners, and they are not classified as movers.

9. Deleting all respondents who change tenure without moving reduces the frequency of own-to-rent transitions. This affects the HRS and AHEAD cohort figures previously presented. In particular, the cohort profiles for one-person AHEAD households (figure 3.6) become flat.

Table 3.4 **Change in the Housing Equity of Initial Owners and Initial Renters, by Change in Household Status**

| Survey and Household Status | Change in Tenure | Means | | Medians | | |
		Change in Housing Equity	Initial Housing Equity	Change in Housing Equity	Initial Housing Equity	N
HRS						
22	OO	6,565	102,893	1,695	81,326	8,919
	OR	−61,073	61,073	−50,905	50,905	164
	RO	64,117	0	35,000	0	215
	RR	0	0	0	0	822
	All	6,192	92,472	0	72,721	10,120
2D	OO	6,223	84,329	1,734	72,721	296
	OR	−75,575	75,575	−52,281	52,281	12
	RO	45,707	0	6,000	0	8
	RR	0	0	0	0	64
	All	3,345	69,176	0	56,928	380
2N	OO	4,203	83,650	2,450	79,994	12
	OR	0	0	0	0	1
	RO					0
	RR	0	0	0	0	5
	All	2,850	56,727	0	34,854	18
11	OO	642	96,874	621	62,333	2,961
	OR	−50,716	50,716	−40,663	40,663	161
	RO	51,883	0	36,361	0	228
	RR	0	0	0	0	2,002
	All	1,126	57,784	0	20,897	5,352
1N	OO	−44,095	77,747	−3,971	33,971	2
	OR					0
	RO					0
	RR	0	0	0	0	3
	All	−25,501	44,964	−3,971	33,971	5
AHEAD						
22	OO	−4,555	116,475	−2,217	90,242	2,309
	OR	−80,472	80,472	−67,682	67,682	74
	RO	79,697	0	45,000	0	31
	RR	0	0	0	0	253
	All	−5,241	103,938	−207	80,217	2,667
2D	OO	−7,182	107,705	−2,631	80,217	354
	OR	−80,749	80,749	−73,322	73,322	50
	RO	70,915	0	58,825	0	11
	RR	0	0	0	0	77
	All	−10,956	86,415	0	62,042	492
2N	OO	−18,869	122,320	−9,941	95,882	35
	OR	−97,003	97,003	−84,602	84,602	14
	RO	13,369	0	13,369	0	1
	RR	0	0	0	0	17
	All	−29,941	90,771	−9,782	62,042	67

(*continued*)

Table 3.4   (continued)

		Means		Medians		
Survey and Household Status	Change in Tenure	Change in Housing Equity	Initial Housing Equity	Change in Housing Equity	Initial Housing Equity	N
11	OO	−4,675	103,232	−1,739	74,869	2,801
	OR	−81,412	81,412	−67,682	67,682	266
	RO	73,623	0	50,269	0	128
	RR	0	0	0	0	1,744
	All	−5,265	64,540	0	37,434	4,939
1N	OO	−13,013	82,910	−6,040	69,521	57
	OR	−72,546	72,546	−56,401	56,401	79
	RO	57,386	0	65,000	0	7
	RR	0	0	0	0	204
	All	−18,043	30,229	0	0	347

Note: N = number of observations.

shown in table 3.5. The key question here is whether continuing homeowners who move and buy another house reduce home equity more than stayers, who can serve as the control group in this comparison. If movers typically wanted to use some of the wealth accumulated in home equity to support other nonhousing consumption, the home equity of movers would be reduced relative to the change in the equity of stayers. The first two panels of table 3.5 show the mean change in housing equity for the HRS and AHEAD; the next two panels show medians. The change in family status is shown on the left margin. Consider the first three rows of the upper panel of the table, which pertain to two-person households in the HRS. The ownership status (tenure) at the end of the interval is shown along the top margin. A household can continue to own or become a renter (or have some other living arrangement) at the end of the interval. The change in home equity is shown for continuing owners, for renters-others, and for both groups combined (all). The initial home value for each group is shown in the right column of the table. On average, the mean home equity of continuing two-person households increased by $3,305. For those who remained home owners, equity increased by $6,569. Initial homeowners whose transition was to the rent-other group reduced home equity by $54,155 on average. The average initial home value of continuing two-person households was $102,310. Thus home equity of the home sellers was only about half of the average equity of all continuing two-person households.

Some of those who continued to own stayed in the same house, others moved and bought a new house. The equity of those who stayed increased

Table 3.5   **Change in Housing Equity of Initial Owners, by Change in Family Status and by Subsequent Tenure**

Change in Household Status	Tenure in Subsequent Period			Number of Observations			Initial Home Equity
	Own	Rent or Other	All	Own	Rent or Other	All	
			Mean Changes				
HRS							
22							
All	6,569	−54,155	5,855	8,918	106	9,024	102,310
Stayer	6,686		6,686	8,295	0	8,295	102,852
Mover	5,074	−54,155	−3,305	623	106	729	96,335
2D							
All	6,288	−28,079	5,547	294	7	301	83,212
Stayer	8,997		8,997	266	0	266	83,939
Mover	−21,935	−28,079	−23,169	28	7	35	77,158
2N							
All	4,203		4,203	12	0	12	83,650
Stayer	4,750		4,750	9	0	9	88,372
Mover	1,863		1,863	3	0	3	63,426
11							
All	642	−48,476	−697	2,961	86	3,047	95,555
Stayer	935		935	2,779	0	2,779	96,012
Mover	−3,739	−48,476	−17,549	182	86	268	90,829
1N							
All	−44,095		−44,095	2	0	0	77,747
Stayer	−44,095		−44,095	2	0	2	77,747
Mover				0	0	0	0
AHEAD							
22							
All	−4,555	−73,974	−5,367	2,309	30	2,339	115,978
Stayer	−4,103		−4,103	2,213	0	2,213	115,103
Mover	−15,877	−73,974	−29,557	96	30	126	132,706
2D							
All	−7,182	−81,900	−13,805	354	39	393	105,418
Stayer	−5,777		−5,777	322	0	322	102,228
Mover	−20,432	−81,900	−51,390	32	39	71	120,352
2N							
All	−18,869	−105,730	−37,168	35	12	47	118,825
Stayer	−18,498		−18,498	33	0	33	123,456
Mover	−24,319	−105,730	−90,020	2	12	14	105,715
11							
All	−4,675	−92,350	−8,446	2,801	126	2,927	102,764
Stayer	−4,011		−4,011	2,671	0	2,671	102,209
Mover	−18,500	−92,350	−55,077	130	126	256	108,598
1N							
All	−13,013	−73,671	−48,315	57	72	129	77,533
Stayer	−13,013		−13,013	57	0	57	82,910
Mover		−73,671	−73,671	0	72	72	73,671

(*continued*)

Table 3.5   (continued)

Change in Household Status	Tenure in Subsequent Period			Number of Observations			Initial Home Equity
	Own	Rent or Other	All	Own	Rent or Other	All	
			Medians				
HRS							
22							
All	693	−50,905	1,474	8,918	106	9,024	81,033
Stayer	1,745		1,745	8,295	0	8,295	81,326
Mover	−360	−50,905	−4,946	623	106	729	72,721
2D							
All	−1,632	−32,530	1,474	294	7	301	71,491
Stayer	2,217		2,217	266	0	266	73,193
Mover	−5,481	−32,530	−10,999	28	7	35	42,594
2N							
All	6,794		2,450	12	0	12	79,994
Stayer	−2,311		−2,311	9	0	9	79,994
Mover	15,899		15,899	3	0	3	87,989
11							
All	125	−40,633	222	2,961	86	3,047	60,493
Stayer	639		639	2,779	0	2,779	62,333
Mover	−389	−40,633	−8,854	182	86	268	49,376
1N							
All	−3,971		−3,971	2	0	0	33,971
Stayer	−3,971		−3,971	2	0	2	33,971
Mover				0	0	0	
AHEAD							
22							
All	−5,179	−64,173	−2,348	2,309	30	2,339	90,242
Stayer	−2,087		−2,087	2,213	0	2,213	89,114
Mover	−8,271	−64,173	−16,869	96	30	126	101,608
2D							
All	−10,008	−73,322	−4,869	354	39	393	80,090
Stayer	−2,303		−2,303	322	0	322	76,706
Mover	−17,712	−73,322	−50,761	32	39	71	80,217
2N							
All	−26,230	−90,242	−13,978	35	12	47	90,242
Stayer	−9,941		−9,941	33	0	33	95,882
Mover	−42,520	−90,242	−54,145	2	12	14	90,242
11							
All	−2,087	−73,322	−2,434	2,801	126	2,927	73,799
Stayer	−1,739		−1,739	2,671	0	2,671	73,322
Mover	−2,434	−73,322	−37,434	130	126	256	74,869
1N							
All	−6,040	−64,173	−39,921	57	72	129	64,173
Stayer	−6,040		−6,040	57	0	57	69,521
Mover		−64,173	−64,173	0	72	72	64,173

by $6,686. The equity of those who moved and bought a new house also increased, by $5,074. In the somewhat more formal estimation in the following we use the change in the equity of the stayers as a measure of the increase the movers would have experienced had they not moved. In this case the decrease for movers was $1,612, about 1.7 percent of the initial home equity of this group. Thus these movers who bought a new home are not typically taking substantial home equity out of housing to support other consumption. By this measure, the greatest decline in home equity occurred in mover households in which a member died, although the sample sizes are small and the means are not precisely measured. For example, the home equity of the small number of two-person households who move but continue to own when one member dies declines by $21,935.

The average equity of continuing one-person HRS households declined by $697, a very small fraction of the average initial home equity of $95,555. Continuing one-person households who moved but continued to own reduced home equity by $3,739, and the stayers increased equity by $935. Using the stayers as a control, the movers reduced equity by 4.8 percent of the initial home equity of this group.

In summary, the average home equity of two-person HRS households increased over this period. This was true for continuing two-person households as well as those in which a member died or in which a member entered a nursing home. The equity of one-person households declined only slightly. Continuing owners who moved typically reduced home equity only marginally, when compared to stayers. The only substantial reduction in the home equity of continuing owners was for households in which one member died.

For the older AHEAD households, changes in home equity are also typically associated with precipitating shocks. But for the older households the shocks are more frequent. Consider continuing two-person households first. The equity of continuing stayer-owners (who do not move) declined by $4,103 and can serve as a base of comparison for other groups. This reduction, if taken at face value, apparently reflects a fall in the value of the homes of the older households as they continue to live in the homes, but not direct withdrawal of housing equity to support other consumption. (Estimates based on housing value rather than equity yields the same result.) This decline is only slightly less than the average reduction for all continuing two-person households, $5,367. Thus on average we conclude that little housing equity is taken from housing to support other consumption.

Continuing homeowners who move reduce home equity by $15,877, which is $11,322 more than the reduction in home equity of the stayers. We take this to represent funds taken from housing that might be used to support other nonhousing consumption. It represents, however, only about 10.5 percent of initial home equity for these households, and less than 4 percent of their initial nonhousing wealth. Remember that the typical older household will only move once from one home to another. So the reduction in housing equity can only be a one-time addition to funds available for other consumption. In the following we show that even this small reduction is probably exaggerated and that in fact the average change is likely positive (an increase in housing equity).

For continuing owners in two-person households in which a member enters a nursing home, the reduction in the home equity of the movers is $5,821 greater than the reduction for the stayers. The reduction in the home equity of continuing one-person households is also small. Particular movers who continue to own reduce home equity by a small fraction of initial home equity.

In summary, among the older AHEAD households, the reduction in home equity of continuing owners is small relative to initial home equity, even among those who move to a different house. Large reductions in home equity are typically observed only for home owners who move and discontinue home ownership. The probability of such a move is larger in cases of precipitating shocks. But as seen in tables 3.3 and 3.4, even in the event of shocks to family status, most households continue to own and thus do not withdraw equity from housing to support other needs. For all HRS groups, the initial home equity of the seller (rent-other) group was much lower than the equity of the continuing owners. For the older AHEAD households, the initial home equity of sellers is also less than the initial home equity of continuing owners, although the difference is much smaller than for the HRS households.

Median changes in home equity are shown in the bottom half of table 3.5. The pattern of change is essentially the same as the pattern for mean changes. The changes, however, are typically smaller than the mean changes, in particular for the older AHEAD households. For example, for continuing two-person households in the HRS, the median increase in home equity is $1,474. The increase for continuing owner-movers is only $2,105 greater than for stayers. For continuing one-person families the median increase is $222. And the reduction for continuing owner-movers is only $1,028 greater than for stayers. Among continuing two-person households in the AHEAD sample, movers reduce equity by $6,184. Continuing one-person households reduce equity by $695. Again, the conclusion is that for the most part housing equity is substantially reduced only after a precipitating shock. In the absence of a shock, the reductions in housing equity by movers represent a small fraction of initial housing equity.

3.2.3   Respondent Estimates of Home Values versus Sales Prices

Before turning to some simple estimation, we emphasize that respondent assessment of home equity likely overestimates home value by a substantial margin. Thus reliance on reported home values yields exaggerated reductions in housing equity when homeowners move. Substantial evidence shows that homeowners overestimate the value of their homes. Kiel and Zabel (1999) surveyed the literature and concluded that self-reported home values exceed actual sale prices or appraisal values by 2 to 16 percent. Their analysis showed that homeowners on average overvalue their home by 8 percent, and that owners with long tenure overvalue their houses even more. In other words, when a family moves the realized sale price is typically less than the family's prior estimate of the home value. This creates a bias in our estimate of the *change* in housing equity among movers. The premove estimate is inflated. The postmove price is presumably accurate because the purchase transaction was recently completed.

The estimates in tables 3.4 and 3.5 on the change in housing equity between waves are based on HRS and AHEAD respondent self-assessment of home values and are affected by such overvaluation. The tendency to overvalue homes confounds mover-stayer comparisons. Recent movers are likely to know the market value of their homes. Stayers, on the other hand, are likely to overvalue their houses.[10] As a result, the change in home equity is more likely to show a larger price decrease for movers than for stayers. Thus in the previous tables movers, relative to stayers, appear to be taking more equity out of their homes than is actually the case.

Information obtained in both the HRS and the AHEAD allows us to gauge the extent of this bias. For households that have recently moved, the surveys inquired about the "selling price" of the house. The sale price can be compared to the reported value of the house in the previous wave. The survey also asks for the month and year of the sale; the month and year of the self-assessed value is the interview date. We index the premove assessed value of movers and the postmove price of movers to obtain measures in 1998 dollars.[11] From these values we obtain estimates of the overvaluation bias.

Mean and median differences between assessed values and sale prices are shown in the table 3.6. The results suggest that both the HRS and the AHEAD respondents overestimated their home values by 15 to 20 percent, based on a comparison of mean values. Based on medians, home values are overestimated by 6 to 7 percent. The mean dollar differences are $20,000 to $30,000, and median dollar differences are $6,000 to $8,000. This suggests that our calculated reductions in the home equity of continuing owner-movers may be due entirely to valuation bias. For example, the mean re-

---

10. We suspect this is most likely to be the case when house prices are not rising rapidly. Another factor that may lead to overestimates by stayers is that most homeowners know the asking price of similar homes in their neighborhood, but may be unaware of the actual selling price.

11. Some movers are missing data for the sale price. The HRS and AHEAD provide no imputations for missing values of the sale price. A bracketing technique is used to obtain ranges for persons unable to provide a sale price, but we have made no attempt here to convert the bracketed amounts to values. The analysis is restricted to observations that specify a sale price.

Table 3.6   Comparison of Estimated Home Values and Sale Prices

Survey	Interval	Estimate of Home Value in Initial Year	Reported Sale Price in Next Year	Mean Difference	Percent Difference
		Means			
HRS	1992–1994				
	(250)	135,607	115,665	19,942	14.7
	1994–1996				
	(233)	157,068	123,883	33,186	21.1
	1996–1998				
	(236)	162,264	138,206	24,048	14.8
AHEAD	1993–1995				
	(163)	101,568	81,625	19,943	19.6
	1995–1998				
	(179)	131,382	109,447	21,935	16.7
		Medians			
HRS	1992–1994				
	(250)	106,151	96,208	7,117	6.7
	1994–1996				
	(233)	109,838	98,347	8,083	7.4
	1996–1998				
	(236)	140,159	122,276	8,290	5.9
AHEAD	1993–1995				
	(163)	83,848	69,094	5,888	7
	1995–1998				
	(179)	89,445	77,081	6,546	7.3

Source: Authors' calculations from the AHEAD and HRS.

Notes: All figures are in 1998 dollars and use household weights. Numbers in parentheses are sample sizes.

duction of $15,887 (or $11,322 using the stayers as a control) in the home equity of two-person AHEAD families who move and continue to own would be more than accounted for by such bias.

3.2.4 More Formal Estimates of Change in Home Equity

Here we consider more formally the change in home equity of movers and stayers. As mentioned above, one way to think about this is to treat movers as the treatment group and stayers as the control group. The home equity of stayers and movers at the beginning and at the end of the interval can be represented by the following table:

	Beginning	End
Stayers	α	$\alpha + t$
Movers	α	$\alpha + t + m$

In this case, a difference-in-difference estimate yields m, the treatment effect. We can estimate this for all households combined, or for any sub-group, by

$$(1) \qquad \Delta E = t + m\mathrm{M},$$

where t is a constant term—and represents a time (inflation) effect—and m is the additional effect for movers, with M a dummy variable identifying movers.

Estimates of this equation, by change in household status, are shown in table 3.7. This table presents estimates for households who owned at both the beginning and at the end of the interval. Data are presented by the subsequent—at the end of the interval—status of the initial homeowners. Ordinary least squares (OLS) estimates are shown in the left portion of the table. Median regression estimates are shown in the right portion of the table. The median regression estimates should be less affected than the OLS estimates by reporting errors or other outliers in the data.

The key mover effect estimate, m, measures the difference between the change in the equity of stayers and the change for movers. The OLS estimates show negative mover effects in each comparison, but only the mover effects for the HRS 2D and AHEAD 11 groups are significantly different from zero at the 5 percent significance level. And, with the possible exception of the estimated mover effect for the 2 to D HRS households, the estimated effect is much lower than the bias suggested in table 3.6. For ex-

Table 3.7   **Estimates of the Mover Equity Effect using Stayers as the "Control" Group, for Initial Homeowners, for Two- and One-Person Households, for the HRS and the AHEAD Households, by Estimation Method**

Change in Household Status	OLS Estimates				Median Regression Estimates			
	Time Effect (t)	t-statistic	Mover Effect (m)	t-statistic	Time Effect (t)	t-statistic	Mover Effect (m)	t-statistic
HRS								
2 to 2	6,686	2.26	−1,612	0.15	1,745	6.98	−2,104	2.24
2 to D	8,997	2.62	−30,931	2.67	2,216	1.66	−7,698	1.76
2 to N	4,750	0.26	−2,887	0.07	−2,311	0.2	18,210	1.16
1 to 1	935	0.45	−4,674	0.57	639	1.8	−1,028	0.73
1 to N								
AHEAD								
2 to 2	−4,103	2.46	−11,774	1.38	−2,087	4.05	−6,185	2.46
2 to D	−5,777	1.5	−14,656	1.18	−2,303	1.51	−15,409	3.16
2 to N	−18,498	2.61	−5,821	0.21	−9,941	3.77	−32,579	4.49
1 to 1	−4,011	2.57	−14,489	1.99	−1,739	5.28	−696	0.47
1 to N								

Note: Too few observations to estimate 1 to N transitions.

ample, the estimated mover effect for continuing two-person households is −$1,612. Referring back to table 3.6, however, we see that the bias estimate for HRS households is between $20,000 and $33,000. Thus because most families are continuing two-person families, a reasonable judgment from these data is that the equity of the continuing two-person households in fact *increased* by about $25,000. Coincidentally, this increase matches the estimated increase for such households based on selling prices, which is discussed in the following. For each of the other groups, with the exception of the HRS 2 to D families, the estimated mover effect is much less than the bias estimates shown in table 3.6, suggesting rather large increases in home equity.

For the HRS households, the median regression mover effect estimates are also small and typically not significantly different from zero. And, the estimates are less than the median bias estimates in table 3.6. Based on the estimated mover effects in conjunction with the bias estimates, we conclude that home equity likely increases substantially when families move and buy another home.

The median estimates for the AHEAD households are larger than the median HRS estimates and are more precisely measured. For the 2D and 2N groups, the estimates are greater than the bias estimates in table 3.6, in particular for the 2N group. Thus these data suggest that for households in which a member dies, and for households in which a member enters a nursing home, home equity is reduced when these households move and buy again. The following analysis is based on selling prices; however, it suggests an increase in the median home equity of these groups as well.

3.2.5   Estimates Based on Selling Price

Each home owner reinterviewed in the HRS and AHEAD is asked whether the home was sold since the previous interview. For many of these households, the selling price is reported.[12] In this section, we estimate the change in the home equity of families who sell and buy another home and the change in equity of those who sell and then choose another tenure. Table 3.8 shows summary data on home equity for adjacent waves of HRS and AHEAD. The first column shows reported home equity from the first of the two waves. The second column shows the reported selling price (obtained from the second wave interview) minus the mortgage reported in the initial wave. The sale occurred sometime between the two waves, but the mortgage pertains to the data of the last interview prior to the sale. The

---

12. There is more missing sale price data than home equity data, used in earlier sections of the paper. Home equity (home value and mortgage balance) is obtained from the housing module. Information on the sale price is obtained from a module on capital gains that has more incomplete responses. There are no imputations for missing or incomplete (bracketed) sale price data. Partly for this reason, we do not use the weights when analyzing the sale price data.

Table 3.8   **Comparison of Initial Reported Home Equity, Selling Price minus Mortgage, and Home Equity at the End of the Interval**

Interval	Initial Reported Equity Prior to Home Sale	Selling Price minus Mortgage	Reported Equity at End of Interval	Sample Size
Mean for Households that Purchased Another House				
HRS				
1992–1994	76,518	64,940	89,317	181
1994–1996	112,382	86,599	126,228	174
1996–1998	108,412	89,038	120,990	166
AHEAD				
1993–1995	108,821	89,284	110,690	71
1995–1998	154,104	114,388	123,737	61
Mean for Households that Did Not Purchase Another House				
HRS				
1992–1994	61,851	55,697	0	55
1994–1996	52,308	57,226	0	48
1996–1998	72,408	86,769	0	38
AHEAD				
1993–1995	75,857	61,543	0	44
1995–1998	78,005	72,313	0	51
Median for Households that Purchased Another House				
HRS				
1992–1994	57,679	49,806	65,903	181
1994–1996	74,941	69,045	88,852	174
1996–1998	82,636	72,082	110,964	166
AHEAD				
1993–1995	78,258	67,826	79,590	71
1995–1998	95,013	70,606	96,000	61
Median for Households that Did Not Purchase Another House				
HRS				
1992–1994	55,137	39,649	0	55
1994–1996	32,819	42,664	0	48
1996–1998	69,561	85,949	0	38
AHEAD				
1993–1995	72,668	65,244	0	44
1995–1998	79,590	73,213	0	51

Notes: No imputed variables are used. All values are in 1998 dollars. The data are not weighted.

third column shows home equity reported in the second of the two waves. For households who purchased another home (the first and third panels of the table), this is the equity in the newly purchased home. For households that did not purchase another home (the second and fourth panels), this column is zero.

Like the data in table 3.6 on reported home values versus selling prices, these data show that households who sell and buy another home substantially overestimate their presale housing equity. For those who sell and do not purchase another home, the overestimation is not so apparent. For several of these groups the reported equity seems to underestimate realized equity, based on selling price minus the mortgage. We believe that the reported selling price is likely to be close to the actual selling price, unlike the presale assessment of home equity. The last column shows reported home equity at the end of the interval. In principle, home equity right after a purchase should also be accurately reported. For each of the intervals, the reported new home equity at the end of the period is substantially greater than gain in home equity from the sale of the prior home, suggesting that equity in the new home is greater than equity in the prior home.

Based on the same data, table 3.9 shows the estimated change in home equity for households that have sold a home and purchased another, by change in family status. These estimates are obtained from simple OLS and median regression estimates of the form

$$(2) \qquad\qquad \Delta E = m + \varepsilon,$$

where ΔE is equity in the new home at the end of the period minus equity from the sale of the prior home. Here, m is the estimated increase in home equity. This specification is estimated for several years separately and for several family status change groups. For all but two groups, there is a substantial increase in home equity. Many of the estimates are for small groups, however, and are not significantly different from zero.

We now consider whether the change in home equity depends on the relationship between income and housing wealth. It might be expected that persons with relatively low income and relatively high housing equity would be more likely to withdraw housing equity. And those with low equity and high income would be more likely to add to housing equity. We begin with estimates of the probability of moving and buying another home, and the probability of moving and discontinuing home ownership, thus withdrawing all housing equity. These outcomes will depend, in particular, on the level of home equity and the level of income in the initial period. Then we show estimates of the relationship between the change in equity, given a move on the one hand, and initial income and home equity levels on the other hand.

Households that own in the initial period can either stay in the same house, move to another house, or discontinue home ownership by moving to a rental apartment or some other arrangement. The probabilities of the latter two transitions may be specified as

$$(3) \quad \Pr[\text{OmO}] = c(2\text{D or 2N or 1N}) + a11 + b22 + \alpha Y + \beta E + \gamma Y \cdot E + \varepsilon$$

$$\Pr[\text{OR}] = c(2\text{D or 2N or 1N}) + a11 + b22 + \alpha Y + \beta E + \gamma Y \cdot E + \varepsilon,$$

where OmO identifies families who sell a home, then move and buy another home (own to move to own), and OR identifies families who discontinue

Table 3.9   **Estimates of the Change in Home Equity for Movers Who Bought Another Home, by Method of Estimations, for HRS and AHEAD Intervals**

Interval	Estimated Change in Home Equity (1998 $)	t-statistic	Sample Size
	OLS Estimates		
HRS			
1992–1994	24,377	3.54	181
1994–1996	39,629	2.86	174
1996–1998	31,952	4.55	166
AHEAD			
1993–1995	21,406	1.37	71
1995–1998	9,349	0.59	61
HRS (pooled waves)			
2 to 2	31,345	6.39	373
1 to 1	40,014	1.73	96
Other	20,742	1.5	52
AHEAD (pooled waves)			
2 to 2	13,887	0.91	63
1 to 1	9,052	0.45	52
Other	43,794	2.01	17
	Median Regression Estimates		
HRS			
1992–1994	6,303	1.86	181
1994–1996	15,455	2.35	174
1996–1998	19,803	3.42	166
AHEAD			
1993–1995	1,066	0.24	71
1995–1998	9,818	1.12	61
HRS (pooled waves)			
2 to 2	17,153	4.01	373
1 to 1	−294	0.04	86
Other	8,856	1.11	52
AHEAD (pooled waves)			
2 to 2	3,438	0.37	63
1 to 1	0	0	52
Other	10,111	0.55	17

ownership (own to rent or other). The parameter a is the effect of a continuing one-person household, and b is the effect of a continuing two-person household. (The estimated parameters are, of course, not constrained to be the same for the OmO and OR groups.) The omitted categories, captured in the constant term c(2D, 2N, and 1N), are the 2D, 2N, and 1N households. Initial period income is denoted by Y and initial home equity is denoted by E. Here, γ indicates whether the effect of Y depends on E (or, equivalently, whether the effect of E depends on Y).

Given the decision to move to another home or to discontinue ownership, we then estimate the conditional change in home equity for the two groups, given that a move occurs. The change in equity equations are in the same format, given by

(4) $\Delta E(\text{OmO}) = c(\text{2D or 2N or 1N}) + a11 + b22 + \alpha Y + \beta E$

$\qquad + \gamma Y \cdot E + \varepsilon$

$\Delta E(\text{OR}) = c(\text{2D or 2N or 1N}) + a11 + b22 + \alpha Y + \beta E$

$\qquad + \gamma Y \cdot E + \varepsilon.$

Given the estimated probabilities and conditional changes in housing equity, we can simulate the expected change in equity for homeowners as

(5) $\Delta E = \Delta E(\text{OmO}) + \Delta E(\text{OR})$

$\qquad = \Pr[\text{OmO}] \cdot E(\Delta E \,|\, \text{OmO}) + \Pr[\text{OR}] \cdot E(\Delta E \,|\, \text{OR}),$

where the expected change is decomposed into its component parts. We present below the simulation for selected quantiles on income and home equity.

Simulated probabilities of moving between the waves are shown in table 3.10. The estimated probit parameter estimates and selected quantiles of home equity and income used to produce this table are shown in table 3A.1. The top three panels of table 3.10 pertain to HRS households, and the bottom three panels pertain to AHEAD households. Simulated probabilities of moving and buying another home are shown on the left side of each panel, and probabilities of moving and discontinuing ownership are shown on the right. The simulations show that initial income and home equity have little effect on the probabilities of moving, although in some instances the estimated parameters are statistically different from zero. For both HRS and AHEAD households, the difference between the probabilities for "house-poor and income-rich" households and for "house-rich and income-poor" households is only a few percentage points. Consistent with the preceding findings, the probability of moving is highest among households that have experienced a disruption in household structure. For example, among AHEAD households the probability of moving and discontinuing ownership is 1.5 percent (evaluated at median income and home equity) for continuing two-person households, 4.4 percent for continuing one-person households, and 21.2 percent for households in which a member has either died or entered a nursing home between the waves.

The simulated change (between the survey waves) in home equity for families who move and buy another home is shown in table 3.11. The associated parameter estimates in table 3A.2 show that initial income and home equity have substantial and statistically significant effects on the change. Both OLS and median regression estimates are shown. The greater the level of initial home equity (based on selling price minus the mortgage), the smaller the increase in equity when the family moves, and the larger the ini-

Table 3.10   **Simulated Move Probabilities at Selected Income and Home Equity Quartiles, for HRS and AHEAD Households**

	Equity					
	Buy Another Home			Discontinue Ownership		
Income	20th	50th	80th	20th	50th	80th
HRS 2 to 2 Households						
20th	0.063		0.063	0.015		0.013
50th		0.065			0.013	
80th	0.069		0.070	0.011		0.009
HRS 1 to 1 Households						
20th	0.055		0.056	0.031		0.027
50th		0.058			0.026	
80th	0.061		0.062	0.023		0.020
HRS Other Households (2D, 2N, 1N)						
20th	0.090		0.091	0.031		0.027
50th		0.094			0.027	
80th	0.099		0.099	0.024		0.021
AHEAD 2 to 2 Households						
20th	0.034		0.041	0.017		0.015
50th		0.037			0.015	
80th	0.037		0.043	0.014		0.011
AHEAD 1 to 1 Households						
20th	0.039		0.047	0.049		0.044
50th		0.043			0.044	
80th	0.042		0.049	0.041		0.035
AHEAD Other Households (2D, 2N, 1N)						
20th	0.049		0.059	0.228		0.211
50th		0.054			0.212	
80th	0.053		0.062	0.204		0.182

tial income, the greater the increase in home equity for households that move. The equity-income interaction, however, is imprecisely measured. The estimated difference in the change in home equity for the 11 or for the 22 groups compared to the 2D-2N-1N groups combined is not statistically significant. These estimates are based on the sample of respondents that report a sale price for the former home and report both the home value and mortgage debt for their current home.[13]

Evaluated at the median (50th quantile) of income and home equity, the simulated change in equity shown in table 3.11 is positive for all family sta-

13. Both the sale price of the old home and the value of and mortgage on the new home are reported in the same wave. The survey does not inquire about the mortgage obligation discharged on the old home. To obtain home equity for the old home we use the mortgage reported in the prior wave.

Table 3.11   Simulated Changes in Housing Equity at Selected Income and Home Equity Quartiles for Households Purchasing Another Home, for HRS and AHEAD Households

	Equity					
	OLS			Median Regression		
Income	20th	50th	80th	20th	50th	80th
	HRS 2 to 2 Households					
20th	38,176		−15,422	24,353		−23,870
50th		25,061			11,929	
80th	54,778		1,854	37,510		−9,537
	HRS 1 to 1 Households					
20th	36,090		−17,508	13,825		−34,397
50th		22,975			1,402	
80th	52,692		−232	26,982		−20,065
	HRS Other Households (2D, 2N, 1N)					
20th	36,041		−17,557	14,588		−33,635
50th		22,926			2,164	
80th	52,644		−280	27,744		−19,303
	AHEAD 2 to 2 Households					
20th	34,548		−28,386	29,758		−46,091
50th		17,970			5,337	
80th	52,781		−9,021	38,129		−33,449
	AHEAD 1 to 1 Households					
20th	27,834		−35,099	8,974		−66,874
50th		11,256			−15,447	
80th	46,067		−15,735	17,345		−54,233
	AHEAD Other Households (2D, 2N, 1N)					
20th	43,547		−19,386	29,526		−46,323
50th		26,970			5,105	
80th	61,781		−22	37,897		−33,681

tus groups, with the exception of the simulation for the AHEAD 11 households, based on median regression estimates. For all family status groups, the greatest simulated reduction in home equity is at the 80th equity quartile and 20th income quantile. The greatest simulated increase in home equity is at the 80th income quartile and the 20th equity quantile. Thus relatively house-rich and income-poor families reduce equity, and relatively house-poor and income-rich households add to home equity when they move and buy another home. For example, based on the OLS estimates for the HRS 22 households, at the high-equity-low-income quantiles, home equity is *reduced* by −$15,422; at the low-equity-high-income quantiles, home equity is *increased* by +$54,778. The pattern of the simulated changes based on the median regression estimates is similar to the pattern based on OLS estimates.

Table 3.12   **Simulated Changes in Housing Equity at Selected Income and Home Equity Quartiles for Households Not Purchasing Another Home, for HRS and AHEAD Households**

	Equity					
	OLS			Median Regression		
Income	20th	50th	80th	20th	50th	80th
	HRS 2 to 2 Households					
20th	−53,822		−53,822	−37,994		−37,994
50th		−58,323			−43,176	
80th	−65,153		−65,153	−51,040		−51,040
	HRS 1 to 1 Households					
20th	−59,492		−59,492	−46,077		−46,077
50th		−63,993			−51,258	
80th	−70,823		−70,823	−59,122		−59,122
	HRS Other Households (2D, 2N, 1N)					
20th	−72,577		−72,577	−56,630		−56,630
50th		−77,077			−61,811	
80th	−83,907		−83,907	−69,675		−69,675
	AHEAD 2 to 2 Households					
20th	−54,127		−54,127	−43,203		−43,203
50th		−60,653			−50,522	
80th	−72,544		−72,544	−63,859		−63,859
	AHEAD 1 to 1 Households					
20th	−54,039		−54,039	−51,688		−51,688
50th		−60,565			−59,007	
80th	−72,455		−72,455	−72,344		−72,344
	AHEAD Other Households (2D, 2N, 1N)					
20th	−78,865		−78,865	−78,698		−78,698
50th		−85,391			−86,017	
80th	−97,281		−97,281	−99,354		−99,354

The change (decrease) in the home equity of the families who discontinue home ownership is shown in table 3.12, and the associated parameter estimates are shown in table 3A.3. In this case, the decline in equity is simply the sale price minus the mortgage. Thus we cannot use the initial home equity to predict the change in equity, as in table 3.11 for those who sell and buy again. Thus estimates of the reduction in equity are based on income only. Essentially the simulated changes show how home equity is related to income. For this selected group of households who sell and do not buy another home, home equity is negatively related to income. The greatest equity reductions occur in families where a household member dies or in which a household member enters a nursing home.

In summary, the move probabilities and change in home equity results reported in tables 3.10–3.12 are combined to calculate expected change in housing equity. These results are reported on an *annual* basis in table 3.13.[14] The top part of the table shows results for movers who sell and buy another house. The bottom part shows results for movers who sell and discontinue ownership. The table shows results by equity-income quantile, as in several of the preceding tables. But in this table, the expected change in equity is decomposed into its component parts: the probability of a move and the change in equity given a move. For example, consider the HRS 22 households. Evaluated at the median of home equity and income, the expected increase in equity through home "upgrading" is $815. Only 3.3 percent of families upgrade each year, but those that do add $12,531 to home equity. Averaged over all HRS households, home equity is increased by $823 through selling and buying a new home. Evaluated at the median of home equity and income, about 1.5 percent of AHEAD 22 households move and buy another home each year. Those that do add $7,426 to home equity. The expected increase in home equity, averaged across all AHEAD household types, is $399. Viewed in this way, the expected changes in the equity of HRS and AHEAD households are not very different at the median: +$823 for the HRS group and +$399 for the AHEAD group.

For HRS 22 households with high initial housing equity and low income (the 80-20 column), the expected annual reduction in equity is –$486: 3.2 percent move and, given a move, the reduction in home equity is –$7,711. Averaged over all HRS households in this high-equity-low-income group, the expected reduction in home equity through selling and buying another home is –$528. The AHEAD households reveal a similar pattern, although again they are less likely to move than the younger HRS households.

The estimates for persons who sell and discontinue ownership are shown in the bottom half of the table. Again consider HRS 22 families evaluated at the median of equity and income. Only 0.7 percent of households discontinue ownership each year. Those that do reduce equity by –$29,162, on average. Averaged over all HRS 22 families, equity is reduced by –$379 through divesting of homes. This reduction can be compared to the +$815 average increase through upgrading. Overall, the average equity of all HRS households is reduced by –$610 in this way, compared to an increase of +$823 through upgrading. For all AHEAD households average equity is reduced by –$1,918 by sellers who discontinue ownership between survey waves, compared with an increase of +$399 through movers who upgrade.

Table 3.14 presents a succinct accounting of the expected *annual* change in the home equity of all HRS initial homeowners combined and of all AHEAD initial homeowners combined. The first column shows the expected change in home equity for households who move and purchase an-

---

14. Waves of the HRS were two years apart. In the AHEAD there were two years between wave 1 and wave 2, and three years between wave 2 and wave 3.

Table 3.13 **Summary of Annual Change in Home Equity of Initial Homeowners, Decomposed into Probability of a Move Times the Change in Equity Given the Move, by Household Status, for Selected Equity and Income Quantiles (based on probit move probability estimates and OLS equity change estimates)**

Survey	Household Status		Equity-Income Quantile				
			50-50	80-20	20-80	80-80	20-20
		Movers Who Sell and Buy a New Home					
HRS	22	Prob OmO	.033	.032	.035	.035	.032
		Change | OmO	12,531	−7,711	27,389	927	19,088
		Expected change	815	−486	1,890	65	1,203
	11	Prob OmO	.029	.028	.031	.031	.028
		Change | OmO	11,488	−8,754	26,346	−116	18,045
		Expected change	667	−490	1,607	−7	993
	Other	Prob OmO	.047	.046	.050	.050	.045
		Change | OmO	11,463	−8,779	26,322	−140	18,021
		Expected change	1,078	−799	2,606	−14	1,622
	All	Expected change	823	−528	1,935	42	1,221
AHEAD	22	Prob OmO	.015	.017	.015	.018	.014
		Change | OmO	7,426	−11,730	21,810	−3,728	14,276
		Expected change	275	−481	807	−160	486
	11	Prob OmO	.018	.019	.017	.020	.016
		Change | OmO	4,651	−14,504	19,036	−6,502	11,502
		Expected change	200	−682	800	−319	449
	Other	Prob OmO	.022	.024	.022	.026	.020
		Change | OmO	11,145	−8,011	25,529	−9	17,995
		Expected change	602	−473	1,353	0	882
	All	Expected change	399	−528	1,045	−130	650
		Movers Who Sell and Discontinue Ownership					
HRS	22	Prob OR	.007	.007	.006	.005	.008
		Change | OR	−29,162	−26,911	−32,577	−32,577	−26,911
		Expected change	−379	−350	−359	−293	−404
	11	Prob OR	.013	.014	.012	.010	.016
		Change | OR	−31,997	−29,746	−35,412	−35,412	−29,746
		Expected change	−832	−803	−815	−708	−922
	Other	Prob OR	.014	.014	.012	.011	.016
		Change | OR	−38,539	−36,289	−41,954	−41,954	−36,289
		Expected change	−1,041	−980	−1,007	−881	−1,125
	All	Expected change	−610	−576	−588	−502	−662
AHEAD	22	Prob OR	.006	.006	.006	.005	.007
		Change | OR	−25,063	−22,367	−29,977	−29,977	−22,367
		Expected change	−376	−336	−420	−330	−380
	11	Prob OR	.018	.018	.017	.014	.020
		Change | OR	−25,027	−22,330	−29,940	−29,940	−22,330
		Expected change	−1,101	−983	−1,228	−1,048	−1,094
	Other	Prob OR	.088	.087	.084	.075	.094
		Change | OR	−35,286	−32,589	−40,199	−40,199	−32,589
		Expected change	−7,481	−6,876	−8,200	−7,316	−7,430
	All	Expected change	−1,918	−1,743	−2,116	−1,849	−1,907

Table 3.14   Accounting for the Overall Change in Home Equity of Initial
                    Homeowners in the HRS and the AHEAD

Survey and Household Status	Expected Annual Change in Home Equity			Initial Home Equity of Sellers ($)	% of Initial Equity
	Move and Purchase New Home[a]	Discontinue Home Ownership[b]	All[c]		
HRS					
22	815	−379	436	75,128	0.58
11	667	−832	−166	81,105	−0.20
Other	1,078	−1,041	37	79,858	0.05
All	823	−610	214	76,952	0.28
AHEAD					
22	275	−376	−101	94,257	−0.11
11	200	−1,101	−901	78,496	−1.15
Other	602	−7,481	−6,879	87,777	−7.84
All	399	−1,918	−1,519	86,445	−1.76

[a]$Pr(OmO) \cdot E(DHE \mid OmO)$
[b]$Pr(OR) \cdot E(DHE \mid OR)$
[c]$E(DHE \mid O)$

other home. (Recall that the expected change is the probability of a move times the average change in home equity given a move.) Both HRS and AHEAD families that move to a new home increase home equity, on average. The second column is the expected reduction in the home equity of households that discontinue ownership. The reduction is largest among households experiencing precipitating shocks. The third column—the sum of the first two columns—is the net annual change in home equity. (Like table 3.13, table 3.14 considers only initial home owners; it does not account for the increase in the home equity that occurs when initial renters buy a home.)

On average, HRS households increase home equity by $214 per year. AHEAD households, on average, reduce home equity by $1,519 annually, which represents an *overall* decline of about 1.76 percent of initial home equity. The percentages in the last column can be used to illustrate the significance of disruptions to family status among AHEAD households: For example, there is almost no decline (−0.11 percent) in the home equity of continuing two-person households. On average, the initial home equity of these households is $94,257. Suppose that this is the average home equity of two-person households at age seventy. At an annual decline of 0.11 percent, the $94,257 would be reduced by only $2,052—to $92,205—by age ninety. The reduction of continuing one-person households is somewhat larger. If the average home equity of one-person households is $78,496 at age seventy, and the annual reduction for one-person households is 1.15

percent, the home equity of continuing one-person households would be reduced by $16,211—to $62,285—by age ninety. Most of the overall reduction of 1.76 percent is accounted for by households who experience precipitating shocks—the "other" group (2N, 2D, or 1N). For these households, home equity falls by 7.84 percent on an annual basis. If each year, the equity of households in this group fell at this rate, average equity of $87,777 at age seventy would be reduced to $17,149 by age ninety. But, only about 12 percent of households are in this group. Thus the reduction for all households is much less than this. Even among households in this group—those experiencing precipitating shocks—only 8.8 percent move in the survey interval in which the shock occurs, as shown in table 3.13. This suggests that the decline in housing equity among continuing one-person households may in part be the delayed consequence of a prior transition from a two-person household to a one-person household.

Thus, as suggested by the results in prior sections of the paper, the summary results in table 3.14 show that in the absence of precipitating shocks there is little systematic reduction in home equity as families age. Families who move to a new home increase home equity, on average. Reductions in equity come from families who sell and discontinue home ownership. And most of these moves are associated with precipitating shocks to family status. We find no systematic withdrawal of home equity to support non-housing consumption.

3.3 Conclusions

Home equity is the principle asset of a large fraction of elderly Americans. In this paper we have used HRS and AHEAD panel data, as well as SIPP data, to understand the change in the home equity of households as they age. We give particular attention to the relationship between changes in home equity and changes in household structure. There are two ways for households to change home equity: by discontinuing home ownership or by selling and moving to another home. We find that, overall, households are unlikely to discontinue home ownership. Ownership terminations are most likely to occur following the death of a spouse or entry of a family member into a nursing home. But even in these circumstances, selling the home is the exception and not the rule. In the absence of a precipitating shock, it is much more likely that a family will sell and buy a new home than discontinue ownership. And, households who sell and buy again tend to increase rather than reduce home equity. That is, assets are transferred to housing.

Overall—combining the effects of discontinuing ownership and moving to another home—we find that housing equity of HRS households increases with age, and the equity of AHEAD households declines somewhat. The overall decline in the housing equity of the older AHEAD households is about 1.76 percent per year, which is accounted for primarily by a 7.84 percent decline among households experiencing precipitating shocks to family status. Families that remain intact reduce housing equity very little, only 0.11 percent per year for two-person households and 1.15 percent per year for one-person households.

We use two approaches to determine whether households wish to reduce home equity as they age. One approach is to compare the change in the home equity of movers to the change for stayers. If households withdraw equity when they sell and move to a new home, the reduction in the equity of the movers will typically be greater than the change for stayers. These comparisons, however, are confounded by the tendency of the self-assessed home values to exceed actual values, as measured by selling prices. A comparison of the selling prices of homes with the prior self-assessment of home values shows that home values reported prior to a sale far exceed realized sales prices. Comparing the change in the home equity of movers and stayers, but accounting for this bias, we conclude that families who sell and buy a new home increase home equity, on average.

The second approach is based on the comparison of the selling price of the old home (minus the mortgage on the home) with the reported equity value in the newly purchased home. We believe that these are the most reliable data on the change in home equity when families move from one home to another. Based on these "sale price" data, we find that, *on average,* households increase home equity when they move to a new house. We also find, however, that equity-rich and income-poor families tend to reduce home values when they sell and buy a new house, while equity-poor and income-rich families tend to increase home equity. For continuing two-person HRS households, for example, we estimate that the between-wave reduction for those at the 80th equity quantile and at the 20th income quantile is −$15,422. On the other hand, we estimate that households at the 20th equity quantile and the 80th income quantile increase equity by +$54,778.

These results suggest that in considering whether families have saved enough to maintain their preretirement standard of living after retirement, housing equity should not, in general, be counted on to support nonhousing consumption. Families apparently do not intend to finance general retirement consumption by saving through investment in housing, as they might through a 401(k) plan or through some other financial form of saving. Rather, we believe the findings here, as well as our earlier findings, suggest that families purchase homes to provide an environment in which to live, even as they age through retirement years. In this case, the typical aging household is unlikely to seek a reverse annuity mortgage to withdraw assets from home equity. It may be appropriate, however, to think of housing as a reserve or buffer that can be used in catastrophic circumstances that result in a change in household structure. In this case, having used the home equity along the way—through a reverse mortgage for example—would defeat the purpose of saving home equity for a rainy day.

Although these results are based largely on new HRS and AHEAD data files, and are based on different methods of analysis, the findings correspond closely to the conclusions we reached in our earlier papers, based on different data sources. These conclusions also correspond closely to the findings of a recent survey of older households sponsored by the American Association of Retired Persons (AARP; 2000, 24), showing that the preponderance of older families agree with the statement: "What I'd really like to do is stay in my current residence as long as possible'."[15] Like our findings, the results of the AARP survey also imply that most households do not intend to liquidate housing equity to support general nonhousing retirement consumption as they age.

Appendix
Mortality Correction

The analyses using the SIPP data are based on cohorts constructed from cross-section surveys. For example, the home ownership (or home equity) profile for a cohort is constructed by combining data for all households aged A in the first survey year with data for households aged $A + T$ from a survey T years later. If the likelihood of survival from A to $A + T$ is related to wealth, then these cohort profiles can be affected by differential mortality. We correct for this problem by reweighting the sample. Households are assigned an adjusted weight that is inversely related to the probability of survival from age A to age $A + T$.

Baseline estimates of these survival probabilities for one- and two-person households are obtained from waves 1 and 2 of AHEAD. A one-person household survives if the person is present in waves 1 and 2. A two-person household survives if both members are present in the second wave. Survival probabilities are estimated from the AHEAD for five year age intervals and for housing equity quartiles. Households that are older and households that have lower levels of housing wealth are less likely to survive. Since the AHEAD only includes households aged seventy and over, published survival rates by age (from the National Center for Health Statistics [NCHS]) were used to extrapolate the AHEAD survival probabilities back to age fifty.

The final step is to reweight the data. For each household observation of age A and housing equity quartile Q, the SIPP frequency weight is multi-

---

15. More detail is presented in Venti and Wise (2001).

Table 3A.1   **Probit Estimates of Move Probabilities and Quantiles Used to Simulate Move Probabilities**

Variable	Buy Another Home		Discontinue Ownership	
	Estimate	t-statistic	Estimate	t-statistic
	HRS Households			
1 to 1	−0.256	−3.24	−0.007	0.06
2 to 2	−0.194	−2.64	−0.303	2.71
Equity	0.001	0.37	−0.006	3.22
Income	0.008	4.09	−0.020	2.66
Equity · Income	−0.000	−1.59	0.000	0.37
Constant	−1.354	−18.92	−1.808	16.81

	Income ($)	Equity ($)
Selected Quantiles of Income and Initial Reported Home Equity		
20th	17,871	30,796
50th	42,986	68,192
80th	81,105	131,984

Variable	Buy Another Home		Discontinue Ownership	
	Estimate	t-statistic	Estimate	t-statistic
	AHEAD Households			
1 to 1	−0.113	1.34	−0.907	13.57
2 to 2	−0.175	1.99	−1.367	15.47
Equity	0.009	3.24	−0.004	0.74
Income	0.014	1.87	−0.024	1.09
Equity · Income	−0.000	2.27	−0.001	0.61
Constant	−1.699	20.83	−0.701	8.89

	Income ($)	Equity ($)
Selected Quantiles of Income and Initial Reported Home Equity		
20th	10,909	37,434
50th	21,433	74,869
80th	40,609	139,042

plied by the inverse of the cumulative survival probability. The survival probabilities are assumed to be one for households less than age fifty. Thus households that are unlikely to survive are given higher weights. For each observation the probability of surviving to age A given equity quartile Q is

$$(6) \qquad S(A, Q) = \prod_{a=50}^{A} s(a, a + 1: Q),$$

where $s(a, a + 1: Q)$ is the one-year survival rate for a household in equity quartile Q. For each household in each year the SIPP frequency weight is multiplied by the inverse of $S(A, Q)$.

Table 3A.2   **OLS and Median Regression Estimates of the Change in Home Equity and Quantiles Used to Simulate Changes in Home Equity for Households Purchasing Another Home**

Variable	OLS		Median Regression	
	Estimate	t-statistic	Estimate	t-statistic
HRS Households				
1 to 1	48.4	0.00	−762.6	0.08
2 to 2	2,134.4	0.16	9,765.2	1.04
Equity	−5,315.7	10.91	−4,798.4	8.53
Income	2,593.1	4.40	2,024.1	2.33
Equity · Income	10.5	1.20	18.4	0.57
Constant	47,719.4	3.64	25,646.6	2.60
	Income ($)	Equity ($)		
Selected Quantiles of Income and Initial Reported Home Equity				
20th	17,871	30,796		
50th	42,986	68,192		
80th	81,105	131,984		
	OLS		Median Regression	
	Estimate	t-statistic	Estimate	t-statistic
AHEAD Households				
1 to 1	−15,713.5	0.49	−20,551.8	0.80
2 to 2	−8,999.6	0.29	231.9	0.01
Equity	−6,234.6	5.21	−7,619.1	4.56
Income	5,998.9	1.83	2,289.0	0.60
Equity · Income	37.5	0.36	141.5	0.64
Constant	60,189.0	1.82	54,972.1	1.77
	Income ($)	Equity ($)		
Selected Quantiles of Income and Initial Reported Home Equity				
20th	10,909	37,434		
50th	21,433	74,869		
80th	40,609	139,042		

Table 3A.3   OLS and Median Regression Estimates of the Change in Home Equity and Quantiles Used to Simulate Changes in Home Equity for Households *Not* Purchasing Another Home

Variable	OLS		Median Regression	
	Estimate	*t*-statistic	Estimate	*t*-statistic
HRS Households				
1 to 1	13,084.3	0.86	10,552.8	0.48
2 to 2	18,754.4	1.37	18,635.4	0.85
Equity	0.0	0.00	0.0	0.00
Income	−1,791.8	2.40	−2,063.0	1.46
Equity · Income	0.0	0.00	0.0	0.00
Constant	−69,374.6	5.16	−51,943.1	2.63
	Income ($)	Equity ($)		
Selected Quantiles of Income and Initial Reported Home Equity				
20th	17,871	30,796		
50th	42,986	68,192		
80th	81,105	131,984		

	OLS		Median Regression	
	Estimate	*t*-statistic	Estimate	*t*-statistic
AHEAD Households				
1 to 1	24,825.9	1.81	27,010.7	2.30
2 to 2	24,737.6	1.66	35,495.2	2.47
Equity	0.0	0.00	0.0	0.00
Income	−6,200.7	2.47	−6,954.9	1.43
Equity · Income	0.0	0.00	0.0	0.00
Constant	−72,100.7	4.79	−71,111.1	6.05
	Income ($)	Equity ($)		
Selected Quantiles of Income and Initial Reported Home Equity				
20th	10,909	37,434		
50th	21,433	74,869		
80th	40,609	139,042		

References

American Association of Retired Persons (AARP). 2000. *Fixing to stay: A national survey of housing and home modification issues.* Washington, D.C.: AARP.

Bernheim, B. Douglas. 1992. *Is the baby boom generation preparing adequately for retirement?* Technical Report. Princeton, N.J.: Merrill Lynch.

Congressional Budget Office. 1993. *Baby boomers in retirement: An early perspective.* Washington, D.C.: GPO.

Engen, Eric, William Gale, and Cori Uccello. 1999. The adequacy of retirement saving. *Brookings Papers on Economic Activity,* Issue no. 2:65–165. Washington, D.C.: Brookings Institution.

Feinstein, Jonathan, and Daniel McFadden. 1989. The dynamics of housing demand by the elderly: Wealth, cash flow, and demographic effects. In *The economics of aging,* ed. David A. Wise, 55–68. Chicago: University of Chicago Press.

Gustman, Alan, and Thomas Steinmeier. 1999. Effects of pensions on savings: Analysis with data from the Health and Retirement Study. *Carnegie-Rochester Conference Series on Public Policy* 50:P271–324.

Hurd, Michael. 2002. Portfolio holdings of the elderly. In *Household portfolios,* ed. Luigi Guiso, Michael Haliassos, and Tullio Jappelli, 431–92. Cambridge, Mass.: MIT Press.

Juster, F. Thomas, and Richard Suzman. 1995. An overview of the Health and Retirement Study. *Journal of Human Resources* 30:PS7–S56.

Kiel, Katherine, and Jeffrey Zabel. 1999. The accuracy of owner-provided house values: The 1978–91 American Housing Survey. *Real Estate Economics* 27 (2): 263–98.

Mayer, Christopher, and Katerina Simons. 1994. Reverse mortgages and the liquidity of housing wealth. *Journal of the American Real Estate and Urban Economics Association* 22 (2): 235–55.

Megbolugbe, Issac, Jarjisu Sa-Aadu, and James Shilling. 1997. Oh, yes, the elderly will reduce housing equity under the right circumstances. *Journal of Housing Research* 8 (1): 53–74.

Merrill, Sally R. 1984. Home equity and the elderly. In *Retirement and economic behavior,* ed. H. Aaron and G. Burtless, 197–225. Washington, D.C.: Brookings Institution.

Merrill, Sally R., Meryl Finkel, and Nadine Kutty. 1994. Potential beneficiaries from reverse mortgage products for elderly homeowners: An analysis of AHS data. *Journal of the American Real Estate and Urban Economics Association* 22 (2): 257–99.

Moore, James F., and Olivia S. Mitchell. 1997. Projected retirement wealth and savings adequacy in the Health and Retirement Study. NBER Working Paper no. 6240. Cambridge, Mass.: National Bureau of Economic Research, October.

Sheiner, Louise, and David Weil. 1993. The housing wealth of the aged. NBER Working Paper no. 4115. Cambridge, Mass.: National Bureau of Economic Research, July.

Venti, Steven F., and David A. Wise. 1989. Aging, moving, and housing wealth. In *The economics of aging,* ed. David A. Wise, 9–48. Chicago: University of Chicago Press.

———. 1990. But they don't want to reduce housing equity. In *Issues in the economics of aging,* ed. David A. Wise, 13–29. Chicago: University of Chicago Press.

———. 1991. Aging and the income value of housing wealth. *Journal of Public Economics* 44:371–97.

———. 2001. Aging and housing equity. In *Innovations for financing retirement.* Pension Research Council Publications, ed. Olivia S. Mitchell, Zvi Bodie, P. Brett Hammond, and Stephen Zeldes, 254–81. Philadelphia: University of Pennsylvania Press.

Comment   Jonathan Skinner

A little more than a decade ago, Venti and Wise dropped an empirical spanner into the machinery of the life-cycle model when they showed that the elderly were as likely to move into a larger house as into a smaller one (Venti and Wise 1989). This puzzling result had been suggested in earlier work (Merrill 1984), and Feinstein and McFadden (1989) similarly demonstrated the remarkable resilience of elderly households to financial downsizing. The Venti and Wise analysis, however, harnessed the panel characteristics of the Retirement History Survey (RHS) to show how robust and pervasive was this finding. The problem for the conventional life-cycle model was that households are supposed to be spending down their accumulated assets as they get older, so as to insure leaving little or nothing when they finally arrive at their terminal (T) year. Because so much of a typical household's assets comprise housing equity, and presumably families are smaller during retirement, the implication of the life-cycle model is to reduce housing consumption, not increase it. How dare these elderly people flout the life-cycle model by moving into bigger houses?

Sheiner and Weil (1992) seemed to provide some reassurance to the conventional life-cycle contingent because they noted that for the older old, that is, people in their eighties and beyond, there was noticeable downsizing of housing, often as a result of widowhood or serious illness. While these findings represented an important step forward, the estimates had wide confidence intervals given the small sample size available to the researchers.

Venti and Wise have returned to the earlier fertile ground, only this time they have come armed with much better data from the HRS and AHEAD on housing choices among the oldest old as well as the younger old. Surprisingly, they continue to find that the elderly are not anxious to downsize even at much older ages, aside from serious transitional changes such as illness or death of a spouse. Their results are not inconsistent with Sheiner and Weil (1992), of course; there are many more of these transitional events for the oldest old, so the overall degree of downsizing tends to be larger for this older group.

The data analysis is careful and extensive, and I have little to quibble about with regard to their analysis. Instead, in these comments I will suggest how their results may be interpreted, and what variants of the life-cycle model fit neatly with their empirical findings and which ones do not.

There are two somewhat separate issues regarding housing of the elderly. The first is why the elderly do not appear to want to move, particularly when their house is large relative to the size of the household (one or two

Jonathan Skinner is John French Professor of Economics at Dartmouth College and a research associate of the National Bureau of Economic Research.

people, typically), and downsizing would free up substantial levels of equity. The second is why the elderly, when they do move, are as likely to move to a larger house as a smaller house. We consider each question in turn.

First, a deep-rooted attachment to one's house (and presumably neighborhood) is a very common reason given for not wanting to move. In a study of one focus group with elderly participants, Curry, Gruman, and Robinson (2001, 39) reported statements showing a strong interest in staying in one's house: "First and foremost, you don't want to give up your home . . . That's a big thing—giving up your home" or "I think the home should be kept sacred." Indeed, one participant made a point of fighting against the urge to stay in one's house: "That sentimental attachment to your home and things that are customary is one of the chronic afflictions of older age and has to be overcome."

This may have as much to do with psychological factors as with an implicit understanding of the fact that housing provides a hedge against future changes in housing prices. Second, cashing out the house and entering the rental market exposes the elderly household to rent hikes that are difficult, if not impossible, to insure against short of home ownership. Sinai and Souleles (2001), for example, suggest that in areas with greater variation in rental price changes, home ownership rates are higher. While Sinai and Souleles point out that the effects of rental variability should be blunted for the elderly, because their horizon tends to be shorter, the larger share of rents in the budgets of the elderly would only serve to strengthen this desire to avoid risk. (A similar story is told for younger households in Banks, Blundell, and Smith [chap. 5 in this vol.] who seek to purchase a house earlier to guard against the risk of future home price increases.) In short, there are very good reasons for elderly homeowners to not sell their houses for both psychological and economic reasons.

Why, then, are elderly people as likely to move into a more costly house as to move into a less costly one? It is important to distinguish between quantity and price here, because it may be the case that the houses they move into are smaller, but cost more. A study by Choi (1996) sheds some light on the motivation for moving among the elderly. Figure 3C.1 displays the primary reasons for moving. The most common reason is poor health, and here presumably downsizing does take place, as is suggested in the Venti and Wise analysis that finds poor health is a common cause for getting out of home ownership altogether. But the second most common reason is to move closer to family. Buying a new house or condominium near one's children can involve spending more for housing, particularly with regard to moving closer to suburban areas. With regard to reasons for moving, "amenities" is not far behind; this includes migration to retirement communities, again which may entail large up-front equity costs.

A fourth reason for not downsizing (both with regard to existing homes and new homes) is that the house provides a "safe haven" for assets with

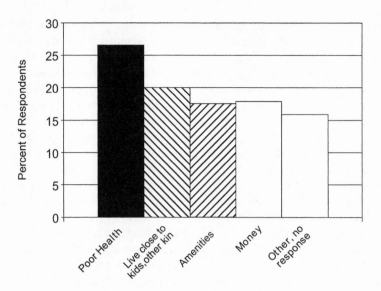

Fig. 3C.1   Reasons given for moving among elderly

Source: Choi (1996)

Notes: Poor health includes health of sample person or spouse, or death/institutionalization of spouse. Amenities includes moving to a retirement/community home.

favorable treatment under Medicaid and other asset-based means tested programs. While states differ with regard to their treatment of home equity, often equity is not included (either on a de facto or de jure basis) in the asset limits used to determine eligibility for Medicaid or Supplemental Social Insurance (SSI). Selling the house and using the resulting interest to pay rent would expose the household to the stringent wealth limitations in the event that a long nursing home stay or chronic illness qualifies them for welfare or Medicaid.

These reasons for holding on to housing wealth are all perfectly consistent with the life-cycle model, albeit one with a few more bells and whistles than the usual perfect certainty model. Housing wealth should be viewed as a particularly valuable insurance for an elderly household (Skinner 1996). In the "good" state of the world, there are no debilitating health or financial downturns, and the elderly can continue to live in their house until death, upon which the house and remaining assets are bequeathed to family members or other worthy recipients. It is important to note, however, that in these "good" states of the world, elderly households do *not* downsize, so in that sense, the simplest life-cycle model, in which households spend down their wealth (both housing and nonhousing) to finance consumption retirement, is simply incorrect.

In the "bad" state of the world, one or more of the spouses qualifies for

Medicaid or another social insurance program with wealth limitations, and while nonhousing assets are depleted under the asset means testing, housing equity is largely preserved, either for the benefit of the healthy spouse or those receiving the bequest. Finally, in the "really bad" state of the world, poor health or adverse financial outcomes results leads to selling the house and moving to a rental or an institutional setting. In this case, the cash is welcome to provide for amenities or a preferred nursing home at the same time that the house no longer remains a viable option for the elderly person; thus the house provides a well-balanced insurance "asset" (Skinner 1996).

This view of the world is one in which assets, including housing assets, are held against future contingencies in later life, so in that sense it can be viewed as a life-cycle model. On the other hand, in the good and bad state of the world, when the assets are not needed directly for very bad adverse outcomes, the household members are happy to pass along a bequest. Only in the "very bad" state of the world are assets largely depleted with regard to bequests.

This approach also makes sense of a seeming paradox in the Survey of Consumer Finances. When asked about why they are saving, more than 40 percent of retirees respond that they are saving against a "rainy day" or emergencies, with only about one-tenth percent responding that they are saving for their children. Yet when asked about bequests, roughly half of all respondents view leaving a financial bequest as "important" or "very important" (Dynan, Skinner, and Zeldes 2002). In other words, one need not choose between a "bequest motive" and a "life-cycle motive" for saving; assets such as housing serve both objectives simultaneously on an *ex ante* basis.

In sum, there is good news and bad news for fans of the conventional life-cycle model. The good news for the fans is that the oldest old do indeed tend to deaccumulate their housing assets. At first blush, this may suggest that the conventional life-cycle model had it right all along. However, the bad news is that, as Venti and Wise demonstrate, the conventional life-cycle model entirely misses the motives for why households are deaccumulating. The motives for why the elderly hold on to housing for so long, and the importance of health-related shocks that cause the elderly to reduce housing equity, should be the major focus of an expanded life-cycle model.

While the Venti and Wise study has provided many pieces of the puzzle, there are still many pieces missing. While I have suggested some reasons why the elderly may wish to purchase more expensive housing, it is not clear why the median should still be essentially no decline in housing value. Are there that many elderly people moving to more expensive or larger houses? What do we know about the characteristics of the houses the elderly are moving into? Are they really larger or just more expensive? Given the long-term importance of housing wealth in the portfolio of the elderly, it would seem that these questions will only become more important in the next several decades as the baby boom generation gears up for retirement.

References

Choi, Namkee G. 1996. Older persons who move: Reasons and health consequences. *Journal of Applied Gerontology* 15 (September): 325–44.

Curry, Leslie, Cynthia Gruman, and Julie Robinson. 2001. Medicaid estate planning: Perceptions of mortality and necessity. *Gerontologist* 21 (1): 34–42.

Dynan, Karen, Jonathan Skinner, and Stephen Zeldes. 2002. The importance of bequests and life cycle saving in capital accumulation: A new view. *American Economic Review* 92 (2): 274–78.

Feinstein, Jonathan S., and Daniel McFadden. 1989. The dynamics of housing demand by the elderly: Wealth, cash flow, and demographic effects. In *The economics of aging,* ed. David A. Wise, 55–86. Chicago: University of Chicago Press.

Merrill, Sally R. 1984. Home equity and the elderly. In *Retirement and economic behavior,* ed. Henry J. Aaron and Gary Burtless, 197–227. Washington, D.C.: Brookings Institution.

Sheiner, Louise M., and David Weil. 1992. The housing wealth of the aged. NBER Working Paper no. 4115. Cambridge, Mass.: National Bureau of Economic Research, July.

Sinai, Todd, and Nicholas Souleles. 2001. Owner-occupied housing as insurance against rent risk. University of Pennsylvania, Wharton School. Mimeograph.

Skinner, Jonathan. 1996. Is housing wealth a sideshow? In *Papers in the economics of aging,* ed. David A. Wise, 241–71. Chicago: University of Chicago Press.

Venti, Steven F., and David A. Wise. 1989. Aging, moving, and housing wealth. In *The economics of aging,* ed. David A. Wise, 9–48. Chicago: University of Chicago Press.

Intergenerational Transfers and Savings Behavior

Jeffrey R. Brown and Scott J. Weisbenner

"If Riches are yours, why don't you take them with you t'other world?"
—Ben Franklin, *Poor Richard's Almanac*

4.1 Introduction

What is the source of household wealth? Economists generally agree that there are two possible sources: households can engage in life-cycle saving by not consuming all of their income, or they can receive bequests or inter vivos transfers from individuals outside of their household. Clearly, both forms of wealth accumulation occur. For at least two decades, however, there has been an ongoing debate about the relative magnitude of these two sources of wealth. This debate was largely started by the seminal paper of Kotlikoff and Summers (1981), which found that life-cycle wealth accounted for only 20 percent of U.S. total net worth. Other authors, notably including Franco Modigliani (1988), the "father" of the life-cycle hypothesis, responded with calculations showing that over 80 percent of net worth can be explained by life-cycle saving.

The source of household wealth is important for many reasons. For example, the behavioral effects of many government programs, such as Social Security, the taxation of savings, and targeted savings programs, will likely depend upon the source of wealth. Debates about the fairness of the wealth distribution in the United States and the extent to which there is intergenerational mobility across this distribution, depend on whether wealth is primarily earned or inherited. The relative importance of life-cycle and transfer wealth also informs the choice of whether to use life-cycle, dynasty, or

Jeffrey R. Brown is assistant professor of finance at the University of Illinois, Urbana-Champaign, and a faculty research fellow of the National Bureau of Economic Research. Scott J. Weisbenner is assistant professor of finance at the University of Illinois, Urbana-Champaign, and a faculty research fellow of the National Bureau of Economic Research.

other models to represent household decision making, and thus has implications for a broad range of policies, such as how we think about household responses to government fiscal policy.

This paper makes two contributions to this literature. First, using the 1998 Survey of Consumer Finances, we provide new evidence suggesting that transfer wealth accounts for approximately 20–25 percent of current household net worth, suggesting a much larger role for life-cycle savings than was found by Kotlikoff and Summers (1981). This figure is calculated in two ways, both of which yield quite similar results: (1) direct survey evidence, and (2) estimating of the flow of transfers in 1998 using an improved methodology that accounts for the correlation between wealth and mortality and converting this into a stock of transfer wealth. In addition to the methodological improvement, new estimates are useful because the composition of household wealth has changed substantially over the past several decades (Juster et al. 1999).

Second, we examine the heterogeneity of the size of transfers received and expected. We demonstrate that while in aggregate, transfer wealth does not appear to be as large as some prior estimates suggest, it is nonetheless quite important for a small subset of the population. Specifically, we show that approximately one-fifth of households report receiving a transfer, and one-eighth expect a substantial transfer in the future. For those households that have received transfers, transfer wealth accounts for, on average, half of current net worth. For lower-wealth households (those with less than $75,000), transfer wealth on average exceeds current wealth.

This paper proceeds as follows. In section 4.2, we review some of the literature relevant to the debate over the relative importance of transfer and life-cycle wealth. We discuss our primary data set, the 1998 wave of the Survey of Consumer Finances (SCF), in section 4.3. Section 4.4 directly estimates transfer wealth using survey questions about the receipt of transfers. Section 4.5 provides an alternative estimate of transfer wealth by calculating the flow of bequests in 1998 using wealth-adjusted mortality rates and converting this into a flow of bequests. In section 4.6, we provide evidence about the degree of heterogeneity in the importance of transfers received and expected. Section 4.7 concludes.

4.2 Literature Review

Modigliani and Brumberg (1954) and Ando and Modigliani (1963) presented the life-cycle hypothesis (LCH), which soon emerged as the principal model of saving behavior and wealth accumulation. According to the LCH, wealth arises from households saving out of current income to finance a future period of retirement. Kotlikoff and Summers (1981) asked whether life-cycle savings alone could explain observed levels of wealth accumulation. They estimated the excess of labor earnings over consumption using aggregate data on a cohort-by-cohort basis and then accumulated the differences to see how the aggregated savings compared to actual observed wealth. They concluded that approximately 20 percent of total wealth was due to life-cycle saving. They also estimated a flow of bequests using the 1962 SCF and a general mortality table, converted it into transfer wealth, and found that the net worth in 1974 was around 150 times the flow of bequests in 1974. This second approach confirmed their primary finding that the majority of aggregate wealth could be attributed to transfers.

The findings of Kotlikoff and Summers (1981) spawned a debate that is still unresolved today. The primary issues in this debate were clearly delineated in a pair of articles by Modigliani (1988) and Kotlikoff (1988). These articles highlighted several important conceptual and methodological differences. For example, should the interest earned from an initial transfer be treated as part of the transfer or as self-accumulated wealth? Should college aid for a dependent child over age eighteen be treated as consumption or as a transfer?

Gale and Scholz (1994) extended the debate further by presenting evidence on the importance of inter vivos gifts, including payment of college tuition, using the 1986 SCF. Using the flow-to-stock conversion methodology (and general mortality tables), they concluded that inter vivos transfers account for at least 20 percent of U.S. wealth (32 percent if college aid is included) and bequests account for at least 31 percent of U.S. wealth.

As surveyed in Gale and Slemrod (2001), there are also a number of overlapping generations model simulations examining this issue (Masson 1986; Laitner 1990; Lord and Rangazas 1991). These models have also produced a wide range of estimates but have made useful conceptual contributions by demonstrating how factors such as credit constraints can affect the shares of life-cycle and transfer wealth.

Finally, some studies estimate transfer wealth directly from survey responses. Hurd and Mundaca (1989), using a 1964 survey of the affluent, estimate that transfers account for roughly one-quarter of total wealth, a substantially smaller share than suggested by Kotlikoff and Summers (1981).

There are several reasons to revisit this well-researched question. First, we are able to bring to bear much more recent data. Several decades have elapsed since the period examined in the Kotlikoff and Summers (1981) study, and over that time we have seen significant changes in the composition of household portfolios. Defined benefit pension plans have been increasingly replaced by bequeathable defined contribution plans, and there is much broader ownership in equities due to the rise in mutual funds. Second, to our knowledge, no prior work measuring aggregate wealth transfers has accounted for the wealth-mortality correlation that is now known to be significant. Third, we focus attention on the concentration of bequests and show that even if bequests are small in aggregate, they are quite significant for the households that receive them.

4.3   Data

This paper uses data from the 1998 SCF, which is a cross-sectional survey that has been conducted every three years since 1983 by the Federal Reserve Board. The data set, which is described in more detail by Kennickell, Starr-McCluer, and Surette (2000), sampled 4,305 households in 1998. The SCF oversamples higher-wealth households because asset ownership is highly skewed, and as a result, it is necessary to weight the data to convert sample averages to population aggregates.

In addition to collecting a rich set of data on household assets and liabilities, the SCF asks households if they have ever given financial support to relatives or friends, and the amount given. It also asks the household to provide details for up to three inheritances, gifts, or trusts that they have received including relation to donor, year received, value when received, and whether it was a bequest or an inter vivos transfer. Additionally, households are asked if they expect to receive a substantial transfer in the future, and if so, how much. Therefore, the SCF provides several different routes one can use to estimate transfer wealth. Two primary methods, self-reported receipts by SCF respondents and the calculation of bequest flows from the SCF respondents, are examined in the next two sections.

4.4   Direct Estimation of Transfer Wealth from Survey Data

The first approach we undertake is to directly estimate transfer wealth based on household reports of transfers received. While this approach is subject to limitations (Kotlikoff 1988), it provides a useful starting point. As we will show, an independent method in section 4.5 will produce similar results.

The SCF asks households to provide details of up to three inheritances/trusts/transfers they have received.[1] Table 4.1 reports inheritances and inter vivos transfers received in the period 1993–September 1998 for people surveyed for the 1998 SCF. Kennickell, Starr-McCluer, and Surette (2000) report that September 1998 is the midpoint of the period during which the 1998 SCF interviews were conducted. In the data set, the date the inheritance is received is rounded to the nearest 5. Thus, "1995" corresponds to inheritances received from 1993 to 1997 and "1998" corresponds to inheritances received during the first nine months of 1998.

After converting the SCF sample averages to population aggregates using the population weights, gross transfers received from 1993 through

---

1. For households that have received more than three substantial transfers, the SCF asks households to value all additional transfers beyond the top three. However, the SCF does not ask the respondent to give the date of receipt or who the donor was for these additional transfers. Households report the value of the additional transfers is $20.3 billion (weighted to reflect the population).

Table 4.1   **Inheritances and Transfers Reported by Recipients over 1993–1998 in 1998 SCF**

	Total	Inheritance and Inherited Trust	*Inter vivos* Transfer/Gift/Trust
1993–Sept. 1998	847	579	268
Amount per year	147	101	47
	1993–September 1998, by Donor		
From parents	590	404	186
From grandparents	88	51	36
From uncle/aunt	40	34	6
From sibling	57	21	37
From friend	42	41	1
From child	23	22	1
Other	8	6	2

Source: Authors' calculations.

Notes: The SCF asks households to give details about three inheritances/gifts/trusts. A bequest/transfer to a spouse is not counted as a bequest/transfer. The year of receipt is rounded to the nearest five, and the reported value is at time of receipt. Transfers received over 1993–1997 are grossed up by a factor of 1.068 to be converted to 1998 dollars. Kennickell, Starr-McCluer, and Surette (2000) report that September 1998 is the midpoint of the period during which the 1998 SCF interviews were conducted. Data weighted to reflect population. Amounts are in billions of 1998 dollars.

September 1998 totaled $847 billion (1998 dollars). Just over two-thirds of the financial support came in the form of a bequest, and the remaining one-third were inter vivos transfers. Not surprisingly, the vast majority (70 percent) of transfers, both bequests and inter vivos gifts, are from parents. Transfers from grandparents constitute 10 percent of total transfers.

Table 4.1 reported gross transfers received since 1993, but some survey respondents report receiving inheritances and inter vivos gifts as far back as 1940. Table 4.2 sums up all inheritances and transfers ever received. By summing up past transfers, we can directly estimate what fraction of current net worth is attributable to transfers received, assuming these transfers had been saved. The remaining part of net worth represents life-cycle wealth (the accumulation of differences between yearly income and consumption).

To be specific, the question we ask is, assuming everyone currently alive had saved all the transfers they received, along with the accumulated interest, how much wealth would that represent? In other words, what is the maximum portion of wealth people hold today that can be attributable to transfers they have received in the past. This is what we will define as transfer wealth throughout the paper. Importantly, our transfer wealth calculation does not represent what is actually left over from transfers received, as we have no way of knowing what fraction of transfers is consumed and what fraction is saved. Rather, it represents what the value would be of all

Table 4.2   Compute Stock of "Transfer" Wealth using 1998 SCF

	Scale Previous Gifts by Inflation	Scale Previous Gifts by Long-Term High-Grade Corporate Bond Return
Total transfer wealth	2,465	5,405
Inheritances/Inherited trust	1,885	4,226
Inter vivos transfer/trust	580	1,178
Transfer Wealth, by Donor		
From parents	1,719	3,863
From grandparents	377	819
From uncle/aunt	134	317
From sibling	109	189
From friend	68	120

	Scale Previous Gifts by 50% Long-Term U.S. Gov't Bond and 50% Large Company Stock	Scale Previous Gifts by Large Company Stock Return
Total transfer wealth	17,326	29,203
Inheritances/Inherited trust	15,057	25,861
Inter vivos transfer/trust	2,269	3,342
Transfer Wealth, by Donor		
From parents	8,488	13,057
From grandparents	7,552	14,310
From uncle/aunt	570	816
From sibling	313	435
From friend	252	382

Source: Authors' calculations.

Notes: Total transfer wealth does not include $20.3 billion of transfers that do not give information on year received, whether was inheritance or *inter vivos* transfer, and who the donor was. Data weighted to reflect population. Amounts in billions of 1998 dollars. Total net worth is equal to $28,794 billion dollars.

the transfers received in the past, plus accumulated interest, had they been saved. This calculation is instructive because it provides an upper bound to the value of what is actually left over from transfers received in the past.

One methodological issue that arises in aggregating past transfers is the decision about how to treat the investment returns on past transfers. Should investment returns be classified as part of transfer wealth or as part of life-cycle saving? It is our view that because life-cycle wealth can be viewed as the value of transfers given minus the value of transfers received, it is sensible to include investment returns on past transfers as part of transfer wealth.[2] Clearly, doing so will result in a higher level of transfer wealth

2. Obviously this need not be a "none or all" decision. For example, one could plausibly argue that returns at the risk-free rate should be included as transfer wealth and any excess returns be included as life-cycle wealth.

than would the alternative. Of course, this raises another methodological issue, the issue of what investment return to apply to past transfers. The choice of return can have a substantial impact on the current size of bequests received many years ago.

Ibbotson Associates reports that average annual inflation from 1926 to 98 was 3.2 percent in the United States, long-term U.S. government bonds had an average nominal return of 5.7 percent, high-grade long-term corporate bonds had an average nominal return of 6.1 percent, and large company stocks had an average nominal return of 13.2 percent. As table 4.2 demonstrates, the choice of scaling factor will have a large effect on the magnitude of gross transfer wealth.[3] The 1998 SCF estimates total net worth in 1998 at $28.8 trillion. When previous gifts are scaled by inflation only (so that investment returns are implicitly included in life-cycle wealth), transfer wealth represents only 9 percent of current net worth.

If instead we gross up past returns by the return offered on corporate bonds (which had a real return of approximately 3 percent over the past seventy years), our estimate of transfer wealth rises to $5.4 billion, or just under one-fifth (19 percent) of current net worth. This estimate is in line with the results of Modigliani (1988). Transfers from parents constitute 71 percent of the value of all transfers received and bequests constitute 78 percent of transfer wealth.

In table 4.2, we show how our estimates of transfer wealth would change if we assumed transfers were invested partially or fully in equities. If transfers are invested 50 percent in government bonds and 50 percent in stocks (an average real return of 6.3 percent), transfer wealth rises to $17.3 trillion (60 percent of current net worth). Finally, if all transfers are invested in large company stocks, then essentially all net worth is due to transfers received (in fact, transfer wealth actually slightly exceeds current net worth). This choice also affects the relative importance of the source of transfers. Because gifts from grandparents were, on average, received longer ago, scaling transfers by equity returns causes grandparent gifts to comprise roughly the same share of transfer wealth as do gifts from parents.

These estimates suggest that the importance of transfer wealth is quite sensitive to the treatment of investment returns. Estimates of the share of transfer wealth vary from 9 percent to 100 percent, as the return is varied from inflation only to a 100 percent equity investment. We believe that a real rate of return of 3 percent seems the most plausible assumption, and thus we will scale past gifts by the corporate bond rate, unless stated otherwise, throughout the remainder of the paper.

In table 4.3 we replicate the algorithm in table 4.2, only this time we use

---

3. When grossing up past transfers, we assume that transfers earn the actual rates of return observed from the date of receipt to the present (rather than assuming the transfer grows at some constant rate).

Table 4.3   **Compute Stock of "Transfer" Wealth using 1989 SCF**

	Scale Previous Gifts by Inflation	Scale Previous Gifts by Long-Term High-Grade Corporate Bond Return
Total transfer wealth	2,670	4,300
Inheritances/Inherited trust	2,121	3,455
Inter vivos transfer/trust	549	845

Source: Authors' calculations.

Notes: Total transfer wealth does not include $39.0 billion of transfers that do not give information on year received, whether was inheritance or inter vivos transfer, and who the donor was. Data weighted to reflect population. Amounts in billions of 1989 dollars. Total net worth is equal to $17,401 billion dollars.

the 1989 SCF. This allows us to test whether the importance of transfers has changed over the past decade. Our estimate of transfer wealth, as a proportion of total net worth, is slightly higher than that calculated using the 1998 survey but is still in the same ballpark. Grossing up past transfers by the corporate bond return, transfer wealth is estimated to be one-quarter of total wealth in 1989, compared to one-fifth a decade later in 1998.

There is a history of studies dating back to the 1960s (for example, Morgan et al. 1962; Projector and Weiss 1964; Barlow, Brazer, and Morgan 1966; and, more recently, Hurd and Mundaca 1989) using survey evidence to elicit the importance of transfer wealth. We believe, however, that this is one of the first studies to calculate transfer wealth directly using recent data such as the SCF. Consistent with most of these past studies, this approach tends to result in shares of transfer wealth that are much smaller than those found by Kotlikoff and Summers (1981; typically on the order of one-fifth to one-fourth).

The SCF is generally regarded as providing the best information on the high-net-worth segment of the population. Of the 4,305 households sampled in its 1998 survey, one-fourth have a net worth over a million dollars, and 245 households have a net worth in excess of $20 million. The maximum net worth in the sample is $501 million, which corresponds to the net worth that a household needed to be included in the *Forbes* 400 richest Americans in 1998. This is by design, as the SCF samples up to the minimum wealth threshold of the *Forbes* 400. This raises the concern that the SCF might be missing the largest large transfers. Perhaps transfers are a more important source of wealth for the superrich.

To address this concern, we examined the source of wealth for the *Forbes* 400 richest Americans in 1998. In their profile, *Forbes* describes the source of wealth (that is, inheritance, Microsoft stock, real estate, etc.). Inheritance was listed as the primary source of wealth for eighty-two members, or about one-fifth, of the *Forbes* 400. For example, the top five wealthiest

Americans in 1998 were all "self-made" (Gates, Buffett, Allen, Dell, Balmer), whereas the next five were Waltons who inherited their wealth from Sam Walton. The total net worth of the eighty-two members whose fortune was inherited constituted 21 percent of the $738 billion total net worth of the *Forbes* 400, surprisingly similar to our estimates in table 4.2.

In the next section, we will estimate the yearly flow of bequests and then under some steady-state assumptions calculate the stock of transfer wealth. We will show how the estimate of the share of transfer wealth is comparable to our best estimate of 20 percent derived directly from reported inheritances (grossing up past transfers by the corporate bond return). It is worth pointing out that our central estimate of transfer wealth does not include college financial aid received from parents (unless SCF respondents report such inter vivos aid as a transfer). Whether college aid represents an inter vivos transfer to another household or whether it should be counted as support for dependent children, and thus consumption of the household, is clearly debatable. We will later, however, discuss how the treatment of college aid as a transfer affects our estimates.

4.5 Estimation of Transfer Wealth from Flow of Transfers

The second approach to estimating transfer wealth involves calculating the flow of transfers for a single year and then converting this flow into a stock of wealth. To adequately capture all sources of transfers, we need to separately estimate the flow of bequests and the flow of inter vivos transfers.

Previous literature (Kessler and Masson 1989; Cox and Raines 1985) has suggested that the magnitude of measured transfers is dependent on whether one asks donors or recipients. Because inheritances are more clearly defined, we should expect close agreement between the amount of inheritances reported by donors and recipients.

With inter vivos transfers, on the other hand, there is more room for differences. A loan, for example, may count as inter vivos "financial support" from the point of view of the donor but not be viewed as a "gift/transfer" by the recipient. There are many other reasons to suspect underreporting bias (Gale and Scholz 1994) that would suggest a discrepancy between the inter vivos transfers reported by donors and recipients.

So how well do the estimates using recipient reports compare to estimates using donor reports? Table 4.4 calculates expected bequests in 1998 using data on net worth and life insurance and various mortality tables. When calculating the bequest, we augment net worth by the face value of life insurance held. As background, using the 1962 SCF and a general mortality table, Kotlikoff and Summers (1981) calculated the ratio of current net worth to expected bequests to be about 150. Specifically, they calculated a total 1962 net worth of $1.75 trillion and a flow of "distant in age" bequests of $12 billion.

Table 4.4   Expected Bequests in 1998 using 1998 SCF and Various Mortality Tables

	1998 Social Security Mortality Table	1998 Annuitant Mortality Table	Attanasio & Hoynes (2000) Mortality
Total	178.1	118.5	126.0
From households with no children	40.3	26.6	30.1
Important to leave inheritance to surviving heirs?			
Very important	72.6	50.8	47.5
(21% of households; 22% of estates)			
Important	39.9	25.9	29.4
(26% of households; 28% of estates)			
Somewhat important	42.5	26.9	31.0
(30% of households; 25% of estates)			
Not important	22.9	14.8	18.1
(21% of households; 25% of estates)			
Do you expect to leave a sizable estate to others?			
Yes	104.7	70.1	66.8
(27% of households; 21% of estates)			
Possibly	28.9	19.3	21.0
(23% of households; 18% of estates)			
No	44.4	29.1	38.2
(50% of households; 61% of estates)			
Expected Bequests in 1995 using 1995 SCF and Various Mortality Tables			
Total	146.4	99.3	100.9

Source: Authors' calculations.

Notes: Amounts are in billions of 1998 dollars. The value of the bequest is household net worth plus the face value of life insurance. If the head of the household has a spouse, both must die for a bequest to occur. Bequests to surviving spouses are not counted. Attanasio and Hoynes (1995) use the SIPP to calculate mortality rates as a function of wealth. They adjust Social Security mortality numbers by a factor d (where $d = .626$ if in top wealth quartile, $d = .789$ if in 2nd wealth quartile, $d = .816$ if in 3rd wealth quartile, and $d = 1.769$ if in bottom wealth quartile). These adjustment factors are taken from Attanasio and Hoynes (1995), table 5.

Previous research on this topic has not adjusted mortality to reflect the correlation with wealth. Recent work by Attanasio and Hoynes (2000) has illustrated the significant mortality differentials across the wealth distribution and the implications of this correlation for studies of consumption and wealth accumulation. In this context, the effect of differential mortality can be illustrated by comparing estimates of the stock of transfer wealth under alternative assumptions about mortality. Using a general population life table provided from the Social Security Administration, we find that net worth is 160 times the estimated flow of bequests (which is $180 billion). This is extremely close to the ratio found in the 1962 SCF.

We explore two alternatives for adjusting the mortality tables. The first is to use annuitant mortality tables that reflect the mortality experience of participants in the individual annuity market who tend to have above average incomes and wealth as discussed by Brown et al. (2001). Because most wealth in the population (and thus in the SCF) is held by such higher income households, we feel this is an appropriate mortality table to use. A similar approach has been used by Poterba (2000) and Poterba and Weisbenner (2001) in studies of the estate tax. Using an annuitant table for 1998, we estimate a flow of bequests of about $120 billion, or about 1/240 of current wealth.

A second alternative is to use the wealth quartile mortality adjustments calculated by Attanasio and Hoynes (2000). Using this adjustment to the general population life table yields an estimate of expected bequests of $126 billion, similar to the estimate using the annuitant mortality table.[4] Therefore, using either approach to correcting the mortality estimates for the wealth-mortality correlation reduces the annual flow of bequests by approximately one-third, thus ultimately reducing our estimate of wealth accumulation from inheritances by roughly one-third as well.

Using the 1995 SCF, we estimate a flow of $100 billion ($107 in 1998 dollars) of bequests during 1995 using the annuitant mortality table. Going back to table 4.1, the average yearly bequest received from 1993 to September 1998, which would roughly correspond to 1995 bequests, was $101 billion in 1998 dollars. Thus, the estimated flow of bequests from both methodologies (direct report of recipient versus estimate based on mortality table) are very similar, once we correct for the correlation between mortality and wealth.

Turning now to inter vivos transfers, table 4.5 reports "financial support" given to non-household members during the year. It is not clear if this includes only gifts, or if it includes loans as well (such as college support). Donors report giving financial support of $64 billion in 1997, a little more than the $47 billion of gifts/trusts that the respondents report receiving annually from 1993 to mid 1998 in table 4.1. This could reflect underreporting of gifts received. It could also reflect an inclusion of loans and college aid when reporting support given but not when reporting gifts received. However, all in all, the inter vivos transfer estimates are not too dissimilar.

We will now follow methodology used by Kotlikoff and Summers (1981) and Gale and Scholz (1994) to convert the flow of bequests/transfers into a stock of net transfer wealth. Net transfer wealth is the difference between the present-day value of transfers received less the present-day value of transfers given for all households currently living. The equations behind this calculation are discussed in the appendix.

The conversion of a flow of transfers to a stock of wealth will depend upon the flow of transfers in the current year (t), the interest rate applied to past transfers (r), the growth rate of transfers (n), the one-year mortal-

---

4. This assumes that all of the estate is bequeathed to a person and not to a charity. Charitable deductions comprised 6.2 percent of gross estate value on estate tax returns filed in 1998. This fraction was 10.4 percent for single decedents (source: Barry Johnson and Jacob Mikow of the Internal Revenue Service).

Table 4.5   Financial Support to Relatives/Friends Who Do Not Live in
                   Household (1997)

	Range (billion $)	Billion $	Percentage
Total	63.7	63.7	100.0
Child	32.3–41.7	36.6	57.4
Niece/Nephew	.9–1.9	1.4	2.2
Grandchild	2.4–9.9	5.8	9.1
Siblings	3.2–9.3	6.1	9.6
Friends	2.3–4.4	3.2	5.0
Parents	6.6–11.6	8.9	13.9
Grandparents	0.1–0.2	.1	.2
Other	1.0–2.5	1.7	2.7

Source: Authors' calculations.

Notes: 1998 SCF asks how much financial support respondents gave in 1997, and then asks respondents to check all the relative-types they gave support without specifying size of gifts across recipients. The first column represents the range of transfers to specific recipients (some donors report that their transfer was given to multiple recipients so we cannot identify how much went to each recipient). $48.8 billion of $62.3 billion of support given by households was given to only one person, so can identify amount of support to a specific recipient for these transfers. It is assumed that if the respondent checks that the transfer went to more than one person, then each recipient received an equal amount. The second and third columns are calculated under this assumption. Data weighted to reflect population.

ity rate δ, the age of recipients of the transfer (I), the age of the donors (G), and the maximum age of an individual (D). A key parameter in the conversion is $r - n - \delta$ (this represents the rate at which past transfers are grossed up to calculate present-day values). Assuming that transfers grow at the rate of income, Kotlikoff and Summers (1981) and Gale and Scholz (1994) suggest that $r - n$ is roughly .01 based on historical averages.[5] If the average one-year mortality rate is between .01 and .02, this would suggest that $r - n - \delta$ is likely close to zero and perhaps even negative.

Table 4.6 presents estimates of the stock of transfer wealth under various assumptions for $r - n - \delta$. Details of the algorithm used to obtain the estimates are in the appendix. The first row of table 4.6 converts the average yearly flow of inheritances reported by recipients over 1993–1998 to a stock of transfer wealth. The second row converts the yearly flow of inter vivos transfers reported by recipients over 1993–1998 to a stock of wealth. Finally, the third row converts the yearly flow of inter vivos transfers reported by donors during 1997 to a stock of wealth.[6]

The average yearly flow of inheritances survey respondents report re-

5. Kotlikoff & Summers (1981) estimate historical averages of the real rate of return of .045 and the real rate of gross domestic product (GDP) growth of .035 ($r - n = .01$). Gale and Scholz (1994) use $r - n = .01$ as their central estimate.

6. It is assumed that parents are thirty years older than their children and sixty years older than their grandchildren. In the second row, if the recipient reports receiving an inter vivos transfers from his parent, it is assumed that the age of the donor is the recipient's age plus thirty years. In the third row, if the donor reports giving inter vivos support to his grandchild, it is assumed that the age of the recipient is the donor's age minus sixty years.

Table 4.6   **Converting a Flow of Transfers into a Stock of Transfer Wealth**

		Stock of Wealth		
	Yearly Flow	$r - n - \delta = 0$	$r - n - \delta = -.01$	$r - n - \delta = .01$
Inheritances (received 1995)	$94 billion	$4.69 trillion	$3.64 trillion	$6.22 trillion
Inter vivos transfers				
(received 1995)	44	1.29	.86	1.98
(given 1997)	64	1.21	.64	2.32

Source: Authors' calculations.

Notes: SCF respondents report inheritances and inter vivos transfers received over 1993–1998. The average amount received over this period (in 1995 dollars) is reported as the flow of inheritances and inter vivos transfers received in 1995. This flow is converted to a stock of transfer wealth in 1995 using the methodology described in the text and the appendix. For comparison, total net worth in 1995 is estimated at $20.68 trillion using the 1995 SCF. SCF respondents also report inter vivos support given in 1997. The bottom row converts this yearly flow to a stock of wealth in 1997. r is the interest rate, n is the growth rate of transfers (usually assumed to be the growth rate of national income), and δ is the one-year mortality rate.

ceiving between 1993 and 1998 is $94 billion (in 1995 dollars). If $r - n - \delta = 0$, converting this flow to a stock of wealth yields transfer wealth of $4.69 trillion (if $r - n - \delta = -.01$, then the estimate falls to $3.64 trillion; if $r - n - \delta = .01$, then the estimate rises to $6.22 trillion). Using the 1995 SCF, net worth held by households in 1995 totaled $20.68 trillion. Taking the average inheritance over 1995–1998 as the yearly flow during 1995, inheritances would account for between 18 and 23 percent of total wealth (3.64 or 4.69/20.68). A similar estimate is obtained when the mortality-adjusted expected flow of bequests during 1998 is converted to a stock of transfer wealth.[7]

The average yearly flow of *inter vivos* transfers SCF respondents report receiving between 1993 and 1998 is $44 billion (in 1995 dollars). If $r - n - \delta = 0$, converting this flow to a stock of wealth yields transfer wealth of $1.29 trillion (if $r - n - \delta = -.01$, then the estimate falls to $.86 trillion; if $r - n - \delta = .01$, then the estimate rises to $1.98 trillion), suggesting that inter vivos transfers account for 4–6 percent of wealth in 1995. Similar estimates are obtained if we instead use inter vivos gifts reported by donors, rather than gifts reported by recipients, to calculate transfer wealth.[8]

---

7. The estimated flow of bequests during 1998 was $120 billion. If $r - n - \delta = 0$, the amount of wealth in 1998 that is attributable to inheritances is $120 · (maximum age – inheritance-weighted age of recipient). See the appendix for this result. The weighted-average age of inheritance recipients over 1993–1998 was fifty-three years based on calculations using the 1998 SCF. If the maximum age is 100, then transfer wealth from inheritances is $5.64 trillion in 1998, or 20 percent of total 1998 net worth.

8. Given the yearly flow of inter vivos support respondents report giving is greater than what they report receiving, one would expect transfer wealth calculated from the flow donor reports to be higher. However, donors report a smaller share of transfers to children and a higher share of transfers to parents than do recipients, which works to offset the higher level of transfers donors report.

The flow-to-stock conversion methodology yields an estimate of transfer wealth in 1995 of $4.50–5.98 billion (assuming $r - n - \delta$ is between $-.01$ and 0). This is 22–29 percent of 1995 net worth. Recall that when we estimated the transfer wealth in table 4.2 by grossing up past transfers by corporate bond returns, we estimated a transfer wealth of 19 percent. Thus, similar estimates are obtained from the two approaches.

So far, in both sets of calculations, we have ignored college support provided by parents. Kotlikoff and Summers (1981) estimate that financial support during college was $10.3 billion in 1974 (total net worth was $3.884 trillion in 1974). Assuming $r - n - \delta = 0$, and using an age gap of thirty years between donors and recipients, this flow of support translates into a stock of transfer wealth that constitutes 8 percent of current net worth.

Gale and Scholz (1994) report, using the 1983 SCF that 13 percent of households report giving college support over 1983–85, with total support over the period totaling $97.4 billion. Using the 1986 SCF, Gale and Scholz (1994) estimate the annual flow of college payments/support from parents at $35.3 billion (1986 net worth was $11.976 billion). Assuming $r - n - \delta = 0$ and using an age gap of thirty years, this flow of support translates into a stock of transfer wealth that constitutes 9 percent of current net worth.

Rather than produce a new estimate of college payments, we argue that the 9 percent figure found by Gale and Scholz (1994) is still approximately correct. In 1986, the flow of college support was converted to a stock of transfer wealth that represented 9 percent of net worth. Net worth has grown from $12.0 trillion to $28.8 trillion from 1986 to 1998 (7.6 percent per year). The College Board reports that tuition and fees have increased at an annual rate of 6.7 percent at four-year private schools, 7.2 percent at four-year public schools, and 7.8 percent at two-year public schools from 1986 to 1998. Because college expenses have grown at nearly the same rate as net worth, it seems reasonable to assume that the present-day value of college aid represents 9 percent of net worth in 1998, just as it did back in 1986.

Thus, assuming that the present-day value of past college aid is on the order of 9 percent of total net worth (just like in 1974 and 1986), then our final estimate of transfer wealth's share would increase from 22–29 percent (which we estimated in table 4.6) to 31–38 percent. Our estimate in table 4.2 would increase from 19 percent to 28 percent, if college payments are included as transfer wealth.

We have so far estimated the stock of transfer wealth two ways. First, we estimated it directly from reported transfer receipts, grossed up to 1998 using the corporate bond rate. Second, we calculated the expected yearly flow of bequests, given wealth adjusted mortality rates for the population, and converted this flow to a stock. Both estimates are fairly close and suggest that transfer wealth accounts for approximately one-fifth to one-fourth of U.S. wealth, and perhaps just over one-third if college support is included.

4.6   Heterogeneity in Transfers Received and Expected

While our estimates suggest that life-cycle saving can explain approximately 80 percent of current net worth, past transfers account for a large fraction of wealth for a nontrivial segment of the population. Table 4.7 shows the unconditional ratio of transfer wealth to total wealth by age and net worth groups, as well as the probability of having received a transfer. In aggregate, transfer wealth accounts for only about one-fifth of total net worth. However, only 22 percent of households report having received a substantial transfer, indicating a high degree of concentration. Both the share of wealth from transfers and the probability of having received a transfer increase with age.

Table 4.8 reports the ratio of transfer wealth to total wealth conditional on having received a transfer. Among households that report having received a transfer, their net worth would be reduced by 50 percent if the present-day value of past transfers were eliminated (among households aged sixty-five and above this fraction rises to 70 percent). For the low to middle net worth households that have received a transfer, that transfer accounts for a large fraction of their current net worth. Among households aged forty to sixty-four, conditional on having received a transfer, 85 percent of wealth accumulated by households in the $75–250K net worth group is due to transfers received. For the low net worth group ($0–75K) aged forty to sixty-four, transfer wealth balloons to over three times larger

Table 4.7   **Ratio of Transfer Wealth to Total Wealth, by Wealth and Age Groups (1998)**

| | Age | | | |
Net Worth	<40	40–64	65+	Total
$0–75	.26	.50	.58	.42
	(.12)	(.14)	(.21)	(.14)
$75–250	.10	.17	.33	.21
	(.16)	(.19)	(.33)	(.23)
$250–500	.09	.18	.19	.17
	(.21)	(.32)	(.36)	(.32)
$500–1000	.14	.13	.40	.22
	(.21)	(.31)	(.45)	(.35)
$1000+	.13	.10	.30	.16
	(.31)	(.41)	(.55)	(.44)
Total	.13	.13	.31	.19
	(.14)	(.22)	(.33)	(.22)

Notes: Transfer wealth was calculated by grossing up past transfers by the corporate bond return. Total net worth is estimated at $28.794 trillion and transfer wealth is estimated at $5.405 trillion. Numbers in parentheses are the fraction of households in group that reported having received a transfer.

Table 4.8   Ratio of Transfer Wealth to Total Wealth for Households Having
                   Received a Transfer, by Wealth and Age Groups (1998)

	Age			
Net Worth	<40	40–64	65+	Total
$0–75	1.44	3.15	2.12	2.26
$75–250	.64	.85	.98	.88
$250–500	.38	.55	.53	.52
$500–1000	.63	.40	.89	.63
$1000+	.47	.25	.60	.37
Total	.60	.37	.70	.50

Source: Authors' calculations.

Notes: Transfer wealth was calculated by grossing up past transfers by the corporate bond return. Total net worth of households that report receiving a past transfer is $10.736 trillion and transfer wealth is estimated at $5.405 trillion (transfer wealth is $.020 billion for households that have negative net worth).

than current net worth, indicating substantial spending out of transfers received. Even for the high net worth group (net worth in excess of $1 million) aged forty to sixty-four, transfers account for one-quarter of their wealth.

The SCF also asks respondents whether they expect to receive a substantial inheritance or transfer in the future and the amount they expect to receive.[9] Tables 4.9 and 4.10 replicate the analysis in tables 4.7 and 4.8, only now we examine the ratio of expected transfers to current net worth. In aggregate, expected future transfers account for only one-tenth of current net worth. However, only 13 percent of households report that they expect a substantial transfer.[10] As expected, both the size of the expected transfer and the probability of expecting a transfer decrease dramatically with age across all net worth groups. Households below the age of forty with a net worth less than $75,000 expect in aggregate to receive future transfers in excess of their current wealth.

Table 4.10 reports the ratio of expected future transfers to total current wealth conditional on expecting a transfer. Among households that report expecting to receive a substantial transfer, their net worth would increase by just over 50 percent if their expectations come to fruition. For the low to middle net worth households that have received a transfer, that transfer accounts for a large fraction of their current net worth. Among households with net worth less than $250K, and conditional on expecting to receive a future transfer, the future transfer is expected to be more than the house-

9. It is not clear whether respondents report the transfer they expect to receive in nominal dollars or 1998 dollars (it is likely, though, that the amount is given in nominal dollars).
10. Using the 1983 SCF, Hurd and Mundaca (1989) also estimate that 13 percent of households expect to receive a large gift/inheritance.

Table 4.9   Ratio of Expected Transfer to Total Wealth, by Wealth and Age Groups (1998)

Net Worth	Age			Total
	<40	40–64	65+	
<$75	1.10	.33	.07	.57
	(.16)	(.09)	(.02)	(.11)
$75–250	.38	.17	.03	.17
	(.21)	(.15)	(.03)	(.13)
$250–500	.42	.15	.01	.14
	(.25)	(.22)	(.05)	(.17)
$500–1000	.24	.10	.00	.08
	(.54)	(.24)	(.02)	(.19)
$1000+	.15	.04	.01	.04
	(.30)	(.25)	(.06)	(.20)
Total	.39	.09	.01	.10
	(.18)	(.15)	(.03)	(.13)

Source: Authors' calculations.

Notes: In the 1998 SCF, households report they expect to receive $2.939 trillion in future transfers. Total net worth is estimated at $28.794 trillion. Numbers in parentheses are the fraction of households in group that expect to receive a transfer.

Table 4.10   Ratio of Expected Transfer to Total Wealth for Households Expecting to Receive a Transfer, by Wealth and Age Groups (1998)

Net Worth	Age			Total
	<40	40–64	65+	
<$75	6.37	2.70	2.29	4.61
$75–250	1.90	1.09	1.11	1.35
$250–500	1.56	.66	.15	.78
$500–1000	.44	.41	.24	.41
$1000+	.37	.18	.15	.20
Total	1.25	.40	.26	.54

Source: Authors' calculations.

Notes: In the 1998 SCF, households reported they expect to receive $2.939 trillion in future transfers ($.172 trillion expected by households with negative net worth). Total net worth of households that report receiving a past transfer is $5.074 trillion.

hold's current wealth (the ratio of expected transfer to current net worth is greater than one). Among relatively affluent (net worth $.25 million to $.5 million) and young households (aged less than forty years), one-quarter of these households expect to receive a substantial future transfer, and the future transfer is expected to be over 1.5 times their current wealth.

Tables 4.7, 4.8, 4.9, and 4.10 raise several interesting questions. Do households that have received a substantial transfer reduce their savings and hence their life-cycle wealth in response to the transfer, that is, is there substitution between transfer wealth and life-cycle wealth? Similarly, do households who expect to receive a transfer in the future save less today? These questions are left for future research.

4.7   Conclusions

There has been a long debate about the importance of life-cycle saving in wealth accumulation. This paper provides new evidence on how important transfers are in wealth accumulation. Using direct survey evidence on transfers received, we calculate that transfer wealth accounts for only about one-fifth of current household net worth. We reach a similar conclusion by estimating the flow of transfers in 1998, accounting for the correlation between wealth and mortality rates, and converting that to a stock of transfer wealth.

While transfers may not account for most of wealth accumulation, they are important for a nontrivial segment of the population. For the one-fifth of households that report having received transfers, the present-day value of those transfers represents half of their current wealth.

Future work will focus on whether past and/or expected future receipts of transfers effect life-cycle savings behavior. For example, do recipients of large transfers reduce the amount of life-cycle savings going forward? Do individuals who expect future transfers engage in less active saving? Another puzzle we leave for future work is reconciling the small role of transfers in explaining wealth accumulation with the fact that consumption tracks income fairly closely. Perhaps growth in unrealized capital gains, which would typically be excluded from measures of income but would increase wealth, can help explain part of this puzzle.

Appendix

Let T be the stock of transfer wealth. Thus T is the present-day value of all transfers received by people currently alive less the present-day value of all transfers given by people still alive. T can be broken down into transfer wealth from bequests and transfer wealth from inter vivos transfers.

Let's focus on bequests/inheritances first. Suppose a forty-year-old receives a $10,000 inheritance in 1995. If we assume that the amount of the inheritance received by the average forty-year-old grows at rate (n), that past inheritances earn interest at rate (r), that the one-year mortality rate is (δ), and that the maximum age a person could live to is (D), then the amount of wealth in the economy attributable to inheritances received when one is forty years old is the integral of (1):

(1)   10,000 · (current population of forty-year-olds) · exponential

[$(x - 40) \cdot (r - n - \delta)$], where the integral is evaluated over x

ranging from forty years to D years.

One can then replicate this calculation for thirty-nine-year-olds, forty-one-year-olds, etc. Thus, more generally, the amount of wealth attributable to inheritances received when one is Y-years-old is the integral of (2):

(2)   (average transfer received by a Y-year-old person)

· (current population of Y-year-olds) · exponential[$(x - Y)$

· $(r - n - \delta)$], where the integral is evaluated over x ranging

from Y years to D years.

To estimate total transfer wealth, we evaluate this integral for each household in the 1998 SCF, using the population weights provided. The sum of all the integrals represents wealth accumulation due to inheritances received. We set the maximum age (D) equal to 100. We first estimate transfer wealth assuming $r - n - \delta = 0$. We also redo the analysis assuming it is $-.01$ and then assuming it is .01.

To calculate wealth accumulated from inter vivos transfers, we want to calculate the present-day value of all inter vivos transfers received by people currently alive less the present-day value of all inter vivos transfers given by people still alive. We calculate the present-day value of all inter vivos transfers received by taking the integral of (2) for each household in the sample. We calculate the present-day value of all inter vivos transfers given by people still alive by taking the integral of (3) for each household in the sample:

(3)   (average transfer given by a Y-year-old person)

· (current population of Y-year-olds) · exponential [$(x - Y)$

· $(r - n - \delta)$], where the integral is evaluated over x ranging

from Y years to D years.

By aggregating the value of [(2) – (3)] across the sample, we get an estimate of wealth accumulation due to inter vivos transfers. Note that for inheritances/bequests, the donor is no longer alive by definition, so integral (3) would be zero.

Inter vivos gifts can be estimated by either using reports from recipients or reports from donors. The SCF asks respondents to report *inter vivos* transfers received and who the donor was. Assuming parents are thirty years older than children, we can estimate the age of the donor. As a robustness check, we also estimate transfer wealth using reports from donors.

Finally, if $(r - n - \delta) = 0$, then integral (1) simplifies to:

transfer $\cdot$ $(D - $ age of recipient).

If $(r - n - \delta) = 0$, then integral (2) $-$ integral (3) simplifies to:

transfer $\cdot$ (age of donor $-$ age of recipient).

Thus, transfer wealth is just the product of aggregate transfers times the some transfer-weighted age gap.

References

Ando, A., and F. Modigliani. 1963. The "life cycle" hypothesis of saving: Aggregate implications and tests. *American Economic Review* 53:55–84.

Attanasio, O., and H. Hoynes. 1995. Differential mortality and wealth accumulation. NBER Working Paper no. 5126. Cambridge, Mass.: National Bureau of Economic Research, May.

———. 2000. Differential mortality and wealth accumulation. *Journal of Human Resources* 35:1–29.

Barlow, R., H. Brazer, and J. Morgan. 1966. *Economic behavior of the affluent.* Washington, D.C.: Brookings Institution.

Brown, J. R., O. S. Mitchell, J. M. Poterba, and M. J. Warshawsky. 2001. *The role of annuity markets in financing retirement.* Cambridge: MIT Press.

Cox, D., and F. Raines. 1985. Inter-family transfers and income redistribution. In *Horizontal equity, uncertainty, and measures of well-being,* eds. M. David and T. Smeeding, 393–421. Chicago: University of Chicago Press.

Gale, W., and J. Scholz. 1994. Intergenerational transfers and the accumulation of wealth. *Journal of Economic Perspectives* 8:145–60.

Gale, W., and J., Slemrod. 2001. Rethinking the estate and gift tax: Overview. In *Rethinking estate and gift taxation,* ed. W. Gale and J. Slemrod, 1–65. Washington, D.C.: Brookings Institution.

Hurd, M., and B. Mundaca. 1989. The importance of gifts and inheritances among the affluent. In *The measurement of saving, investment, and wealth,* ed. R. Lipsey and H. Tice, 737–58. Chicago: University of Chicago Press.

Juster, F. T., J. Lupton, J. P. Smith, and F. Stafford. 1999. The decline in household saving and the wealth effect. University of Michigan. Working Paper.

Kennickell, A., M. Starr-McCluer, and B. Surette. 2000. Recent changes in U.S. family finances: Results from the 1998 Survey of Consumer Finances. *Federal Reserve Bulletin* 86 (January): 1–29.

Kessler, D., and A. Masson. 1989. Bequest and wealth accumulation: Are some pieces of the puzzle missing? *Journal of Economic Perspectives* 3:141–52.

Kotlikoff, L. 1988. Intergenerational transfers and savings. *Journal of Economic Perspectives* 2:41–58.

Kotlikoff, L., and L. Summers. 1981. The role of intergenerational transfers in aggregate capital accumulation. *Journal of Political Economy* 89:706–32.

Laitner, J. 1990. Random earnings differences, lifetime liquidity constraints, and altruistic intergenerational transfers. University of Michigan. Mimeograph.

Lord, W., and P. Rangazas. 1991. Savings and wealth in models with altruistic bequests. *American Economic Review* 81:289–96.

Masson, A. 1986. A cohort analysis of age-wealth profiles generated by a simulation model in France (1949–1975). *Economic Journal* 96:173–90.

Modigliani, F. 1988. The role of intergenerational transfers and life cycle saving in the accumulation of wealth. *Journal of Economic Perspectives* 2:15–40.

Modigliani, F., and R. Brumberg. 1954. Utility analysis and the consumption function: An interpretation of cross-section data. In *Post-Keynesian economics,* ed. K. Kurihara, 388–436. New Brunswick, N.J.: Rutgers University Press.

Morgan. J., M. David, W. Cohen, and H. Brazer. 1962. *Income and welfare in the United States.* New York: McGraw-Hill.

Poterba, J. 2000. The estate tax and after-tax investment returns. In *Does Atlas shrug? The economic consequences of taxing the rich,* ed. J. Slemrod, 333–53. Cambridge: Harvard University Press.

Poterba, J., and S. Weisbenner. 2001. The distributional burden of taxing estates and unrealized capital gains at the time of death. In *Rethinking estate and gift taxation,* ed. W. Gale and J. Slemrod, 422–49. Washington, D.C.: Brookings Institution.

Projector, D., and G. Weiss. 1964. *Survey of financial characteristics of consumers.* Washington, D.C.: GPO.

Comment   Alan J. Auerbach

This paper takes up, once again, the important and controversial question of the role of bequests in capital formation. There can be few more timely topics, given the current U.S. flirtation with estate tax repeal.

Since the influential paper by Kotlikoff and Summers (1981) argued that the majority of U.S. assets were attributable to bequests, researchers have used alternative approaches and different data sets to reassess these findings. Brown and Weisbenner are the latest to venture into this debate. Their paper repeats some earlier calculations that allow one to assess the impact of data differences and then moves on to provide estimates based on a new approach to assessing the way in which bequests, both past and anticipated, affect private saving. The paper is carefully written and easy to follow, even for a tyro in this murky area. In my comments, I will first offer an overview of the paper and then move on to some selective comments on methodology and results.

The paper consists of two main parts. In the first, the authors adopt two alternative approaches from the literature to estimate the magnitude of what they label *transfer wealth,* which we should think of as the wealth that exists because individuals received bequests at some point in the past. The second part of the paper disaggregates the population by age and wealth

Alan J. Auerbach is Robert D. Bursh Professor of Economics and Law at the University of California, Berkeley, and a research associate of the National Bureau of Economic Research.
This is a substantially shortened version of my discussion of the original version of the paper, much of which was devoted to material that has been omitted from the published version.

and considers the importance of transfer wealth for each cell. As indicated, the first part of the paper provides updated estimates of the share of transfer wealth in total wealth. The key finding here is that transfer wealth accounts for perhaps 20–25 percent of total wealth. This is consistent with some earlier findings, although it is well below the estimates originally provided by Kotlikoff and Summers (1981).

But, as the past literature has made clear, it is necessary to be careful in specifying what one means by *transfer wealth*. Put another way, the paper provides two alternative calculations of transfer wealth, but it is useful to go back one step and identify the question to which each of these calculations is the answer. The first approach looks at the population currently alive and, using information on past transfers received, asks how much wealth would have accumulated to the current date as a result if these transfers, and all of the accumulated interest on them, had been saved. The second approach makes the same assumption about all inheritances being saved but reduces the need for data on past transfers. It does so by invoking a smooth-growth assumption that allows one to translate information on transfers received by a cohort today into transfers received by cohorts of the same age in prior years. The two methods, then, aim at answering the same question but use different mixes of data and assumptions to do so. It is heartening that the results are similar, so one can have some confidence in the answer. But why are we asking this question?

I see two problems with equating these estimates and transfer wealth. First, it is not clear that reported transfers, the basic input to both calculations, include all transfers. There are many transfers that parents provide to children that the latter might not think of as outright transfers, even if they have the same economic effect. Thus, transfer wealth might be understated by the calculations based on reported transfers. On the other hand, why should one assume that all transfers received are fully saved? This wouldn't be optimal behavior except under restrictive assumptions and, more to the point, it is also quite inconsistent with the empirical results reported later in the paper that life-cycle wealth is fully crowded out by past transfers. If we really believe these estimates, then why shouldn't our estimates of transfer wealth be zero, if *transfer wealth* is defined as the increment to wealth because of past transfers.

Let me turn next to the disaggregate estimates of transfer wealth provided in tables 4.7 through 4.10. These results are certainly interesting, as they show that transfer wealth is a larger share of wealth for lower-wealth households. But, as with the previous calculations, it is hard to draw further conclusions without a better understanding of the behavior associated with these cross-section relationships. The implication here is that transfer wealth acts to mitigate differences in the wealth distribution. But consider the following hypothetical situation. Suppose that all individuals were identical with respect to their own earnings and transfers received but that they differed in their propensity to consume inherited wealth. Then, all would have the same transfer wealth based on the methodology used here, but those with a high propensity to consume transfers would be observed to have lower overall wealth. The result would be the pattern observed in table 4.7, with lower-wealth individuals having a larger share of their wealth accounted for by transfer wealth. But transfer wealth would be playing no role in reducing the dispersion of total wealth.

Where that leaves us, I am afraid, is the subject for future research, but we should be grateful to Brown and Weisbenner for doing this careful groundwork.

Reference

Kotlikoff, L., and L. Summers. 1981. The role of intergenerational transfers in aggregate capital accumulation. *Journal of Political Economy* 89:706–32.

5

Wealth Portfolios in the United Kingdom and the United States

James Banks, Richard Blundell, and James P. Smith

Introduction

In this paper, we document and attempt to explain differences between the U.S. and U.K. household wealth distributions, with an emphasis on the quite different portfolios held in stock and housing equities in the two countries. As a proportion of their total wealth, British households hold relatively small amounts of financial assets—including equities in stock—compared to American households. In contrast, British households appear to move into home ownership at relatively young ages, and a large fraction of their household wealth is concentrated in housing. Finally, the age gradient in home equity appears to be much steeper in the United Kingdom whereas U.S. households exhibit a steeper age gradient in stock equity.

Moreover, these portfolio differences between the two countries are not

James Banks is reader in economics at University College London and deputy research director of the Institute for Fiscal Studies where he also directs the Centre for Economic Research on Ageing. Richard Blundell is Leverhulme Research Professor of Economics at University College London, and director of the ESRC Centre for the Microeconomic Analysis of Fiscal Policy and director of research at the Institute for Fiscal Studies. James P. Smith is a senior economist at RAND.

Banks acknowledges the financial support of the Leverhulme Trust through the research program The Changing Distribution of Consumption, Economic Resources and the Welfare of Households. Blundell would like to thank the ESRC Centre for the Microeconomic Analysis of Fiscal Policy. Smith's research was supported by a grant from the National Institute on Aging. This paper benefited from the expert programming assistance of David Rumpel and Patty St. Clair. Many thanks are due to François Ortalo-Magne and John Shoven for useful discussions and comments. We are also grateful to participants at the National Bureau of Economic Research (NBER) Economics of Aging conference (June 2001) and the British Household Panel Survey (BHPS) Annual Conference (July 2001) for comments. The usual disclaimer applies.

temporally static, as important changes have been taking place in both countries in their housing and equity markets. Especially in Britain, there have been some fundamental changes in national policies that have been aimed at encouraging wider rates of home ownership and greater participation in the equity market.

As well as large volatility in real rates of return in housing and corporate equity markets, the last few decades have also witnessed periods of unusually large capital gains in both the housing and stock market. Besides the large background risk in their incomes, young householders in Britain and the United States face considerable housing price and stock price risks when deciding on their desired portfolio balances. While price risk in the equity market appears to be historically similar in the two countries, housing price risk may be much higher in the United Kingdom in recent decades.

In addition, institutional differences between the countries imply much younger new home buyers in the United Kingdom than in the United States. In this paper, we argue that the higher housing price volatility in the United Kingdom combined with much younger entry into home ownership is an important factor accounting for the relatively small participation of young British householders in the stock market. We show it is important to acknowledge the dual role of housing—providing both wealth and consumption services—in understanding wealth accumulation differences between the United States and the United Kingdom. Institutional differences, particularly in housing markets, that affect the demand and supply of housing services turn out to be important in generating portfolio differences between the two countries. In particular, these differences in housing price risk imply steeper life-cycle accumulations in housing and less steep accumulations in stock equity over the life cycle in the United Kingdom.

This paper is divided into six sections. The first describes the data sources used, whereas section 5.2 presents some basic facts about the distribution of total wealth as well as the housing and financial asset components that make up that total. The third section highlights some salient differences between British and American housing and equity markets. The next section summarizes some theoretical reasons why young British people may desire not to hold much of their household wealth in the form of corporate equity. Section 5.5 tests some implications of this theoretical perspective using comparative international data on the characteristics of young homeowners. The final section summarizes our conclusions.

5.1 Data Sources

To make wealth comparisons, for the United States we primarily use the Panel Study of Income Dynamics (PSID), which has gathered almost thirty years of extensive economic and demographic data on a nationally representative sample of approximately 5,000 (original) families and 35,000 individuals who live in those families. Unlike many other prominent American wealth surveys, the PSID is representative of the complete age distribution. Wealth modules were included in the 1984, 1989, 1994, and 1999 waves of the PSID and all four waves are examined here. In addition, questions on housing ownership, value, and mortgage were asked in each calendar year wave of the PSID.

For the United Kingdom, we use the British Household Panel Survey (BHPS). The BHPS has been running annually since 1991 and, like the PSID, is also representative of the complete age distribution. The wave 1 sample consisted of some 5,500 households and 10,300 individuals, and continuing representativeness of the survey is maintained by following panel members wherever they move in the United Kingdom and also by including in the panel the new members of households formed by original panel members.

The BHPS contains annual information on individual and household income and employment as well as a complete set of demographic variables. Data are collected annually on primary housing wealth and occasionally on secondary housing wealth and vehicle wealth. In 1995 the BHPS included an individual wealth module which forms the basis of the wealth information used here. Since some components of wealth are collected at the household level, we construct a household wealth definition from wave 5 to use in what follows. Hence we draw a subsample of BHPS households for whom the head and the spouse (where relevant) remain present and who successfully complete the 1995 wealth module. This results in a total of 4,688 households observed in the panel for between one and eight waves.

Appendix table 5A.1 contains a side-by-side account of the elements that comprise household wealth in the two surveys. Besides housing equity, PSID nonhousing assets are divided into seven categories: other real estate (which includes any second home); vehicles; farm or business ownership; stocks, mutual funds, investment trusts, and stocks held in individual retirement accounts (IRAs); checking and savings accounts, certificates of deposit (CDs), treasury bills, savings bonds, and liquid assets in IRAs; bonds, trusts, life insurance, and other assets; and other debts. The PSID wealth modules include transaction questions about purchases and sales so that active and passive (capital gain) saving can be distinguished.

While the BHPS detail on assets is similar to the PSID, there are some differences. Most important, no questions were asked about business equity in the BHPS. To make wealth concepts as comparable as possible, business equity was excluded from total wealth in the PSID.[1] Neither survey

---

1. To the extent that omitted components vary across countries, and particularly for groups converting business wealth to personal wealth, these may be important issues that deserve further investigation. Given that the majority of our analysis will be most pertinent to young households, however, pension wealth will be important only in the context of long-term

oversamples high income or wealth households, which—given the extreme skew in the wealth distribution—implies that both surveys understate the concentration of wealth among the extremely wealthy. While this lack of a high wealth oversample is typically a limitation in describing wealth distributions, it has the advantage here of greater comparability between the data sets. Another limitation common to both countries is that neither provides any measure of private pension or government pension wealth.

There are also differences in the way financial asset wealth was collected. Both surveys collect wealth information in four broad classes, but the classes are somewhat different in each country. The PSID uses checking accounts, stocks, other saving (predominantly bonds), and debts, whereas the BHPS uses bank accounts, savings accounts, investments, and debts. For each of the BHPS classes, there are also a series of dummy variables recording whether each individual has funds in a particular component of each category. In addition, for investments a variable records which of the various subcomponents is the largest.

The following procedure makes the wealth categories as comparable as possible when disaggregated data are necessary. Bank and savings accounts are aggregated in the BHPS. The investments category is subdivided as follows: For individuals who report no ownership of either national savings bonds, national savings certificates, or premium bonds, we code their entire investment wealth as shares (27 percent who report owning investment wealth). For those who report no share ownership, mutual funds, personal equity plans or "other" investments, we code the investment wealth as bonds (44 percent of those with investment wealth). For those reporting both "types" of investment wealth (28 percent, we allocate wealth entirely to either shares or bonds, according to asset type of the largest asset.

Finally, an issue of comparability arises over the unit of assessment to which the wealth module applies. More specifically, it is not possible to get a single estimate of household wealth in any subcategory of financial wealth from the BHPS. This is because every individual was asked to complete the wealth questionnaire and having reported a total amount for, say, investments was simply asked "Are any of your investments jointly held with someone else?" This framework creates obvious problems in generating a measure of household wealth. We address this issue by using a bounding approach. For each of the financial wealth categories in the BHPS, two measures are reported. First, we compute an upper bound under the assumption that any jointly held asset classes are actually held solely by the individual (the limit of the case where the individual owns "most" of the asset). Second, we compute a lower bound under the assumption that an individual only owns $1/N$th of the asset class in which joint ownership is re-

---

saving. As such, it will be relatively small in present discounted value terms, relatively safe, and important for us, inaccessible for short- or medium-run smoothing purposes. Hence in what follows we do not control for what pension differences there are across countries.

ported, where N is the number of adults in the household. To compute the upper bound of net financial wealth, we add the upper bounds for the asset components and subtract the lower bound of the debt component and vice versa for the lower bound. In this paper, both lower- and upper-bound estimates are presented. Fortunately, our conclusions appear not be sensitive to how this problem is resolved, and the availability of individual-level wealth holdings will be an advantage for certain later aspects of our analysis.

5.2   Comparing the Wealth Distribution in the United States and Britain

We describe here the main characteristics of wealth distributions in the United Kingdom and United States, highlighting similarities and differences. We use two concepts of household wealth—total household wealth (excluding business equity) and total financial assets. Since the BHPS wealth module was only fielded in 1995, we confine our cross-section comparisons to the 1994 wave of the PSID. To deal with currency differences, the U.K. data (collected in September 1995) are converted into U.S. dollars using the then exchange rate of 1.5525, and all financial statistics for both countries are presented in 1995 U.S. dollars.[2]

Table 5.1 lists mean values of wealth and its components for both countries. Total household wealth is about one-third higher in the United States, but within-asset category differences are far larger. Total nonfinancial assets held by households are reasonably similar in the United Kingdom and United States. Within that subaggregate, British households actually have greater absolute and relative amounts of wealth in home equity than American households do. Converted to a common currency, mean housing equity is almost $10,000 more than their American counterparts. Similarly, British households hold 62 percent of their total household wealth as home equity: The comparable percent for American households is only 34 percent.

The other striking difference between the United Kingdom and United States lies instead in financial wealth where mean values in America are more than twice those in Britain. These differences exist in all components of financial wealth, but they are particularly large in stock market equity. On average, in the mid-1990s American households owned about $20,000 more in corporate equity than their British counterparts.

Given the extreme skew in wealth distributions, means can be poor summary statistics for wealth. In a previous paper (Banks, Blundell, and Smith 2000), we have shown that total net wealth and financial wealth distributions in both countries were extremely unequally distributed. Turning to

2. Given that this is close to the Organization for Economic Cooperation and Development (OECD) purchasing power parity (PPP) conversion rates for this time (1.55 in 1994 and 1.53 in 1995) our comparisons are unaffected by the use of exchange rate as opposed to PPP conversion factors.

Table 5.1   Household Wealth and Components in the United States and the United Kingdom (1995 US$, thousands)

Wealth Category	1994 PSID	1995 BHPS	
		Lower	Upper
Net Home Equity	44.8	54.3	54.3
Other Real Estate	24.2	9.5	9.5
Net Vehicle Wealth	10.9	3.8	3.8
Net Tangible Assets	79.9	67.7	67.7
Stocks and Mutual Funds	28.8	7.7	10.3
Liquid Assets	19.5	10.0	12.8
Other Financial Assets	9.5	4.7	5.2
Other Debts	6.1	1.6	2.0
Net Financial Assets	51.7	19.4	26.7
Total Wealth	131.6	87.2	94.4

differences between countries, large differences did not emerge for the typical household. Median total net worth was slightly higher among British households, whereas median financial assets were somewhat greater among American households. Rather, the critical differences lie in the upper tails of the wealth distribution, especially in financial assets. No matter which assumption about joint or separate ownership of assets is made in the BHPS, the top fifth of American households have considerably more financial wealth than the top fifth of British households. The between country discrepancy in financial wealth expands rapidly as we move up the respective financial wealth distributions.

These wealth differences are not due to age and income differences between the countries. Banks, Blundell, and Smith (2000) demonstrate that, within age groups, net financial wealth in both countries increases with household income albeit in a highly nonlinear way and that at almost all points in the age–income distribution, U.S. households are holding more financial wealth than their U.K. counterparts. The same breakdown for net total wealth shows that for almost all of the younger age–income groups, U.K. households have at least as much wealth, if not slightly more, than their U.S. counterparts.

5.3 A Comparison of Four Markets—Housing and Stock Markets in the United States and the United Kingdom

To set a background for this paper, we first describe the most salient trends in housing and equity markets in these two countries during the last few decades. Our description includes trends and differences in rates of ownership, rates of return, and amounts of wealth held in these forms.

Table 5.2 **Proportion of Households Who are Homeowners in Year *t*, by Age of the Head**

Age Range	1969	1974	1979	1984	1989	1994	1997	1999
United Kingdom								
20–29	0.418	0.456	0.508	0.537	0.518	0.489		0.424
30–39	0.529	0.596	0.648	0.692	0.729	0.688		0.669
40–49	0.476	0.568	0.615	0.718	0.772	0.787		0.755
50–59	0.476	0.489	0.517	0.631	0.711	0.770		0.779
60–69	0.446	0.443	0.490	0.527	0.624	0.702		0.722
70+	0.411	0.419	0.425	0.486	0.553	0.585		0.615
Total	0.465	0.498	0.537	0.603	0.655	0.676		0.673
United States								
20–29	0.326	0.310	0.288	0.246	0.233	0.272	0.277	
30–39	0.604	0.661	0.665	0.590	0.530	0.528	0.530	
40–49	0.737	0.751	0.760	0.738	0.766	0.704	0.695	
50–59	0.700	0.770	0.778	0.806	0.799	0.811	0.810	
60–69	0.785	0.736	0.756	0.776	0.796	0.830	0.870	
70+	0.639	0.751	0.760	0.681	0.699	0.717	0.770	
Total	0.639	0.631	0.624	0.601	0.609	0.626	0.651	

5.3.1   Rates of Asset Ownership: Housing

Table 5.2 lists the proportion of households who are homeowners, by the age of head of household, for selected years in both countries. While aggregate rates of home ownership are now not that dissimilar (around two-thirds in both countries in the most recent year listed), there are striking differences by age.[3] Home ownership rates amongst young households are far higher in the United Kingdom than in the United States, with differences as big as 20 percentage points for householders between the ages of twenty and twenty-nine. While not as large, the fraction of households aged thirty–thirty-nine is currently double digit larger in the United Kingdom. The offset to the greater rates of home ownership among young British householders is the much lower historical rates among older households in the United Kingdom. For example, among those over age sixty, the prevalence of owning a home in 1984 was more than 20 percentage points larger in the United States than in the United Kingdom.

Table 5.2 also suggests that there are stronger cyclic and trend effects on home ownership rates in the United Kingdom compared to the United States. Although the levels are always above their U.S. counterparts, there was a sharp upswing in home ownership among the youngest British household heads (those between the ages of twenty and twenty-nine),

3. Figures for the United Kingdom are computed from the FES microdata to enable the comparison with 1985. However, calculations confirm that home ownership rates in the 1995 BHPS data match those in the 1995 FES to well within 1 percentage point for all age groups and for the population as a whole.

which reached its peak between 1984 and 1988, during the height of a housing boom. Since that year, the trend reversed, and the proportion of homeowners amongst the youngest group in the United Kingdom fell. With lower amplitude, a similar pattern exists among those aged thirty–thirty-nine. We return below to the question of why cyclic variation in home ownership may be larger in the United Kingdom.

There are impressive cohort effects in U.K. home ownership with secular changes concentrated among older households. For example, among British households aged fifty–fifty-nine, home ownership rates increased by almost 30 percentage points after 1974. While not confined to that time period, the size of the increase in home ownership is largest in the five-year interval between 1979 and 1984.

Table 5.3 presents the same data separately for U.K. households based on whether the head had some postcompulsory education. This dramatic secular increase in home ownership in Britain is concentrated among those with less education. Once again examining those aged fifty–fifty-nine, there was a 32 percentage point increase in home ownership among those with no post-compulsory schooling compared to a 12 percentage point increase among those households whose head had moved beyond compulsory schooling levels.

The structure of these differences in home ownership between the United Kingdom and United States raise several questions. One question is what accounted for the magnitude and structure of the dramatic secular shift in the United Kingdom. Given its timing, one contributing factor is the "right-to-buy" scheme for public housing tenants that was introduced

Table 5.3	U.K. Home Ownership Rates by Age, Year, and Schooling Level of Head				
Age Range	1979	1984	1989	1994	1999
	No Post Compulsory Education				
20–29	0.384	0.450	0.468	0.421	0.341
30–39	0.526	0.567	0.590	0.598	0.596
40–49	0.515	0.645	0.681	0.680	0.679
50–59	0.413	0.540	0.648	0.699	0.739
60–69	0.410	0.447	0.549	0.634	0.680
70+	0.376	0.425	0.454	0.471	0.583
Total	0.436	0.508	0.559	0.579	0.622
	With Post Compulsory Education				
20–29	0.617	0.677	0.623	0.594	0.525
30–39	0.814	0.803	0.844	0.795	0.767
40–49	0.792	0.842	0.874	0.861	0.868
50–59	0.766	0.802	0.826	0.865	0.887
60–69	0.729	0.736	0.788	0.828	0.916
70+	0.660	0.689	0.793	0.802	0.816
Total	0.735	0.771	0.807	0.803	0.785

in 1980. Under this scheme those households who had been renting in government owned housing for a certain minimum duration were given an automatic right to buy their home from the local authorities. The house was valued at current market value but discounts, varying between 30 percent and 60 percent, were applied according to how long they had been living there.

The right-to-buy program is consistent with the main features of the data in tables 5.2 and 5.3. Most important, public housing tenants are concentrated among the less educated where most of the increase in home ownership occurred. Secondly, the concentration of change was among middle-age and older households who had longer tenure and could meet the minimum tenure requirement and who also may have accumulated a bit of savings for a down payment.

The more difficult question arising from table 5.2, and one on which we focus in this paper, is why rates of home ownership are much higher among younger U.K. households. One possibility is the structure of mortgages themselves. The typical U.K. model is characterized by a low down payment (5 percent to 10 percent), variable interest rates, and a fairly low take-up of mortgage interest insurance. The typical U.S. mortgage has a higher down payment (20 percent), fixed interest rates,[4] and often is accompanied by mortgage interest insurance, generating a more stable intertemporal financial commitment (see Chiuri and Jappelli 2000) for an institutional differences discussion). Differences in down payment requirements alone shorten the time (compared to American households) it takes young British households to save in order to reach their required down payments.[5]

Differences in housing wealth accumulation could be driven by other factors in the housing market. Rental market rigidities or failures commonly thought to exist in the United Kingdom could be one issue. Renters' right rules are far more common in the United Kingdom, making it difficult to evict existing tenants. This may explain differences in ownership rates among the young but not differences in the amount and growth of net equity in housing held by homeowners. The low ownership rates among older British most likely lie in a combination of the widespread availability

---

4. In the 1996 PSID sample, only 20.8 percent of households with mortgages had variable rate mortgages.

5. The role of cross-country differences in tax treatment is interesting since the U.S. tax treatment is actually more favorable than in the United Kingdom. While mortgage interest payments had been tax deductible in the United Kingdom, over the past twenty years this has been gradually phased out and all tax relief has been abolished from April 2000. U.S. households still receive full tax deductibility on all mortgage interest payments. Capital gains on primary residences are untaxed in both countries. These tax differences may affect ownership rates and equity payments differently. Importantly, there is no tax advantage to carrying mortgage debt in the United Kingdom, whereas this advantage is substantial in the United States.

Table 5.4   PSID Housing Equity and Its Components: Homeowners Only
(1984–1996; in thousands of 1995 US$)

	House Value		Mortgage Outstanding		
Year	Mean	Median	Mean	Median	Net Equity Mean
1984	94.1	78.1	25.8	11.4	68.3
1985	97.6	82.3	27.6	11.0	70.0
1986	101.8	80.4	28.4	11.4	73.4
1987	108.4	84.0	31.1	12.9	77.3
1988	112.6	80.9	33.2	13.4	79.4
1989	115.6	83.4	35.3	14.3	80.3
1990	115.3	79.8	35.2	15.4	80.1
1991	110.6	79.3	34.8	14.3	75.8
1992	109.5	80.4	35.0	12.9	74.5
1993	112.0	83.5	38.4	15.6	73.6
1994	114.7	86.9	42.0	14.8	72.7
1995	114.5	90.0	39.7	15.0	74.8
1996	116.0	88.2	39.9	15.7	76.1

of public housing to their generations as well as their much lower levels of economic status compared to U.S. households.

Tables 5.4 and 5.5 provide another view of the housing market dynamics in the two countries by listing yearly values of home values and outstanding mortgages for homeowners.[6] The value of British homes is always above that of their American counterparts. For example, in 1994 the median value of a home in the United Kingdom is about 14 percent higher than the median value of a home in the United States. Unless one has a strong prior that British homes are in some sense "better" than American homes, this price differential may simply indicate that the price of housing is higher in the United Kingdom. If so, the advantage of British households in housing wealth raises some conceptual questions of whether this type of wealth advantage should be treated on a par with wealth differences that emerge in other assets. If British homes are more expensive for the same quality, and demand is inelastic, British households will spend more on housing as discussed in section 5.4.

Tables 5.4 and 5.5 also indicate that the higher net equity held in British homes in part reflects higher housing prices in the United Kingdom but also the smaller outstanding mortgages in the United Kingdom. This mortgage differential prevails in spite of the fact that initial down payment requirements are lower in the United Kingdom than in the United States.

6. Over the years in common the time series of home values among homeowners in table 5.3 captures the swings in home prices contained in figure 5.3. No questions were asked in the BHPS about housing in 1992, and no mortgage questions were asked in 1991.

Table 5.5   **BHPS Housing Equity and Its Components: Homeowners Only**
                       (1991–1998; in thousands of 1995 US$)

Year	House Value		Mortgage Outstanding		Net Equity Mean
	Mean	Median	Mean	Median	
1991	137.8	112.9	n.a.	n.a.	n.a.
1993	122.3	98.9	34.4	13.2	88.0
1994	120.0	96.7	34.4	14.5	85.6
1995	115.2	93.2	34.9	18.6	80.2
1996	117.6	95.8	32.9	16.7	84.7
1997	119.4	95.4	37.8	20.5	81.6
1998	124.5	99.6	35.5	19.9	89.0

Note: n.a. = not available.

This in turn suggests that compared to their U.S. counterparts, British households may not engage in significant amounts of refinancing their homes as real housing prices rise and capital gains are accumulated. Consistent with this view, note the significant increase in outstanding mortgages in the United States at a pace that parallels that of real housing prices so that net housing equity has remained flat. While the refinancing of homes has become reasonably commonplace in the United States over the last decade or so (data from the 1996 PSID indicate that 37 percent of households with existing mortgages had refinanced), this phenomenon appears to be much less important in the United Kingdom. British households seem to be far more cautious in using wealth accumulated through capital gains in housing for other purposes.

5.3.2   Rates of Asset Ownership: Stock

Using the PSID, one-quarter of U.S. households directly owned some stock in 1984, a fraction that grows to 40 percent by 1999. Direct share ownership was far less common among British households, especially in the early 1980s. Figure 5.1 plots the time-series pattern of equity ownership in the United Kingdom between 1978 and 1996. By the mid-1980s, British household equity ownership rates had been stable and hovered just below 10 percent—well less than the U.S. figure in 1984. Starting in 1984, equity ownership grew more rapidly in the United Kingdom than in the United States. While the gap in equity ownership has narrowed, by the mid-1990s almost one-quarter of British households directly owned stock compared to one-third of American households.

Table 5.6 lists stock ownership rates by age in a form similar to that displayed in tables 5.4 and 5.5. Consistent with figure 5.1, secular changes in British stock ownership look much like classic calendar year effects. There

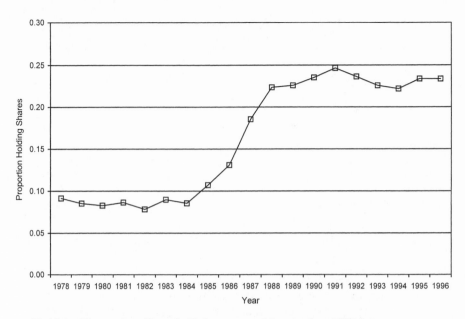

Fig. 5.1   Time series of household share-ownership rates from FES data

was almost no change between 1979 and 1984, followed by a sharp increase during the next five years with very little change thereafter. These increases in stock ownership were slightly larger among middle-age households, but in general one is struck by the near uniformity in increases in prevalence across all age groups. Not shown in table 5.6, stock ownership expanded by a somewhat greater amount among more educated British households.[7]

The same questions asked about home ownership are relevant to equity markets as well. Why the intercountry differences, and why the massive secular shifts in the United Kingdom? In the United Kingdom most of this increase was concentrated in a four-year period from 1985 to 1989, coinciding with the flotation of previously nationalized public utilities such as British Telecom (1984) and British Gas (1986). Around this time, the U.K. government introduced also a further set of measures aimed at promoting a "share-owning democracy"—namely tax-favored employee share ownership schemes. In the United States the increase in share ownership was more gradual throughout the 1980s, no doubt induced by rising rates of return. One result of these trends was that although the stock market boom was relatively similar across the countries, the fraction of American households benefiting was far higher than in Britain throughout the 1980s and 1990s.

7. For example, between 1984 and 1989, stock ownership rates increased by 11 percentage points among those who stopped at the compulsory schooling level while it increased by 17 percentage points among household heads with more than a compulsory school education.

Table 5.6   **Proportion of Households Who are Stock Owners, by Year and Age of the Head**

Age	1979	1984	1989	1994	1999
United Kingdom					
20–29	0.032	0.032	0.102	0.119	0.113
30–39	0.054	0.051	0.187	0.174	0.211
40–49	0.087	0.076	0.262	0.237	0.258
50–59	0.103	0.127	0.312	0.276	0.333
60–69	0.126	0.110	0.288	0.293	0.351
70+	0.109	0.111	0.205	0.236	0.283
Total	0.086	0.086	0.277	0.222	0.262
United States					
20–29		0.144	0.160	0.188	.230
30–39		0.262	0.258	0.310	.350
40–49		0.306	0.358	0.409	.412
50–59		0.340	0.374	0.473	.486
60–69		0.288	0.336	0.416	.456
70+		0.208	0.247	0.271	.399
Total		0.248	0.279	0.341	.398

Source: U.K. data from Family Expenditure Survey (see Banks and Tanner 1999).
Note: Blank cells indicate not available.

The differences between the two countries in stock ownership are again more difficult to answer. One possible explanation is that market conditions, in particular transaction costs, taxes, or information, differ across the two countries. Certainly prior to the mid-1980s in Britain there was a tax bias away from direct holdings of equity toward wealth held in housing or occupational pensions, because equity was more heavily taxed than consumption, and housing and pensions benefited from tax advantages relative to consumption. Given the structure of the tax system these differences were significantly greater in times of high inflation.[8] However, the introduction of personal equity plans and employee share ownership schemes meant that, from 1987 onward, equity could be held in a more favorably taxed manner by British households. Indeed, personal equity plans give holdings of equity an identical tax treatment to IRAs or 401(k)s, that

8. For equity, interest income tax was levied on dividend income at the investor's marginal rate (which could be as high as 83 percent during the 1970s and 60 percent during the 1980s). In addition, investment income over a certain threshold (around £2,000 per year in mid-1970's prices) was also subject to a 15 percent investment income surcharge, although this was paid by only very few tax payers. Capital gains tax was levied on nominal capital gains until 1985 and then real gains after that date at a flat rate of 30 percent. Since 1988 real capital gains were taxed at the investor's marginal income tax rate. Since 1983 the ceiling on which mortgage interest payments were tax exempt was fixed in nominal terms, thus rapidly reducing the tax advantage to housing relative to other assets. See Banks and Blundell (1994) for details.

is, neutral with respect to consumption.[9] These tax differences are discussed in section 5.4.

Another pertinent difference is stamp duty, where a 0.5 percent charge is levied on all share transactions in the United Kingdom. But for infrequently traded portfolios, such a difference is unlikely to be behind the marked differences in share ownership observed across the two countries. Finally, there could be differences in the information individuals have about stock market investment opportunities. While this is a plausible explanation for differences in the middle of the income distribution, there are cross-country differences even in the very highest percentiles of the income or wealth distribution, where such information differences are unlikely to be so pronounced.

An alternative explanation for these differences, and possibly for higher accumulations of financial wealth in America compared to most of Europe (including the United Kingdom) more generally, involves differences in attitudes toward capitalist financial institutions (see Banks, Blundell, and Smith 2000). Especially during the 1970s and early 1980s, it is probably a fair characterization that there was more distrust of the fairness of capitalism as an economic system, at least among significant segments of the European population. The stock market is one of most vivid capitalist symbols, so this distrust may have resulted in lower average participation in equity markets among Europeans. This could be one reason why the equity boom that eventually occurred in the United Kingdom affected fewer households. However, the results obtained by Banks, Blundell, and Smith (2000) suggest that only a part of the differences in equity ownership can be explained by ideology differences between the countries.

If transaction costs, taxes, and ideology cannot fully explain the low rates of stock ownership in the United Kingdom, where do we go from there? In the following we provide a new explanation for these low rates of equity ownership that are founded not in the institutional character of the equity markets in the two countries but rather in differences in the two housing markets.

5.3.3 Rates of Return on Assets

Figure 5.2 plots inflation adjusted equity price indexes for both countries, each expressed relative to a 1980 base.[10] The magnitude of the recent

9. On direct holdings of equity or mutual funds held outside of personal equity plans (PEPs) or IRAs, the tax treatment is also comparable across the United States and United Kingdom. Dividend income is taxed as income in both countries, and realized capital gains are taxable in both countries. However, in the United Kingdom capital gains are taxed only above a fairly sizeable annual exemption (around $10,000 per year). In the United States capital gains are taxed at a rate lower than that in the United Kingdom (also varying with the length of the time the asset is held, but with no exemption).

10. The U.S. index is the S&P500 while the U.K. index is the Financial Times All Share index. For an analysis of the impact of the American stock market on wealth distributions and savings behavior, see Juster et al. (2000).

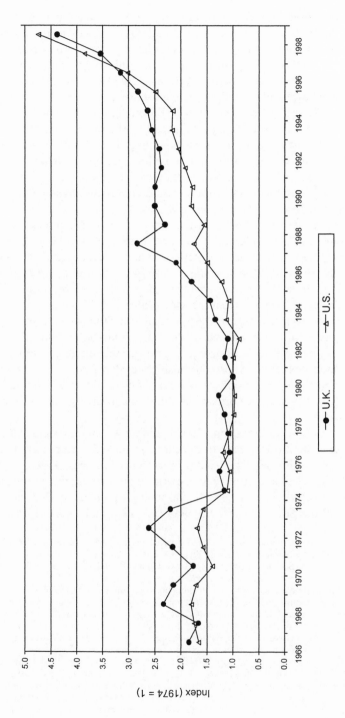

Fig. 5.2 Stock prices

stock market boom in both countries is impressive even compared to historical equity premiums. For example, real equity prices in the United Kingdom are about two and one-half times larger in real terms in 1995 as they were in 1980—slightly larger than the equity appreciation in the United States over the same period. Yet, measured from this 1980 base, it is remarkable how similar equity appreciation has been in both countries. The U.S. equity rates of return would be higher than those in the United Kingdom if the mid-1970s was used instead as the reference, suggesting that up to 1980 the (recent) historical experience in the stock market was more favorable in America. Still, the compelling message from figure 5.2 is that differential rates of return in each country's equity markets during the 1980s and 1990s cannot explain the quite different levels of financial wealth holdings in each country by the mid-1990s.[11]

Similarly, figure 5.3 shows real indices of average house prices for the United States and United Kingdom over the period 1974 to 1998. As with the indices for equity returns, both series are normalized to unity in 1980. Immediately apparent is the much larger volatility of housing prices in the United Kingdom, with real prices rising by 50 percent over the period 1980 to 1989 and then falling back to its previous value by 1992. Over the period as a whole, however, real returns were similar across the two countries and much smaller than those realized in the equity market. In addition, the highly volatile returns to housing equity and variable interest rates leaves British households much exposed to business-cycle vagaries. This should make them much more cautious than Americans would be of refinancing their homes during housing price upswings and converting the funds into financial assets.[12]

The U.K. index also hides considerable differences across regions, with some being much more volatile than others. In table 5.7 we present summary statistics for house prices from the regional subindices, showing both average house prices and average house price inflation over the period as a whole, along with the corresponding variances. Immediately clear is that London and the South East of England (in which almost 30 percent of

11. For simplicity, our comparison relates to stock prices as opposed to stock returns, but dividend yields are comparable or, if anything, higher in the United Kingdom, so this cannot account for higher U.S. stock holdings (see Bond, Chennels, and Devereux 1995, for example).

12. To this point we have discussed income, housing price, and stock price risk in isolation. In deciding on the composition of their wealth portfolios, households will also consider the correlation of these risks. This is a complicated subject, and we just scratch the surface here. To examine how these risks are correlated over time, using yearly data we estimated in each country correlations between the proportional change in real gross domestic product, proportional changes in real house prices, and proportional changes in real stock prices. Proportional changes were used to attempt to isolate the risk and eliminate the deterministic component. In neither country is there any correlation between stock price risk and either housing price or gross domestic product (GDP) risk, but a significant positive correlation exists between housing price risk and GDP risk. Moreover, this correlation is significantly higher in the United Kingdom than in the United States, consistent with our view that housing supply elasticity is much smaller in the United Kingdom.

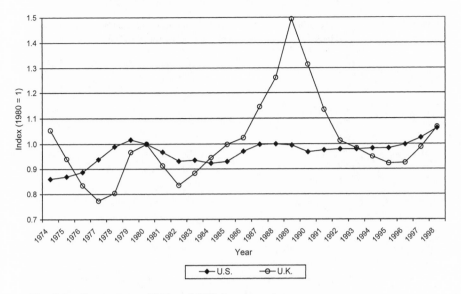

Fig. 5.3   Comparison of U.S. and U.K. housing prices

Table 5.7   **Regional House Price Volatility in the United Kingdom, 1978–2000**

Region	Fraction of Households in Region (1995)	Average Real House Price (1980 = 1)	Variance of Real House Price	Average Real House Price Inflation	Variance of Real House Price Inflation
Inner London	10.38	1.1386	0.3049	0.0280	0.0174
Outer London		1.1316	0.2860	0.0245	0.0156
South East	19.40	1.0974	0.2724	0.0209	0.0159
East Anglia	4.18	1.0645	0.2689	0.0164	0.0170
South West	9.11	1.0937	0.2368	0.0178	0.0128
East Midlands	7.47	1.0798	0.2092	0.0101	0.0118
West Midlands	9.45	1.0489	0.1917	0.0109	0.0107
North West	10.42	1.0394	0.1815	0.0120	0.0097
Yorkshire	8.91	0.9867	0.1473	0.0028	0.0115
Wales	4.99	0.9750	0.1327	0.0047	0.0130
North	6.32	1.0224	0.1217	0.0051	0.0073
Scotland	9.37	1.0021	0.0576	0.0041	0.0026

Source: Nationwide house price indices (1978q1–2000q2).

U.K. households are located) face considerably higher volatility than the average U.K. index. We return to this in the following.

5.3.4   Differences in Wealth Holdings in Housing and Stock

In tables 5.8 and 5.9 we report percentiles of net primary housing wealth and stock wealth, in both the United States and the United Kingdom, by home ownership and stock ownership status. Note that in this table and

Table 5.8   Percentiles of U.K. Net Primary Housing Wealth and Stock Wealth, by
                   Home Ownership and Stock Ownership Status (BHPS 1995)

Percentile	All (100%)	Homeowners (65.6%)	Stock Holders (24.0%)	Homeowners with Stock (20.7%)
	Net Primary Housing Wealth			
Mean	54.3	82.2	89.0	104.5
10	0.0	9.3	0.0	11.6
25	0.0	32.6	17.1	45.0
50	32.6	68.3	73.0	85.4
75	85.4	108.7	125.8	139.7
90	136.6	155.3	201.8	217.4
95	186.3	225.1	279.5	310.5
	Stock Wealth (lower)			
Mean	7.8	11.3	32.8	35.5
10	0.0	0.0	0.6	0.7
25	0.0	0.0	2.3	2.3
50	0.0	0.0	9.2	9.3
75	0.0	1.6	31.1	38.8
90	13.2	23.3	77.6	93.2
95	41.9	60.6	139.7	155.3
	Stock Wealth (upper)			
Mean	10.3	14.8	43.5	46.5
10	0.0	0.0	0.8	0.8
25	0.0	0.0	3.1	3.1
50	0.0	0.0	10.9	14.0
75	0.0	1.6	46.6	50.5
90	15.5	31.0	116.4	116.4
95	50.5	77.6	156.8	186.3

those that follow, we use the upper bound of household stock wealth in the United Kingdom. Because the United Kingdom has less stock wealth, if anything, differences between the United States and the United Kingdom will be underestimated. For all types of households the distribution of wealth held in the form of primary housing is higher at each point in the United Kingdom than in the United States, although the differences are largest in the bottom three-quarters of the distribution.

In contrast, stock holdings are much higher among American households. In the mid-1990s, the mean value of shares in America was three times as large as in Britain and was about twice as large when considering shareholders only. In both countries, distributions of stock values are highly skewed, with extreme concentrations in 5 to 10 percent of households. But at all points in the distributions, the value of American holdings are multiples of two or three of those held by British households.[13]

13. Banks, Blundell, and Smith (2000) show that the comparison between the 1995 BHPS and the 1984 PSID reveals that, both for the full population of households and for share-

Table 5.9   **Percentiles of U.S. Net Primary Housing Wealth and Stock Wealth, by Home Ownership and Stock Ownership Status (PSID 1994)**

Percentile	All (100%)	Homeowners (62.6%)	Stock Holders (34.1%)	Homeowners with Stock (27.6%)
		Net Primary Housing Wealth		
Mean	45.2	72.1	80.5	99.7
10	0.0	8.2	0.0	14.3
25	0.0	22.5	10.2	34.5
50	17.9	51.1	51.1	71.6
75	66.5	92.0	102.2	122.7
90	125.8	153.4	184.0	204.5
95	178.9	224.9	256.6	286.3
		Stock Wealth		
Mean	31.0	46.1	90.5	104.8
10	0.0	0.0	1.2	2.0
25	0.0	0.0	5.1	7.2
50	0.0	0.0	23.5	28.6
75	6.1	20.4	66.5	81.8
90	51.1	102.2	204.5	230.0
95	153.4	204.5	347.6	409.0

The conditional distributions contained in tables 5.8 and 5.9 hint at a greater separation of stock and housing holdings among British households. Among stockholders, the mean value of stock holdings in the United Kingdom is only $3,000 higher if British households are also homeowners. The "effect" of home ownership on stock wealth is much higher in the United States, especially among large stock values.

Tables 5.10 and 5.11 present means and medians of stock and housing wealth by age band in the two countries, split according to whether households have stocks, housing wealth, or both. Looking at the patterns by age, a striking difference emerges. Homeowners in the United Kingdom demonstrate a substantial age gradient in their housing wealth, at both the mean and median. Median net housing wealth for the forty–forty-nine-year-olds is seven times higher than that for the twenty–twenty-nine-year-olds. This gradient is much flatter in the United States, with the corresponding ratio being just over three. The reverse is true for stock wealth—the age gradient of stock wealth for stock owners in the United Kingdom is

holders only, the distribution of share values held by households are virtually identical. That is, after the stock market surge in both countries, British households had stock wealth similar to American households ten years earlier. In the early 1980s, however, we know that in light of the subsequent extremely large increase in share ownership, British households' stock holdings were considerably smaller than their American counterparts. This initial condition difference between the two countries would have profound impacts on wealth distributions by the mid-1990s.

Table 5.10   **Mean U.K. Net Primary Housing Wealth and Stock Wealth, by Age, Home Ownership, and Stock Ownership Status (BHPS 1995)**

Age Range	All (100%) Mean	Homeowners (65.6%) Mean	Homeowners (65.6%) Median	Stock Holders (24.0%) Mean	Stock Holders (24.0%) Median	Homeowners with Stock (20.7%) Mean	Homeowners with Stock (20.7%) Median
Housing Wealth							
20–29	6.3	16.7	10.9	5.6	3.1	10.3	11.6
30–39	26.8	38.7	31.0	36.6	24.8	43.5	31.0
40–49	63.3	82.7	68.3	95.2	69.9	104.5	74.5
50–59	83.7	109.6	96.3	122.2	112.9	131.2	121.1
60–69	82.1	119.5	93.2	117.4	105.6	143.9	132.0
70+	57.4	104.2	86.9	112.0	100.9	139.0	108.7
Stock Wealth (lower)							
20–29	1.5	1.8	0.0	10.2	4.7	9.5	3.7
30–39	3.9	5.1	0.0	15.0	5.4	16.0	5.8
40–49	6.1	7.5	0.0	23.2	7.8	24.1	7.8
50–59	11.0	13.5	0.0	32.4	9.3	32.6	10.9
60–69	15.3	21.4	0.0	55.4	20.2	65.5	38.8
70+	8.2	15.4	0.0	50.7	10.1	57.0	115.5
Stock Wealth (upper)							
20–29	1.6	2.0	0.0	10.7	4.7	10.2	3.7
30–39	4.7	6.2	0.0	17.9	6.2	19.3	6.2
40–49	7.5	9.3	0.0	28.5	9.3	29.6	9.3
50–59	18.0	20.0	0.0	53.0	15.5	48.1	15.5
60–69	19.5	27.2	0.0	70.0	30.0	83.3	50.5
70+	9.8	18.9	0.0	60.8	12.4	69.7	15.5

Table 5.11   **U.S. Net Primary Housing Wealth and Stock Wealth, by Age, Home Ownership, and Stock Ownership Status (PSID 1994)**

Age Range	All (100%) Mean	Homeowners (62.6%) Mean	Homeowners (62.6%) Median	Stock Holders (34.1%) Mean	Stock Holders (34.1%) Median	Homeowners with Stock (27.6%) Mean	Homeowners with Stock (27.6%) Median
Housing Wealth							
20–29	9.9	36.4	15.3	23.6	0.0	55.0	18.4
30–39	21.4	40.5	28.6	33.7	21.5	46.1	33.7
40–49	43.1	61.3	48.4	80.7	48.1	96.8	63.4
50–59	81.1	100.0	62.4	114.5	76.7	128.6	81.8
60–69	86.0	104.0	81.8	132.1	102.2	139.1	112.5
70+	60.0	84.3	71.6	92.2	76.7	108.2	91.0
Stock Wealth							
20–29	2.4	4.6	0.0	12.6	3.6	15.5	4.1
30–39	12.5	20.1	0.0	40.2	10.2	47.0	11.2
40–49	25.4	32.9	0.0	62.0	21.5	67.7	25.6
50–59	51.1	61.0	1.0	108.2	35.8	117.6	35.8
60–69	88.7	105.6	0.0	213.0	61.3	221.2	61.3
70+	33.4	41.1	0.0	123.3	51.1	127.9	51.1

extremely shallow,[14] whereas in the United States stock wealth rises by a factor of almost ten for stock holders aged fifty in comparison to those aged twenty–twenty-nine. Looking at just those who own both homes and stocks, the differences still emerge. It is these differences that we will explore in more detail later in the paper and that motivate the design of our modeling exercise.

5.4   A Model of Housing Tenure Choice and Portfolio Decisions

5.4.1   The Demand for Housing Services

In the simplest model, housing demand is purely a function of family size. It will therefore increase over the early period of the adult life cycle as family size increases. In figure 5.4, we present profiles for house size, with each line representing a thirty-year time series of the average number of rooms for a year-of-birth cohort over the time period 1968–98. The figure shows that in the United Kingdom there is a strong increase in house size, as measured by the number of rooms, as the head of household grows older, flattening out around age forty but rising steeply from the twenties to the thirties. For this reason we can frame our discussion in terms of a stylized model with three stages in an early adult life cycle: leaving home, living as a couple without children, and living as a couple with children. There is also little evidence of strong cohort effects during the early part of the adult life cycle, as evidenced by the lack of vertical differences between each cohort's profiles up to age forty. Hence this rise is the same whether we look at the individual date of birth cohorts, as in the figure, or pool across cohorts.

In general, housing demand will also depend on the unit price of services, the level of (expected) wealth, and the degree of uncertainty over all these variables. It is likely that demand for housing services is price inelastic. Consequently, *expenditure* on housing services will be increasing in the price of housing services. According to our numbers, the median value of a U.S. owned home in 1994 is about 14 percent less than the median price (value) of a U.K. owned home. Unless we think that there is 14 percent more utility involved, this is evidence of a higher unit price in the United Kingdom. A higher unit price in the United Kingdom will induce a higher level of expenditure, conditional on all the other factors.

5.4.2   The Choice of Housing Tenure

At the start of the adult life cycle, housing tenure decisions occur in two stages: first, a choice of when to leave the parental home and second,

14. Note that for stock wealth the mean profiles are substantially affected by a cluster of extremely high-wealth young individuals. Age gradients at all but the 99th percentile and above display the same increasing pattern as the median.

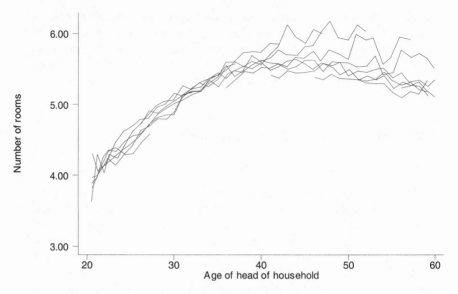

Fig. 5.4   Average number of rooms over the life cycle, by age and cohort, from FES data (1968–1998).

whether to rent or to buy. Strictly speaking, the latter is *not* a portfolio decision because, if a house is bought and continuously remortgaged, there
is no necessity to hold any housing equity. Yet, ownership is a prerequisite
for securing housing equity, and so the decision to own may be influenced
by portfolio choices as well as pure service-flow considerations. A house
may also be owned without any desire to accumulate housing equity simply
because it is an efficient way to achieve a desired flow of housing services.
For a household with little expected mobility and heterogeneity of tastes,
owning can be the least costly way of achieving a desired level of housing
service.

Young households who first decide to rent remain potential purchasers
of a starter home as soon as they are able to secure a down payment. In the
decision to leave the parental home, credit constraints will also play an important role as such constraints are typically binding on young adults who
must accumulate sufficient wealth to meet down payment and collateral requirements. Consequently, the income of the young will be important, and
the volatility of incomes of young people rather than per capita income per
se, will be critical in generating swings in housing transactions.[15] Higher
down payments lengthen the time required to build up enough wealth to
satisfy lenders and will make first-time home buyers older, on average. Sim-

15. This also accords with the property ladder model of Ortalo-Magne and Rady (1998),
which views the housing market as a step-function.

ilarly, inadequate rental markets may delay the age at which one leaves the parental home but lower the age at which one buys the first home. This last point is explored, using the BHPS data used in our analysis, in Ermisch (1999) who finds empirical support for the economic conditions of the housing market relating to the household formation choices of the young in Britain.

In light of the data in figure 5.4 and of empirical and theoretical models of housing market dynamics (see, e.g., Di Salvo and Ermisch 1997 and Ortalo-Magne and Rady 1998, respectively), the initial home purchase is best seen as the first step in a property ladder. If there is some job or demographic mobility expected then, because of lower transaction costs, the rental market may provide a less costly way of choosing an optimal path for housing services. If house prices are variable, the rental market may also provide a contract insuring against some of that risk. But by leaving equity in their home, first-time homeowners are partially self-insuring against price fluctuations in the housing market. While a price increase will raise the price (and required down payment) on the second home, the price of the first home is also increasing, providing additional resources for that now larger down payment. A symmetric argument obtains during periods of housing price declines.

As incomes and family sizes grow, these now slightly older young adults hope to buy a larger, more expensive home. The time interval between these purchases is once again governed by the length of time it takes to secure the larger down payment needed on the bigger house. Low down payment requirements will shorten the interval between home purchases. In addition, any capital gains on the first house may be used to help buy the second. Capital gains during booms will tend to shorten the time interval between the first and second home purchase, whereas capital losses during downturns will lengthen this interval.

5.4.3   House Price Uncertainty and the Choice between Stock and Housing Equity

Each household has a desired level of total wealth. This level will depend on expected future income and consumption streams as well as the returns on assets. First, consider the portfolio demand for housing equity. If house prices are variable and uncertain then, given the increased demand over the early part of the life cycle, housing equity will be an important source of insurance against house price risk. The larger the uncertainty in house prices and the steeper the demand over the life cycle, the more important is the insurance aspect of housing equity.

Conditional on being an owner, therefore, the higher the level of house price uncertainty the larger the demand to pay down the mortgage and to hold wealth in housing equity. This will be particularly the case for households early in their life cycle as they anticipate stepping up the property ladder. It would make little sense for risk-adverse young households who face housing price volatility to invest their assets in the stock market even if stock price and housing price risks are uncorrelated.

The tax treatment of mortgage repayments will also influence the level of mortgage held and the desire to hold equity in housing. A tax advantage to borrowing via a mortgage will make it optimal to consume more housing services and to use ownership as a vehicle for that consumption but not necessarily to pay down the mortgage. Rather, it might be optimal to invest in another risky asset rather than pay down the outstanding mortgage or even to remortgage a housing equity capital gain.

5.4.4   The Supply of Housing Services

There are two aspects of the supply of housing services that are central to our model. First, a more inelastic supply will induce a larger sensitivity of house prices to fluctuations in demand, in particular to fluctuations in the income of young, first-time buyers. The second aspect relates to the rental market. Imperfections and/or regulation of the private rental market may make it difficult for the young to use rental housing as the step between leaving the parental home and acquiring a house. The rental market may also be dominated by the public sector in which case the allocation mechanism may be less sensitive to the demand of young households.

A consequence of inelastic demand is that *expenditure* on housing services will be increasing in the price of housing services.

5.4.5   Model Predictions

The model predictions for the United Kingdom relative to the United States as households move through their early life-cycle profile are clear. The demand for housing services will increase as family size increases. Consider the three stages of our stylized life-cycle profile: leaving home, living independently without children, and living with children. The model predicts that the level of owner occupation at the second stage should be lower in the United States relative to the United Kingdom if the deposit and mobility motivations dominate the tax advantage. This is reinforced by the higher house price volatility in the United Kingdom which makes owner occupation more likely for those in the second stage of this life-cycle profile.

This prediction could also be rationalized by an inefficient rental market in the United Kingdom. However, the arguments also suggest that the United Kingdom would have a higher level of housing equity for volatility reasons but that this would be reduced once full household size is reached at stage three in the early life-cycle profile because the positive volatility effect would disappear. Other things being equal, the tax advantage in the United States would make households more likely to be owners in the

United States and less likely to pay down capital—and less likely to accumulate housing equity.

The higher volatility in the United Kingdom increases the desire to hold housing equity in the United Kingdom for those households in the second stage of their demographic profile, that is, those who expect to increase their family size. In turn, this increases the desire to be an owner for such households in the United Kingdom. We expect more owners and a higher paying down of outstanding housing debt in the United Kingdom and a higher level of housing equity in the United Kingdom. The latter, but not the former, of these is predicted by the tax advantage.

5.5 The Housing Market and Income Risk of the Young

5.5.1 The Housing Market

Our model on housing markets places great weight on the role of young households and on the role of housing and stock in portfolios over the life cycle. To evaluate whether the young merit such an emphasis, we examine individuals who purchased a new home between waves of the PSID and BHPS samples. Across all ages, about one in twenty household heads in both countries are observed to have bought a new home since the previous wave of the panel. It is also clear that young people were far more active in the housing market. For example, 12 percent of British household heads between the ages of twenty and twenty-nine had bought a new home during the last year. The comparable number in the United States was 9 percent.

Table 5.12 lists the age distribution of household heads who purchased a home between the annual waves of each survey.[16] Besides describing all home buyers, these data are stratified by whether household heads were "first-time" buyers or "repeat" buyers. Repeat buyers represent those who had lived in a home that they owned before this new purchase, whereas first-time buyers were not living in a home that they had personally owned right before this new purchase.[17]

Consistent with our view that they constitute the active part of the housing market, new home buyers are much younger than the average homeowner.[18] Moreover, the typical purchaser of a new home is a good deal younger in the United Kingdom than in the United States. For example, 63 percent of all new buyers in the United Kingdom are less than forty years old with a median age of thirty-five. The comparable numbers for the

16. To provide adequate sample sizes on home buyers, the data were pooled across years.
17. More precisely, "first-time" buyers consist of those who lived in a rental house in the previous survey wave and those who lived in an owned home with their parents.
18. For example, in 1994 the mean age of all homeowners was 50.4 in the United Kingdom and 51.3 in the United States.

Table 5.12   **Age Distribution of Home Buyers (%)**

	All Buyers		First Time Buyers		Repeat Buyers	
Age	U.K.	U.S.	U.K.	U.S.	U.K.	U.S.
20–29	30.1	21.5	47.4	31.6	15.7	9.9
30–39	32.5	35.8	26.8	36.2	37.3	35.3
40–49	16.0	19.8	9.7	16.4	21.3	23.7
50–59	9.2	9.8	5.3	7.6	12.4	12.3
60–69	5.5	7.5	3.6	4.6	7.1	10.8
70+	6.7	5.7	7.2	3.6	6.2	8.1
Total	100.0	100.0	100.0	100.0	100.0	100.0
Median	35.0	37.0	30.0	34.0	38.0	41.0
Mean	39.3	41.1	35.9	37.6	42.2	45.1

Notes: Rows for each country should add up to 100.0. Sample comprised of home buyers who are heads in period *t*; all years pooled.

United States are 57 percent and a median age of thirty-seven. The differences between the two countries are most striking among those household heads between the ages of twenty and twenty-nine, who constitute 30 percent of all new U.K. buyers compared to 22 percent in the United States.

First-time buyers are especially young, with median ages of only thirty (United Kingdom) and thirty-four (United States). Household heads less than thirty years old comprise almost half (47 percent) of all first time buyers in Britain, much higher than the comparable U.S. proportion of about one-third (32 percent). Not surprisingly, repeat buyers are somewhat older in both countries, but even here the median ages are only thirty-eight (United Kingdom) and forty-one (United States). More than half of repeat home buyers in the United Kingdom are less than forty years old.

Age is one dimension in which new home buyers differ in the two countries.[19] Table 5.13 tries to illuminate an additional dimension by listing prevalence rates of new owners by their joint ownership and headship status in the previous survey wave. A similar fraction of new buyers in both countries had owned their own home in the prior wave. The principal difference emerges in the third column where there exists a far greater fraction of American households who made a transition from renting a place of their own to buying one. These intercountry differences are especially large among young people (aged twenty–twenty-nine). In particular, 64 percent

19. As documented in section 5.3, over recent years the relative tax status of housing and stock wealth has been changing markedly. Broadly speaking, both assets are now taxed neutrally with respect to current consumption, while in the past housing was tax-favored, and wealth held in the form of stocks was tax-penalized. In contrast, since the introduction of IRAs both assets have received a relatively stable tax treatment in the United States.

Table 5.13   **Make Up of New Homebuyers, by Age**

Age Range	Status in Previous Year				
	Head and Owner	Nonhead in an Owned House	Head and Renter	Nonhead in a Renter House	All
United Kingdom					
20–29	0.196	0.380	0.250	0.174	100.0
30–39	0.530	0.132	0.261	0.077	100.0
40–49	0.615	0.125	0.210	0.051	100.0
50–59	0.639	0.102	0.252	0.007	100.0
60–69	0.625	0.080	0.250	0.045	100.0
70+	0.449	0.065	0.467	0.019	100.0
United States					
20–29	0.202	0.125	0.635	0.038	100.0
30–39	0.439	0.030	0.517	0.014	100.0
40–49	0.538	0.023	0.422	0.017	100.0
50–59	0.575	0.010	0.396	0.019	100.0
60–69	0.657	0.015	0.320	0.008	100.0
70+	0.639	0.026	0.329	0.005	100.0

Note: Sample comprised of home buyers who are heads in period t; all years pooled.

of new buyers in this age group in the United States were previously household heads who were renters. The comparable British figure is only one-quarter. The counterweight is the large fraction of young home buyers in Britain who were not heads of household in the prior year (55 percent in the United Kingdom compared to 16 percent in the United States). These young British nonhousehold heads were more than twice as likely to live in an owned as opposed to a rented home—it was simply not a home that they owned.

Among those who had lived previously in an owned home, the dominant situation for those between the ages of twenty and twenty-nine was that they departed the parental home. While this is true for both countries, this is a far larger group of young people in the United Kingdom than it is in the United States. A key difference between the two countries concerns what happens when a young person first leaves the parental home. Across the years we examined, about one-fifth of British adults aged twenty–twenty-nine who were living in the parental home moved out the next year. The U.S. number is only slightly larger (about one-fourth). While the likelihood of leaving the parental home was roughly similar, where these British and American young adults went could not have been more different. This is illustrated in table 5.14, which shows that almost half of all young adults aged twenty–twenty-nine in Britain who left the parental nest bought their own home. In sharp contrast, this fraction is only 18 percent in the United States. While much smaller numbers are making this transition among

Table 5.14   **Proportion of Those Moving Out of Family Home Who Become Owners, by Age**

Age Range	United Kingdom	United States
20–29	0.466	0.180
30–39	0.557	0.231
All ages	0.486	0.191

Note: Sample comprised of all adults who are child of head in $t-1$ and not child of head in t; all years pooled.

those aged thirty–thirty-nine, the differences in the type of transition between the two countries remain.[20]

The data in this section document the following important differences between new home buyers in the United Kingdom and the United States. New home buyers are disproportionately very young adults with a particularly pronounced tilt toward the young in Britain. When they leave their parents' home, Americans first tend to live in rental housing either on their own or with their spouse or partner. No doubt due to difficulties in the British rental market, when British youth leave their parents they tend to skip over this intermediate step and go immediately on to purchasing their own house. Finally, these trends have interacted with massive compositional changes in household population so that increasing fractions of young homeowners are not currently married.

5.5.2 Income Risk

Our emphasis on the young also points to a potentially important role for income risk in this model. There are two aspects of income risk that will be useful to distinguish. The first is the systematic variation in aggregate first-time buyer income or shocks to income. As we noted previously, it is this that generates variation in the demand for first-time purchases. The second possible measure of income variance is the level of within-period income risk for each age group. We focus on the former since the latter will act as background risk and will only indirectly affect the demand curve

---

20. Another key demographic phenomenon—the delay, decline, and disruption of marriage, especially among the young—was also affecting the attributes of homeowners. In 1969, 98 percent of British home owners less than thirty years old were married. Thirty years later, one-third of young British home owners were not currently married. These rates currently appear similar within age groups in the two countries, but because there are more young homeowners in Britain, there are far more unmarried homeowners there. This large and growing fraction of young home owners who are not currently married may be another important element of the story. One impact of marriage is that it is an individual income risk reducing institution as one partner insures the other against the vagaries of life. With increasing numbers of young householders not currently married, they may be exposed to more income risk even if the structure of income risk by age did not change.

through risk aversion. A higher level of the first will create fluctuations in the price of housing provided supply is inelastic.

To investigate this we need to examine whether the variation of the age-specific aggregate shocks is larger for the young. The framework we adopt follows Banks, Blundell, and Brugiavini (2001) and separates aggregate from idiosyncratic risk. To estimate the aggregate variance for each age band, we regress average log income for each cohort on its lagged value for the same cohort and a list of changes in observable demographic characteristics. We then compute the variance of the time- and cohort-specific income shocks from this regression for each age group. The results of this regression using the repeated cross sections from the U.K. Family Expenditure Survey (FES) (1978–99) are presented in table 5.15.

In a simple liquidity constrained model, the variance of income itself, rather than the variance of income shocks, would determine fluctuations in demand. A comparison of the two measures of the aggregate variance for broad age bands in the United Kingdom is presented in the first two columns of table 5.16. For both measures there is a steep decline in aggregate income variation as we move from households whose heads are in their twenties to those households where the heads are in the thirties age band.

Table 5.15   **Log Income Model for the United Kingdom: Quarterly Income by Cohort (1968–1992)**

Variable	Coefficient	Standard Error
Log income $(t-1)$	1.0070	0.0088
Δ number employed	0.1277	0.0500
Δ number adults	0.7455	0.0344
Δ number children	0.0534	0.0288
Δ number female	−.4004	0.0318
Regions	Yes	
Seasonals	Yes	
Sargan	17.07 (3)	
GR^2	0.9178	0.0049

Notes: IV estimation using lagged variables as instruments. Household income equivalized by the number of adults.

Table 5.16   **Measures of the Variance of Log Income in the United Kingdom, by Age Group (1968–1992)**

Age	Aggregate Variance of Income	Aggregate Variance of Income Shocks	Within Age Group Income Variance
20s	0.0263	0.0074	0.2301
30s	0.0155	0.0034	0.2362
40s	0.0185	0.0049	0.2713

Note that the level of income variation rises systematically over time, especially in the 1980s, so that younger cohorts face a higher aggregate variation than older cohorts did at the same age. Finally, note that our measure of risk for the young may be an underestimate because the young will presumably also face more risk as a result of uncertainty about future demographics and household formation.

5.6   How Well Does the Model Explain the Data?

The model developed in section 5.4 was motivated by a number of facts relating to housing tenure choice, to housing equity, and to the stock of wealth holdings by households over their life cycle in the United Kingdom and the United States. In this section we ask whether the model can provide a convincing explanation and whether it can do better than other competing explanations.

5.6.1   Implications of the Model

The principal implications of our model stem from the significantly higher volatility of house prices in the United Kingdom. This starting point is fundamental, and we have two underlying explanations for it. First, the supply of housing is likely to be more inelastic in the United Kingdom, in part due to the greater population density there. This is most clearly seen in the dominance of the greater London area in the British housing market. Around 30 percent of all homes in England are located within the Southeast (including Greater London). Not only is the available space limited there, but new housing construction or conversion is heavily regulated and costly to build. This more inelastic supply implies that for any given demand side fluctuations, housing prices will be more volatile in the United Kingdom than in the United States.

Second, house prices are more sensitive to the variation in first-time buyer demand and therefore the volatility of first-time buyer incomes. Because new British home buyers are younger and therefore positioned on the more volatile part of the income risk–age curve, income fluctuations inducing demand side swings will also contribute to the greater price volatility in the British housing market.

In addition to more volatile prices, down payment requirements are less onerous in the United Kingdom, and the rental market is less efficient. In our model, these conditions all conspire to lead young U.K. households to move into owner occupation rather than to rent and to do this at an earlier age. This pattern of home ownership is borne out by the data. We find a significantly lower use of the rental market in the United Kingdom among younger households and a much higher probability in the United Kingdom of transiting from parental home to owner occupation. Of those adults aged twenty–twenty-nine observed to leave the parental home in the BHPS, 46.6 percent became owner-occupiers directly, as opposed to only 15.0 percent for their PSID counterparts. Although the group is much smaller, similar differences pertain for the thirty–thirty-nine age group.

Our model also had implications for portfolio choice. The higher house price volatility in the United Kingdom makes it optimal for those young households who expect to move up the property ladder to hold housing equity. Young homeowners in the United Kingdom who plan to upgrade their housing by purchasing a larger, newer home as their incomes and families expand may face considerable housing price risk. One method of self-insuring against housing price volatility would be to maintain a large fraction of household wealth in housing equity thereby matching possible variation in the value of one's current home with the price of any desired home upgrade.[21] In contrast, a quite risky strategy among young homeowners would be to hold much of their wealth in stock. Even if housing price and stock price risks are uncorrelated, a downturn in the equity market could make it quite difficult for young homeowners (who have limited amounts of household wealth) to reach their down payment goals for the new home.

For young U.K. households facing higher house price risk and lower down payment requirements, the model predicts that they enter the housing owning market earlier, cover a very large percentage of the house price by mortgage, and then pay down the mortgage as a saving instrument for future movements up the property ladder. Early in their adult life cycle we would expect to see a higher proportion of young owner-occupier households in the United Kingdom. At this point they would have little equity in housing and hold relatively large mortgages. But as they move through the early part of their adult life cycle they would, rather, accumulate housing equity than stock. Consequently, we predict that compared to the United States, in the United Kingdom age gradients in housing equity will be steeper and in stock equity less in the early part of the life cycle. From figure 5.4 we might expect this comparison to be particularly strong in the twenties and thirties and then to dampen out in the forties and fifties as the property ladder reaches a plateau.

The housing and stock wealth numbers reported in tables 5.10 and 5.11 would appear to be most relevant for testing these predictions. Tables 5.10 and 5.11 show, as predicted, that U.K. households indeed have a much steeper gradient in the accumulation of wealth in housing equity. The strong gradient for U.K. households is evident in both the mean and the

---

21. The downside of this risk, the so-called "negative equity" phenomenon that was widespread in the late 1980s and early 1990s, is only a problem if households cannot meet the monthly mortgage payments and are forced out of the market by repossession.

median of housing wealth in the first panel of table 5.10. The model also implies that the gradient should be even steeper among homeowners, especially those facing high housing price risk. Mean housing wealth rises by a factor of two between the twenties and thirties and then again by the same factor between the thirties and forties for homeowners in the United Kingdom. The reverse is true for stock wealth. Compared to the United States, the United Kingdom shows little gradient in stock wealth for those households early in their adult life cycle. For stock, due to a few large outliers, the median is probably a more robust measure, but even for the median there is little evidence of a gradient in the United Kingdom. In the United States the gradient in stock wealth is even more striking than it is for housing wealth in the United Kingdom.

5.6.2   Biases in Age Gradients for the Portfolios of the Young

There are potential problems with our reliance on the data in tables 5.10 and 5.11. First, cohort effects that we have seen are quite real in housing, and equity markets may confound them. Second, they describe the pattern of wealth holdings by age of household heads and many young adults are in households headed by their parents and thus appear in households with older heads.

Cohort Effects

The data in tables 5.10 and 5.11 are cross-sectional age profiles and may be contaminated by year and cohort effects. If cohort and time effects are the same across the two countries, our comparisons of age profiles may be less affected by this issue than for each individual country age profile. Yet the evidence in tables 5.2 and 5.6—listing ownership age profiles by country and year—suggests this may not be the case.

There are two types of cohort-year effects that may well affect our comparisons. The first are unique events that differentially affected the incentives to own homes or stocks in the two countries. The second results from the possible contamination of home and stock equity age profiles due to capital gains.

We first examine the impact of capital gains. For stocks, average rate of returns have been high and approximately the same in both countries, but there remains a possibility that middle-aged American cohorts benefited by being differentially exposed to the stock market (in comparison to the United Kingdom) in the mid-1980s. Fortunately, because questions are included on new stock purchases and sales we are able, in the United States data, to separate out that part of wealth accumulation in stock that is due to capital gains. To examine the impact of capital gains, we list in the first column of table 5.17 the cross-sectional holdings of stock wealth by age in the United States in 1984. The next column labeled shows the actual stock wealth of these 1984 age groups ten years later. The large within-cohort increases in stock wealth are certainly suggestive of significant capital gains in stocks. While these adjusted profiles indicate a much less steep pure life-cycle increase in stock wealth, even the capital gains adjusted data for the United States exhibit a larger age gradient than the unadjusted U.K. age gradient. Because the British stock age gradient is also exaggerated by capital gains, we conclude that the steeper U.S. age gradient for stock wealth is not solely a consequence of capital gains in stocks. For housing, however, the time series of returns suggests that over the period as a whole (particularly to 1994) returns were similar in both countries but more volatile in the United Kingdom.

In addition to the impact of differential capital gains, there are other cohort-year effects that differentially impact both stock and housing markets in the United Kingdom. However, these year effects are specific to a very narrow time period, allowing us to control for their impact. For example, the large increase in stock ownership rates in the United Kingdom due to the flotation of national industries was concentrated during the time period 1984–89. By limiting our comparisons to the post-1989 period, we can minimize the impact of this effect. We do so in table 5.18 by listing in the first column 1989 age profiles of stock ownership in both countries. In the adjacent column are listed the ownership rates of these age groups ten

Table 5.17   Fraction of U.S. Change in Stock Wealth between 1984 and 1994 Due to Capital Gains

Age Range	1984	Realized 1994	Realized Adjusted for Capital Gains
20–29	0.9	12.5	7.0
30–39	4.8	25.4	15.1
40–49	8.7	51.1	23.7
50–59	19.6	88.7	42.3

Table 5.18   Life-Cycle Changes in Stock Ownership (1989–1999)

Age Range	1989	1999
United Kingdom		
20–29	0.102	0.211
30–39	0.187	0.258
40–49	0.262	0.333
50–59	0.312	0.351
United States		
20–29	0.160	0.350
30–39	0.258	0.412
40–49	0.358	0.486
50–59	0.374	0.456

years later. In all cases, there was a much more rapid buildup in stock ownership in the United States compared to the United Kingdom.

Household Composition

So far we have been considering age profiles of housing and stock wealth computed by the age band of the head of the household. The head of the household is in turn defined by the owner of the property, and in the case of joint ownership, the oldest of the joint owners. Given the higher frequency of young adults living in households with older heads in the United Kingdom, tables 5.10 and 5.11 could display serious differential bias in the age pattern of housing and stock holdings of the United Kingdom relative to the United States. These biases apply to a considerably wider set of problems and relationships of interest than this one alone.

There are two potential biases due to household composition in looking at differences in life-cycle age profiles across countries. The very notion of a household (defined by the age of the head) results in the consideration of a selected sample. In both countries there will be young adults, at the beginning of their life cycles, who are still in the parental home or in other nonspousal living arrangements, many of whom will not be picked up in our calculations in the appropriate age band. To the extent that this group is differentially sized in the two countries the age profiles will be differentially affected.

Table 5.19 examines this issue by considering all adults in each age band (as opposed to just household heads) and looking at the distribution of relationships to the head of the household in which they live. Roughly one-quarter of adults aged twenty–twenty-nine in each country are still living with their parents (i.e., they are children of the head). But this is where the similarities end. A higher proportion of young adults in the United Kingdom are married or cohabiting with the household head, considerably fewer adults in the United Kingdom are actually household heads, and considerably more are in "other" arrangements, where among the young this group is predominantly made up of nonrelatives.

This means that the country-specific age profiles may well be influenced by the fact that when working at the household level we do not count many young individuals at the start of their life cycles. These children of household heads will crop up instead in our tables as members of the households aged forty–forty-nine or fifty–fifty-nine. These omitted young adults from the early age bands will tend to have lower housing (in fact zero) and stock wealth so that age gradients will tend to be understated.

Table 5.19 indicates a second bias—there are substantially more single heads of household among the young in the United States than in the United Kingdom. Individuals in single and married households are treated quite differently in a household unit analysis. The combined assets of the

Table 5.19   All Adults: Distribution of Relationships to Head of Household, by Age (%)

Age Range	Head	Married Spouse	Cohabiting Spouse	Child	Other	Total
United Kingdom						
20–29	37.3	17.6	11.2	25.0	9.0	100.0
30–39	55.7	33.7	5.5	4.0	1.1	100.0
40–49	58.9	35.9	2.7	2.0	0.7	100.0
50–59	62.6	33.8	1.7	1.0	1.0	100.0
60–69	66.0	31.4	0.6	0.3	1.6	100.0
70+	80.6	25.8	0.4	0.0	3.2	100.0
All	58.1	28.1	4.3	6.5	3.0	100.0
United States						
20–29	47.0	21.2	5.0	24.3	2.5	100.0
30–39	59.0	33.1	3.0	4.0	1.0	100.0
40–49	59.2	35.6	1.8	2.2	1.1	100.0
50–59	59.7	36.9	1.0	1.2	1.4	100.0
60–69	62.7	33.6	0.5	0.7	2.6	100.0
70+	73.4	18.6	0.2	0.3	7.5	100.0
All	58.7	30.0	2.3	6.7	2.4	100.0

Note: Sample comprised of adults over age seventy; all years pooled.

two individuals in a married household are summed and treated as one.[22] When there are many young married households, average assets are inflated and the age gradient of wealth is affected.[23]

The magnitude of the impacts of these biases on age profiles for wealth will depend to some extent on the amounts of wealth held by each group identified in table 5.19. The discussion above makes it clear that there is some reason to believe that even if there were no underlying differences in wealth between young heads and other young adults, we would still observe an unduly flat age profile. In fact, the situation is exacerbated because young heads (particularly when coupled with their spouses) typically have more assets than their peers. Taking data at the individual level once more from the BHPS, the rate of stock ownership among young (twenty–twenty-nine) heads and spouses is 14.7 percent, compared with 8.6 percent for young adults living in the parental home. Correspondingly, asset stocks are around 33 percent higher for this group also ("upper" estimates are $4,034

22. Individuals in married households may also individually accumulate more wealth due to marriage selection effects (being more prudent) or if marriage encourages savings.
23. A further issue is that the way in which the BHPS data is collected; with asset stocks asked individually and then questions about joint ownership following, one might expect this to impact on the difference between our "upper" and "lower" bounds for the youngest age group, in particular. We use the upper bounds in table 5.15.

Table 5.20   The Effect of Household Composition on Stock and Home Equity Age
Gradients: Median Values of Stocks (Stockholders), by Age (in
thousands of US$)

	United Kingdom			
Age Range	Households	Tax Units	Individuals	United States
20–29	4.7	3.1	1.6	3.6
30–39	6.2	4.7	3.0	10.2
40–49	9.3	9.0	4.7	21.5
50–59	15.5	15.6	7.8	35.8
60–69	30.0	32.6	17.1	61.3
70+	12.4	15.6	8.1	51.1

for heads, $3,120 for children of heads, and $612 for non-relatives; "lower" estimates are $2,496, $1,160 and $545, respectively).

Using the U.K. data, in which asset values are actually collected from individual household members, we can begin to understand the importance of such biases on our age–wealth profiles.[24] In table 5.20 we recomputed age profiles for stock in the United Kingdom on a tax unit and an individual basis, as opposed to a household basis. For the tax unit we define as *separate* units all adults except spouses as opposed to just looking at all households. Spouses' assets are added to those of the heads, and the combined unit is counted only once. For the individual analysis, we divide the assets in a married household by two and count each adult in an age band as a distinct unit.

The final two columns of table 5.20 repeat the household-level medians from tables 5.10 and 5.11. The differences in age profiles across different types of units are not trivial. In particular, stock wealth is differentially lower for the youngest tax units so that the resulting tax unit and individual age gradients are much steeper than household unit gradients. For example, at a household unit in the United Kingdom the ratio of median stock wealth of the sixty–sixty-nine age band is 6.4 times that of the twenty–twenty-nine age band. The comparable U.K. number at the tax unit or individual unit level is about 10.6. These ratios are sufficiently different to raise serious questions about the sensitivity of tests of the life-cycle model to the widespread use of household unit analysis. However, no matter which U.K. unit of analysis is used, the stock age gradients are always much less than the household unit in the United States where the comparable ratio of these two age groups is 17. The U.S. number itself would be much higher at the tax or individual unit level. Thus, we conclude

24. Due to the data collection process in PSID, it is not possible to carry out this exercise on the U.S. data.

that while household composition is an extremely important issue, the biases it creates do not substantively affect our conclusion that age gradients of housing equity are steeper in the United Kingdom, while age gradients of stocks are steeper in the United States.

5.6.3   Other Potential Explanations

This combination of differences in ownership and the gradient of stock versus housing equity between the United Kingdom and United States gives support to our proposed model. However, it may well be that there are many other explanations of the same phenomena that could perform equally well. We now turn to these. The first and most obvious potential candidate for these differences between the United Kingdom and the United States is the tax differentials, that is, the possibility that the preferential treatment of mortgage debt in the United States could drive all the observed differences in net housing wealth. It is certainly true that tax differences can explain why homeowners in the United States maintain a relatively large mortgage debt. However, such a difference in tax advantages will also make ownership more attractive over renting, thus making it difficult to explain the high demand for home ownership in the United Kingdom, relative to the United States, among young households.

A second possibility is that rental market inefficiencies alone could drive the observed differences. In this case, rental market inefficiencies could explain the lower use of the rental sector among younger households in the United Kingdom. However, such an explanation taken on its own cannot explain why, once one is an owner, there is a strong demand in the United Kingdom for one to pay down the mortgage and to save heavily in housing equity.

A third potential explanation is that the right-to-buy policy is in line with the predictions of our model because it makes home ownership more attractive for lower- to middle-income groups in the United Kingdom. These are certainly people who can be expected to want to insure against house price risk. However, they will typically not be the young. The right-to-buy is available to existing public sector renters; consequently, it was most important in getting middle-aged public sector renters to move into home ownership in the mid-1980s when the policy was enacted.

Finally, we consider the possibility that differences are driven solely by differences in the fixed costs or transactions costs associated with stock ownership. Extensive privatization and demutualization in the United Kingdom over this period created many middle-income stock owning households who typically held very small values of one or two privatized stocks. This could explain the relatively low share of wealth held in stock in the United Kingdom, but again it cannot explain the high fraction of wealth held in housing equity and why this is particularly the case among the young.

Of course, there is always the possibility that previously discussed factors could be combining to yield the observed international differences in age gradients across the dimensions we have identified in our analysis. The full evaluation of this possibility and the corresponding inferences about the role of risk in housing decisions, in comparison to the role of tax incentives or the failure of the rental market, for example, is left as an important topic for future research in understanding U.S.-U.K. differences in household wealth portfolios.

5.7 Conclusions

In this paper we have attempted to address an interesting housing equity puzzle. Why do younger households in the United Kingdom accumulate so much of their wealth in housing equity rather than diversifying in stock as is true for their U.S. counterparts? In trying to address this puzzle we have built up a detailed picture of housing choices and wealth accumulation in both countries. Using available microdata sources, we have documented how this has evolved for different age groups, for different demographic groups, and for different education groups in both countries. We have shown that young adults in the United Kingdom leave their parental home later than in the United States, and when they do leave they are much more likely to become a homeowner rather than use the rental market. Once a homeowner they are much more likely to accumulate wealth in housing equity rather than in other investment instruments.

Why so? Is it just the differential tax treatment of mortgages or the different institutional structures of the housing and stock markets in the two countries? We argue that although these differences are real and can go some way to explaining the observed facts, something more is needed. The higher volatility of house prices in the United Kingdom was the clue. We derived a modeling framework that explains the higher volatility and uses this to explain the different gradients in housing equity and stock holdings across the countries. Importantly, this model separates three dimensions of housing wealth outcomes—the demand for housing services, the owner occupation decision, and the housing equity decision.

The inefficient rental market places many more U.K. households in the owner-occupier sector at an earlier age than in the United States. The higher volatility of house prices in the United Kingdom adds to this incentive because, for those expecting to move up the house-size ladder, housing equity is an efficient insurance vehicle for house price uncertainty. The only way to invest in housing equity is to become an owner. Once an owner, this insurance mechanism increases the incentive to hold a higher proportion of wealth in housing equity rather than in some other risky asset. Where house prices are less volatile, as in the United States, this incentive is much reduced. Consequently, as households age and wish to accumulate wealth, they will do this more through housing equity in the United Kingdom than in the United States. We predict a higher gradient in the accumulation of stock in the United States and conversely a high gradient in the accumulation of housing equity in the United Kingdom, precisely the "puzzle" we see in the data and a fact that alternative explanations have difficulty predicting.

Appendix

Table 5A.1   Comparisons of PSID and BHPS Asset Categories

PSID	BHPS
1. Other Real Estate—second home, land, rental real estate, money owed in land contract	1. Value of second home
2. Net Vehicle Equity—wheels, cars, trucks, motor home, trailers, boats	2. Net value of car(s)
3. Net Equity in farm or business	3. Not available
4. Stocks—corporate, mutual funds, investments trusts, stocks in IRAs	4. "Investments": stocks, shares, mutual funds and investment trusts, bonds
5. Checking, savings accounts, funds in IRAs, money market funds, treasury bills, CDs	5. Savings in accounts at bank, building society, including TESSAs
6. Other Savings—bonds, life insurance, valuables, trust or estate rights	6. Not available
7. Other Debts—credit card, student loans, loans from relatives, medical or legal bills	7. Other loans outstanding: credit card, bank loan, hire purchase, store card, credit union, etc.
8. Net Home Equity (home value—all mortgages)	8a. Value of residence 8b. Outstanding mortgage on all property

Net Financial Assets:

$4 + 5 + 6 - 7$	$4 + 5 - 7$

Net Worth:

$1 + 2 + 3 + 8 +$ Net Financial Assets	$1 + 2 + 8 +$ Net Financial Assets

Questionnaire Methods:

Unfolding brackets	1: banded 2, 8a, 8b: value requested 4, 5, 7: value requested, then unfolding brackets

References

Banks, J. W., and R. W. Blundell. 1994. Taxation and savings incentives in the UK. In *Household saving and public policy,* ed. James M. Poterba, 57–80. Chicago: University of Chicago Press.

Banks, J. W., R. W. Blundell, and A. Brugiavini. 2001. Risk pooling, precautionary saving and consumption growth. *Review of Economic Studies* 68 (4): 757–79.

Banks, J. W., R. W. Blundell, and J. Smith. 2000. Wealth inequality in the United States and Great Britain. Working Paper no. 2000/20. Institute for Fiscal Studies.

Bond, S., L. Chennels, and M. Devereux. 1995. Company dividends and taxes in the UK. *Fiscal Studies* 16 (3): 1–18.

Chiuri, M. C., and T. Jappelli. 2000. Financial markets imperfections and home-ownership: An international comparison. Working Paper no. 44. CSEF, University of Salerno.

Di Salvo, P., and J. Ermisch. 1997. Analysis of the dynamics of housing tenure choice in Britain. *Journal of Urban Economics* 42:1–17.

Ermisch, J. 1999. Prices, parents, and young people's household formation. *Journal of Urban Economics* 45:47–71.

Juster, T., J. Lupton, F. Stafford, and J. P. Smith. 2001. Savings and wealth: Then and now. University of Michigan and RAND. Unpublished Manuscript, June.

Ortalo-Magne, F., and S. Rady. 1998. Housing market fluctuations in a life-cycle economy. Discussion Paper no. 296. London: Financial Markets Group, London School of Economics.

Comment   John B. Shoven

This is a tremendously valuable paper with lots of interesting facts and an innovative model to explain them. The paper compares the portfolio holdings of British and American households. They find a significant number of noteworthy differences: (1) British households have greater home equity in both absolute and relative terms in their portfolios, (2) wealth is more concentrated in the United States, (3) American households hold more financial assets in their portfolios, particularly those higher up in the wealth distribution, (4) direct participation in equity markets is greater in the United States than in Britain, but British participation increased in the 1980s, (5) homeownership increased in the United Kingdom in the 1980s, particularly among the middle aged and relatively uneducated, (6) homeownership is much higher among young adults in the United Kingdom than in the United States, (7) housing prices are higher and have been much more volatile in the United Kingdom, (8) down payment requirements for homes are much lower in the United Kingdom, (9) mortgage interest is not tax deductible in the United Kingdom as it is in the United States, and (10) U.S. and U.K. equity markets performed similarly between 1979 and 1999. That is quite a list of facts, and Banks, Blundell, and Smith deserve credit for highlighting them and developing a model that can explain many of them.

The facts that the authors concentrate on are that young people in the

John B. Shoven is Charles R. Schwab Professor of Economics at Stanford University, and a research associate of the National Bureau of Economic Research.

United Kingdom are much more likely to own a house, they accumulate housing equity more rapidly, and they are much less likely to participate in equity markets. The authors relate these facts to others, particularly the lower down payment requirements and the more volatile housing prices in the United Kingdom. In their model, young people desire to trade up in housing as they age and as their families get larger. With volatile housing prices, a way to partially insure against price changes in the larger house you desire in the future is to own a smaller house in the same market. The assumption is that house prices are much more closely correlated with other houses in the same market than they are with equity returns. In such a situation, saving for your next house by investing in equities is far riskier than saving by accumulating equity in your own home. Once you purchase a home, paying down the mortgage is advantageous in the United Kingdom because of the lack of mortgage interest deductibility. In the United States, with less volatile housing prices, with a better rental market, and with mortgage interest deductibility, the pattern of homeownership is quite different. I found the Banks, Blundell, and Smith model quite ingenious in that (1) it makes sense, and (2) it implies that riskier house prices actually stimulate the demand for owner occupation.

Banks, Blundell, and Smith have some explanations for why house prices are more volatile in the United Kingdom (e.g., lower supply elasticity due to higher population density), but they don't explain why down payment requirements on homes are lower in the United Kingdom. One would think that lending institutions would require higher down payments in more volatile markets. So, one question that they left unanswered was whether the higher downpayment requirements in the United States were the result of some form of market failure.

A bigger problem that I have with the paper is that it is difficult to put the portfolio differences between the United States and the United Kingdom into perspective when the paper only includes information on the two countries being examined. It isn't surprising that portfolio behavior is different in the United Kingdom and the United States; the more interesting question is whether these differences are unusually large. For instance, how do the observed differences compare with California versus Idaho, the United Kingdom versus Sweden, or the United States versus Canada? I am still wondering whether the United States and the United Kingdom are more similar than most countries or regions, or more different.

Another matter worthy of further study is the extent to which private portfolio differences reflect different government policies. The two countries differ in whether they offer public health insurance, in the cost of higher education, and in the public and private retirement systems. Private saving and portfolios presumably reflect the different government and institutional policies in the two countries. Are the tastes and preferences of Americans and the British similar, with their behavior differences simply reflecting the different institutional environments in which they live? I couldn't answer this question from reading the paper.

Despite my desire for even more analysis and information, I think that this paper adds a lot to the literature. It identifies some of the significant factors accounting for the portfolio differences between U.S. and U.K. households. In fact, it is so successful that I hope that these or other researchers will ask these same questions for additional countries and regions of the world. Then we will learn whether the United Kingdom and the United States are really that (relatively) different.

6

Mortality, Income, and Income Inequality over Time in Britain and the United States

Angus Deaton and Christina Paxson

6.1 Introduction

This paper is concerned with the time-series patterns of mortality, income, and income inequality in the United States and in Britain. One starting point is Deaton and Paxson (2001), in which we used pooled time-series and cross-sectional data from the United States to estimate a strong protective effect of income across birth cohorts that closely matched estimates from individual-level data from the National Longitudinal Mortality Study. We found no evidence for the proposition that year and age-specific income inequality is a health hazard; indeed, our regressions found *protective* effects of higher inequality, essentially because for adults aged thirty-five and over in the United States, mortality declined more rapidly during the period of rapid increase in income inequality in the 1980s than it did in the 1970s, before income inequality began to increase.

In this paper, we extend our analysis to British data, and to a comparative examination of the British and American mortality experience, over time and across age groups. The comparison between the two countries is interesting in part because of the different systems of health care, one

Angus Deaton is the Dwight D. Eisenhower Professor of International Affairs and professor of economics and international affairs at the Woodrow Wilson School of Public and International Affairs and the economics department at Princeton University, and a research associate of the National Bureau of Economic Research. Christina Paxson is professor of economics and public affairs and director of the Center for Health and Wellbeing at Princeton University, and a research associate of the National Bureau of Economic Research.

We are grateful to the National Institute on Aging for its support through the NBER, and to the John D. and Catherine T. MacArthur Foundation for support for its network on inequality and poverty in broader perspectives. We thank Thu Vu for research assistance and Sir George Alleyne, James Banks, Anne Case, David Cutler, Victor Fuchs, Joe Newhouse, and Jim Smith for comments and suggestions.

country with universal, albeit often rationed, coverage and the other with largely private provision until Medicare at age sixty-five. Comparative analysis is also useful because there are both similarities and differences in patterns of income in the two countries. Although changes in income inequality are similar in Britain and the United States, patterns of income growth are not. According to purchasing power parity (PPP) estimates, incomes are higher in the United States than in Britain, but in recent years real incomes have been growing more rapidly in Britain. Both countries experienced historically large increases in income inequality in the 1980s.

Section 6.2 presents an examination of the patterns of income, income inequality, and mortality in the two countries over the last half century. Section 6.3 is concerned with an age-specific and time-series analysis of mortality and income in Britain and with the comparison of the results with those from the United States.

6.2   Patterns of Mortality in Britain and the United States since 1950

We begin our discussion with an examination of changes in mortality in the United States and in Britain over the period 1950 to 2000, particularly in relation to changes in income and income inequality. In this section, we rely entirely on graphical analysis. Figure 6.1 shows the data on income and income inequality. The top panels show measures of real income in the two countries, and the bottom panels show measures of income inequality. The two panels on the left are for the United Kingdom, and the two panels on the right are for the United States. The top left panel shows two indicators of real income. The lower curve shows real personal disposable income in pounds per capita at 1999 prices; this series is taken from the national income and product accounts. The upper curve, available for a shorter time period, and calculated from survey data, shows median *household* disposable income. Apart from the different methodologies and the fact that households typically contain more than one person, the two series show similar business cycle and trend behavior over the period when both are available.

Data on income inequality are more controversial than data on income levels. There are many different estimates of the Gini coefficient of income inequality in the United Kingdom, differing by concept and by source. The earlier Gini coefficient shown in the bottom left panel, Gini (a), comes from Deininger and Squire (1996). This series is identical to that reported in Goodman and Webb (1994) and Gottschalk and Smeeding (2000), and is one of the several series reported in Brandolini (1998) and Atkinson and Brandolini (2001). We also show a more recent series, Gini (b). (A range of Gini coefficients for the United Kingdom is given by Brandolini (1998). Although the series differ among themselves and with the Gini coefficients shown in figure 6.1, the pattern we are about to describe is consistent with

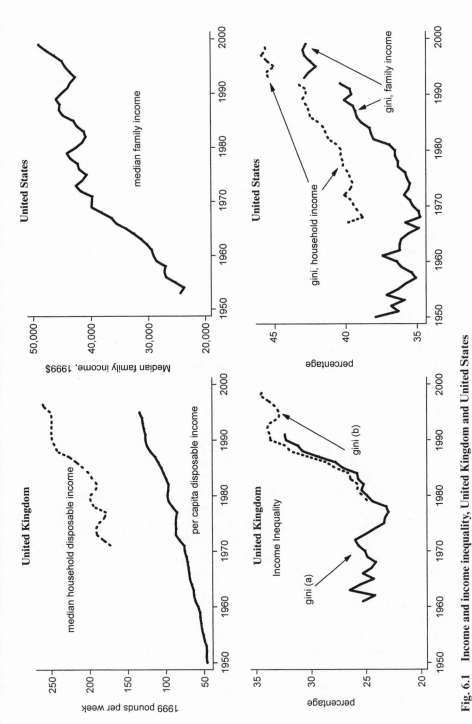

Fig. 6.1 Income and income inequality, United Kingdom and United States

Sources: U.K. National Statistics website (http://www.statistics.gov.uk/); Institute for Fiscal Studies, London (http://www.ifs.org.uk/election/ebn4.pdf)—supplied to us by James Banks.

the full range of data.) Income inequality in Britain changed relatively little until the early 1970s, though there is some evidence of a narrowing of inequalities during the second World War. During the 1970s, income inequality seems to have declined, after which, from about 1978, there was a rapid increase. By about 1985, the decline of the early 1970s had been undone, and the rate of growth of income inequality accelerated. Depending on the time frame, it is therefore possible to date the beginning of the increase from either the late 1970s or the mid-1980s. By 1990, the increase appears to have stopped, and income inequality did not increase during the 1990s, remaining at the high level established by 1990.

Given the lack of movement in income inequality in Britain until the 1970s, we can safely suppose that median incomes tracked mean incomes before the early 1970s. We can therefore conclude from the top left panel that median real income growth was somewhat faster after the early 1970s than before it. As we shall see, this is in sharp contrast to what happened in the United States, and this lack of any slowdown in British income growth will play an important role in our interpretation of the mortality data.

The right-hand panels of figure 6.1 show the income and income inequality data for the United States. On the top panel we present the U.S. Census Bureau's estimate of real *median* family income, in 1999 dollars. The Census Bureau also publishes official estimates of the Gini coefficient based on (partly unpublished) survey data from the Current Population Survey (CPS). These numbers, for both families and households (which can contain unrelated individuals), are shown in the lower left-hand panel. Both series have discontinuities between 1992 and 1993. The Census Bureau changed its questionnaires between those years, allowing a higher top value of income to be reported, and is unable to estimate how much of the change between 1992 and 1993 is real (see Jones and Weinberg 2000).

The experience of income inequality in the United States is remarkably similar to that in the United Kingdom. Until the mid-1970s, there is little perceptible trend, though perhaps some narrowing. After 1972, income inequality increases, with the rate of increase accelerating in the mid-1980s. If we were to extrapolate across the breaks in the series, the increase goes on into the 1990s. However, it is also possible that the two detached arms should be lowered onto the earlier series, in which case, as in Britain, there is little or no increase in income inequality in the 1990s. In any case, there is no increase except across the disputed years 1992 and 1993.

Median incomes behave as the mirror image of income inequality. Prior to 1972, there was steady growth in real family incomes, and inequality, though varying from year to year, showed no trend. After 1972, the situation was reversed, with little growth in real median family incomes and a rapid growth in income inequality. In the 1990s, and especially if we discount the apparent increase in income inequality, the earlier pattern appears to have resumed, with real growth in incomes and stable income inequality, albeit at a higher level than in the 1950s and 1960s.

The different patterns of income growth in the two countries and the similar patterns of income inequality provide a useful background within which to examine how long-term patterns of income and inequality growth have conditioned changes in mortality.

Figure 6.2 turns to the mortality data, beginning with infant mortality rates. Mortality data for England and Wales are available from 1851 to 1998.

Although infant mortality is not our main concern here, it is a useful

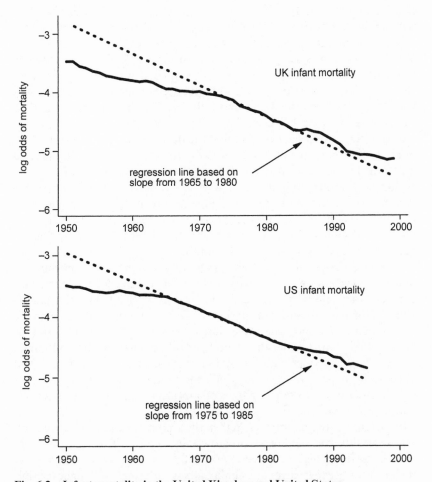

Fig. 6.2   Infant mortality in the United Kingdom and United States

Sources: U.K. Government Actuaries Department (http://www.gad.gov.uk/b2/b2div6 .htm#life); U.K. National Statistics website (http://www.statistics.gov.uk/); Berkeley Mortality Database (http://www.demog.berkeley.edu/wilmoth/mortality/).

starting point because of its place in the previous literature; because it is likely to respond more rapidly than adult mortality to changes in the environment, including any effects of income and income inequality; and because it will illustrate several of the themes that will recur in the discussion of mortality among adults and the elderly. In his 1996 book, *Unhealthy Societies,* Richard Wilkinson implicates the rise of income inequality in Britain in infant mortality, arguing that mortality rates fell less rapidly after 1985 than would have been the case had income inequality remained constant. Figure 5.10 of Wilkinson (1996, 97) plots a time series of mortality, not only of infants, but also of children and young adults, and shows that the sum of age-adjusted mortality rates fell less rapidly after 1985 than it did in the decade from 1975 to 1985. A good deal of the effect comes from changes in infant mortality, and the top panel of figure 6.2 replicates Wilkinson's analysis using the log odds of mortality. We fit a regression line to the data from 1975 to 1985 and plot the predicted values together with the full series from 1950 to 1999. After 1985, when income inequality was increasing in earnest, the infant mortality rate was indeed above the 1975 to 1985 trend. Note, however, that 1975 to 1985 saw the most rapid decrease in the postwar period and that the decline was also relatively slow, not only after 1985, but also prior to 1975, when income inequality showed no upward trend. Note also that there has been no resumption of the more rapid downward trend in the years after 1990 when inequality stopped increasing, indeed rather the reverse. So the case against income inequality is less than overwhelming, although it is true that the ten-year trend in infant mortality decline in Britain was broken around 1985 at the time that income inequality began to rise most rapidly.

A similar analysis for the United States is shown in the bottom panel of figure 6.2. The graphs for the two countries show marked similarities, with two periods of relatively slow decline bracketing a period of more rapid decline. In the United States, the period of rapid decline is earlier than in the United Kingdom and lasts rather longer; it starts about 1965 and ends around 1980. Once again, the second period of slower decline (although not the first) coincides with the period of rapid inequality increase. And once again, there is no inequality episode to match the earlier period of slow decline, nor are there any signs of a return to more rapid progress after inequality stopped growing.

If we take the two countries together, there is no obvious link between infant mortality and the long-term growth in incomes. The pre- and post-1972 histories of real income are quite different in the two countries, yet their mortality experiences are similar, albeit with some differences in timing. Furthermore, the rapid mortality decline in the United States from 1965 to 1980 continued unabated, notwithstanding the halt in the growth of real median family income after 1972. Instead, the most obvious feature of the two graphs is their similarity, especially if the British data are matched against lags of the American data. Indeed, if the British series is regressed on the contemporaneous and four lagged values of the American series, only the fourth lag is significantly different from zero, and it attracts a coefficient of 0.98. A regression of British infant mortality on the fourth lag of American mortality, with a coefficient of unity, cannot be rejected against the alternative with current American mortality and all four lags. Such evidence is suggestive, not of any simple link between mortality, income, and income inequality, but rather of the importance of technological change, with US technological innovations reaching Britain with about a four year lag.

Figure 6.3 shows plots of the log odds of mortality for England and Wales by five-year age groups from twenty–twenty-four to sixty-five–sixty-nine. Females are shown on the left and males on the right, both drawn on the same scale. The top panels are for the younger groups, from twenty to twenty-four through to forty to forty-four, and the bottom panels for the age groups from forty-five to forty-nine through to sixty-five to sixty-nine. The mortality experience among those aged seventy and above is not shown here (but see figure 6.6); its behavior over time is similar to the mortality rates of those aged sixty-five to sixty-nine. It is important to look at younger and older groups separately, and also at males and females separately, because mortality of the four groups behaves quite differently. This differentiation by age is also an important reason for differentiating income and income inequality by age, which is one of the main motivations for our work on cohorts in section 6.3.

Men always have higher mortality rates than women in the same age group. This is particularly true for young men under thirty. However, the most important difference between the younger and older groups, between the top and bottom panels, is in the behavior of their mortality rates over time. The younger groups, like infants in figure 6.2, have more rapid mortality decline in the early years, before 1970 and much less rapid mortality declines—and in some cases (young men and the youngest women) mortality even *increases*—in the later years. The story is quite different for age groups over forty. There is a steady decline in mortality throughout the period, and the trend *accelerates* after the early 1970s. The acceleration in mortality decline is more pronounced for older and middle-aged men than for women and more rapid among middle-aged than older women. The transition from the "young" pattern of deceleration to the "older" pattern of acceleration takes place gradually over age groups. In males aged from thirty-five to forty-four, for example, we see evidence of both patterns, with the acceleration setting in and then being reversed at the end of the period.

Whatever is the cause of these patterns, income inequality is an unlikely candidate, unless there is some ex ante reason to suppose that the young are more affected than the middle-aged and the elderly. Otherwise, the pattern of mortality and income inequality is wrong for those over forty, just

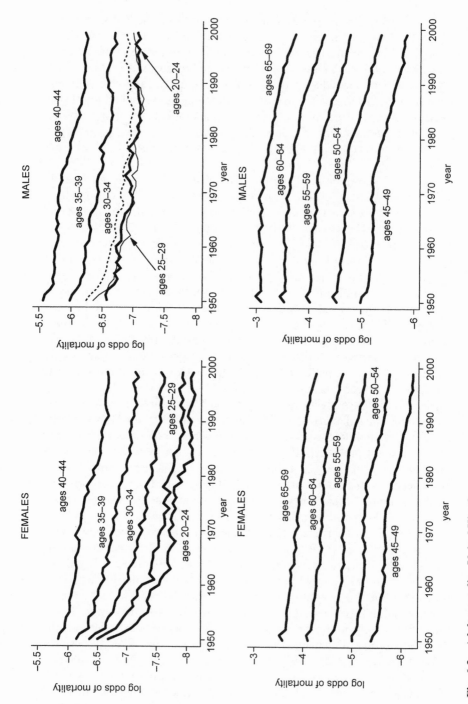

Fig. 6.3   Adult mortality, United Kingdom

as it is right for the younger groups and for the infant mortality rate. Deaths from AIDS account for almost all of the increase in mortality rates among young men and of the elimination of mortality decline among the youngest groups of women. It is unclear that the AIDS epidemic would have been very different had there been no increase in income inequality.

Figure 6.4 shows mortality rates by age for men and women in the United States using the same format as in figure 6.3. As was the case with the infant mortality rates, there are marked similarities between the British and American experiences, though once again there are important differences in timing. The elimination of the decline in mortality rates among younger age groups and its subsequent reversal are more pronounced in the American data. Rising mortality rates among the youngest groups are more common and are apparent even in the forty–forty-four age group of men. In the older groups, we see the same acceleration in mortality decline as in Britain. As before, it is more pronounced among men than among women and more apparent for middle-aged women than for those aged over sixty.

Because the pattern of income inequality in the United States is so similar to that in Britain, income inequality is no more likely a cause of the American patterns than it is of the British ones. The American data also help us cast a good deal of doubt on the hypothesis that income is the main driving force behind mortality decline. The productivity slowdown in the United States, and its associated decline in the rate of growth of real median incomes, is almost coincident with the *acceleration* in mortality decline among the middle-aged and elderly. Although it is undoubtedly possible to muddy the waters by thinking about income operating at a lag, perhaps of many years, any simple story is precluded by the fact that the histories of income growth and mortality decline both break into two prolonged and sharply different periods and that the associations over these two periods are precisely the wrong way round.

If the mortality patterns are not driven by income and income inequality, what are their causes? There are many competing explanations. The differences between men and women may have something to do with their different histories of smoking, with women taking up the habit later than men, and with the long lags between smoking and its health consequences in heart disease and lung cancer. There was a worldwide decrease in coronary heart disease from the early 1970s, which one line of thought takes as evidence for the (co-)involvement of an infectious agent (*chlamydia pneumoniae*). This hypothesis is controversial, with some evidence indicating it is not correct (Wald et al. 2000; Danesh et al. 2000). The decline may instead have been due to major technical improvements in the treatment of heart disease, particularly the spread of angioplasty and of coronary bypass grafts as well as the increased use of drugs including aspirin and clotbusters.

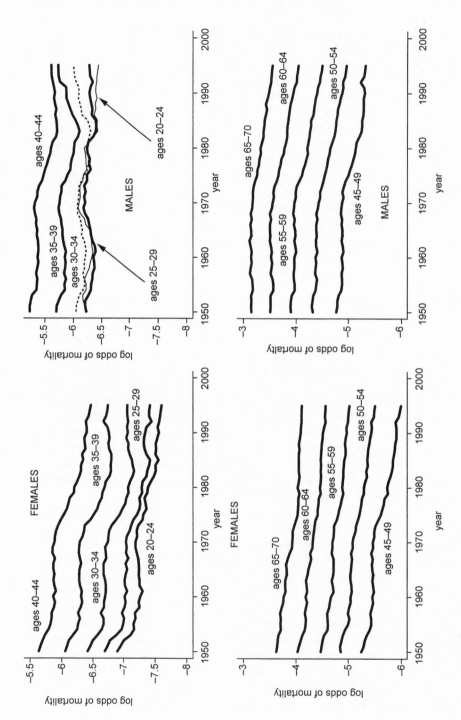

Fig. 6.4 Adult mortality, United States

The role of medical technology in mortality decline is clarified by direct comparison of the British and American experiences. These are provided in figure 6.5 for infant mortality and for middle-aged adults and in figure 6.6 for the elderly. As always, we disaggregate by sex and here show selected five-year age groups. With the exception of 1950 and 1951 for infant mortality, American mortality rates are higher than British mortality rates up to age sixty-five. For the elderly, mortality rates are higher in the United Kingdom. Aside from their levels, and as was the case for infant mortality, the development of mortality rates over time is similar in the two countries, though once again developments in the United States—particularly the acceleration in mortality decline around 1970 and its more recent slowing—appear to lead the same developments in Britain. This evidence further serves to strengthen the supposition that variations in the rate of decline in these mortality rates is driven, not by income or income inequality, but by technological change, much of which is first seen in the United States and is subsequently transmitted to Britain. For the middle-aged groups, from ages forty-five to sixty and for both men and women, we replicate the result that we found for infant mortality; in a regression of British on contemporaneous and four lags of American mortality rates, the fourth lag has a coefficient close to unity, while the contemporaneous and earlier lags are insignificantly different from zero.

Although it appears to benefit from technical progress first, the United States has higher levels of mortality than Britain. One obvious explanation is the more or less universal access to health care in Britain in contrast to the United States, a hypothesis that might seem to be further supported by the cross-over after age sixty-five, at which point most Americans are covered by Medicare. According to this story, the elderly in the United States have the best of both worlds, with both good access and superior technology. The superior technology in the United States benefits younger Americans less because of limited access. While there may be some truth in this account, it faces two immediate problems. First, the difference between British and American mortality rates is steadily diminishing with age. Although the cross-over takes place around age sixty-five, the graphs for those aged fifty-five to fifty-nine are closer than those aged forty-five to forty-nine. Similarly, after the crossover has taken place, the gap between elderly Americans and elderly Britons proceeds to increase with age. Although exposure to better technology may plausibly have an effect that cumulates with age, it is hard to see why age should narrow the gap prior to the availability of Medicare. The second problem with the access story is that the differences between British and American mortality rates do not seem to have changed after the introduction of Medicare in the late 1960s. The pattern of relative mortality by age was established prior to the introduction of Medicare.

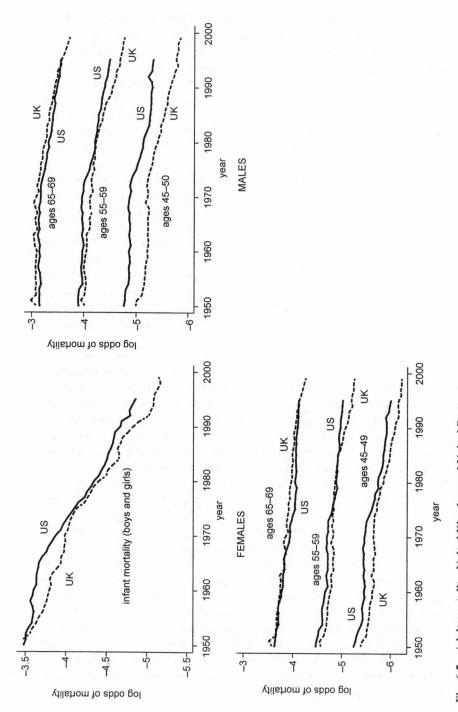

Fig. 6.5 Adult mortality, United Kingdom and United States

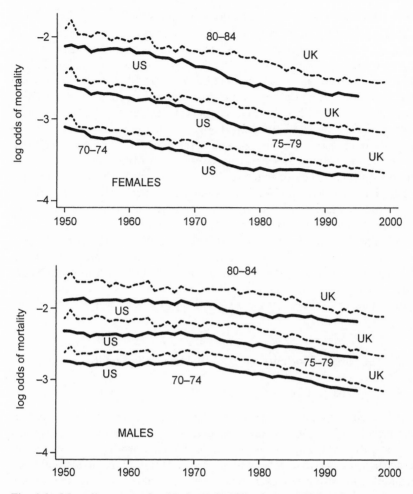

Fig. 6.6   Mortality among the elderly, United Kingdom and United States

A more satisfactory account of relative mortality in the two countries recognizes the benefits of universal access but notes the low levels of health-care financing in Britain, not only relative to the United States, but also relative to other Organization for Economic Cooperation and Development (OECD) countries; see, for example, Gerdtham and Jönsson (2000, table 1). The consequent rationing of health care in Britain is in many cases based on age, with the elderly (with elderly generously defined) frequently denied access to expensive technologies from which they are likely to benefit, kidney dialysis being only the clearest example; see Aaron and Schwartz (1984). As Aaron and Schwartz also make clear, there are great differences in the way that new technologies are introduced in the two countries. In the competitive health care industry in the United States, there is great pressure to adopt new technologies as soon as they are feasible, essentially irrespective of cost. This certainly happened with the technologies that are important for the mortality changes discussed in this paper, the construction of neonatal facilities for low birth weight babies and the adoption of angioplasty and bypass surgery. In Britain, by contrast, with its centralized National Health Service, expensive new technologies cannot be adopted without central government approval, which needs to wait for demonstrated effectiveness and the release of funding. Even then, access to the technologies is restricted, especially by age. These differences in institutional structure generate about a four-year lag between the introduction of expensive new technologies in the United States and in Britain, and this provides us with the opportunity to assess the effects of these technological changes on mortality.

We should note that our analysis, although helping to explain the patterns in the data, is silent on the relative merits of the two systems. Although the American system generates lower mortality rates at higher ages, the increases in life expectancy will sometimes be small and the cost very great. The British system spends relatively little and has higher life expectancy at birth.

6.3   Age Specific Mortality, Incomes, and Income Inequality

6.3.1   Summary of Previous Work

We begin with a brief summary of the theory that motivated our earlier empirical work in Deaton and Paxson (2001). In that paper, we examined the extent to which income is protective against mortality and whether income inequality is associated with higher mortality. Our starting point was a simple model in which each person's health status (h) is assumed to be a function of his or her income (y) *relative* to the average income of those in the person's reference group (z). Assuming a linear relationship between health and (the logarithm of) income, the expected value of health conditional on y and z is

$$(1) \qquad E(h \mid y, z) = \alpha + \beta(y - z).$$

The reference group could be defined by geography or other characteristics. If z is a fixed number for all individuals, then (1) collapses to a model in which health is determined solely by own-income.

Equation (1) has several implications for the relationship between health, income, and income inequality. First, given that reference groups are not observable, (1) is not estimable. Instead, we must work with the expectation of health conditional on own-income. Assuming that y and z are jointly normal, this conditional expectation can be expressed as

(2) $$E(h \mid y) = \alpha + \frac{\beta\sigma_\varepsilon^2}{\sigma_\varepsilon^2 + \sigma_z^2}(y - \mu) = \alpha + \beta^*(y - \mu),$$

where the marginal distribution of z is assumed to be $N(\mu, \sigma_z^2)$, and the distribution of y conditional on z is $N(z, \sigma_\varepsilon^2)$ so that σ_ε^2 and σ_z^2 are measures of within–reference group and between–reference group inequality.

Two main conclusions are drawn from equation (2). First, if the reference group model is correct, estimates of β^* will differ from β, with the extent of the bias a function of the relative sizes of the within- and between-group variances. If within–reference group inequality is small, then individual income is a poor measure of relative income, and the estimated income gradient in health will be small. If, on the other hand, within–reference group inequality is large relative to between–reference group inequality—which might be the case if reference groups are defined by large geographical areas, entire birth cohorts, or by entire populations of countries—then β^* will be close to β.

The second conclusion is that models in which health is determined by relative income do *not* necessarily imply that inequality will be harmful to health. In equation (2), inequality affects the slope of the gradient, but does not appear as a separate determinant of health outcomes. This result is driven by the assumption that individuals compare themselves to the *mean* income level in the reference group. If, instead, what matters is income relative to income at the top of the distribution within the reference group, a mean-preserving spread in income will harm the health of all those with incomes below the top of the distribution. Although this assumption delivers the result that inequality is harmful to health, other assumptions and outcomes are possible. For example, if rank within the reference group is what matters for health, then changes in inequality will not increase or reduce health (given income). Likewise, if what matters is income relative to the lowest income within the reference group, then mean-preserving spreads in income will improve the health of all but the poorest.

In our American and British work, we estimate models that relate the mortality experiences of birth cohorts to income and income inequality with the cohort. Aggregation within cohorts can introduce a relationship between mortality and inequality even if there is no relationship at the individual level. By Jensen's inequality, if health is increasing but concave in income (or, conversely, if the relationship between the probability of mortality and income is decreasing but convex), then a mean-preserving spread in within-cohort income will reduce average health. Aggregation to the cohort level also has implications for the slope of the gradient. If reference groups lie "within" cohorts—so that what matters for health is own-income relative to income of some group of individuals born in the same year—then aggregation will annihilate the relationship between health and income. On the other hand, if reference groups cut across cohorts, then estimation using the aggregated data will provide information on the gradient, although the slope of the gradient may be attenuated as in (2). These points are discussed in more detail in Deaton and Paxson (2001).

6.3.2 Data

In the following section we extend our earlier work on mortality, income, and income inequality from the United States to Britain, or more precisely to England and Wales. (Britain is England and Wales plus Scotland; the United Kingdom is Britain plus Northern Ireland.) Income measures are drawn from the 1971 to 1998 rounds of the British *Family Expenditure Survey* (FES). The FES has information on households in England, Wales, Scotland, and Northern Ireland. We excluded households from Scotland and Northern Ireland so as to match the income to the mortality data.

As in the American work, we combine the mortality and income data together at the level of the birth cohort. We restrict our analysis to groups of individuals aged twenty-five to eighty-five. There are approximately 11,000 observations on individuals (both men and women) in this age range in any single survey year of the FES, and there are, on average, eighty-five observations within each cohort-age-gender cell. The FES is used to compute averages (or medians, variances, etc.) of income and education variables for each cohort-age-gender cell. These data are then merged with the mortality data by cohort, age, and gender. When the two data sources are combined, we are left with individuals born from 1886 (aged eighty-five in 1971) to 1973 (aged twenty-five in 1998). For a small number of birth cohorts at some advanced ages, there are no individuals in the FES. Our final data set upon merging consists of 1,680 cohort-age cells for men and 1,706 cohort-age cells for women.

The income measure we use is normal gross weekly household income. We adjust for household size by dividing income by the number of "adult equivalents" in the household, where children under the age of eighteen count as one-half an adult. In most of our analyses we use the average of the logarithm of income per adult equivalent as our measure of the income level. For measures of dispersion we use the Gini coefficient and the variance of the logarithm of income per adult equivalent. The education variables we use require discussion. From 1978, the FES has information on the age at which the individual left full-time schooling. We convert this to years of schooling by assuming that education starts at age five. There were a small number of cases of individuals who reporting finished full-time schooling after the age of twenty-five (with one seventy-two-year-old reporting that full-time schooling did not end until age fifty-two). In these cases we restricted our measure of years of schooling to twenty. Because information on education was not available prior to 1978, our sample period is 1978–1998 when we use information on education.

The FES also contains some information on tobacco use, which is an important determinant of health. The FES does not directly ask respondents if they currently smoke nor does it collect any information on smoking history. However, it does collect individual-level data on tobacco purchases during the reference period. We construct an indicator for smoking that is set to one if the individual purchased any tobacco. This smoking measure is far from perfect. Individuals may purchase tobacco for others or have it purchased for them. In addition, there is evidence that tobacco purchases in the FES are underreported (Goodman and Webb 1999). Finally, previous as well as current tobacco use may affect mortality. These factors are likely to attenuate our estimates of the relationship between tobacco and mortality. Nevertheless, when looking at the influence of income on mortality, it is useful to be able to control for tobacco use, albeit imperfectly.

In many of the results that follow, we contrast British results with results from the United States, drawn from Deaton and Paxson (2001). The U.S. data are constructed in the same way as the British data. The mortality data are from the Berkeley mortality data base, and the income information is calculated from the 1976–1996 waves of the March CPS. The variable definitions are similar, with a few small exceptions. One is that income is annual before–tax household income, rather than normal gross weekly household income. Another is that schooling is based on questions about the grade level attained rather than the age at which schooling was completed. Further details on the data are in Deaton and Paxson (2001).

6.3.3   An Empirical Formulation

There are several possible ways of using age and year data to examine the effects of income and income inequality on mortality. An important requirement for a suitable empirical model is that age and time trends be flexibly incorporated so that their effects are not inappropriately projected onto the income variables. Beyond age twenty or so, mortality increases monotonically with age. Income inequality also increases with age, and income has the characteristic life-cycle pattern of increase and decline. If age-specific mortality is not flexibly modeled, there is a danger that we ascribe some of the effects of age to income or income inequality. Similar arguments apply to time trends. Mortality has a background underlying downward trend, and it makes little sense to spuriously match this to the trends in income and income inequality.

To avoid these difficulties, we start from the specification

$$(3) \qquad \ln o_{at} = \beta_0 + \beta_1 t + \alpha_a + \gamma_{at} + \varepsilon_{at},$$

where $\ln o_{at}$ is the log odds of mortality for the group aged a and observed in year t. β_0 and β_1 are parameters; t is a time trend; α_a is an unrestricted set of age dummies, one for each year of age; and ε_{at} is a residual. The term γ_{at} needs to be further specified in order to give the model content. One possibility would be a cohort model in which $\gamma_{at} = \theta_{t-a}$ and thus varies only by year of birth; versions of this model were explored in Deaton and Paxson

(2001). Alternatively, we can use γ_{at} as a vehicle for the economic variables. For example, one model that we explore is where γ_{at} is a linear function of (for example) mean family income and mean years of education for people aged a in year t, and of income inequality within the age group in that year so that

(4)
$$\gamma_{at} = \gamma_1 \bar{y}_{at} + \gamma_2 \bar{s}_{at} + \gamma_3 gini_{at}.$$

We shall also estimate such models separately for different age groups, which effectively allows the coefficients in equations (3) and (4) to be functions of age. Such a specification is very close to the leading statistical model of mortality in the demographic literature of Lee and Carter (1992). Their model is for the logarithm of the mortality rate itself, rather than the log odds, but the two measures are close when the probability of death is small, and they write

(5)
$$\ln p_{at} = \tilde{\alpha}_a + \tilde{\beta}_a k_t + u_{at},$$

where $\tilde{\alpha}_a$ and $\tilde{\beta}_a$ are unrestricted age coefficients, and k_t is a random walk with (downward) drift so that with innovation v_t

(6)
$$k_t = k_{t-1} + \tilde{\beta}_1 + v_t.$$

In their estimations, the random walk with drift is very close to a time trend so that equation (5) is in practice very close to equation (3) with age-specific coefficients on the time trend and γ_{at} omitted.

Although models such as equations (1) and (5) fit the data well, they have a number of deficiencies for our purposes and, indeed, more generally. Because all age-specific mortality rates are assumed to share the same trend, either a simple linear trend in equation (1) or a random trend in equation (5), these models cannot recognize episodes in which age-specific mortality rates deviate for a substantial period from their long-run trends. In our current data, this is a problem for the younger adult groups whose long-term mortality decline has been interrupted in recent years by mortality related to AIDS (see figures 6.3 and 6.5). As a result, we run some risk of spuriously attributing the spread of an infectious disease to any economic events that happen to coincide with it; again, see the discussion in section 6.2. More generally, equations (3) and (4) allow economic variables to play a role only once unrestricted age effects and time trends have been eliminated. But as Lee and Carter's work (1992) makes clear, these variables by themselves give a good account of the data so that, given our concern not to impute too much to economic variables, the specification may allow them too little information to work with. While recognizing the problem, we currently see no way of dealing with it.

Figure 6.7 shows long-term information on cohort mortality in the United Kingdom and United States and highlights some of the difficulties of modeling the time-series properties of mortality. The graph shows the

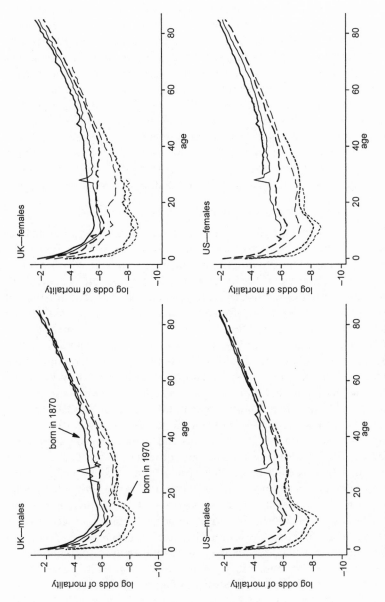

Fig. 6.7   Log odds of mortality by cohort, United Kingdom and United States

log odds of mortality for every twentieth cohort, starting with those born in 1870 and ending with those born in 1970. The U.K. and U.S. patterns share many of the same features. The log odds of mortality decline sharply after infancy, and after age thirty increase roughly linearly with age. Although there were mortality declines at all ages for both sexes over this period, the patterns differ across age groups. The declines were particularly rapid for women of child-bearing age in the early part of the twentieth century. In addition, mortality declines at older ages are more pronounced for women than for men. The mortality experience of both countries shows evidence of the influenza pandemic of 1919 (and, for British males, deaths associated with the first World War). Finally, in both countries there is a marked slowing of mortality decline among young men born in the latter half of the twentieth century. In many of the results that follow, we omit the youngest groups of men (aged twenty-five to thirty-four) so that the slowdown in mortality decline due to HIV/AIDS does not affect the analysis.

6.3.4   Income, Income Inequality, and Mortality

We start by examining the relationship between mortality and the level of income. Table 6.1 contains the first set of regression results using the specification shown in equation (3), in which we assume that γ_{at} is a linear function of the average of the logarithm of income per adult equivalent. The regressions are estimated separately for men and women, for the full sample of twenty-five–eighty-five-year-olds, and for four smaller age ranges. We report only the estimates of the coefficient on income. The first three columns of estimates and t-values are for the United States, with and without the time trend, and in the third column, with an interaction of the time trend with age. This last specification is similar to Lee and Carter's (1992) formulation in that it allows the effects of a common trend to vary across ages. The last three columns repeat these equations for Britain.

When time trends are excluded from the regressions, the estimates are closely comparable for the United States and Britain. For all age groups combined, the logarithm of income per equivalent is protective against mortality, with a coefficient of –0.56 (men) and –0.53 (women) in the United States and –0.64 (men) and –0.77 (women) in the United Kingdom. Apart from the twenty-five–thirty-nine-year-old group of males in the United States, whose mortality rates have been increasing in recent years (again, see figure 6.4) and whose mortality rate is estimated to respond positively to increases in income, the age group estimates are also similar across the two countries. In both cases, income is most strongly protective in middle-age. As we showed in Deaton and Paxson (2001), these protective effects of income are close to those estimated from the individual-level data from the National Longitudinal Mortality Study in the United States. We also argued, based on the model of reference groups, that this correspondence of the two sets of estimates was to be expected if, as seems likely, reference groups cut across cohorts rather than being confined within them.

Table 6.1   Log Odds of Dying as a Function of Income, by Age Range

	United States, 1975–1995			United Kingdom, 1971–1998		
Age Range	No Time Trend (1)	Time Trend (2)	Trend + Trend/Age Interaction (3)	No Time Trend (4)	Time Trend (5)	Trend + Trend/Age Interaction (6)
Males						
All ages	-0.559 (24.14)	-0.281 (8.81)	-0.079 (2.48)	-0.642 (34.74)	0.085 (4.00)	0.072 (3.84)
25–39	0.452 (5.05)	0.168 (1.79)	-0.075 (0.83)	-0.171 (7.64)	-0.048 (1.07)	-0.005 (0.12)
40–54	-0.770 (17.80)	-0.261 (3.85)	-0.229 (4.43)	-0.979 (26.15)	0.030 (0.86)	-0.051 (1.86)
55–69	-0.941 (19.37)	0.107 (5.92)	0.048 (3.08)	-0.914 (19.47)	0.060 (2.66)	-0.009 (0.37)
70–85	-0.430 (19.02)	0.035 (1.67)	0.057 (4.18)	-0.609 (22.73)	0.002 (0.12)	0.019 (1.39)
Females						
All ages	-0.528 (27.44)	-0.125 (5.35)	-0.130 (5.49)	-0.774 (44.53)	0.019 (1.01)	0.023 (1.24)
25–39	-0.362 (6.08)	-0.174 (2.65)	-0.197 (2.49)	-0.691 (19.89)	-0.035 (0.71)	-0.032 (0.64)
40–54	-0.850 (23.50)	-0.022 (0.50)	-0.010 (0.22)	-1.039 (27.86)	-0.011 (0.34)	-0.026 (0.77)
55–69	-0.322 (10.79)	0.207 (9.26)	0.117 (7.55)	-0.671 (21.46)	0.117 (3.62)	0.010 (0.33)
70–85	-0.370 (14.61)	0.059 (2.84)	0.036 (1.93)	-0.686 (21.42)	0.033 (1.89)	-0.004 (0.26)

Notes: T-statistics in parentheses. Each regression includes the mean of the logarithm of household income per adult equivalent (mean $\ln(y/ae)$) and a set of age dummies. The regressions are estimated for the full sample and for four different age groups. Each cell in the table reports a coefficient on the mean of log of income per adult equivalent from a single regression.

The inclusion of time trends upsets this conformity of results across countries and data sets. (Similar results are obtained when a complete set of year dummies are included instead of a time trend.) In the United States, when all ages are pooled, the time trend reduces the estimated effect of log income but does not eliminate it. However, including the time trend does change the sign of the income coefficient for the older age groups. Results in Deaton and Paxson (2001) indicate that when a time trend is included but income is instrumented with a set of cohort dummies and with a measure of schooling, the effect of income is similar to that originally estimated with no trend. It is questionable whether the cohort dummies and years of schooling are valid instruments for income in a mortality regression. Schooling, in particular, may have independent effects on health. However, the fact that the use of these instruments yielded sensible results that lined up with those found in microdata (from the National Longitudinal Study) provided some ex post justification for their use.

The results for the United Kingdom with the trend included are quite different from results with no trend included and from the U.S. results. In Britain, the inclusion of a time trend essentially eliminates any estimated role for income, a result which will not be reversed in any of the other specifications we report in the following. Indeed, in most cases (men of all age groups and both men and women aged fifty-five to sixty-nine) higher cohort income appears to be associated with *higher* mortality rates. The addition of the interaction term between the trend and age has some effect on these results—specifically, the positive and significant association between mortality and income for those aged fifty-five to sixty-nine disappears. However, in no case is income estimated to be significantly protective. Finally, using the British data, the instrumentation strategy described previously did not restore the protective effect of income.

Figures 6.8 and 6.9 explore why the results are so different in the two countries. The starting point for these graphs are two matching regressions, one of the log odds of mortality on a set of age dummies and a time trend and another of the logarithm of income per adult equivalent on the same variables. The residuals of these regressions are averaged (by year in figure 6.8 and by birth year in figure 6.9) and then plotted against one another so that we can see how the behavior of the mortality rates matches the behavior of log income, once allowance has been made for age effects and time trends in both. Both figures show plots for males on the left and for females on the right, with Britain on the top and the United States on the bottom. In figure 6.8 the residuals are plotted against time so that the graphs show the average residuals over all cohorts in each year of the log odds of mortality and the logarithm of income. In figure 6.9, the plot is against year of birth so that the averaging is over all years for each cohort.

Figure 6.8 indicates that the year-averaged mortality and income residuals are not negatively related for either country. Regressions of one on the

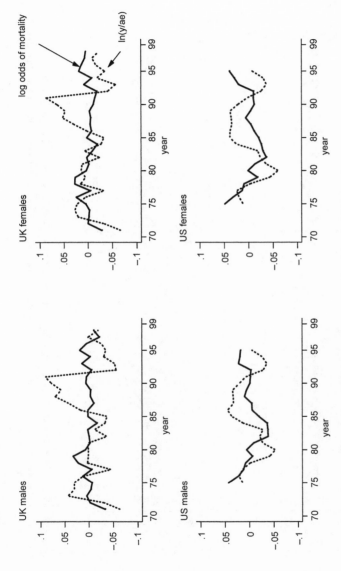

Fig. 6.8   Year-averaged residuals of log odds mortality, United Kingdom and United States

Note: Graphed lines are of residuals, averaged over years, of a regression of the variable on a set of age dummies and a time trend.

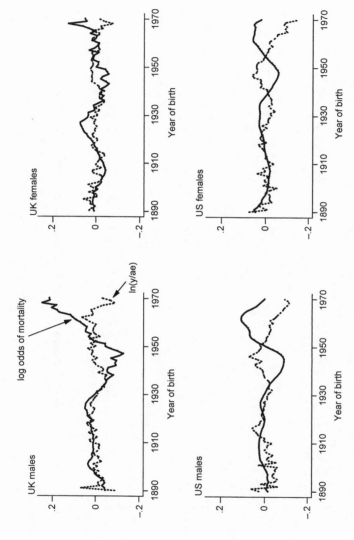

Fig. 6.9 Cohort-averaged residuals of log odds mortality, United Kingdom and United States

Note: Graphed lines are of residuals, averaged over birth years, of a regression of the variable on a set of age dummies and a time trend.

other yield coefficients for income that are small—sometimes positive and sometimes negative—and not significantly different zero for males and females in both countries. The cohort-averaged residuals in figure 6.9 have different patterns. For the United States, there is a negative relationship between the income and mortality residuals. The coefficient on income from a regression is -0.54 ($t = 4.6$) for males and -0.45 ($t = 6.2$) for females. For the U.K. these coefficients are -0.05 ($t = 0.18$) for males and -0.15 ($t = .89$) for females. Note, however, that these results hinge on the experience of cohorts born after 1930. For those born earlier (many of whom were retired by the start of our sample period) there is no apparent relationship between income and mortality in either country.

We do not have an explanation for the differences in results across Britain and the United States. It is especially difficult to piece together a story that reconciles these differences and is also consistent with existing evidence from micro-level data for both countries. For example, one possible explanation of the cohort-level results shown here is that the relationships between income and health in the United States and Britain are genuinely different from each other. The provision of national health care may break the link between health and income in Britain so that income is important in the United States but not in Britain. Although plausible, this explanation is at odds with micro-level evidence from the Whitehall studies (Marmot 1994) that show a strong positive relationship between socioeconomic status and health. The Whitehall results typically use occupation or education rather than income as an indicator of socioeconomic status. However, education and occupation are highly correlated with income, and because we do not control for education or occupation in table 6.1, we would expect income to capture the general effects of socioeconomic status.

Another possible explanation is that our earlier conclusions about the United States were wrong and that income is not important for health in either country. The results in table 6.1 do not provide very strong evidence that income affects mortality in either country, at least when the time trend is included. In Deaton and Paxson (2001), the U.S. results with a trend were consistent with the micro evidence only after applying a set of instruments of questionable validity. And the relationships between income and mortality found in the microdata could be due to the effect of health on income so that individuals in poorer health both earn less and are more likely to die. However, it is difficult to dismiss the micro evidence so easily. For example, Case, Lubotsky, and Paxson (2002) indicate that the income gradient in health begins early in childhood, a time period during which simple stories in which health drives income are not plausible.

It may be more sensible to focus on the relationship between mortality and education rather than income. Education is a better measure of long-run resources than current income, and it may be that it is long-run rather than current incomes that matter for health. Education may also affect how well individuals are able to make use of new medical technologies and information. Our earlier work from the United States indicates that controlling for education eliminates the protective effect of income when using the cohort-aggregated data (although not when using the microdata from the National Longitudinal Mortality Study). Evidence from Deaton and Lubotsky (2003) using U.S. city-level data indicates that the association between income and mortality vanishes once controls for education are introduced.

Table 6.2 shows regressions of the log odds of mortality on both income and mean years of schooling. Age dummies and a time trend are included in each regression. The first column shows U.S. results. As in Deaton and Paxson (2001), schooling has a large, negative, and significant association with mortality. When education is included, income appears to be hazardous for males, possibly reflecting the countercyclical pattern in mortality discussed by Ruhm (2000). Income is either hazardous or insignificant for females. The British results show a very similar pattern. However, the

Table 6.2   **Log Odds of Dying as a Function of Income, Education, and Smoking**

	United States (all males)	United Kingdom (all males)		United States (all females)	United Kingdom (all females)	
Mean ln(y/ae)	0.093	0.057	0.071	−0.012	0.013	0.019
	(2.91)	(2.36)	(2.97)	(0.47)	(0.67)	(0.98)
Mean years of schooling	−0.115	−0.020	−0.018	−0.065	−0.022	−0.017
	(22.0)	(3.07)	(2.74)	(10.6)	(4.08)	(3.05)
Fraction smokers			0.203			0.154
			(5.55)			(4.92)
	Males Aged 35–59			Females Aged 35–59		
Mean ln(y/ae)	0.201	0.070	0.079	0.001	−0.022	−0.015
	(3.49)	(1.83)	(2.03)	(0.02)	(0.71)	(.049)
Mean years of schooling	−0.260	−0.029	−0.027	−0.191	0.008	0.012
	(21.0)	(2.54)	(2.35)	(13.92)	(0.86)	(1.26)
Fraction smokers			0.135			0.146
			(2.06)			(2.86)
	Males Aged 60–85			Females Aged 60–85		
Mean ln(y/ae)	0.095	0.035	0.034	0.121	0.043	0.052
	(5.00)	(2.46)	(2.37)	(7.19)	(2.28)	(2.81)
Mean years of schooling	0.002	−0.018	−0.018	−0.022	−0.031	−0.030
	(0.52)	(4.51)	(4.55)	(4.84)	(5.98)	(5.95)
Fraction smokers			−0.013			0.128
			(0.65)			(4.68)

Notes: *T*-statistics in parentheses. Each regression includes a set of age dummies and a time trend. The regressions are estimated for the full sample, and for subsets of cohorts in different age groups. The data for the United States are for 1975–1995, and for the United Kingdom are for 1978–1998.

effects of both income and education are much smaller than in the United States. For example, a one-year increase in education is predicted to reduce the odds of mortality for all males by 11.5 percent in the United States and only 2.0 percent in the United Kingdom. These results could be due to genuine differences in the provision of health care between Britain and the United States. However, they are also consistent with the hypothesis that it is neither education nor income that matters, but some third factor that is less correlated with education in Britain, where the variation in education is much less. More work using micro-level data is required before drawing this conclusion.

The third column adds a control for the fraction of the individuals in the cohort that reports purchases of tobacco. These regressions can only be run for Britain, not for the United States. We include tobacco not only because it is likely to be associated with mortality, but also because its use may be correlated with income and education, and it is useful to see whether its inclusion affects the results. As expected, mortality is usually higher in cohorts where the fraction of smokers is high. One exception is among men aged from sixty to eighty-five where smoking has no effect on mortality; perhaps those at risk have already been selected out by this age. However, the treatment of tobacco does not change the behavior of the estimates of income or education. As before, income is estimated to be either insignificantly different from zero or hazardous, and education is generally protective.

In table 6.3 we turn to the role of inequality, measured by the Gini coefficient for incomes within the cohort. We also look at the fraction of the cohort that is unemployed, following the literature that argues that unemployment raises the risk of death. As is the case for inequality in the United States, the estimated effects of inequality on mortality are perverse. Higher income inequality in both countries is associated with *lower* mortality, though note that the effect is only significantly different from zero for younger and older men in the United States. Adding years of schooling and smoking does not affect this conclusion, nor does adding the unemployment rate. There is no clear pattern in the association between the fraction unemployed and mortality. Unemployment is estimated to be protective of health for all women and hazardous to health only for the group of older men, most of whom are retired. Unemployment has no effect on mortality for the younger working-aged groups for whom the effects might be expected to be the largest.

Taken together, the results for Britain are not supportive of the idea that either income or income inequality affect mortality. The only consistent patterns we find are that education is (mildly) protective and that smoking is a health hazard. Part of the reason for these findings may simply be that we are asking too much of the data. Including the time trend may be removing most of the variation in the data in which we are most interested,

Table 6.3   **Log Odds of Dying as a Function of Income, Education, and Smoking**

	United States (all males)	United Kingdom (all males)			United States (all females)	United Kingdom (all females)		
Mean ln(y/ae)	−0.279	0.040	0.069	0.086	−0.125	0.004	0.025	0.016
	(8.74)	(1.65)	(2.81)	(2.99)	(5.39)	(0.21)	(1.23)	(0.69)
gini ln(y/ae)	−0.159	−0.020	0.028	0.026	−0.116	−0.078	−0.053	−0.017
	(1.64)	(0.40)	(0.57)	(0.45)	(1.54)	(2.08)	(1.40)	(0.36)
Mean years of schooling			−0.019	−0.020			−0.015	−0.021
			(2.80)	(2.67)			(2.72)	(3.22)
Fraction smokers			0.204	0.250			0.154	0.147
			(5.57)	(5.92)			(4.94)	(4.11)
Fraction unemployed				0.047				−0.086
				(0.75)				(2.11)
	Males Aged 35–59				Females Aged 35–59			
Mean ln(y/ae)	−0.435	0.051	0.078	0.069	−0.255	−0.016	−0.015	−0.022
	(6.49)	(1.33)	(2.02)	(1.63)	(5.93)	(0.54)	(0.48)	(0.71)
gini(y/ae)	−1.367	−0.022	0.011	0.026	−0.234	0.001	−0.007	0.006
	(5.92)	(0.24)	(0.13)	(0.28)	(1.46)	(0.02)	(0.011)	(0.08)
Mean years of schooling			−0.027	−0.028			0.012	0.012
			(2.34)	(2.39)			(1.26)	(1.16)
Fraction smokers			0.135	0.136			0.146	0.148
			(2.06)	(2.07)			(2.85)	(2.90)
Fraction unemployed				−0.057				−0.101
				(0.55)				(1.16)
	Males Aged 60–85				Females Aged 60–85			
Mean ln(y/ae)	0.115	0.015	0.033	0.078	0.102	0.008	0.053	0.055
	(6.33)	(1.02)	(2.13)	(4.35)	(6.04)	(0.41)	(2.67)	(2.11)
gini (y/ae)	−0.175	−0.016	0.009	0.015	−0.032	−0.010	−0.006	0.093
	(3.80)	(0.59)	(0.33)	(0.47)	(0.66)	(0.30)	(0.19)	(2.26)
Mean years of schooling			−0.018	−0.027			−0.030	−0.055
			(4.52)	(5.71)			(5.91)	(8.80)
Fraction smokers			−0.013	−0.018			0.128	0.118
			(0.63)	(0.76)			(4.67)	(3.64)
Fraction unemployed				0.083				−0.021
				(2.55)				(0.80)

Notes: T-statistics in parentheses. Each regression includes a set of age dummies and a time trend. The regressions are estimated for the full sample, and for subsets of cohorts in different age groups. The data for the United States are for 1975–1995, and for the United Kingdom are for 1978–1998.

making it possible to identify the effects of income. However, excluding the trend is not a sensible option because secular changes in mortality are likely to load onto trends in income or income inequality.

6.3.5   Pooling Data from Britain and the United States

All of the results so far analyze the United States and Britain separately. In this final subsection, we ask whether anything can be learned by pooling the data and exploiting differences in income and mortality between the United States and Britain. Pooling the data may, in theory, solve the problem of identification in the presence of trends. Under the (strong) assumption that the two countries share the same technologically-driven trends in mortality, it is possible to identify the effects of income by examining how changes in the relative incomes of same-aged individuals in the two countries are related to relative differences in mortality.

Table 6.4 shows estimates of models of the following form:

$$(7) \qquad \ln o_{cat} = \delta_c + \gamma_y + \lambda_a + \beta \ln\left(\frac{y}{ae}\right)_{cat} + \varepsilon_{cat},$$

where $\ln o_{cat}$ is the log odds of mortality for those in country c at age a and year t, the first three terms on the right-hand side are country, year, and age-fixed effects, and $\ln (y/ae)_{cat}$ is the logarithm of income per adult equivalent. This equation is estimated separately for men and women. The sample is restricted to the years 1975–1995 so that both countries are represented in all years. We report results with all ages pooled, although the results are similar when we break the sample into older and younger age groups.

The first four columns of table 6.4 show estimates that are not pooled and replicate the basic findings discussed previously. (Differences from previous results reflect the different sample period for Britain and the use of a complete set of year dummies rather than a time trend.) In the first two columns, we estimate the model separately for each country, with no year

Table 6.4   **Pooled U.S. and U.K. Regressions, Log Odds of Mortality (1975–1995)**

	United States	United Kingdom	United States	United Kingdom	Pooled U.S. and U.K. Regressions	
			Males			
ln(*y/ae*)	−0.559	−0.462	−0.375	0.099	−0.874	−0.885
	(24.2)	(16.7)	(11.0)	(3.9)	(27.0)	(20.5)
			Females			
ln(*y/ae*)	−0.528	−0.602	−0.186	0.028	−0.813	−0.636
	(27.4)	(20.0)	(7.7)	(1.2)	(32.7)	(20.6)
Age dummies	Yes	Yes	Yes	Yes	Yes	Yes
Year dummies	No	No	Yes	Yes	No	Yes
U.K. dummy	No	No	No	No	Yes	Yes

F-tests on Restrictions of Equality of Coefficients Across Countries in Pooled Regression

Men

Age effects for United Kingdom = Age effects for United States – $F(60,2379)$ 161.84

Year effects for United Kingdom = Year effects for United States – $F(20,2379)$ 22.51

Women

Age effects for United Kingdom = Age effects for United States – $F(60,2397)$ 138.33

Year effects for United Kingdom = Year effects for United States – $F(20,2397)$ 33.23

Note: T-statistics in parentheses. Each cell shows a coefficient for ln(*y/ae*) from a single regression.

dummies. As before, income is protective in both countries for both men and women. The American and British results are remarkably similar. The second two columns add year dummies. In line with all of our results so far, this has the effect of reducing but not eliminating the estimated gradient for the United States, but reversing the sign of the income to health gradient for Britain.

In the final two columns we present pooled results. With no year effects, we obtain the usual large negative and significant coefficients for income: –0.89 for men and –0.64 for women. Adding year effects does *not* alter this result: The coefficient on income for males is essentially unchanged and that for females declines by less than one-quarter.

Figure 6.10 presents the data in way that elucidates these results. We computed the difference in the log odds of mortality between Britain and the United States for each age-cohort cell and also the differences in the logarithm of income within each age-cohort cell; the currencies were converted to common units using PPP exchange rates. The top two panels average these differences by year (males are on the left and females are on the right). The bottom two panels average these differences by year of birth. The birth-year averaged figures are especially illuminating. For males and females, the difference between British and American mortality declines steadily over time so that more-recently-born British cohorts have lower mortality relative to their American counterparts than do cohorts born earlier in the twentieth century. Similarly, although British incomes are always below American incomes, the relative difference has declined so that the most recently-born cohorts of British males have incomes that are similar to their counterparts in the United States. The opposite slopes of these two curves account for the large negative relationship between mortality and income in the pooled regressions. The picture is much the same for females, although for this group there is an initial decline in relative British incomes between those born in 1890 and those born around 1910. (This decline also appears for men but is more muted.) The negative relationship is less apparent in the top year-average figures in which the income differences are dominated by the sharp British recession in the early 1990s.

Although these results indicate that there is a negative association between income and mortality, there are reasons to treat them with some skepticism. First, they are based on the assumption that health technology is identical in the two countries: In the regression results and (implicitly) in the graphs we are assuming that year and age effects are identical across the two countries. In fact they are not. The bottom panel of table 6.4 presents F-tests for the equality of the age and year effects in the pooled model. The hypothesis that the age effects are identical is strongly rejected for both men and women. Consistent with the time-series results discussed in section 6.2, the unrestricted age effects indicate that mortality increases faster with age in Britain than in the United States for both men and women

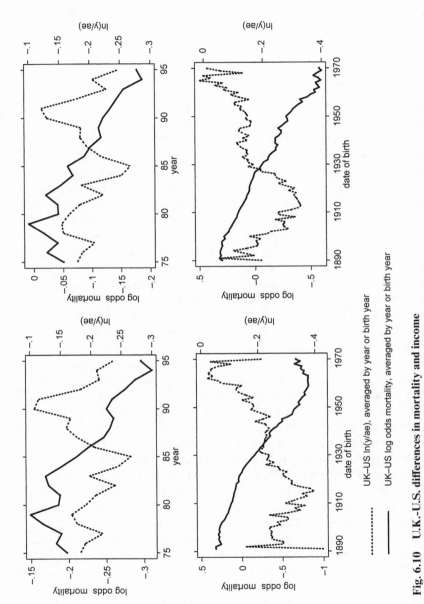

Fig. 6.10 U.K.–U.S. differences in mortality and income

Note: The currencies were converted to common units using PPP exchange rates from the OECD website (http://www.oecd.org/std/nadata.htm).

(although somewhat more so for men). It is also invalid to restrict the year effects to be the same across the two countries—which is not surprising, given our results in figures 6.2 and 6.3 that suggest that British technology lags that of the United States. The unrestricted year effects show mortality declines over the period that are somewhat larger in Britain than the United States.

6.4   Conclusions

In both Britain and America, for men and for women and for most age groups, there has been a very substantial decline in mortality rates since 1950. Our examination of these rates, by sex and age group and in relation to the evolution of incomes and income inequality, does not suggest any simple relationship between income growth and the decline in mortality, nor between income inequality and mortality rates. In the United States, the period of slowest income growth saw substantial accelerations in the rate mortality decline, particularly among middle-aged and older men and women. In both the United States and Britain, the increase in income inequality took place at the same time as a deceleration in mortality decline at the younger ages, including infant mortality. But there are previously slow rates of decline when nothing was happening to income inequality, and the later rise in income inequality was associated with the acceleration in mortality decline among middle-aged and older adults in both countries. A more plausible account of the data is that over time declines in mortality are driven by technological advances or by the emergence of new infectious diseases, such as AIDS. These advances and retreats are associated with specific conditions and specific treatments, and so affect men and women differently and different age groups differently. They also happen first in the United States, with the British experience following with a lag of several years. Clearly this hypothesis needs a great deal more investigation, for example, by looking at more countries.

If changes in mortality over time are driven by technology and not by income, there must be some doubt as to whether our previous analysis in Deaton and Paxson (2001) came to the correct conclusions about the role of cohort incomes in the decline of cohort mortality. Certainly, our results cannot be replicated on the British data. Simple regressions of the log odds of mortality on log income per equivalent and on age dummies give similar results in both countries, with income estimated to be strongly protective, but the addition of time trends destroys the result in the Britain, although not in the United States. Education reduces mortality among British cohorts, and smoking increases it. But neither these sensible results, nor the inclusion of other variables, repairs our inability to produce coherent and stable effects of income on mortality at the cohort level. We suspect—but have been unable to demonstrate decisively—that the cohort analysis is flawed by the necessity to make the almost certainly invalid assumption that age effects in mortality are constant through time. This is contradicted, for example, by the spread of AIDS that has almost certainly raised the early life relative to later life mortality rates among recently born men and women compared with their seniors. If this is a serious problem, the cohort method may not be useful in this context, or at least it will require substantial modification in order to give sound results.

More substantively, we suspect that our time-series results in section 6.2 are more reliable and that this comparative international work is a productive direction for future research. Even so, there remains a major puzzle about the role of income. Income growth seems to play little role in the decline of mortality at the national level. At the cohort level, the same is possibly true, as argued previously. Yet in the individual-level data from the National Longitudinal Mortality Study, as from many other data sets, income is protective against mortality, even when education and other socioeconomic variables are controlled. Why there should be such a contrast between the individual and national effects of income is a topic that requires a good deal of further thought and analysis.

References

Aaron, Henry J., and William B. Schwartz. 1984. *The painful prescription: Rationing hospital care.* Washington, D.C.: Brookings Institution.

Atkinson, Anthony B., and Andrea Brandolini. 2001. Promise and pitfalls in the use of 'secondary' data-sets: Income inequality in OECD countries as a case study. *Journal of Economic Literature* 39 (3): 771–99.

Brandolini, Andrea. 1998. Pareto's law and Kuznet's curve: A bird's eye view of long-run changes in income distribution. Rome: Banca d'Italia, Research Department.

Case, Anne, Darren Lubotsky, and Christina Paxson. 2002. Economic status and health in childhood: The origins of the gradient. *American Economic Review* 92 (5): 1308–34.

Danesh, John, Peter Whincup, Mary Walker, Lucy Lennon, Andrew Thomson, Paul Appleby, Yuk-ki Wong, Martine Bernardes-Silva, and Michael Ward. 2000. *Chlamydia pneumoniae* IgG titres and coronary heart disease: Prospective study and meta-analysis. *British Medical Journal* 321:208–13.

Deaton, Angus, and Darren Lubotsky. 2003. Mortality, inequality and race in American cities and states. *Social Science and Medicine* 56 (6): 1139–53.

Deaton, Angus, and Christina Paxson. 2001. Mortality, education, income, and inequality among American cohorts. In *Themes in the economics of aging,* ed. David A. Wise, 129–70. Chicago: Chicago University Press.

Deininger, Klaus, and Lyn Squire. 1996. A new data set measuring income inequality. *World Bank Economic Review* 10:565–91.

Gerdtham, Ulf-G., and Bengt Jönsson. 2000. International comparisons of health expenditure. In *Handbook of health economics,* Vol. 1A, ed. Anthony J. Culyer and Joseph P. Newhouse, 11–53. Amsterdam: North-Holland.

Goodman, Alissa, and Steven Webb. 1994. For richer, for poorer; The changing distribution of income in the United Kingdom 1961–1991. Commentary no. 42. London: Institute for Fiscal Studies.

————. 1999. The distribution of UK household expenditure, 1979–92. *Fiscal Studies* 16 (3): 55–80.

Gottshcalk, Peter, and Timothy Smeeding. 2000. Empirical evidence on income inequality in industrial countries. In *Handbook of income distribution,* Vol. 1, ed. Anthony B. Atkinson and François Bourguignon, 261–307. Amsterdam: North-Holland.

Jones, Arthur F., and Daniel H. Weinberg. 2000. The changing shape of the nation's income distribution. P60–204. Washington, D.C.: Bureau of the Census. http://www.census.gov/ftp/pub/hhes/www/p60204.html.

Lee, Ronald D., and Lawrence R. Carter. 1992. Modeling and forecasting U.S. mortality. *Journal of the American Statistical Association* 87:659–71.

Marmot, Michael G. 1994. Social differences in health within and between populations. *Daedalus* 123:197–216.

Ruhm, Christopher. 2000. Are recessions good for your health? *Quarterly Journal of Economics* 115 (2): 617–50.

Wald, N. J., M. R. Law, J. K. Morris, X. Zhou, Y. Wong, and M. E. Ward. 2000. *Chlamydia pneumoniae* infection and mortality from ischaemic heart disease: Large prospective study. *British Medical Journal* 321:204–207.

Wilkinson, Richard G. 1996. *Unhealthy societies: The affliction of inequality.* London: Routledge.

Comment   James Banks

This paper adds to the large and growing body of evidence on the relationship between socioeconomic status (SES) and health, or in this case mortality, outcomes. The key innovation here is the detailed comparison of identical research questions, specified in the same way in both the United States and the United Kingdom using directly comparable data and methodology. The exploiting of comparative microdata in a genuinely integrated manner is beginning to be a fruitful avenue for research, and the analysis in this paper is a further example of potential gains from this type of research. The authors' conclusions provide a strong case for more of such work to be undertaken, addressing not only this particular research question (where the gains would seem to be unquestionable) but also the issue more widely.

The United States and United Kingdom are natural starting points for a comparative evaluation of the links between SES and health because a good fraction of what is known, either in the health economics or epidemiological literature, has been established in these two countries. Two

James Banks is reader in economics at University College London and deputy research director of the Institute for Fiscal Studies where he also directs the Centre for Economic Research on Ageing.

relevant background studies in this respect (as they can be directly compared) are those of Hurd, McFadden, and Merrill (2000) and Attanasio and Emmerson (2003) who investigate links between SES and mortality using comparable data on comparable cohorts, taken from the Asset and Health Dynamics among the oldest old survey (AHEAD) and the U.K. Retirement Survey, respectively. The former find that wealth and income (rankings) are correlated with mortality outcomes, as expected, but that the relationship does not hold when controlling for subjective mortality probabilities and initial health. The latter study shows that wealth ranking affects mortality outcomes in the United Kingdom, even controlling for initial health status, although in this instance the authors do not have the option of including subjective measures. In this paper Deaton and Paxson show that when turning to data on all cohorts at all ages over a number of years the relationship between income and mortality in the United Kingdom disappears when put under detailed scrutiny. This in turn is argued to be sufficient to cast doubt on the findings (presented both here and in their previous paper) for the United States over the same period. There is certainly something to this argument, and it is hard to disagree with the authors' resulting assessment of the drawbacks of the cohort methodology employed in the paper. Some of these issues will be touched on in what follows, but I will also point out a number of places where it is clear that more needs to be known before one can really evaluate the hypothesis that SES and, in particular, inequalities in SES maybe associated with differences in health outcomes.

The U.S.-U.K. Comparison

The comparative analysis in section 6.2 of the paper throws up both similarities and differences between the time path of income, income inequality, and (age-specific) mortality rates in the two countries that lie at the crux of the issue. On the economic side, trends in income inequality are argued to be similar, although trends in incomes are shown to be quite different, particularly at and below the median. With respect to mortality, trends in infant mortality are remarkably similar, even though the U.S. time-series appears to lead the United Kingdom by a couple of years,[1] and trends in adult age-specific mortality rates appear similar. Here it may be worth pointing out two points where one could take an alternative interpretation of the authors' figures.

With respect to income inequality, while it is certainly true that inequality in the United States and the United Kingdom broadly speaking followed the same trends—being flat until the late 1970s and then rising be-

---

1. The authors' point about possible technology lags between the two countries is an important and potentially attractive explanation that demands a more detailed investigation.

fore flattening out in the 1990s—the magnitude and speed of these changes was very different across the two countries. Inequality, as measured by the Gini coefficient, was considerably higher in the United States than in the United Kingdom throughout the sample period, and the time path is strikingly different. The degree of inequality rose by almost 10 percentage points (40 percent) through the 1980s in the United Kingdom, during which time U.S. inequality rose by 3 to 4 percentage points (less than 10 percent). Of course there are measurement and comparability issues here, but the possible consequences of such extreme and rapid change in the United Kingdom, as opposed to the more gradual change experienced in the United States, could be interesting to explore, particularly given the nature of transmission mechanisms typically talked about for the inequality–health relationship (see Marmot and Wilkinson 1999, for example).

There are also a set of differences between the time paths of age-specific mortality rates in the two countries that could be important. It is certainly true that mortality rates for the old show very similar time paths across the two countries. For younger adults, however, this is less the case, to my eye at least, with quite different trends and patterns for males and females between ages twenty and forty over the whole sample, but particularly in the period from the late 1980s onward.

Methodology

The use of data on all cohorts at all ages adds substantially to the analysis and allows the authors to examine grander research questions than a single cohort or cross-sectional study. But the drawback, as is well known, is that identifying assumptions need to be made to separate out the effects of interest, whether these be age, cohort, or time. As is pointed out in the paper, age profiles (for income and mortality) are assumed to be the same for all cohorts, and Deaton and Paxson discuss the fact that it could be the violation of this assumption that lies behind the breakdown of the SES–health relationship at the cohort level. This assessment seems sensible on two grounds. Firstly, the assumption implies that advances in medical technology benefit all age groups (relatively) equally, such that they can be captured in a trend effect leaving the age profile unaffected. Second, and highly related, the implication is that health technology effects (or for that matter other changes, including income and income and income inequality) must operate contemporaneously. For example, were some health event or technology to change mortality rates at one particular age then that cohort's mortality experiences will likely differ at later ages, either as a result of dynamic effects of the event itself or as a result of selection, thus changing the age relativities for the cohort in comparison to its predecessors.

For this reason, and with respect to this particular international comparison, the role of the "access to health services" story may be hard to evaluate. Consider again the age-specific mortality rates in the two countries discussed previously. Even those aged fifty at the end of the sample period will have been born in the late 1940s. Yet the biggest innovation in U.K. healthcare—the National Health Service (NHS), discussed at a number of points in the paper—was only introduced in 1948. One possibility is that the NHS, through changing the nature and distribution of health interventions in early life, will have led to changes in later life that will only show up as international differences in those cohorts born after its introduction. Similar arguments could apply in reverse to more recent years, when the United Kingdom has not had the expansion in (aggregate) health care spending of the United States.[2]

Even with a less restrictive framework for cohort-age profiles, the international comparison in this paper also points to a methodological issue about the role and nature of inequality itself that could maybe be taken further. There is some discussion in this paper, but particularly elsewhere, of mechanisms that might underlie links between inequalities in SES and health, often relating to psychosocial factors, such as stress, control, and so on. It is quite possible, however, that such underlying psychosocial factors are changing differentially across the two countries, or at least are being picked up differentially in the two income inequality series. Essentially income and income inequality may be a better proxy for underlying changes in the variables of interest in one country than the other. We know, for example, that in the United Kingdom the rise in inequality has been paralleled by marked changes in living arrangements (with many more single adult households and a doubling in the proportion of households who are single parents), work patterns (with an increasing polarization of households into no-earner or two-earner couples), and by changes in the returns to education, all of which could be thought to be important changes that would in turn be channeled into health through inequalities in SES. Evidence on similar changes in the United States is also available, but it would be particularly interesting to address these mechanisms directly in the microdata for the two countries and simultaneously control for the differences in the changing nature of the income inequality in the two countries.

A more difficult dimension of changes in inequality to control for is the degree to which cross-sectional variances in incomes measure permanent inequality or transitory uncertainty in incomes and any potential difference in trends of each component across countries. Evidence from the United Kingdom (Blundell and Preston 1998) suggests an important role for both components in the rise of income dispersion over recent years, but

2. For example, in 1997, health care spending was 13.9 percent of the gross domestic product (GDP) in the United States, of which around half (6.5 percent) was public, and in contrast, spending in the United Kingdom was only 6.8 percent of GDP, of which almost all (5.8 percent) was public (Emmerson, Frayne, and Goodman 2000).

each component might be thought to be distinct in the sense of the mechanisms by which it could lead to changes in health. The instrumenting of income and the variance of income in the analysis of this paper begin to go some way to addressing the stripping out of the inequality component, although choice of instruments is always a problem, as pointed out in the authors' analysis.

Comparative Issues

If more comparative work is to be undertaken in the future it is worth pointing out that, by definition, such analysis has to deal with the comparability (and relevance) of the measures employed in the individual countries and, indeed, of the populations themselves. Given broad similarities between the United States and the United Kingdom, this is probably not a particularly important issue for the analysis in this particular paper although I would still like to have seen more on this issue. But, in general, the definition of income (gross or net, annual or weekly), equivalence scale, or education could have differential effects across countries, particularly to the extent that international differences differ across cohorts or change over time. Nevertheless, this paper shows clearly that comparative avenues do look very promising. One possible country to add into the picture would be Germany, which research has shown to have important differences with respect to the U.K.-U.S. model. In particular, West Germany has had the income growth and technical progress of the United States and United Kingdom but notably without the rise in (wage) inequality during the 1980s that is common to both countries in this current comparison (see Giles, Gosling, Laisney, and Geib 1998). Such additional variation could be crucial in understanding the relationships in this paper.

One of the authors' main conclusions is unchanged between this paper and its predecessor—there is still much research (and in particular comparative research) to be done in this area. The evidence here, coupled with the promise of further detailed international comparative exercises addressing potential transmission mechanisms linking SES, mortality, and morbidity, and the increasing availability of microdata specifically designed to target this research question, suggests that such future work will lead to important advances in our understanding of the issue.

References

Attanasio, Orazio, and Carl Emmerson. 2003. Mortality, health status and wealth. *Journal of the European Economics Association,* forthcoming.
Blundell, Richard, and Ian Preston. 1998. Consumption inequality and income uncertainty. *Quarterly Journal of Economics* 113 (2):603–40.
Emmerson, Carl, Chris Frayne, and Alissa Goodman. 2000. *Pressures in UK healthcare: Challenges for the NHS.* London: Institute for Fiscal Studies.

Giles, Chris, Amanda Gosling, Francois Laisney, and Thorsten Geib. 1998. *The distribution of income and wages in the UK and West Germany, 1984–1992.* London: Institute for Fiscal Studies.

Hurd, Michael, Dan McFadden, and Angela Merrill. 2000. Predictors of mortality among the elderly. NBER Working Paper no. 7440. Cambridge, Mass.: National Bureau of Economic Research, December.

Marmot, Michael, and Richard Wilkinson, eds. 1999. *Social determinants of health.* Oxford: Oxford University Press.

Does Money Protect Health Status?
Evidence from South African Pensions

Anne Case

7.1 Introduction

A strong, positive association between income and health status has been documented between countries, within countries at points in time, and within countries over time with economic development. The channels by which better health leads to higher income, and those by which higher income protects health status, are of interest to both researchers and policy makers. However, quantifying the impact of income on health and documenting the mechanisms through which income leads to better health are difficult, given the simultaneous determination of health and income.

In this paper, we quantify the impact of a large, exogenous increase in income—that associated with the South African state old age pension—on health status. We find, in households that pool income, that the pension protects the health of all household members, working in part to protect the nutritional status of household members, in part to improve living conditions, and in part to reduce the stress under which the adult household members negotiate day-to-day life.

We begin in section 7.2 with a discussion of an integrated family survey run in 1999, one that captured information on individuals' health, mental health, social connectedness, and economic status. In section 7.3 we document the relationship between income and health status and then turn to the pension as an instrument, allowing us to identify the causal impact of

Anne Case is professor of economics and public affairs and director of the Research Program in Development Studies at the Woodrow Wilson School of Public and International Affairs, Princeton University, and a research associate of the National Bureau of Economic Research.

I thank Angus Deaton and Robert Jensen for comments on an earlier draft.

income on health status. In section 7.4 we document some of the pathways through which higher incomes lead to better health.

7.2 The Langeberg Survey

In 1999, the South African Labour and Development Research Unit (SALDRU) at the University of Cape Town ran a survey on a racially stratified random sample of 300 households (1,300 individuals) in the Langeberg Health District, which is comprised of three magisterial districts (county-sized administrative units) in the Western Cape in South Africa[1] (see Case and Wilson 2001 for additional details on the survey).

The survey instrument used was one that had been developed over a four-year period and was the joint product of researchers at the University of Cape Town (Monica Ferreira, Human Sciences Research Council/University of Cape Town (HSRC/UCT) Centre for Gerontology; Karen Charlton, nutrition and dietetics unit; and Francis Wilson, economics and SALDRU); the University of the Western Cape (Pieter le Roux, economics); the University of the Witwatersrand (Merton Dagut and Martin Wittenberg, faculty of commerce); Rhodes University (Valerie Moller); the Medical Research Council (Krisela Steyn and Debbie Bradshaw); Princeton University (Anne Case and Angus Deaton, economics and Woodrow Wilson School); Harvard University (Robert Jensen, Kennedy School of Government; David Bloom and Larry Rosenberg, School of Public Health; and Lakshmi Reddy Bloom); Massachusetts Institute of Technology (MIT; Courtney Coile, economics); and Steven Low (University of Cape Town), John Gear (Health Systems Trust), Najma Shaikh and Ingrid le Roux (Western Cape Provincial Department of Health), together with other persons in the medical community of South Africa. This team of gerontologists, economists, public health experts, and physicians grappled with the survey design, both structure and content, through many rounds of piloting, until there was consensus that the questionnaire worked well in the field. Funding for the pilot surveys was provided by the National Institute of Aging, through a grant to David Bloom and the National Bureau of Economic Research; by the John D. and Catherine T. MacArthur Foundation, through a grant to Princeton University; and through the HSRC/UCT Centre for Gerontology at the University of Cape Town. Funding for

1. The survey was carried out under the auspices of SALDRU, the Southern African Labour and Development Research Unit of the School of Economics at the University of Cape Town, under the direction of Francis Wilson. The survey manager was Jaqui Goldin, who organized the interviews, which were conducted by students of the School of Social Work at the University of Cape Town and community workers who had been specially trained in the process. Sampling and listing was done by Matthew Welch and Faldie Esau, with generous advice from Jim Lepkowski of the Institute for Social Research at the University of Michigan.

the Langeberg survey was provided by the Mellon Foundation, through a grant to the University of Cape Town.

A key component of the survey design was that every adult identified as a household member would be interviewed separately. In South Africa, as elsewhere, household members often have private information to which other members do not have access. A household member's earnings, for example, or whether she has a bank account, is often information that she would protect from others in the household. In addition, conflict between household members can lead to very different accounts of life in the household. In one pilot household, the head of household reported that no one in the household drank "too much." His adult children, interviewed separately, spoke of the fear they lived with because their father was regularly drunk and abusive. In another pilot household, the female household head refused to recognize the presence of her son's child as a member of her household, although this grandchild was living in her house with her son. Relying only on the account of one "knowledgeable household member," as do most household surveys, the child's presence (or the head's drinking problem) would have been entirely overlooked. Moreover, mental and physical health status relate to individuals, not to households, and should be asked at the individual level.

The survey had four modules. The first was a household module, which collected information from the person in the household identified as "most knowledgeable about how income is spent by this household" on household composition, income, and expenditures. We added experimental questions on whether and how often adults and, separately, children in the household had to skip meals because there was not enough money for food. We also added experimental questions on how the household would classify its financial situation (on a five point scale from "very comfortable" to "extremely poor") and, when the household respondent gave an answer that was not at least "comfortable," the question was asked how much money in total the household would need per month to be comfortable.

The survey also had a module for younger adults (aged eighteen to fifty-four), in which questions were asked on work histories, earnings, health status, mental health status, and social connectedness. A module for older adults (aged fifty-five or greater) asked additional questions on activities of daily living and about South Africa's unique old age pension. Weight and height were recorded for all adults. The fourth module in the survey collected information on vaccines from children's health cards, interviewed an adult about whether and for how long the child was breast fed, and weighed and measured all children aged twelve and under.

Summary statistics for the survey are provided in table 7.1, where we present means by race for health status, individual incomes, and household and individual characteristics that are important in what follows.

All adults aged eighteen and above were asked to rate their health, in an-

Table 7.1   **The Langeberg Survey: Variable Means and Standard Errors (adults, aged eighteen and above)**

	Blacks	Coloreds	Whites
Self-reported health status[a]	2.80	2.34	2.22
	(.091)	(.060)	(.124)
Respondent's total income	489	921	2,968
	(82.8)	(145)	(538)
Respondent's age	37.1	38.8	49.6
	(1.41)	(.756)	(2.29)
Respondent's completed education	6.95	6.52	11.7
	(.276)	(1.07)	(.465)
Indicator: Respondent is a pensioner	.100	.076	.220
	(.044)	(.015)	(.057)
Indicator: Respondent lives with a pensioner	.232	.213	.326
	(.074)	(.059)	(.083)
Indicator: Respondent lives with someone aged 55 or above	.361	.337	.512
	(.080)	(.061)	(.088)
Indicator: Respondent lives in a household that does not pool income	.186	.244	.104
	(.075)	(.052)	(.039)
No. of observations	229	316	136

Notes: Sample means are weighted using weights based on the 1996 South African census, taking into account the stratification of the sample (by race), and the clustering of observations (by enumerator area). Standard errors are presented in parentheses.

[a] 1 = Excellent; 2 = Good; 3 = Average; 4 = Poor; 5 = Very Poor.

swer to the following questions: "How would you describe your health at present? Would you say it is excellent, good, average, poor or very poor?" Answers are scored from 1 to 5, with "excellent" equal to 1 and "very poor" equal to 5. Self-reported health has been shown to be a strong predictor of mortality, even when one controls for current health status and behaviors. Poor self-ratings of health are also a significant predictor of change in functioning among the elderly (see Idler and Kasl 1995 for findings on changes in functioning and for extensive references on the studies of self-reported health and mortality). In the Langeberg survey, we find blacks report themselves to be in significantly worse health (2.80) than coloreds (2.34) and whites (2.22), with mean self-reported health for blacks closer to "average" than to "good." The median response among blacks was "average," whereas that among coloreds and whites was "good."

Table 7.1 also makes clear that blacks have significantly lower incomes than do colored and white respondents in the Langeberg survey. On average, black incomes are one-half of colored incomes, and colored incomes are one-third of white incomes. Whites are significantly older than blacks or coloreds in the Langeberg survey—in part due to the fact that this area of the Western Cape is a popular retirement area for whites. Whites also have markedly higher levels of education; whites, on average, have completed twelve years of schooling, whereas blacks and coloreds, on average, have completed fewer than seven. Roughly 10 percent of our adult black and colored sample are pensioners, and more than 20 percent of the black and colored adults in our sample live with a pensioner.

7.3   The Impact of Income on Health Status

A strong association between income and health status can be seen in table 7.2, which examines the relationship between self-reported health status and income, while controlling for age, sex, and education. Self-reported health status is an ordinal measure, and regressions that treat the difference between "excellent" and "good" (say) as equal to that between "poor" and "very poor" are unlikely to be appropriate. For that reason, we quantify the relationship between income and health status using ordered probits. For blacks and coloreds, a doubling of income is associated with an improvement in self-reported health of roughly 0.2 points. For whites, a doubling of income is associated with an improvement in health status of 0.3 points.

For all races, older adults report worse health, on average. However, results in table 7.2 show that the health status of whites erodes more slowly with age (.023 points per year of age) than does that of blacks (.035), bearing in mind that higher numbers are associated with worse health. For blacks, a doubling of income is associated with the same improvement in

Table 7.2   **Income and Health Status**

	South Africa			United States	
	Blacks	Coloreds	Whites	Blacks	Whites
Log(own income)	−.229	−.222	−.325	−.176	−.209
	(.071)	(.068)	(.130)	(.004)	(.002)
Age	.035	.032	.023	.019	.017
	(.005)	(.004)	(.012)	(.0002)	(.0001)
Education	−.049	.014	−.155	−.052	−.077
	(.024)	(.015)	(.064)	(.001)	(.001)
Female	.136	.006	−.019	.153	.079
	(.216)	(.166)	(.247)	(.008)	(.003)
No. of observations	122	243	86	83,427	544,256

Sources: The Langeberg Survey 1999 (columns [1]–[3]; http://web.uct.ac.za/depts/saldru/lang .htm) and the U.S. NHIS 1986–1995 (columns [4]–[5]; http://ww.cdc.gov/nchs/nhis.htm).

Notes: Standard errors are presented in parentheses. Dependent variable = self-reported health status (1 = Excellent, 5 = Very Poor). South African ordered probits are weighted using weights based on the 1996 South African census, taking into account the stratification of the sample (by race), and the clustering of observations (by enumerator area). Income for the NHIS is total household income. Both the U.S. and South African samples restricted to adults aged eighteen and older.

health status we would expect to see if we could roll back the respondent's age by six years: Both are associated with an improvement in health of just over 0.2 points. Education is associated with better health, particularly for whites. We find a much smaller effect for blacks and no effect for colored respondents. This may be due to the fact that blacks and coloreds would have been forced to attend schools that were inferior to white schools in virtually every dimension (see Case and Deaton 1999).

For comparison, the last two columns in table 7.2 present ordered probits for blacks and whites in the United States, using data from the National Health Interview Survey (NHIS) from 1986 to 1995. The association between income and health status in the United States is very similar to that observed in the Langeberg survey for blacks and coloreds, with a doubling of income being associated with roughly a 0.2 point improvement in health status. The self-reported health status of Americans erodes more slowly with age than that of South Africans. As was true in the South African data, we find health status in the United States eroding more quickly with age for blacks than for whites. Education in the United States appears to be protective of health status and, again as was true in the South African data, education appears to be more protective for whites than for blacks. Women in the United States report worse health on average, controlling for age, education, and log of household income. The "female" coefficient is very similar for the black samples of the Langeberg (.136) and the NHIS (.153), although in the Langeberg its standard error is large.

That there is a strong association between income and health status does not by itself demonstrate that income has a causal effect on health. Threads run from income to health, and from health to income, with third factors potentially influencing them both (Smith 1999; Fuchs 1982). We must have a sharp knife with which to cut the knot between health and income. The South African old age pension is just that sort of instrument.

The state old age pension was originally intended as a safety net for the small numbers of whites who reached retirement age without an adequate employment-based pension. The pension was first extended to the colored and Indian population in an attempt to make the three-chamber parliament politically palatable (van der Berg 1994), and payments were gradually equalized across all racial groups during the disintegration of the apartheid regime in the early 1990s. Complete parity in payment between races was reached, and the system was fully in place at the end of 1993.

The pension appears to be a modest amount of money when measured using a yardstick of white incomes but looks like quite a large amount of money when measured against black incomes: At the time of the Langeberg survey, the pension was 520 rands per month, an amount equal to the median colored income and 2.5 times the median black income in the Langeberg survey. On paper, the pension is means-tested. In practice, women aged sixty or above and men aged sixty-five or above generally receive the full amount of the pension if they do not have a private pension. The take-up rate for the state pension is roughly 80 percent for blacks and coloreds. For whites, who are generally covered by private pensions, the take-up rate is less than 10 percent (Case and Deaton 1998).

7.3.1 Identification

We identify the impact of money on health status by comparing the self-reported health status of black and colored adults who live with pensioners and those that do not. For children, we use height for age as a measure of long-term nutritional status and compare heights of children living in households with and without a pensioner. For most of the analysis, we will focus on black and colored households and will identify pensioners based on age eligibility in order to avoid issues of take-up.

If all black and colored elderly receive the pension, we cannot identify the impact of the pension separately from the impact of having an elderly person in the household. Perhaps grannies have more time to care for small children, leading to healthier children among those who live with a granny. Alternatively, if older adults require a good deal of care and attention, then their presence may prove to be a burden on other adults in the household.

We propose two strategies to disentangle the impact of the pension income from the impact of the pensioner. First, the Langeberg survey asked a "knowledgeable" household member whether people in the household pool their incomes. If incomes are pooled, then the pension income should protect the health status of all household members. However, if incomes aren't pooled, then we should find no effect of pension receipt on the health of other household members. Table 7.1 shows that roughly 20 to 25 percent of black and colored adults in the Langeberg survey are living in households that do not pool income. (The strongest predictor of nonpooling is the presence in the household of a young adult—male or female—who is currently working for money. In pilot surveys, we found that these young men and women are often not willing to put their money into a common household pool.) We will use the difference in the impact of pension income in households that pool and those that do not as one strategy to identify the effect of money on health status.

The second strategy is to control for the number of older household members (aged fifty-five and above) in our analysis. If as adults get older they become more helpful (harmful) to the health of other members, then we should be able to quantify that effect by adding a control for the number of members aged fifty-five and above. This second strategy, then, quantifies the difference made by the presence of older members who are receiving the pension (aged sixty and above for women, sixty-five and above for men) and those who are not (aged fifty-five to pension age). Table 7.1 shows that roughly one-third of the black and colored adults in the Langeberg survey were living with someone aged fifty-five or above.

In what follows, we do not present results controlling for household or individual income because these are likely to be determined jointly with the health status of household members. Each pensioner brings 520 rands per month into the household, and the tables that follow can be read as the estimated effect of this extra income on respondents' health status.

7.3.2   The Effect of Income on Health Status

We estimate the effect of pension income on health status by running ordered probits of self-reported health status on the number of pensioners in the household and on an indicator that the respondent is a pensioner, controlling for age, sex, race, and race interacted with sex, for black and colored adults in the Langeberg survey. Results for these probits are presented in table 7.3.

We present results separately for respondents from households where incomes are pooled (columns [1] and [2]), not pooled (columns [3] and [4]), and for all respondents regardless of pooling status (columns [5] and [6]).

Table 7.3 shows that in households that pool income the pension protects the health status of all adults. All else being equal, adding an additional pensioner to the household improves the health status of all adults by 0.5 points. In households that pool income, pensioners receive no additional health protection above that which all adults receive: The coefficient on the indicator that the respondent is a pensioner is positive (suggesting worse health), but never significantly different from zero. In contrast, in households that do not pool income, having pensioners in the household is

Table 7.3   **Pensioners, Income Pooling, and Health Status: Colored and Black Respondents Only**

	Household Pools Income		Household Does Not Pool Income		All Households	
No. of pensioners	−.503	−.586	.148	.182	−.291	−.357
	(.259)	(.383)	(.278)	(.264)	(.154)	(.269)
Indicator: Respondent	.262	.314	−1.03	−1.03	−.195	−.161
is a pensioner	(.612)	(.682)	(.450)	(.448)	(.480)	(.523)
No. of members aged	—	.089	—	−.033	—	.070
55 or above		(.179)		(.149)		(.163)
Indicator: Household	—	—	—	—	−.019	−.009
does not pool income					(.087)	(.075)
No. of observations	422	422	95	95	517	517

Notes: Standard errors are presented in parentheses. Ordered probits are weighted using weights based on the 1996 South African census, taking into account the stratification of the sample (by race), and the clustering of observations (by enumerator area). All probits include indicators for age, sex, race, and age interacted with race. Results are robust to estimation separately by race, and to the inclusion of the respondent's years of completed education. Dashes indicate that this variable was not included in the ordered probit.

not protective of health status, unless the respondent is the pensioner. In nonpooling households, pensioners report health status that is one full point better (1.03) than other household members, on average, controlling for age, race, and sex. That pension income has a larger effect on pensioners' health in nonpooling households is consistent with a model in which money protects health status. In nonpooling households, the pensioner may retain a greater share of the pension income for his or her personal use, which then would have a larger effect on personal health.

The number of members aged fifty-five or above is not a significant determinant of health status in either pooling or nonpooling households. The coefficient on this measure of the number of older members is small and insignificant in all specifications. The presence of an older member has no significant effect on health status, unless that older person brings resources in the form of a pension.

When we group together respondents from households that pool and those that do not, we find that the presence of pensioners is still protective of health status, although the coefficient has been attenuated by grouping together respondents who are protected by pension income (those from pooling households) and those who are not (those from nonpooling households).

Overall, we take the results in table 7.3 as evidence that pension income protects health status of all adult household members in pooling households and the health status of the pensioners (and pensioners only) in nonpooling households.

We turn to the impact of pension income on health outcomes for black and colored children in table 7.4, where we present results of regressions of height for age, controlling for the number of pensioners in the household. We restrict our sample to children born after January 1, 1994, the date at which the pension was fully operational. We find, with or without controls

Table 7.4   **Pensioners and Children's Height: Colored and Black Children Born after January 1, 1994**

	Black Children		Colored Children	
No. of pensioners	5.10	8.09	6.03	5.74
	(2.62)	(3.87)	(1.51)	(1.62)
No. of members aged 55 or above	—	–3.11	—	.574
		(3.55)		(.907)
No. of observations	37	37	44	44

Notes: Standard errors are presented in parentheses. Ordinary least squares regressions are weighted using weights based on the 1996 South African census, taking into account the stratification of the sample (by race), and the clustering of observations (by enumerator area). All regressions contain an indicator for female children. Dependent variable = children's height in centimeters.

for the number of members aged fifty-five and above, that a pensioner is associated with roughly a five centimeter increase in a child's height for age, controlling for sex, household size, the number of members aged zero to seventeen, and a complete set of quarter-since-birth indicator variables to capture the effect of age on height. This effect is roughly equal to one half-year's growth for black and colored children aged zero to six in the Langeberg data and is roughly 1 standard deviation increase in height for age (this estimate is, then, slightly higher than that estimated by Duflo, 2000, who found that grandmothers' pensions increased heights for age for granddaughters by 0.7 standard deviations, using data from a period before the pension was entirely operational).

The evidence in section 7.3 shows that cash, in the form here of the South African old age pension, improves the health status of all adults in households where income is pooled and the heights of children living with pensioners. We turn in section 7.4 to discuss ways by which rands might lead to better health outcomes.

7.4   Mechanisms Leading to Better Health

The mechanisms through which money may be used to foster better health may be many. We begin with a look at the answers to open-ended questions asked of pensioners: "What did you start doing differently when you received your pension?" and "In what ways did your life become better when your pension started, if any?" We present the answers to these questions (for the pensioners who provided answers) in table 7.5. Some respondents note that the pension is smaller than the amount of money they had been earning, but many report the pension to be a greater amount. Food figures prominently in the pensioners' responses. One respondent replies, for example, that he now "looked after the children and made sure that there was always something to eat." In addition, many respondents report that they upgraded their housing, putting in a kitchen unit, or a phone, or a paraffin stove. Finally, some pensioners report they have fewer worries.

We can quantify some of these mechanisms by examining the impact of the pension on nutrition, on sanitation, on psychosocial stress, and on the health consequences of limitations in activities of daily living.

7.4.1   Activities of Daily Living

One mechanism through which the old age pension appears to improve health is through protecting the health status of the older household members who report limitations in their activities of daily living (ADLs). The Langeberg survey asked all household members aged fifty-five and older about their level of difficulty in carrying out the following activities by themselves:

Table 7.5   **Respondent Reports on Life after Pension Receipt: Black and Colored Pensioners**

	PANEL A
	"What did you start doing differently when you received your pension?"

Race	Sex	Open-Ended Response
		In Households that Do Not Pool Income
Black	F	Yes things became different because the money that I earned was smaller than the pension.
Colored	F	Still the same.
Black	F	Bought furniture and renovated the house.
Black	F	I had to start budgeting. I never budgeted before.
Black	F	Relieved poverty a bit.
Black	M	No
Black	F	Opened a bank account.
Colored	M	The household were more easier when she got the pension.
Colored	M	His lifestyle changed—better living conditions.
Colored	F	Nothing.
		In Households that Pool Income
Colored	M	They bought less food now because of the expense of some things.
Colored	M	The hours of work was reduced and he could pay his burial money up to date.
Colored	F	All necessities—such as bed linen and enough food for the household.
Colored	M	A telephone put in.
Colored	M	Were able to pay off his burial.
Colored	F	Nothing changed as the money became more, the price of groceries increased.
Black	M	He gave it to his wife.
Black	F	She started to suffer; bought less food because she got less money.
Black	M	Financially it went worse because the pension is less than what he earned.
Black	M	Doing odd jobs on own time.
Black	M	Pay debts, pay municipality.
Black	F	Lifestyle improved.
Black	F	I buy kitchen unit.
Black	F	Could afford a better life, like buying more food for children.
Black	M	Cannot recall.
Black	M	Looked after the children and made sure that there was always something to eat.
Colored	F	Bought personal things.
Colored	M	Life gets better and could save money.
Colored	F	Nothing changed. Her salary wasn't much less than her pension.
Colored	F	The household were more easier when she got the pension.
Black	M	In the household things goes much better. I could bought a parafin stove.
Colored	M	Worked a less than before.
Colored	M	Expenses needed to decrease with a strict budget.
Colored	F	Sick—asthma.
Colored	F	TO BUY MORE BEDDING.
Colored	F	Nothing—too many expenses.

(continued)

Table 7.5 (continued)

PANEL B
"In what ways did your life become better when your pension started, if any?"

Race	Sex	Open-Ended Response
		In Households that Do Not Pool Income
Black	F	It become better because pension money was more that make my life to be better.
Colored	F	None wise my life became better.
Black	F	It is better. I'm more independent.
Black	F	It was better cause they could buy food though not yet enough.
Black	M	Still the same.
Black	F	I could open my own bank account and my life has improved.
Colored	M	She could buy more food.
Colored	M	Residentiality improved and conditions in house seems to be stable.
Colored	F	Went worse.
		In Households that Pool Income
Colored	M	Did not become better at all.
Colored	M	He has always food to eat now.
Colored	F	Lifestyle improved now.
Colored	M	Yes converted.
Colored	M	Is able to buy himself some things.
Colored	F	Can now buy more groceries and other specialities.
Black	M	It didn't get better because while he was working he earned more money.
Black	F	When she stopped working she draw UIF money.
Black	M	Life did not get better.
Black	M	None.
Black	F	Could buy more food.
Black	F	My life become better than before because the pension money is more.
Black	F	Could maintain children better than before.
Black	M	Nothing changed.
Black	M	None.
Colored	F	Could buy better food for the house hold.
Colored	M	I could buy any thing I need and to give money for household.
Colored	F	It did not improve much.
Colored	F	She could buy more food.
Black	M	With the income.
Colored	M	Don't have to work anymore.
Colored	M	There were less worries, and they didn't need to work anymore and could rest.
Colored	F	No money.
Colored	F	NONE.
Colored	F	Not better.

dressing
bathing
eating
toiletting
taking a bus, taxi, or train
doing light work in or around the house
managing money (if they had to)
climbing a flight of stairs
lifting or carrying a heavy object
walking 200–300 meters

If an older respondent reported difficulty with an activity (answering "difficult, but can do with no help," "can do but only with help," or "can't do"), then the respondent was given a value of "1" for having a limitation in that activity. The number of limitations was then summed over all activities. For black and colored respondents, the number of limitations in ADLs are plotted in figure 7.1, where we find a great deal of variation in limitations within this population.

That limitations in ADLs are significantly correlated with health status can be seen in table 7.6, where we report estimates from ordered probits of self-reported health status as a function of the number of limitations in ADLs—by sex of respondent, an indicator that the respondent is a pensioner, the number of ADLs interacted with the respondent being a pensioner, and the number of ADLs interacted with the household size—for black and colored respondents aged fifty-five and older. All probits in table 7.6 also control for the respondent's sex, race, age, race interacted with age,

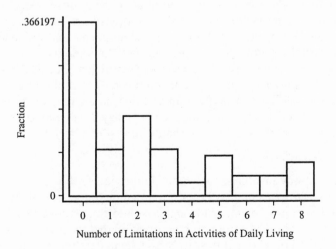

Fig. 7.1   **Limitations in activities of daily living (ADLs)**

Table 7.6   Activities of Daily Living (ADLs) and Self-Reported Health Status

No. of ADL limitations					
Male respondent	.152	.376	.481	.381	.535
	(.087)	(.159)	(.198)	(.156)	(.190)
Female respondent	.235	.576	.791	.585	.896
	(.129)	(.189)	(.274)	(.186)	(.239)
Indicator: Respondent				.251	.890
is a pensioner				(.388)	(.385)
No. of ADL limitations			−.249		−.335
× pensioner			(.120)		(.112)
No. of ADL limitations		−.044	−.048	−.044	−.050
× household size		(.026)	(.028)	(.025)	(.027)

Notes: The ADL questions were asked only in the older adult module (aged fifty-five and above), and sample is restricted to black and colored respondents aged fifty-five and above. Number of observations = 70. Standard errors are presented in parentheses. Ordinary least squares regressions are weighted using weights based on the 1996 South African census, taking into account the stratification of the sample (by race), and the clustering of observations (by enumerator area). All regressions include indicators for sex, race, age, race interacted with age, and controls for the number of household members and the number of members aged zero to seventeen. Dependent variable = self-reported health status (1 = Excellent, 5 = Very Poor); ordered probits.

and include the number of household members and the number of members aged zero to seventeen.

We find that limitations in ADLs are associated with significantly worse health status. Limitations for women are associated with larger erosions in health status than are those for men (although the difference between women and men is not statistically significant). Pensioners with limitations in ADLs report better health status than do older adults with limitations who do not receive the pension. In addition, older adults in larger households report better health status with limitations in ADLs than do other older adults. It appears that both the pension income and residence in a large household is protective for members with limitations.

These results are consistent with a model in which money (in the form of a pension) brings help (purchased or volunteered) when respondents cannot dress or bathe by themselves. In addition, in a large household, it is possible that additional household members may be at hand to help when an older adult is unable to dress or bathe himself or herself.

7.4.2   Sanitation

A second way in which money may influence health is through better sanitation. The pension may be used to upgrade household facilities, and some of the improvements made may have health consequences. In table 7.7, we present evidence from probit estimation that the presence of a pensioner in the household is positively and significantly correlated with a flush toilet in the dwelling and negatively correlated with an indicator that

Table 7.7   **Sources of Water**

	Source of Household's Water is Off-Site		Indicator: Flush Toilet in Dwelling	
Someone in household is eligible	−.001		.187	
for a state pension	(.039)		(.118)	
No. of years of pension receipt		−.008		.031
(based on pensioner's age)		(.007)		(.014)
Urban	−.066	−.064	.111	.111
	(.087)	(.087)	(.950)	(.193)

Source: The Langeberg survey 1999.

Notes: Standard errors are presented in parentheses. Sample restricted to black and colored households. All probits include household size, and an indicator that the household is colored. Probits are weighted using weights based on the 1996 South African census, taking into account the stratification of the sample (by race), and the clustering of observations (by enumerator area). Numbers reported in the table are the change in the probability of the household having this type of sanitation, given a change in the right side variable. Number of observations = 220.

the household's source of water is off-site. Roughly 40 percent of the black and colored households in our sample have a flush toilet; 10 percent do not have water on-site. Obtaining water on-site, or a flush toilet, may take time to accomplish. We allow for this possibility in table 7.7 by regressing these water-related variables on the number of years the pensioner should have been receiving his or her pension (based on age) interacted with an indicator that a pensioner is present. We find that the presence of a flush toilet is significantly more likely the greater the number of years of pension receipt in the household.

7.4.3   Nutrition

Results in table 7.8 suggest that the pension is also useful in protecting the nutritional status of adults within the household. A knowledgeable household member was asked in each household whether in the past year an adult in the household had skipped a meal or had the size of a meal reduced because of lack of funds. Probit results in table 7.8 show that, in households where pensions are pooled, the pension significantly reduces the probability that an adult has skipped a meal. In households that pool income, the presence of a pensioner reduces the probability that an adult has skipped a meal by roughly 25 percent (with or without controls for the number of members aged fifty-five and above.) These results are consistent with the answers given to open-ended questions (reported in table 7.5), where many pensioners reported that life had changed upon pension receipt because the pensioner could now purchase enough food.

That skipping meals is associated with poorer health can be seen in table 7.9, where we regress health status on an indicator that meals were skipped,

Table 7.8   **Meals Missed for Lack of Money and the Old Age Pension**

	Household Pools Income		Household Does Not Pool Income		All Households	
No. of pensioners in	−.256	−.210	−.161	−.047	−.242	−.186
household	(.107)	(.150)	(.203)	(.209)	(.069)	(.123)
No. of members aged 55		−.051		−.124		−.063
or above		(.090)		(.080)		(.080)
Indicator: Household					−.029	−.037
does not pool income					(.080)	(.084)
No. of observations	186	186	34	34	220	220

Notes: Dependent variable = 1 if the "knowledgeable" household member reported that in the past twelve months an adult in the household skipped a meal or had the size of a meal reduced because there was not enough money for food. Numbers reported in the table are the change in the probability that a member has missed a meal, given a change in the right side variable. Also included in each probit are household size and an indicator for the household's race. The sample contains one observation per household. Sample restricted to black and colored households.

together with information on the number of pensioners in the household. In a pooling household, when an adult is reported to have skipped a meal, health status of respondents is 0.20 points worse. In nonpooling households, the coefficient on missing a meal is also large (.23), but is not significantly different from zero, given the large standard error the coefficient attracts. Adding the information on meal skipping reduces the pensioner coefficient in pooling households by roughly 5 percent. With enough information on how pension income is spent, we may be able to parse out the effect of having a pensioner in the household on household health into its component parts.

7.4.4   Psychological Risk Factors

Pension receipt may also reduce the level of psychosocial stress faced by household members. Adler et al. (1994) and Marmot (1999), among others, have argued that the lack of adequate resources may reduce people's ability to cope with stressful life events and may put people at risk for depression, hostility, and psychosocial stress.

We explore this channel using data collected in the Langeberg survey on depression, a close correlate of stress (Sapolsky 1994). Each adult respondent was asked how often in the past week they

felt that they could not stop feeling miserable
felt depressed
felt sad
cried a lot
did not feel like eating
felt that everything was an effort

Table 7.9   Hunger and Health Status

	Pooled			Not Pooled			All		
Indicator: An adult in the household skipped meals	—	.199 (.078)	.197 (.078)	—	.226 (.236)	.220 (.231)	—	.200 (.088)	.197 (.085)
No. of pensioners in household	-.606 (.409)	-.586 (.399)	-.477 (.282)	.189 (.171)	.232 (.150)	.375 (.303)	-.387 (.283)	-.357 (.277)	-.253 (.164)
Indicator: Respondent is a pensioner	.319 (.684)	.332 (.680)	.266 (.605)	-.864 (.526)	-.916 (.524)	-.958 (.511)	-.151 (.526)	-.159 (.522)	-.211 (.473)
No. of members aged 55 or above	.123 (.202)	.125 (.191)	.145 (.238)	.157 (.249)	.157 (.249)		.113 (.186)	.118 (.178)	.118 (.178)
Household size	-.026 (.058)	-.020 (.061)	-.004 (.059)	-.112 (.123)	-.124 (.128)	-.110 (.111)	-.030 (.061)	-.028 (.065)	-.014 (.057)
Household does not pool income	—	—	—	—	—	—	.020 (.083)	.014 (.085)	-.009 (.104)
No. of observations	413	413	413	95	95	95	508	508	508

Source: The Langeberg survey 1999.

Notes: Standard errors are presented in parentheses. Sample restricted to black and colored households. All regressions are weighted using weights based on the 1996 South African census, taking into account the stratification of the sample (by race), and the clustering of observations (by enumerator area). Included in all regressions are indicators that the respondent is colored, female, respondent's age, and age interacted with colored, and the number of members aged zero to seventeen. Dashes indicate that this variable was not included in this ordered probit.

Table 7.10   The Depression Index and the Old Age Pension

Indicator: Household contains at least on pensioner	−.529	
	(.266)	
Indicator: Household contains one pensioner		−.518
		(.238)
Indicator: Household contains two or more pensioners		−.942
		(.517)
Indicator: Respondent is a pensioner	−.316	−.188
	(.302)	(.356)
No. of members aged 55 or above	.072	.113
	(.177)	(.204)
Indicator: Household does not pool income	.100	.079
	(.294)	(.313)

Notes: Standard errors are presented in parentheses. Ordinary least squares regressions are weighted using weights based on the 1996 South African census, taking into account the stratification of the sample (by race), and the clustering of observations (by enumerator area). Sample restricted to black and colored respondents aged eighteen and above. Number of observations = 528. All regressions include indicators for sex, race, age, race interacted with age, and controls for the number of household members and the number of members aged zero to seventeen. Dependent variable = Depression Index (with values from 0 to 8). Blank cells indicate that this variable was not included.

experienced restless sleep
felt they could not get going

We use a respondent's answers to these questions to create a depression index. Specifically, for each, if the respondent reported that he or she felt this way "most of the time" we coded their answer as a "1," and our depression index is the simple sum of these responses. Table 7.10 shows that the depression index is significantly lower the greater the number of pensioners in the household. The presence of members aged fifty-five and above has no significant effect on the index, suggesting that it is not the presence of older members, but the money they bring with them, that reduces stress for all adults within the household.

7.5   Conclusions

Income, in the form of an old age pension, has been shown here to improve the health status of all household members in households that pool income. This improvement provides a benchmark against which governments and international organizations interested in improving health status can evaluate other health-related interventions. In those cases in which the lack of capacity, organizational ability, or political will makes improvement in health systems difficult to deliver, the delivery of cash may be a better option if the goal is improvement in health.

References

Adler, Nancy E., Thomas Boyce, Margaret A. Chesney, Sheldon Cohen, Susan Folkman, Robert L. Kahn, and S. Leonard Syme. 1994. Socioeconomic status and health, the challenge of the gradient. *American Psychologist* 49 (1): 15–24.

Case, Anne, and Angus Deaton. 1998. Large cash transfers to the elderly in South Africa. *Economic Journal* 108:1330–61.

————. 1999. School inputs and educational outcomes in South Africa. *Quarterly Journal of Economics* 458:1047–84.

Case, Anne, and Francis Wilson. 2001. Health and wellbeing in South Africa: Evidence from the Langeberg Survey. Princeton University. Mimeograph.

Duflo, Esther. 2000. Grandmothers and granddaughters: Old age pension and intra-household allocation in South Africa. NBER Working Paper no. 8061. Cambridge, Mass.: National Bureau of Economic Research, December.

Fuchs, Victor R. 1982. Time Preference and Health: An Exploratory Study. In *Economic aspects of health*, ed. Victor R. Fuchs, 93–120. Chicago: University of Chicago Press.

Idler, Ellen L., and Stanislav V. Kasl. 1995. Self-Ratings of health: Do they also predict change in functional ability? *Journal of Gerontology: Social Sciences* 508 (6): S344–53.

Marmot, Michael. 1999. Epidemiology of socioeconomic status and health: Are determinants within countries the same as between countries? In *Socioeconomic status and health in industrial nations,* ed. Nancy E. Adler, Michael Marmot, Bruce S. McEwen, and Judith Stewart, 16–29. New York: The New York Academy of Sciences.

Sapolsky, Robert M. 1994. *Why zebras don't get ulcers, A guide to stress, stress-related diseases and coping.* New York: W. H. Freeman.

Smith, James P. 1999. Healthy bodies and thick wallets: The dual relationship between health and economic status. *Journal of Economic Perspectives* 13 (2): 145–66.

van der Berg, Servaas. 1994. *Issues in South African social security.* Washington, D.C.: World Bank.

Comment   Robert T. Jensen

There has been a surge of interest in the relationship between socioeconomic status (SES) and health. Much of this evidence has drawn on data from wealthy, industrialized nations. The present paper makes an important contribution because it both presents evidence from a low-income country and uses a unique strategy to isolate the effect of income on health. The latter point is particularly important since most studies that find a cross-sectional correlation between health and SES are unable to rule out

Robert T. Jensen is associate professor of public policy at the John F. Kennedy School of Government, Harvard University, and a faculty research fellow of the National Bureau of Economic Research.

the possibility that causality runs in the opposite direction (from health to SES) or that there are unobservable "third factors" affecting both health and SES. Direction of causality is clear in this paper because it examines the impact of a large, exogenous income source, namely the South African old age pension system.

The author finds that pension income has a large effect on health, especially improving measures of self-reported health status. Further, pensions improve the health of not only the elderly recipients, but also of other household members living with pensioners. However, the others only benefit in households which "pool," or share, income. This result provides a significant sophistication and refinement beyond what is typically seen in studies of the SES–health relationship. If income is not pooled perfectly within households, the correct measure of SES for an individual is not total household income (per capita), but only the amount of income actually available to that person. Recent empirical evidence, especially from developing countries, has confirmed that distribution within households is not always equal and that household decision making cannot be treated as though it arises from a single household utility function with pooled income.

The results isolating the effects of income on health can serve as a useful benchmark for evaluating health interventions. In low-income countries, the effectiveness of health interventions (such as construction of health clinics or the provision of medicines) is often limited. A number of factors often inhibit success of these interventions, including difficulties in distribution, delivery, and maintenance, as well as funding for ongoing costs, such as medicines and medical personnel. Quite simply, it is often too difficult to maintain a well-functioning system of health clinics adequately supplied with medicines and trained personnel, especially when much of the population is dispersed in low-density rural areas, and funding is poor. In this context, finding that increases in income improve health suggests that perhaps the best (or most cost-effective) health intervention may be direct cash grants. Therefore, the results of this report carry great significance. In an effort to refine and strengthen these results, I offer the following comments:

Can Income be a Mixed Blessing?

The reduced-form relationship between health and SES tells an interesting story but to some extent may not tell the whole story. Income surely has some effect on health but examining the reduced-form relationship ignores critical and important individual factors and dynamics. In particular, while income may bring improved health through the purchase of adequate nutrition, medical care, and services, it may bring adverse consequences as well. For example, obesity is a problem in South Africa, especially among women (the *mean* value of the body mass index among older women is 32, which qualifies as obese). This is a significant public health concern because obesity is a risk factor for conditions such as hypertension, heart disease, and diabetes. If more income leads to more food intake or a diet that is higher in sodium, fat, or cholesterol (for example, increases in income may be associated with increases in meat consumption; see Jensen in this volume), then we might expect income to ultimately have adverse consequences on health. The measurable effects on health (and mortality) may not show up for many years but are something that should be monitored.

It is also possible that increases in income could be associated with increases in smoking and drinking because there is some evidence (from developed countries) that alcohol and tobacco are normal goods. These behavioral factors could also ultimately lead to worse health. For the South African case in particular, there might be a difference between men and women in terms of what effect the increased pension income has on alcohol and tobacco consumption.

The interesting aspects of focusing on both the positive and negative effects on health would be to offer insight into the design of strategies that capture the positive benefits of improvements in income but avoid the negative consequences, for example, subsidizing certain foods or lowering fees for health clinics (though these strategies are often problematic in themselves).

What are the Direct Channels through which Income Affects Health?

Ultimately, the paper and ink that make up currency have no direct health-promoting or curative properties. The value of such an in-depth, integrated household survey like the one used in this paper is that it provides information on a variety of topics that might assist in trying to uncover the specific channels through which income affects health (again, in both positive and negative directions). For policy purposes, it is these direct channels that may be of most interest. The paper investigates a few specific channels: assistance in daily living, meals missed, and depression/psychosocial stress. However, there are numerous other channels through which income might affect health:

- Living environment (moving to a safer or cleaner living environment);
- Sanitation/water (greater access to sanitation or clean water);
- Medical services (more likely to get a checkup, to see a doctor if ill, to pay for a higher-quality private doctor; more able to afford medicines if necessary);
- Labor supply: Increases in nonlabor income could lead to reductions in working hours, which would reduce physical strain on the body (although a more sedentary lifestyle could adversely affect health);
- Diet and nutrition (intake of foods with higher nutritional content,

that is, moving away from low-cost staples [like grains] that are filling and provide calories, and toward foods with higher levels of other nutrients): However, again, some of these foods could also have higher levels of fat, sodium, or cholesterol.

Given all these potential channels linking SES and health, and given how much detail the survey collects, it would be interesting to see more direct evidence. For example, it should be possible to track health effects through increases in food expenditure and changes in food consumption patterns, alcohol and tobacco use, working hours, and use of medical services.

Limiting Factors: Is Income Necessary, Sufficient, Both, or Neither?

Income is likely to have an effect on health through the various channels mentioned previously but there are likely to be factors that limit the extent to which income can help. For example, if medicine and medical care are important factors in the production of health, which they are likely to be, then large increases in income won't help much unless there are accessible health facilities nearby with well-trained personnel and an adequate supply of medicines. Income likewise will not clean the water one pulls from a stream or contaminated well (unless the person moves to a new area or buys a filter or some other mechanism for treating water). Income also will not drain a swamp or spray to clear an area of malaria-carrying mosquitoes or prevent other vector-borne illnesses, though they may allow one to purchase vaccines or medicines or prophylactics, such as mosquito netting or repellent. Given that some of the major illnesses and leading causes of death in low-income countries arise from greater environmental and health threats that a person may not be able to control on their own or that are not specifically related to income(for example, infectious diseases, parasites, and AIDS), understanding the limiting factors and the interaction of income with these other factors and with other health interventions may provide important insights for health policy.

The Use of Subjective Measures of Health Status

As a complex and multidimensional concept, defining "good health" is extremely challenging and measuring it even more difficult. Measures such as overall, self-reported health status (self-ranking on a scale of 1 to 5, from very bad to very good) have gained widespread popularity. These measures have been shown to have good predictive power for mortality (in developed countries), as individuals are likely able to recognize the state of their health, perhaps even in ways sophisticated tests cannot detect. However, there are a few possible problems with these measures; first, awareness of health conditions in low-income countries is much lower than in wealthy nations. Individuals in wealthy nations may have a lot of information about their health status due to the much higher use (and quality) of medical services, which would allow them to provide meaningful answers to questions about overall perceived health status. Another problem is that individuals may norm their responses relative to a reference group; if I live among other people who are mostly very poor and my health is slightly better, I may say that my health is very good. Similarly, a rich person may norm their health relative to a reference group of other rich people. But differences in averages across the groups may make the comparisons in self-reported health status by income less appropriate. If the rich are, on average, healthier than the poor, a rich person's report of "bad" may actually reflect better true health status than a poor person's "good" due to these reference group effects.

Also, while such measures may be good predictors of mortality, it is possible that systematic errors arise precisely along the specific lines of SES, which would cause problems for studies of the SES–health relationship. The rich and poor are likely to have differential awareness or knowledge of health conditions, and thus there would arise differences in the extent to which self-reports are good measures of true health. Of course, to the extent this is true, it would most likely only strengthen the association between SES and health because the rich are more likely to be aware of health conditions or illnesses they have due to greater use of (higher quality) medical services. But if the goal is to get a valid estimate of the effects of income on health, especially for use as a benchmark against which to compare the impacts of other policies, any biases should be a cause of concern.

One potential specific problem with the use of self-assessed health in the present case is that the data show that the pension income is associated with reductions in a "depression index." Figure 7C.1 demonstrates the main con-

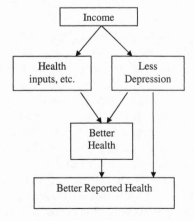

Fig. 7C.1   A potential problem with self-reported health status

cern. Income leads to improvements in health (for example, through greater inputs into health), but also leads to lower depression. Reduced depression, aside from possibly affecting health itself, may change reported health status, even in the absence of any true changes in health. People who are less depressed are likely to report everything more positively, and thus even without changes in health status there could be changes in *reported* health status. This would again affect the extent to which we can use income as a benchmark.

Overall, it is certainly possible that subjective, self-reported health measures are just as meaningful in developing as in developed nations and valid even for use in SES-health studies. However, there is a need for validation studies. Confirming their validity would provide a great value to researchers interested in health in developing countries because a single, easy question that captures meaningful information on such a hard-to-measure but important attribute as health could be used widely in a variety of surveys and studies.

Pooling

Some of the most intriguing results of the paper are the differences in the impacts of the pension on the health of nonpensioners, for pooling versus nonpooling households. The finding that the health of children and other adult members improves in pension households only when income is pooled provides powerful evidence that (1) income matters for health, (2) the distribution of income within households, sharing, and pooling matter for the well-being of individuals within households, and (3) even a simple question asking whether the household pools income captures a meaningful characteristic of household behavior. Empirical and theoretical research in development economics has taken quite seriously (perhaps because of the prevalence of extended households) the notion of resource sharing and decision making within households, moving beyond the simple notion that a household behaves as though there were a single utility function and budget constraint. This paper provides yet another example of the power and relevance of such analysis. It would seem that studies from wealthier nations should follow suit or at least test for the validity of the assumptions of the conventional model of household behavior.

There should also be more research on how better to infer resource sharing within households. Asking only whether income is pooled at all (0 or 1) may ignore some important "shades" of sharing between complete sharing and no sharing. There may be domains and areas of decision making in which households behave more like a single entity, and others where they act more like a collection of individual optimizers. A further issue is that individuals within households may be differentially aware of the extent to which income is pooled within the household. In the present paper, only one "knowledgeable" person in the household is asked about pooling. As is emphasized in the paper with regard to the need to collect information on individual health and incomes, certain information within households is private. It is possible that there may not be perfect pooling, but only the person holding back some of their money is aware of it. In general, further probing and research on distribution and decision making within households is likely to yield important information about individual well-being and its distribution.

8

Socioeconomic Status, Nutrition, and Health among the Elderly

Robert T. Jensen

8.1 Introduction

There has been a great deal of research on the relationship between socioeconomic status (SES) and health.[1] This relationship is of interest for several reasons; first, there is increasing recognition that in assessing living standards and well-being in a society, and its distribution among members, measures such as health may represent more appropriate indicators than income or expenditure. Second, understanding the relationship between SES and health is important because it can shed light on what may be a self-reinforcing cycle of poverty; low SES leads to worse health, which in turn reduces earnings capacity.

Much of the literature has focused on adults (especially those of working-age), though there has recently been increasing attention paid to children (Case et al. 2002; Meara 2001; Jensen and Richter 2001) and the elderly (Hurd, McFadden, and Merrill 1999; Jensen and Richter 2003, Smith and Kington 1997a,b). For the elderly, the health–SES relationship is particularly important because of increasing life expectancies, increasing fragility of many pension and social security systems throughout the world, and declines in extended families and traditional systems of support for the elderly.

In this paper, we apply data from a nationally representative household-level survey to explore the relationship between health and SES for the

Robert T. Jensen is associate professor of public policy at the John F. Kennedy School of Government, Harvard University, and a faculty research fellow of the National Bureau of Economic Research.

I would like to thank David Cutler, Lindsey Knapp, and Kaspar Richter for comments, suggestions, and assistance.

1. For summaries of this vast literature, see Feinstein 1993 and Smith 1999.

elderly in Russia. In doing so, we have two main objectives; first, we explore the basic relationship, which is valuable because there has been little evidence on the health–SES relationship for transition economies. Further, we add to the literature by presenting evidence from a variety of measures of health and health risk factors, including measurements of blood pressure, weight, and height conducted by trained enumerators, as well as nutrient intake derived from twenty-four- and forty-eight-hour food intake diaries. Therefore, we need not rely exclusively on self-reports of health status, where response choices may have different interpretations for different people (as in self-reported overall health status), or where there may be problems of differential reporting by SES (for example, due to differential knowledge or awareness of health conditions). We use these data to show that the relationship between health and SES in Russia can't be adequately described by simple statements, such as the poor are less healthy than the rich; although, on net, the rich are healthier than the poor in some overall sense, there are important ways in which the rich face greater health risks.

But the most interesting questions in the study of the relationship between health and income, and the biggest challenges, involve trying to decompose the health differentials into the root causes. As others have noted, there are numerous channels through which the two could be linked; first, SES could affect health through the purchase of inputs that produce health (medical services, nutrition, safe and clean living environment, for example). The poor may also have more stress due to, say, greater economic volatility and uncertainty, and this greater stress could lead to worse health directly or through changes in health-related behaviors. It is also quite possible that causality runs in the opposite direction, where health affects earnings capacity and thus SES. Finally, it could also be that there are factors which cause both low SES and poor health (for example, rates of time preference or attitudes towards risk).

Therefore, our second objective is to narrow down and focus on one particular mechanism—nutrition—through which SES may affect health. The role of nutrition as a factor in the differential health status between rich and poor is often overlooked when examining middle- and upper-income countries because widespread hunger and starvation, even among the poorest, have largely been eliminated, and in fact widespread obesity is considered a greater public health concern. However, nutrition must be viewed as more complex than hunger or simply sufficient caloric intake. In particular, there are important micronutrients beyond calories that are important for good health, especially for the elderly. And the intake of these nutrients may be sensitive to income, as the lowest cost staple foods in most countries (for example, bread or rice) may yield sufficient "bulk" or calories, but (unless fortified) may have low levels of vitamins, minerals, and protein. On the other hand, these foods tend to be low in fat, cholesterol, and sodium, compared to foods which may be more expensive and eaten in larger quantities by the rich, for example, meat. Therefore, it is quite possible that nutrition plays a role in the relationship between health and SES, even in countries where calorie malnutrition is scarce and obesity is widespread.

We use detailed data on food intake to analyze nutrient intake for elderly Russians and how it varies with income, and the consequences for health and the relationship between health and SES. We do so by exploring (1) differences in the diets of the rich and poor, (2) how differences in diet translate into differences in nutrient intake, and (3) the impact of nutrient intake on health.

8.2   The "Health-SES" Gradient

We begin by documenting the relationship between SES and health in Russia. We do not, however, attempt to deal with the extremely important issue of reverse causality, that is, determining whether low SES causes bad health or vice versa, or both—a problem that plagues all studies of health and SES. Thus, the results should not be seen as suggesting causality, only establishing an empirical relationship in which there is much interest. Some studies have attempted to overcome this problem using exogenous changes in the income of the elderly (Case, chap. 7 in this vol.; Jensen and Richter 2003). However, in the present case we have no such exogenous variation.

8.2.1   The Data

We use data from various rounds of the Russian Longitudinal Monitoring Survey (RLMS), a nationally representative survey of approximately 4,000 households collected between 1992 and 1998.[2] The data are well-suited to the present purposes, containing detailed information on income, expenditures, and a variety of measures of health. For the later rounds of the survey there is also a twenty-four- or forty-eight-hour food recall diary, where all individuals report everything they have eaten. Furthermore, trained enumerators administered medical measurements during the surveys, including measuring weight and height, hip and thigh circumference, and blood pressure.[3]

For assessing health status and health risk factors, we analyze systolic and diastolic blood pressure (which can be used to assess hypertension, a leading factor in heart attack and strokes), as well as construct the body mass index (BMI),[4] which is an important predictor of mortality. In addition, we consider the following set of health indicators: self-assessed

2. The survey is coordinated by the Carolina Population Center at the University of North Carolina at Chapel Hill. Further description of the data can be found at www.cpc.unc.edu/projects/rlms/rlms_home.html.

3. Blood pressure measurements were taken three times in order to adhere to the clinical standard.

4. BMI is weight (in kilograms) divided by squared height (in meters).

health, which is the response to a question asking the respondent to evaluate their overall health, with possible responses ranging from 1 to 5 (1 = very good; 2 = good; 3 = average; 4 = bad; 5 = very bad). We also use an indicator for whether the respondent reports in the past twelve months having experienced strong chest pains lasting half an hour or more. Finally, we construct an index of the respondent's ability to perform various activities of daily living (ADL). The ADL index ranges from 0 to 50, with the responses from ten questions about specific activities scored on a scale of 1 to 5, where the possible responses represent 1 (not at all difficult); 2 (slightly difficult); 3 (somewhat difficult); 4 (very difficult, but possible); and 5 (cannot do it). Thus, a higher score indicates greater functional limitations. Activities included are run one kilometer; walk one kilometer; walk 200 meters; walk across a room; sit for two hours; stand up after sitting; climb several flights of stairs; climb one flight of stairs; lift and carry a weight of about five kilograms; and squat, crouch or kneel.

8.2.2   The Gradient

Table 8.1 presents evidence on the gradient between health and SES. To represent SES, we divide the sample of persons aged sixty and older into quartiles of income per capita (we make no adjustments for economies of scale or adult equivalents because there is no rigorous theoretical basis or obvious choice for specific adjustment factors).

The initial evidence from Russia is comparable to what is found elsewhere; for both men and women, on measures like self-assessed health, ADL limitations, and whether the person was ill in the past thirty days, the poor are less healthy than the rich. Elderly men and women in the highest income quartile report better health status (0.3 for men and 0.2 for women, on a five point scale) than individuals in the lowest quartile. The wealthiest also report fewer physical limitations; for men, the ADL index is almost five points lower for individuals in the upper quartile. Because the minimum score for each of the ten areas of functioning is 1, this indicates that the wealthiest, on average, are half a point better able to perform every task, on a scale of 1 to 5. For women, the gradient is smaller but still present. Again, it should be emphasized that causality could run in either direction (or both directions); the poor could have greater physical limitations because of their income, or their limitations could diminish their work capacity and thus their income.

There is a sharp decline in the reported incidence of chest pains (lasting greater than thirty minutes) with income; 16 percent of the poorest men and 30 percent of the poorest women report having experienced chest pains in the past month lasting for more than half an hour, compared to 12 and 19 percent of those in the top income quartile.

However, the other health variables show that the gradient is much more complex, and in fact along some dimensions the gradient favors the poor, especially with regard to health risk factors. Men and women in the lowest

Table 8.1   Health and SES among the Elderly in Russia

Quartile	Self-Assessed	ADL Index	Systolic (mm HG)	Diastolic (mm HG)	BMI (kg/m2)	Sick in last 30 days?	Chest Pains >30 mins.?	Workers Only	
								Systolic (mm HG)	Diastolic (mm HG)
Men									
I	3.3	20.1	132	84	25.4	.58	.16	130	84
II	3.3	20.6	135	85	26.0	.54	.18	130	83
III	3.3	19.5	136	85	25.0	.55	.18	132	85
IV	3.0	15.4	137	86	26.2	.47	.12	135	85
Women									
I	3.6	25.8	135	86	27.6	.74	.30	131	83
II	3.6	25.8	138	86	28.5	.75	.24	133	85
III	3.5	24.0	140	86	28.9	.69	.24	134	84
IV	3.4	22.4	139	85	28.7	.66	.19	134	84

Source: Based on data from 1995 RLMS.

Notes: Quartile refers to quartile of income per household member; no adjustments made for economies of scale. Sample restricted to persons aged sixty and above. Self-assessed health is the response to a question asking the respondent to evaluate their health, with possible responses ranging from 1 to 5 (1 = Very Good; 2 = Good; 3 = Average; 4 = Bad; 5 = Very Bad). "Chest pains > 30 mins." is whether in the past twelve months the person has experienced strong pains in the chest, lasting half an hour or more. The ADL Index ranges from 0 to 50, with responses from ten questions about specific activities of daily living scored on a scale of 1 to 5 (1 = Not at all difficult; 2 = Slightly difficult; 3 = Somewhat difficult; 4 = Very difficult, but possible; 5 = Cannot do it). Activities included were walk across a room; walk 200 meters; walk one kilometer; run one kilometer; sit for two hours; stand up after sitting; lie down and get up from a bed unassisted; climb one flight of stairs; climb several flights of stairs; lift and carry a weight of about five kilograms; squat, crouch, or kneel. Thus, a higher score indicates greater functional limitations.

Table 8.2   Health Inputs/Behaviors and SES among the Elderly in Russia

Quartile	Drink?	Amount drink, if >0 (g)	Smoke?	Amount smoke, if >0 (g)
		Men		
I	.53	24.1	.44	16
II	.53	19.1	.40	14
III	.62	23.9	.39	14
IV	.64	29.9	.39	15
		Women		
I	.18	4.9	.08	6.3
II	.16	8.0	.12	5.6
III	.27	5.7	.13	6.7
IV	.26	9.5	.10	7.0

Source: Based on data from 1995 RLMS.

Notes: Quartile refers to quartile of income per household member, no adjustments made for economies of scale. Sample restricted to persons aged sixty and above.

income quartile have lower (4–5 mm HG) systolic blood pressure than those in the upper quartile; this could be due to a number of factors; for example, wealthier people may face more work-related stress. We will also see later, however, that the rich have higher levels of sodium intake and consume more fat, both of which would also be associated with higher blood pressure. Further, the incidence of drinking is higher among the wealthier (shown in the following). Part of the differences in blood pressure between rich and poor may be due to greater employment rates among the rich, which could affect blood pressure.[5] In the final two columns of the table, we present data only on working persons; overall, systolic blood pressure is lower for those who are working compared to nonworkers, but we see that the working-poor still have lower blood pressure than the working-rich. These results are also interesting in light of the results in Jensen (2001), who finds that individuals who are more concerned about job loss (which typically the poor are) have higher blood pressure and are more likely to report having chest pains and other health problems.

The BMI data show wealthier individuals are also heavier than poorer persons, which is a health risk in itself and could also explain the higher blood pressure among the rich. However, the lower BMI of the poor could be related to illness, which in itself leads to lower income.

Table 8.2 presents information on behaviors that influence health, by in-

---

5. Though the direction of correlation is ambiguous, some work may create greater stress due to work-related responsibilities and pressures, or due to concern over job security. By contrast, the physical activities of work, provided it is not too strenuous, and the social contact provided could also have beneficial effects on blood pressure compared to being idle or spending most time alone.

come quartile. For both men and women, the wealthy are approximately 10 percentage points more likely to say they have drunk alcohol in the past week and report drinking more the last time they drank. Smoking declines slightly with income for men, but the difference is small. There is no difference for either men or women in the number of cigarettes smoked, conditional on smoking.

Thus, overall, the relationship between health and SES needs to be seen as far more complex than simply stating that the poor are less healthy than the rich. The poor are less healthy on many outcome measures of health (mostly self-reported), but, for example, blood pressure and BMI are higher among the richest persons, which leads to increased risk of heart disease, stroke, and mortality. The important conclusion is that while there may be scope for policies to improve the health of the poor, policies should also not ignore the potential for improving the health of the wealthy.

8.3 The Role of Nutrition

We now turn to the issue of nutrition in the relationship between health and SES. One direct channel through which income may affect health is through nutrition. This channel is often overlooked in most settings of industrialized nations, where obesity is more of a concern than malnutrition. In fact, the Russian data are consistent with these observations, showing that obesity is very high, and the incidence of insufficient caloric intake is rare, even among the poorest.

However, proper nutrition is much more than adequate energy intake. While the exact linkages and magnitude of effects have not been precisely determined by medical researchers, it has long been understood that proper nutrition has a large effect on health. Energy (calories) is important for all aspects of functioning, but other nutrients (vitamins, minerals, and protein) are nearly as important, and long-term deficiency of certain nutrients can affect health through disease, or musculoskeletal maintenance. With age, people need fewer calories (energy from food), both because the basal metabolic rate (calories needed for involuntary work like breathing, heartbeat, and food digestion) declines, and because people tend to become less active. But while the elderly typically need fewer calories, they still need nearly the same amount of important nutrients such as protein, vitamins, and minerals.

To explore the role of nutrition in the relationship between health and SES, we first examine how diet varies with income, then how nutrition varies with diet, and then how nutrition affects health and physical functioning.

8.3.1   From Income to Diet

Table 8.3 presents data on dietary patterns by income quartile. For households in the various quartiles, we report raw quantities consumed on

Table 8.3   Income and Nutrient Intake among the Elderly in Russia

Quartile	Meat/Fish/ Eggs	Dairy	Bread	Cereals	Vegetables	Fruit	Fats	Sugar	Borsch/ Shchi
				Men					
I	102	125	219	93	242	45	17	31	401
II	114	116	231	77	256	78	14	35	396
III	114	116	231	77	258	78	14	35	396
IV	159	160	246	73	280	66	15	40	357
				Women					
I	60	107	168	62	209	69	10	30	285
II	57	97	169	76	187	57	12	29	277
III	69	122	162	72	204	74	13	32	260
IV	90	156	159	80	244	85	10	33	268

Source: Based on data from 1995 RLMS.
Notes: See table 8.2.

a daily basis, in grams, for ten food groupings.[6] Overall, for both men and women, the largest categories of consumption by weight are borsch/shchi (a vegetable soup), bread and vegetables, and much smaller quantities of fruit and cereals. But additionally, the diets of the rich and the poor differ noticeably. While the rich eat more of most every food group except borsch/ shchi, there is a difference across the various food groups in how much more they consume. For men, the wealthiest quartile consume fifty-seven more grams (56 percent) of meat per day than the poorest, fifty-nine more grams (21 percent) of fruits and vegetables (combined), and thirty-five grams (28 percent) more dairy. On the other side, daily consumption of borsch/shchi is forty-four grams (11 percent) lower for the wealthy, and ce-reals are twenty grams (22 percent) lower. For women, the largest differ-ences between the top and bottom quartiles are that the rich consume more dairy (forty-nine grams, 46 percent), and meat (thirty grams, 33 percent). Borsch/shchi is seventeen grams (6 percent) lower for the richest women, but most other categories are largely the same.

The upper half of table 8.5 presents estimates of elasticities from regres-sions of quantities consumed of the various foods on total household ex-penditure per person, whereas additional regressors that we include are age, gender, education, family size, and twenty-five food price variables, gathered from community-level price surveys. We estimate the regressions, both cross-sectionally (columns [1] and [3]) and while exploiting the panel nature of the data, to regress changes in consumption on changes in in-come. The results confirm what is observed in the data in the previous

6. An important issue, which we do not treat here, is quality substitution within food cate-gories. See, for example, Subramanian and Deaton 1996.

tables on means, namely that the largest positive elasticities are on meat, dairy, and fruit, and borsch/shchi has a large, negative elasticity. Another important lesson from this table is that the cross-sectional elasticities are very close to those obtained using the fixed-effects specification. If the elasticities were larger in cross section compared to changes, then we would be more likely to conclude that the differences in consumption patterns were due to other differences—in tastes or other attributes—between rich and poor (or that there is a degree of inertia in consumption, for example, due to habits). These results therefore suggest that economic resources are an important factor in the differential diets of rich and poor and that, with increases in income, diet changes in significant ways.

8.3.2 From Diet to Nutrition

From the food intake data, we can calculate daily intake of a variety of micro- and macro-nutrients by merging intake with Russia-specific conversion tables that list the nutrient content (approximately twelve macro- and micronutrients) of nearly 2,600 individual food items.[7] In addition, we also have information in the survey on whether individuals are taking specific vitamin or mineral supplements, which we can use to calculate total nutrient intake.[8] Table 8.4 presents nutrient intake by income quartile, along with the (U.S.) recommended levels of daily intake for the elderly.[9]

The first thing to notice is that for all income groups, the intake of several key nutrients is well below recommended levels. For men, intake of niacin, vitamin C, magnesium, potassium, and calcium are low. Women are low on intake of these same nutrients, as well as protein, thiamin, and riboflavin. Further, both men and women have extremely high daily sodium intakes.

In terms of the gradient with income, for men, higher income is associated with increased intake of important micronutrients such as calories, protein, niacin, vitamin C, potassium, calcium, and iron. Women additionally increase intake of thiamin and riboflavin. However, for both men and women, increases in income are also associated with increased intake

---

7. The food items for which we have nutrient information are extremely detailed and match the level of detail provided in the food intake data. For example, there are entries for prepared and packaged foods; nearly thirty different entries for potatoes, which vary along several dimensions, including method of preparation (boiling, frying—for seven different types of oil/ lard); and entries for several hundred specific meals and entrees.

8. However, since we do not know the exact content of specific vitamin supplements, for persons who report taking vitamins we add to their daily intake the recommended daily level for the specific nutrient (we add the required amount for all nutrients if the person takes a multivitamin).

9. Guidelines are for individuals aged fifty or older, drawn from the 1997–1998 U.S. Dietary Reference Intakes, which includes Recommended Dietary Allowances (RDA) for thiamin, riboflavin, niacin, and magnesium and Adequate Intakes (AI) for calcium; 1989 RDA for energy, protein, vitamin A, vitamin C, and iron; 1995 Dietary Guidelines for Americans, published by the U.S. Department of Agriculture and the U.S. Department of Health and Human Services (for sodium).

Table 8.4   Income and Nutrient Intake among the Elderly in Russia as compared to U.S. Dietary Guidelines

Quartile	Energy (kcal)	Protein (g)	Fat (%)	Thiamin (mg)	Riboflavin (mg)	Niacin (mg NE)	Vitamin C (mg)	Magnesium (mg)	Calcium (mg)	Potassium (mg)	Iron (mg)	Sodium (mg)
Men												
I	1,991	62	29.5	1.2	.77	13.4	49	269	494	2,818	15.6	4,336
II	1,898	60	29.6	1.1	.84	12.5	43	258	568	2,835	15.0	4,192
III	2,041	68	32.2	1.1	.96	13.8	47	367	577	2,852	16.2	4,542
IV	2,110	69	31.8	1.2	1.0	15.0	56	385	623	3,292	17.4	4,752
U.S. Guideline	2,000	63	30	1.2	1.3	16	60	420	1,000	3,500	10	2,400
Women												
I	1,712	42	28.2	.81	.71	8.9	46	243	415	2,220	11.8	2,946
II	1,751	45	29.3	.82	.81	9.3	45	242	458	2,202	12.0	2,958
III	1,831	44	29.6	.80	.84	9.0	46	255	476	2,187	12.2	2,939
IV	1,810	49	32.2	.86	.91	10.4	50	245	499	2,392	13.2	3,137
U.S. Guideline	1,800	50	30	1.1	1.1	14	60	320	1,000	3,500	10	2,400

Sources: Based on data from 1995 RLMS. Guidelines for intake are for individuals aged 50 or older, drawn from: 1997–1998 U.S. Dietary Reference Intakes (which includes Recommended Dietary Allowances [RDA] for thiamin, riboflavin, niacin, and magnesium and Adequate Intakes [AI] for calcium); 1989 Recommended Dietary Allowances [RDA] for energy, protein, vitamin C, and iron); 1995 Dietary Guidelines for Americans, published by the U.S. Department of Agriculture and the U.S. Department of Health and Human Services (for sodium). U.S.D.A. website (http://www.nal.usda.gov/fnic/etext/000105.html).

Notes: See table 8.2.

of sodium and a greater percent of calories from fat. Thus the wealthy have diets which yield more of several important nutrients, but the diets are less desirable from a health perspective in other ways.

It should be kept in mind that these data simply represent intake through food or vitamin supplements. The actual levels of the various vitamins and minerals available in a person's body may differ from these intakes for several reasons. First, the body can produce some nutrients (for example, the body can produce vitamin D through exposure to sunlight, though the elderly often have reduced time spent outside). Also, individuals vary in their ability to absorb vitamins. Furthermore, insufficient intake of some nutrients inhibits the absorption and effective use of other nutrients; for example, vitamin D is important for the body's ability to absorb calcium properly. There are also important interactions between nutrients; for example, an imbalance in the levels of potassium and sodium may be as harmful to blood pressure as simply an excess of sodium. Finally, it should also be mentioned that levels that vastly exceed the recommended levels could be just as harmful as deficiencies. For instance, the elderly are less able to effectively clear vitamin A from the body, and thus are at risk of vitamin A toxicity, which can lead to adverse reactions.

The lower half of table 8.5 provides estimates of the elasticities of intake of the various nutrients. For both men and women, the greatest elasticities are on the intake of calcium, fat, protein, vitamin C, and sodium. And as with consumption of foods, the cross-sectional and first-differenced elasticities are similar, suggesting income itself plays a role in the differential level of nutrient intake between the rich and poor. However, an important point which emerges from all of these results is that while nutritional status will improve (in some ways) with income, even large increases in income would not lead to completely adequate nutrition. The elasticities of many of the nutrients are quite small, and even among the wealthiest quartile, there are still deficiencies in the intake of calcium, potassium, magnesium, and vitamin C (for women). Therefore, it will take more than growth in incomes to arrive at adequate nutritional status among the elderly.

8.3.3 From Nutrition to Health

We saw earlier that on several measures, for instance, ADL's, the poor were less healthy than the rich. An important question we address now is whether the lower nutrient intake of the poor is directly associated with the lower health status of the poor. We focus on the particular case of the greater physical limitations of the poor, because the measure is slightly more objective than overall self-reported health status and because there is a clear link between the intake of certain nutrients and physical functioning, especially for the elderly. The macro- and micro-nutrients considered most important for maintenance of bones and muscles in old age, and thus those most likely to affect physical limitations, are protein—for muscle

Table 8.5   **Nutrient Elasticities with Respect to Expenditure**

	Men		Women	
	Cross-Section (1)	First-Diffs. (2)	Cross-Section (3)	First-Diffs. (4)
Foods				
Meat/Fish/Eggs	.31***	.20***	.14***	.11***
Dairy	.18**	.14*	.28**	.19*
Bread	.12***	.10**	.10***	.09*
Cereals	−.06*	.03	.08	−.02
Vegetables	.11***	.19*	.09**	.08
Potatoes	−.08	.03	−.03	.08
Fruit	.16*	.10*	.14*	.13**
Fats	.18	.10**	.10	.08
Sugar	.04*	−.03	.09**	.02
Borsch/Shchi	−.20**	−.15***	−.11	−.10*
Nutrients				
Energy (kcal)	.14**	.10*	.19**	.15*
Protein (g)	.20*	.15*	.21***	.13**
Fat (g)	.19*	.30**	.28***	.25**
Thiamin (mg)	.11	.06	.08	.14
Riboflavin (mg)	.19*	.08	.16	.11
Niacin (mg NE)	.16	.03	.12	.06
Vitamin C (mg)	.19**	.16**	.12**	.17***
Magnesium (mg)	.16***	.20***	.09	.03
Calcium (mg)	.29***	.41***	.31***	.22***
Potassium (mg)	.13**	.08	.08	−.04
Iron (mg)	.14	.07	.11	.03
Sodium (mg)	.18**	.31***	.09	.14*

Notes: Numbers in the tables are elasticities from regressions where food or nutrient consumed (or changes in amount consumed) is the dependent variable, and age, gender, education, family size, and twenty-five food prices, obtained from community-level surveys.

***Significant at the 1 percent level.
**Significant at the 5 percent level.
*Significant at the 10 percent level.

maintenance, repair, and growth—and calcium, vitamin A, vitamin D (the latter of which we do not measure in our data), and possibly magnesium— for maintaining bone density and strength. For example, there is in particular a well-established link between low calcium intake and osteoporosis, a loss of bone density/mass. The main sources of calcium are dairy products and dark, leafy vegetables, and the last section revealed that the poor consume much lower quantities of these foods.

In order to assess the effect of nutrition on physical functioning, we regress the level of the ADL index on the intake of these nutrients (this assumes that the intake in the survey adequately reflects typical nutrient intake over a longer period of time). We also include total calories consumed, because there is evidence that in the presence of calorie deficiency, protein will be burned as energy rather than being used for muscle maintenance and repair. Other control variables that we include are income, age, education, BMI, and whether the person smokes or drinks. We focus exclusively on nonworkers to eliminate some of the feedback from ADLs to health (alternate regressions that include workers and add hours worked to the regression yield similar results).

The results are presented in table 8.6. In the first and fourth columns, we see the basic result that higher income is associated with a better ADL functioning (that is, a smaller number for the index, signifying fewer limitations) for both men and women. There is also a decline with age, with a worsening of approximately three-quarters of a point for men and women with every year of age. In the second and fifth columns, we add nutrient intake. Additional protein, calcium, and vitamin A are all associated with statistically significant reductions in ADL limitations. The results suggest that an increased intake of 300 mg of calcium per day (an eight ounce glass of milk) is associated with a reduced ADL index of 5 points for men, or roughly half a point for each of the ten measures, and 1 point for women.

Table 8.6   **Effects of Nutrition on Change in Limitations to Daily Functioning**

	Men			Women		
	(1)	(2)	(3)	(4)	(5)	(6)
log income per capita	−.10	−.062	−.070	−.12	−.084	−.12
	(.065)	(.067)	(.25)	(.061)	(.074)	(.104)
Age	.88	.60	.69	.73	.64	.70
	(.30)	(.22)	(.30)	(.22)	(.044)	(.054)
Calories		−.0020	−.004		−.004	−.002
		(.0012)	(.003)		(.001)	(.0012)
Protein		−.017	−.004		−.04	−.048
		(.010)	(.006)		(.025)	(.034)
Calcium		−.013	−.018		−.006	−.004
		(.007)	(.008)		(.001)	(.001)
Vitamin A		−.012	−.015		−.018	.031
		(.008)	(.008)		(.042)	(.042)
Magnesium		−.012	−.021		−.003	−.004
		(.019)	(.008)		(.012)	(.002)
BMI			.45			.62
			(.18)			(.072)
Smokes?			2.3			5.3
			(1.2)			(3.0)
Drinks?			1.0			2.2
			(.70)			(.97)
Minutes exercise			−.021			−.013
			(.013)			(.055)
No. of observations	570	570	570	745	745	745

The coefficient on income is also now much smaller and no longer statistically significant, because excluding nutrient variables created an omitted variable bias. In columns (3) and (6), we add in whether the person drinks or smokes and their BMI. As would be expected, drinking, smoking, and higher body weight are associated with greater declines in activity functioning. Calcium remains negative and statistically significant for both men and women. Some of the other minerals are no longer statistically significant individually, but an *F*-test reveals that we would not reject the hypothesis of the joint significance of protein, vitamin A, and magnesium at conventional levels of significance.

8.4   Conclusion

The problem of correlation between poverty and poor health exists for Russia as elsewhere. Numerous studies have documented this relationship for other countries. However, the relationship is not entirely one-dimensional, and along some dimensions the wealthy are worse-off than the poor, or face greater health risks. There are numerous empirical problems which can't be overcome with existing data. However, exploring the specific channels linking SES and health, such as nutrition, provides insight on where to investigate further for causal links.

There are several important directions along which future research should proceed: First, for the SES-health link, the main objective now should be to focus on the implications for policy. The general implications of this research so far have been too broad; as mentioned previously, there are numerous reasons why the health of the poor can be worse than that of the rich. And each of these mechanisms implies different corrective policy instruments. This holds for the results of this paper as much as any other; assessing that nutrition plays a role in the disparities in health between rich and poor focuses the search for policy prescriptions somewhat, but also yields the need for further investigation. The important factor for policymakers to determine is whether the differences in nutritional intake are due to the relative costs of foods and thus the ability to afford proper nutrition; preferences (and especially the tradeoff between nutritional and nonnutritional attributes of food); knowledge; quality of medical advising with emphasis on diet; willingness to sacrifice/forgo nonnutritional attributes of food for nutritional content; or possibly some other reason. In the present case, the estimates of the elasticities from the panel data closely match those using cross-sectional variation, suggesting that with changes in income, the current poor would consume like the current rich, which will both improve their health in some ways, but hurt it in others.

From a methodological perspective, there is also a need for more research on how to correctly measure the quantities of interest. For health, this means greater analysis of the validity of subjective or self-reported measures, and the increased use of physically measured quantities or survey questions that are less subject to differences in interpretation or reporting. Likewise, measuring SES requires additional research; most studies in this literature assume that all income is pooled within households, so household income per person (or perhaps adjusted for economies of scale or adult equivalents) is used to represent access to resources by individuals. An exception is Case (chap. 7 in this vol.), who directly examines income pooling within households and the implications for health. This line of inquiry is related to research on intrahousehold decision making bargaining, and income pooling. The results from some of the literature in this field tell us that distribution within households is important for understanding the well-being of the elderly. We need additional survey methods and new data that gather more information on what goes on inside households.

References

Case, Anne, Darren Lubotsky, and Christina Paxson. 2002. Economic status and health in childhood: The origins of the gradient. *American Economic Review* 92 (5): 1308–34.

Feinstein, Jonathan. 1993. The relationship between socioeconomic status and health: A review of the literature. *The Milbank Quarterly* 71:279–322.

Hurd, Michael, Daniel McFadden, and Angela Merrill. 1999. Predictors of mortality among the elderly. NBER Working Paper no. W7440. Cambridge, Mass.: National Bureau of Economic Research, December.

Jensen, Robert T. 2001. Job security, stress and health. Harvard University, John F. Kennedy School of Government. Mimeograph.

Jensen, Robert T., and Kaspar Richter. 2001. Understanding the relationship between poverty and children's health. *European Economic Review* 45 (4-6): 1031–39.

———. 2003. The health implications of Social Security failure: Evidence from the Russian pension crisis. *Journal of Public Economics,* forthcoming.

Meara, Ellen. 2001. Why is health related to socioeconomic status? NBER Working Paper no. W8231. Cambridge, Mass.: National Bureau of Economic Research, April.

Smith, James P. 1999. Healthy bodies and thick wallets: The dual relation between health and socioeconomic status. *Journal of Economic Perspectives* 13:145–66.

Smith, James P., and Raynard Kington. 1997a. Demographic and economic correlates of health in old age. *Demography* 34 (1): 159–70.

———. 1997b. Race socioeconomic status, and health in late life. In *Racial and ethnic differences in the health of older Americans,* ed. Linda Martin, G. Soldo, and J. Beth, 106–62. Washington, D.C.: National Academy Press.

Subramanian, Shankar, and Angus Deaton. 1996. The demand for food and calories. *Journal of Political Economy* 104 (1): 133–62.

Comment   David M. Cutler

Rob Jensen's paper is very interesting. It examines income and health in Russia, a country where income variability and health differences between rich and poor are large. Jensen's data are clear, his analysis sound, and his results intriguing.

Indeed, Jensen may even underestimate the importance of his results. At the time of economic transition in Russia, mortality rates increased by staggering amounts. Between 1990 and 1994, male life expectancy at birth fell from sixty-four to fifty-eight years, and female life expectancy fell from seventy-four to seventy-one years. This is an enormous regression, the likes of which the world may never have seen before, at least not in the modern era.

A natural question arises—how much of this setback is a result of people getting poorer as the economy became turbulent, and how much is a result of other factors? The start to answering this question is to understand how and why income affects health. There are other questions as well: What type of social safety net can prevent such situations? What explains the difference between the experience of Russia and other Eastern European countries who went through transition with much less difficulty?

I interpret Jensen's results slightly differently than he does. Jensen shows that when looking at physical measures of health, the rich are in better health than the poor. For example, the rich have fewer ADL impairments than the poor, they have higher self-reported health status, and they report fewer incidents of chest pain in the previous thirty days. Jensen does not examine mortality differences between rich and poor, which could confirm and supplement these measures, but he could do so.

But when Jensen looks at the risk factors that would lead to health differences, he finds no clear message. The rich have better nutrition than the poor, but have worse risk factors along other dimensions. Blood pressure is higher for the rich than the poor, and the rich smoke more than the poor. Jensen finds that in total, risk factors do not explain much of the link between income and health. Only 30 percent of the effect of income on health for men is explained by this wealth of risk factors, and none of the link for women. The average effect is thus about 15 percent. At the end of the day, these results do not tell us much in total about why income and health status are linked in Russia. It is not that nothing matters, just that what matters does not paint a clear picture. Unfortunately, these results also make it more difficult to know how to interpret the link between income and

David M. Cutler is professor of economics in the Department of Economics and the John F. Kennedy School of Government, Harvard University, and a research associate of the National Bureau of Economic Research.

health, and how to explain the Russian mortality crisis at the time of privatization.

The issue that this research faces is how to answer the pressing question—why do the rich have better health than the poor? Jensen has made a start, but I think he can push further. I have several comments about the data employed and the results presented that are intended to aid in this effort.

First, Jensen does not look at disease onset. One theory about the link between income and health is that richer people are less likely to develop severe conditions, perhaps because they have a better risk factor profile. A second theory is that the rich are less impaired by the same diseases than the poor. Perhaps they have better access to medical care, they can afford nonmedical goods that improve health, or they have better social situations that allow them to recover from disease more rapidly.

Jensen shows that the risk factor explanation is not entirely supported in the diseases he looks at. But Jensen has just a subset of the relevant risk factors. This is not to be critical. Measuring risk factors is complex, and we don't even know all the risk factors for disease. So any set of data is by necessity a subset of the true risk factors. Still, it is important to keep this in mind.

One way to differentiate these explanations is to look at the incidence of disease and health conditional on disease separately. The risk factor explanation argues that rich people should be less likely to experience serious diseases such as heart attacks, strokes, or cancers. The alternative is that the rich are less impaired when they have these diseases. I believe doing this decomposition is possible using the data that Jensen has, and it would be a welcome addition.

Jensen may be able to go even further. For example, other data might indicate how the rich and poor are treated in the medical sector when they have certain diseases. This would allow us to learn whether the medical system explains part of the link between income and health.

The second comment is that it would be nice to have more information on the quality of the data. The data on food and nutrition come from diet surveys that people fill out. They are self-reported surveys kept for two days. Such a methodology is common to many countries, including the United States. But it is not without problems. In the United States, for example, diet surveys indicate that the average woman consumes about 1,500 calories per day and the average male consumes about 2,500 calories per day. This is far below levels of caloric intake consistent with stable weight, even in a time period in which weight has been increasing rapidly. The diet surveys are underreporting average consumption by a substantial amount.

I should note that underreporting is not the same as lying. The act of keeping a diary may induce people to consume less than they would otherwise. We do not know how much of the underreporting is lying, mis-recording of information, or behavioral change in response to keeping the diary. What we do know is that those nutrition totals almost certainly can-not be correct for the average person on the average day.

I have no idea if the Russian data is better or worse than the U.S. data. Reported caloric intake for women is higher in Russia than in the United States, but reported caloric intake for males is lower. One would need to compare these caloric intakes to changes in weight to see if they make sense. Jensen should be able to do this. It would add enormously to the credibility of the findings.

There is another data quality issue worth addressing. It is not clear to me that the data record the true quality of the food consumed, even if the food intake is correctly reported. For example, one hears stories about the brew-ing of homemade vodka in bad economic times. Such vodka may be far worse for health than commercially sold vodka. I don't know if the survey is able to capture this. The same is true potentially about all of the food measures. Is meat the same for the rich and poor? What about borsch? Jensen notes that the survey has more than one category for each food item, but in the U.S. context these are typically different items of food (hamburger versus steak, for example), not different qualities of the same item. Maybe the beef consumed by the poor is lower quality than the beef consumed by the rich, even when officially the same type of meat? More in-formation about the quality of the food consumed is clearly warranted. Given how different the observable measures of nutrition are by income, the unobservable differences may be just as great.

The final comment is that Jensen should look at additional risk factors to see how they relate to income. Several factors come to mind that may ex-plain the difference in health between rich and poor. First, the poor might experience more stress than the rich. Jensen has shown in other work that increased stress from the privatization of industry increases blood pres-sure, which may explain some of the overall increase in mortality during the transition. Stress may also differ cross-sectionally, with the poor facing more stress than the rich.

A second risk factor is the nature of jobs. Lower income people have different jobs from higher income people that may directly influence their health. For example, blue collar workers may naturally have more ADL impairments than white collar workers because they work in manual jobs, and this may be correlated with income. Jensen has information about the jobs that people are employed in and could control for this.

A third risk factor is the environment. Is the person living in a polluted or clean area? What infectious diseases are or were in the area? This again may influence health and is likely to differ systematically between rich and poor. There are almost certainly other risk factors that are relevant in the Russian context that would be interesting to explore.

I do not know if any of these factors will explain the link between income and health that Jensen finds. But the issue is an important one, with potential applications for Russia, Eastern Europe, and developed countries more generally. More exploration on why income is related to health and what this says about economic transition could enhance research and policy making in many contexts.

9

Changes in the Age Distribution of Mortality over the Twentieth Century

David M. Cutler and Ellen Meara

Mortality rates decline extremely rapidly in the United States over the twentieth century, as they did in all developed countries. Figure 9.1 shows the magnitude of the decline. In 1900, 1 in 42 Americans died annually. On an age-adjusted basis, the share in 1998 was 1 in 125 people, for a cumulative decline of 67 percent. Given such a substantial improvement in mortality, it is natural to ask how we achieved such gains in health and which innovations or policies contributed most to these gains.

Such a task is clearly large. One way to start is to analyze major trends in mortality over the century and to consider how mortality declines differ by age and cause of death. By providing detailed information on which demographic groups experienced the largest mortality improvements and for what causes of death, these analyses motivate hypotheses to explain the overall improvement in mortality in the twentieth century.

The mortality decline shown in figure 9.1 seems approximately linear over the time period. Mortality decreased at a relatively constant rate of 1 percent per year between 1900 and 1940. There was then a period of rapid decline from 1940 to 1955 in which mortality declined 2 percent per year, followed by essentially flat mortality rates until 1965. Since 1965, mortality rates have fallen at roughly 1 to 1.5 percent per year. This relative constancy of mortality decline suggests that perhaps a single factor can

David M. Cutler is professor of economics in the Department of Economics and the John F. Kennedy School of Government, Harvard University, and a research associate of the National Bureau of Economic Research. Ellen Meara is assistant professor of health economics in the Department of Health Care Policy at Harvard Medical School, and a faculty research fellow of the National Bureau of Economic Research.

We are grateful to Brian Kim and Mariko Golden for research assistance; to David Meltzer, Angus Deaton, Chris Paxson, and Anne Case for comments; and the National Institutes on Aging for research support.

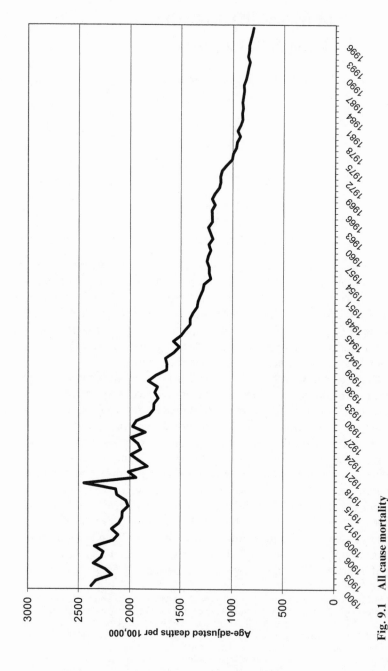

Fig. 9.1   All cause mortality

Source: United States Vital Statistics data.

Note: Death rates shown are adjusted to the standard population of the United States in 1940.

explain the trend in longer life; the popular Lee and Carter (1992) model of mortality posits a driving force of mortality that is approximately constant over time.

But the aggregate trends mask as much as they reveal. While mortality declines have been relatively continuous over the twentieth century, the age distribution of mortality decline has not. We start off the paper by highlighting a basic fact about mortality declines in the past century: Mortality reduction used to be concentrated at younger ages but is increasingly concentrated among the aged. In the first four decades of the century, 80 percent of life expectancy improvements resulted from reduced mortality for those below age forty-five, with the bulk of this for infants and children. In the next two decades, life expectancy improvements were split relatively evenly by age. In the latter four decades, about two-thirds of life expectancy improvements resulted from mortality reductions for those over age forty-five; only one-third was from the younger population.

This change has been accompanied by several important epidemiological trends. Throughout the first half of the twentieth century, infectious diseases were the leading cause of death. Changes in the ability to avoid and withstand infection were the prime factors in reduced mortality in the first part of the century. This disease-fighting ability was not predominantly medical. Nutrition (Fogel 1994) and public health measures (Preston 1996) were vastly more important in reduced mortality over this time period than were medical interventions, as substantial research documents. Nutrition and public health were particularly important for the young, and so mortality reduction was concentrated at younger ages.

Between 1940 and 1960, infectious diseases continue to decline, but was due more to medical factors. Antibiotics, including penicillin and sulfa drugs, became important contributors to mortality reduction in this era. Antibiotics help the elderly as well as the young, and so mortality reductions became more widespread across the age distribution.

Since 1960, mortality reductions have been associated with two new factors: the conquest of cardiovascular disease in the elderly, and the prevention of infant death due to low birth weight. While it is not entirely clear what factors account for the reduction in cardiovascular disease mortality, the traditional roles of nutrition, public health, and antibiotics are certainly less important. Taking their place are factors related to individual behaviors, such as smoking and diet and high-tech medical treatment. We term this change the "medicalization" of death: Increasingly, mortality reductions are attributed to medical care and not social or environmental improvements.

The medicalization of death does not imply that medicine is the only factor influencing mortality. For several important causes of death, income improvements and social programs have had and continue to have a large impact on mortality. For example, Medicare likely has a direct impact on mortality by increasing elderly access to medical care, but it also may have important income effects since it reduced out of pocket spending by the elderly for medical care. Social Security and civil rights programs may also be important in better health. We do not quantify the role of medicine, income, social programs, and other factors in improved mortality in the last half century, but we show examples where each is important as a first step in this research process.

The paper is structured as follows. The first section presents the basic facts about changes in the age distribution of mortality change and life expectancy improvements, highlighting the growing role of mortality reductions among the elderly. The next three sections examine why this trend has occurred, discussing in particular the epidemiology of mortality reduction at different points in time and for different causes. The fifth section then presents limited evidence on the nonmedical factors that influence mortality.

9.1   Changes in the Age Distribution of Longer Life

We start the analysis by summarizing changes in the age distribution of mortality improvements over time. One can summarize mortality rates in many ways. We consider a relatively simple measure: life expectancy at birth $[LE_0(t)]$. This measure has the advantage that it weights mortality changes by how important they are to overall survival. Mortality reductions in an age range where few people die will not contribute as much to improvements in life expectancy at birth as mortality reductions in an age range where there are more deaths.

Because it is helpful for our analysis, let us be more precise about the measure. Consider a cohort of people born in year t. At age 0, the share of people who die is $p(0, t)$. Suppose the initial population had $S(0, t)$ people. The number of people alive at the end of year t and entering next year is $S(1, t + 1) = S(0, t) \cdot [1 - p(0, t)]$. To forecast life expectancy, we need to forecast the share of people who will die in year $t + 1$, at age 1, and more generally the share of people who will die at age a, in year $t + a$. Following standard conventions, we use a period life table and assume that the probability of death at any age a in the future will be equal to the probability of death of people aged a in year t, or $p(a, t + a) = p(a, t)$. This estimate is static; it assumes no change in mortality in the future. Although this is not the best forecasting technique—mortality rates have fallen over time—it is appropriate for our purposes of decomposing changes over time.

People who die at age a are assumed to have died halfway through the year. Thus, life expectancy for a person dying at age a is $a - 1/2$. Adding across all possible ages of death, up to maximum longevity T, life expectancy at birth is then

(1) $$\mathrm{LE}_0(t) = \sum_{a=0}^{T} p(a, t) \cdot S(a - 1, t) \cdot \left(\frac{a - 1}{2}\right),$$

where

(2) $$S(a, t) = S(0, t) \cdot \prod_{s=0}^{a-1} [1 - p(s, t)],$$

and for simplicity, we assume that the cohort, $S(0, t)$, equals 1.

Figure 9.2 shows life expectancy at birth in the United States in the twentieth century. In 1900, the average infant could expect to live forty-eight years. By the end of the century, life expectancy was near eighty years.

We want to understand how changes in mortality at different ages contribute to overall life expectancy improvements. To do this, we compare t with another year t'. If we substitute t' for t in equations (1) and (2), equation (1) will give us life expectancy at birth in year t'. But we can also substitute selectively. For example, suppose we replace $p(a, t)$ with $p(a, t')$ just for the elderly. We denote $p'(a, t)$ as the new mortality probability at any age. Life expectancy at birth is then

(3) $$\mathrm{LE}_0'(t) = \sum_{a=0}^{T} p'(a, t) \cdot S'(a - 1, t) \cdot \left(\frac{a - 1}{2}\right),$$

where $S'(a - 1, t)$ is defined analogously to equation (2), substituting $p'(a, t)$ for $p(a, t)$. The difference between equations (3) and (1), $\mathrm{LE}_0'(t) - \mathrm{LE}_0(t)$ is the effect of mortality changes between t and t' on overall years of life expectancy at birth.

If we estimate equation (3), replacing different age groups sequentially and then add up the life expectancy improvements attributable to each age group, the resulting improvement in life expectancy will be close to, but not exactly the same as, the effect of considering changes for all age groups together. The reason for the discrepancy has to do with the covariance of benefits from mortality reduction at different ages. Saving more babies has a greater impact on life expectancy at birth when the elderly also live longer than when elderly mortality is assumed constant, because more people reach their older years as infant mortality falls and thus benefit from the improvements in elderly mortality. We group the covariance effects between mortality reductions in different age groups into one term.

We estimate equations (1) through (3) empirically by considering mortality changes for five groups in the population: infant mortality (<one); child mortality (one–fourteen); young adult mortality (fifteen–forty-four); older adult mortality (forty-five–sixty-four); and elderly mortality (sixty-five+). We consider the impact of mortality changes in each of these age groups over three time periods: 1900–40; 1940–60; and 1960–90. The reason for choosing these time periods will become apparent later. Thus, our first estimate is how much of the overall improvement in life expectancy at

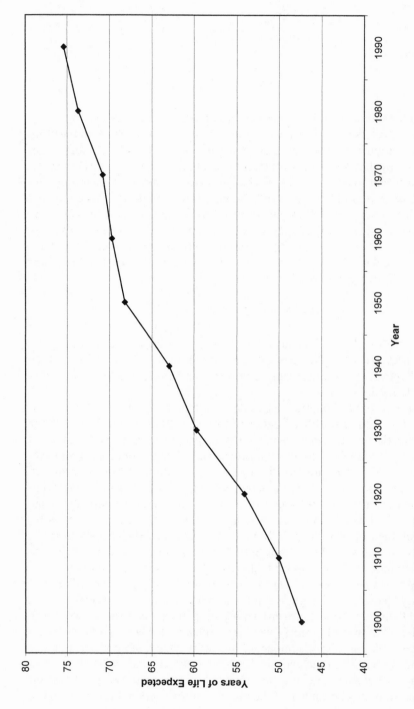

Fig. 9.2 Life expectancy at birth
Source: United States Vital Statistics data.

birth between 1900 and 1940 is a function of reduced mortality for each of those five age groups and so on for the different time periods.

Figure 9.3 and table 9.1 show the results. Throughout the paper, total mortality estimates are age-adjusted to the 1990 population age distribution unless otherwise noted. Our results are not sensitive to our choice to age-adjust based on the 1990 population. The first bars of figure 9.3 and column (1) of table 9.1 shows the contributors to life expectancy improvements at birth in the 1900–40 time period; the second bars and column are for the 1940–60 time period; and the third bars and column are for the 1960–90 time period. In the 1900–40 era, life expectancy improvements were concentrated at younger ages. Reduced infant mortality, for example, contributed 4 and a half years to overall improvements in life expectancy. Reduced child mortality contributed nearly as much, and reduced young adult mortality contributed about 3 and a half years. Together, these three changes account for nearly thirteen of the sixteen-year increase in expected longevity. Mortality reductions among older adults and the elderly, in contrast, explain just 1 and a half years of increased longevity combined. About 80 percent of longevity improvements, therefore, are attributable to reduced mortality among the under-forty-five population.

The next bars of the figure and column of the table are for the two decades in the middle of the century, 1940–60. The overall improvement in life expectancy at birth is smaller in this time period than in the 1900–40 time period. The change between 1940 and 1960, for example, is 6.4 years, compared to 15.9 years in the previous four decades. Part of the smaller improvement is due to the fact that the time interval is only half as large, but that is not all of the explanation.

More important for our analysis, the contribution of mortality declines at different ages to overall improvements in life expectancy is very different from the earlier time period. In the 1940–60 time period, the different age groups all contributed roughly equally to improvements in life expectancy at birth. The effect of mortality reductions in each age group is about 1 to 1 and a half years of additional life. Only 60 percent of overall improvements resulted from reduced mortality among the under-forty-five population; 35 percent is from the older population.

The third bars and last column of the table show the results for the 1960–90 time period. Once again, the situation changed greatly. Infant mortality was still an important source of increased longevity in the latter three decades, but child and young adult mortality were substantially less important. Taking their place were older adult and elderly mortality reductions. Reduced mortality among older adults and the elderly contributed in total about three years to overall improvements in life expectancy at birth. Changes in mortality for these age groups explain two-thirds of the overall improvement in life expectancy at birth.

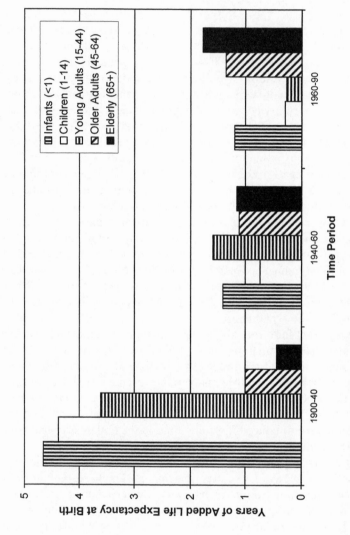

Fig. 9.3 Sources of life expectancy improvement by age
Source: Authors' calculations.

Table 9.1   **Contributions to Life Expectancy at Birth**

Change in Life Expectancy at Birth	1900–1940	1940–1960	1960–1990
Total change (%)	15.9	6.4	5.1
Change attributable to:			
Infant mortality (<1)	4.7	1.4	1.2
Child mortality (1–14)	4.4	0.7	0.3
Young adult mortality (15–44)	3.6	1.6	0.3
Older adult mortality (45–64)	1.0	1.1	1.4
Elderly mortality (65+)	0.4	1.2	1.8
Covariance terms	1.8	0.4	0.1

Notes: The text describes the decomposition. Ages in parentheses.

The greater relative contribution of mortality reductions for the older population in the post-1960 period can be explained by two factors. The first is that mortality reductions for the elderly were more rapid in the later time period than in the earlier one. Figure 9.4 and table 9.2 shows the annual rate of decline in mortality for the different population groups. Where mortality among the elderly declined by only 0.3 percent per year between 1900 and 1940, mortality declined by 1.1 percent per year after 1960.

The second explanation is that overall mortality rates among the young were already very low by 1960 so that even large continued increases in the *rate* of decline translated into much smaller changes in the absolute *level* of mortality. Compared to 1900, mortality among infants was only 15 percent as high in 1960. Even when mortality rates for infants continued to decline at their pre-1960 level, as table 9.2 shows, the absolute changes corresponding to these declines were much smaller. By 1960, 70 percent of infants were already surviving to age sixty-five; this share could not increase that rapidly in subsequent generations.[1]

For both of these reasons, the nature of longevity improvements shifted over time. Where longevity improvements were concentrated at younger ages early in the century, they were increasingly pronounced among the elderly in the latter decades. Overall survival still increased, but the timing of those changes was very different.

---

1. This fact leads to a third potential explanation for the shift in longevity improvements toward the elderly, but one that is not empirically so consequential. Since the probability that an infant survived to older ages was greater in 1960 than in 1900, the same reduction in mortality rates for the elderly would have a larger impact on life expectancy at birth in the later time period. But the dominant factor in the increased contribution of mortality declines among the elderly is the more rapid reduction in mortality rates for the elderly, not the increased survival to older ages.

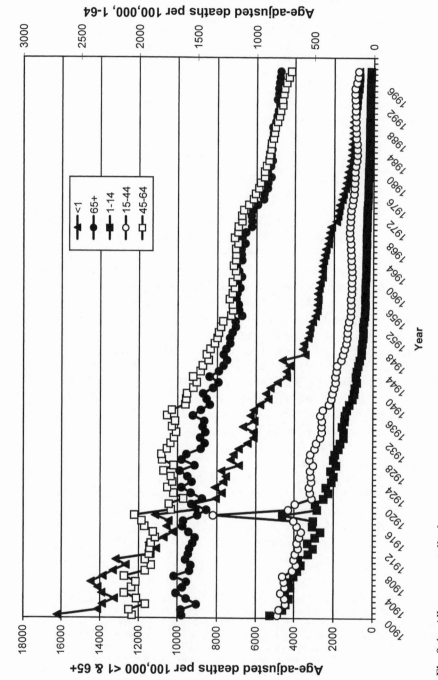

Fig. 9.4 All cause mortality by age
Source: United States Vital Statistics data.

Table 9.2   **Change in Mortality Rates, by Age (annual rate of decline for each age group)**

Age Groups	1900–1940	1940–1960	1960–1990
Total change (%)	0.9	1.5	1.2
Decline by age:			
Infant mortality (<1)	2.7	3.5	3.3
Child mortality (1–14)	4.2	4.4	2.5
Young adult mortality (15–44)	2.1	3.1	0.6
Older adult mortality (45–64)	0.6	1.4	1.3
Elderly mortality (65+)	0.3	1.1	1.1

9.2   The First Four Decades: Public Health and Nutrition

Our goal in the next several sections is to understand why longevity improvements have shifted towards the elderly. There are two ways to understand this. The first is at the epidemiological level—what factors about mortality changed over the twentieth century that led to the shifting pattern of mortality decline? The second level of understanding is at the economic and social level—what is the underlying reason for the change in those causes of death?

An example illustrates the difference. Since the late eighteenth century, mortality rates have been declining in most developed countries. The cause of this is reduced death from infectious disease. That is the basic epidemiological fact. But the real issue is why infectious disease mortality declined. Was it improved nutrition that allowed people to avoid and withstand infections better, public health measures that reduced the spread of diseases, or did diseases become less virulent? The latter questions are the subject of substantial research in historical demography and are the ultimate object of interest.

We do not answer the questions we ask at the detailed level. Indeed, it has taken decades of work to distinguish between public health, nutritional, and medical explanations for mortality reductions over the course of the eighteenth and nineteenth centuries, so attempting such an analysis here for the twentieth century would be an act of supreme hubris. Rather, we concentrate first on the epidemiology of changes in the mortality distribution and use that to suggest hypotheses about why they are occurring. Even this is difficult, though. Cause of death changes over time, as does physician coding. It is not possible to put together an entirely consistent mortality record over time. We present here what is most readily comparable and save less comparable data for future analysis.

A first way to approach the sources of mortality reduction is to look at what causes of death declined most rapidly over time. Table 9.3 shows information on this. The rows of the table show the various causes of death.

Table 9.3   Contribution of Different Diseases to Mortality and Mortality Change

| | 1900–1940 | | 1940–1960 | | 1960–1990 | |
Cause	Mortality Rate at Beginning	Annual Change (%)	Mortality Rate at Beginning	Annual Change (%)	Mortality Rate at Beginning	Annual Change (%)
Total	2,376	-0.9	1,649	-1.5	1,228	-1.2
Infectious disease	764 (32)	-3.2 (76)	208 (13)	-5.7 (34)	64 (5)	—
Pneumonia, influenza	282	-2.4	107	-3.9	48	-1.4
Tuberculosis	208	-3.5	49	-9.2	7	-7.4
Dysentery, enteritis, & diarrheal diseases	137	-5.8	13	-4.9	5	—
Vaccine preventable	84	-3.5	21	-11.2	2	—
Other infections	53	-2.7	18	-9.9	2	—
Cardiovascular disease	512 (22)	0.9 (-29)	725 (44)	0.02 (-1)	728 (59)	-2.3 (98)
Neoplasms	108 (5)	1.2 (-9)	176 (11)	0.2 (-1)	182 (15)	0.4 (-6)
Respiratory neoplasms	—	—	9	5.3	25	2.9
Chronic nephritis[a]	132 (6)	0.2 (-1)	141 (13)	-13.0 (32)	9 (1)	-9.1 (2)
Accidents	87 (4)	0.3 (-1)	99 (6)	-2.4 (9)	61 (5)	-1.6 (6)
Diabetes	17 (1)	2.2 (-3)	40 (2)	-3.0 (4)	21 (2)	-0.4 (1)
Other	757 (32)	-2.6 (68)	260 (16)	-2.3 (23)	164 (13)	0.7 (-10)

Notes: Death rates are age-adjusted to 1990 age distribution. The numbers in parentheses in the mortality rate column are the percentages of the share of total mortality attributable to that cause. The numbers in parentheses in the annual change column are the percentages of the share of change in total mortality.
[a]Includes chronic nephritis, nephritis not specified as chronic or acute, and unspecified renal sclerosis.

The columns are the different time periods. In each case, we report mortality rates at the beginning of the sample and the annual change in mortality rates attributable to that cause. We separate these changes into the three time periods analyzed previously: 1900–40, 1940–60, and 1960–90.

Infectious diseases were the leading causes of death in 1900. Together, infectious diseases accounted for 32 percent of total deaths. Pneumonia and influenza were the biggest killers, accounting for 12 percent of total deaths by themselves. Tuberculosis was also important, and to a lesser extent dysentery, enteritis, diarrheal diseases, and diseases where vaccinations are today possible. The leading killers of today—cardiovascular disease and cancer—together accounted for fewer deaths than infectious diseases in 1900.

Infectious diseases also saw the most rapid mortality declines in the 1900–40 period. Deaths from pneumonia and influenza fell by 2.4 percent annually between 1900 and 1940. Deaths from tuberculosis and vaccine-preventable illness both fell 3 to 6 percent annually. In total, reduced death from infectious diseases accounts for three-quarters of total mortality reduction in this period. Figures 9.5, 9.6, and 9.7 show mortality from pneumonia and influenza, tuberculosis, and vaccine-amenable conditions graphically. Death from all of these causes was falling markedly throughout the time period.

The figures make another important point—most of the mortality reductions for these conditions occurred well before the first medical treatment was available. Pneumonia and influenza are mostly treated with penicillin, and before that with sulfa drugs. But sulfa drugs were discovered in 1935, and essentially all of the decline in pneumonia- and influenza-attributable deaths occurred well before sulfa drugs were available. Tuberculosis mortality fell long before antituberculosis drugs came into use in the mid-1940s. And vaccine-preventable deaths declined well before there were vaccines.

We are by no means the first to notice this finding. Thomas McKeown (1976) and McKeown, Record, and Turner (1975) first brought the issue to prominence, and it has been a well-recognized fact ever since. Indeed, substantial research has been devoted to understanding why these diseases declined prior to the advent of effective medical care. The two leading hypotheses are that nutritional improvements allowed people to avoid contracting disease and withstand disease once it was contracted (Fogel 1994), and that public health measures reduced the spread of disease (Preston 1996). In each case, preventing disease among some people may limit its spread among others as well. We do not have any additional evidence to bring to bear on this issue. Rather, the focus of our analysis is on the transition from this period to later ones.

In contrast to infectious diseases, diseases of old age—cardiovascular disease and cancer most prominently—were increasing over the 1900 to

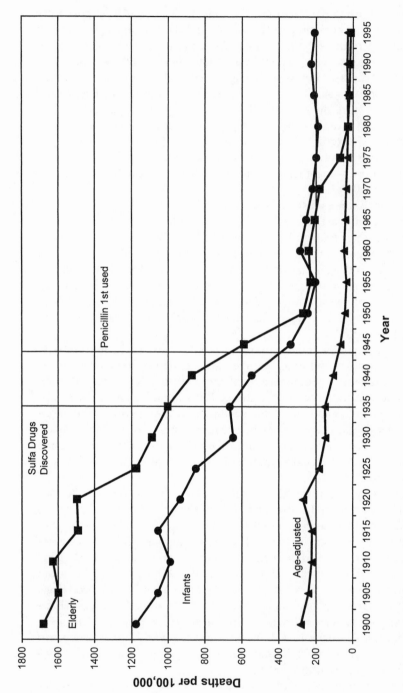

Fig. 9.5　Pneumonia and influenza deaths

Source: United States Vital Statistics data.

Note: Pneumonia and influenza deaths are not reported separately prior to 1965. Influenza accounts for less than 3 percent of total deaths in this category in 1965.

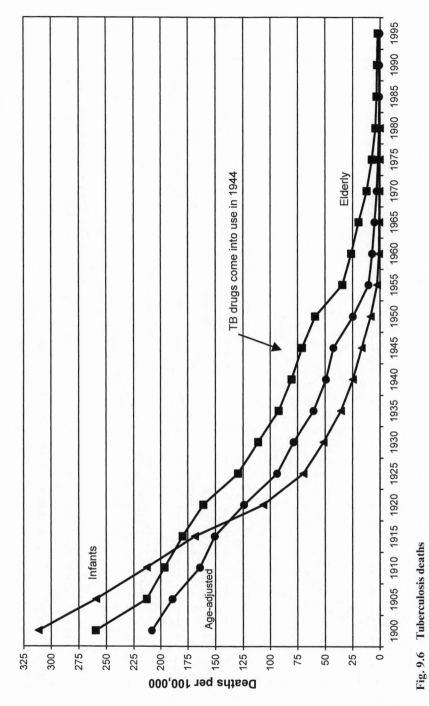

Fig. 9.6 Tuberculosis deaths
Source: United States Vital Statistics data.

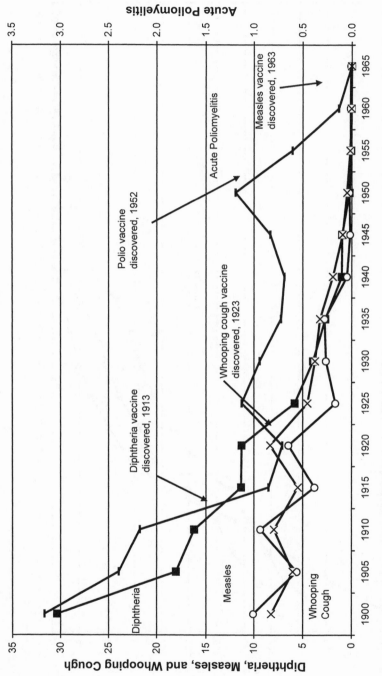

Fig. 9.7 Age-adjusted deaths per 100,000, diseases sensitive to vaccines

Source: United States Vital Statistics data.

1940 period, as figures 9.8 and 9.9 show. Cardiovascular disease mortality increased by 0.9 percent annually from 1900 to 1940, and cancer mortality increased by 1.2 percent annually. It is not completely known whether the increase in cardiovascular disease mortality results from better diagnosis or a true rise in cardiovascular deaths, but it is believed by most to be at least partly a true increase. We know, for example, that smoking rates were increasing over this time period and smoking is a leading risk factor for cardiovascular disease and cancer. Thus, there are identifiable factors that would lead to increased mortality for these conditions.

The net effect is that cardiovascular disease accounted for 22 percent of mortality in 1900 but 44 percent of deaths in 1940. Cancer accounted for 5 percent of total deaths in 1900 and 11 percent of deaths in 1940.

9.3   Midcentury: First Medical Advance

Even with the dramatic decline in mortality from infectious diseases between 1900 and 1940, infectious diseases were still prominent killers in 1940. Thirteen percent of deaths resulted from infectious disease in 1940, more than cancer but far below the now dominant cardiovascular disease.

Infectious disease mortality continued its substantial decline in the 1940–60 time period. Between 1940 and 1960, deaths due to infectious disease declined 5.7 percent per year, well above the 3.2 percent annual rate between 1900 and 1940. In total, the decline in infectious disease mortality accounted for 34 percent of the total decline in mortality in this period.

What is different about the decades in midcentury is the growing importance of medical care in this mortality decline. Midcentury saw the development and widespread diffusion of drugs to treat many infectious diseases, most importantly sulfa drugs and penicillin. These drugs are used most prominently in treating pneumonia but also other infectious diseases as well. Following the introduction of sulfa drugs and penicillin, mortality for conditions where penicillin is effective declined particularly rapidly. For example, pneumonia and influenza deaths declined at an annual rate of 2.4 percent per year between 1900 and 1940, but by 3.9 percent per year between 1940 and 1960. As figure 9.5 shows, the timing of the more rapid mortality reduction is coincident with the development of these medications. It is therefore a reasonable inference that medical innovation explains part of this more rapid decline.

We can be more formal about this conclusion. Because we believe that much of the decline in pneumonia and influenza before 1940 stemmed from better nutrition and public health measures, one way to more formally test whether penicillin and sulfa drugs had a significant impact on these diseases is to compare pneumonia and influenza mortality to another disease or set of diseases that are sensitive to public health and nutrition, but not sensitive to penicillin or sulfa drugs. Dysentery, enteritis, and

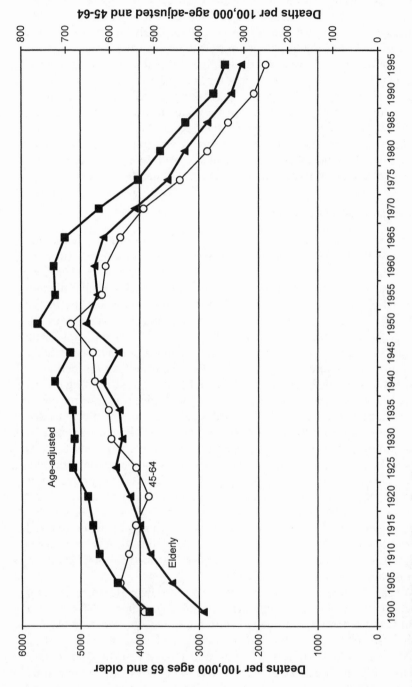

Fig. 9.8 Deaths due to cardiovascular disease

Source: United States Vital Statistics data.

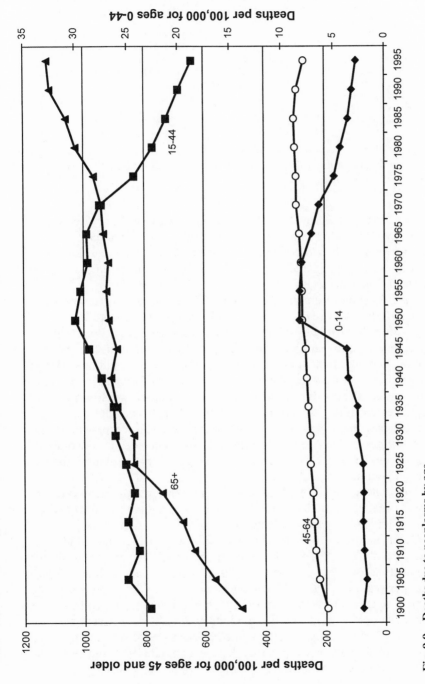

Fig. 9.9 Deaths due to neoplasms by age
Source: United States Vital Statistics data.

Table 9.4   Difference-in-Difference of Effect of Medications on Mortality (%)

| | Annual Change in Mortality | | |
Disease	Before Sulfanomides and Penicillin (1915–1935)	After Sulfanomides and Penicillin (1945–1965)	Difference
Pneumonia/influenza	–1.9	–2.4	–0.5
Dysentery, enteritis, diarrheal disease	–6.1	–2.8	3.3
Difference-in-difference			–3.8

Note: Because death rates are based on entire U.S. population, standard errors are negligible and therefore omitted.

diarrheal diseases provide such an example because these diseases are largely viral and thus do not respond to antibiotics. Individuals with better nutrition will be more resistant to these diseases, and better sanitation, cleaner water supply, and better hygiene in general helps to prevent the spread of these diseases.

Table 9.4 shows a simple difference-in-difference calculation of the trend in deaths due to these diseases during the twenty years before and twenty years after the advent of sulfanomide drugs and penicillin. Deaths due to dysentery, enteritis, and diarrheal diseases declined in both time periods but much more rapidly during the 1915–35 time period than the 1945–65 time period. The slowdown in the rate of decline was 3.3 percent per year. In contrast, deaths due to pneumonia and influenza witnessed a more rapid decline during the postantibiotic period, by 0.5 percent per year. If one believes that deaths due to these diseases would have experienced similar declines in the absence of antibiotics, this difference-in-difference of 3.8 percent per year following antibiotics suggests that antibiotics did significantly impact mortality.

This conclusion also finds support in the literature. McDermott (1978) noted the rapid decline in infectious disease mortality after 1937 and attributed it to pharmaceutical advance as well.

Other important diseases declined significantly midcentury, and medical care plays a clear role in these cases as well. For example, chronic nephritis accounted for 13 percent of deaths in 1940, but declined 4.7 percent per year until 1960. This decline alone accounts for 32 percent of the decline in total mortality. Figure 9.10 shows deaths from nephritis over time. The decline in mortality from kidney disease is coincident with the advent of kidney dialysis in the United States in 1948. While there was a small decline in deaths from kidney disease in the late 1920s and 1930s, the rate of mortality decline increased dramatically in the 1940s.

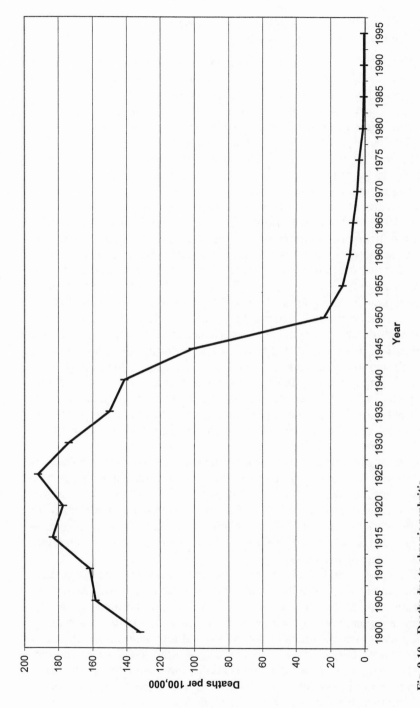

Fig. 9.10 Deaths due to chronic nephritis
Source: United States Vital Statistics data.

9.4   The Later Decades: Cardiovascular Disease and Low Birth Weight Infants

By 1960, infectious disease mortality was extremely low. The cumulative decline in infectious disease deaths from 1900 to 1960 was 92 percent. And even though infectious disease mortality continued to decline, further declines did not contribute greatly to overall improvements in life expectancy at birth. After all, even a large decline in mortality from a cause that does not kill many people has little impact on overall longevity. The leading killers in 1960 were cardiovascular disease (59 percent of the total) and cancer (15 percent of the total). Infectious disease mortality was only 5 percent of total mortality.

It was around this time that mortality reductions as a whole slowed. Between 1955 and 1965, overall mortality was flat. The already low level of infectious disease mortality, combined with the lack of progress in mortality from the chronic diseases of old age, was a leading reason for this. The realization that the traditional killers had largely been eliminated led to pessimism about future improvements in longevity. It was feared that technological progress had done all for health that it was able to do and that the limits of longevity had been reached. Famed biologist Rene Dubos was among those who believed that "Modern medicine has little to offer for the prevention or treatment of chronic and degenerative diseases that dominate the pathological picture of technologic societies" (Dubos 1969, 328).

Beginning in the mid-1960s, though, cardiovascular disease mortality began to decline. The decline, shown in figure 9.8, was rapid, about 2 percent per year through the end of the century. The cumulative decline in cardiovascular disease mortality between 1960 and 1995 was close to two-thirds.

Cardiovascular disease is most prominent among the elderly, so the mortality gains were concentrated there. Indeed, cardiovascular disease is so prominent among the elderly that the decline in cardiovascular disease mortality explains essentially all of the overall reduction in mortality for the elderly since 1965. For the population as a whole, 98 percent of mortality reductions between 1960 and 1990 were a result of reduced cardiovascular disease mortality.

There are several causes of reduced cardiovascular disease mortality. Cutler and Kadiyala (2001) document the sources and provide a rough attribution. According to their findings, medical care accounts for a relatively large share of cardiovascular disease mortality reduction. A major component of such care is high-tech medical interventions for the treatment of acute heart disease, particularly heart attacks. These interventions include drugs to dissolve blood clots and restore blood flow to the heart, surgical procedures such as bypass surgery and angioplasty, and specialized equipment such as coronary care units and trained emergency response teams. A related component is low-tech medical care, largely pharmaceuticals. Medications to reduce blood pressure, manage cholesterol, control the heart rhythm, reduce the heart's workload in times of stress, and similar goals have reduced mortality for patients with heart disease and prevented serious occurrences of heart disease for patients who have not yet experienced a severe episode.

Cutler and Kadiyala (2001) also highlight the importance of behavioral changes. Principal among these is the reduction in smoking. As figure 9.11 shows, smoking rates fell after 1960, after six decades of continuous increase. Between 1960 and 1990, the number of cigarettes smoked declined by one-third. Reductions in fat intake have also played a role in better health.

This decomposition of mortality reductions for cardiovascular disease is not as accurate as one would like. Issues such as changes in childhood disease and birth weight, which may affect cardiovascular disease in later life, are not explicitly accounted for. Still, even this rough decomposition of mortality makes clear the growing medicalization of better health. A significant part of reduced mortality is directly attributable to medical interventions, either for acute disease or in a chronic setting. Another large part is behavioral, but has roots in medical knowledge about the origins of disease.

Indeed, the medicalization of mortality reduction extends even to ages where medicine traditionally had a very small role. It was noted earlier, for example, that infant mortality reductions contributed to improved life expectancy at birth in the 1960 to 1990 time period just as they did in the pre-1960 time period. But the nature of these changes after 1960 was very different.

Figure 9.12 divides infant mortality into two components: neonatal mortality, or death in the first twenty-eight days of life; and postneonatal mortality, or death in the subsequent eleven months. In the first half of the century, postneonatal mortality declines were substantially more important than neonatal mortality declines. Between 1915 and 1960, postneonatal mortality declined by 4.4 percent per year, compared to a 1.9 percent annual decline in neonatal mortality. Postneonatal mortality is generally attributable to the infectious diseases noted previously, so this is consistent with the aggregate evidence on mortality change.

Since 1960, however, most of the decline in infant mortality has been in neonatal mortality. In the 1960 to 1998 period, neonatal mortality declined by 3.5 percent annually, compared to 2.9 percent for postneonatal mortality. Death in the first month of life is generally not a result of infectious disease. It is predominantly due to low birth weight and the adverse consequences of low birth weight for infant development. In fact, our earlier analysis of the issue (Cutler and Meara 2000) suggested that essentially all of the reduction in neonatal mortality since 1960 can be attributed to medical progress.

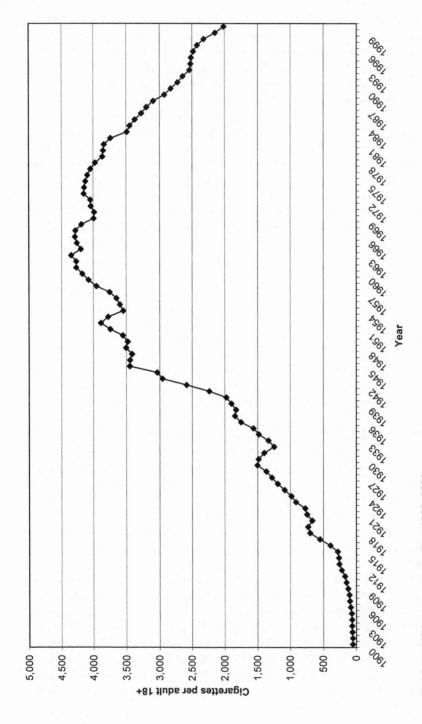

Fig. 9.11 Tobacco consumption, 1900–2000

Sources: United States Department of Agriculture; United States Centers for Disease Control and Prevention.

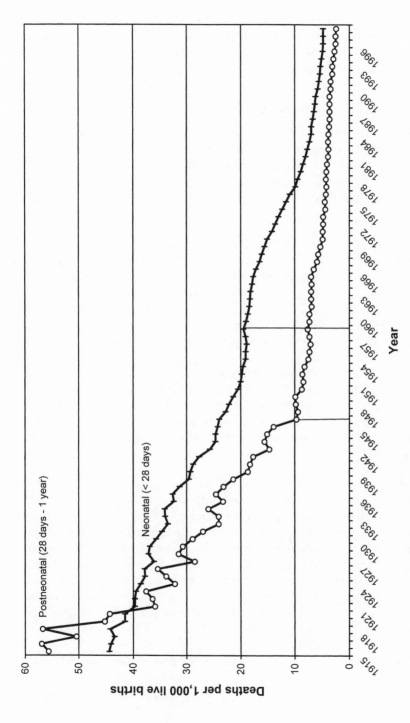

Fig. 9.12 Neonatal and postneonatal mortality
Source: United States Vital Statistics data.

The decline in mortality in the latter part of the twentieth century therefore seems attributable in substantial measure to medical progress. That is very different from the reasons why mortality declined earlier in the century and has enormous implications for the value of medical care.

9.5   Other Factors Influencing Mortality

Still, medicine is not the only factor influencing health. Understanding mortality reductions requires us to disentangle many different causes. We discuss in this section several additional causes of mortality reduction and some evidence on their importance. The logical next step—estimating how important the different factors are—we leave to future work.

9.5.1   Behavior

Some behaviors promote health and others worsen it. Behavioral change is a key component of health changes. The most significant behavioral change of the twentieth century was the rise and decline of smoking. Figure 9.11 shows smoking trends over the century. From essentially no cigarette consumption in 1900, per capita consumption of cigarettes rose to over 4,000 per year in 1960, or over two packs per smoker per day. Since then, cigarette consumption has declined to about 2,000 per year, a reduction of over 50 percent.

The most important health consequences of smoking are heart disease and cancer, particularly cancer of the lung, thorax, and bronchus.[2] The trend in cardiovascular disease mortality was discussed above. The trend in smoking-sensitive cancers is shown in figure 9.13. Trends in mortality from both of these conditions mirror the change in smoking, with a ten- to twenty-year lag.

9.5.2   Socioeconomic Status

Socioeconomic status may affect health in several ways. Medical technology is expensive, and income increases have been instrumental in financing that care. Further, socioeconomic status is associated with better behaviors. Better educated, and thus richer, people smoke less than less educated people (at least currently—they used to smoke more), perhaps because they know more about the true risks of disease. Education has a slightly stronger relationship to smoking than income, but this could be either because education truly matters more or because education picks up measures of permanent income not well captured by current income in most surveys on smoking.

But there are other links as well. Richer people may demand better

---

2. While many cancers are attributable in some part to smoking, smoking accounts for the greatest share of these three cancers.

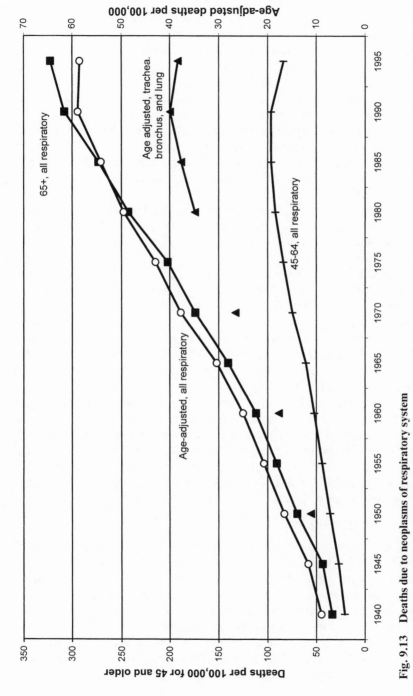

Fig. 9.13 Deaths due to neoplasms of respiratory system
Source: United States Vital Statistics data.

health, just as there is an income elasticity to many goods. The link between behavior and education suggests such an effect. Some direct evidence on this question comes from looking at suicide rates, shown in figure 9.14. Since 1930, suicide rates among the elderly have fallen by 56 percent, while rates among teens have tripled. The decline in suicide among the elderly is coincident with the large absolute increase in income for the elderly stemming from transfer programs such as Social Security and the programs that preceded it. Following the introduction of formal Social Security benefits, benefits rose rapidly over the period from 1950 until 1970, with a particularly rapid rise in the late 1960s. During these same time periods, suicide rates among the elderly fell most rapidly. It is less clear that the rise in youth suicide reflects falling income, although it may be due to other social pressures that are influencing youths (Cutler, Glaeser, and Norberg 2001).

Finally, income may affect health in other, indirect ways. A large literature on income inequality and health finds a correlation between adverse health outcomes and high levels of income inequality, even after controlling for mean income (Wilkinson 1996; Berkman and Kawachi, 2000). This literature has been questioned as being not particularly robust (Mellor and Milyo 2001) and as inconsistent with posited mechanisms for action (Deaton 2001). Overall, therefore, it is difficult to tell if this mechanism is important in practice.

Some of the most compelling research on social status and health comes from the Whitehall study of British civil servants (Marmot et al. 1984, 1987, 1991). In a series of studies following civil servants over time, it has been well documented that professionals in the British civil service experience better health than their counterparts in lower-level occupations within the civil service. This is true for mortality and a variety of health measures related to cardiovascular disease and other major morbidities. It is also true for risk factors such as smoking, sedentary lifestyle, and related behavioral variables, although these lifestyle factors cannot explain the entire difference in health outcomes across occupation. As income gaps widen over time, disparities in health have also widened (Menchik 1993).

9.5.3 Social Policies

Social policy is a third additional factor influencing mortality. Social policy is a vast term, and it is helpful to disaggregate it. Some social policies are clearly oriented to health improvements. Medicare and Medicaid are prime examples. Both programs were designed to increase access to health care for vulnerable populations, the elderly, and the poor, with the ultimate goal of improving health for these groups.

Other social policies such as Social Security affect income and may affect health through that channel. Income may have direct effects on health by increasing the purchase of medical care services and financing

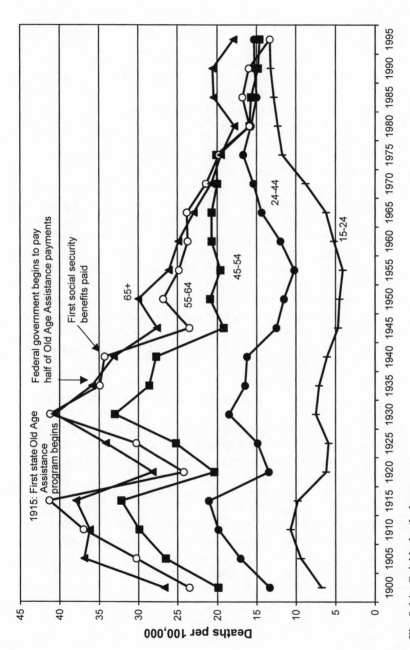

Fig. 9.14 Suicide deaths by age
Source: United States Vital Statistics data.

The following labels appear on the figure:

Deaths per 100,000

45 40 35 30 25 20 15 10 5 0

1900 1905 1910 1915 1920 1925 1930 1935 1940 1945 1950 1955 1960 1965 1970 1975 1980 1985 1990 1995

1915: First state Old Age Assistance program begins

Federal government begins to pay half of Old Age Assistance payments

First social security benefits paid

65+

55-64

45-54

24-44

15-24

consumption of items such as nutritious food that contributes to good health, or indirect effects by increasing the desire for healthy behaviors to enjoy a longer and higher quality life. It may be difficult to measure the precise impact of Social Security benefits on overall health, but evidence, such as that presented on suicide in figure 9.14, suggests that income benefits can have a substantial impact on the well-being of the elderly.

Finally, some social policies may affect health by changing the access that people have to already-established resources. One example of such policies would be the combination of civil rights legislation and improved health programs for the poor during the mid-1960s, especially through Medicaid. Ongoing work by Almond, Chay, and Greenstone (2001) suggests that the Civil Rights Act, along with expansions in the Medicaid program, led to substantial improvements in access to care, and ultimately in health outcomes for the poor. They show this by comparing white and nonwhite infant mortality disparities over time, presented in figure 9.15.

There is a clear decline in the ratio of nonwhite to white infant mortality following the 1966 Civil Rights Act. However, the considerable change in the nonwhite to white ratio of infant deaths over the century suggests that there are many factors that influenced health differentially for the different races. For example, the period during World War II shows a big fall in the ratio of nonwhite to white infant mortality. This shrinking infant mortality gap mirrors the shrinking racial wage gaps that occurred during World War II. It is also interesting to note that the ratio of nonwhite to white infant mortality is higher during the last decade of the century than at any other point in the past 100 years.

9.6   Conclusion

Mortality has declined continuously in most developed countries over the course of the twentieth century. In the United States, mortality rates declined every decade, and with the exception of a single ten-year period, did so at relatively constant rates.

But the constancy of mortality reductions masks significant heterogeneity by age, cause, and source. Early in the twentieth century, mortality declines resulted from public health and economic measures that improved peoples' ability to withstand disease. Formal medical care was unimportant for longer life. Because nutrition and public health were more important for the young than the old, mortality reductions were concentrated at younger ages. By midcentury, medical care became more significant and other factors less so. Penicillin and sulfa drugs brought the first mortality reductions at older ages, which were coupled with continuing improvements in health at younger ages. The pattern of mortality reduction was relatively equal by age.

In the latter part of the twentieth century, death became increasingly

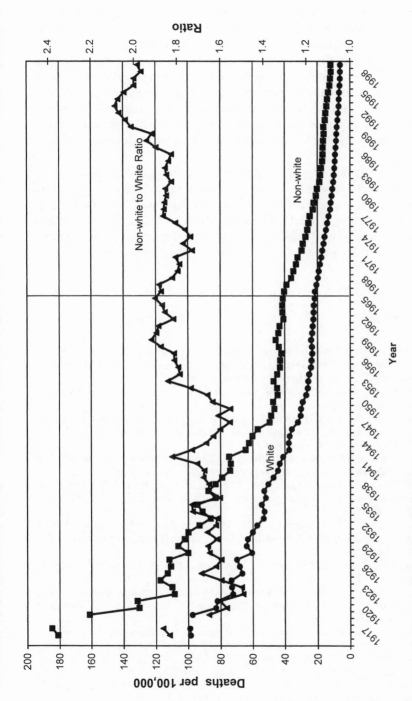

Fig. 9.15 Nonwhite and white infant mortality

Source: United States Vital Statistics data.

Note: Race is determined by race of child until 1970 when race is race of mother.

medicalized. Cardiovascular disease mortality was prevented in significant part through medical intervention. Traditional killers such as pneumonia in the young continued to decline, but mortality from these causes was already so low that further improvements did not add greatly to overall longevity. Rather, infant mortality declined because medical advances kept alive infants born of low birth weight. Still, there was a significant shift in the nature of longevity improvements away from improvements at younger ages and toward improvements at older ages. Most of the additional years added to life in the last few decades of the twentieth century were at older ages.

Medical care is an important, but not the only important, factor in reduced mortality. In addition to nutrition and public health, health insurance programs, income changes, and social policies more generally have all contributed to longer life. Disentangling the role of these different factors in reduced mortality is a difficult task but one that is increasingly important in light of the vast fiscal consequences of an aging society.

References

Almond, Douglas, Kenneth Chay, and Michael Greenstone. 2001. Civil rights, the war on poverty, and black-white convergence in infant mortality in Mississippi. University of California, Berkeley. Mimeograph.

Berkman, Lisa, and Ichiro Kawachi, eds. 2000. *Social epidemiology.* New York: Oxford University Press.

Cutler, David, Edward Glaeser, and Karen Norberg. 2001. Explaining the rise in youth suicide. In *Risky behavior among youths,* ed. Jonathan Gruber, 219–69. Chicago: University of Chicago Press.

Cutler, David, and Srikanth Kadiyala. 2001. The economics of better health: The case of cardiovascular disease. Harvard University. Mimeograph.

Cutler, David, and Ellen Meara. 2000. The technology of birth: Is it worth it? In *Frontiers in health policy research,* Vol. 3, ed. Alan Garber, 33–67. Cambridge, Mass.: MIT Press.

Deaton, Angus. 2001. Relative deprivation, inequality, and mortality. NBER Working Paper no. 8099. Cambridge, Mass.: National Bureau of Economic Research, January.

Dubos, Rene. 1969. The Diseases of Civilization. *Milbank Memorial Fund Quarterly,* 47:327–29.

Fogel, Robert W. 1994. Economic growth, population theory, and physiology: The bearing of long-term processes on the making of economic policy. *American Economic Review* (84): 369–95.

Lee, Ronald, and Lawrence Carter. 1992. Modeling and forecasting U.S. mortality. *Journal of the American Statistical Association* 87 (419): 659–71.

Marmot, Michael, M. Kogevinas, and M. A. Elston. 1987. Social/economic status and disease. *Annual Review of Public Health* 8:111–35.

Marmot, Michael, M. J. Shipley, and G. Rose. 1984. Inequalities in death—specific explanations of a general pattern? *Lancet* 1 (8384): 1003–06.

Marmot, Michael, G. D. Smith, S. Stansfeld, C. Patel, F. North, J. Head, I. White, E. Brunner, and A. Feeney. 1991. Health inequalities among British civil servants: The Whitehall II Study. *Lancet* 337 (8754): 1387–93.

McDermott, Walsh. 1978. Medicine: The public good and one's own. *Perspectives in Biology and Medicine* 21 (2): 167–87.

McKeown, Thomas. 1976. *The modern rise of population.* New York: Academic Press.

McKeown, Thomas, R. G. Record, and R. D. Turner. 1975. An interpretation of the decline of mortality in England and Wales during the twentieth century. *Population Studies* 29:391–422.

Mellor, Jennifer, and Jeffrey Milyo. 2001. Income inequality and health. *Journal of Policy Analysis and Management* 20 (1): 151–55.

Menchik, Paul L. 1993. Economic status as a determinant of mortality among black and white older men: Does poverty kill? *Population Studies* 47 (3): 427–36.

Preston, Sam. 1996. *American longevity: Past, present, and future.* Syracuse University Policy Brief no. 7/1996. Distinguished Lecturer in Aging Series. Syracuse, N.Y.: Syracuse University, Center for Policy Research.

Wilkinson, Richard. 1996. *Unhealthy societies.* London: Routledge.

Area Differences in Utilization
of Medical Care and Mortality
among U.S. Elderly

Victor R. Fuchs, Mark McClellan, and
Jonathan Skinner

10.1 Introduction

The two most important, most enduring questions in health economics
are (1) what are the determinants of expenditures? and (2) what are the determinants of health? Extensive research over the last thirty-five years has
produced a variety of answers to these questions, depending in large part
on the specific context within which the questions are posed. One crucial
distinction is between explaining changes over time and explaining cross-
sectional differences at a given time. With regard to secular changes in the
United States in recent decades, most health economists now believe that
advances in medical technology provide the major explanation for both increases in expenditures and improvements in health.[1] With regard to cross-
sectional differences, the focus of this paper, there is less agreement. By exploiting a rich body of data from the Centers for Medicare and Medicaid

Victor R. Fuchs is Henry J. Kaiser, Jr. Professor of Economics (Emeritus) at Stanford University, and a research associate of the National Bureau of Economic Research. Mark Mc-
Clellan is commissioner of the U.S. Food and Drug Administration, associate professor of
economics at Stanford University, associate professor of medicine at Stanford Medical
School, and a research associate of the National Bureau of Economic Research. Jonathan
Skinner is John French Professor of Economics at Dartmouth College, and a research associate of the National Bureau of Economic Research.

For development of the variables used in this paper we are indebted to Jeffrey Geppert,
Chris Kagay, Hoon Byun, and Sarah Rosen. We also thank Deborah Kerwin-Peck and Sarah
Rosen for preparation of the tables and Dan Gottlieb for additional research assistance. Fi-
nancial support was provided to Fuchs by the Robert Wood Johnson and Kaiser Family
Foundations and to Mark McClellan and Jonathan Skinner by the National Institute on Ag-
ing. Helpful comments from David Cutler, Angus Deaton, Ed Glaeser, and especially Joseph
Newhouse are gratefully acknowledged.

1. See, for example, Cutler et al. (1998), Pardes et al. (1999), Currie and Gruber (1996), and
Schneider (1999).

Services (formerly HCFA), the U.S. Census of Population, and other sources, we hope to narrow that disagreement, at least with respect to area differences in utilization of care and mortality of the elderly.

Our focus on the elderly is motivated in part by the fact that they account for a disproportionate share of national health care expenditures and an even greater share of government health care expenditures. Moreover, the elderly experience the bulk of the major health problems of the population. Approximately one-half of all deaths occur between ages sixty-five and eighty-four, and another one-fourth occur at ages eighty-five and above. These shares are based on the current age distribution of the U.S. population. For a stationary population experiencing current age-specific mortality rates, deaths at ages sixty-five–eighty-four would still account for almost one-half the total; the share at eighty-five and above would rise to one-third. The focus on the elderly is facilitated by the fact that the Medicare program generates a large, detailed body of data on utilization and mortality.

One reason for focusing on area differences is that the large number of metropolitan and nonmetropolitan areas in the United States provide a convenient framework for aggregating individual data in the search for variables that may be related to utilization and mortality. Moreover, many health policy analysts believe that an understanding of area differences may suggest opportunities to limit expenditures and/or improve health (for example, Wennberg, Fisher, and Skinner 2002).

This paper has two main sections: utilization and mortality. In most markets an interest in expenditures would require attention to prices as well as quantities, but given universal insurance coverage through Medicare and administrative price setting by HCFA, utilization is a natural subject for study. Mortality is only one of many possible measures of health, but there are several reasons to concentrate on it. First, mortality is by far the most objective measure. Second, it is, for most people, the most important health outcome. Third, it is probably significantly correlated with morbidity because most deaths are preceded by illness.

In this paper we focus on whites, aged sixty-five–eighty-four, or more specifically, those people not identified as African-American. We exclude blacks because at those ages both utilization and mortality of blacks are higher than for whites, and the percentage black in an area is correlated with other variables of interest. Moreover, preliminary research by Donald Nichols suggests that the relationship between those other variables and utilization and mortality may be significantly different for blacks than for whites. We exclude anyone eighty-five and over because it is more difficult to obtain accurate measures for self-reported variables such as education and income. About one-half the population eighty-five and over suffer from some form of dementia, and about one-fifth are in nursing homes where measurement of income is particularly problematic. Moreover, most nursing home utilization is not covered by Medicare, the source of our data on utilization.

Briefly, we find wide variation in the utilization of health services across regions. It is not simply that some regions are higher along all dimensions of care, but that in some regions (Florida, for example) there is much more diagnostic testing, even while per capita inpatient services are comparable to the national average. In general, utilization is strongly positively associated with mortality across areas—in other words, areas with more sick elderly use more health care, other things being equal. There remains, however, substantial variation in utilization after controlling for factors such as education, income, and mortality.

Cross-area variations in mortality rates among this elderly group are not as large as variations in utilization, but they are still substantial. The 10 percent of metropolitan statistical areas (MSAs) with the highest mortality (age-sex adjusted) have an average death rate 38 percent greater than the 10 percent of MSAs with the lowest mortality. The comparable differential between the high and low utilization areas is 49 percent.

Education, real income, cigarettes, obesity, air pollution, and the percent black account for more than half of the variation in mortality across areas, but there is still substantial differences across regions unexplained by these variables. Florida, in particular, has death rates significantly below the national average; the differential is particularly large for areas in the southern portion of the state. The final section of the paper explores two puzzles revealed by regression analyses: (1) why Florida is so different from the rest of the country with respect to utilization and mortality; and (2) why the presence of more blacks in an area should be associated with higher mortality among elderly whites. We considered several possible solutions to these puzzles, including differential migration patterns of the elderly, but ultimately we are left with conjectures rather than robust explanations.

10.2   Previous Studies

10.2.1   Spatial Variations in Health Care Utilization

There is an extensive literature on geographic variations in health care spending and how it might be explained; we consider here a selective overview of these studies.

Researchers have documented variations across regions in health care utilization beginning with the studies by Glover in the 1930s, the work by Wennberg and associates in the 1970s and 1980s, and more recent studies by a wide variety of researchers.[2] There is a general consensus that the variations are real and persistent over time. The *Dartmouth Atlas of Health*

---

2. For an excellent review of some of this earlier literature, see Eisenberg (1986). More recently, see Wennberg and Cooper (1999), Escarce (1992), Green and Becker (1994), Chassin et al. (1986), and references therein.

Care provides extensive documentation of the differences across regions for a variety of utilization measures (Wennberg and Cooper 1999). In the *Atlas* studies, regions are defined based on Hospital Referral Regions (HRRs), each of which has at least one hospital with a tertiary cardiovascular or neurological surgical center. The geographical boundary of the HRR is based on the migration patterns of Medicare patients who use the hospitals inside the HRR, of which there are 306 in the United States. Average 1995–96 fee-for-service Medicare per capita expenditures ranged from $3,506 in Eugene, Oregon, $3,700 in Minneapolis, $7,783 in Miami, to $9,033 in McAllen, Texas; these are all adjusted for age, sex, race, and regional price differences using a variant of the part B price adjuster. Utilization rates of specific interventions that are not subject to the difficulties of price adjustment also show dramatic variations across regions. These differences are therefore best thought of as differences in quantities—hospital admissions, physician visits, and procedures—for the enrollees who live in each region, regardless of where they actually get their care.

Most of the controversy comes in how these variations can be interpreted. One clear possibility is factors related to demand; a sicker population, for example, should lead to greater demand for health care. Health status is clearly a critical determinant of health care utilization. Average annual spending for Medicare beneficiaries with "poor" self-assessed health is $8,743, but only $1,656 for those in excellent health (Wennberg and Cooper 1996).

While regional differences in health status are clearly important determinants of health care spending (as we demonstrate in the following), they do not fully explain the two-fold differences in Medicare spending across regions. Even after accounting for differences across regions in underlying health measures such as stroke, heart attacks, hip fractures, cancer incidence, income, poverty rates, and behavioral factors such as the percentage of smokers and seatbelt users, one cannot explain more than 42 percent of the overall variation across regions in expenditures (Skinner and Fisher 1997; Skinner, Fisher, and Wennberg 2001). Longitudinal cohort studies also reveal differences in resource use across both hospitals and regions after controlling for patient health status and function.[3]

A related "demand" based explanation is that patient preferences (ow-

---

3. Cutler and Sheiner (1999) found that regional measures of the age/sex/race composition of the population explained 70 percent of regional differences in (age-sex-race adjusted) Medicare expenditures. The factors providing the additional explanatory power included the age-composition of deaths in the region and the age-specific mortality rates. Here we raise a cautionary note about "ecological fallacy" in which aggregated data are used to make inferences about individual causal pathways, a concern of particular importance to any research on geographic variation (Susser 1994a,b). For example, the percentage of the elderly population that is Hispanic is predicted to increase regional Medicare expenditures (Cutler and Sheiner 1999), yet average Medicare expenditures for Hispanics is roughly equal to expenditures for non-Hispanics.

ing to unmeasured illness or preferences for care, holding illness constant) determine health care utilization, so that health care resources move to areas with the greatest demand as measured by initial physician visits or other indicators, such as health (Escarce 1992; Escarce 1993; Folland and Stano 1989; Green and Becker 1994). In many of these studies, demand is inferred by the frequency of initial visits to the physician (as opposed to subsequent referrals, which are viewed as supply-driven). It remains an interesting, and largely untested, question as to whether visits to physicians reflect demand (patient preferences) or supply (how often the physician schedules office visits). Clearly, these demand-related factors can potentially explain some of the variation we observe, particularly in Florida where rates of utilization are higher than the rest of the country.

Another explanation is based on the supply of health care resources. The earliest incarnation of this link is "Roemer's Law," which states that if a hospital bed is built, it will be filled. In this view, the preexisting resource capacity of the area, which arose out of historical accident, in turn determines the intensity of care in the region. In regions with greater supplies of hospital beds, inpatient expenditures are higher. A similar story holds for physician supply; larger populations of physicians per capita are associated with higher levels of per capita physician expenditures (Wennberg and Cooper 1996, 1999).

However, correlation does not establish causation. One could expect more hospital beds to be built where there is greater demand, and one would expect physicians to move to regions where the demand of physician services is high. Furthermore, the correlations are not very strong. For example, using *Dartmouth Atlas* data, just one-quarter of the variation in part B (physician) expenditures across the United States can be explained by physician supply. And while the supply of specialists in Miami is 45 percent higher than the supply in Minnesota, the number of visits by specialists to people in their last six months of life in Miami is more than four times larger. In other words, there appear to be significant nonlinearities in treatment patterns across regions that cannot be explained solely by differences in resource supply.

Another hypothesis, closely related to Wennberg's "practice style" theory is that some physicians show greater "enthusiasm" for specific procedures (Wennberg, Barnes, and Zubkoff 1982; Chassin 1993). A recent study surveyed both orthopedic surgeons and referring physicians with regard to their propensity to perform surgery (in the former case) and their perceptions of outcomes and propensity to refer (in the latter case), and found that these factors were highly significant in explaining overall knee replacement rates in the population, even after controlling for the underlying clinical conditions of the patients (Wright et al. 1999). The study did not, however, test patient preferences conditional on health needs.

A number of studies seeking to explain physician behavior have examined associations between specific physician psychosocial attributes or physician training or practice characteristics (years in practice, diversity of diagnoses managed, specialty) and measures of utilization (Allison et al. 1998; Franks et al. 2000; Pearson et al. 1995; Selby et al. 1999). Although associations were generally weak, physicians with greater fear of malpractice, anxiety due to uncertainty, and less willingness to take risks were more likely to spend more per patient or more likely to refer. However, the magnitudes of these differences are not large enough to explain, by themselves, the wide regional variation in utilization.

As a statistical proposition, differences in physician enthusiasm by themselves are not enough to generate regional variations. Most regions include a large number of physicians, and if physicians are endowed with differing but randomly distributed levels of enthusiasm, they would average out over the large number of physicians in the area. (Of course, for some surgical procedures, one or two specialists could exert a strong influence on regional rates.) The interesting question therefore is why enthusiasm should be correlated across physicians within a given region.

Finally, factors that operate at the level of the hospital and market are also known to influence spending. Teaching status, membership in multi-hospital chains, degree of competition, and hospital ownership (for example, for-profit ownership) have all been associated with differences in resource use (Gray and McNerney 1986; Kessler and McClellan 1999; Silverman, Skinner, and Fisher 1999; Taylor, Whellan, and Sloan 1999). The extent to which these factors contribute to regional differences in spending is not well understood.

10.2.2 Spatial Variations in Mortality

Spatial variations in mortality have not been studied as extensively as variations in utilization, and many studies have focused heavily on the influence of one or two variables such as air pollution or income inequality. The earliest investigations typically used states or a limited number of MSAs as the units of observation, thus suffering from the problem of few degrees of freedom (Auster, Leveson, and Sarachek 1969; Silver 1972). Considerable effort has been devoted to studying the effects of income and education and to sorting out the relative importance of these closely related variables. Both variables are usually found to be related to mortality, but their importance can vary greatly with age and cause of death. Income, for instance, is much more highly correlated with infant mortality than with deaths at other ages.

Attempts to discover the impact of medical care have produced mixed results (Fuchs and Kramer 1972; Hadley 1988). More recently, Skinner, Fisher, and Wennberg (2001) used as an instrument physician visits in the last six months. This geographical variable was highly correlated with overall Medicare expenditures but uncorrelated with predicted survival based on regional measures of health. This study found "flat of the curve" effects of Medicare expenditures on survival, at least for the expenditures explained by physician visits in the last six months. Similar results were found using cohort data of heart attack patients controlling for detailed chart data using the Cooperative Cardiovascular Project data (Fisher et al. 2003).

Several studies have found a positive association between air pollution and mortality.[4] More recently, numerous investigators have focused on income inequality (rather than low income per se) as a major cause of higher mortality.[5] In two comprehensive reviews of this literature Deaton (2001) and Deaton and Paxson (1999) critique the theoretical foundations of these studies and their empirical implementations. In a study of changes over time in Britain and the United States, Deaton and Paxson (2001) find no support for an effect of income inequality on mortality. Deaton and Lubotsky (2001) find that when they control for percent black, the effect of income inequality is eliminated. They also find that percent black is positively related to white mortality at nearly all ages.

10.3   Data and Estimation Strategy

In this paper utilization is measured using a weighted index of quantities of services. We adopt this approach, instead of using Medicare expenditures, because it sidesteps the difficult problem of deflating Medicare expenditures across regions to "undo" differential payments made by Medicare for the same service in different areas. These differentials are introduced to offset differences in costs experienced by the providers of care and for other reasons. Deflated expenditures are also problematic to the extent that the residents of an area receive services in another area. In such cases, the price index of the area of residence is not the appropriate deflator.[6]

We count the number of specific services received by the resident of an area, regardless of the area where the services were provided. Each detailed service is then weighted by the national reimbursement rate for that service; the sum of the weighted quantities divided by the number of Medicare enrollees is the total utilization for each area. Because this approach relies on billing codes for thousands of detailed services, systematic differences across areas in coding could introduce inaccuracies into this measure. Also, services not covered by Medicare are not included.

The year of the study is 1990, with the utilization and mortality measures based on an average of 1989–91. Many of the other measures are obtained

---

4. See Evans, Tosteson, and Kinney (1984), Chappie and Lave (1982), and Ozkaynak and Thurston (1987).

5. See Kennedy, Kawachi, and Prothrow-Stith (1996), Kaplan et al. (1996), and Lynch et al. (1998).

6. The Medicare records define residence as the location where the individual receives Social Security retirement checks.

from the 1990 Census of Population. There are 224 MSAs with populations exceeding 100,000.[7] In addition, residents of MSAs with less than 100,000 are aggregated to one group within each state and residents outside MSAs are also aggregated to one group per state. The result is 313 areas.[8]

In this paper the areas are aggregated into seven regions:

Region	Census Divisions and States
North	New England, Middle Atlantic, and East North Central
Upper South	Delaware, Maryland, Washington, D.C., Virginia, and West Virginia
Deep South	North Carolina, South Carolina, Georgia, and East South Central
Florida	Florida
West South	West South Central
Big Sky	West North Central, Montana, Idaho, Wyoming, and Colorado
West	Pacific, Arizona, New Mexico, Utah, and Nevada

This regional breakdown was developed by a geographer, Ge Lin, who found it to be more useful than the conventional census regions, or divisions, in studying disability among the elderly (Lin 2000). We find this breakdown intuitively appealing, especially for the distinctions it makes among the southern states and among the mountain states and its treatment of Florida as a separate region.

We also aggregate areas according to their total population size in the following manner: (1) over 500,000, (2) 250,000 to 500,000, (3) 100,000 to 250,000, (4) under 100,000 (aggregated to a single area within a state), and (5) non-MSAs (aggregated to a single area within each state). When regions and population size are used as dummy variables, the omitted categories are "North" and "over 500,000."

10.4 Results

Table 10.1 presents a list of variables included in this paper, giving the short name, definition, and source. For a fuller explanation of the derivation of the utilization measures, see the appendix. The utilization measure, mortality, percent high school dropout (LOED), and real income have all been adjusted for age and sex. Cigarette use and obesity are state measures; the same value is assigned to every area within each state. Particulate concentration (Pollution) is only available for MSAs > 100,000.

Table 10.2 provides summary statistics for each variable. The means and standard deviations are calculated by weighting each area by its share of the population white aged sixty-five–eighty-four. Looking first at the

7. One other MSA > 100,000, St. Cloud, Minnesota, was excluded from the study because of problems with the mortality data.
8. Some states do not have any MSAs with less than 100,000 or do not have any non-MSA residents.

Table 10.1   **Names, Definitions, and Sources of Variables**

Variable	Definition	Source
TOTUTIL	Total health care utilization, per white Medicare enrollee 65–84[a] (1989–1991)	HCFA[e,f,g] (1989–1991)
INUTIL	Inpatient utilization (including institutional reimbursement and physician services), per white Medicare enrollee 65–84[a] (1989–1991)	HCFA[e,f,g] (1989–1991)
OUTUTIL	Outpatient utilization (including institutional reimbursement for same day services, physician, and miscellaneous services), per white Medicare enrollee 65–84[a] (1989–1991)	HCFA[e,f,g] (1989–1991)
TOTADM	Weighted total hospital admissions, per white Medicare enrollee 65–84[a] (1989–1991)	HCFA[e,f] (1989–1991)
MEDADM	Weighted hospital medical admissions, per white Medicare enrollee 65–84[a] (1989–1991)	HCFA[e,f] (1989–1991)
SURGADM	Weighted hospital surgical admissions, per white Medicare enrollee 65–84[a] (1989–1991)	HCFA[e,f] (1989–1991)
TOTPHYS	Total physician utilization (inpatient and outpatient), per white Medicare enrollee 65–84[a] (1989–1991)	HCFA[e,g] (1989–1991)
EANDM	Physician utilization for evaluation and management services (inpatient and outpatient), per white Medicare enrollee 65–84[a] (1989–1991)	HCFA[e,g] (1989–1991)
DIAG	Physician utilization for diagnosis (inpatient and outpatient), per white Medicare enrollee 65–84[a] (1989–1991)	HCFA[e,g] (1989–1991)
TREAT	Physician utilization for procedures/treatment (inpatient and outpatient), per white Medicare enrollee 65–84[a] (1989–1991)	HCFA[e,g] (1989–1991)
MORT	Deaths, per 1,000 whites 65–84[a] (average 1989–1991)	HCFA[e] (1989–1991)
LOED	Percent of whites 65–84[a] with less than 12 years of schooling (1990)	U.S. Census of Population (1990)
REALINC	Mean income for whites aged 65–84[a] (1990) deflated by cost of living index[c] (1991)	U.S. Census of Population (1990)
CIGS	Per capita sales by state (packs) (average 1984–1989)	Tobacco Institute (1998)
OBESE	Percent obese[d] by state, adjusted for race (1991)	Mokdad et al. (1999)
POLUTN	Mean PM-10 concentration (particulate matter 10 microns or smaller in diameter, $\mu g/m^3$; average	Shprentz (1996)
BLACK	Percent of total population black (1990)	Area Resource File (1992)

[a]Standardized for age and sex.
[b]HCFA 5 percent samples (MEDPAR, Outpatient SAF, BMAD, HHA SAF, Hospice SAF).
[c]COL predicted from a regression of U.S. Chamber of Commerce cost-of-living index for 109 metropolitan areas (1991) on standardized wage index and median property values (1990).
[d]Body mass index (weight divided by square of height) $\geq 30 \text{ kg/m}^2$.
[e]Hiskew 20 percent random sample.
[f]MEDPAR 20 percent random sample.
[g]BMAD 5 percent random sample.

Table 10.2   **Summary Statistics**

	Mean[a]	SD[a]	CV[a]	25th	50th	75th	Minimum	Maximum
				Percentile				
Part A: All Areas (N = 313)								
TOTUTIL	3,265	368	11.3	2,870	3,088	3,375	2,316	4,368
INUTIL	2,132	207	9.7	1,903	2,063	2,231	1,576	2,931
OUTUTIL	1,133	254	22.4	930	1,051	1,169	691	1,998
TOTADM	1,783	178	10.0	1,589	1,735	1,888	1,352	2,423
MEDADM	933	138	14.8	793	904	1,004	567	1,518
SURGADM	849	65	7.7	789	840	889	615	1,083
TOTPHYS	1,195	237	19.9	975	1,096	1,226	797	1,976
EANDM	400	82	20.5	318	359	397	235	660
DIAG	210	61	29.2	157	185	222	100	460
TREAT	585	120	20.6	488	546	637	377	1,011
MORT	38.3	3.1	8.1	36.1	38.8	41.1	29.2	51.8
LOED	0.382	0.098	25.7	0.318	0.388	0.459	0.134	0.691
REALINC	14,022	1,570	11.2	12,772	13,995	15,373	9,473	21,105
CIGS	114.7	16.2	14.1	107.3	112.6	124.3	62.4	193.4
OBESE	0.118	0.018	15.1	0.103	0.120	0.132	0.082	0.158
BLACK	0.108	0.088	81.0	0.018	0.061	0.143	0.001	0.425
Part B: MSAs > 100,000 (N = 224)								
TOTUTIL	3,340	388	11.6	2,880	3,113	3,484	2,316	4,368
INUTIL	2,136	215	10.1	1,874	2,056	2,238	1,576	2,931
OUTUTIL	1,204	267	22.2	955	1,084	1,218	691	1,998
TOTADM	1,766	179	10.1	1,567	1,710	1,889	1,352	2,423
MEDADM	906	126	13.9	777	872	980	567	1,518
SURGADM	859	71	8.3	787	850	914	615	1,083
TOTPHYS	1,274	243	19.1	1,012	1,132	1,273	797	1,976
EANDM	430	83	19.3	328	373	410	235	660
DIAG	230	63	27.2	165	195	235	117	460
TREAT	613	127	20.8	503	566	652	377	1,011
MORT	38.2	3.1	8.2	36.2	38.9	41.3	29.2	51.8
LOED	0.345	0.080	23.2	0.305	0.368	0.425	0.167	0.691
REALINC	14,464	1,536	10.6	13,221	14,402	15,679	9,473	21,105
CIGS	112.9	13.8	12.2	107.3	112.6	124.3	62.4	193.4
OBESE	0.116	0.017	14.8	0.103	0.120	0.133	0.082	0.151
POLUTN	29.3	6.1	20.9	23.7	26.4	29.1	17.2	60.4
BLACK	0.124	0.077	62.2	0.028	0.076	0.154	0.001	0.425

Notes: SD = standard deviation; CV = coefficient of variation; N = number of observations; MSA = metropolitan statistical area. For explanations of variables, see table 10.1.

[a]Weighted by population: whites aged sixty-five to eighty-four.

means, we see that inpatient utilization accounts for about two-thirds of the total and outpatient utilization one-third. Admissions are approximately evenly divided between medical and surgical. Approximately one-half of total physician utilization is accounted for by treatment (procedures), about one-third by evaluation and management, and about one-sixth by diagnostic interventions.

The utilization measure shows considerably more variation across areas than does mortality. The relative variation in outpatient utilization is more than double that for inpatient utilization. As between medical admissions and surgical admissions, the former has twice the variation of the latter. Diagnosis has the most variation of the three types of physician services; all three have much greater variation than hospital admissions. This difference may be explained in part by more random variation in the measure of outpatient utilization, which has a smaller mean and is calculated from a smaller sample.

10.4.1   Utilization Indexes by Region and Population Size

Tables 10.3 and 10.4 show indexes of utilization for areas grouped by region or population size for various types of utilization. All indexes are based on U.S. = 100. All are adjusted for age and sex, and areas are weighted by their population of whites sixty-five–eighty-four. The first column of table 10.3 shows that total utilization is much greater in Florida than in the rest of the country. Utilization is lowest in Big Sky. Across areas grouped by population size, total utilization is highest in the areas with over 500,000 population, and the 250,000–500,000 population group is second highest. The other three categories all have below-average utilization, with little difference among them.

Comparisons between indexes for inpatient (INUTIL) and outpatient (OUTUTIL) utilization (table 10.3 columns [2] and [3]) show many substantial differences, both for regions and population size. Most noteworthy is Florida, where the inpatient index is slightly below the national average, but outpatient utilization is approximately 55 percent above. In Big Sky the direction of difference is reversed; the inpatient index exceeds the outpatient index by more than 20 percentage points. Areas of large population size tend to show relatively more utilization of outpatient care; the reverse is true for MSAs < 100,000 and the areas that are not MSAs.

Substantial regional and population size differences in the indexes for medical admissions and surgical admissions can be seen in table 10.4. In Florida, the index for surgical admissions is 15 percentage points higher than for medical admissions; the West region also has relatively more surgical admissions. In the three southern regions, medical admissions tend to be relatively higher than surgical admissions, but the only big differential is in the Deep South.

The final utilization comparisons in table 10.4 are among three types of

Table 10.3   Utilization Indexes, by Region and Population Size (U.S. = 100)

	TOTUTIL	INUTIL[a]	OUTUTIL[b]
Part A: All Areas (N = 313)			
Region			
North	96.8	97.8	95.1
Upper South	101.2	102.4	98.9
Deep South	102.7	104.8	98.6
Florida	117.5	97.4	155.3
West South	101.8	104.9	95.9
Big Sky	91.8	99.3	77.7
West	101.8	100.3	104.5
Population size			
>500,000	103.6	101.4	107.9
250,000–500,000	99.5	95.8	106.4
100,000–250,000	94.8	95.7	93.2
<100,000	96.9	100.3	90.5
Not MSA	94.9	99.2	86.7
U.S. expenditure per enrollee	3,265	2,132	1,133
Part B: MSAs > 100,000 (N = 224)			
Region			
North	96.1	98.1	92.5
Upper South	100.1	99.2	101.8
Deep South	100.5	102.3	97.1
Florida	116.0	97.2	149.3
West South	101.6	104.9	95.8
Big Sky	93.1	101.6	78.1
West	102.2	102.2	102.0
U.S. expenditure per enrollee	3,340	2,136	1,204

Notes: All indexes standardized for age and sex. Area values weighted by population: whites aged sixty-five to eighty-four. N = number of observations; MSA = metropolitan statistical area. See table 10.1 for explanations of variables.

[a]Includes hospital and physician.

[b]Includes hospital, physician, and miscellaneous services.

physician services: evaluation and management, diagnosis, and treatment (surgical and nonsurgical procedures). The differences for Florida are huge, with the index for diagnostic tests 63 percent above the U.S. average, while evaluation and management is only 27 percent above. The procedures/treatment index is intermediate at 45 percent above the U.S. average. When only the areas above 100,000 are compared, the differentials are slightly smaller. In Big Sky the diagnostic test index is particularly low: 14 percentage points below the procedures/treatment index in the same region.

10.4.2   Correlations among the Different Measures of Utilization

Most measures of utilization are positively correlated, suggesting that the forces that influence variation in utilization across areas are stronger

Table 10.4   Hospital Admissions Indexes, by Region and Population Size (U.S. = 100)

	TOTADM	MEDADM	SURGADM	TOTPHYS	EANDM[a]	DIAG[a]	TREAT[a]
			Part A: All Areas (N = 313)				
Region							
North	98.5	98.8	98.2	94.0	100.1	95.4	89.3
Upper South	102.2	105.4	98.8	98.5	99.6	95.5	98.9
Deep South	107.3	113.5	100.4	92.7	91.0	91.0	94.5
Florida	92.3	84.8	100.7	142.0	126.6	162.8	145.0
West South	105.8	107.0	104.4	97.5	91.7	99.0	101.0
Big Sky	101.1	101.9	100.2	85.3	80.5	77.2	91.6
West	97.8	94.4	101.4	111.2	110.3	104.9	114.0
Population size							
>500,000	100.0	98.4	101.7	109.0	111.6	112.8	105.8
250,000–500,000	95.4	91.1	100.1	102.7	96.6	104.4	106.2
100,000–250,000	96.2	94.0	98.6	92.4	87.7	92.1	95.7
<100,000	102.1	105.2	98.6	89.5	88.5	83.3	92.4
Not MSA	101.6	105.5	97.3	86.3	84.2	80.5	89.8
U.S. expenditure per enrollee	1,783	933	849	1,195	400	210	585
			Part B: MSAs > 100,000 (N = 224)				
Region							
North	99.4	100.8	98.0	91.7	97.7	93.3	86.9
Upper South	97.7	98.1	97.3	102.1	100.0	101.6	103.8
Deep South	104.6	106.7	102.2	91.5	86.4	90.1	95.6
Florida	92.6	86.3	99.2	136.4	121.7	153.6	140.3
West South	105.7	105.9	105.6	97.6	91.1	97.1	102.3
Big Sky	103.3	105.2	101.4	85.3	81.7	77.6	90.8
West	100.3	99.0	101.7	108.3	108.1	100.7	111.3
U.S. expenditure per enrollee	1,766	906	859	1,274	430	230	613

Note: See table 10.3.

[a] Includes inpatient and outpatient.

than the possibilities for substitution between various types of utilization. For example, the coefficient of correlation between inpatient and outpatient utilization is 0.27, even though there are surely some opportunities for substitution between inpatient and outpatient care. Similarly, although some health problems can be treated either medically or surgically, the correlation between medical admissions and surgical admissions is 0.47. The largest negative correlation, –0.13, is between medical admissions and physicians' diagnostic services. (For a full set of correlation coefficients see 10A.1.)

10.4.3   Mortality Indexes

Table 10.5 presents mortality indexes for areas grouped by region or by population size. As in the utilization tables, all indexes have been adjusted for age and sex, and areas are weighted by the population of whites aged sixty-five–eighty-four in those regions. The most striking result is the low mortality in Florida, which is slightly more than 10 percent below the U.S.

Table 10.5   **Mortality Indexes, by Region and Population Size (U.S. = 100)**

	MORT	Ages 65–74	Ages 75–84	Men	Women
Part A: All Areas (N = 313)					
Region					
North	102.2	102.3	102.0	101.9	102.5
Upper South	106.4	107.4	105.5	106.3	106.5
Deep South	108.5	109.7	107.5	112.0	104.5
Florida	89.5	90.0	89.2	90.3	88.7
West South	103.9	104.0	103.8	104.3	103.4
Big Sky	94.0	93.2	94.6	95.4	92.4
West	94.0	92.8	94.9	91.0	97.3
Population size					
>500,000	99.8	99.7	99.9	98.7	101.1
250,000–500,000	98.1	97.1	98.8	97.8	98.4
100,000–250,000	100.7	100.6	100.8	101.4	100.0
<100,000	101.7	102.0	101.4	102.8	100.4
Not MSA	99.8	100.1	99.5	101.6	97.7
Deaths per 1,000	38.31	26.16	59.68	48.95	30.72
Part B: MSAs > 100,000 (N = 224)					
Region					
North	102.9	103.4	102.6	103.1	102.8
Upper South	104.4	103.8	104.8	103.6	105.2
Deep South	108.7	110.2	107.6	112.0	105.1
Florida	88.9	89.8	88.2	90.5	87.1
West South	104.7	103.5	105.6	105.4	103.9
Big Sky	97.7	96.8	98.3	98.1	97.2
West	94.5	93.4	95.3	92.2	97.1
Deaths per 1,000	38.20	26.03	59.60	48.41	30.92

Note: See table 10.3.

average. Also below the U.S. average are Big Sky and West regions. The other four regions all have above average mortality, with the Deep South experiencing the highest rate at more than 8 percent above the U.S. average. When areas are grouped by population size, the most notable result is that the mortality indexes are approximately the same across all the groups. Apparently despite the many socioeconomic and other differences that exist between the large and the small metropolitan and nonmetropolitan areas, white death rates at ages sixty-five–eighty-four do not vary with population size.

The second and third columns of table 10.5 allow comparisons of mortality between ages sixty-five–seventy-four and seventy-five–eighty-four (adjusted for sex mix). On the whole, the indexes are very similar. The regional rankings of mortality for the two age groups are almost identical. There is a slight tendency for the regional differentials to be smaller at ages seventy-five–eighty-four than at sixty-five–seventy-four. When age-adjusted mortality rates for men and women are compared (columns [4] and [5] of table 10.5), two substantial regional differentials are evident. In Deep South the relative mortality index is more than 7 percentage points higher for men than for women. In West, the index for men is 6 percentage points lower than for women.

10.4.4 Socioeconomic and Other Indexes

Differentials in socioeconomic and other indexes across areas grouped by population size and region are shown in table 10.6. Florida again stands out from the rest of the country in several respects. The percentage of high school dropouts is the lowest and real income the highest of all the regions. Only the West rivals Florida in having a low percentage of elderly with less than twelve-years schooling. By contrast, the percent of dropouts is particularly high in the Deep South. Across the population size groups, the patterns for the percentage of high school dropouts and real income are quite systematic, with the former indexes rising and the latter falling as population size falls.

Regional differences in cigarette use and obesity are not as large as for the percentage with low education and have distinctive patterns of their own. Cigarette use is highest in the Deep South and lowest in the West. Obesity is highest in the North and West South and lowest in Florida. Both cigarette use and obesity are lowest in the two largest population size groups and highest in the three other groups. In this respect, the pattern is similar to that for low educational attainment.

The reasons for including the percent of total black population in 1990 (BLACK) in the study will become apparent in discussion of the mortality regressions. For the present, we note that this variable has great regional variation, with extremely high rates in the Upper South and Deep South and extremely low rates in Big Sky and West. The index is much above av-

Table 10.6   Socioeconomic and Other Indexes, by Region and Population Size
(U.S. = 100)

	LOED[a]	REALINC[a]	CIGS	OBESE	BLACK	POLUTN
Part A: All Areas (N = 313)						
Region						
North	102.2	95.6	102.0	108.0	94.1	
Upper South	109.6	107.5	105.9	95.9	167.8	
Deep South	131.0	96.3	118.3	97.6	195.2	
Florida	73.3	112.3	106.4	83.0	121.6	
West South	115.4	104.0	97.3	105.3	126.0	
Big Sky	100.1	104.1	94.8	101.0	38.5	
West	75.9	100.7	83.9	88.1	48.9	
Population size						
>500,000	88.4	103.3	97.9	98.0	125.5	
250,000–500,000	95.1	103.1	99.4	98.9	78.8	
100,000–250,000	100.4	101.8	100.9	102.2	74.1	
<100,000	116.0	94.0	104.1	102.8	77.4	
Not MSA	119.6	94.2	102.2	102.9	68.3	
U.S. average	0.382	14,022	114.7	0.118	0.108	
Part B: MSAs > 100,000 (N = 224)						
Region						
North	109.7	94.8	102.6	109.1	106.6	97.2
Upper South	95.6	118.0	107.1	90.5	203.0	90.2
Deep South	121.4	101.9	118.3	98.3	168.3	99.0
Florida	79.8	108.5	108.1	84.2	105.3	81.7
West South	110.9	108.8	97.6	107.9	118.9	87.3
Big Sky	94.9	103.8	98.8	97.3	64.7	96.4
West	80.9	99.0	85.4	89.1	49.2	120.8
U.S. average	0.345	14,464	112.9	0.116	0.124	29.3

Note: See table 10.3.
[a]Standardized for age and sex.

erage in the largest metropolitan areas and considerably below average in all the others.

The last variable in table 10.6, pollution, is only measured for the MSAs greater than 100,000. The index for the West is 21 percent above the U.S. average; all other regions are below the U.S. average, with the lowest rate in Florida. Across population size groups, the pollution index declines steadily from the largest to the smallest.

10.4.5   Correlations among Variables

Some variables, such as low education and real income, are highly correlated with one another; the coefficient is –0.61. Low education is also significantly correlated with cigarettes (0.38) and obesity (0.37). All three variables are significantly correlated with mortality: low education (0.49), cigarettes (0.44), and obesity (0.41). For a full matrix of correlation coefficients among all the variables, see 10A.2.

10.4.6   Regression Analysis: Utilization

In this section, we consider what factors appear to explain the various measures for utilization. All variables are in natural logs except for the region and population size dummy variables. All regressions are run across the 313 areas and across the 224 MSAs > 100,000. At a theoretical level, the relation between low education and utilization is uncertain. It might be negative because individuals with less than twelve years of schooling might lack information about health care or might have less easy access to care. On the other hand, the relationship might be positive to the extent that those with less education are in worse health and require more care.

The predictive relation between income and utilization is also uncertain. If higher-income individuals are in better health, the relationship might be negative, but the relationship could be positive if there is a strong positive income elasticity of demand for care. Among other considerations, higher-income individuals are more likely to have private insurance that supplements Medicare.

Finally, because poor health usually results in increased utilization of health care, we expect mortality to be positively related to utilization to the extent that mortality is a good indicator of poor health. The relationship could be negative if this effect is outweighed by a reverse causality running from greater utilization to lower mortality. Because of the possibility of reverse causality, the parameter estimate for deaths per 1,000 whites aged sixty-five–eighty-four, average 1989–91 (MORT) should be regarded as a lower-bound estimate of the true coefficient.

Table 10.7 presents regression results for our measure of total utilization for three specifications. The first includes only the region and population size dummies, the second the two socioeconomic variables and mortality, and the third all the variables together. The results for the 224 MSAs are similar to those for the 313 areas and are available in table 10A.3. Probably the most striking result is the large coefficient for MORT: With all variables included, it is 0.51 (0.08). Under the reasonable assumption that the mortality rate is a good indicator of the health of the population, we infer that variation in health status across areas is a major determinant of health care utilization among whites aged sixty-five–eighty-four. Another notable result is the large increase in the Florida coefficient when the other variables are added to the regression. All the population size dummies have significant negative coefficients; that is, utilization is greater in MSAs larger than 500,000 than in any of the other areas. One likely interpretation is that patients in large metropolitan areas find it easier to obtain care (because of closer proximity to hospitals and physicians and the availability of a wide range of specialists).

Table 10.7   **Utilization Regression Results, OLS**

	Ln TOTUTIL			Ln INUTIL	Ln OUTUTIL
R^2	0.366	0.090	0.450	0.343	0.652
Upper South	0.053		0.029	0.022	0.036
	(0.025)		(0.025)	(0.024)	(0.037)
Deep South	0.080		0.040	0.027	0.063
	(0.018)		(0.019)	(0.018)	(0.027)
Florida	0.193		0.270	0.113	0.496
	(0.021)		(0.023)	(0.022)	(0.034)
West South	0.064		0.049	0.064	0.021
	(0.019)		(0.020)	(0.019)	(0.029)
Big Sky	−0.028		0.014	0.092	−0.148
	(0.018)		(0.019)	(0.018)	(0.028)
West	0.038		0.091	0.094	0.087
	(0.015)		(0.017)	(0.016)	(0.025)
250,000–500,000	−0.064		−0.058	−0.053	−0.065
	(0.020)		(0.019)	(0.018)	(0.027)
100,000–250,000	−0.090		−0.090	−0.074	−0.118
	(0.021)		(0.020)	(0.019)	(0.029)
<100,000	−0.061		−0.060	−0.027	−0.117
	(0.016)		(0.016)	(0.015)	(0.024)
Not MSA	−0.082		−0.079	−0.041	−0.152
	(0.014)		(0.015)	(0.015)	(0.022)
Ln LOED		−0.080	0.036	0.043	0.020
		(0.033)	(0.036)	(0.034)	(0.052)
Ln REALINC		0.151	0.026	−0.032	0.147
		(0.072)	(0.074)	(0.071)	(0.108)
Ln MORT		0.361	0.515	0.694	0.216
		(0.086)	(0.084)	(0.080)	(0.122)
Intercept	8.086	5.247	5.986	5.458	4.853
	(0.009)	(0.730)	(0.763)	(0.729)	(1.113)

Notes: MSA = metropolitan statistical area. See table 10.1 for explanations of variables. Numbers in parentheses are standard errors. Number of observations = 313.

Table 10.7 also presents regression results for inpatient utilization and outpatient utilization for the specification that includes all the variables. The coefficient for mortality is very large for inpatient care, but much smaller for outpatient care. For Florida, the reverse is true, with a huge coefficient for outpatient care and a much smaller (but still statistically significant coefficient) for inpatient care. In contrast, the Big Sky region has a large, statistically significant positive coefficient for inpatient care and a negative one for outpatient care. Clearly, regions differ both with regard to overall utilization as well as with respect to specific components of care. Neither low education nor real income are significantly related to utilization after controlling for the other variables. This result may reflect the offsetting theoretical considerations discussed previously.

Table 10.8   **Utilization Regression Results, by Type of Service, OLS**

	Ln MEDADM	Ln SURGADM	Ln EANDM	Ln DIAG	Ln TREAT
R^2	0.526	0.261	0.549	0.570	0.609
Upper South	0.024	−0.019	0.035	0.025	0.076
	(0.031)	(0.020)	(0.040)	(0.054)	(0.037)
Deep South	0.046	0.001	−0.029	0.033	0.064
	(0.023)	(0.015)	(0.030)	(0.040)	(0.028)
Florida	0.058	0.077	0.264	0.499	0.464
	(0.029)	(0.018)	(0.037)	(0.049)	(0.034)
West South	0.063	0.051	−0.030	0.080	0.112
	(0.025)	(0.016)	(0.032)	(0.042)	(0.029)
Big Sky	0.139	0.064	−0.115	−0.138	0.042
	(0.024)	(0.015)	(0.030)	(0.041)	(0.028)
West	0.081	0.067	0.078	0.062	0.242
	(0.021)	(0.013)	(0.027)	(0.036)	(0.025)
250,000–500,000	−0.067	−0.013	−0.156	−0.140	−0.039
	(0.023)	(0.015)	(0.030)	(0.040)	(0.028)
100,000–250,000	−0.087	−0.036	−0.213	−0.184	−0.083
	(0.025)	(0.016)	(0.032)	(0.042)	(0.029)
<100,000	0.007	−0.023	−0.196	−0.254	−0.060
	(0.020)	(0.013)	(0.026)	(0.034)	(0.024)
Not MSA	0.009	−0.039	−0.235	−0.280	−0.110
	(0.019)	(0.012)	(0.024)	(0.032)	(0.022)
Ln LOED	0.084	0.013	−0.009	0.064	0.043
	(0.044)	(0.028)	(0.057)	(0.076)	(0.053)
Ln REALINC	−0.147	0.083	−0.126	0.170	0.304
	(0.092)	(0.059)	(0.118)	(0.157)	(0.109)
Ln MORT	1.100	0.466	0.190	−0.116	0.106
	(0.104)	(0.067)	(0.133)	(0.178)	(0.123)
Intercept	4.272	4.250	6.560	4.239	3.046
	(0.945)	(0.605)	(1.212)	(1.618)	(1.122)

Notes: See table 10.7.

Table 10.8 presents similar regression results for medical and surgical admission and the three types of physician services. The coefficient for mortality is extremely large for medical admissions, no doubt reflecting the severe illness of many patients with neoplastic, cardiovascular, and cerebrovascular diseases who are admitted to medical services with little hope of altering the final outcome. The mortality coefficient for surgical admissions is less than half that for medical admissions, but still highly significant. In contrast, none of the three types of physician utilization has a mortality coefficient that is significantly different from zero.

The relationship between mortality and utilization reported in this paper is echoed in a study by Frohlich, Fransoo, and Roos (2001) of twelve communities in Winnipeg, Manitoba. They found that age-sex adjusted deaths before age seventy-five, their Premature Mortality Rate (PMR), was positively correlated with most types of care. However, PMR was not correlated with visits to specialists and negatively correlated with "high profile" procedures such as magnetic resonance imagings (MRIs), coronary artery bypass grafts (CABGs), hip and knee replacements, and preventive services.

The coefficients for Florida are particularly large for diagnostic and treatment services, smaller but still highly significant for evaluation and management, and smallest for hospital admissions. The Big Sky region has notably large negative mortality coefficients for evaluation and management and diagnostic services and a notably large positive coefficient for medical admissions. In comparisons of utilization across areas grouped by population size, the most striking result is the much higher utilization of evaluation and management and diagnostic services in MSAs > 500,000 relative to those with 250,000–500,000, and especially in areas with less than 250,000 or areas not classified as MSAs. The only significant result for the socioeconomic variables is a large, positive relation between real income and treatment. Result of regressions similar to those in table 10.8 but restricted to MSA > 100,000 are presented in table 10A.4.

Because there may be some causality running from utilization to mortality, we also ran two-stage least squares regressions. The results are reported in table 10A.5. The coefficients for predicted Ln mortality are typically much larger than in the ordinary least squares (OLS) regressions, but the standard errors are also much larger, raising questions about the reliability of the estimates.

10.4.7   Regression Analysis: Mortality

In addition to the dummy variables for region and population size, the mortality regressions include the percentage of individuals who did not finish high school and mean real income. Education and income have been shown to exhibit strong associations with mortality. Similarly, the harmful effects of cigarettes and obesity on health have been well established. Finally, given the Deaton and Lubotsky results, we also include a variable measuring the fraction of the population that is African American.

The mortality regression results are presented in table 10.9 in three specifications similar to those shown for utilization. First we note that the R^2s are considerably higher for mortality than for utilization regressions. This is despite the fact that none of the population-size dummies are significantly different from zero either when just the geographical dummies are included or when the other variables are entered into the regression. This is unlike the utilization regressions where there is a significant differential between the largest areas and the others.

Inclusion of the other variables results in a significant reduction in the negative coefficients for Big Sky and West. There is also a small reduction in the negative coefficient for Florida. Nevertheless, even after controlling

Table 10.9   **Mortality Regression Results, All Areas**

	(1)	(2)	(3)
R^2	0.485	0.521	0.627
Upper South	0.041		0.045
	(0.017)		(0.016)
Deep South	0.064		0.025
	(0.012)		(0.013)
Florida	−0.134		−0.096
	(0.014)		(0.015)
West South	0.019		0.020
	(0.013)		(0.013)
Big Sky	−0.079		−0.026
	(0.012)		(0.012)
West	−0.085		−0.009
	(0.010)		(0.012)
250,000–500,000	−0.013		0.001
	(0.013)		(0.012)
100,000–250,000	−0.004		0.009
	(0.014)		(0.013)
<100,000	−0.009		−0.004
	(0.011)		(0.011)
Not MSA	−0.016		−0.010
	(0.009)		(0.011)
Ln LOED		0.076	0.036
		(0.018)	(0.023)
Ln REALINC		−0.141	−0.121
		(0.042)	(0.049)
Ln CIGS		0.098	0.133
		(0.027)	(0.031)
Ln OBESE		0.148	0.111
		(0.024)	(0.025)
Ln BLACK		0.027	0.021
		(0.003)	(0.004)
Intercept	3.671	4.992	4.507
	(0.006)	(0.428)	(0.510)

Note: Number of observations = 313.

for all the other variables, Florida has a coefficient (relative to North) of −0.096 (0.01). It is the region with by far the lowest mortality. After controlling for the other variables, the highest regional mortality is in the Upper South.

Looking at the other variables we find that the percentage of high school dropouts has a positive coefficient until the geographic variable dummies are entered into the equation. Then the coefficient, while still positive, is not significantly different from zero. In the full regression, real income has a negative coefficient that is significantly different from zero. Cigarette use has the expected positive coefficient, which becomes larger when the geographic dummies are included. Obesity has the expected positive coefficient, but it becomes smaller when the geographic dummies are included. Finally, the percent black has a positive coefficient and also remains relatively unchanged by inclusion of the geographic dummies. In the regressions across the 224 MSAs > 100,000, shown in table 10A.7, the results are similar. In addition, the pollution index has the expected positive coefficient and remains relatively unchanged in the presence of the geographic dummies.

Preliminary efforts to find an effect of income inequality were unsuccessful. In fact, in a variety of specifications, the coefficient for inequality was always negative. Similarly, we found no evidence of a relationship between religiosity and mortality whether measured by percent of religious adherents or by frequency of church attendance.

10.5   Two Puzzles

Here we consider two specific puzzles regarding patterns of mortality and utilization. The first puzzle is why the percentage of African Americans in an area is positively related to the mortality of whites aged sixty-five–eighty-four. The second puzzle concerns the unusually low mortality and unusually high utilization in Florida relative to the rest of the country.

10.5.1   Percent Black and Mortality

Why should the mortality of whites aged sixty-five–eighty-four be significantly positively related to the percent of the total population of an area that is black? The possible answers fall into two main categories. First, there may be health differences *among the elderly whites* that are correlated with BLACK, differences that are not accounted for by the other variables in the mortality regression. Such differences could arise as a result of selective in- and out-migration under the reasonable assumption that the movers are healthier than the stayers.

Second, there may be differences *among the areas* that are correlated with the white mortality. Some of these differences could take the form of fewer, *locally* provided services or a different mix of services that affect white mortality. Some differences could be psychosocial, such as racial tension or the fear of crime.

In order to learn more about the relationship between percent black and percent white mortality, we tested to see whether it is stronger in areas of high or low segregation. Using three Cutler-Glaeser measures of segregation—centralization, isolation, and dissimilarity—we divided the areas into equal groups of high segregation and low segregation and ran the basic mortality regression for each group. In none of the three trials did the coefficient for Ln BLACK differ significantly between the high- and the low-segregation group. The mean coefficient for the three high-segregation groups regressions was 0.018 and for the low segregation groups 0.022. It appears that the relation between BLACK and MORT is about the same for areas of high and low segregation.

Another attempt to gain insight into the percent black effect produced more significant results. We divided the 224 MSAs > 100,000 into two equal groups based on the percentage change in the population of whites aged sixty-five–seventy-four between 1980 and 1990. The two groups are designated as "high-growth" and "low-growth," respectively. We then ran identical, full specification regressions for each group with the following results for the percent black coefficient: In the high-growth areas, the coefficient is 0.051 (0.010); in low-growth areas, the coefficient is 0.008 (0.009). The fact that percent black is not significantly related to mortality in the low-growth areas suggests rejection of explanations that rely on *differences among the areas.* If such differences were causal, it is not easy to see why they would not also be operative in the low-growth areas.

The large coefficient in the high-growth areas suggests the possibility of unmeasured differences in selective migration, with the healthier (or more health conscious) migrants moving to the areas with lower percent blacks. However, if there is also a selective out-migration, why doesn't that produce a significant coefficient for BLACK in the low-growth areas? One possible answer is that much of the out-migration probably comes from a relatively few, very large areas such as New York, Chicago, Philadelphia, Boston, and Detroit, whereas the destination of the migrants is more dispersed with many going to areas with relatively small populations. This means that the effect of out-migration on the mortality rates of the remaining populations could be much less than the effect of in-migration on mortality rates in the high-growth areas.

10.5.2   Floridian Exceptionalism

The data examined in this paper reveal that Florida is exceptional in three respects: (1) Among whites aged sixty-five–eighty-four utilization of care is much higher than in any other region, and the differential increases when other variables are introduced as controls; (2) mortality is by far the lowest in the country; (3) the positive relation between mortality and utilization that is evident in the rest of the country is not present in Florida.

Above-average Medicare spending in Florida has been well established in previous studies, for example, Wennberg and Cooper (1999). Our direct, detailed measures of utilization of services (rather than nominal or deflated Medicare spending) show that the Florida differential from the North of 0.193 (0.021) when only population size is controlled for rises to 0.270 (0.023) when education, real income, and mortality are included in the regression. Depending on the type of care, the size of the Florida differential varies enormously, from 0.058 (0.029) for medical admissions to 0.499 (0.049) for diagnostic services.

With respect to mortality the introduction of other variables reduces the negative coefficient for Florida from –0.134 (0.014) to –0.096 (0.015), but it still remains much larger than Big Sky, the region with the next lowest mortality of –0.026 (0.012).

The combination of low mortality and high utilization is one of the most intriguing aspects of Floridian exceptionalism. When total utilization in Florida is regressed on mortality (controlling for education and income, all variables in logs) the coefficient is slightly negative albeit not significantly different from zero. For the country as a whole, including Florida, the coefficient is 0.515 (0.084); when Florida is excluded the coefficient rises to 0.636 (0.092).

In order to gain some insight into Floridian exceptionalism, we examined each Florida MSA > 100,000 separately as shown in table 10.10. Predicted levels of utilization and mortality, obtained for each MSA from regressions that exclude Florida, are compared to actual levels, and the percent differential between actual and predicted calculated. We see that utilization is above predicted in every Florida MSA, but the differentials

Table 10.10   **Percent Differential between Actual and Predicted Values for Florida MSAs > 100,000**

Degrees North Latitude		TOTUTIL		MORT		Percent Differential	
		Actual	Predicted	Actual	Predicted	TOTUTIL	MORT
30.26	Pensacola	3,724	3,197	41.1	37.9	16.5	8.4
30.2	Jacksonville	4,084	3,310	40.5	37.8	23.4	7.0
29.4	Gainesville	3,548	3,190	42.7	36.7	11.2	16.4
29.11	Daytona Beach	3,342	2,524	30.7	37.4	32.4	–17.9
29.1	Ocala	3,331	2,610	33.1	38.8	27.6	–14.7
28.33	Orlando	4,074	3,120	37.8	37.7	30.6	0.3
28.04	Melbourne	3,858	2,843	35.8	36.9	35.7	–2.8
28.02	Lakeland	3,129	2,814	35.0	38.5	11.2	–8.9
27.58	Tampa	3,874	2,992	35.7	37.5	29.5	–4.7
27.29	Bradenton	3,442	2,800	36.3	36.7	23.0	–1.1
27.28	Fort Pierce	3,661	2,690	33.3	37.1	36.1	–10.4
27.2	Sarasota	3,667	2,478	30.1	35.3	48.0	–14.6
26.42	West Palm Beach	4,030	2,607	30.2	35.7	54.6	–15.4
26.39	Fort Meyers	3,769	2,435	29.3	36.9	54.8	–20.5
25.45	Miami	4,130	2,820	33.0	37.7	46.5	–12.5

Notes: MSA = metropolitan statistical area. See table 10.1 for explanations of variables. Percent differential is calculated by running regressions across 209 MSAs > 100,000 (Florida excluded), then predicting utilization and mortality for each Florida MSA using the regression equations and the MSA values, then calculating the percentage differential between observed and predicted.

tend to be largest in the southern portion of the state. The mortality differentials also tend to be greatest in the southern MSAs; indeed, the three most northern MSAs have actual mortality that is above the levels predicted from the regression. Two exceptions to the North versus South differences are Daytona Beach and Ocala; these relatively northern MSAs have utilization and mortality differentials that resemble those of the southern MSAs.

Is Florida the only state with exceptional results? To answer this question we examined several other states that have been mentioned in health policy discussions as being unusual with respect to utilization or mortality or both. With methods analogous to those used to obtain the results presented in table 10.10, we calculated percentage differentials between actual and predicted values for MSAs > 100,000 in Arizona, Minnesota, Nevada, Oregon, and Utah. The results presented in table 10.11 show some differentials, but nothing that comes close to challenging the characterization of Florida as "exceptional."

Another possible explanation for the low mortality rates in Florida is migration. Suppose that people who move to Florida are, on average,

Table 10.11   **Percent Differential between Actual and Predicted Values for MSAs > 100,000 in Selected States**

	TOTUTIL	MORT
Arizona		
Phoenix	17.8	−3.6
Tucson	5.7	6.0
Yuma	4.7	1.2
Minnesota		
Duluth	−5.8	10.9
Minneapolis	−5.5	−0.7
Rochester	19.5	−4.1
Nevada		
Las Vegas	−5.0	6.5
Reno	−5.4	0.2
Oregon		
Eugene-Springfield	−6.8	−7.1
Medford	−9.7	−10.3
Portland-Vancouver	−13.6	7.0
Salem	−12.6	−7.4
Utah		
Provo-Orem	−12.8	7.2
Salt Lake City-Ogden	−24.6	10.5

Notes: MSA = metropolitan statistical area. See table 10.1 for explanations of variables. Percent differential is calculated for each state by running regressions across MSAs > 100,000 (excluding the state in question), then predicting utilization and mortality for each MSA in that state using the regression equations and the MSA values, then calculating the percentage differential between actual and predicted.

healthier than their counterparts who did not move. Given the large share of Florida residents who have moved from other states, one would expect that Florida would be a very healthy region simply because of this selection effect.

To test this hypothesis, we used the Medicare claims database for 1998 in Miami and Tampa, Florida, two regions with large populations of retirees. We first compared mortality rates of current residents of these areas as a function of where they were living three years previously. The sample was limited to nonblacks aged sixty-eight–eighty-four, with a cutoff age of sixty-eight to ensure that we could match Medicare denominator information on zip code of residence from three years before when they were sixty-five. Migrants from the North experience a lower mortality probability (odds ratio equal to 0.80, 95 percent confidence interval of 0.71 to 0.91), which is consistent with the hypothesis that migrants tend to be somewhat healthier than nonmigrants. Migrants from other parts of the country, however, showed if anything slightly elevated mortality rates, although individually the effects were not significant. In any case, the overall influence of recent migrants (during the past three years) is minimal with regard to overall mortality rates because the proportion of recent movers—just 4.2 percent of the sample—is so small. Weighting the odds ratios by the proportion of people who migrated implies that the influence of this recent migration on overall mortality rates in the region is to reduce it by only about 0.5 percent.

The three-year window is probably too restrictive. Another approach is to use the first three digits of the individual's Social Security number. For this cohort, Social Security numbers were most likely issued while in their adult years, particularly during the 1940s through the 1960s when eligibility of Social Security gradually expanded to cover most employment sectors. This approach runs the risk of including in the "migrant" category individuals who may have been living in Florida for several decades. In any case, the results do not support the migration explanation; the one-third of the sample who received their Social Security number in Florida had slightly lower mortality than those who received their number in some other region.

If selective in-migration does not explain low mortality in the southern Florida MSAs, there are two other possibilities that need to be explored. First, the relatively benign climate for most of the year allows the elderly residents to pursue a great deal of physical activity, including golf, tennis, swimming, walking, and so on. Such activity is undoubtedly conducive to better health. Second, the low mortality in the southern Florida MSAs may result from a high level of social interaction among the elderly, as well as public services directed toward this very large voting bloc. Many of them live in communities populated primarily by other elderly where there is a great deal of eating out together, participating in social functions, and helping one another at times of physical or emotional stress.

Many social critics deplore age-restricted living arrangements and argue that the elderly would derive health and other benefits from interactions with members of younger generations. Reconciliation of these two points of view could lie in the classic quantity-quality trade-off. Holding the quantity of social interaction constant, the social critics may be correct that interactions across generations are more beneficial. But it also may be true that the greater quantity of social interactions in the elderly segregated communities more than offsets the lower value of a given unit of interaction.

As is apparent from the previous discussion, it is much easier to document Floridian exceptionalism than it is to explain it. We do not think that the high utilization is the cause of the low mortality because there is no support for this view in data for the rest of the country. When we tried utilization as a right-hand-side (RHS) variable in the mortality regression, the coefficient was positive in both OLS and two-stage least squares (2SLS) specifications. Nor do other studies find in comparisons between Florida and other regions that reductions in mortality are attributable to greater levels of care (Skinner, Fisher, and Wennberg 2001). One "demand-driven" explanation for both high utilization and low mortality is that Floridians are very concerned about health, and this concern may also be expressed in exercise, diet, and other behaviors that are demonstrably linked to longevity, as well as increased demand for medical care.

10.6 Summary

This paper examines 313 U.S. areas for differences in medical care utilization and mortality of whites aged sixty-five–eighty-four in 1990. Areas are grouped into seven regions and five groups based on population size. Utilization is measured by direct count of detailed services, weighted by the national reimbursement for each service.

Probably the most noteworthy result of the utilization regressions is the extent to which cross-area variation in utilization is related to variation in mortality. For total utilization, the elasticity is 0.515 (0.084) after controlling for region, population size of area, education, and real income. This is a lower-bound estimate; the true coefficient would be larger to the extent that there is a negative relationship running from utilization of care to mortality. The elasticity is especially large for medical admissions and especially small for physicians' diagnostic services and treatments.

Also noteworthy is the extent to which the well-known propensity for higher utilization in Florida is even larger after controlling for socioeconomic variables and mortality. The coefficient for Florida is 40 percent (8 percentage points) higher when the other variables are in the regression.

A third result worthy of comment is the much higher utilization in MSAs of over 500,000 population relative to other areas. The average differential is about 8 percent. Among the other areas there is no strong pattern related to population size. Similarly, there is no consistent pattern for the socioeconomic variables in their relationship to total utilization of care (although see McClellan and Skinner 1999).

The mortality regressions produced several noteworthy results. First, we find no relationship between mortality and population size. Elderly residents of large MSAs enjoy no advantage in life expectancy over their peers who live in small MSAs or outside MSAs, despite the well publicized differentials in the availability of medical care. Secondly, we find a very large negative coefficient for Florida. This region has by far the lowest mortality of any large region regardless of whether other variables are controlled for. Cigarette smoking, air pollution, and obesity have their expected positive coefficients. Last, we note a robust positive relationship between percent black and mortality of whites aged sixty-five–eighty-four. This relationship is particularly strong among areas with above-average growth of the elderly population between 1980 and 1990. Among low-growth areas, the coefficient is not significantly different from zero. This puzzle, and the exceptional results for Florida for utilization and mortality, requires further investigation.

Appendix

Procedures for Estimating Total Health Care Utilization (TOTUTIL) and Its Components

Inpatient Hospital Utilization

The hospital admissions measures of utilization are created using the Medicare Provider Analysis and Review File (MEDPAR) 20 percent sample. They are 1989–91 averages for nonblack Medicare enrollees, aged sixty-five–eighty-four.

Hospital admissions claims are weighted by the national average cost of the diagnosis related group (DRG). (There are over 500 diagnosis related groups, as coded using the International Classification of Diseases, 9th revision.) This average cost is calculated for each DRG by dividing the total national charges for a given DRG by the number of claims. Charges include the DRG price (sum of the reimbursement, primary payor reimbursement, primary payor amount, coinsurance amount, inpatient deductible, and blood deductible noncovered charges), the total per diem amount, and the amount paid over the DRG allowance.

The measure of utilization is calculated by summing the weighted number of claims for each area and dividing by the total number of enrollees in that area. The index is adjusted for sex and age using the indirect method. Each claim is classified as "medical" or "surgical" based on its DRG code.

Physician Utilization

The physician utilization measures are created using the part B Medicare Annual Data (BMAD) Procedure File 5 percent sample. They are 1989–91 averages for nonblack Medicare enrollees, aged sixty-five–eighty-four.

The physician claims are weighted by the national Medicare reimbursement amount, based on the HCFA Common Procedure Coding System (HCPCS) code. (This coding system is used primarily for billing Medicare for supplies, materials, injections, and services performed by health care professionals. There are over 12,000 HCPCS codes.) Four Medicare payment schedules are used to determine the reimbursement amount:

- Anesthesiology uniform relative value guide, 1999: The weight is set as the prevailing charge conversion factor (16.0) multiplied by the sum of the uniform base unit plus time units.
- Clinical Diagnostic Laboratory Fee Schedule (CLAB), 1999: The weight is set as the 60 percent national limitation amount (equal to 74 percent of the 1999 median) and adjusted to 1992 for inflation.
- Durable Medical Equipment, Prosthetics/Orthotics, and Supplies Fee Schedule (DMEPOS), 1999: The weight is set as the maximum fee schedule amount (equal to the midpoint of the statewide fee schedule amounts) and adjusted to 1992 for inflation.
- Relative Value Unit (RVU), 1992: The weight is set as the total relative value unit with a conversion factor of 31.001.

Some of the HCPCS codes in the claims data were adjusted because the earliest RVU schedule was published in 1992; however, many HCPCS codes changed between 1991 and 1992. In order to match the 1989–1991 BMAD data to the 1992 RVUs, we reassigned some of the HCPCS codes in the claims data to their respective 1992 codes. This reassignment was based on a crosswalk published by HCFA in the *Federal Register* (Vol. 56, No. 227).

The measure of utilization is calculated by summing the weighted number of claims for each area and dividing by the total number of enrollees. The index was adjusted for sex and age using the indirect method. Using the 1999 Berenson-Eggers Type of Service (BETOS) Public Use File, the physician claims were classified into four categories: evaluation & management; procedures/treatment; diagnosis (imaging and tests); and miscellaneous (durable medical equipment and other).

Hospital Outpatient

The utilization measure for institutional expenditures on outpatient care is extrapolated by calculating the ratio of national outpatient (outpatient hospital and freestanding surgery centers) physician expenditures to national institutional expenditures for outpatient care. This ratio is applied to the area outpatient physician expenditures to obtain area institutional outpatient utilization.

Denominator

The enrollment numbers, used as a denominator for all of the utilization measures, are calculated from the Health Insurance Skeleton Eligibility Write-Off File (hiskew) 20 percent sample. They are 1989–91 averages of nonblack people aged sixty-five–eighty-four who were ever enrolled in Medicare.

In order to remove HMO members, we delete anyone who has "ever been enrolled in an HMO" as reported in the hiskew file. This measure alone, however, removes too many people. To obtain a more accurate count of enrollees in an HMO at a moment in time, we use HCFA statistics published in the 1995 *Health Care Financing Review Statistical Supplement* for the percent of Medicare enrollees in an HMO for each state. This measure cannot be used alone because of the large difference in HMO membership between large and small cities in states with a high HMO rate.

To correct these problems, we combine the published HCFA state rates with the variation across MSAs in a given state as calculated from hiskew. We calculate the ratio of the HCFA state HMO rate to the hiskew state rate (a weighted average of the MSA HMO rates). We then apply this ratio to the individual MSA HMO rates. Finally, the utilization measures are adjusted by dividing by the percent of Medicare enrollees not in an HMO.

Table 10A.1   Coefficients of Correlation[a] among Ten Measures of Utilization

	TOTUTIL	INUTIL	OUTUTIL	TOTADM	MEDADM	SURGADM	TOTPHYS	EANDM	DIAG	TREAT
					Part A: All Areas (N = 313)					
TOTUTIL	1.000	0.748	0.842	0.562	0.420	0.651	0.836	0.728	0.738	0.778
INUTIL	0.748	1.000	0.272	0.947	0.856	0.780	0.338	0.352	0.222	0.314
OUTUTIL	0.842	0.272	1.000	0.046	-0.086	0.310	0.938	0.770	0.890	0.873
TOTADM	0.562	0.947	0.046	1.000	0.947	0.730	0.058	0.103	-0.014	0.051
MEDADM	0.420	0.856	-0.086	0.947	1.000	0.472	-0.087	0.027	-0.134	-0.122
SURGADM	0.651	0.780	0.310	0.730	0.472	1.000	0.346	0.227	0.250	0.400
TOTPHYS	0.836	0.338	0.938	0.058	-0.087	0.346	1.000	0.873	0.910	0.915
EANDM	0.728	0.352	0.770	0.103	0.027	0.227	0.873	1.000	0.807	0.630
DIAG	0.738	0.222	0.890	-0.014	-0.134	0.250	0.910	0.807	1.000	0.736
TREAT	0.778	0.314	0.873	0.051	-0.122	0.400	0.915	0.630	0.736	1.000
					Part B: MSAs > 100,000 (N = 224)					
TOTUTIL	1.000	0.751	0.847	0.588	0.484	0.623	0.861	0.727	0.724	0.813
INUTIL	0.751	1.000	0.285	0.954	0.888	0.828	0.391	0.411	0.213	0.373
OUTUTIL	0.847	0.285	1.000	0.086	-0.011	0.238	0.935	0.725	0.879	0.880
TOTADM	0.588	0.954	0.086	1.000	0.950	0.833	0.141	0.192	0.006	0.141
MEDADM	0.484	0.888	-0.011	0.950	1.000	0.619	0.051	0.193	-0.056	-0.002
SURGADM	0.623	0.828	0.238	0.833	0.619	1.000	0.267	0.143	0.117	0.359
TOTPHYS	0.861	0.391	0.935	0.141	0.051	0.267	1.000	0.857	0.892	0.911
EANDM	0.727	0.411	0.725	0.192	0.193	0.143	0.857	1.000	0.776	0.601
DIAG	0.724	0.213	0.879	0.006	-0.056	0.117	0.892	0.776	1.000	0.706
TREAT	0.813	0.373	0.880	0.141	-0.002	0.359	0.911	0.601	0.706	1.000

Notes: N = number of observations; MSA = metropolitan statistical area. See table 10.1 for explanations of variables.

[a]Weighted by population: whites aged sixty-five to eighty-four.

Table 10A.2   **Coefficients of Correlation[a] among Utilization, Mortality, and Other Variables**

	TOTUTIL	MORT	LOED	REALINC	OBESE	BLACK	CIGS	POLUTN
				Part A: All Areas (N = 313)				
TOTUTIL	1.000	0.119	-0.145	0.191	-0.158	0.383	0.055	
MORT	0.119	1.000	0.490	-0.275	0.411	0.398	0.443	
LOED	-0.145	0.490	1.000	-0.610	0.366	0.067	0.379	
REALINC	0.191	-0.275	-0.610	1.000	-0.193	0.288	-0.136	
OBESE	-0.158	0.411	0.366	-0.193	1.000	-0.081	0.209	
BLACK	0.383	0.398	0.067	0.288	-0.081	1.000	0.262	
CIGS	0.055	0.443	0.379	-0.136	0.209	0.262	1.000	
				Part B (N = 224)				
TOTUTIL	1.000	0.001	-0.170	0.143	-0.153	0.244	0.096	0.302
MORT	0.001	1.000	0.526	-0.216	0.531	0.395	0.403	0.086
LOED	-0.170	0.526	1.000	-0.547	0.474	0.127	0.336	-0.012
REALINC	0.143	-0.216	-0.547	1.000	-0.149	0.287	0.048	-0.214
OBESE	-0.153	0.531	0.474	-0.149	1.000	0.085	0.311	-0.040
BLACK	0.244	0.395	0.127	0.287	0.085	1.000	0.391	-0.047
CIGS	0.096	0.403	0.336	0.048	0.311	0.391	1.000	-0.273
POLUTN	0.302	0.086	-0.012	-0.214	-0.040	-0.047	-0.273	1.000

Notes: N = number of observations. See table 10.1 for explanations of variables.

[a]Weighted by population: whites aged sixty-five to eighty-four.

Table 10A.3 **Utilization Regression Results, OLS, MSAs > 100,000**

	Ln TOTUTIL			Ln INUTIL	Ln OUTUTIL
R^2	0.309	0.043	0.418	0.343	0.581
Upper South	0.037		0.021	0.003	0.058
	(0.036)		(0.037)	(0.034)	(0.055)
Deep South	0.053		0.011	0.006	0.022
	(0.027)		(0.027)	(0.025)	(0.040)
Florida	0.197		0.289	0.121	0.533
	(0.024)		(0.028)	(0.026)	(0.041)
West South	0.063		0.043	0.063	0.010
	(0.026)		(0.028)	(0.026)	(0.042)
Big Sky	−0.020		0.012	0.090	−0.146
	(0.028)		(0.027)	(0.025)	(0.040)
West	0.056		0.115	0.108	0.130
	(0.017)		(0.021)	(0.019)	(0.031)
250,000–500,000	−0.062		−0.055	−0.049	−0.062
	(0.021)		(0.019)	(0.018)	(0.029)
100,000–250,000	−0.087		−0.083	−0.066	−0.116
	(0.022)		(0.021)	(0.019)	(0.031)
Ln LOED		−0.090	0.025	−0.004	0.073
		(0.047)	(0.048)	(0.044)	(0.072)
Ln REALINC		0.093	0.066	−0.035	0.232
		(0.094)	(0.102)	(0.095)	(0.153)
Ln MORT		0.186	0.627	0.799	0.343
		(0.114)	(0.106)	(0.099)	(0.159)
Intercept	8.083	6.441	5.172	5.053	3.624
	(0.010)	(0.921)	(1.019)	(0.948)	(1.526)

Notes: MSA = metropolitan statistical area. See table 10.1 for explanations of variables. Number of observations = 224.

Table 10A.4   **Utilization Regression Results, by Type of Service, OLS, MSAs > 100,000**

	Ln MEDADM	Ln SURGADM	Ln EANDM	Ln DIAG	Ln TREAT
R^2	0.452	0.289	0.410	0.443	0.615
Upper South	−0.017	−0.041	0.040	0.034	0.137
	(0.044)	(0.029)	(0.061)	(0.079)	(0.052)
Deep South	0.006	0.003	−0.091	−0.037	0.057
	(0.032)	(0.021)	(0.044)	(0.058)	(0.038)
Florida	0.046	0.091	0.274	0.511	0.527
	(0.033)	(0.022)	(0.045)	(0.059)	(0.039)
West South	0.056	0.050	−0.036	0.022	0.132
	(0.033)	(0.022)	(0.046)	(0.060)	(0.039)
Big Sky	0.129	0.060	−0.130	−0.170	0.060
	(0.032)	(0.021)	(0.044)	(0.058)	(0.038)
West	0.085	0.084	0.107	0.089	0.284
	(0.024)	(0.016)	(0.034)	(0.044)	(0.029)
250,000–500,000	−0.060	−0.011	−0.154	−0.131	−0.038
	(0.023)	(0.015)	(0.032)	(0.041)	(0.027)
100,000–250,000	−0.073	−0.033	−0.205	−0.171	−0.085
	(0.025)	(0.016)	(0.034)	(0.045)	(0.029)
Ln LOED	−0.001	−0.002	0.012	0.078	0.072
	(0.056)	(0.038)	(0.078)	(0.102)	(0.067)
Ln REALINC	−0.144	0.109	−0.105	0.293	0.244
	(0.120)	(0.080)	(0.167)	(0.217)	(0.142)
Ln MORT	1.162	0.613	0.174	0.081	0.330
	(0.125)	(0.084)	(0.174)	(0.226)	(0.148)
Intercept	3.924	3.447	6.436	2.371	2.815
	(1.200)	(0.803)	(1.672)	(2.173)	(1.422)

Notes: See table 10A.3.

Table 10A.5 Utilization Regression Results for Total Health Care, Inpatient, and Outpatient Utilizations, Two-Stage Least Squares

	Part A: All Areas ($N = 313$)			Part B: MSAs > 100,000 ($N = 224$)		
	Ln TOTUTIL	Ln INUTIL	Ln OUTUTIL	Ln TOTUTIL	Ln INUTIL	Ln OUTUTIL
R^2	0.422	0.246	0.637	0.381	0.260	0.528
Upper South	0.018	0.022	0.009	0.000	-0.007	0.017
	(0.027)	(0.025)	(0.040)	(0.041)	(0.036)	(0.065)
Deep South	0.028	0.027	0.032	-0.022	-0.009	-0.043
	(0.021)	(0.020)	(0.031)	(0.031)	(0.027)	(0.049)
Florida	0.295	0.114	0.557	0.369	0.156	0.687
	(0.029)	(0.027)	(0.043)	(0.038)	(0.033)	(0.060)
West South	0.045	0.063	0.011	0.031	0.058	-0.013
	(0.020)	(0.019)	(0.031)	(0.031)	(0.027)	(0.049)
Big Sky	0.030	0.092	-0.109	0.036	0.100	-0.098
	(0.022)	(0.021)	(0.033)	(0.030)	(0.026)	(0.048)
West	0.105	0.094	0.122	0.153	0.124	0.204
	(0.020)	(0.019)	(0.030)	(0.025)	(0.022)	(0.040)
250,000-500,000	-0.054	-0.053	-0.054	-0.042	-0.043	-0.038
	(0.019)	(0.018)	(0.029)	(0.022)	(0.019)	(0.034)
100,000-250,000	-0.087	-0.074	-0.111	-0.072	-0.061	-0.095
	(0.020)	(0.019)	(0.030)	(0.023)	(0.020)	(0.037)
<100,000	-0.053	-0.027	-0.100			
	(0.017)	(0.016)	(0.025)			
Not MSA	-0.070	-0.041	-0.128			
	(0.017)	(0.016)	(0.025)			
Ln LOED	0.015	0.042	-0.031	-0.048	-0.036	-0.067
	(0.039)	(0.037)	(0.058)	(0.056)	(0.049)	(0.089)
Ln REALINC	0.034	-0.032	0.166	0.063	-0.037	0.225
	(0.075)	(0.071)	(0.112)	(0.112)	(0.097)	(0.177)
Predicted Ln MORT	0.758	0.703	0.811	1.332	1.106	1.702
	(0.185)	(0.174)	(0.276)	(0.229)	(0.198)	(0.362)
Intercept	5.000	5.424	2.438	2.549	3.907	-1.438
	(1.020)	(0.961)	(1.525)	(1.339)	(1.160)	(2.116)

Notes: First stage used to predict regressions can be found in table 10.9. See table 10.1 for explanations of variables. N = number of observations; MSA = metropolitan statistical area. Numbers in parentheses are standard errors.

Table 10A.6   **Utilization Regression Results for Hospital Admissions and Physician Utilizations, Two-Stage Least Squares**

	Ln MEDADM	Ln SURGADM	Ln EANDM	Ln DIAG	Ln TREAT
Part A: All Areas (N = 313)					
R^2	0.450	0.204	0.544	0.564	0.608
Upper South	0.023	−0.029	0.019	0.001	0.080
	(0.033)	(0.021)	(0.043)	(0.057)	(0.039)
Deep South	0.044	−0.010	−0.047	0.007	0.069
	(0.025)	(0.017)	(0.033)	(0.044)	(0.030)
Florida	0.060	0.100	0.301	0.551	0.455
	(0.035)	(0.023)	(0.046)	(0.061)	(0.042)
West South	0.063	0.048	−0.036	0.071	0.114
	(0.025)	(0.016)	(0.032)	(0.043)	(0.030)
Big Sky	0.141	0.079	−0.091	−0.105	0.036
	(0.027)	(0.018)	(0.035)	(0.047)	(0.032)
West	0.082	0.080	0.099	0.092	0.236
	(0.024)	(0.016)	(0.031)	(0.042)	(0.029)
250,000–500,000	−0.067	−0.009	−0.150	−0.131	−0.040
	(0.024)	(0.015)	(0.031)	(0.041)	(0.028)
100,000–250,000	−0.086	−0.033	−0.208	−0.178	−0.084
	(0.025)	(0.016)	(0.032)	(0.043)	(0.030)
<100,000	0.008	−0.017	−0.186	−0.240	−0.063
	(0.021)	(0.014)	(0.027)	(0.036)	(0.025)
Not MSA	0.010	−0.030	−0.220	−0.260	−0.114
	(0.021)	(0.013)	(0.027)	(0.036)	(0.024)
Ln LOED	0.082	−0.006	−0.039	0.021	0.051
	(0.047)	(0.031)	(0.062)	(0.082)	(0.056)
Ln REALINC	−0.147	0.090	−0.115	0.187	0.301
	(0.092)	(0.060)	(0.119)	(0.159)	(0.109)
Predicted Ln MORT	1.123	0.684	0.553	0.392	0.011
	(0.225)	(0.147)	(0.293)	(0.391)	(0.268)
Intercept	4.181	3.366	5.087	2.176	3.432
	(1.246)	(0.812)	(1.617)	(2.162)	(1.481)
Part B: MSAs > 100,000 (N = 224)					
R^2	0.358	0.229	0.394	0.419	0.587
Upper South	−0.024	−0.053	0.012	−0.008	0.111
	(0.044)	(0.031)	(0.065)	(0.086)	(0.056)
Deep South	−0.004	−0.015	−0.136	−0.102	0.016
	(0.034)	(0.023)	(0.050)	(0.065)	(0.043)
Florida	0.071	0.133	0.380	0.666	0.626
	(0.041)	(0.028)	(0.060)	(0.079)	(0.052)
West South	0.052	0.044	−0.052	−0.002	0.117
	(0.033)	(0.023)	(0.049)	(0.065)	(0.042)
Big Sky	0.137	0.073	−0.097	−0.121	0.090
	(0.033)	(0.023)	(0.048)	(0.064)	(0.042)
West	0.098	0.105	0.158	0.164	0.331
	(0.027)	(0.019)	(0.040)	(0.053)	(0.034)
250,000–500,000	−0.056	−0.004	−0.137	−0.107	−0.023
	(0.023)	(0.016)	(0.035)	(0.046)	(0.030)
100,000–250,000	−0.069	−0.027	−0.191	−0.150	−0.072
	(0.025)	(0.017)	(0.037)	(0.049)	(0.032)
Ln LOED	−0.024	−0.041	−0.085	−0.064	−0.018
	(0.061)	(0.042)	(0.090)	(0.118)	(0.077)

Table 10A.6   (continued)

	Ln MEDADM	Ln SURGADM	Ln EANDM	Ln DIAG	Ln TREAT
Ln REALINC	−0.145	0.107	−0.110	0.285	0.240
	(0.121)	(0.084)	(0.178)	(0.235)	(0.153)
Predicted Ln MORT	1.385	0.989	1.113	1.456	1.199
	(0.247)	(0.172)	(0.365)	(0.481)	(0.313)
Intercept	3.096	2.044	2.941	−2.750	−0.423
	(1.445)	(1.005)	(2.132)	(2.815)	(1.833)

Notes: First stage used to predict regressions can be found in table 10A.7. See text for explanations of variables. N = number of observations; MSA = metropolitan statistical area. Numbers in parentheses are standard errors.

Table 10A.7   **Mortality Regression Results, MSAs > 100,000**

	(1)	(2)	(3)
R^2	0.473	0.517	0.645
Upper South	0.011		0.055
	(0.022)		(0.023)
Deep South	0.056		0.043
	(0.017)		(0.018)
Florida	−0.147		−0.088
	(0.015)		(0.017)
West South	0.017		0.051
	(0.016)		(0.016)
Big Sky	−0.053		0.004
	(0.017)		(0.016)
West	−0.087		−0.008
	(0.011)		(0.016)
250,000–500,000	−0.012		0.008
	(0.013)		(0.012)
100,000–250,000	−0.006		0.016
	(0.014)		(0.013)
Ln LOED		0.115	0.021
		(0.025)	(0.029)
Ln REALINC		−0.031	−0.178
		(0.055)	(0.064)
Ln CIGS		0.088	0.142
		(0.039)	(0.044)
Ln OBESE		0.169	0.138
		(0.032)	(0.036)
Ln POLUTN		0.057	0.045
		(0.021)	(0.024)
Ln BLACK		0.024	0.026
		(0.005)	(0.006)
Intercept	3.672	3.879	4.900
	(0.006)	(0.578)	(0.692)

Notes: MSA = metropolitan statistical area. See table 10.1 for explanations of variables. Numbers in parentheses are standard errors. Number of observations = 224.

References

Allison, J. J., C. I. Kiefe, E. F. Cook, M. S. Gerrity, E. J. Orav, and R. Cenor. 1998. The association of physician attitudes about uncertainty and risk taking with resource use in a Medicare HMO. *Medical Decision Making* 18:320–29.

Auster, R., I. Leveson, and D. Saracheck. 1969. The production of health, an exploratory study. *Journal of Human Resources* 4 (4): 411–36.

Chappie, M., and L. Lave. 1982. The health effects of air pollution: A reanalysis. *Journal of Urban Economics* 12:346–76.

Chassin, M. R. 1993. Explaining geographic variations: The enthusiasm mypothesis. *Medical Care* 31: YS37–44.

Chassin, M. R., R. H. Brook, R. E. Park, J. Keesey, A. Fink, J. Kosecoff, K. Kahn, N. Merrick, and D. H. Solomon. 1986. Variations in the use of medical and surgical practices by the Medicare population. *New England Journal of Medicine* 314:285–90.

Currie, J., and J. Gruber. 1996. Saving babies: The efficacy and cost of recent changes in the Medicaid eligibility of pregnant women. *Journal of Political Economy* 104 (6): 1263–96.

Cutler, D., M. McClellan, J. Newhouse, and D. Remler. 1998. Are medical prices declining? Evidence from heart attack treatments. *Quarterly Journal of Economics* 113 (4): 991–1024.

Cutler, D., and L. Sheiner. 1999. The geography of Medicare. *American Economic Review* 89 (2): 228–33.

Deaton, A. 2001. Health, inequality, and economic development. NBER Working Paper no. 8099. Cambridge, Mass.: National Bureau of Economic Research, June.

Deaton, A., and D. Lubotsky. 2001. Mortality, inequality and race in American cities and states. NBER Working Paper no. 8370. Cambridge, Mass.: National Bureau of Economic Research, July.

Deaton, A., and C. Paxson. 1999. Mortality, education, income, and inequality among American cohorts. NBER Working Paper no. 7140. Cambridge, Mass.: National Bureau of Economic Research, May.

———. 2001. Mortality, income, and income inequality over time in Britain and the United States. NBER Working Paper no. 8534. Cambridge, Mass.: National Bureau of Economic Research, July.

Eisenberg, J. A. 1986. *Doctors' decisions and the cost of medical care: The reasons for doctors' practice patterns and ways to change them.* Ann Arbor, Mich.: Health Administration Press Perspectives.

Escarce, J. 1992. Explaining the association between surgeon supply and utilization. *Inquiry* 29:403–15.

———. 1993. Medicare patients' use of overpriced procedures before and after the Omnibus Budget Reconciliation Act of 1987. *American Journal of Public Health* 83:349–55.

Evans, J. S., T. Tosteson, and P. L. Kinney. 1984. Cross-sectional mortality studies and air pollution risk assessment. *Environmental International* 10:55–83.

Fisher, E. S., D. E. Wennberg, T. A. Stukel, D. J. Gottlieb, F. L. Lucas, and E. L. Pinder. 2003. The implications of regional variations in Medicare spending. Part 2: Health outcomes and satisfaction with care. *Annals of Internal Medicine* 138 (4): 288–98.

Folland, S., and M. Stano. 1989. Sources of small area variation in the use of medical care. *Journal of Health Economics* 8:85–107.

Franks, P., G. C. Williams, J. Zwanziger, C. Mooney, and M. Sorbero. 2000. Why do physicians vary so widely in their referral rates? *Journal of General Internal Medicine* 15:163–68.

Frohlich, N., R. Fransoo, and N. Roos. 2001. Indicators of health status and health service use for the Winnipeg Regional Health Authority. Winnipeg, Manitoba: Manitoba Center for Health Policy and Evaluation, Department of Community Health Sciences, March.

Fuchs, V. R., and M. J. Kramer. 1986. Determinants of expenditures for physicians' services in the United States, 1948–1968. In *The health economy,* ed. Victor R. Fuchs, 67–107. Cambridge, Mass.: Harvard University Press.

Gray, B. H., and W. J. McNerney. 1986. For-profit enterprise in health care: The Institute of Medicine Study. *New England Journal of Medicine* 314:1523–28.

Green, L. A., and M. P. Becker. 1994. Physician decision making and variation in hospital admission rates for suspected acute cardiac myocardial infarction. A tale of two towns. *Medical Care* 32:1086–97.

Hadley, J. 1988. Medicare spending and mortality rates of the elderly. *Inquiry* 25:485–93.

Health Care Financing Administration. 1989–91. *Five percent random sample of Medicare enrollment, 1989–91.* Baltimore, Md.: Health Care Financing Administration.

Kaplan, G. A., E. R. Pamuk, J. W. Lynch, R. D. Cohen, and J. L. Balfour. 1996. Inequality in income and mortality in the United States: Analysis of mortality and potential pathways. *British Medical Journal* 312:999–1003.

Kennedy, B. P., I. Kawachi, and D. Prothrow-Stith. 1996. Income distribution and mortality: Cross-sectional ecological study of the Robin Hood Index in the United States. *British Medical Journal* 312:1004–07.

Kessler, D., and M. McClellan. 1999. Is hospital competition socially wasteful? NBER Working Paper no. 7266. Cambridge, Mass.: National Bureau of Economic Research, July.

Lin, G. 2000. A regional assessment of elderly disability in the U.S. *Social Science and Medicine* 50:1015–24.

Lynch, J. W., et al. 1998. Income distribution and mortality in metropolitan areas of the United States. *American Journal of Public Health* 88 (7): 1074–80.

McClellan, M., and J. Skinner. 1999. Medicare reform: Who pays and who benefits? *Health Affairs* 18 (1): 48–62.

Mokdad, A. H., M. K. Serdula, W. H. Dietz, B. A. Bowman, J. S. Marks, and J. P. Koplan. 1999. The spread of the obesity epidemic in the United States, 1991–1998. *Journal of the American Medical Association* 282 (16): 1519–22.

Ozkaynak, H., and G. D. Thurston. 1987. Associations between 1980 U.S. mortality rates and alternative measures of airborne particle concentration. *Risk Analysis* 7 (4): 449–61.

Pardes, H., K. G. Manton, E. S. Lander, H. D. Tolley, A. D. Ullian, and H. Palmer. 1999. Effects of medical research on health care and the economy. *Science* 283 (January): 36–37.

Pearson, S. D., L. Goldman, E. J. Orav, E. Guadagnoli, T. B. Garcia, P. A. Johnson, and T. H. Lee. 1995. Triage decisions for emergency department patients with chest pain: Do physicians' risk attitudes make the difference? *Journal of General Internal Medicine* 10:557–64.

Schneider, E. L. 1999. Aging in the third millennium. *Science* 283 (February): 796–97.

Selby, J. V., K. Grumbach, C. P. Quesenberry, Jr., J. A. Schmittdiel, and A. F. Truman. 1999. Differences in resource use and costs of primary care in a large HMO according to physician specialty. *Health Services Research* 34:503–18.

Silver, M. 1972. An econometric analysis of spatial variations in mortality rates by race and sex. In *Essays in the economics of health and medical care,* ed. Victor R. Fuchs, 161–227. New York: Columbia University Press.

Silverman, E., J. Skinner, and E. Fisher. 1999. The association between for-profit hospital ownership and increased Medicare spending. *New England Journal of Medicine* 341 (August): 420–26.

Skinner, J., and E. Fisher. 1997. Regional disparities in Medicare expenditures: An opportunity for Medicare reform. *National Tax Journal* 50 (September): 413–25.

Skinner, J., and E. Fisher, and J. Wennberg. 2001. The efficiency of Medicare. NBER Working Paper no. 8395. Cambridge, Mass.: National Bureau of Economic Research, July.

Shprentz, D. S. 1996. *Breath-taking: Premature mortality due to particulate air pollution in 239 American cities.* New York: Natural Resources Defense Council.

Susser, M. 1994a. The logic in ecological: I. The logic of analysis. *American Journal of Public Health* 84:825–29.

———. 1994b. The logic in ecological: II. The logic of design. *American Journal of Public Health* 84:830–35.

Taylor, D. H., Jr., D. J. Whellan, and F. A. Sloan. 1999. Effects of admission to a teaching hospital on the cost and quality of care for Medicare beneficiaries. *New England Journal of Medicine* 340:293–99.

Tobacco Institute. 1998. *The tax burden on tobacco: Historical compilation*, Vol. 33. Washington, D.C.: Tobacco Institute.

U.S. Bureau of the Census. 1990. *U.S. Census of Population, 1990.* Washington, D.C.: U.S. Bureau of the Census.

U.S. Bureau of Health Professions. 1992. *Area resource file.* Washington, D.C.: U.S. Bureau of Health Professions, Office of Data Analysis and Management.

Wennberg, J. E., B. A. Barnes, and M. Zubkoff. 1982. Professional uncertainty and the problem of supplier-induced demand. *Social Science and Medicine* 16:811–24.

Wennberg, J. E., and M. M. Cooper. 1996. *The Dartmouth atlas of health care in the United States.* Chicago: American Health Association Press.

———. 1999. *The quality of medical care in the United States: A report on the Medicare Program. The Dartmouth atlas of health care in the United States.* Chicago: American Health Association Press.

Wennberg, J. E., E. Fisher, and J. Skinner. 2002. Geography and the debate over Medicare reform. *Health Affairs* 21 (2, Suppl. Web Exclusive): W96–114.

Wright, J. G., G. A. Hawker, C. Bombardier, R. Croxford, R. S. Dittus, D. A. Freund, and P. C. Coyte. 1999. Physician enthusiasm as an explanation for area variation in the utilization of knee replacement surgery. *Medical Care* 37:946–56.

Comment   Joseph P. Newhouse

Fuchs, McClellan, and Skinner (FMS) have several findings:

1. Using metropolitan and rural areas as units of observation, mortality is an important explanatory variable for both Medicare spending and

Joseph P. Newhouse is John D. MacArthur Professor of Health Policy and Management at Harvard University, and a research associate of the National Bureau of Economic Research.

use of services among whites aged sixty-five–eighty-four, and is quantitatively more important in explaining the variation in that spending than are economic and demographic variables.

2. Florida is very different from the remainder of the country in having observed rates of use that are much higher than predicted and observed mortality that is much lower than predicted.

3. There is a city size gradient in use; metropolitan areas with populations between 250,000 and 500,000 have higher rates of use than smaller cities and nonmetropolitan areas, and areas with more than 500,000 people have still higher use.

4. Even with measures specific to whites aged sixty-five–eighty-four, the following three variables do not exert an important or robust effect on use or on mortality: real income; a measure of inequality or dispersion in income; and the proportion of individuals with less than a high school education.

5. Even with measures not specific to whites aged sixty-five–eighty-four, and indeed measured at the state level, cigarette consumption, obesity, and air pollution affect mortality measured across metropolitan areas.

6. The percentage of the area's total population that is black is significantly associated with elderly white mortality.

This paper is in the tradition of literature from some of the earliest days of health economics, including several papers by the first author (for example, Fuchs and Kramer 1972; Bombardier et al. 1977; Fuchs 1978; Auster, Leveson, and Sarachek 1969). The canonical paper in that literature made use of data at the state level, and the variation was mostly or entirely cross-sectional. Much of the older literature, however, was more concerned with explaining use of medical services than explaining mortality. Utilization was typically measured in partial or crude fashion, such as a count of physician visits or hospital admissions. If mortality was measured, it was usually total mortality or infant mortality. The standard finding was that the marginal unit of medical service had little effect on mortality but that lifestyle variables did importantly affect mortality; the classic paper in this genre was Fuchs' comparison of Nevada and Utah, showing large differences in mortality relating to lifestyle (Fuchs 1974).

This paper makes several advances over the earlier literature, primarily exploiting the availability of detailed information on the use of services from Medicare claims data. Such data enable one to measure the intensity of services per medical encounter (for example, per visit or per hospital admission), and it is the change in intensity that has driven the sustained increase in medical spending. Real per capita spending on medical care rose on average 4.4 percent per year in the United States between 1940 and 1998, a factor of 12. It rose 4.2 percent per year between 1980 and 1998, a factor of 2. Virtually the entire rise has been in increased services per encounter. For example, the rise in total spending since 1980 occurred despite a decline of hospital days per person by about one-third and approximately unchanged physician visit rates (U.S. Department of Health and Human Services 2000). Thus, the measures of utilization used in the older literature are simply not helpful in understanding why spending rose.

Fuchs, McClellan, and Skinner also use the detailed claims data to disaggregate spending into finer categories. For example, they classify physician services into evaluation and management services, surgical and other treatment procedures, and diagnostic interventions. Finally, unlike most all of the earlier literature, FMS restrict their measure of mortality to the elderly, where mortality is believed to be more sensitive to medical care.

I begin my comments with some additional or different interpretations of the results then add some caveats. I next comment on possibilities for future extensions along the lines of this paper, but I conclude with a skeptical comment on the overall research strategy for the questions at issue that are posed at the outset of the paper: What determines medical spending? What determines health?

Other Interpretations

I think more can be said about four results: the positive effect of mortality rates on spending; the smoking and obesity results; the city size gradient; and the relationship between the percentage black and elderly white mortality rates.

Mortality and Spending

Some of the relationship between mortality and spending represents a mechanical effect of spending at the end of life. Between 5 and 6 percent of the Medicare beneficiaries die each year (these numbers include those aged over eighty-five, who are excluded from FMSs results), and decedents spend about five to six times as much as nondecedents (Lubitz and Riley 1993; Hogan et al. 2000). Using these figures, one can show that at the mean a 1 percent rise in the mortality rate adds about 0.13 percent to spending. Because the FMS estimated elasticity of spending with respect to mortality is 0.82, well above 0.13, this solidifies their conclusion that mortality is a proxy for general health status. That is, the estimated relationship is not simply additional spending at the end of life.

Disproportionate spending at the end of life, however, is consistent with FMSs findings that mortality has much greater effects on medical than on surgical spending, on inpatient than on outpatient spending, and on evaluation and management services rather than procedures, because surgical procedures and aggressive treatment are less likely among the terminally ill or those predictably near the end of life.

Smoking, Obesity, and Pollution

FMS's estimated elasticities for mortality with respect to smoking, obesity, and pollution variables are in the range of 0.05 to 0.15. But there is surely large random measurement error in these variables because the smoking and obesity variables pertain to both the elderly and nonelderly, are statewide rather than specific to the metropolitan or rural area, and do not account for migration (for example, the nonsmoker from Massachusetts who retires to North Carolina is given the smoking habits of a North Carolinian). As a result, the estimated elasticities understate the true elasticities, potentially by a large amount.

The City Size Gradient

The city size gradient may partly reflect the location of most teaching hospitals in larger cities. Teaching hospitals treat given cases more intensively than community hospitals, and most of their patients are from the local area. I do not suppose that this could account for all of the city size effect, but it may be possible to control for the share of teaching hospital use with the Medicare claims data. I have more to say about the city size gradient in the following.

One result in table 10.10 is provocative; Gainesville, whose medical delivery system is dominated by a major teaching hospital, has much higher predicted mortality than other Florida metropolitan areas. There is no obvious explanation for why a primarily university town should have high mortality, and one wonders whether this might have something to do with the teaching hospital or whether it is simply a random event from small numbers of deaths. Fuchs, McClellan, and Skinner attribute mortality to place of residence, and not to place of death, which raises the question of how residence is determined. For example, if someone moves to Gainesville for an extended period to undertake an experimental cancer treatment, does that person's measured residence change?

The Black Variable

Fuchs, McClellan, and Skinner treat the black variable as more causally related to race than I would. They divide areas with many blacks into those with high and low segregation, but find an approximately equal effect in both kinds of areas. This, of course, simply shows that the black variable is not measuring the effect of segregation. They also hypothesize that migrating whites may avoid metropolitan areas with a large black population. They test this by omitting California, Arizona, and Florida from their sample, but their result is robust, contrary to the migration hypothesis.

These results leave open that the black variable is simply a proxy for omitted variables (or possibly functional form misspecification) that are correlated with the within-region variation in the black variable. Any omitted variable that affects mortality in those areas within a region that have a high percentage of blacks and that are also extreme on the omitted variable will load onto the black variable. Furthermore, if these areas have extreme values for several of the variables that are included, any nonlinearity in the functional form will also be picked up by the black variable.

Possibilities for Future Extensions

Fuchs, McClellan, and Skinner's data are from the 1989–1991 period. In its mix of services Medicare was unstable in the 1990s; for example, postacute care grew from less than 2 percent of total spending to around 15 percent of spending between 1988 and 1997. I show in figures 10C.1 and 10C.2 the time series for skilled nursing facility days and home health visits per 1,000 beneficiaries. Moreover, reimbursement for physician services, hospital outpatient departments, and postacute care providers all changed markedly in the 1990s (Newhouse 2002). Although it is possible that the distribution of services across areas remained relatively invariant to these changes, it seems improbable. Thus, if this line of work is pursued further, it would be worthwhile reestimating these equations on data from a decade later. One problem in doing so is that in the 1990s enrollment in managed care roughly tripled, from 3 to 15 percent, and detailed claims data for that group are not available.

Problems

Deflators

Despite its correlation of 0.8 with the quantity variable, the measure of deflated spending has substantial measurement error, stemming from the deflator used, the Geographic Practice Cost Index (GPCI) for the area. The GPCI is a measure of physician office input costs. Half of total physician spending is the professional component (that is, physician take-home pay), but the GPCI underweights this by a factor of four for political reasons. Thus, even for physician spending the weights are in error. And physicians account for only about 30 percent of Medicare spending, a figure that includes their in-hospital services; the market basket of inputs for institutional providers differs.

Furthermore, nonlabor input shares, many of which do not vary in price locally, differ across providers. For example, hospitals and skilled nursing facilities differ by about 10 percentage points in their nonlabor share. This error introduces a systematic bias in an unknown direction. Suppose there are some inputs purchased in local markets, primarily labor, and some inputs purchased in national markets, such as supplies and drugs. These pro-

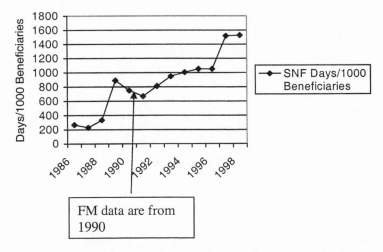

Fig. 10C.1   Skilled nursing facility (SNF) days per 1,000 Beneficiaries, 1986–1998
Source: Newhouse 2002.

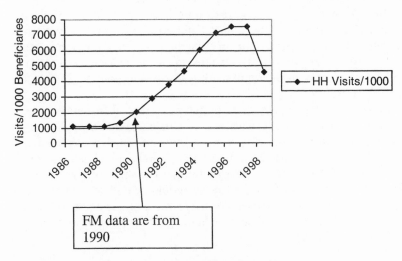

Fig. 10C.2   Home health visits per 1,000 beneficiaries
Source: Newhouse 2002.

portions of local and national inputs will differ across types of providers. Only that portion of costs attributable to the local inputs should be deflated.

To bring out the problem, suppose the weight on the portion that is local errs by treating all dollars as local. Thus, the variable used in this hypothetical example is ln(Total$/D$), where D is the deflator, and the deflator only measures local prices. The proper variable is ln(Local$/$D$ + National$), where Local$ and National$ are spending on locally and nationally purchased inputs, respectively. One can manipulate this latter expression to show that it equals ln[D(1 − L) + L] + ln(Total$/$D$), where L is the proportion of inputs purchased locally.

If one uses ln(Total$/$D$) as a dependent variable instead of ln(Local$/$D$ + National$), ln[$D$(1 − L) + L] is in the error term. But the D will cause the error term to covary with a number of right-hand-side variables. For example, larger cities have higher values of D. In this example the deflator overweights local inputs and one can sign the bias; in the FMS regression it is not clear whether the GPCI over- or underweights local inputs, and that will determine the direction of the bias.

Furthermore, as FMS say, this deflator is incorrect for out-of-area services, which are also systematic by city size, being more prevalent in nonmetropolitan areas. Among nonmetropolitan residents, physician visits are twice as likely to be outside the country of residence as among metropolitan residents (25 versus 13 percent); 12 percent of visits by nonmetropolitan residents were to metropolitan physicians, but only 1 percent of visits by metropolitan residents were to nonmetropolitan physicians (Kleinman and Makuc 1983). I suspect the data for hospitalization are even more disparate. Thus, nonmetropolitan area spending is overdeflated, and consequently the city size gradient is overstated. This is consistent with the gradient's being smaller in the total quantity regression than in the deflated spending regression.

Another issue related to the deflator is whether real income of the elderly should be deflated for property values. To the degree that the elderly own their own homes, they are receiving a stream of housing services from home equity, which should be imputed to their income. This income will generally be greater in areas with higher property values. As a result, I am not persuaded the income of the elderly should be deflated for property values. After deflating for variation in wages, an elderly person who owns her own home with a $25,000 income in Palo Alto may be as well-off as a similar person in Dubuque.

Exclusion of the Nursing Home Population

Fuchs, McClellan, and Skinner excluded the nursing home population. I would not have done this because of possible selection bias. Given that they were excluded, it would be useful to show that this proportion does not vary much across their areas.

The Research Strategy

Although this paper follows in a long tradition of work to explain area differences—indeed, the words *Area Differences* are in the title—I am not persuaded that this is the best strategy to use to answer the questions of what affects health care spending and mortality. Rather, I think person- or household-level data are more suitable.

My guess is that the health economics literature started with area data three decades ago largely because of data availability. Additionally, one of the burning questions at that time was whether physicians induced demand, and for that question area data lost little to person- or household-level data.

But for purposes of understanding the relationship between health status and lifestyle habits, price (including for Medicare beneficiaries the presence of supplementary insurance), and income, person- or household-level data would seem superior. Otherwise one loses all the within-area variation, which is where much of the variation is. Person-level data are now available through the Medicare Current Beneficiary Survey and through the Medical Care Expenditure Survey. I suspect that in the future these data would be more fruitful to exploit.

References

Auster, Richard, Irving Leveson, and Deborah Sarachek. 1969. The production of health: An exploratory study. *Journal of Human Resources* 4 (4): 412–36.
Bombardier, Claire, Victor R. Fuchs, Lee A. Lillard, and Kenneth E. Warner. 1977. Socioeconomic factors affecting the utilization of surgical operations. *New England Journal of Medicine* 297 (13): 699–705.
Fuchs, Victor R. 1974. Some economic aspects of mortality in developed countries. In *The economics of health and medical care,* ed. Mark Perlman, 174–93. London: Macmillan.
———. 1978. The supply of surgeons and the demand for operations. *Journal of Human Resources* 13 (Supplement): 35–56.
Fuchs, Victor R., and Marcia J. Kramer. 1972. Determinants of expenditures for physicians' services in the United States, 1948–68. NBER Occasional Paper no. 117. Cambridge, Mass.: National Bureau of Economic Research.
Hogan, Christopher, Joanne Lynn, Jon Gabel, June Lunney, Ann O'Mara, and Anne Wilkinson. 2000. Medicare beneficiaries' costs and use of care in the last year of life. Washington, D.C.: Medicare Payment Advisory Commission.
Kleinman, Joel C., and Diane Makuc. 1983. Travel for ambulatory medical care. *Medical Care* 21 (5): 543–57.
Lubitz, James, and Gerald F. Riley. 1993. Trends in Medicare payments in the last year of life. *New England Journal of Medicine* 328 (15): 1092–96.
Newhouse, Joseph P. 2002. Medicare policy in the 1990s. In *Economic performance during the 1990s,* ed. Jeffrey Frankel and Peter Orszag, 899–955. Cambridge, Mass.: MIT Press.
U.S. Department of Health and Human Services, National Center for Health Statistics. 2000. Health, United States, 2000 with adolescent health chartbook. Washington, D.C.: Government Printing Office.

Healthy, Wealthy, and Wise?
Tests for Direct Causal Paths between Health and Socioeconomic Status

Peter Adams, Michael D. Hurd, Daniel McFadden,
Angela Merrill, and Tiago Ribeiro

This chapter consists of four components: (1) the paper *Healthy, Wealthy and Wise? Tests for Direct Causal Paths between Health and Socioeconomic Status* by Peter Adams, Michael D. Hurd, Daniel McFadden, Angela Merrill, and Tiago Ribeiro, which originally was presented at the conference and then appeared in the *Journal of Econometrics,* Vol. 112: (2003); (2) a new addendum that describes updates in data and analysis since its publication; (3) additional appendix tables; and (4) the authors' response to comments on the paper.

11.1 Introduction

11.1.1 The Issue

The links between health, wealth, and education have been studied in a number of populations, with the general finding that higher socioeconomic status (SES) is associated with better health and longer life.[1] In a survey of

Peter Adams is affiliated with the Department of Economics at the University of California, Berkeley; Michael D. Hurd is affiliated with RAND Corporation; Daniel McFadden is affiliated with the Department of Economics at the University of California, Berkeley; Angela Merrill is affiliated with Mathematica; and Tiago Ribeiro is affiliated with the Department of Economics at the University of California, Berkeley.

We gratefully acknowledge financial support from the National Institute on Aging through a grant to the NBER Program Project on the Economics of Aging. Tiago Ribeiro acknowledges support from scholarship PRAXIS XXI/BD/16014/98 from the Portuguese Fundação para a Ciência e a Tecnologia. We thank Laura Chioda, Victor Fuchs, Rosa Matzkin, James Poterba, and Jim Powell for useful comments.

1. See Backlund, Sorlie, and Johnson (1999); Barsky et al. (1997); Bosma et al. (1997); Chandola (1998, 2000); Davey-Smith, Blane, and Bartley (1994); Drever and Whitehead (1997); Ecob and Smith (1999); Elo and Preston (1996); Ettner (1996); Feinstein (1992);

this literature, Goldman (2001) notes that this association has been found in different eras, places, genders, and ages, and occurs over the whole range of SES levels, so that it is not linked solely to poverty. The association holds for a variety of health variables (most illnesses, mortality, self-rated health status, psychological well-being, and biomarkers such as allostatic load) and alternative measures of SES (wealth, education, occupation, income, level of social integration).[2] There has been considerable discussion of the causal mechanisms behind this association, but there have been relatively few natural experiments that permit causal paths to be definitively identified.[3] In this paper, we test for the *absence* of direct causal links in an elderly population by examining whether *innovations* in health and wealth in a panel are influenced by features of the historical state.

Figure 11.1 depicts possible causal paths for the health and SES innovations that occur over a short period. An individual's life history is built from these period-by-period transitions. First, low SES may lead to failures to seek medical care and delay in detection of conditions, reduced access to medical services, or less effective treatment.[4] Also, increased risk of health problems may result from increased stress or frustration, or increased exposure to environmental hazards, that are associated with low

---

Fitzpatrick et al. (1997); Fitzpatrick and Dollamore (1999); Fox, Goldblatt, and Jones (1985); Goldblatt (1990); Haynes (1991); Hertzman (1999); Humphries and van Doorslaer (2000); Hurd (1987); Hurd and Wise (1989); Kaplan and Manuck (1999); Karasek et al. (1988); Kitawaga and Hauser (1973); Lewis et al. (1998); Leigh and Dhir (1997); Luft (1978); Marmot et al. (1991); Marmot, Bobak, and Davey-Smith (1995); Marmot et al. (1997); Martin and Preston (1994); Martin and Soldo (1997); McDonough et al. (1997); Murray, Yang, and Qiao (1992); Power, Matthews, and Manor (1996); Power and Matthews (1998); Rodgers (1991); Ross and Mirowsky (2000); Schnall, Landsbergis, and Baker (1994); Seeman et al. (2002); Shorrocks (1975); Stern (1983); Wadsworth (1991); Whitehead (1988); Wilkinson (1998); and Woodward et al. (1992).

2. The associations can become more complex when multiple health conditions and multiple SES measures are studied. Competing risks may mask the hazard for late-onset diseases; for example, elevated mortality risk from cardiovascular diseases in low SES groups may induce an apparent reverse relationship between SES and later-onset cancer in the surviving population (Adler and Ostrove 1999). Longer-run measures of SES such as education, occupation, and wealth appear to have a stronger association with health status than current income (Fuchs 1993). Using carefully measured wealth, we find that it explains most of the association with health, and education conditioned on wealth is not systematically correlated with health.

3. Papers examining explicit causal mechanisms include Chapman and Hariharran (1994); Dohrenwend et al. (1992); Evans (1978); Felitti et al. (1998); Fox, Goldblatt, and Johnson (1985); Goldman (1994); Kelley, Hertzman, and Daniels (1997); and McEwen and Stellar (1993).

4. There may be an important distinction between direct causal mechanisms influencing mortality, conditioned on health status, and direct causal mechanisms influencing onset of health conditions. For mortality, an SES gradient could be due to differentially effective treatment of acute health conditions. For morbidity, an SES gradient could reflect differentials in prevention and detection of health conditions. These involve different parts of the health care delivery system, and differ substantially in the importance of individual awareness and discretion, and allocation of costs between Medicare and the individual.

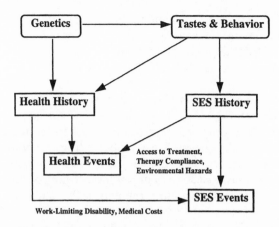

Fig. 11.1   Possible causal paths for SES and health

SES.[5] These factors could provide direct causal links from SES history to health events. Second, poor health may reduce the ability to work or look after oneself, and increase medical care expenditures, leading to reduced income and less opportunity to accumulate assets. This could provide a direct causal link from health to changes in SES.

There may also be hidden *common factors* that lead to ecological association of health and SES. For example, unobserved genetic heterogeneity may influence both resistance to disease and ability to work. Causal links may be reinforced or confounded by behavioral response. Behavioral factors such as childhood nutrition and stress, exercise, and smoking may influence both health and economic activity level. For example, tastes for work and for "clean living," whether genetic or learned, may influence both health and earnings. Finally, rational economic decision making may induce robust consumers to accumulate in order to finance consumption over a long-expected retirement, or unhealthy individuals to spend down assets.

Preston and Taubman (1994), Smith and Kington (1997a, b), and Smith (1998, 1999) give detailed discussions of the various causal mechanisms that may be at work and the role of behavioral response from economic consumers. The epidemiological literature (Goldman 2001) uses a different terminology for the causal paths: Links from SES to health innovations are termed *causal mechanisms,* while links from health to SES are termed *selection* or *reverse causation* mechanisms. Apparent association due to measurement errors, such as overstatement of the SES of the healthy or under-

5. For example, industrial and traffic pollution, and poor dwelling ventilation are risk factors for lung disease, and housing prices and household income are negatively correlated with air pollution levels in census data (Chay and Greenstone 1998).

detection of illnesses among the poor, are called *artifactual mechanisms.*[6] This literature classifies all common factors in terms of their implicit initial action as either causal or selection mechanisms.[7]

11.1.2   This Study

We study the population of elderly Americans aged seventy and older, and in this population test for the *absence* of direct causal paths from SES to innovations in health, and from health status to innovations in SES. These hypotheses will in general be accepted *only* if no causal link is present *and* there are no persistent hidden factors that influence both initial state and innovations. Rejection of one of these hypotheses does not demonstrate a direct causal link, because this may be the result of common hidden factors. However, in an elderly population persistent hidden factors will often be manifest in observed covariates, so that once these covariates are controlled, the residual impact of the hidden factors on innovations will be small. For example, genetic frailty that is causal to both health problems and low wages, leading to low wealth, may be expressed through a health condition such as diabetes. Then, onset of new health conditions that are also linked to genetic frailty may be only weakly associated with low wealth, once diabetic condition has been entered as a covariate. Thus, in this population, *rejection* of the hypotheses *may* provide useful diagnostics for likely causal paths.

The objectives and conclusions of this paper are limited. We study only elderly Americans, for whom Medicare provides relatively homogeneous and comprehensive health care at limited out-of-pocket cost to the individual. This population is retired, so new health problems do not impact earnings. Statements about the presence or absence of direct causal mechanisms in this population, given previous health and SES status, say nothing about the structure of these mechanisms in a younger population, where associations of health and SES emerge as a result of some pattern of causation and operation of common factors.

Our tests for the *absence* of causality do *not* address the question of how to identify invariant models and causal links when these tests fail. If a test

6. Consider phenomena such as underestimation of the hazard of a disease due to competing risks from other illnesses or death. In an unfortunate discrepancy in terminology, economists would call this a selection effect, while epidemiologists would classify it as an artifactual mechanism rather than a selection mechanism.

7. Usually, one can argue that observed association must originate from some initial causal action so that common factors originate from some initial direction of causation. However, there is no apparent initial causal action for genetically linked conditions such as Down syndrome, which increase mortality risk and preclude work. Further, as a practical matter, it is often impossible to make observations at the high frequencies that would be required to identify causal chains when feedbacks are nearly instantaneous. Then common factors will appear at feasible levels of detection to operate simultaneously, and their true causal structure will not be identified. For these reasons, there would be considerable merit in adding *common mechanisms* to the epidemiologist's classification.

for the absence of a direct causal path is rejected, it may be possible through natural or designed experiments to separate causal and ecological effects; see Angrist, Imbens, and Rubin (1996), Heckman (2000, 2001). Suppose a strictly exogenous variable is causal to SES, and clearly not itself directly causal to health or causal to common factors. Then, an association of this variable with innovations in health conditions can only be through a direct causal link from SES to health. A variable with these properties is termed a *proper instrument* or *control variable* for SES. Proper instruments are hard to find. They can be obtained through designed experiments, where random treatment assignment precludes the possibility of confounding by common factors, provided recruitment and retention of experimental subjects does not reintroduce confounding. For example, an experiment that randomly assigned co-payment rates and coverage within Medicare for prescription drugs or assisted living could provide evidence on direct causal links from SES to health conditions, provided attrition and compliance are not problems. Occasionally, natural experiments may provide random treatment assignment. Economic events that impact individuals differently and that are not related to their prior SES or health are potentially proper instruments. For example, a tax change that affects wealth differently in different states is arguably a proper instrument, as is a change in mandated Medicaid coverage that has a differential impact across states. Individual events such as receipt of inheritances may be proper instruments, although they would be confounded if they are anticipated, or if the probability of their occurrence is linked to health status; see Meer, Miller, and Rosen (2001). Weak association between SES and a proper instrument for it makes it difficult to obtain precise estimates of direct causal effects; see Staiger and Stock (1997).

Section 11.2 of this paper discusses the foundation for econometric causality tests, and sets out the models for the dynamics of health and SES that will be used for our analysis. Section 11.3 describes the panel study and data that we use. Section 11.4 describes the association of SES and prevalence of health conditions in the initial wave of the panel. Section 11.5 analyzes incidence of new health conditions, and presents tests for noncausality of SES for the incidence of health innovations. Section 11.6 tests for the absence of a causal link from health conditions to wealth accumulation and other SES indicators. Section 11.7 uses our estimated models for prevalence and incidence to simulate life histories for a current population aged seventy under counterfactual (and unrealistically simplistic) interventions that assume a major health hazard can be removed, or SES shifted for the entire population. This simulation accounts consistently for comorbidities and competing hazards over the life course. The purpose of this exercise is to demonstrate the feasibility of using our modeling approach for policy applications when the models pass the causality tests described in next section. Finally, section 11.8 gives conclusions and outlines

topics for future research. The appendix to this paper, containing tables
11A.1 to 11A.11 with detailed estimation results and the data and com-
puter routines we use, are posted on the internet at http://elsa.berkeley.edu/
wp/hww/hww202.html.

11.2   Association and Causality in Panel Data

11.2.1   Testing Causality

The primary purpose of this study is to test for direct causal links between SES and health. There is a large literature on the nature of causality
and the interpretation of "causality tests."[8] Our analysis fits generally
within the approach of Granger (1969), Sims (1972), and Hoover (2001),
but our panel data structure permits some refinements that are not available in a pure time series setting.

Let Y_t denote a K-vector of demographic, health, and socioeconomic
random variables for a household at date t and interpret a realization of
these variables as an observation in one wave of a panel survey. Let Y_t be
the information set containing the history of this vector through date t. Let

(1) $f(Y_t | Y_{t-1})$

$$\equiv f_1(Y_{1t} | Y_{t-1}) \cdot f_2(Y_{2t} | Y_{1t}, Y_{t-1}) \cdot \ldots \cdot f_K(Y_{Kt} | Y_{1t}, \ldots, Y_{K-1,t}, Y_{t-1})$$

denote a model of the conditional distribution of Y_t given Y_{t-1}. Without loss
of generality, we have written this model as a product of one-dimensional
conditional distributions, given history and given components of Y_t determined previously. Writing the model in this way does not imply that the
components of Y_t form a causal chain, as they may be simultaneously determined, or determined in some causal sequence other than the specified
sequence. However, the model structure simplifies if the current components of Y_t in the specified order do form a causal chain or are conditionally independent. If one takes Wold's view that causal action takes time,
then for sufficiently brief time intervals, $f_K(Y_{Kt} | Y_{1t}, \ldots, Y_{K-1,t}, Y_{t-1})$ will not
depend on contemporaneous variables, and what Granger calls *instanta-
neous causality* is ruled out. In practice, time aggregation to observation intervals can introduce apparent simultaneous determination. Conversely, in
applications where time aggregation is an issue, one can treat observed
variables as indicators for some latent causal chain structure defined for
very short time intervals.

---

8. See Dawid (2000); Freedman (1985, 2001); Granger (1969); Sims (1972); Zellner (1979);
Swert (1979); Engle, Hendry, and Richard (1983); Geweke (1984); Gill and Robins (2001);
Heckman (2000, 2001); Holland (1986, 1988); Pearl (2000); Robins (1999); Sobel (1997,
2000); Hendry and Mizon (1999); and Woodward (1999).

We shall focus on first-order Markov processes, specializations of (1) in which only the most recent history conveys information,

$$(2) \qquad f(Y_t \,|\, Y_{t-1}) \equiv f(Y_t \,|\, Y_{t-1})$$

$$\equiv f_1(Y_{1t} \,|\, Y_{t-1}) \cdot f_2(Y_{2t} \,|\, Y_{1t}, \, Y_{t-1})$$

$$\cdots \cdots f_K(Y_{Kt} \,|\, Y_{1t}, \ldots, Y_{K-1,t}, \, Y_{t-1}).$$

Note that if (1) is a higher-order Markov process, then (2) can be obtained by expanding the variables in Y_t to include higher-order lags. Greater generality could be achieved via a hidden Markov structure in which the observed Y_t are deterministic functions of a latent first-order Markov process.[9] We leave this extension for future research.

Model (2) is *valid* for a given history Y_{t-1} if it is the true conditional distribution of Y_t given this history. Term f a *structural* or *causal* model, or a (*probabilistic*) *law,* for Y_t relative to a family of histories if it has the *invariance* property that it is valid for each history in the family. Operationally, this means that within specified domains, f has the *transferability* property that it is valid in different populations where the marginal distribution of Y_{t-1} changes, and the *predictability* or *invariance under treatments* property that it remains valid following policy interventions that alter the marginal distribution of Y_{t-1}. By including temporal or spatial variables in Y, it is possible to weaken invariance requirements to fit almost any application. Done indiscriminately, this creates a substantial risk of producing an "overfitted" model that will be invalid for any "out-of-sample" policy interventions. Then, proposed models should be as generic as possible. However, it may be necessary in some applications to model "regime shifts" that account for factors that are causal for some populations or time periods, and not for others.

Suppose the vector $Y_t = (H_t, S_t, X_t)$ is composed of subvectors H_t, S_t, and X_t, which will later be interpreted as health conditions, SES status, and strictly exogenous variables, respectively. We say that S is *conditionally noncausal* for H, given X, if $f(H_t \,|\, H_{t-1}, X_{t-1})$ is a valid model; that is, given H_{t-1} and X_{t-1}, knowledge of S_{t-1} is *not needed* to achieve the invariance properties of a causal model. Conversely, if $f(H_t \,|\, H_{t-1}, S_{t-1}, X_{t-1}) \not\equiv f(H_t \,|\, H_{t-1}, X_{t-1})$, then knowledge of S_{t-1} *contributes to the predictability* of H_t. Note that either one or both conditional noncausality of S for H and conditional noncausality of H for S may hold. If either holds, then H and S can be arrayed in a (block) causal chain, and if both hold, then H and S are conditionally independent. Writing model (2) as a product of univariate conditional

9. Any discrete-time stationary stochastic process can be approximated (in distribution for restrictions to a finite number of periods) by a first-order hidden Markov model so there is no loss of generality in considering only models of this form; see Kunsch, Geman, and Kehagias (1995).

probabilities $f_i(H_{it} \mid H_{1t}, \ldots, H_{i-1,t}, H_{t-1}, S_{t-1}, X_{t-1})$, one can test for conditional noncausality of S for each component H_i. It is possible to have a causal chain in which S is conditionally causal to a previous component of H, and this component is in turn "instantaneously" causal to H_j, yet there is no direct causal link from S to H_i. Placing S after H in the vector Y, we have conditional probabilities $f(S_t \mid H_t, H_{t-1}, S_{t-1}, X_{t-1})$. There may be instantaneous conditional independence of H and S, with the conditional distribution of S_t not depending on H_t or conditional noncausality of H for S, with the conditional distribution not depending on H_{t-1}, or both. The statement that X is *strictly exogenous* in a valid model (2) is equivalent to the condition that H and S are conditionally noncausal for X in this model.[10]

The conventional definition of a *causal model* or *probabilistic law* requires that f be valid for the universe of possible histories (except possibly those in a set that occurs with probability zero); see Pearl (2000). It is possible to reject statistically a proposed causal model by showing that it is highly improbable that an observed sample with a given history was generated by this model. It is far more difficult using statistical analysis to conclude inductively that a proposed model is valid for the universe of possible histories. We have the far more limited objective of providing a foundation for policy analysis, where it is the invariance property under policy interventions that is crucial to predicting policy consequences. We have defined *validity* and *noncausality* as properties of a *model,* and of the outcomes of a *process* of statistical testing that could in principle be conducted on this model. Only within the domain where the model is valid, and invariance confirms that the model is accurately describing the true data generation process, can these limited positivistic model properties be related to the causal structure embedded in the true data generation process. Further, we can choose the domain over which invariance will be tested to make the definition operational and relevant for a specific analysis of policy interventions. Similarly, our definition of conditional noncausality is a positivistic construct in the spirit of the purely statistical treatment of "causality" by Granger (1969), and the test we will use is simply Granger's test for the absence of causality, augmented with invariance conditions. Thus, for example, if our analysis using this framework concludes that SES is not conditionally causal for new health events within the domain where the Medicare system finances and delivers health care, then this finding would support the conclusion that policy interventions in the Medicare system to increase access or reduce out-of-pocket medical expenses will not alter the conditional probabilities of new health events, given the health histories of enrollees in this system. It is unnecessary for this policy purpose to answer

---

10. Econometricians have traditionally used the term *strictly exogenous* to refer to properties of variables in the true data generation process, a stronger nonpositivistic version of this condition.

the question of whether the analysis has uncovered a causal structure in any deeper sense. Econometric analysis is better matched to the modest task of testing invariance and noncausality in limited domains than to the grander enterprise of discovering universal causal laws. However, our emphasis on invariance properties of the model, and on tests for Granger causality within invariant families, is consistent with the view of philosophers of science that causality is embedded in "laws" whose validity as a description of the true data generation process is characterized by their invariance properties; see Pearl (2000), Feigl (1953), and Nozick (2001).

11.2.2   Some Specific Formulations

Starting from class (2), we consider operational models of the linear latent variable form

$$(3) \qquad Y_{it}^* = Y_{1,t}\alpha_{1i} + \ldots + Y_{i-1,t}\alpha_{i-1,i} + Y_{t-1}'\beta_i + \delta_i - \sigma_i\varepsilon_{it}$$

with

$$(4) \qquad\qquad\qquad Y_{it} = \psi_i(Y_{it}^*, Y_{t-1}),$$

where Y^* is a latent variable, ε_{it} is an unobserved disturbance that is standard normal and independent across i and t, and ψ is a partial observability mapping that depends on the latent variable, and possibly on the lagged variables. For example, for a chronic health condition such as diabetes, Y_{it} will indicate whether there has ever been a diagnosis of the disease, with $Y_{it} = \max\{Y_{i,t-1}, 1(Y_{it}^* \geq 0)\}$. For an acute condition such as a heart attack, $Y_{it} = 1(Y_{it}^* \geq 0)$ indicates a new occurrence. Components of Y may be binomial or ordered discrete variables such as health status, or continuous variables such as household income. In this model, the α's, β, δ, and σ are parameters; restrictions are imposed as necessary for identification. In (3), the linearity in variables and parameters, the first-order Markov property, and the triangular dependence of Y_{it}^* on previous components of Y_t are not, in themselves, particularly restrictive, as one can approximate any continuous Markov model of form (2) by a form (3) in which Y_t is expanded to include transformations and interactions to sufficient order. The normality assumption is also not restrictive in principle. A latent random variable with conditional cumulative distribution function (CDF) $F(Y_{1t}^* \mid Y_{t-1})$ and the partial observability transformation (4) can be redefined using the standard normal CDF Φ as $Y_{1t}^{**} = \Phi^{-1}(F(Y_{1t}^* \mid Y_{t-1}))$ and $Y_{1t} = \psi_1(F^{-1}(\Phi(Y_{1t}^{**}) \mid Y_{t-1}), Y_{1,t-1})$; this gives a version of models (3) and (4) in which the disturbance is standard normal.[11] The same construction can be

---

11. For the CDF F of a random variable Y, define $F(y-) = \sup_{y'<y}F(y')$ and $F^{-1}(p) = \min\{x' \mid F(x') \geq p\}$. Define the random variable $Z \equiv h(Y) = \Phi^{-1}(F(Y-) + U[F(Y) - F(Y-)])$, where U is a uniform $(0, 1)$ random variable. Then Z is a.s. standard normal. Define $Y^* = F^{-1}(\Phi(Z))$. Then, $Y^* = Y$ a.s., so that Y is given a.s. by a nondecreasing transformation of a standard normal random variable.

applied to the remaining components of Y_t. The causal chain assumption is innocuous when the time interval is too short for most causal actions to operate, and the components of Y_t are conditionally independent. However, the causal chain assumption is a more substantive restriction when the time interval is long enough for multiple events to occur, as it precludes even the feedbacks that would appear in multiple iterations of a true causal chain. Of course, the generally nonrestrictive approximation properties of models (3) and (4) do not imply that a particular specification chosen for an application is accurate, and failures of tests for invariance can also be interpreted as diagnostics for inadequate specifications.

In models (3) and (4), a binomial component i of Y_t with the partial observability mapping $\max\{Y_{i,t-1}, \mathbf{1}(Y_{it}^* \geq 0)\}$ and the identifying restriction $\sigma_i = 1$ satisfies $Y_{it} = 1$ if $Y_{i,t-1} = 1$, and otherwise is one with the probit probability

$$(5) \quad f_i(Y_{it} = 1 \mid Y_{1t}, \ldots, Y_{i-1,t}, Y_{t-1})$$
$$= \Phi(Y_{1,t}\alpha_{1i} + \ldots + Y_{i-1,t}\alpha_{i-1,i} + Y_{t-1}'\beta_i + \delta_i).$$

Analogous expressions can be developed for ordered or continuous components.

11.2.3   Measurement Issues

A feature of the panel we use is that the waves are separated by several years, and the interviews within a wave are spread over many months, with the months between waves differing across households. If model (2) applies to short intervals, say months, then the transition from one wave in month t to another in month $t + s$ is described by the probability model

$$(6) \qquad f(Y_{t+s} \mid Y_t) = \sum_{Y_{t+1}, \ldots, Y_{t+s-1}} f(Y_{t+1} \mid Y_t) \cdot \ldots \cdot f(Y_{t+s} \mid Y_{t+s-1}).$$

Direct computation of these probabilities will generally be intractable, although analysis using simulation methods is possible.

A major additional complication in our panel is that interview timing appears to be related to health status, with household or proxy interviews delayed for individuals who have died or have serious health conditions. This introduces a spurious correlation between apparent time at risk and health status that will bias estimation of structural parameters. To study empirical approximations to (6) and corrections for spurious correlation, we consider a simple model of interview delay. Let $p = \Phi(\alpha + \beta x)$ denote the monthly survival probability for an individual who was alive at the previous wave interview, where x is a single time-invariant covariate that takes the value $-1, 0, +1$, each with probability $1/3$. Counting from the time of the previous wave interview, let k denote the number of months this individual lives, and c denote the month that interviews begin for the current wave.[12] There is a distribution of initial contact times; let q denote the probability of a month passing without being contacted, and let m denote the month of initial contact. Assume that an individual who is living at the time of initial contact is interviewed immediately, but for individuals who have died by the time of initial contact, there is an interview delay, with r denoting the probability of an additional month passing without a completed interview with a household member or proxy. Let n denote the number of months of delay in this event. Assume that m and n are not observed, but the actual interwave interval t, equal to m if the individual is alive at time of initial contact, and equal to $m + n$ otherwise, is observed. The density of k is $p^{k-1}(1 - p)$ for $k \geq 1$. The density of m is $q^{m-c}(1 - q)$ for $m \geq c$. Let d be an indicator for the event that the individual is dead at the time of initial contact. The probability of t and $d = 0$ is $h(0, t) = q^{t-c}(1 - q)p^t$, the product of the probability of contact at t and the probability of being alive at t. The probability of t and $d = 1$, denoted $h(1, t)$, is the sum of the probabilities that the individual is dead at an initial contact month m, with $c \leq m \leq t$, and the subsequent interview delay is $n = t - m$, or

$$(7) \qquad h(1, t) = \sum_{m=c}^{t} (1 - p^m)q^{m-c}(1 - q)r^{t-m}(1 - r).$$

If $r < pq$, then $h(1, t) = (1 - q)(1 - r)\{(q^{t-c+1} - r^{t-c+1})/(q - r) - p^c((pq)^{t-c+1} - r^{t-c+1})/(pq - r)\}$. Then, the probability of an observed interwave interval t is $h(t) = h(0, t) + h(1, t)$, and the conditional probability of $d = 1$, given t, is $P(1 \mid t) = h(1, t)/h(t)$. Absent interview delay, the conditional probability of $d = 1$ given t would be simply $p^{t-1}(1 - p)$. The parameter values $\alpha = -2.47474$, $\beta = 0.3$, $c = 22$, $q = 0.85$, and $r = 0.5$ roughly match our panel. For these values, the median interwave interval is 25.5 months, and at $t = 34$, 87 percent of the interviews have been completed.

Figure 11.2 plots the inverse normal transformations of the true death rate $p^{t-1}(1 - p)$ and the apparent death rate $P(1 \mid t)$ against $\log(t)$ for each value of the covariate x. The *true* relationship is to a reasonable empirical approximation linear in x and in $\log(t)$. Then, in the absence of interview delay, one could approximate p, given x, with reasonable accuracy by estimating a probit model for death of the form $\Phi(\theta + \gamma x + \lambda \log(t))$, and then estimating p using the transformation $p = (1 - \Phi(\theta + \gamma x + \lambda \log(t)))^{1/t}$ for the observed interwave interval t.[13] However, the figure shows that interview delay induces a sharp gradient of apparent mortality hazard with interwave interval, so that an estimated model will not extrapolate to realistic mortality hazards over shorter periods. A simple imputation of time at

12. It does not matter for the example if the previous wave interview month is fixed or has a distribution, provided the *relative* interwave interval c is fixed, and current wave outcomes are independent of the timing of the previous wave interview.

13. A Box–Cox transformation of time at risk, $z = 4(t^{1/4} - 1)$, gives a somewhat better approximation in the probit model than $\log(t)$, but has no appreciable effect on the accuracy of estimated monthly transition probabilities.

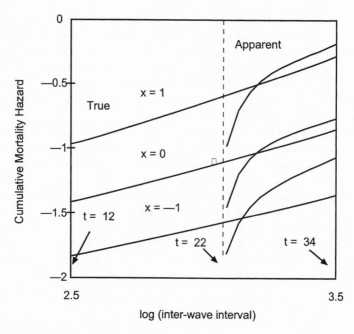

Fig. 11.2   Effect of interview delay (cumulative mortality hazard = Φ^{-1} [death probability])

risk up to initial contact leads again to models that work well with the procedure just outlined for estimation of p conditioned on x. A simple imputed time of initial contact for those who have died is the observed interwave interval less the difference in the mean interwave interview times for dead and living respondents. This imputation can be adjusted further so that the extrapolated annual death rate, $\Phi(\theta + \lambda \log(12) + \gamma x)$, matches the sample average mortality rate. We do the additional adjustment for our panel, with results that are almost identical to the simple imputation of time of initial contact.

We conducted a Monte Carlo calculation of the approximations above in a sample of 50,000. In this simulation, the empirical approximation to observed mortality in the absence of interview delay is $\Phi(-3.1053 + 0.5327x + 0.652 \log(t))$. With interview delay and the simple imputation described above, $\Phi(-2.9900 + 0.5349x + 0.6174 \log(t))$ is the empirical approximation.[14] Table 11.1 gives the annual mortality rates implied by these approximations. From these results, we conclude first that in the absence of interview delay, the probit model $\Phi(\theta + \lambda \log(t) + \gamma x)$ provides an adequate approximation to exact annual mortality rates as a function of time

14. The model estimated with interview delay and without imputation, is $\Phi(-4.6639 + 0.5349x + 1.1178 \log(t))$.

Table 11.1   **Approximation Accuracy with Interview Delay (%)**

x	Exact Annual Mortality Rate	Approximate Annual Mortality Rate without Interview Delay	Error	Approximate Annual Mortality Rate with Interview Delay and Imputed Contact Time	Error
0	7.71	7.90	2.41	7.93	2.79
−1	3.27	3.06	−6.55	3.07	−6.03
+1	16.41	16.71	1.80	16.75	2.05
Avg.	9.13	9.22	0.98	9.25	1.34

Note: The approximate annual mortality rate is given by $1 - (1 - \Phi(\theta + \gamma x + \lambda \log(t)))^{12/t}$, where t is the exact or imputed initial contact time and the model is estimated from the data generated by the Monte Carlo experiment.

at risk, across values of the covariate x that substantially change relative risk, and second that this remains true in the presence of interview delay when one imputes the initial contact time for dead subjects.

These conclusions on the accuracy of the approximation should extend to the exact interwave transition probabilities (6) in our Markov model, supporting use of the probit approximation

$$(8) \quad f_i(Y_{i,t+s} = 1 \mid Y_{1t+s}, \ldots, Y_{i-1,t+s}, Y_t)$$

$$= \Phi(Y_{1,t+s}\alpha_{1i} + \ldots + Y_{i-1,t+s}\alpha_{i-1,i} + Y_t'\beta_i + \delta_i + \lambda_i \log(s)),$$

where $s = t_{i2} - t_{i1}$ is the imputed months between initial contact for a wave and previous wave interview, for estimation of incidence between waves. For simulation of yearly transitions, we use the approximation

$$(9) \quad f_i(Y_{i,t+12} = 1 \mid Y_{1t+12}, \ldots, Y_{i-1,t+12}, Y_t)$$

$$= 1 - (1 - \Phi(Y_{1,t+1}\alpha_{1i} + \ldots + Y_{i-1,t+1}\alpha_{i-1,i} + Y_t'\beta_i + \delta_i + \lambda_i \log(s)))^{12/s}$$

$$\approx \Phi(Y_{1,t+1}\alpha_{1i} + \ldots + Y_{i-1,t+1}\alpha_{i-1,i} + Y_t'\beta_i + \delta_i + \lambda_i \log(s))12/s,$$

where s is the median interwave interval, and the final approximation holds when the probability of a transition is small. Formula (9) generalizes to any probability of a transition from the status quo, with the probability of remaining at the initial state defined so that all the transition probabilities sum to one. We expect this formula to approximate well the probabilities of no new health conditions in a sample population over periods corresponding to the observed interwave intervals.

Estimation of models based on (2)–(8) is straightforward. Because of the independence assumption on the disturbances and the absence of common parameters across equations, the estimation separates into a probit, ordered probit, or ordinary least-squares regression for each component of Y, depending on whether the partial observability mapping is binary, ordered, or linear. Conventional likelihood ratio tests can be used for the significance of explanatory variables.

11.3   The AHEAD Panel Data

11.3.1   Sample Characteristics

Our data come from the Asset and Health Dynamics among the Oldest Old (AHEAD) study.[15] This is a panel of individuals born in 1923 or earlier and their spouses. At baseline in 1993 the AHEAD panel contained 8,222 individuals representative of the noninstitutionalized population, except for oversamples of blacks, Hispanics and Floridians. Of these subjects, 7,638 were over age sixty-nine; the remainder were younger spouses. There were 6,052 households, including individuals living alone or with others, in the sample. The wave 1 surveys took place between October 1993 and August 1994, with half the total completed interviews finished before December 1993. The wave 2 surveys took place approximately twenty-four months later, between November 1995 and June 1996, with half the total completed interviews finished by the beginning of February 1996. The wave 3 surveys took place approximately twenty-seven months after that, between January 1998 and December 1998, with half the total completed interviews finished near the beginning of March 1998. In each wave, there was a long but thin tail of late interviews, heavily weighted with subjects who had moved, or required proxy interviews due to death or institutionalization. Subjects never interviewed, directly or by proxy, are excluded from the calculation of the distribution of interview months. The AHEAD is a continuing panel, but it has now been absorbed into the larger Health and Retirement Study (HRS), which is being interviewed on a three-year cycle.

The AHEAD panel has substantial attrition, with death being the primary, but not the only, cause. A significant effort has been made to track attritors, and identify those who have died through the National Death Register. Figure 11.3 describes outcomes for the full age-eligible sample. For subjects where a proxy interview was possible, an "exit interview" gives information on whether decedents had a new occurrence of cancer, heart attack, or stroke since the previous wave. From the 6,743 age-eligible individuals who did not attrit prior to death, we formed a working sample for analysis consisting of 6,489 by excluding 254 additional individuals with critical missing information. Figure 11.4 describes their outcomes. In a few cases, attritors in wave 2 rejoined the sample in wave 3, but we treat these as permanent attritors because the missing interview makes the observation unusable.

---

15. The AHEAD survey is conducted by the University of Michigan Survey Research Center for the National Institute on Aging; see Soldo et al. (1997).

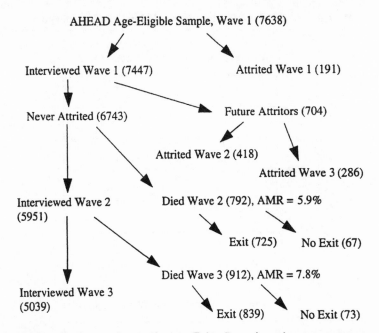

AMR = Crude annual mortality rate, Exit = Proxy interview following death

Fig. 11.3   Age-eligible sample outcomes

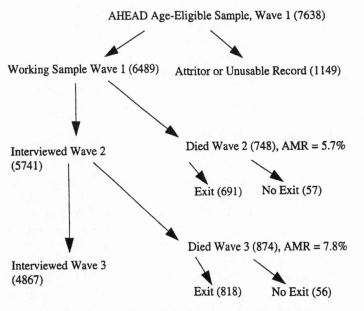

AMR = Crude annual mortality rate, Exit = Proxy interview following death

Fig. 11.4   Working sample outcomes

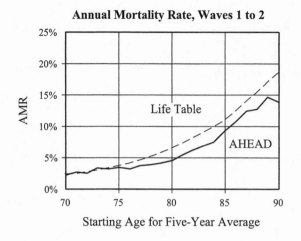

Annual Mortality Rate, Waves 1 to 2

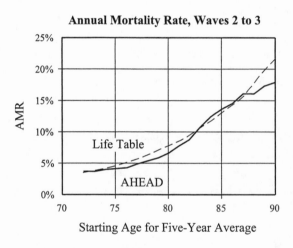

Annual Mortality Rate, Waves 2 to 3

Fig. 11.5   **Mortality hazard for AHEAD white females**

The restriction of the AHEAD panel to the noninstitutionalized elderly in wave 1 selects against those with the highest mortality risk, particularly at the oldest ages, but the impact of this selection attenuates over time. For white females, figure 11.5 compares the observed annual mortality rate in the AHEAD panel with the expected annual mortality rate from the 1997 life tables for the United States (U.S. Census 1999).[16] Between waves 1 and 2, the AHEAD mortality risk is substantially below the life table for ages above seventy-five, reflecting the selection effect of noninstitutionalization.

16. The AMR for the AHEAD sample is the actual death rate between waves for each five-year segment of ages in the initial wave, annualized using the median 25.5 month interval between the waves. The AMR from the life tables is obtained by applying life table death rates by month to the actual months at risk for each individual in the five-year segment of ages in

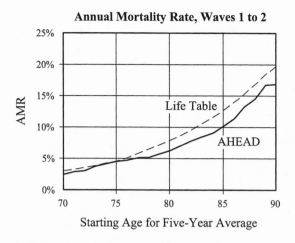

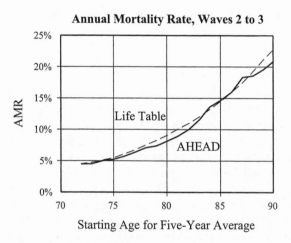

Fig. 11.6   **Mortality hazard for AHEAD working sample**

Between waves 2 and 3, this effect has essentially disappeared. There is a persistent divergence of the mortality risks above age ninety. In this range, the AHEAD data is sparse, so the curve is imprecisely determined. However, the life tables derived from historical mortality experience may overstate current mortality risk at advanced ages. Figure 11.6 makes the same mortality experience comparisons for the full AHEAD working sample and draws the same conclusions.[17]

the initial wave to calculate expected deaths between waves. This is annualized. For these calculations, the distribution of months at risk for decedents is assumed to be the same as that for survivors.

17. The construction mimics figure 11.5, with life table rates applied using the age, sex, and race of each subject.

11.3.2   Descriptive Statistics

The AHEAD survey provides data on health and socioeconomic status, as well as background demographics. A list of the health conditions we study, with summary statistics, is given in table 11.2. A list of the socioeconomic conditions and demographic variables we use is given in table 11.3. Table 11A.2 lists the variable transformations used in our statistical analysis.[18] In setting up causality tests, using the framework set out in section 11.2, we will use the health conditions, followed by the socioeconomic conditions, in the order given in these tables. We list cancer, heart disease, and stroke first because they may be instantaneously causal for death, and because we have information from decedent's exit interviews on new occurrence of these diseases. We group the remaining health conditions by degenerative and chronic conditions, then accidents, then mental conditions, because if there is any contemporaneous causality, it will plausibly flow in this order. Similarly, if there is contemporaneous causality between health and socioeconomic conditions, it plausibly flows from the former to the latter.

11.3.3   Constructed Variables

The collection and processing of some of the variables requires comment. The AHEAD has an extensive battery of questions about health conditions, including mental health. Most health conditions are asked for in the form "Has a doctor ever told you that you had . . . ?" However, for cancer, heart disease, and stroke, subjects are also asked if there was a new occurrence since the previous interview, and for some conditions such as arthritis, incontinence, and falls, the questions in wave 1 ask for an occurrence in the past twelve months. We note that there are some major groups of health conditions that were not investigated in AHEAD: degenerative neurological diseases, kidney and liver diseases, immunological disorders other than arthritis, sight and hearing problems, back problems, and accidents other than falls. The body mass index (BMI) index is calculated from self-reported height and weight. Information is collected on the number of limitations for six activities of daily living (ADL), and on the number of limitations for five instrumental activities of daily living (IADL). A high ADL limitation count indicates that the individual has difficulty with personal self-care, while a high IADL limitation count indicates difficulty in household management. The study collects data on self-assessed health status, where the subject is asked to rate his or her health as excellent, very good, good, fair or poor. We use an indicator for a poor/fair response. No reference is made to other groups such as "people your age." The study contains the Center for Epidemiologic Studies Depression scale (CESD)

18. All appendices can be found at http://elsa.berkeley.edu/wp/hww/hww202.html.

Table 11.2   **Health Condition Variables in AHEAD**

| | Wave 1 | | | | Wave 2 | | | | Wave 3 | | | |
Label	Variable	N	Mean	SD	Variable	N	Mean	SD	Variable	N	Mean	SD
Health condition prevalence												
Doc ever told had cancer?	CANCER1	6,489	0.137	0.344	CANCER2	6,432	0.176	0.381	CANCER3	5,685	0.188	0.391
Doc ever told had heart attack/disease?	HEART1	6,489	0.317	0.465	HEART2	6,432	0.364	0.481	HEART3	5,685	0.321	0.467
Doc ever told had stroke?	STROKE1	6,489	0.089	0.285	STROKE2	6,432	0.123	0.329	STROKE3	5,685	0.143	0.350
Doc ever told had lung disease?	LUNG1	6,489	0.115	0.318	LUNG2	6,432	0.124	0.330	LUNG3	5,685	0.127	0.333
Doc ever told had diabetes?	DIABET1	6,489	0.134	0.340	DIABET2	5,741	0.147	0.354	DIABET3	4,867	0.158	0.365
Doc ever told had high blood pressure?	HIGHBP1	6,489	0.502	0.500	HIGHBP2	5,741	0.525	0.499	HIGHBP3	4,867	0.553	0.497
Seen Doc for arthritis in last 12 m?	ARTHRT1	6,489	0.267	0.442	ARTHRT2	5,741	0.278	0.448	ARTHRT3	4,867	0.279	0.448
Incontinence last 12 m?	INCONT1	6,489	0.202	0.402	INCONT2	5,741	0.301	0.459	INCONT3	4,867	0.371	0.483
Fall in last 12 m require treatment?	FALL1	6,489	0.080	0.271	FALL2	6,432	0.180	0.384	FALL3	5,685	0.267	0.443
Ever fractured hip?	HIPFRC1	6,489	0.050	0.219	HIPFRC2	6,432	0.068	0.252	HIPFRC3	5,685	0.084	0.278
Proxy interview	PROXYW1	6,489	0.104	0.306	PROXYW2	5,741	0.132	0.339	PROXYW3	4,867	0.154	0.361
Age-educ. adjust cognitive impairment?	COGIM1	6,489	0.257	0.437	COGIM2	5,741	0.349	0.477	COGIM3	4,867	0.403	0.491
Ever seen Doc for psych prob?	PSYCH1	6,489	0.109	0.312	PSYCH2	5,741	0.128	0.334	PSYCH3	4,867	0.143	0.350
Depressed (cesd8 > 4)	DEPRES1	6,488	0.099	0.299	DEPRES2	5,741	0.086	0.280	DEPRES3	4,862	0.108	0.310
Body mass index (Quetelet)	BMI1	6,475	25.4	4.5	BMI2	5,740	25.1	4.6	BMI3	4,866	25.0	4.6
Low BMI spline = max(0, 20 − bmi)	LOBMI1	6,475	0.155	0.654	LOBMI2	5,740	0.198	0.763	LOBMI3	4,866	0.223	0.810
High BMI spline = max(0, bmi −25)	HIBMI1	6,475	1.889	3.164	HIBMI2	5,740	1.808	3.143	HIBMI3	4,866	1.740	3.037
Current smoker?	SMOKNOW1	6,489	0.102	0.303	SMOKNOW2	5,741	0.078	0.267	SMOKNOW3	4,867	0.066	0.249
No. of ADLs (needs help/difficult)	NUMADL1	6,489	0.725	1.391	NUMADL2	6,432	0.882	1.652	NUMADL3	5,444	1.035	1.774
No. of IADLs (needs help/difficult)	NUMIADL1	6,489	0.618	1.166	NUMIADL2	6,432	0.582	1.204	NUMIADL3	5,685	0.711	1.253
Poor/fair self-reported health	DHLTH1	6,483	0.373	0.484	DHLTH2	5,739	0.368	0.482	DHLTH3	4,859	0.434	0.496
Health condition incidence												
Cancer[a]					JCANCER2	6,432	0.050	0.218	JCANCER3	5,685	0.061	0.239
Heart attack/condition[a]					JHEART2	6,432	0.087	0.281	JHEART3	5,685	0.154	0.361
Stroke[a]					JSTROKE2	6,432	0.050	0.219	JSTROKE3	5,685	0.069	0.254
Died since last wave?					TDIED2	6,489	0.115	0.319	TDIED3	5,741	0.152	0.359
(continued)												

Table 11.2 (continued)

Label	Wave 1				Wave 2				Wave 3			
	Variable	N	Mean	SD	Variable	N	Mean	SD	Variable	N	Mean	SD
Lung disease[a]					ILUNG2	6,432	0.024	0.154	ILUNG3	5,685	0.032	0.177
Diabetes[a]					IDIABET2	5,741	0.024	0.153	IDIABET3	4,867	0.025	0.156
High blood pressure (HBP)[a]					IHIGHBP2	5,741	0.053	0.225	IHIGHBP3	4,867	0.055	0.229
Arthritis[a]					IARTHRT2	5,741	0.112	0.316	IARTHRT3	4,867	0.117	0.321
Incontinence *in last 12 months*					JINCONT2	5,741	0.233	0.423	JINCONT3	4,867	0.258	0.438
Fall requiring treatment[a]					JFALL2	6,432	0.128	0.335	JFALL3	5,240	0.165	0.371
Hip fracture[a]					JHIPFRC2	6,432	0.02	0.150	JHIPFRC3	5,681	0.033	0.178
Proxy interview					PROXYW2	5,741	0.132	0.339	PROXYW3	4,867	0.154	0.361
Cognitive impairment					ICOGIM2	5,741	0.121	0.326	ICOGIM3	4,867	0.100	0.300
Psychiatric problems[a]					IPSYCH2	5,741	0.046	0.210	IPSYCH3	4,867	0.040	0.196
Depression					IDEPRES2	5,741	0.051	0.220	IDEPRES3	4,862	0.072	0.259
BMI better indicator					BMIBT2	5,740	0.197	0.397	BMIBT3	4,866	0.190	0.392
BMI worse indicator					BMIWS2	5,740	0.167	0.373	BMIWS3	4,866	0.188	0.391

Notes: N = number of observations; SD = standard deviation.

[a] AHEAD Waves 2 and 3: "Since the last interview . . . ?".

Table 11.3   SES and Demographic Variables in AHEAD

Label	Wave 1				Wave 2				Wave 3			
	Variable	N	Mean	SD	Variable	N	Mean	SD	Variable	N	Mean	SD
SES variables												
Wealth 97 Dol (V.2) (000)	C.2W1	6,489	176.6	297.8	C.2W2	5,741	237.5	527.3	C.2W3	4,867	247.7	736.2
Nonliquid wealth (000)	C.2N1	6,489	112.0	191.8	C.2N2	5,741	121.2	312.1	C.2N3	4,867	119.2	400.7
Liquid wealth (000)	C.2L1	6,489	64.7	185.2	C.2L2	5,741	116.3	309.6	C.2L3	4,867	128.6	560.6
Income 97 Dol (V.2) (000)	C.2I1	6,489	23.8	28.8	C.2I2	5,741	24.5	58.6				
1st quartile wealth indicator	Q1WB1	6,489	0.261	0.654	Q1WB2	5,741	0.228	0.419	Q1WB3	4,867	0.255	0.436
4th quartile wealth indicator	Q4WB1	6,489	0.216	0.412	Q4WB2	5,741	0.273	0.446	Q4WB3	4,867	0.268	0.443
1st quartile income indicator	Q11B1	6,489	0.260	0.439	Q11B2	5,741	0.246	0.431				
4th quartile income indicator	Q41B1	6,489	0.247	0.431	Q41B2	5,741	0.246	0.431				
Change residence?					NMOVED2	5,642	0.068	0.251	MOVED3	4,867	0.102	0.303
Own residence?	DNHOUS1	6,489	0.732	0.443	DNHOUS2	5,741	0.721	0.449	DNHOUS3	4,867	0.707	0.455
Neighborhood safety poor/fair	HOODPF1	6,489	0.147	0.354	HOODPF2	5,741	0.107	0.309	HOODPF3	4,867	0.101	0.301
House condition poor/fair	CONDPF1	6,489	0.146	0.354	CONDPF2	5,741	0.109	0.312	CONDPF3	4,867	0.123	0.328
Demographic variables												
Widow?	WIDOW1	6,489	0.416	0.493	WIDOW2	5,741	0.443	0.497	WIDOW3	4,867	0.434	0.496
Divorced/separated?	DIVSEP1	6,489	0.054	0.226	DIVSEP2	5,741	0.054	0.226	DIVSEP3	4,867	0.055	0.228
Married	MARRIED1	6,489	0.498	0.500	MARRIED2	5,741	0.465	0.499	MARRIED3	4,867	0.477	0.500
Never married?	NEVMARR1	6,489	0.032	0.176	NEVMARR2	5,741	0.035	0.172	NEVMARR3	4,867	0.031	0.172
Age at interview in months	AGEM1	6,489	939.2	72.0	AGEM2	6,432	962.9	71.9	AGEM3	5,741	984.8	68.7
Mother's death age	MAGEDIE1	6,489	73.9	17.4								
Father's death age	PAGEDIE1	6,489	71.5	15.1								
Ever smoke?	SMOKEV	6,489	0.526	0.499								
Education (years)	EDUC	6,489	10.7	3.8								
Educ > 10 years indicator	HS	6,489	0.605	0.489								
Educ > 14 years indicator	COLL	6,489	0.143	0.350								

Notes: N = number of observations; SD = standard deviation.

battery of questions measuring general mood, and from this we form an indicator for depression.

The AHEAD is linked to Medicare records. There is insufficient detail to permit reconciliation of self-reports on objective health conditions against diagnoses in the medical records, but errors in self-reports are an issue. We find small, but significant, inconsistencies across waves of AHEAD in reported chronic conditions. A study of Canadian data for a younger population finds substantial discrepancies between self-reported conditions and diagnoses from medical records, particularly for chronic conditions such as arthritis; see Baker, Stabile, and Deri (2001). These authors also find support for a "self-justification" hypothesis that non-workers are more likely to make false positive claims for health conditions. If this reporting behavior carries into old age, then the reduction in SES as a consequence of spotty employment would induce an artifactual association of self-reported health conditions and SES.

The study measures cognition using a battery of questions which test several domains (Herzog and Wallace 1997): Learning and memory are assessed by immediate and delayed recall from a list of ten words that were read to the subject; reasoning, orientation, and attention are assessed from serial 7s, counting backwards by 1, and the naming of public figures, dates, and objects.[19] This score reflects both long-term native ability and health-related impairments due to health events. We carry out the following statistical analysis to reduce the effect of native ability so that we can concentrate on health-related loss of cognitive function. First, we analyze a "nonimpaired" sample of younger individuals, born between 1942 and 1947, who were administered the same cognitive battery in the 1998 Health and Retirement Study (HRS) as were the AHEAD subjects. For these younger individuals, where health-related impairment of cognitive function is rare, we carry out a least absolute deviation (LAD) regression of the cognitive score on education level, sex, and race. We use this fitted regression to predict a "baseline" nonimpaired cognitive score for each member of the AHEAD sample. An additional adjustment is required because average education levels were rising rapidly early in the twentieth century, due to changes in child labor laws and introduction of compulsory education. We assign each AHEAD subject a "1923 cohort equivalent" education level by first regressing education on sex, race, and birth cohort, using a specification search to find interactions and nonlinearities, and then adding to their actual years of education the difference in the mean years of education for their sex–race cohort and the corresponding 1923 sex–race cohort. We then calculate for each AHEAD sample member the deviation of their cognitive score from this adjusted baseline. As a normaliza-

19. Serial 7s asks the subject to subtract 7 from 100, and then to continue subtracting from each successive difference for a total of five subtractions.

tion, we assign a threshold such that 15 percent of AHEAD subjects aged seventy–seventy-four in wave 1 fall below the threshold. We then use the same threshold in other age groups and other waves to define an indicator for cognitive impairment.[20]

11.3.4   Measurement of Wealth

The AHEAD individuals and couples are asked for a complete inventory of assets and debts, and about income sources. Subjects are asked first if they have any assets in a specified category, and, if so, they are asked for the amount. A nonresponse to the amount is followed by unfolding bracket questions to bound the quantity in question, and this may result in complete or incomplete bracket responses. Through the use of unfolding brackets, full nonresponse to asset values was reduced to levels usually less than 5 percent, much lower than would be found in a typical household survey. Generally, median responses among full respondents for an asset category are comparable to other economic surveys, such as the Survey of Consumer Finance (SCF). However, changes in reported assets between waves contain outliers that suggest significant response errors between waves. For couples, where both members are asked the questions on assets, there is also substantial intersubject response variation. It is possible that these repeated reports could be used to control statistically for response error in couples. However, there are systematic differences between respondents, and we use the asset responses only from the individual that a couple says manages the household finances. There may also be an issue of bias in responses recovered by unfolding brackets. Hurd et al. (1998) used experimental variation in the bracket sequences for two financial questions on wave 2 of AHEAD, and found that anchoring to the bracket quantities was significant.

For complete or incomplete bracket responses in an asset category, we impute continuous quantities using hot deck methods. In wave 1, if information on ownership of an asset is missing for a subject, but this subject does give ownership status in wave 2, then we impute wave 1 ownership by drawing from the conditional empirical distribution of those who have the same response in wave 2 and give a response in wave 1. For subjects missing ownership in both waves 1 and 2, we draw an ownership pair from the empirical distribution of ownership pairs for those giving responses. Given ownership and complete or incomplete bracket information, we draw from the empirical distribution of wave 1 continuous responses that are consistent with the subject's bracket. In later waves, we have adopted a first-order

20. When an interview was done with a proxy, the cognitive battery was not given, but the interviewee was asked if the respondent was cognitively impaired. In our analysis, we treat proxy interview status as a component of the state that appears as a contemporaneous explanation of cognitive impairment; the coefficient on this variable compensates for differences in the definitions of cognitive impairment.

Markov cross-wave hot deck imputation procedure that assigns a continuous quantity within the given response bracket. First, missing ownership is imputed by choosing randomly from respondents, conditional on ownership in the previous wave. Then, given ownership, we impute a quantitative *change* in the item from the previous wave by drawing from the empirical distribution of subjects with complete responses that fall in the corresponding brackets in the current and the previous wave. This assures that imputed changes will have the same empirical distribution as observed changes, given the conditioning information available. This procedure does not revise previous wave imputations, so analyses based on earlier waves are not affected. We have experimented with cross-item imputation methods, where bracket information on some asset categories would be used to refine the conditioning used in the imputation of other asset categories. We have found that this has very little effect on the imputed variables or on the results obtained from analyses that use these variables. Therefore, we carry out all imputations one item at a time.

Measured wealth is accumulated over eleven asset categories, including imputed items. We distinguish *liquid wealth,* composed of IRA balances, stocks, bonds, checking accounts, and certificates of deposit, less debt; and *nonliquid wealth,* composed of net homeowner equity, other real estate, vehicles and other transportation equipment, businesses, and other assets. The variation in reported wealth of AHEAD households by asset category is substantial from wave to wave, suggesting that in addition to real volatility and reallocation of wealth portfolios, there are serious reporting problems with assets. Values of businesses owned and real estate are problematic items, because current market valuations may be unavailable to respondents, and subjective valuations may be unreliable. Suppose that W_t is measured wealth of household in wave t, in 1997 dollars, and that $W_t = W_t^* + \eta_t$, where W_t^* is true wealth and η_t is reporting error. To minimize the impact of extreme outliers in wealth and wealth changes, which we believe are a particular problem due to gross reporting errors, our statistical analysis will use bounded transformations of measured wealth.

The equations of motion for real wealth satisfy $dW_i^*/dt = rW_i^* + S_i$, where $i = T, N, L$ indexes total wealth or its nonliquid and liquid components, r is the instantaneous real rate of return, including unrealized capital gains, and S_i is the flow of savings to the wealth component. Make the logistic transformation $Z_i = 1/(1 + \exp(-c_i W_i + d_i))$, where c_i and d_i are chosen so that in AHEAD wave 1 the median and the semi-interquartile range of Z_i are one-half. Then, Z_i is a monotone transformation of measured wealth that is less sensitive to extremes. The equation of motion for Z_i is $dZ_i/dt - rZ_i(1 - Z_i)(\log(Z_i/(1 - Z_i)) + d_i) = c_i Z_i(1 - Z_i)S_i + c_i Z_i(1 - Z_i)(d\eta/dt - r\eta)$. We assume that over an inter-wave interval, this equation of motion can be approximated by

$$(10) \quad \frac{Z_{it} - Z_{i,t-1} - R_{t-1}Z_{i,t-1}(1 - Z_{i,t-1})(\log(Z_{i,t-1}/(1 - Z_{i,t-1})) + d_i)}{m_t}$$

$$= S_{it}^{\#} + \sigma v_{it},$$

where t indexes the wave, m_t is the interval in months between waves $t - 1$ and t, R_t is the S&P real rate of return over the given interval, $S_{it}^{\#}$ is the measured part of $c_i Z_{i,t-1}(1 - Z_{i,t-1})S_{i,t-1}$, attenuated at extreme values of $Z_{i,t-1}$, and the disturbance v_{it} includes the measurement error $c_i Z_{i,t-1}(1 - Z_{i,t-1})((\eta_{it} - \eta_{i,t-1})/m_{t-1} - r\eta_{t-1})$ and the unmeasured part of $c_i Z_{i,t-1}(1 - Z_{i,t-1})S_{i,t-1}$. We assume v is homoskedastic. This is consistent with a measurement error in observed wealth that is heteroskedastic, with gross measurement errors more likely when true wealth is near its extremes.[21] The disturbance in (10) may be serially correlated; however, we have not incorporated this into our analysis. The effect of the transformation is to substantially reduce the influence of outliers in the distribution of changes in measured wealth. In application, we specify $S_{it}^{\#}$ to be a linear function of transformed nonliquid and liquid wealth, $Z_{T,t-1}(1 - Z_{T,t-1}) \log(Z_{N,t-1}/(1 - Z_{N,t-1}))$ and $Z_{T,t-1}(1 - Z_{T,t-1}) \log(Z_{L,t-1}/(1 - Z_{L,t-1}))$, and of other SES, demographic, and health variables, scaled by $Z_{T,t-1}(1 - Z_{T,t-1})$.

11.3.5   Mortality and Observed Wealth Change

A problem with the analysis of wealth changes is that terminal wealth is not observed following the death of a single, or the death of both members of a household, introducing a selection effect. A second problem is that a household death may have a direct impact on the wealth of a survivor, due to the expenses associated with a death and the disposition of the estate. There are also severe wealth measurement problems following a household death, because a death typically requires a valuation of assets, and in many cases changes the financially responsible respondent. For this reason, we will analyze separately wealth changes for singles and for couples, allow a regime shift following the death of one member of a couple, and account for the selection that occurs when there are no survivors.

For a single female, we adopt a bivariate selection model,

$$(11) \quad Y_{ft}^* = Y_{f,t-1}\beta_f + \varepsilon, \quad y_{ft} = \mathbf{1}(Y_{ft}^* > 0), \quad Y_{wt} = Y_{w,t-1}\beta_w + Y_{w,t}'\gamma_w + \lambda\varepsilon + \kappa\eta,$$

$$Y_{wt} \text{ observed if } y_{ft} = 1,$$

---

21. Heteroskedasticity in (10) will arise from selection effects, described later, as well as possibly from a failure of the transformation to fully control the effects of gross reporting errors. When working with this model, we use standard error estimates that are robust with respect to heteroskedasticity of unknown form and do not attempt direct tests of the implicit error specification underlying transformation (10).

where the first latent equation determines survival, $y_{ft} = 1$, the second equation corresponds to the transformed wealth change equation (10) with dependence on the previous state $Y_{w,t-1}$ and the previously determined components $Y'_{w,t}$ of the current state, with the wealth change observed for survivors. The disturbance ε_f has mean zero, variance one, and a density $f(\varepsilon)$. The disturbance η is independent of ε, and has mean zero and variance one. The correlation of the disturbances in the selection and wealth change equations is $\rho = \lambda/(\lambda^2 + \kappa^2)^{1/2}$, and the unconditional variance of the wealth change equation is $\sigma^2 = \lambda^2 + \kappa^2$. When ε and η are standard normal, this is the conventional bivariate normal selection model. However, specification tests for normality fail, and for robustness we adopt a more flexible specification, approximating the density $f(\varepsilon)$ by an Edgeworth expansion,

$$(12) \qquad f(\varepsilon) = \sum_{j=0}^{J} \gamma_j H_j(\varepsilon)\phi(\varepsilon),$$

where the γ_j are parameters and $H_j(\varepsilon)$ are Hermite orthogonal polynomials; see Newey, Powell, and Walker (1990). Let $\Psi_{jk}(a) = \int_a^\infty \varepsilon^k H_j(\varepsilon)\phi(\varepsilon)d\varepsilon$. Then, the polynomials $H_j(\varepsilon)$ and the partial moment functions $\Psi_{jk}(a)$ can be constructed using the recursions

(13) $H_0(\varepsilon) = 1$, $H_1(\varepsilon) = \varepsilon$, and $H_j(\varepsilon) = \varepsilon H_{j-1}(\varepsilon) - (j-1)H_{j-2}(\varepsilon)$ for $j > 1$,

$\Psi_{00}(a) = \Phi(-a)$, $\Psi_{01}(a) = \phi(a)$, and

$\Psi_{0k}(a) = a^{k-1}\phi(a) + (k-1)\Psi_{0,k-2}(a)$ for $k > 1$,

$\Psi_{j0}(a) = H_{j-1}(a)\phi(a)$ and $\Psi_{jk}(a) = a^k H_{j-1}(a)\phi(a) + k\Psi_{j-1,k-1}(a)$

for $k > 0$, for $j > 0$.

Table 11A.1 derives these results and gives the leading terms for H_j and Ψ_{jk}: We require that f integrate to one and have unconditional mean zero and variance one; this forces $\gamma_0 = 1$, $\gamma_1 = 0$, and $\gamma_2 = 0$. The free parameters γ_j for $j > 2$ determine higher-order moments of ε. For example, skewness and kurtosis are determined by $E\varepsilon^3 = 6\gamma_3$ and $E\varepsilon^4 = 3 + 24\gamma_4$. With these restrictions, we have, finally

$$(14) \qquad E(\varepsilon \mid \varepsilon > a) = \frac{\phi(a) + \sum_{j=3}^{j} \gamma_j \Psi_{j1}(a)}{\Phi(-a) + \sum_{j=3}^{J} \gamma_j \Psi_{j0}(a)} \quad \text{and}$$

$$E(\varepsilon^2 \mid \varepsilon > a) = \frac{\Phi(-a) + a\phi(a) + \sum_{j=3}^{j}\gamma_j \Psi_{j2}(a)}{\Phi(-a) + \sum_{j=3}^{j}\gamma_j \Psi_{j0}(a)}.$$

We use the Edgeworth approximation and these conditional expectations with $J = 4$. We then have

(15) $E(Y^*_{wt} | \varepsilon > - Y_{f,t-1}\beta_f)$

$$= Y_{w,t-1}\beta_w + Y'_{w,t}\gamma_w + \lambda \frac{\phi(Y_{f,t-1}\beta_f) + \sum_{j=3}^{4} \gamma_j \Psi_{j1}(- Y_{f,t-1}\beta_f)}{\Phi(Y_{f,t-1}\beta_f) + \sum_{j=3}^{4} \gamma_j \Psi_{j0}(- Y_{f,t-1}\beta_f)} .$$

We estimate this conditional expectation in a two-step procedure. First, the parameters β_f of the selection equation are estimated by maximum likelihood, and substituted into expression (15) for the expectation of the wealth change equation.[22] Then, the parameters in this conditional expectation are estimated using nonlinear least squares. The disturbance $\zeta = \lambda\varepsilon + \kappa\eta - E(\varepsilon | \varepsilon > - Y_{f,t-1}\beta_f)$ has mean zero and variance:

(16) $E(\zeta^2 | \varepsilon > - Y_{f,t-1}\beta_f)$

$$= \kappa^2 + \lambda^2 \left(\frac{\sum_{j=0}^{J} \gamma_j \Psi_{j2}(- Y_{f,t-1}\beta_f)}{\sum_{j=0}^{J} \gamma_j \Psi_{j0}(- Y_{f,t-1}\beta_f)} - \left[\frac{\sum_{j=0}^{J} \gamma_j \Psi_{j1}(- Y_{f,t-1}\beta_f)}{\sum_{j=0}^{J} \gamma_j \Psi_{j0}(- Y_{f,t-1}\beta_f)} \right]^2 \right).$$

We regress the squared residuals from the estimation of (15) on the right-hand-side variables in (16) to obtain an estimate of κ^2. Finally, we estimate the covariance matrix for the parameter estimates using the generalized method of moments "sandwich" formula, with the Eicker-White procedure used for robustness against heteroskedasticity of unknown form, and the delta method used to incorporate the effects of variance in the first-stage selection parameter estimates.

Next consider the effects of death and selection on couples. We adopt a trivariate selection model with selection equations

(17) $Y^*_{ft} = Y_{f,t-1}\beta_f + \varepsilon_f, \quad Y^*_{mt} = Y_{m,t-1}\beta_m + \varepsilon_m, \quad y_{ft} = 1(Y^*_{ft} > 0),$

$y_{mt} = 1(Y^*_{mt} > 0)$

for the female and male members of the couple, respectively, where ε_f and ε_m are assumed to be independent with zero mean and unit variance, and densities $g_f(\varepsilon_f)$ and $g_m(\varepsilon_m)$. The independence assumption could fail if there are hidden common factors in mortality risk for both household members; for example, indirect effects of smoking. However, the frequency of multiple deaths in a household between waves is sufficiently rare in the AHEAD data so that mortality risk interactions are empirically not identified. We distinguish three regimes (y_f, y_m) in which wealth change is observed: intact couples where both members survive (1,1), the female survives the death of her spouse (1,0), and the male survives the death of his

---

22. We find that the coefficients of the index in the mortality model are not sensitive to the Edgeworth generalization, and in estimation of the model for wealth change use the first-stage probit models for mortality estimated earlier, with invariance imposed, to obtain the indices that appear in the selection effects.

spouse $(0,1)$. We will let $Y_t^0 = [Y_{ht-1} Y_{mt-1} y_{ft} \cdot Y_{ft}' y_{mt} \cdot Y_{mt}']$ denote the vector of variables that explain wealth change, where Y_{ht-1}, Y_{ft-1}, and Y_{mt-1} are, respectively, previous wave common, female, and male variables, Y_{ft}' are previously determined components of the current state for females, observed only for survivors and hence zeroed out for nonsurvivors, and Y_{mt}' are the analogous previously determined components of the current state for males, again observed only for survivors. We assume that in an observed regime jk the wealth change model takes the form

$$(18) \quad Y_{wt} = Y_t^0 \beta_{wjk} + (\lambda_f - \theta_f 1(j + k = 1))\varepsilon_f + (\lambda_m - \theta_m 1(j + k = 1))\varepsilon_m + \kappa_{jk}\eta,$$

where η is independent of ε_f and ε_m, with zero mean and unit variance. For intact couples, unobserved dependence of wealth change on selection is reflected in the parameters λ_f and λ_m, a direct extension of the bivariate selection model to the trivariate case with two independent selection effects. For intact couples, the correlations of the disturbances in the selection and wealth change equations are $\rho_f = \lambda_f/(\kappa_{11}^2 + \lambda_f^2 + \lambda_m^2)^{1/2}$ and $\rho_m = \lambda_m/(\kappa_{11}^2 + \lambda_f^2 + \lambda_m^2)^{1/2}$. The coefficients β_{jk} and the standard deviation κ_{jk} are allowed to vary by regime, to capture the observed and unobserved economic effects of a death on valuation and reporting of assets. In addition, the selection effects are allowed to shift, from λ_f to $\lambda_f - \theta_f$ for the female selection disturbance, and from λ_m to $\lambda_m - \theta_m$ for the male selection disturbance. We incorporate these effects to accommodate an apparent interaction in which unexpected survival of a couple (for example, ε_f and ε_m large positive) increases dissaving, perhaps due to additional medical and living expenses linked to overcoming high mortality hazards, but the unexpected death of a spouse (for example, ε_f large negative) also increases dissaving, perhaps because revaluations of assets tend to be more drastic in circumstances where mortality hazard is low.

We adopt the Edgeworth approximation (12) for each of the densities $g_f(\varepsilon_f)$ and $g_m(\varepsilon_m)$. In regime jk with $j + k > 0$, letting $s_f = 2y_f - 1$ and $s_m = 2y_m - 1$, one has

$$(19) \quad E(Y_{wt} | jk) = Y_t^0 \beta_{wjk} + s_f(\lambda_f - y_f \theta_f)$$

$$\cdot \frac{\phi(Y_{f,t-1}\beta_f) + \sum_{j=3}^{4} \gamma_j \Psi_{j1}(-Y_{ft-1}\beta_f)}{\Phi(s_f Y_{f,t-1}\beta_f) + s_f \sum_{j=3}^{4} \gamma_j \Psi_{j0}(-Y_{f,t-1}\beta_f)}$$

$$+ s_m(\lambda_m - Y_m \theta_m)$$

$$\cdot \frac{\phi(Y_{m,t-1}\beta_m) + \sum_{j=3}^{4} \gamma_j \Psi_{j1}(-Y_{m,t-1}\beta_m)}{\Phi(s_m Y_{m,t-1}\beta_m) + s_m \sum_{j=3}^{4} \gamma_j \Psi_{j0}(-Y_{m,t-1}\beta_m)}.$$

As in the case of singles, we estimate the conditional expectation (19) by nonlinear least squares after plugging in estimates of β_f and β_m from the earlier mortality models. A final stage, analogous to (16), regresses the squared residuals from (19) for each regime on an intercept, $E(\varepsilon_f^2 \mid s_f) - (E(\varepsilon_f \mid s_f))^2$, and $E(\varepsilon_m^2 \mid s_m) - (E(\varepsilon_m \mid s_m))^2$; the coefficient on the intercept is an estimate of κ_{jk}^2. Because the number of deaths among couples is relatively small, we impose the constraints $\beta_{w10} = \beta_{w01}$ for empirical identification.

Household income in AHEAD is also susceptible to measurement error, and to minimize its effect, we use income quartiles as explanatory variables. These are obtained by converting all incomes to 1997 dollars, determining the quartiles for the pooled incomes of all subjects in all waves, and using the thresholds thus established to classify each observed subject income. AHEAD respondents rate the safety of their neighborhood and the condition of their dwelling on a five-point scale, from poor to excellent; we use indicators for poor or fair responses.

11.4   Socioeconomic Status and Prevalence of Health Conditions

11.4.1   Descriptive Statistics

We first give some descriptive statistics on the prevalence of health conditions in the AHEAD population. Table 11.4 shows prevalence rates in the AHEAD sample in wave 1, classified by age and sex, for the health conditions listed in table 11.2. Generally, prevalence of health conditions does not show a strong age gradient, indicating broadly that morbidity rates among survivors do not increase much with age. Selection effects from initial noninstitutionalization and from mortality may be responsible. The major exception is cognitive impairment, which rises as age increases. The prevalence of acute and degenerative conditions among survivors fall after about age eighty, reflecting the effect of selection due to deaths from these conditions. Males have higher prevalence of acute and degenerative diseases than do females, but females have higher prevalence of mental and chronic conditions, and accidents.

Figure 11.7 shows the age gradients of wealth, income, and education in wave 1 of the AHEAD sample. These gradients reflect substantial cohort effects, as well as life-cycle and composition effects. Work, income, and asset accumulation patterns of the AHEAD population were impacted by World War II, and those over age eighty experienced the Great Depression during their prime working years. The United States was substantially rural when the AHEAD population was born, and education was truncated for work for many members of this population. In addition to cohort effects, the curve for assets reflects life-cycle decumulation of assets through the retirement years, and the curve for income reflects the rising proportion of widows in the survivors to older ages. There is an additional compositional effect from the association of SES and mortality: Higher SES is selected preferentially among survivors. However, in aggregate cross section, the life-cycle and cohort effects dominate the compositional effects.

Table 11.4   **Prevalence of Health Conditions, by Age and Sex**

	White Females					White Males				
Condition	70–74	75–79	80–84	85–89	90+	70–74	75–79	80–84	85–89	90+
Cancer[a]	0.122	0.137	0.168	0.141	0.127	0.132	0.185	0.202	0.187	0.093
Heart disease[a]	0.244	0.275	0.361	0.339	0.370	0.361	0.390	0.423	0.368	0.296
Stroke[a]	0.051	0.069	0.104	0.121	0.133	0.066	0.12	0.102	0.130	0.148
Lung disease[a]	0.109	0.123	0.108	0.082	0.055	0.151	0.171	0.173	0.093	0.056
Diabetes[a]	0.121	0.097	0.107	0.088	0.055	0.133	0.145	0.112	0.104	0.074
High blood pressure[a]	0.481	0.510	0.537	0.582	0.448	0.433	0.477	0.418	0.321	0.167
Arthritis[b]	0.222	0.285	0.267	0.328	0.254	0.167	0.205	0.196	0.161	0.167
Incontinence[b]	0.228	0.263	0.266	0.331	0.365	0.085	0.138	0.145	0.161	0.259
Fall[b]	0.082	0.096	0.116	0.138	0.133	0.044	0.046	0.048	0.088	0.056
Hip fracture[a]	0.032	0.052	0.079	0.127	0.138	0.020	0.031	0.041	0.067	0.056
Cognitive impairment	0.120	0.149	0.338	0.452	0.635	0.137	0.173	0.291	0.446	0.500
Psychiatric disease[a]	0.149	0.137	0.105	0.082	0.044	0.094	0.092	0.071	0.036	0.056
Depression	0.070	0.117	0.131	0.099	0.116	0.048	0.050	0.071	0.083	0.093
Smoker	0.133	0.095	0.058	0.040	0.017	0.142	0.123	0.082	0.041	0.093
ADL impairment[c]	0.375	0.544	0.829	1.266	2.16	0.285	0.499	0.691	1.114	1.444
IADL impairment[c]	0.293	0.340	0.662	1.099	2.011	0.304	0.422	0.658	0.964	1.426
Self-reported health	0.273	0.348	0.387	0.393	0.42	0.263	0.364	0.437	0.332	0.296

[a]AHEAD 1993 (wave 1) question: "Has a doctor ever told you . . . /Do you have . . . /Have you ever . . . ?."

[b]AHEAD 1993 (wave 1) question: "During the last 12 months, have you . . . ?".

[c]Average number; max(ADL) = 6, max(IADL) = 5.

11.4.2   Models of Association

To examine the association of SES and health conditions, we estimate a series of binomial probit models of the form

$$(20) \qquad P(Y_{it} = 1 \mid Y_{1t}, \ldots, Y_{i-1,t}, W_t, X_t),$$

where the Y_{it} are indicators for the prevalence of various health conditions, W_t denotes a vector of SES conditions, and X_t denotes other demographic variables. The health conditions appear in the same sequence as in table 11.2, with previous conditions in (20) providing information on association among health conditions. Included in W_t are indicators for the top and bottom quartiles of wealth and income, indicators for ten or more years of education (high school) and for fourteen or more years of education (college), and indicators for poor or fair neighborhood safety and dwelling condition.

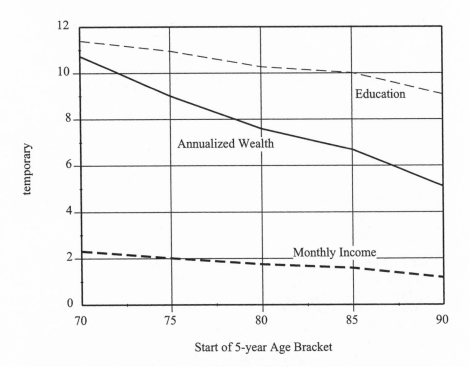

Fig. 11.7   Cohort gradients (education, wealth, and income)

The detailed estimation results can be found at http://elsa.berkeley.edu/
wp/hww/hww202.html. Sample sizes are not adequate for comparable
models for non-whites. We find the expected patterns of comorbidity, with
a strong association of heart disease, stroke, lung disease, and arthritis, and
a strong association of diabetes, heart disease, and high blood pressure. Incontinence is associated with cancer and stroke, and for women with diabetes, high blood pressure, and arthritis. Falls, hip fractures, and strokes
are associated. Psychiatric diseases and depression are associated with
arthritis and falls. BMI is positively associated with diabetes, high blood
pressure, and arthritis, and negatively associated with lung disease. Current smokers have lower BMI, are less likely to have diabetes, and are more
likely to be depressed. Numbers of ADLs and IADLs are positively associated with most acute diseases, arthritis, falls, hip fractures, cognitive impairment, and psychiatric disease. A poor or fair self-reported health status is associated with most acute and chronic diseases, with ADLs and
IADLs, and with depression.

Some covariates are associated with health conditions, and may be risk
factors for these conditions. Widowhood is associated with increased cancer and heart disease for women, increased psychiatric disease for men,
and increased lung disease and depression for both men and women. For

Table 11.5   Summary of Associations of SES and Health Conditions AHEAD Wave 1

SES Association	White Females	White Males
1 percent level	Heart disease, stroke, lung disease, diabetes, cognitive impairment, depression, BMI, IADL impairment, self-reported health status	Lung disease, cognitive impairment, BMI, current smoker, ADL impairment, IADL impairment, self-reported health status
5 percent level	Cancer, HBP, Arthritis	HBP, depression
Not significant	Incontinence, fall, hip fracture, psychiatric condition, current smoker, ADL impairment	Cancer, heart disease, stroke, diabetes, arthritis, incontinence, fall, hip fracture, psychiatric condition

Note: HBP = high blood pressure; BMI = body mass index (high or low); ADL = activities of daily living (impairment requiring assistance with personal care); IADL = instrumental activities of daily living (impairment requiring assistance with household management).

women, father's age at death is associated with heart disease, and mother's age at death is associated with high blood pressure. For men, father's age at death is associated with high blood pressure and arthritis.

We generally find a statistically significant association of SES and prevalence of health conditions, as summarized in table 11.5. It is noteworthy that for males the prevalence of the acute diseases, cancer, heart disease, and stroke are not strongly associated with SES, contrary to literature findings for younger populations. This may be the result of early onset of these diseases, particularly among the poor and among smokers, that selects out of the AHEAD population those males most at risk for these diseases. Overall, wealth is the SES component most commonly associated with health conditions. Education, neighborhood rating, and dwelling rating are occasionally significant, and income is almost never significant. Table 11.6 summarizes the SES components that are individually significant in their association with various health conditions and indicates the sign of the correlation. For a number of these conditions, prevalence rates are insufficient to detect the effects of SES components with satisfactory power. However, for heart disease, high blood pressure, arthritis, cognitive impairment, and self-rated health status, sample sizes should guarantee reliable indicators of association.

11.4.3   Relative Risk

To provide an indication of the direction and magnitude of the association of health conditions and SES, we calculate *relative risk* for low SES versus high SES, where the definition of *low SES* is bottom quartiles for income and wealth, less than a high school education, and a poor/fair neighborhood and dwelling, and the definition of *high SES* is top quartiles for income and wealth, a college education, and a good or better neighborhood and dwelling. Relative risk is defined as the AHEAD sample average of the ratio of the two probabilities, all other variables remaining at the ob-

Table 11.6   **Significant Associations of SES Components and Health Conditions, by Gender**

Condition	Wealth F	Wealth M	Income F	Income M	Education F	Education M	Unsafe Neighborhood F	Unsafe Neighborhood M	Dwelling Poor/Fair F	Dwelling Poor/Fair M
Cancer						↗	↘			
Heart disease	↘↘								↗↗	
Stroke	↘↘				↘↘					
Lung disease		↘								
Diabetes	↘	↘		↘						
HBP										↗↗
Arthritis	↘	↘								
Incontinence							↗		↗	↗↗
Fall	↘						↗			
Hip fracture										
Cognitive impairment	↘↘		↘↘		↘↘	↘↘		↗		↗↗
Psychiatric condition					↘					
Depression				↘	↘				↗↗	
BMI	↘↘				↘↘	↘↘				
Current smoker		↘↘								↗
ADL impairment		↘↘								
IADL impairment	↘↘				↘↘					
Poor/Fair self-rated health	↘↘				↘↘	↘	↗	↗↗	↗↗	↗↗

Notes: The table summarizes 180 two-tailed significance tests, so that if the tests were independent, one would expect about 9 of the 41 significant coefficients at the 5 percent level by chance, and about 2 of the 23 significant coefficients at the 1 percent level by chance.

    ↗ = positive at 5 percent level; ↗↗ = positive at 1 percent level; ↘ = negative at 5 percent level; ↘↘ = negative at 1 percent level. See table 11.5 notes for explanations of abbreviations.

Table 11.7   **Relative Risk of High vs. Low SES for Various Health Conditions, by Gender**

Condition	Relative Risk F	Relative Risk M	Condition	Relative Risk F	Relative Risk M	Condition	Relative Risk F	Relative Risk M
Cancer	1.97	0.98	HBP	0.76**	0.65**	Cognitive impairment	0.53**	0.17**
Heart disease	0.46**	0.75**	Arthritis	0.80	0.60**	Psychiatric	1.14	0.64
Stroke	0.61	0.43**	Incontinence	0.83	0.71	Depression	0.34**	0.21**
Lung disease	0.30**	0.33**	Fall	0.68	0.44**	Smoke now	0.27**	0.23**
Diabetes	0.19**	0.65	Hip fracture	0.82	0.83	Health poor/fair	0.31**	0.34**

Notes: High SES is defined as top quartile in wealth and income, college education, and good neighborhood and welling; low SES is defined as bottom quartile in wealth and income, less than a high school education, and poor neighborhood and welling. Associations in AHEAD wave 1. See table 11A.3 for an pdated version of these results.

**Relative risks that are significantly different from one at the 5 percent level.

served levels for the subjects. Table 11.7 summarizes the relative risks for the various health conditions. Note that the prevalence models are describing only association, not causation, so that relative risk numbers cannot be interpreted causally. With the statistically insignificant exception of cancer and psychiatric conditions for females, high SES is associated with lower prevalence. Thus, we confirm in the AHEAD population the literature findings of a systematic association of SES with mortality and morbidity risk and show that this association extends across a variety of acute, degenerative, chronic, and mental health impairments.

11.5   Incidence of Health Conditions and Tests for Causality in the AHEAD Panel

11.5.1   Models of Incidence

Following the format described in section 11.2, we use the incidence of new health problems (or recurrence of cancer, heart disease, stroke, incontinence, falls, and hip fractures), conditioned on initial demographic, health, and SES status, to test for the absence of direct causal pathways. We define incidence for a group of health conditions to be the occurrence of a condition that was not previously reported, or a recorded reoccurrence in the case of an acute condition (cancer, heart disease, stroke). The descriptive statistics in table 11.2 provide information on rates of incidence of these conditions between waves.[23]

We estimate models for incidence of each health condition, conditioned on previously considered incidences of health conditions, the prevalence of health conditions in the previous wave of the panel, and on SES and demographic variables in the previous wave. The models are binomial probit except for BMI, which is fitted with a linear model using ordinary least squares (OLS), and numbers of ADL and IADL impairments, which are fitted as ordered probits. Detailed parameter estimates can be found at http://elsa.berkeley.edu/wp/hww/hww202.html. Again, the data do not permit the same analysis of nonwhites. The models are estimated by stacking the data for wave 1 to wave 2 transitions above the data for wave 2 to wave 3 transitions. Table 11.8 summarizes the health conditions and covariates that are significant risk factors for the incidence of health conditions. The associations reflect a number of known comorbidities, but show relatively few associations of SES components and incidence of health conditions.

11.5.2   Causality Tests

Figure 11.8 gives the structure of the invariance and causality tests we report. We test only whether the model parameters are invariant between the

---

23. The incidence rates in table 11.2 can be converted to crude annual rates via the formula $0.4706 \cdot \log(1 + \text{rate})$. These rates are uncorrected for population composition effects.

Table 11.8   Statistically Significant Risk Factors for Incidence of Health Conditions

	Health Conditions and Comorbidities		SES Covariates	
Incidence	Female	Male	Female	Male
Cancer	Cancer ($\nearrow$), BMI ($\searrow$),		Ever smoke ($\nearrow$)	
Heart disease	Lung disease ($\nearrow$), diabetes ($\nearrow$), poor/fair self-rated health ($\nearrow$)	Diabetes ($\nearrow$), poor/fair self-rated health ($\nearrow$)		
Stroke	Stroke ($\nearrow$), new heart ($\nearrow$)	Stroke ($\nearrow$), HBP ($\nearrow$), psychiatric ($\nearrow$), new heart ($\nearrow$)	Income ($\nearrow$)	
Mortality	Cancer ($\nearrow$), HBP ($\nearrow$), arthritis ($\searrow$), cognitive impairment ($\nearrow$), BMI ($\searrow$), ADL ($\nearrow$), poor/fair self-rated health ($\nearrow$), new cancer ($\nearrow$), new heart ($\nearrow$), new stroke ($\nearrow$)	Cancer ($\nearrow$), lung ($\nearrow$), diabetes ($\nearrow$), incontinence ($\searrow$), cognitive impairment ($\nearrow$), BMI[a], ADL ($\nearrow$), poor/fair self-rated health ($\nearrow$), new cancer ($\nearrow$), new heart ($\nearrow$), new stroke ($\nearrow$)		Mother's death age ($\searrow$)
Lung disease	Heart ($\nearrow$), current smoker ($\nearrow$), poor/fair self-rated health ($\nearrow$)	Poor/fair self-rated health ($\nearrow$)		Wealth ($\searrow$)
Diabetes	BMI ($\nearrow$)	Lung disease ($\searrow$), BMI ($\nearrow$)	Ever smoke ($\searrow$)	Education ($\searrow$)
HBP	BMI ($\nearrow$), new heart ($\nearrow$), new stroke ($\nearrow$), new diabetes ($\nearrow$)	Heart ($\nearrow$), arthritis ($\nearrow$), new heart ($\nearrow$), new stroke ($\nearrow$)		
Arthritis	Lung ($\nearrow$), depression ($\nearrow$), BMI ($\nearrow$), ADL ($\nearrow$), poor/fair self-rated health ($\nearrow$)	HBP ($\nearrow$), BMI ($\nearrow$)	Education ($\searrow$), mother's death age ($\nearrow$)	
Incontinence	Arthritis ($\nearrow$), incontinence ($\nearrow$), fall ($\nearrow$), BMI ($\nearrow$), ADL ($\nearrow$), IADL ($\nearrow$), new heart ($\nearrow$), new stroke ($\nearrow$), new arthritis ($\nearrow$)	Lung ($\nearrow$), incontinence ($\nearrow$), IADL ($\nearrow$), new stroke ($\nearrow$)		

(*continued*)

Table 11.8   (continued)

Incidence	Health Conditions and Comorbidities		SES Covariates	
	Female	Male	Female	Male
Fall	Fall (↗), hip fracture (↗), cognitive impairment (↗), psychiatric (↗), new incontinence (↗)	Fall (↗), new stroke (↗), new incontinence (↗)		
Hip fracture	Fall (↗), hip fracture (↗), new fall (↗)	Hip fracture (↗), new incontinence (↗)		
Cognitive impairment	New stroke (↗), new hip fracture (↗)	HBP (↘), IADL (↗)	Education (↘)	
Psychiatric	Heart (↗), hip fracture (↘), cognitive impairment (↗), depression (↗), new incontinence (↗), new cognitive impairment (↗),	Arthritis (↗), BMI (↘), new HBP (↗), new incontinence (↗)	Income (↘), widow (↘), divorced/separated (↘)	
Depression	Cancer (↘), heart (↗), poor/fair self-rated health (↗), new arthritis (↗), new incontinence (↗), new psychiatric (↗)	Lung (↗), new incontinence (↗)	Ever smoke (↗)	
Self-rated health	Heart (↗), lung (↗), diabetes (↗), arthritis (↗), cognitive impairment (↗), depression (↗), poor/fair self-rated health (↗), new cancer (↗), new heart (↗), new stroke (↗), new lung (↗), new arthritis (↗), new depression (↗), new ADL (↗)	Heart (↗), lung (↗), HBP (↗), poor/fair self-rated health (↗), new cancer (↗), new heart (↗), new stroke (↗), new lung (↗), new cognitive impairment (↗), new psychiatric (↗), new depression (↗), new BMI (ᵃ), new ADL (↗)	Dwelling poor/fair (↗)	

Notes: One percent significance level. new = incidence since last wave. The table summarizes approximately 1000 tests of individual coefficients, so that if they were independent, one would expect approximately 10 of the listed associations reflect type 1 errors. See table 11.5 for explanations of abbreviations.

[a] Any change in BMI (body mass index), up or down, lowers self-rated health.

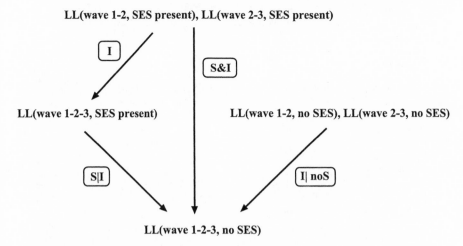

LL(wave 1-2, SES present), LL(wave 2-3, SES present)

I

S&I

LL(wave 1-2-3, SES present)   **LL(wave 1-2, no SES), LL(wave 2-3, no SES)**

S|I   I| noS

LL(wave 1-2-3, no SES)

Fig. 11.8   Invariance and causality tests

Note: LL denotes log likelihood for specified condition, an unconditional invariance test is denoted by "I," a conditional test for no direct SES causality, given invariance, is denoted by "S | I" and a joint test of invariance and no direct SES causality is denoted by "S&I."

wave 1 to 2 transitions and the wave 2 to 3 transitions. We exclude intercepts, age splines, and log of time at risk terms from the invariance test. The reason for doing so is that these terms will capture variations in survey recontact procedure across waves. However, we find in most cases that there is no significant difference in the age spline coefficients across the different transitions. The models are estimated unconstrained, and with the imposition of invariance, noncausality of SES, or both. Likelihood ratio tests are conducted for invariance, with and without noncausality imposed, and for noncausality conditioned on invariance. Because the invariance test without noncausality of SES imposed and the noncausality test conditioned on invariance are nested, they should give the same conclusion, at compatible significance levels, and as a joint test of invariance and noncausality. In accordance with section 11.2, we take acceptance of the joint hypothesis as evidence that there is *not* a direct causal path from SES to incidence of the given health condition and take this as support for the proposition that differential access to medical care and SES-linked environmental hazards are not causing incidence rates to vary with SES.

The test results are given in table 11.9. The columns of numbers in these tables are, respectively, significance levels for the invariance test with SES variables included, the invariance test with SES variables excluded, the noncausality test conditioned on invariance, and the joint test of invariance and noncausality. The final columns in the table give the relative risk for high versus low SES (see section 11.4.3), and the significance level of a *T*-test of the null hypothesis that the relative risk is one.

Table 11.9   Health Innovations, Tests for Invariance and Causality

Condition	Condition occurred previously?	Sex	Significance Levels				Relative Risk	
			Invariance with SES Variables	Invariance w/o SES Variables	No SES Causality, Given Invariance	Joint Invariance and No SES Causality	High vs. Low SES	Significance
Cancer	All	F	0.056	0.023	0.311	0.057	1.260	0.568
	No	F	0.856	0.865	0.315	0.777	1.234	0.633
	Yes	F	0.133	0.335	0.949	0.313	3.729	0.608
	All	M	0.000	0.000	0.225	0.000	0.569	0.045
	No	M	0.122	0.071	0.059	0.044	0.467	0.008
	Yes	M	0.002	0.046	0.021	0.000	14.731	0.645
Heart	All	F	0.000	0.000	0.812	0.000	0.889	0.617
	No	F	0.214	0.075	0.447	0.240	0.814	0.480
	Yes	F	0.690	0.832	0.623	0.744	0.963	0.927
	All	M	0.017	0.020	0.290	0.018	1.321	0.412
	No	M	0.802	0.571	0.007	0.240	1.698	0.350
	Yes	M	0.472	0.601	0.250	0.382	1.225	0.710
Stroke	All	F	0.068	0.034	0.056	0.023	0.765	0.410
	No	F	0.371	0.239	0.104	0.205	0.748	0.413
	Yes	F	NC	0.529	0.597	NC	1.999	0.755
	All	M	0.086	0.042	0.290	0.080	1.179	0.717
	No	M	0.248	0.162	0.641	0.336	0.874	0.756
	Yes	M	NC	0.002	0.200	NC	8.300	0.584
Mortality		F	0.010	0.006	0.812	0.030	0.680	0.122
		M	0.021	0.032	0.228	0.018	1.196	0.664
Lung disease		F	0.493	0.479	0.381	0.470	0.341	0.000
		M	0.603	0.620	0.013	0.174	0.225	0.000
Diabetes		F	0.110	0.177	0.246	0.091	0.847	0.778
		M	0.243	0.199	0.043	0.085	2.649	0.941

HBP	F	0.004	0.009	0.777	0.012	1.109	0.779
	M	0.220	0.121	0.668	0.310	0.886	0.809
Arthritis	F	0.041	0.017	0.042	0.012	1.126	0.623
	M	0.187	0.276	0.145	0.116	0.415	0.000
Incontinence	F	0.357	0.329	0.080	0.183	0.867	0.324
	M	0.161	0.486	0.237	0.129	0.980	0.943
Fall	F	0.864	0.763	0.515	0.861	1.016	0.940
	M	0.402	0.383	0.507	0.438	0.944	0.871
Hip fracture	F	0.604	0.470	0.275	0.520	0.413	0.048
	M	0.056	0.051	0.305	0.055	0.198	0.003
Proxy	F	0.345	0.442	0.250	0.283	0.414	0.000
	M	0.424	0.326	0.019	0.131	0.447	0.001
Cognitive	F	0.020	0.007	0.001	0.000	0.759	0.162
	M	0.429	0.245	0.022	0.140	0.522	0.003
Psychiatric	F	0.075	0.031	0.012	0.012	0.342	0.000
	M	0.194	0.546	0.110	0.108	0.102	0.000
Depression	F	0.299	0.347	0.078	0.151	0.411	0.000
	M	0.767	0.856	0.302	0.695	0.352	0.001
BMI	F	0.419	0.330	0.738	0.531		
	M	0.010	0.002	0.249	0.009		
Smoke now	F	0.509	0.242	0.838	0.650	0.649	0.530
	M	0.366	0.146	0.064	0.182	6.448	0.841
ADL	F	0.010	0.018	0.818	0.027		
	M	0.004	0.044	0.370	0.005		
IADL	F	0.673	0.514	0.368	0.636		
	M	0.016	0.003	0.006	0.002		
Self-rated health	F	0.151	0.111	0.001	0.009	0.670	0.000
	M	0.581	0.570	0.034	0.282	0.656	0.000

Note: See table 11.5 for explanations of abbreviations.

In a majority of cases, our test for invariance is accepted. For cancer and heart disease incidence, it is necessary to separate models for those with and without a previous occurrence of the condition. For females, exceptions where invariance is rejected at the 1 percent level are mortality and ADL count. Exceptions for males are cancer with a previous occurrence, mortality, ADL count, BMI, and IADL count. The failure of the mortality models to satisfy invariance may be related to the initial selection of a noninstitutionalized population in wave 1 of the AHEAD panel. Of course, in addition to the question of the power of our test to detect invariance failures, our single test of invariance across waves falls considerably short of the battery of invariance tests that would be desirable to establish that the model system has the stability and sensitivity required for policy applications.

For females, the tests for noncausality of the SES variables, conditioned on a maintained hypothesis of invariance, are rejected for arthritis and psychiatric disease at the 5 percent level and for cognitive impairment and self-rated health at the 1 percent level. Notably, these are all chronic or mental conditions where Medicare coverage is limited and the cost of drugs or assistance may be substantial. For males, this test for noncausality is rejected for cancer with a previous occurrence, heart disease with no previous occurrence, lung disease, diabetes, cognitive impairment, and self-rated health at the 5 percent level, and for IADL count at the 1 percent level. The results of the joint test for invariance and noncausality are roughly consistent with the separate tests. For conditions such as cancer with a previous occurrence and IADL count for males, cognitive impairment for females, and mortality for both females and males, the noncausality test results may be confounded by the failure of invariance.

The relative risks in table 11.9 should *not* be interpreted causally, since again the cases where noncausality is rejected and the relative risks are substantially different from one may be due to a common unobserved effect rather than a direct causal link. The pattern of fifteen relative risks exceeding one and eighteen less than one suggests no broad linkage between SES and health changes, *given prior health,* and the direct links that may be indicated from the significance levels (lung disease and hip fractures for males and females, some cancers and arthritis for males) appear to be related to specific features of poverty, such as smoking history and poor dwelling environment. There are a few cases where the relative risk for high versus low SES is substantially less than one, irrespective of statistical significance, indicating an unproven link of sufficient magnitude to warrant further investigation: lung disease, hip fracture, and the mental diseases for females, and lung disease, diabetes, arthritis, and the mental diseases for males. Large deviations in relative risk from one that are not statistically significant suggest that acceptance of the joint hypothesis of invariance and noncausality could be due to low power. Notably, death shows no relation to SES, once previous health state is controlled, and the relative risks are insignificantly different from one. This indicates that there are no strong direct causal links from SES to mortality, which at the level of resolution of this study rules out differential access to medical treatment for life-threatening illness. Thus, the association of SES and mortality among the elderly appears to come primarily from variation in the prevalence of health conditions with SES, and more weakly from indirect causal links from SES to incidence of health conditions that increase mortality risk.

The pattern of failures of the noncausality test for mental diseases suggests the possibility of a direct causal link related to differential access. Medicare limits the scope of care for mental conditions, so ability to pay may indeed be an important factor in efficacy of treatments that prevent or control these conditions.

11.6   Tests for Noncausality from Health Status to Asset Accumulation

11.6.1   Models of Incidence

Health may influence asset accumulation of elderly households because of the cost of medical treatment and related services. Medicare covers acute conditions with limited copayments, but there is the possibility of direct effects from uncovered costs of drugs and living assistance. Also, health conditions may limit the consumption of other goods, and because health status is an indicator of longevity, an individual planning consumption and precautionary reserves over remaining life may adjust target wealth based on altered perceptions of longevity and anticipated medical costs; see Alessie, Lusardi, and Kapteyn (2000), Attanasio and Hoynes (2000), Hurd (1987), Hurd and Wise (1989), Hurd and McGarry (1997), Hurd, McFadden, and Gan (1998). These effects could induce an association of SES and health status even if there were no causal links from SES to health. In the elderly AHEAD population, we will not observe the most likely direct causal link from health status to accumulation among workers, the effect of health on current labor market participation and productivity.

We analyze transitions in wealth from wave to wave using the framework of section 11.2 and model (11) for singles and (17) and (18) for couples, with demographics, previous wave health conditions, and current wave incidence of new health conditions as explanatory variables. Statistically significant selection coefficients are consistent with a direct causal link from death to a change in household wealth, but also consistent with ecological factors that induce an association of mortality risk and SES. Total, nonliquid, and liquid wealth are analyzed separately, with transformation (10) applied to each component.

Tables 11A.5, 11A.6, and 11A.7 give the detailed incidence models for total, nonliquid, and liquid wealth change. As in previous studies of savings, we find that most of the variance in wealth changes over the population is not explained by observed economic variables. This remains true after introduction of health conditions. We find dissaving rates out of liquid wealth, before realization of returns calculated from the S&P 500, that are 5.3 percent for couples, 4.8 percent for singles, and 6.0 percent for survivors whose spouses have died. The dissaving rates from nonliquid wealth, again before realization of returns, are, respectively, 6.9 percent, 6.3 percent, and 8.0 percent for intact couples, singles, and survivors. The higher dissaving rates from nonliquid assets indicates that the wealth portfolios of the elderly are rebalanced to become more liquid as they age. These dissaving rates can be compared to an average rate of dissaving of 8.3 percent of remaining wealth in an age seventy-plus population with life-table survival probabilities who consume the expected annuitized value of their wealth.[24] Then, observed dissaving rates out of wealth are not grossly lower than would be expected with pure life-cycle consumption averaging over retirement and full pooling of mortality risk. We find that low income couples and individuals have significantly higher dissaving rates than their high income counterparts, but the differences are not quantitatively large. Home ownership is associated with significantly less dissaving for intact couples.

The models for both singles and couples show significant departures from normality in the selection equations. The Edgeworth expansion parameters show positive skewness and smaller than normal kurtosis for female singles, negative skewness and insignificantly different from normal kurtosis for male singles. For couples, both males and females have negative skewness and larger than normal kurtosis. We also find significant selection effects, with $\rho_f = -0.49$ for couples and -0.21 for singles, and $\rho_m = -0.51$ for couples and -0.89 for singles. These imply that households that survive despite unfavorable mortality risks have increased dissaving, either because of increased cost of overcoming health problems or because households at elevated risk spend down more rapidly. Equation (18) includes shift parameters that modify the dependence of the wealth change disturbance on the unobserved selection effects in regimes where a spouse dies. These are statistically significant, and sufficiently large to reverse the direction of the intact couple selection effects.

Table 11.10 summarizes the health conditions and other covariates that are individually significant in explaining changes in wealth. For intact couples, we find some acute conditions *increase* saving, perhaps because they restrict consumption, or perhaps because couples conserve assets for a potential surviving spouse. For the conditions that are associated with in-

---

24. This calculation is made from the 1996 life tables and assumes the historical S&P rate of return from 1993 to 1997, and a 7 percent real rate of return on assets after 1997.

Table 11.10   **Statistically Significant Risk Factors for Wealth Changes**

Component	Health Conditions	Covariates
Intact couple		
Total wealth	M self-rated health poor/fair ($\nearrow$), M new heart ($\nearrow$), M new hip fracture ($\searrow$), F new cancer ($\nearrow$)	Nonliquid wealth ($\searrow$), liquid wealth ($\searrow$), income ($\nearrow$), homeowner ($\nearrow$)
Nonliquid wealth		Nonliquid wealth ($\searrow$), liquid wealth ($\nearrow$), homeowner ($\nearrow$)
Liquid wealth	M new heart ($\nearrow$), M BMI worse ($\searrow$)	Nonliquid wealth ($\nearrow$), liquid wealth ($\searrow$), income ($\nearrow$), dwelling poor/fair ($\searrow$)
Spouse died		
Total wealth		Nonliquid wealth ($\searrow$), liquid wealth ($\searrow$), income ($\nearrow$)
Nonliquid wealth		Nonliquid wealth ($\searrow$)
Liquid wealth	F new stroke ($\searrow$)	Nonliquid wealth ($\nearrow$), liquid wealth ($\searrow$), income ($\nearrow$)
Single		
Total wealth	M new cancer ($\nearrow$), F new cancer ($\searrow$), F new depression ($\searrow$)	M,F nonliquid wealth ($\searrow$), M,F liquid wealth ($\searrow$), M,F income ($\nearrow$)
Nonliquid wealth	M hip fracture ($\nearrow$), M new cancer ($\nearrow$), M new heart ($\nearrow$)	M,F nonliquid wealth ($\searrow$), M liquid wealth ($\nearrow$), F income ($\nearrow$), F homeowner ($\nearrow$)
Liquid wealth	F cognitive impairment ($\searrow$), F new stroke ($\searrow$), F new cognitive impairment ($\searrow$)	M,F nonliquid wealth ($\nearrow$), M,F liquid wealth ($\searrow$), M,F income ($\nearrow$), F dwelling poor/fair ($\searrow$)

Notes: One percent significance level. M = male; F = female; new = incidence since last wave; $\nearrow$ indicates increased saving; $\searrow$ indicates decreased saving.

creased dissaving (cognitive impairment and stroke for single females), costs of maintenance associated with these conditions may be directly causal to wealth changes.

11.6.2   Causality Tests

Table 11.11 summarizes our tests for invariance and absence of direct causal links. We test for common parameters in the wealth change models between waves 1–2 and waves 2–3, excepting intercepts and age effects to allow for the effects of sample timing. Invariance is convincingly rejected for each demographic group and wealth category, indicating that our model fails to capture the structural determinants of wealth change. As a consequence, our noncausality tests to follow may produce rejections due to model misspecification, confounding the detection of direct causal

Table 11.11   **Wealth Changes, Tests for Invariance and Causality**

| Demographic Group Wealth Component | Invariance | Significance Levels | | |
| | | Noncausality | | |
		Previous Health Conditions	Current Health Conditions	All Health Conditions
Intact couple				
Total wealth	0.000	0.036	0.001	0.000
Nonliquid wealth	0.000	0.014	0.028	0.001
Liquid wealth	0.000	0.006	0.012	0.000
Spouse died				
Total wealth	0.000	0.811	0.776	0.074
Nonliquid wealth	0.000	0.071	0.814	0.037
Liquid wealth	0.000	0.676	0.456	0.023
Single				
Total wealth	0.000	0.004	0.022	0.001
Nonliquid wealth	0.000	0.100	0.347	0.235
Liquid wealth	0.000	0.000	0.028	0.000

links. A deconstruction of the invariance failures, detailed in appendix table 11A.8, shows that for nonliquid and liquid wealth, invariance passes for demographic and health prevalence and incidence variables, but fails for female SES variables, and for all male variables including SES taken together. Thus, there was an unexplained regime shift before and after wave 2 of AHEAD. Possible explanations for this are an interaction between the criterion of noninstitutionalization in the initial panel recruitment and economic behavioral response; a wealth-linked interaction in panel retention; problems in the measurement of wealth in the AHEAD population, which exhibits unexplained mean reversion; or a true behavioral shift with age in a single cohort that is not captured accurately by a model that pools wealth change observations across cohorts.

We expect that terminal medical and burial expenses, estate taxes and other estate settlement costs, insurance payments, and bequests will have a substantial impact on the size of a decedent's estate and surviving spouse's reported wealth. We easily reject the hypothesis that the model coefficients for intact couples and for surviving spouses are the same, but note that measurement problems associated with a change in financially responsible respondent could also produce this rejection.

The hypothesis of no direct causality of health conditions for total wealth changes is rejected at the 1 percent level for intact couples and singles. For nonliquid wealth, the hypothesis is rejected for intact couples, and for liquid wealth, the hypothesis is rejected for all demographic groups.

The failure of the invariance tests, and the possibility of confounding by persistent common factors and selection suggest that conclusions on the health to wealth link be interpreted with caution. Table 11A.9 deconstructs the causality tests and identifies the health conditions and genders responsible for rejections. The pattern of results suggest that if there is indeed a direct causal link, then it is most likely to involve liquid wealth and health conditions that require assisted living.

Table 11A.10 estimates models of income change, given health conditions and other covariates. One would not expect health status to have a significant impact on the incomes of retirees, conditioned on previous wealth, and the empirical results are generally consistent with this expectation. We have not done formal tests of invariance or causality for income. Also included in the state vector Y_t that describes individuals are changes in home ownership status, and dwelling and neighborhood conditions. We estimate incidence models for these components; results are in table 11A.11.

11.7   Simulation of Life Courses under Counterfactual Conditions

11.7.1   The Simulation Experiment

For policy analysis of interventions that alter delivery or cost of medical services, or retirement financing, one would like to trace through the direct and indirect causal links between wealth, health, and mortality. If Markov models of the sort developed in sections 11.2–11.6 satisfy the required invariance properties, then they can be used to simulate the impacts of these interventions on the life courses of a synthetic population. In this section, we develop such a simulation analysis and apply it to illustrative interventions. Because we have not uniformly accepted invariance, and in a number of cases find associations that may be either direct causal links or hidden common factors, this simulation analysis assumes more than our estimates support. It should be interpreted only as an exercise that shows how a model of this general structure might be used in a policy application to unravel the dynamics of comorbidities and forecast condition-specific morbidity and mortality and life expectancy.

We simulate the life courses of a synthetic population in which heads of household are initially aged seventy–seventy-four. To synthesize this population, we start from the 1,612 households in AHEAD wave 1 whose heads are white and aged seventy–seventy-four. Using the SES and demographic variables for each household in this subsample, we make ten Monte Carlo draws from the prevalence models in section 11.4 to create synthetic initial health profiles for the household head, and spouse if present. This gives an initial synthetic sample of 16,120 households. We then create life courses for the members of each household by drawing recursively from the Markov incidence models in sections 11.5 and 11.6, adjusted to annual transitions using (9) to approximate the probabilities of moving to new states.

We first consider a base scenario (S0) in which initial prevalence and incidence transitions are given by our models estimated on the AHEAD data. We note that the simulation outcomes can be expected to differ to some degree from the cross-cohort patterns found in AHEAD, because the distribution of conditions at ages seventy–seventy-four will differ from the distributions of prevalence that actually prevailed for older individuals in AHEAD when they were aged seventy–seventy-four. They should also differ to some degree from the actual experience that the aged seventy–seventy-four cohort in AHEAD will have through the remainder of their lives, because the simulation cannot anticipate the realized future distribution of exogenous variables and because our models do not allow for drift-in disease incidence or condition-specific mortality hazards that will result from changes in medical care. Historically, these drifts have been very significant, reducing morbidities and increasing life expectancies. If these trends continue, then the baseline simulations will underestimate actual survival experience.

We next consider two stylized policy interventions. The first alternative scenario (S1) examines the impact on life courses of the introduction of a hypothetical medical treatment that cures diabetes, for example, by stem cell and immune system therapy that rejuvenates the pancreas for both type I and type II diabetics. In this scenario, we assume that prevalence of diabetes at the start of the simulated panel drops to zero, and that there is zero incidence of this condition as the cohort ages. We do not alter the historical prevalence of conditions associated with diabetes. Thus, we assume that the historical impact on individuals of type I diabetes, notably increased prevalence of heart disease and stroke at ages seventy–seventy-four, is not altered. The second alternative scenario (S2) examines the impact on life courses of reducing the entire population from their current SES to our definition of a low-SES individual: bottom quartile for wealth and income, less than a high school education, and a poor or fair neighborhood and dwelling. This alternative is obviously hypothetical and is not even a stylized approximation to any real policy alternative. However, it provides an extreme in which the interactions of health and SES are permitted maximum play, giving an upper bound on the effect that SES could possibly have on health outcomes, and providing a finger exercise that tests the plausibility of our model system.

11.7.2   Baseline Simulation

Table 11.12 summarizes the survival probabilities and prevalence of health conditions among survivors in the simulated cohort as it ages, under

Table 11.12   **Simulation Outcomes**

		Age					
	Scenario	70	75	80	85	90	95
White females							
Survival probability[a]	S0	1.000	0.905	0.743	0.500	0.240	0.079
	S1	1.000	0.906	0.757	0.517	0.257	0.087
	S2	1.000	0.884	0.662	0.359	0.125	0.027
Cancer[b]	S0	0.112	0.174	0.219	0.245	0.257	0.262
	S1	0.112	0.169	0.217	0.243	0.258	0.252
	S2	0.112	0.208	0.273	0.298	0.302	0.336
Heart disease[b]	S0	0.224	0.322	0.442	0.538	0.588	0.594
	S1	0.224	0.321	0.429	0.515	0.569	0.608
	S2	0.224	0.344	0.495	0.608	0.663	0.679
Stroke[b]	S0	0.042	0.105	0.191	0.272	0.326	0.341
	S1	0.042	0.104	0.186	0.260	0.317	0.351
	S2	0.042	0.105	0.196	0.274	0.320	0.366
Lung disease[b]	S0	0.105	0.151	0.179	0.190	0.168	0.143
	S1	0.105	0.150	0.183	0.190	0.175	0.154
	S2	0.105	0.193	0.258	0.278	0.276	0.286
Diabetes[b]	S0	0.114	0.161	0.198	0.199	0.170	0.157
	S1	0.114	0.000	0.000	0.000	0.000	0.000
	S2	0.114	0.181	0.231	0.233	0.207	0.231
High Blood Pressure[b]	S0	0.467	0.583	0.678	0.738	0.761	0.778
	S1	0.467	0.585	0.678	0.742	0.783	0.804
	S2	0.467	0.597	0.701	0.764	0.786	0.810
Arthritis[b]	S0	0.232	0.501	0.677	0.791	0.857	0.901
	S1	0.232	0.501	0.670	0.784	0.856	0.905
	S2	0.232	0.567	0.769	0.876	0.925	0.965
Incontinence[b]	S0	0.232	0.416	0.601	0.751	0.843	0.891
	S1	0.232	0.427	0.611	0.749	0.844	0.906
	S2	0.232	0.444	0.664	0.814	0.891	0.917
Fall[b]	S0	0.071	0.271	0.464	0.635	0.759	0.837
	S1	0.071	0.268	0.456	0.628	0.754	0.846
	S2	0.071	0.260	0.460	0.640	0.759	0.822
Hip fracture[b]	S0	0.030	0.046	0.070	0.109	0.153	0.215
	S1	0.030	0.043	0.069	0.109	0.156	0.190
	S2	0.030	0.056	0.104	0.160	0.224	0.258
Proxy interview	S0	0.038	0.056	0.103	0.163	0.230	0.294
	S1	0.038	0.063	0.095	0.155	0.222	0.271
	S2	0.038	0.103	0.211	0.316	0.409	0.521
Cognitive impairment[b]	S0	0.104	0.253	0.437	0.609	0.736	0.818
	S1	0.104	0.251	0.435	0.602	0.722	0.803
	S2	0.104	0.405	0.669	0.838	0.910	0.952
Psychiatric disease[b]	S0	0.154	0.215	0.307	0.376	0.421	0.434
	S1	0.154	0.219	0.305	0.379	0.416	0.426
	S2	0.154	0.316	0.508	0.634	0.704	0.762
Depression[b]	S0	0.068	0.183	0.305	0.429	0.515	0.575
	S1	0.068	0.179	0.305	0.424	0.521	0.596
	S2	0.068	0.247	0.434	0.574	0.665	0.749

(continued)

Table 11.12 (continued)

	Scenario	Age					
		70	75	80	85	90	95
Body Mass Index[c]	S0	25.7	24.7	23.6	22.3	21.0	20.5
	S1	25.7	24.7	23.6	22.3	21.1	20.3
	S2	25.7	24.7	23.4	22.2	21.2	20.8
Current smoker[b]	S0	0.128	0.088	0.063	0.043	0.027	0.017
	S1	0.128	0.091	0.063	0.048	0.031	0.016
	S2	0.128	0.109	0.084	0.056	0.039	0.020
ADL limits[c]	S0	0.31	0.27	0.66	1.18	1.68	2.14
	S1	0.31	0.26	0.59	1.08	1.63	1.99
	S2	0.31	0.45	1.21	2.08	2.77	3.33
IADL limits[c]	S0	0.25	0.11	0.29	0.58	0.85	1.14
	S1	0.25	0.10	0.27	0.53	0.81	1.04
	S2	0.25	0.25	0.73	1.34	1.84	2.30
Poor/fair self-rated health[b]	S0	0.254	0.305	0.441	0.540	0.585	0.613
	S1	0.254	0.293	0.416	0.501	0.574	0.582
	S2	0.254	0.507	0.711	0.811	0.841	0.860
White males							
Survival probability[a]	S0	1.000	0.828	0.558	0.279	0.091	0.019
	S1	1.000	0.844	0.586	0.304	0.105	0.025
	S2	1.000	0.827	0.485	0.170	0.032	0.004
Cancer[b]	S0	0.145	0.242	0.320	0.400	0.478	0.514
	S1	0.145	0.248	0.321	0.395	0.482	0.546
	S2	0.145	0.281	0.391	0.479	0.555	0.596
Heart[b]	S0	0.352	0.490	0.611	0.709	0.774	0.733
	S1	0.352	0.488	0.626	0.701	0.752	0.766
	S2	0.352	0.443	0.554	0.627	0.632	0.681
Stroke[b]	S0	0.075	0.140	0.213	0.282	0.317	0.310
	S1	0.075	0.142	0.213	0.287	0.323	0.351
	S2	0.075	0.190	0.317	0.423	0.517	0.596
Lung disease[b]	S0	0.150	0.185	0.205	0.203	0.183	0.152
	S1	0.150	0.184	0.206	0.212	0.200	0.184
	S2	0.150	0.183	0.201	0.195	0.190	0.085
Diabetes[b]	S0	0.135	0.171	0.183	0.190	0.177	0.171
	S1	0.135	0.000	0.000	0.000	0.000	0.000
	S2	0.135	0.135	0.119	0.095	0.085	0.128
High Blood Pressure[b]	S0	0.443	0.553	0.636	0.699	0.719	0.743
	S1	0.443	0.551	0.637	0.702	0.740	0.784
	S2	0.443	0.565	0.643	0.689	0.692	0.638
Arthritis[b]	S0	0.175	0.405	0.582	0.718	0.801	0.848
	S1	0.175	0.419	0.602	0.719	0.792	0.865
	S2	0.175	0.581	0.806	0.913	0.948	0.915
Incontinence[b]	S0	0.097	0.259	0.433	0.603	0.748	0.852
	S1	0.097	0.252	0.414	0.582	0.707	0.840
	S2	0.097	0.309	0.528	0.703	0.849	0.872
Fall[b]	S0	0.041	0.162	0.300	0.435	0.547	0.667
	S1	0.041	0.163	0.292	0.440	0.559	0.681
	S2	0.041	0.214	0.410	0.588	0.728	0.809

Table 11.12   (continued)

		Age					
	Scenario	70	75	80	85	90	95
Hip fracture[b]	S0	0.025	0.032	0.044	0.066	0.119	0.167
	S1	0.025	0.030	0.044	0.068	0.108	0.138
	S2	0.025	0.076	0.147	0.247	0.357	0.447
Proxy Interview	S0	0.111	0.110	0.114	0.125	0.155	0.157
	S1	0.111	0.109	0.120	0.147	0.170	0.170
	S2	0.111	0.223	0.303	0.382	0.429	0.468
Cognitive impairment[b]	S0	0.146	0.326	0.505	0.662	0.768	0.857
	S1	0.146	0.329	0.509	0.657	0.772	0.897
	S2	0.146	0.484	0.743	0.881	0.934	0.936
Psychiatric disease[b]	S0	0.085	0.133	0.186	0.240	0.268	0.291
	S1	0.085	0.135	0.187	0.240	0.263	0.319
	S2	0.085	0.237	0.430	0.557	0.621	0.660
Depression[b]	S0	0.038	0.105	0.184	0.233	0.262	0.281
	S1	0.038	0.110	0.196	0.259	0.263	0.344
	S2	0.038	0.199	0.344	0.421	0.445	0.404
Body Mass Index[c]	S0	26.1	25.5	24.9	24.6	24.4	24.4
	S1	26.1	25.6	25.0	24.7	24.6	24.1
	S2	26.1	24.6	23.6	23.2	23.2	22.9
Current smoker[b]	S0	0.131	0.063	0.035	0.015	0.009	0.005
	S1	0.131	0.061	0.041	0.014	0.003	0.000
	S2	0.131	0.075	0.038	0.013	0.000	0.000
ADL limits[c]	S0	0.33	0.36	0.75	1.33	1.84	2.45
	S1	0.33	0.38	0.79	1.37	1.88	2.46
	S2	0.33	0.94	2.11	3.24	4.15	4.51
IADL limits[c]	S0	0.34	0.16	0.33	0.63	0.94	1.24
	S1	0.34	0.15	0.34	0.64	0.95	1.23
	S2	0.34	0.52	1.22	2.00	2.65	2.85
Poor/fair self-rated health[b]	S0	0.282	0.355	0.445	0.487	0.514	0.543
	S1	0.282	0.352	0.448	0.488	0.482	0.500
	S2	0.282	0.586	0.760	0.818	0.871	0.830

Notes: S0 = baseline; S1 = no diabetes; S2 = all low SES. See table 11.5 for explanation of abbreviations.
[a]Proportion of age 70 population surviving to the specified age.
[b]Proportion of surviving population at specified age who ever had condition.
[c]Mean in surviving population.

the baseline scenario (S0), the no-diabetes scenario (S1), and the low-SES scenario (S2). Keeping in mind that we expect the simulation model to differ from the historical cross-cohort record in AHEAD, the success of this model in plausibly mimicking observed conditions in the AHEAD population can be judged by comparing the results for scenario S0 with life table survival probabilities. Life expectancy for a cohort of white females aged seventy–seventy-four is 13.15 years from the 1996 life tables and 14.36 years in our baseline simulation. The life table probability of survival for fifteen years for the aged seventy–seventy-four cohort is 0.535, while the corresponding survival probability in the simulation model is 0.500. For white males, the life expectancy at age seventy is 11.31 years from the life tables and 10.81 years from the S0 simulation. The fifteen-year survival probability is 0.381 from the life tables and 0.279 from the simulation model. Thus, relative to the life tables, the simulation model underpredicts female mortality and overpredicts male mortality. The comparison of annual mortality rates for white females given in figure 11.5 indicates that actual AHEAD mortality experience was more favorable than the life tables between waves 1 and 2, presumably due to selection in panel recruitment, and very close to the life tables between waves 2 and 3. Then, the baseline simulation appears to reproduce relatively accurately the cross-cohort survival experience in AHEAD. This provides a reality check for the simulation model, but also suggests that if the survival experience of a current cohort differs from the historical cross-cohort pattern, then the simulation model will miss the drift in mortality hazards that a single cohort will face in the future.

A comparison of prevalence rates for various health conditions among survivors of various ages can be made between AHEAD at wave 1, given in table 11.4, and the baseline simulation in table 11.12. There are issues of comparability in the definition of prevalence for some conditions, but the pattern that emerges is that the simulated prevalences are systematically higher than the historical prevalences and increasingly so at older ages. For example, for white females aged eighty–eighty-four, the historical and simulated prevalence rates are 0.168 versus 0.219 for cancer, 0.361 versus 0.442 for heart disease, and 0.338 versus 0.437 for cognitive impairment. One possible explanation for this is that the links from morbidity to mortality are stronger than the mortality model detects, perhaps because of underreporting of health conditions that arise prior to death, so that the simulation model underestimates the selection effect of mortality that reduces prevalence among survivors. A second possible explanation is that there is strong unobserved heterogeneity in susceptibility to various health conditions, so that cumulative prevalence is overestimated by our first-order Markov models which describe prevalence for most conditions as the result of one or more positives in a series of Bernoulli trials. It is possible to test for persistent unobserved heterogeneity by asking whether the frequency of a negative for a condition between waves 1 and 3 of AHEAD is the product of the frequencies of a negative between successive waves. When we do this, we do not find persistent unobserved heterogeneity. However, the power of the test is modest, and it is possible that even a limited degree of persistent unobserved heterogeneity is enough to explain the differences in AHEAD and the simulation.

A comparison is given in table 11.13 between median wealth and income by age in the AHEAD panel and in the baseline simulation. The historical

Table 11.13   **Wealth and Income in AHEAD and in the Baseline Scenario, by Age**

	70–74	75–79	80–84	85–89	90+
AHEAD cross-cohort data					
Total wealth (000)					
1st quartile	64.38	46.92	32.76	14.05	2.17
Median	144.04	112.76	94.35	71.34	40.13
3rd quartile	314.27	242.68	203.20	185.91	117.93
Nonliquid wealth (000)					
1st quartile	47.72	28.20	10.81	0.86	0.00
Median	94.94	80.48	62.01	44.19	5.44
3rd quartile	178.96	151.68	113.88	109.12	65.47
Liquid wealth (000)					
1st quartile	2.18	1.31	0.54	0.33	0.00
Median	26.19	15.97	11.89	9.73	5.40
3rd quartile	98.21	70.93	70.93	55.31	37.83
Income (000)					
1st quartile	14.15	11.97	9.76	8.68	6.74
Median	22.78	19.59	15.26	13.77	9.76
3rd quartile	34.92	31.65	28.06	25.10	15.29
Baseline simulation data					
Total wealth (000)					
1st quartile	56.67	65.69	37.07	16.08	8.22
Median	136.20	121.43	79.94	51.86	41.59
3rd quartile	299.13	206.63	136.38	91.16	74.29
Nonliquid wealth (000)					
1st quartile	42.72	37.39	17.56	2.97	–3.77
Median	91.53	74.34	47.13	29.17	21.21
3rd quartile	171.34	118.09	78.90	55.44	45.07
Liquid wealth (000)					
1st quartile	1.64	19.16	10.91	4.96	3.61
Median	22.79	43.77	31.16	22.01	19.38
3rd quartile	95.90	80.05	58.58	42.39	36.69
Income (000)					
1st quartile	13.56	13.57	11.25	8.62	7.92
Median	21.82	18.19	15.89	13.58	11.92
3rd quartile	34.70	29.58	23.12	17.81	15.85

cross-cohort data shows sharply declining wealth and income with age, and a less liquid portfolio with age, reflecting strong cohort effects as well as life-cycle and selection effects. The simulation results, which exclude cohort effects, nevertheless show even more sharply declining wealth with age and a strong shift toward a more liquid portfolio mix. If the simulation is correctly describing portfolio balance of a single cohort over its life course, then there is a strong cross-cohort effect, with older cohorts starting from retirement portfolios that are more heavily invested in housing equity and other nonliquid forms. The simulated semi-interquartile range is narrower than its historical counterpart, particularly for older households. In the simulation, variability (defined as the ratio of the semi-interquartile range divided by the median) falls with age, whereas in the historical cross-cohort data variability rises with age. This suggests that in addition to cross-cohort effects, that there may be persistent heterogeneity in savings behavior that is not captured in our model.

11.7.3   Alternative Scenarios

Table 11.12 gives the survival probabilities and prevalences of various health conditions under our alternative no-diabetes scenario (S1) and the low-SES scenario (S2). In the no-diabetes simulation, the direct mortality risk from diabetes, and the incidence of comorbidities with diabetes are eliminated, although our simulated population will display elevated prevalence of heart disease and stroke at age seventy among former diabetics. Life expectancy at age seventy under this scenario increases from 14.36 to 14.69 years for females, and from 10.81 to 11.26 years for males. These rates imply in turn that a former diabetic's life expectancy increases by 2.72 years for females and 3.32 years for males. Other health condition prevalences that fall in the absence of diabetes are heart disease, stroke, cognitive impairment, ADL and IADL impairment, and poor/fair self-rated health. While reduction in mortality risk from one source must as a matter of accounting eventually lead to more deaths from competing risks, there are no substantial movements in prevalences of the remaining health conditions.

The alternative low-SES scenario reduces our entire aged seventy simulated population to the bottom quartile for wealth and income, gives them less than a high school education and places them in a dwelling in poor condition in an unsafe neighborhood. They are kept in this low-SES status for the remainder of their lives; that is, there is no opportunity in this simulation for households to escape low SES by a lucky change in wealth or income. However, our population displays the patterns of prevalence of health conditions established in their earlier lives with their historical SES status. This scenario is quite artificial, but it demonstrates the holistic effect on the broad spectrum of health conditions of low SES. Life expectancies at age seventy in this scenario drop dramatically, from 14.36 to 12.27 years for females, and from 10.81 to 9.56 years for males. Prevalences of cancer, heart disease, lung disease, diabetes, arthritis, incontinence, hip fractures, cognitive impairment, psychiatric disease, and depression all increase sharply, as do the number of ADL and IADL impairments. Conditions whose prevalence is not affected substantially by low SES are stroke, high blood pressure, and falls. These results indicate that *if* the associations of SES and incidence of health conditions that we find in AHEAD *were entirely* the result of direct causal links from wealth to health, then the protective effect of the prevailing pattern of higher SES is 1.26–2.08 years of added life expectancy. Thus, our findings that for most health conditions the evidence is against direct causal links from SES to incidence do not appear to rule out a substantial cumulative effect of SES over conditions and time that induce a noticeable SES gradient in mortality. Given our specific findings against direct causal links from SES to incidence of acute conditions and mortality, the most obvious possible source for this gradient are SES-linked differences in genetic susceptibility and behavior.

We have emphasized that our stylized, hypothetical policy intervention and the changes in health they produce over the life course are strictly illustrative and should be interpreted with great caution. These finger exercises *cannot* be used to draw conclusions about any real policy initiatives. This is particularly true since we have included within our model system components that fail the invariance tests that we have emphasized must be met by a valid policy model, and because in many cases our models display *some* wealth or income gradients for incidence that we cannot with our statistical methods identify as the sole result of direct causal links. While most of these effects are not statistically significant, it is possible that in a larger or longer panel with greater statistical power, they will prove to be significant. Then, it is essential to turn to the more advanced statistical methods of Heckman (2001) and others to identify the direct causal components in these incidence associations and improve the models to achieve invariance. Only after this is done, and realistically detailed policy scenarios are considered, could policy makers take our model system seriously as a policy tool. However, we believe that our results do demonstrate that it would be useful for health policy analysis to utilize a system of invariant models with a causal chain structure to simulate policy impacts, in a framework that takes into account indirect impacts, competing hazards, and direct causal links between SES and health. We believe that analysis of the broad sweep of comorbidities and wealth effects over the life course is an important complement to the diseasecentric orientation of many medical and epidemiological studies of health outcomes.

11.8   Summary and Speculations for Further Research

This paper has used innovations in health conditions and in wealth in the AHEAD panel to carry out tests for the absence of direct causal links from SES to health, and from health conditions to wealth. By advancing beyond the detection of association to a framework in which there is some possibility of detecting the absence of causal links, this paper provides a methodology that may be useful in winnowing the list of possible direct causal mechanisms, or delimiting their domain of action. For the AHEAD sample, a panel of U.S. elderly aged seventy and older in 1993, we conclude generally that for mortality and for acute, sudden-onset diseases, the hypothesis of *no* causal link from SES is accepted, and for incidence of mental problems the hypothesis is rejected. The results for chronic and degenerative diseases are mixed. We generally reject the hypothesis of no direct causal link from health conditions to total wealth changes but cannot rule out confounding of the test by invariance failures.

The pattern of results suggests that incidence of acute, sudden onset health conditions, conditioned on existing health conditions, does not exhibit a significant SES gradient, while incidence of some mental, chronic, and degenerative conditions appear to have an association to SES due to some combination of direct causal links and common unobserved behavioral or genetic factors. The results suggest that there may be an SES gradient in seeking treatment for the second class of conditions that may influence detection, or for maintaining preventative regimens that may maintain some conditions below the reporting thresholds. Our findings are not inconsistent with the possibility that for mental and chronic illnesses where the acute care procedures covered by Medicare are often inapplicable, ability to pay may be a causal factor in seeking and receiving treatment. We do not find systematic persuasive associations of health conditions and changes in total wealth, except for surviving spouses. Problems in measuring and modeling wealth changes suggest caution in concluding from these results that there is generally no direct causal link from health conditions to wealth changes.

We emphasize that our results apply only to elderly individuals in the United States, where Medicare and Medicaid programs limit out-of-pocket medical costs, particularly for acute care, and where retired status eliminates a possible direct causal link from health status to ability to work. Further, in an elderly population, common factors may be manifest in prior health conditions and economic status, so they have little impact once incidence is conditioned on prior state. Our results provide no evidence on the nature of the causal links at younger ages, during the stages of life where association of health and wealth is emerging as a consequence of some causal structure.

Future waves of the AHEAD (HRS) panel will allow the hypotheses of invariance and noncausality to be tested with greater power. This will particularly be the case when full tracking of decedents, and determination of cause of death from medical records, become part of the data. It seems likely that some of the associations we have found between changes in health and wealth will survive more detailed analysis, and that suitably defined natural or designed experiments are likely to be needed to fully unravel the causal structure underlying these associations.

The modeling structure used in this paper is parametric, and the high dimensionality of the vector of possible explanatory variables and the relatively limited information contained in binomial outcomes in the AHEAD panel make it difficult to move to a more robust nonparametric analysis.

However, we have been flexible in specifying the variable transformations that appear in our models, and we interpret our analysis as conforming in spirit, if hardly in fact, to a method of sieves approach to nonparametric analysis. One of the major limitations of our models, which would be likely to lead them to fail invariance tests in situations where a sharp test is possible, is that they do not account adequately for the multiple risk structure of health conditions and its implications for the duration patterns that can emerge, particularly over the relatively long intervals between waves. Some outcomes, such as mortality and nonfatal heart disease, are competing risks, while others, like diabetes and heart conditions, are complementary risks. For future research, we are investigating hidden Markov models in which a latent vector of propensities for all health and SES conditions follows a first-order Markov process, conditioned on demographic state, and all possible causal links across the components of this latent vector appear in the model. Given thresholds that trigger observed states, this model provides a consistent but computationally demanding data generation process for the vector of Markov states month-by-month. Within this model, it is possible to carry out joint tests for the absence of classes of causal links. The next wave of this research, incorporating wave 4 of AHEAD, will include full development of flexible multiple-risk duration models.

Appendix

Table 11A.1   Functions Related to Partial Moments of an Edgeworth Expansion

j/k	(0)	(1)	(2)	(3)	(4)
0	$\Phi(-a)$	ϕ	$a\phi + \Phi(-a)$	$(a^2 + 2)\phi$	$(a^3 + 3a)\phi + 3\Phi(-a)$
1	ϕ	$a\phi + \Phi(-a)$	$(a^2 + 2)\phi$	$(a^3 + 3a)\phi + 3\Phi(-a)$	$(a^4 + 4a^3 + 12a)\phi + 12\Phi(-a)$
2	$H_1\phi$	$(aH_1 + 1)\phi$	$(a^2H_1 + 2a)\phi + 2\Phi(-a)$	$(a^3H_1 + 3a^2H_1 + 6a)\phi + 6\Phi(-a)$	$(a^4H_1 + 4a^3H_1 + 12a^2H_1 + 24a)\phi + 24\Phi(-a)$
3	$H_2\phi$	$(aH_2 + 2aH_1 + 2)\phi$	$(a^2H_2 + 2aH_1 + 2)\phi$	$(a^3H_2 + 3a^2H_1 + 6aH_1 + 6)\phi$	$(a^4H_2 + 4a^3H_1 + 12a^2H_1 + 24a)\phi + 24\Phi(-a)$
4	$H_3\phi$	$(aH_3 + H_2)\phi$	$(a^2H_3 + 2aH_2 + 2H_1)\phi$	$(a^3H_3 + 3a^2H_2 + 6aH_2 + 6H_1)\phi$	$(a^4H_3 + 4a^3H_2 + 12a^2H_1 + 24a)\phi + 24\Phi(-a)$
5	$H_4\phi$	$(aH_4 + H_3)\phi$	$(a^2H_4 + 2aH_3 + 2H_2)\phi$	$(a^3H_4 + 3a^2H_3 + 6aH_3 + 6H_2)\phi$	$(a^4H_4 + 4a^3H_2 + 24a^2H_2 + 24H_1)\phi$
6	$H_5\phi$	$(aH_5 + H_4)\phi$	$(a^2H_5 + 2aH_4 + 2H_3)\phi$	$(a^3H_5 + 3a^2H_4 + 6aH_3 + 6H_2)\phi$	$(a^4H_5 + 4a^3H_4 + 24a^2H_3 + 24H_2)\phi$

Note: Let $H_j(\varepsilon)$ denote Hermite polynomials, defined by $H_j(\varepsilon)\phi(\varepsilon) = (-1)^j\phi^{(j)}(\varepsilon)$, where $\phi^{(j)} \equiv d^j\phi/d\varepsilon^j$. This definition implies the recursion $H_j(\varepsilon) = \varepsilon H_{j-1}(\varepsilon) - dH_{j-1}(\varepsilon)/d\varepsilon$ with $H_0(\varepsilon) = 1$ and $H_1(\varepsilon) = \varepsilon$. A useful recursion for computation is $H_j(\varepsilon) = \varepsilon H_{j-1}(\varepsilon) - (j-1)H_{j-2}(\varepsilon)$. Other leading polynomials are $H_2(\varepsilon) = \varepsilon^2 - 1$, $H_3(\varepsilon) = \varepsilon^3 - 3\varepsilon$, $H_4(\varepsilon) = \varepsilon^4 - 6\varepsilon^2 + 3$, $H_5(\varepsilon) = \varepsilon^5 - 10\varepsilon^3 + 15\varepsilon$, and $H_6(\varepsilon) = \varepsilon^6 - 15\varepsilon^4 + 45\varepsilon^2 - 15$. For $j \le k$, repeated integration by parts yields

$$\int_{-\infty}^{\infty} H_j(\varepsilon)H_k(\varepsilon)\phi(\varepsilon)d\varepsilon = (-1)^k\int_{-\infty}^{\infty} H_j(\varepsilon)\phi^{(k)}(\varepsilon)d\varepsilon = (-1)^{k-j}\int_{-\infty}^{\infty} H_j^{(j)}(\varepsilon)\phi^{(k-j)}(\varepsilon)d\varepsilon = (j!)\int_{-\infty}^{\infty} H_{k-j}(\varepsilon)\phi(\varepsilon)d\varepsilon.$$

Then, $\int_{-\infty}^{\infty} H_j(\varepsilon)^2\phi(\varepsilon)d\varepsilon = j!$, and for $j < k$, $\int_{-\infty}^{\infty} H_j(\varepsilon)H_k(\varepsilon)\phi(\varepsilon)d\varepsilon = 0$, since $\int_{-\infty}^{\infty} H_{k-j}(\varepsilon)\phi(\varepsilon)d\varepsilon = (-1)^{k-j}\int_{-\infty}^{\infty} \phi^{(k-j)}(\varepsilon)d\varepsilon = 0$. Define $\Psi_{jk}(a) = \int_{a}^{\infty} \varepsilon^k H_j(\varepsilon)\phi(\varepsilon)d\varepsilon$. One has $\Psi_{00}(a) = \Phi(-a)$, $\Psi_{01}(a) = \phi(a)$, $\Psi_{0k}(a) = a^{k-1}\phi(a) + (k-1)\Psi_{0,k-2}(a)$. For $j > 0$, one has $\Psi_{j0}(a) = \int_{a}^{\infty} H_j(\varepsilon)\phi(\varepsilon)d\varepsilon = \int_{a}^{\infty} (-1)^j\phi^{(j)}(\varepsilon)d\varepsilon = -(-1)^j\phi^{(j-1)}(a) = H_{j-1}(a)\phi(a)$. Integration by parts for $k > 0$ gives $\Psi_{jk}(a) = \int_{a}^{\infty} \varepsilon^k(-1)^j\phi^{(j)}(\varepsilon)d\varepsilon = -a^k(-1)^j\phi^{(j-1)}(a) - k\int_{a}^{\infty} \varepsilon^{k-1}(-1)^j\phi^{(j-1)}(\varepsilon)d\varepsilon = a^k H_{j-1}(a)\phi(a) + k\Psi_{j-1,k-1}(a)$. The table below gives $\Psi_{jk}(a)$ for $k \le 4$ and $j \le 6$. An expansion $f(\varepsilon) = \sum_{j=0}^{J} \gamma_j H_j(\varepsilon)\phi(\varepsilon)$ satisfies $\int_{-\infty}^{\infty} \varepsilon^k f(\varepsilon)d\varepsilon = \sum_{j=0}^{J} \gamma_j \Psi_{jk}(a)$. Then, $\int_{-\infty}^{\infty} f(\varepsilon)d\varepsilon = \gamma_0$, $\int_{-\infty}^{\infty} \varepsilon f(\varepsilon)d\varepsilon = \gamma_1$, $\int_{-\infty}^{\infty} \varepsilon^2 f(\varepsilon)d\varepsilon = \gamma_0 + 2\gamma_2$, $\int_{-\infty}^{\infty} \varepsilon^3 f(\varepsilon)d\varepsilon = 3\gamma_1 + 6\gamma_3$, and $\int_{-\infty}^{\infty} \varepsilon^4 f(\varepsilon)d\varepsilon = 3\gamma_0 + 12\gamma_2 + 24\gamma_4$. When $J = 4$, $\gamma_0 = 1$, and $\gamma_1 = \gamma_2 = \gamma_3 = 0$, a sufficient condition for f to be positive is $0 \le \gamma_4 < 1/6$.

The appendix tables published in this chapter are an *updated* version of those originally cited in the 2003 *Journal of Econometrics* article. As such, some of the numerical results reported in the paper do not directly match those presented in the appendix as published in this chapter. The original appendix containing detailed parameter estimates can be found at http://elsa.berkeley.edu/wp/hww/hww202.html.

Table 11A.2   Transformed Variables

	Wave 1–2				Wave 2–3			
	Variable	N	Mean	SD	Variable	N	Mean	SD
Demographic/SES variables			*Females*					
1st quartile income indicator	XQ1I1	3,992	0.0655	0.1068	XQ1I2	3,580	0.0613	0.1043
4th quartile income indicator	XQ4I1	3,992	0.0385	0.0825	XQ4I2	3,578	0.0339	0.0771
Neighborhood safety poor/fair	XHOODPF1	3,992	0.0366	0.0859	XHOODPF2	3,580	0.0324	0.0814
House condition poor/fair	XCONDPF1	3,992	0.0361	0.0858	XCONDPF2	3,580	0.0334	0.0827
Own residence?	XDNHOUS1	3,992	0.1306	0.1150	XDNHOUS2	3,578	0.1209	0.1139
Educ > 10 yrs indicator	XHS1	3,992	0.1270	0.1147	XHS2	3,578	0.1218	0.1135
Educ > 14 yrs indicator	XCOLL1	3,992	0.0222	0.0665	XCOLL2	3,580	0.0201	0.0626
	XAS701S	3,992	23.2281	18.2049	XAS702S	3,578	26.2357	18.1556
	XAS801S	3,992	5.4289	10.3034	XAS802S	3,579	6.6345	11.1556
Never married?	XNEVMARR1	3,992	0.0082	0.0434	XNEVMARR2	3,580	0.0076	0.0413
Widow?	XWIDOW1	3,992	0.1297	0.1180	XWIDOW2	3,579	0.1309	0.1168
Divorced/Separated?	XDIVSEP1	3,992	0.0135	0.0550	XDIVSEP2	3,580	0.0133	0.0547
Mother's death age	XMAGEDI1	3,992	16.0466	5.7117	XMAGEDI2	3,578	15.4259	6.2546
Father's death age	XPAGEDI1	3,992	15.6112	5.3007	XPAGEDI2	3,578	15.0117	5.8754
Ever smoke?	XSMOKEV1	3,992	0.0814	0.1115	XSMOKEV2	3,579	0.0778	0.1096
Health condition prevalence								
Cancer[a]	XCANCER1	3,992	0.0274	0.0754	XCANCER2	3,579	0.0284	0.0760
Heart attack/Condition[a]	XHEART1	3,992	0.0657	0.1057	XHEART2	3,579	0.0698	0.1072
Stroke[a]	XSTROKE1	3,992	0.0186	0.0636	XSTROKE2	3,580	0.0209	0.0667
Lung disease[a]	XLUNG1	3,992	0.0225	0.0694	XLUNG2	3,580	0.0211	0.0672
Diabetes[a]	XDIABET1	3,992	0.0300	0.0787	XDIABET2	3,580	0.0331	0.0819
HBP[a]	XHIGHBP1	3,992	0.1209	0.1177	XHIGHBP2	3,580	0.1195	0.1167

(*continued*)

Table 11A.2 (continued)

	Wave 1–2				Wave 2–3			
	Variable	N	Mean	SD	Variable	N	Mean	SD
Arthritis[a]	XARTHRT1	3,992	0.0672	0.1064	XARTHRT2	3,580	0.0690	0.1067
Incontinence in last 12 months[a]	XINCONT1	3,992	0.0536	0.0984	XINCONT2	3,579	0.0729	0.1073
Fall requiring treatment[a]	XFALL1	3,992	0.0210	0.0669	XFALL2	3,580	0.0434	0.0903
Hip fracture[a]	XHIPFRC1	3,992	0.0133	0.0545	XHIPFRC2	3,580	0.0149	0.0570
Proxy interview	XPROXYW1	3,992	0.0197	0.0652	XPROXYW2	3,580	0.0274	0.0755
Cognitive impairment	XCOGIM1	3,992	0.0604	0.1033	XCOGIM2	3,580	0.0785	0.1109
Psychiatric problems[a]	XPSYCH1	3,992	0.0275	0.0755	XPSYCH2	3,580	0.0320	0.0806
Depression	XDEPRES1	3,992	0.0263	0.0745	XDEPRES2	3,580	0.0226	0.0693
Low BMI	XLOBMI1	3,992	0.0445	0.1704	XLOBMI2	3,579	0.0557	0.2012
High BMI	XHIBMI1	3,983	0.4588	0.7938	XHIBMI2	3,578	0.4180	0.7682
Current smoker	XSMOKNOW1	3,992	0.0186	0.0635	XSMOKNOW2	3,580	0.0154	0.0583
No. of ADLs	XNUMADL1	3,992	0.1836	0.3375	XNUMADL2	3,580	0.1884	0.3572
No. of ADLs	XNUMIADL1	3,992	0.1473	0.2755	XNUMIADL2	3,580	0.1202	0.2619
Fair/Poor self-reported health	XDHLTH1	3,992	0.0865	0.1143	XDHLTH2	3,580	0.0832	0.1125
Health condition incidence								
Cancer[a]	XJCANCER2	3,951	0.0094	0.0459	XJCANCER3	3,547	0.0092	0.0449
Heart attack/Condition[a]	XJHEART2	3,951	0.0292	0.0780	XJHEART3	3,548	0.0316	0.0801
Stroke[a]	XJSTROKE2	3,951	0.0126	0.0533	XJSTROKE3	3,548	0.0154	0.0578
Lung disease[a]	XILUNG2	3,951	0.0050	0.0339	XILUNG3	3,548	0.0068	0.0393
Diabetes[a]	XIDIABET2	3,580	0.0054	0.0352	XIDIABET3	3,090	0.0052	0.0345
HBP[a]	XIHIGHBP2	3,580	0.0120	0.0513	XIHIGHBP3	3,090	0.0119	0.0512
Arthritis[a]	XIARTHRT2	3,580	0.0274	0.0758	XIARTHRT3	3,090	0.0244	0.0708

Variable	Code	N			Code	N		
Incontinence *in last 12 months*[a]	XJINCONT2	3,951	0.0588	0.1015	XJINCONT3	3,547	0.0631	0.1029
Fall requiring treatment[a]	XJFALL2	3,951	0.0340	0.0826	XJFALL3	3,548	0.0362	0.0845
Hip fracture[a]	XJHIPFRC2	3,951	0.0066	0.0389	XJHIPFRC3	3,548	0.0074	0.0409
Proxy interview	XPROXYW2	3,580	0.0279	0.0762	XPROXYW3	3,090	0.0331	0.0819
Cognitive impairment	XICOGIM2	3,992	0.0233	0.0705	XICOGIM3	3,580	0.0174	0.0611
Psychiatric problems[a]	XIPSYCH2	3,580	0.0114	0.0506	XIPSYCH3	3,090	0.0096	0.0464
Depression	XIDEPRES2	3,580	0.0131	0.0539	XIDEPRES3	3,090	0.0151	0.0575
BMI better Indicator	XBMIBT2	3,992	0.0402	0.0889	XBMIBT3	3,580	0.0378	0.0863
BMI worse Indicator	XBMIWS2	3,992	0.0341	0.0829	XBMIWS3	3,579	0.0360	0.0844
Current smoker	XSMOKNOW2	3,580	0.0154	0.0582	XSMOKNOW3	3,090	0.0127	0.0531
No. of ADLs	XNUMADL2	3,951	0.2544	0.4351	XNUMADL3	3,548	0.2994	0.4731
No. of ADLs	XNUMIADL2	3,951	0.1760	0.3337	XNUMIADL3	3,548	0.2038	0.3522
Fair/Poor self-reported health	XDHLTH2	3,580	0.0846	0.1135	XDHLTH3	3,089	0.0948	0.1149

Males

Demographic/SES variables

Variable	Code	N			Code	N		
1st quartile income indicator	XQ1I1	2,497	0.0525	0.0988	XQ1I2	2,161	0.0529	0.0992
4th quartile income indicator	XQ4I1	2,497	0.0419	0.0830	XQ4I2	2,158	0.0355	0.0764
Neighborhood safety poor/fair	XHOODPF1	2,497	0.0310	0.0797	XHOODPF2	2,161	0.0294	0.0777
House condition poor/fair	XCONDPF1	2,497	0.0318	0.0810	XCONDPF2	2,161	0.0297	0.0783
Own residence?	XDNHOUS1	2,497	0.1430	0.1087	XDNHOUS2	2,158	0.1323	0.1089
Educ > 10 yrs indicator	XHS1	2,497	0.1126	0.1111	XHS2	2,158	0.1065	0.1091
Educ > 14 yrs indicator	XCOLL1	2,497	0.0267	0.0695	XCOLL2	2,158	0.0233	0.0642
	XAS701S	2,497	19.4711	16.6014	XAS702S	2,158	21.5620	16.5232
	XAS801S	2,497	3.8552	8.2739	XAS802S	2,160	4.5202	8.8800
Never married?	XNEVMARR1	2,497	0.0055	0.0349	XNEVMARR2	2,161	0.0048	0.0330
Widow?	XWIDOW1	2,497	0.0399	0.0882	XWIDOW2	2,161	0.0426	0.0895

(continued)

Table 11A.2 (continued)

	Wave 1–2				Wave 2–3			
	Variable	N	Mean	SD	Variable	N	Mean	SD
Divorced/Separated?	XDIVSEP1	2,497	0.0104	0.0486	XDIVSEP2	2,159	0.0102	0.0478
Mother's death age	XMAGEDI1	2,497	15.1925	6.3133	XMAGEDI2	2,158	14.4231	6.8565
Father's death age	XPAGEDI1	2,497	14.7368	6.0174	XPAGEDI2	2,158	13.9436	6.5630
Ever smoke?	XSMOKEV1	2,497	0.1589	0.1064	XSMOKEV2	2,159	0.1496	0.1077
Health condition prevalence								
Cancer[a]	XCANCER1	2,497	0.0306	0.0779	XCANCER2	2,161	0.0333	0.0801
Heart attack/Condition[a]	XHEART1	2,497	0.0740	0.1072	XHEART2	2,160	0.0748	0.1068
Stroke[a]	XSTROKE1	2,497	0.0214	0.0674	XSTROKE2	2,161	0.0231	0.0692
Lung disease[a]	XLUNG1	2,497	0.0308	0.0792	XLUNG2	2,161	0.0284	0.0759
Diabetes[a]	XDIABET1	2,497	0.0290	0.0765	XDIABET2	2,161	0.0298	0.0772
HBP[a]	XHIGHBP1	2,497	0.0916	0.1127	XHIGHBP2	2,160	0.0927	0.1117
Arthritis[a]	XARTHRT1	2,497	0.0457	0.0927	XARTHRT2	2,161	0.0442	0.0911
Incontinence *in last 12 months*[a]	XINCONT1	2,497	0.0273	0.0744	XINCONT2	2,159	0.0433	0.0891
Fall requiring treatment[a]	XFALL1	2,497	0.0119	0.0510	XFALL2	2,160	0.0218	0.0671
Hip fracture[a]	XHIPFRC1	2,497	0.0079	0.0424	XHIPFRC2	2,161	0.0090	0.0450
Proxy interview	XPROXYW1	2,497	0.0293	0.0778	XPROXYW2	2,161	0.0325	0.0810
Cognitive impairment	XCOGIM1	2,497	0.0545	0.0995	XCOGIM2	2,160	0.0705	0.1069
Psychiatric problems[a]	XPSYCH1	2,497	0.0179	0.0622	XPSYCH2	2,161	0.0210	0.0668
Depression	XDEPRES1	2,497	0.0168	0.0609	XDEPRES2	2,161	0.0136	0.0548
Low BMI	XLOBMI1	2,492	0.0179	0.1042	XLOBMI2	2,161	0.0214	0.1199
High BMI	XHIBMI1	2,492	0.3524	0.6063	XHIBMI2	2,160	0.3318	0.6056
Current smoker	XSMOKNOW1	2,497	0.0283	0.0762	XSMOKNOW2	2,161	0.0196	0.0645

	Variable	N	Mean	SD	Variable	N	Mean	SD
No. of ADLs	XNUMADL1	2,497	0.1310	0.2918	XNUMADL	2,160	0.1323	0.3130
No. of ADLs	XNUMIADL1	2,497	0.1253	0.2654	XNUMIADL2	2,161	0.0860	0.2264
Fair/Poor self-reported health	XDHLTH1	2,497	0.0804	0.1113	XDHLTH2	2,161	0.0768	0.1091
Health condition incidence								
Cancer[a]	XJCANCER2	2,481	0.0162	0.0591	XJCANCER3	2,137	0.0160	0.0588
Heart attack/Condition[a]	XJHEART2	2,481	0.0291	0.0769	XJHEART3	2,137	0.0347	0.0821
Stroke[a]	XJSTROKE2	2,481	0.0125	0.0524	XJSTROKE3	2,137	0.0141	0.0552
Lung disease[a]	XILUNG2	2,481	0.0061	0.0373	XILUNG3	2,137	0.0074	0.0408
Diabetes[a]	XIDIABET2	2,162	0.0047	0.0323	XIDIABET3	1,781	0.0053	0.0341
HBP[a]	XIHIGHBP2	2,162	0.0103	0.0470	XIHIGHBP3	1,781	0.0099	0.0463
Arthritis[a]	XIARTHRT2	2,162	0.0202	0.0655	XIARTHRT3	1,780	0.0211	0.0649
Incontinence in last 12 months[a]	XJINCONT2	2,481	0.0378	0.0854	XJINCONT3	2,135	0.0398	0.0865
Fall requiring treatment[a]	XJFALL2	2,481	0.0185	0.0629	XJFALL3	2,135	0.0191	0.0629
Hip fracture[a]	XJHIPFRC2	2,481	0.0033	0.0280	XJHIPFRC3	2,137	0.0029	0.0256
Proxy interview	XPROXYW2	2,162	0.0329	0.0817	XPROXYW3	1,781	0.0342	0.0825
Cognitive impairment	XICOGIM2	2,497	0.0228	0.0690	XICOGIM3	2,161	0.0171	0.0596
Psychiatric problems[a]	XIPSYCH2	2,162	0.0087	0.0444	XIPSYCH3	1,781	0.0065	0.0383
Depression	XIDEPRES2	2,162	0.0086	0.0442	XIDEPRES3	1,780	0.0111	0.0492
BMI better Indicator	XBMIBT2	2,497	0.0355	0.0833	XBMIBT3	2,161	0.0316	0.0788
BMI worse Indicator	XBMIWS2	2,497	0.0300	0.0781	XBMIWS3	2,161	0.0282	0.0748
Current smoker	XSMOKNOW2	2,162	0.0204	0.0660	XSMOKNOW3	1,780	0.0169	0.0603
No. of ADLs	XNUMADL2	2,481	0.2103	0.4204	XNUMADL3	2,136	0.2252	0.4362
No. of ADLs	XNUMIADL2	2,481	0.1463	0.3154	XNUMIADL3	2,137	0.1594	0.3159
Fair/Poor self-reported health	XDHLTH2	2,162	0.0790	0.1106	XDHLTH3	1,780	0.0883	0.1115

Notes: N = number of observations; SD = standard deviation. See table 11.5 for explanations of abbreviations.

Table 11A.3   Prevalence Regressions—Causality Tests and Relative Odds

| | No. of Observations | | Noncausality | | Relative Odds (high vs. low SES) | | | |
| | | | | | Female | | Male | |
Variable	Female	Male	Female (p-value)	Male (p-value)	Odds	SE	Odds	SE
CANCER	3,153	2,028	0.0148	0.1963	1.92	0.59	0.97	0.28
HEART	3,153	2,028	0.0000	0.0971	0.46**	0.07	0.74**	0.10
STROKE	3,153	2,028	0.0061	0.4981	0.70	0.23	0.41**	0.15
LUNG	3,153	2,028	0.0005	0.0007	0.31**	0.10	0.42**	0.12
DIABETES	3,153	2,028	0.0000	0.4123	0.19**	0.07	0.61	0.21
HIGH BLOOD PRESSURE	3,153	2,028	0.1024	0.0153	0.82**	0.08	0.63**	0.08
ARTHRITIS	3,153	2,028	0.0076	0.0770	0.76**	0.12	0.61**	0.15
INCONTINENCE	3,153	2,028	0.0114	0.2886	0.87	0.14	0.77	0.24
FALL	3,153	2,028	0.0034	0.1508	0.60**	0.17	0.43**	0.25
HIP FRACTURE	3,153	2,028	0.7840	0.5262	0.70	0.28	0.81	0.63
PROXY INTERVIEW	3,153	2,028	0.0000	0.0000	0.90	0.44	0.16**	0.06
COGNITIVE IMPAIRMENT	3,153	2,028	0.0000	0.0000	0.55**	0.09	0.14**	0.04
PSYCHIATRIC	3,153	2,028	0.2938	0.3554	1.16	0.31	0.56	0.23
DEPRESSION	3,153	2,028	0.0000	0.0098	0.36**	0.11	0.19**	0.10
BODY MASS INDEX	—	—	0.0000	0.0122				
CURRENT SMOKER	3,145	2,027	0.0591	0.0001	0.21**	0.27	0.23**	0.09
ACTIVITIES DAILY LIVING	—	—	0.4505	0.0008	—	—	—	—
INSTRUMENTAL ACTIVITIES DAILY LIVING	—	—	0.0000	0.0092	—	—	—	—
SELF REPORTED HEALTH	3,147	2,027	0.0000	0.0000	0.32**	0.05	0.37**	0.06

Note: SE = standard error.

**Relative risks that are significantly different from one at the 5 percent level.

Table 11A.4   Incidence Regressions—Tests (*p*-values)

| | Invariance | | | |
| | With SES | | Without SES | |
Variable	Female	Male	Female	Male
CANCER	0.5275	0.0155	0.3088	0.0071
CANCER—no previous	0.8573	0.1291	0.8116	0.0639
CANCER—previous	0.0682	0.0443	0.0789	0.0835
HEART	0.0854	0.6901	0.0517	0.6188
HEART—no previous	0.1704	0.8228	0.0604	0.4982
HEART—previous	0.5468	0.6925	0.4918	0.7248
STROKE	0.3842	0.2036	0.2663	0.1351
STROKE—no previous	0.1719	0.2584	0.1603	0.1799
STROKE—previous	0.9073	0.0448	0.7838	0.0866
MORTALITY	0.2212	0.3777	0.3153	0.4915
LUNG	0.5518	0.6892	0.4825	0.5021
DIABETES	0.1893	0.2340	0.2810	0.1282
HIGH BLOOD PRESSURE	0.0066	0.3934	0.0244	0.1718
ARTHRITIS	0.0461	0.0709	0.0319	0.1665
INCONTINENCE	0.7809	0.3505	0.5968	0.6817
INCONTINENCE—no previous	0.7057	0.1019	0.4261	0.5548
INCONTINENCE—previous	0.9620	0.7931	0.8921	0.7303
FALL	0.9035	0.2626	0.7904	0.2072
FALL—no previous	0.7918	0.1401	0.6119	0.1332
FALL—previous	0.3649	0.0000	0.3576	0.0000
HIP FRACTURE	0.4915	0.1261	0.2803	0.0530
HIP FRACTURE—no previous	0.9297	0.2997	0.7237	0.1227
PROXY INTERVIEW	0.3008	0.5908	0.4646	0.3777
PROXY INTERVIEW—no previous	0.1275	0.7948	0.4442	0.6064
COGNITIVE IMPAIRMENT	0.0053	0.2878	0.0083	0.1425
PSYCHIATRIC	0.1266	0.2949	0.0516	0.3647
DEPRESSION	0.2109	0.9437	0.2989	0.9343
BODY MASS INDEX	0.2599	0.0089	0.2511	0.0020
CURRENT SMOKER	0.4203	0.7097	0.2140	0.5042
CURRENT SMOKER—no previous	0.1331	0.0328	0.0783	0.0401
CURRENT SMOKER—previous	0.7966		0.7332	
ACTIVITIES DAILY LIVING	0.0010	0.0211	0.0069	0.0377
INSTRUMENTAL ACTIVITIES DAILY LIVING	0.6031	0.0077	0.3883	0.0027
SELF RATED HEALTH	0.3761	0.6342	0.3408	0.6065
SELF RATED HEALTH—no previous	0.5144	0.2515	0.5578	0.2151
SELF RATED HEALTH—previous	0.2395	0.1652	0.1763	0.1886

(*continued*)

	Noncausality					
	Wave 1–2		Wave 2–3		Wave 1–3	
	Female	Male	Female	Male	Female	Male
CANCER	0.9874	0.5883	0.4080	0.1653	0.6133	0.1980
CANCER—no previous	0.7038	0.6584	0.2886	0.1730	0.3130	0.1658
CANCER—previous	0.1428	0.2277	0.4719	0.0168	0.2989	0.0359
HEART	0.5398	0.0538	0.3963	0.9964	0.3978	0.2430
HEART—no previous	0.8722	0.3444	0.7495	0.4118	0.7360	0.0393
HEART—previous	0.1040	0.0707	0.1533	0.7372	0.0192	0.1716
STROKE	0.7567	0.8367	0.5845	0.0278	0.6573	0.0593
STROKE—no previous	0.4147	0.9546	0.6708	0.0639	0.7128	0.2035
STROKE—previous	0.8239	0.3012	0.8819	0.1548	0.7986	0.3827
MORTALITY	0.0980	0.2753	0.8830	0.3056	0.6516	0.3636
LUNG	0.1657	0.1739	0.8663	0.1224	0.3431	0.0097
DIABETES	0.6152	0.1413	0.0197	0.2361	0.1096	0.0250
HIGH BLOOD PRESSURE	0.3422	0.9956	0.0831	0.9409	0.5339	0.9897
ARTHRITIS	0.1786	0.0285	0.2423	0.7129	0.0848	0.3947
INCONTINENCE	0.7627	0.0191	0.2536	0.7999	0.1628	0.4632
INCONTINENCE—no previous	0.9140	0.0369	0.6018	0.1970	0.4530	0.6408
INCONTINENCE—previous	0.8996	0.2471	0.1675	0.6643	0.1490	0.2440
FALL	0.5325	0.6875	0.953	0.4539	0.6003	0.5918
FALL—no previous	0.5015	0.6973	0.9435	0.2509	0.5576	0.5321
FALL—previous	0.3286	0.0000	0.8034	0.0000	0.6959	0.0529
HIP FRACTURE	0.6125	0.5974	0.3700	0.6656	0.1586	0.4304
HIP FRACTURE—no previous	0.4606	0.4610	0.7058	0.7249	0.1277	0.2344
PROXY INTERVIEW	0.0172	0.4856	0.8700	0.1267	0.2540	0.0317
PROXY INTERVIEW—no previous	0.0016	0.7935	0.5408	0.1207	0.0874	0.0732
COGNITIVE IMPAIRMENT	0.0007	0.2587	0.2591	0.1995	0.0016	0.0262
PSYCHIATRIC	0.0428	0.2376	0.2138	0.0685	0.0036	0.0649
DEPRESSION	0.0071	0.1433	0.2605	0.3770	0.0113	0.0653
BODY MASS INDEX	0.1876	0.8388	0.9308	0.7108	0.6729	0.6640
CURRENT SMOKER	0.6031	0.2821	0.9741	0.6927	0.6251	0.1286
CURRENT SMOKER—no previous	0.3355	0.1965	0.8744	0.9802	0.5148	0.9615
CURRENT SMOKER—previous	0.3750	0.3248	0.5473	0.3248	0.2736	0.0249
ACTIVITIES DAILY LIVING	0.0771	0.0137	0.3460	0.9714	0.8278	0.3577
INSTRUMENTAL ACTIVITIES						
DAILY LIVING	0.3738	0.0510	0.8166	0.2426	0.2408	0.0085
SELF RATED HEALTH	0.0133	0.0476	0.0996	0.3006	0.0013	0.0204
SELF RATED HEALTH—no previous	0.0149	0.1874	0.2022	0.1210	0.0071	0.0337
SELF RATED HEALTH—previous	0.2250	0.1955	0.5565	0.2555	0.1934	0.1752

Table 11A.4 (continued)

| | Joint (Invariance + Noncausality) | | Relative Odds (high vs. low SES) | | | |
| | | | Female | | Male | |
	Female	Male	Odds	SE	Odds	SE
CANCER	0.5999	0.0124	1.3099	0.4606	0.7316	0.2699
CANCER—no previous	0.7778	0.0844	1.2423	0.4835	0.6733	0.2934
CANCER—previous	0.0666	0.0110	5.8494	7.7533	2.6866	3.4206
HEART	0.0986	0.5708	0.9739	0.2107	1.0196	0.2379
HEART—no previous	0.2780	0.4464	0.8190	0.2525	1.3003	0.5022
HEART—previous	0.1686	0.5161	1.1323	0.3180	0.8778	0.2629
STROKE	0.4812	0.0800	0.7308	0.2537	0.9363	0.3517
STROKE—no previous	0.2711	0.1893	0.6787	0.2666	0.8182	0.3603
STROKE—previous	0.9477	0.0537	1.1538	0.9298	1.6050	1.2472
MORTALITY	0.3076	0.3596	0.6881	0.2069	1.1677	0.4066
LUNG	0.5039	0.2032	0.3272	0.1731	0.5043	0.4315
DIABETES	0.1013	0.0622	0.6932	0.4119	1.4837	3.1948
HIGH BLOOD PRESSURE	0.0127	0.6660	0.8959	0.2884	0.7425	0.3568
ARTHRITIS	0.0204	0.0816	1.0309	0.2177	0.5433	0.1596
INCONTINENCE	0.6148	0.3733	0.8501	0.1268	1.1093	0.3031
INCONTINENCE—no previous	0.6954	0.1583	0.7738	0.1983	1.0196	0.3574
INCONTINENCE—previous	0.8574	0.6836	0.9398	0.0903	1.1258	0.2871
FALL	0.9133	0.3285	0.9845	0.1947	0.9228	0.3132
FALL—no previous	0.8079	0.1809	1.0259	0.2536	0.8638	0.3220
FALL—previous	0.4700	0.0000	1.0032	0.2718	89.6130	267.8210
HIP FRACTURE	0.3475	0.1434	0.3270	0.2205	0.2096	0.2770
HIP FRACTURE—no previous	0.7845	0.2381	0.2289	0.1690	0.1397	0.1924
PROXY INTERVIEW	0.2482	0.2610	0.4587	0.1610	0.4756	0.1750
PROXY INTERVIEW—no previous	0.0610	0.5310	0.2666	0.1094	0.3992	0.2009
COGNITIVE IMPAIRMENT	0.0002	0.0888	0.7795	0.1721	0.5920	0.1852
PSYCHIATRIC	0.0123	0.1372	0.3942	0.1529	0.1589	0.1243
DEPRESSION	0.0422	0.7534	0.3753	0.1453	0.2856	0.1530
BODY MASS INDEX	0.3452	0.0190				
CURRENT SMOKER	0.4918	0.5276	0.4609	0.3702	0.9187	1.1083
CURRENT SMOKER—no previous	0.1652	0.0970	0.1055	0.1581	19.9184	132.7460
CURRENT SMOKER—previous	0.7141		0.9262	0.1595	0.9499	0.1758
ACTIVITIES DAILY LIVING	0.0036	0.0240				
INSTRUMENTAL ACTIVITIES DAILY LIVING	0.5089	0.0008				
SELF RATED HEALTH	0.0444	0.2784	0.6749	0.0780	0.6445	0.0919
SELF RATED HEALTH—no previous	0.1380	0.0907	0.5892	0.1224	0.5066	0.1290
SELF RATED HEALTH—previous	0.1773	0.1159	0.8500	0.0754	0.9227	0.0824

Notes: SE = standard error. NC = nonconvergence.

Table 11A.5　　　**Total Wealth Regressions—(*t*-statistics)**

Variable	Couples		Spouse Died		Single	
	Estimate	*t*-statistic	Estimate	*t*-statistic	Estimate	*t*-statistic
XONE1	0.0610	12.72	0.0917	5.35	0.0552	4.70
XONE2	0.0487	9.94	0.0755	3.46	0.0430	3.45
XLWLTH12	−0.0528	−10.98	−0.530	−4.23	−0.0503	−7.93
XNWLTH12	−0.0673	−8.23	−0.1033	−5.61	−0.0629	−5.52
XQ1I12	−0.0037	−3.88	−0.0052	−1.58	−0.0014	−0.53
XQ4I12	0.0098	6.98	0.0040	0.58	0.0066	2.68
XHOODPF12	−0.0001	−0.05	0.0066	1.59	0.0030	1.02
XCONDPF12	−0.0031	−2.48	−0.0027	−0.52	0.0000	0.01
XDNHOUS12	0.0085	5.29	0.0124	2.74	0.0015	0.66
M_XHS12	0.0007	0.79	0.0019	0.51	0.0035	1.67
M_XCOLL12	0.0008	0.57	0.0034	0.62	0.0034	0.86
M_XAS701S	0.0000	1.69	0.0001	0.67	0.0001	1.94
M_XAS801S	0.0000	−0.80	0.0000	0.05	−0.0001	−1.29
M_XAS702S	0.0000	1.22	0.0000	−0.37	0.0001	1.82
M_XAS802S	0.0000	−0.58	0.0001	0.47	−0.0001	−0.76
M_XNEVMARR12					0.0131	1.62
M_XWIDOW12					0.0123	1.64
M_XDIVSEP12					0.0138	1.73
M_XMAGEDI12	0.0000	1.24	−0.0001	−1.06	0.0000	−0.89
M_XPAGEDI12	0.0000	−0.10	0.0001	0.86	−0.0001	−1.40
M_XSMOKEV12	−0.0012	−1.17	−0.0046	−1.40	0.0012	0.44
M_XCANCER12	0.0003	0.24	0.0025	0.76	0.0004	0.15
M_XHEART12	−0.0004	−0.45	0.0009	0.28	−0.0007	−0.33
M_XSTROKE12	−0.0003	−0.16	−0.0024	−0.47	−0.0015	−0.49
M_XLUNG12	0.0039	2.15	−0.0057	−1.51	−0.0009	−0.33
M_XDIABET12	−0.0013	−1.13	−0.0004	−0.11	0.0024	0.91
M_XHIGHBP12	−0.0003	−0.36	0.0035	1.19	−0.0002	−0.09
M_XARTHRT12	−0.0007	−0.56	0.0015	0.41	−0.0011	−0.54
M_XINCONT12	0.0012	0.87	−0.0061	−1.77	−0.0008	−0.30
M_XFALL12	−0.0018	−1.26	−0.0021	−0.39	−0.0051	−0.151
M_XHIPFRC12	−0.0029	−0.84	0.0042	0.57	0.0059	1.49
M_XPROXYW12	−0.0004	−0.20	−0.0027	−0.69	0.0055	1.04
M_XCOGIM12	0.0011	0.88	−0.0048	−1.69	−0.0024	−1.10
M_XPSYCH12	−0.0012	−0.61	0.0055	1.25	0.0015	0.43
M_XDEPRES12	−0.0001	−0.02	0.0033	0.69	−0.0015	−0.54
M_XLOBMI12	−0.0009	−0.20	−0.0002	−0.09	0.0020	0.99
M_XHIBMI12	0.0000	0.25	0.0002	0.44	−0.0003	−0.88
M_XSMOKNOW12	−0.0029	−1.71	−0.0030	−0.54	−0.0045	−1.59
M_XNUMADL12	0.0001	0.17	−0.0001	−0.03	−0.0010	−1.05
M_XNUMIADL12	−0.0010	−0.93	0.0002	0.05	0.0014	1.16
M_XDHLTH12	0.0000	−0.04	0.0022	0.53	0.0039	1.62
M_XJCANCER23	0.0007	0.22	0.0011	0.10	0.0091	2.21
M_XJHEART23	0.0007	0.29	−0.0023	−0.19	0.0029	1.00
M_XJSTROKE23	0.0043	1.22	−0.0024	−0.22	0.0051	1.33
M_XILUNG23	−0.0021	−1.08	−0.0051	−0.35	−0.0033	−1.22
M_XIDIABET23	−0.0012	−0.48	0.0250	1.94	−0.0015	−0.35
M_XIHIGHBP23	−0.0006	−0.18	−0.0174	−1.15	0.0009	0.34
M_XIARTHRT23	−0.0008	−0.53	−0.0016	−0.25	−0.0020	−0.67

Table 11A.5 (continued)

Variable	Couples Estimate	_t_-statistic	Spouse Died Estimate	_t_-statistic	Single Estimate	_t_-statistic
M_XJINCONT23	−0.0006	−0.39	0.0015	0.17	0.0007	0.31
M_XJFALL23	0.0003	0.24	0.0048	0.34	−0.0029	−1.30
M_XJHIPFRC23	−0.0044	−0.57	−0.0006	−0.02	−0.0009	−0.14
M_XPROXYW23	−0.0005	−0.29	0.0017	0.20	−0.0010	−0.27
M_XICOGIM23	0.0001	0.06	−0.0057	−0.48	0.0020	0.84
M_XIPSYCH23	−0.0003	−0.18	0.0008	0.06	0.0046	1.54
M_XIDEPRES23	−0.0016	−0.72	0.0009	0.11	−0.0032	−1.07
M_XBMIBT23	0.0004	0.36	−0.0020	−0.26	0.0022	1.14
M_XBMIWS23	−0.0013	−1.00	−0.0031	−0.34	0.0008	0.39
M_XSMOKNOW23	0.0040	2.08	−0.0069	−0.38	−0.0006	−0.24
M_XNUMADL23	−0.0001	−0.12	−0.0055	−1.63	−0.0003	−0.56
M_XNUMIADL23	0.0004	0.41	0.0006	0.20	−0.0008	−1.06
M_XDHLTH23	−0.0007	−0.67	−0.0118	−1.32	0.0015	0.90
F_XONE1					0.0753	12.84
F_XONE2					0.0656	10.87
F_XLWLTH12					−0.0503	−16.12
F_XNWLTH12					−0.0640	−11.29
F_XQ1I12					−0.0006	−0.81
F_XQ4I12					0.0089	7.79
F_XHOODPF12					−0.0010	−1.12
F_XCONDPF12					−0.0012	−1.36
F_XDNHOUS12					0.0035	3.54
F_XHS12	0.0008	0.75	0.0069	1.66	0.0016	2.16
F_XCOLL12	0.0019	1.34	0.0029	0.49	0.0026	1.80
F_XAS701S	0.0000	1.14	−0.0001	−0.83	0.0000	−0.09
F_XAS801S	−0.0001	−0.75	0.0000	0.04	0.0000	0.04
F_XAS702S	0.0000	−1.88	0.0000	0.66	0.0000	−0.35
F_XAS802S	0.0001	1.96	−0.0001	−0.37	0.0000	0.51
F_XNEVMARR12					0.0023	0.50
F_XWIDOW12					0.0010	0.23
F_XDIVSEP12					0.0001	0.01
F_XMAGEDI12	0.0000	1.08	0.0000	−0.02	0.0000	0.44
F_XPAGEDI12	0.0000	−0.79	0.0000	−0.40	0.0000	−0.47
F_XSMOKEV12	0.0024	2.58	0.0007	0.17	0.0007	0.88
F_XCANCER12	−0.0012	−0.87	−0.0049	−0.86	−0.0007	−0.69
F_XHEART12	0.0002	0.21	−0.0025	−0.77	−0.0010	−1.42
F_XSTROKE12	−0.0010	−0.52	0.0021	0.29	−0.0002	−0.20
F_XLUNG12	0.0002	0.10	−0.0033	−0.71	−0.0015	−1.48
F_XDIABET12	−0.0027	−1.99	0.0041	0.86	−0.0018	−1.89
F_XHIGHBP12	0.0006	0.61	0.0047	1.55	−0.0010	−1.35
F_XARTHRT12	0.0008	0.73	−0.0018	−0.40	0.0004	0.44
F_XINCONT12	−0.0013	−1.01	0.0001	0.03	0.0006	0.66
F_XFALL12	0.0001	0.09	−0.0002	−0.05	0.0010	0.99
F_XHIPFRC12	0.0011	0.33	0.0018	0.28	−0.0005	−0.40
F_XPROXYW12	−0.0013	−0.40	−0.0013	−0.20	−0.0004	−0.25
F_XCOGIM12	−0.0003	−0.17	−0.0050	−1.11	−0.0023	−2.70

(_continued_)

Table 11A.5 (continued)

Variable	Couples		Spouse Died		Single	
	Estimate	t-statistic	Estimate	t-statistic	Estimate	t-statistic
F_XPSYCH12	−0.0005	−0.44	0.0007	0.14	−0.0010	−0.97
F_XDEPRES12	−0.0016	−0.91	−0.0012	−0.24	−0.0007	−0.61
F_XLOBMI12	0.0007	0.34	0.0013	0.58	0.0001	0.10
F_XHIBMI12	−0.0003	−1.79	−0.0011	−2.61	−0.0002	−1.47
F_XSMOKNOW12	−0.0014	−0.60	−0.0013	−0.20	−0.0026	−1.48
F_XNUMADL12	0.0013	1.58	0.0015	0.63	−0.0005	−1.64
F_XNUMIADL12	0.0002	0.20	−0.0016	−1.00	−0.0006	−1.37
F_XDHLTH12	0.0002	0.15	−0.0012	−0.21	−0.0004	−0.44
F_XJCANCER23	0.0019	0.71	−0.0002	−0.01	−0.0077	−3.19
F_XJHEART23	0.0033	1.69	−0.0045	−0.80	−0.0023	−2.00
F_XJSTROKE23	0.0041	1.77	−0.0185	−2.60	−0.0034	−1.98
F_XILUNG23	0.0044	1.15	−0.0039	−0.49	−0.0004	−0.26
F_XIDIABET23	−0.0011	−0.37	−0.0002	−0.03	0.0000	0.02
F_XIHIGHBP23	0.0023	1.09	0.0010	0.15	0.0001	0.06
F_XIARTHRT23	0.0012	0.81	0.0029	0.44	0.0010	1.09
F_XJINCONT23	0.0024	2.50	−0.0009	−0.24	0.0011	1.37
F_XJFALL23	−0.0011	−0.60	−0.0036	−0.75	0.0003	0.35
F_XJHIPFRC23	0.0010	0.27	0.0067	0.82	0.0006	0.036
F_XPROXYW23	−0.0017	−0.67	−0.0036	−0.52	−0.0011	−0.82
F_XICOGIM23	−0.0001	−0.05	−0.0023	−0.48	−0.0024	−2.42
F_XIPSYCH23	−0.0014	−0.70	−0.0158	−2.49	0.0012	0.93
F_XIDEPRES23	−0.0026	−1.52	0.0005	0.07	−0.0011	−0.78
F_XBMIBT23	0.0006	0.39	0.0017	0.34	−0.0001	−0.19
F_XBMIWS23	−0.0001	−0.10	0.0013	0.22	0.0001	0.11
F_XSMOKNOW23	−0.0038	−1.56	0.0013	0.13	0.0012	0.70
F_XNUMADL23	−0.0002	−0.33	0.0020	1.22	−0.0002	−0.93
F_XNUMIADL23	0.0006	0.73	−0.0014	−0.65	−0.0003	−0.84
F_XDHLTH23	−0.0032	−2.68	−0.0028	−0.60	−0.0003	−0.33
CF4	−0.2411	−0.18	−0.2411	−0.18	−0.0128	−0.27
CF3	−1.1433	−1.38	−1.1433	−1.38	0.5102	6.01
CM4	0.1903	1.40	0.1903	1.40	−0.1306	−1.97
CM3	−0.3582	−2.24	−0.3582	−2.24	−0.4368	−3.62
AM	−0.0025	−1.87	0.0012	2.80	−0.0076	−4.39
AF	−0.0008	−0.30	0.0004	0.45	−0.0019	−10.04
C	0.0000	21.10	0.0000	7.74	0.0000	6.11
VARM	0.0000	−0.88	0.0000	−0.89	0.0000	−0.81
VARF	0.0000	−2.53	0.0000	1.20	0.0000	0.48
SIGMA	0.0043	42.20	0.0000	7.74	0.0088	6.12
THETA	2.4733	19.10				
RHOM	−0.4882	−6.31			−0.8641	−17.28
RHOF	−0.1606	−3.11			−0.2103	−5.32

Notes: Prefixes M_ and F_ refer to males and females, respectively. For couples and spouse died regressions household-level variables are common for males and females. We report the estimates under the male section. CF3, CF4 = third/fourth order Edgeworth expansion terms for females; CM3, CM4 = third/fourth order Edgeworth expansion terms for males; AF, AM = estimates of λ in equations (15) and (19); C = estimate of k^2 in equation (16); VARM, VARF = estimates of λ^2 in equation (16) for males and females; SIGMA = estimate of σ as defined in page 440 of paper; THETA = estimate of θ in equation (19); RHOF, RHOM = estimate of ρ as defined in page 442 of paper.

Table 11A.6   Nonliquid Wealth Regressions—(*t*-statistics)

Variable	Couples		Spouse Died		Single	
	Estimate	*t*-statistic	Estimate	*t*-statistic	Estimate	*t*-statistic
XONE1	0.0582	14.64	0.0752	4.68	0.0482	4.74
XONE2	0.0459	11.33	0.0655	3.13	0.0438	3.94
XLWLTH12	0.0046	1.03	0.0041	0.40	0.0128	2.56
XNWLTH12	−0.1311	−15.98	−0.1646	−8.65	−0.1138	−8.91
XQ1I12	−0.0010	−1.19	−0.0011	−0.37	−0.0012	−0.50
XQ4I12	0.0021	2.17	0.0032	0.53	0.0015	0.66
XHOODPF12	−0.0017	−1.47	0.0050	1.27	0.0002	0.07
XCONDPF12	−0.0014	−1.19	−0.0008	−0.17	−0.0001	−0.03
XDNHOUS12	0.0068	4.45	0.0074	1.80	0.0013	0.50
M_XHS12	0.0000	0.04	0.0005	0.14	0.0010	0.47
M_XCOLL12	0.0000	−0.01	0.0021	0.44	−0.0008	−0.25
M_XAS701S	0.0000	0.22	0.0001	0.82	0.0001	2.71
M_XAS801S	−0.0001	−1.73	−0.0001	−0.43	−0.0001	−1.88
M_XAS702S	0.0000	0.48	0.0000	0.10	0.0001	2.01
M_XAS802S	0.0000	−1.16	0.0000	−0.19	−0.0001	−0.91
M_XNEVMARR12					0.0078	1.13
M_XWIDOW12					0.0078	1.26
M_XDIVSEP12					0.0101	1.45
M_XMAGEDI12	0.0000	0.33	−0.0001	−1.63	−0.0001	−1.64
M_XPAGEDI12	0.0000	0.23	0.0000	0.37	−0.0001	−1.20
M_XSMOKEV12	−0.0011	−1.33	−0.0044	−1.36	−0.0016	−0.67
M_XCANCER12	−0.0004	−0.35	0.0037	1.44	0.0032	1.20
M_XHEART12	0.0003	0.36	−0.0011	−0.42	0.0002	0.10
M_XSTROKE12	0.0015	0.83	−0.0013	−0.29	0.0012	0.44
M_XLUNG12	0.0022	1.30	−0.0018	−0.50	0.0001	0.05
M_XDIABET12	−0.0019	−1.89	0.0024	0.83	0.0044	1.87
M_XHIGHBP12	−0.0005	−0.71	0.0041	1.52	0.0007	0.37
M_XARTHRT12	0.0019	1.62	0.0052	1.52	−0.0012	−0.60
M_XINCONT12	0.0004	0.33	−0.0040	−1.48	−0.0034	−1.29
M_XFALL12	−0.0002	−0.14	−0.0025	−0.50	−0.0059	−1.90
M_XHIPFRC12	−0.0015	−0.48	0.0068	0.91	0.0100	2.32
M_XPROXYW12	0.0025	1.43	−0.0049	−1.35	0.0057	1.14
M_XCOGIM12	0.0024	2.07	−0.0018	−0.71	0.0017	0.81
M_XPSYCH12	−0.0007	−0.41	−0.0058	−1.62	0.0009	0.35
M_XDEPRES12	0.0018	0.48	−0.0027	−0.65	0.0018	0.57
M_XLOBMI12	0.0010	0.21	−0.0025	−1.25	0.0061	2.21
M_XHIBMI12	0.0003	2.04	0.0002	0.32	−0.0003	−0.70
M_XSMOKNOW12	−0.0006	−0.44	0.0006	0.10	−0.0050	−1.98
M_XNUMADL12	−0.0002	−0.24	0.0010	0.49	0.0004	0.51
M_XNUMIADL12	−0.0013	−1.31	0.0007	0.22	0.0008	0.76
M_XDHLTH12	−0.0017	−1.53	−0.0029	−0.81	0.0033	1.37
M_XJCANCER23	0.0012	0.42	0.0022	0.22	0.0170	3.07
M_XJHEART23	0.0020	0.93	0.0046	0.40	0.0097	2.51
M_XJSTROKE23	0.0024	0.69	−0.0077	−0.65	0.0066	1.62
M_XILUNG23	−0.0025	−1.54	−0.0010	−0.07	−0.0062	−2.39
M_XIDIABET23	0.0001	0.06	0.0212	2.97	−0.0003	−0.07

(*continued*)

Table 11A.6   (continued)

Variable	Couples		Spouse Died		Single	
	Estimate	t-statistic	Estimate	t-statistic	Estimate	t-statistic
M_XIHIGHBP23	−0.0025	−0.80	−0.0254	−1.90	0.0004	0.16
M_XIARTHRT23	−0.0010	−0.80	0.0058	0.96	−0.0023	−0.82
M_XJINCONT23	0.0000	0.00	−0.0069	−0.97	0.0014	0.78
M_XJFALL23	0.0000	0.01	−0.0034	−0.23	−0.0009	−0.49
M_XJHIPFRC23	−0.0038	−0.50	0.0221	0.91	−0.0040	−1.09
M_XPROXYW23	0.0002	0.11	−0.0017	−0.23	0.0012	0.34
M_XICOGIM23	0.0008	0.59	−0.0026	−0.20	−0.0013	−0.70
M_XIPSYCH23	−0.0004	−0.27	0.0027	0.28	0.0036	1.37
M_XIDEPRES23	−0.0007	−0.36	−0.0088	−1.15	−0.0001	−0.04
M_XBMIBT23	−0.0001	−0.15	−0.0057	−0.86	0.0005	0.31
M_XBMIWS23	−0.0004	−0.29	−0.0078	−0.97	0.0014	0.78
M_XSMOKNOW23	0.0015	0.97	−0.0128	−0.64	0.0038	1.72
M_XNUMADL23	0.0004	0.53	−0.0070	−2.30	−0.0005	−0.87
M_XNUMIADL23	−0.0002	−0.15	0.0037	1.36	−0.0008	−1.17
M_XDHLTH23	−0.0005	−0.55	−0.0044	−0.52	0.0015	0.92
F_XONE1					0.0688	12.20
F_XONE2					0.0619	10.64
F_XLWLTH12					0.0033	1.42
F_XNWLTH12					−0.1257	−20.66
F_XQ1I12					0.0004	0.59
F_XQ4I12					0.0030	3.13
F_XHOODPF12					−0.0010	−1.21
F_XCONDPF12					0.0002	0.26
F_XDNHOUS12					0.0045	4.66
F_XHS12	0.0004	0.41	0.0034	0.89	0.0001	0.21
F_XCOLL12	0.0005	0.44	0.0095	1.88	0.0016	1.36
F_XAS701S	0.0000	−0.51	0.0000	−0.32	0.0000	−1.70
F_XAS801S	0.0000	0.69	−0.0001	−0.81	0.0000	0.28
F_XAS702S	0.0000	−0.45	0.0000	0.45	0.0000	−1.09
F_XAS802S	0.0001	1.26	0.0000	0.03	0.0000	0.54
F_XNEVMARR12					0.0001	0.02
F_XWIDOW12					0.0000	0.01
F_XDIVSEP12					−0.0001	−0.01
F_XMAGEDI12	0.0000	0.64	0.0000	0.73	0.0000	0.74
F_XPAGEDI12	0.0000	−0.31	0.0000	0.32	0.0000	0.47
F_XSMOKEV12	−0.0003	−0.40	−0.0025	−0.63	0.0001	0.20
F_XCANCER12	0.0007	0.57	−0.0052	−1.00	0.0001	0.07
F_XHEART12	−0.0009	−0.89	−0.0046	−1.51	−0.0006	−0.96
F_XSTROKE12	0.0029	1.83	0.0010	0.13	−0.0005	−0.44
F_XLUNG12	0.0000	−0.01	−0.0008	−0.20	−0.0012	−1.45
F_XDIABET12	−0.0002	−0.13	0.0064	1.36	−0.0012	−1.38
F_XHIGHBP12	0.0001	0.15	0.0046	1.82	−0.0014	−2.16
F_XARTHRT12	−0.0002	−0.18	0.0029	0.68	0.0004	0.59
F_XINCONT12	0.0000	−0.02	−0.0014	−0.42	0.0000	0.02
F_XFALL12	0.0005	0.33	0.0012	0.31	0.0010	1.12
F_XHIPFRC12	0.0039	1.29	−0.0018	−0.33	−0.0008	−0.69
F_XPROXYW12	−0.0007	−0.24	−0.0011	−0.19	−0.0005	−0.32

Table 11A.6 (continued)

Variable	Couples Estimate	Couples t-statistic	Spouse Died Estimate	Spouse Died t-statistic	Single Estimate	Single t-statistic
F_XCOGIM12	0.0005	0.33	−0.0043	−1.04	−0.0014	−1.70
F_XPSYCH12	0.0000	−0.01	0.0033	0.66	−0.0013	−1.48
F_XDEPRES12	0.0006	0.40	−0.0025	−0.51	−0.0008	−0.83
F_XLOBMI12	0.0017	0.90	0.0004	0.20	−0.0004	−1.16
F_XHIBMI12	0.0000	0.17	−0.0012	−3.19	−0.0001	−0.87
F_XSMOKNOW12	−0.0004	−0.18	0.0038	0.61	−0.0033	−2.14
F_XNUMADL12	0.0001	0.18	0.0011	0.49	−0.0004	−1.28
F_XNUMIADL12	0.0008	0.89	0.0000	0.00	0.0003	0.89
F_XDHLTH12	0.0006	0.47	−0.0011	−0.21	−0.0008	−1.00
F_XJCANCER23	−0.0010	−0.46	0.0028	0.33	−0.0063	−2.60
F_XJHEART23	0.0007	0.38	−0.0039	−0.79	−0.0019	−1.76
F_XJSTROKE23	0.0015	0.83	−0.0032	−0.44	−0.0022	−1.33
F_XILUNG23	0.0060	1.74	−0.0070	−1.11	−0.0019	−1.41
F_XIDIABET23	−0.0028	−1.41	−0.0050	−0.58	−0.0005	−0.31
F_XIHIGHBP23	0.0002	0.09	−0.0009	−0.15	0.0002	0.14
F_XIARTHRT23	0.0004	0.27	0.0001	0.01	0.0010	1.14
F_XJINCONT23	0.0007	0.86	−0.0006	−0.17	0.0005	0.78
F_XJFALL23	−0.0006	−0.32	−0.0042	−1.04	−0.0005	−0.73
F_XJHIPFRC23	−0.0045	−1.86	−0.0025	−0.39	−0.0003	−0.23
F_XPROXYW23	0.0006	0.23	−0.0043	−0.61	−0.0008	−0.61
F_XICOGIM23	−0.0007	−0.41	−0.0016	−0.34	−0.0016	−1.98
F_XIPSYCH23	−0.0005	−0.28	−0.0047	−0.65	−0.0001	−0.08
F_XIDEPRES23	0.0007	0.42	−0.0041	−0.65	−0.0010	−0.88
F_XBMIBT23	0.0033	0.24	0.0044	1.00	0.0024	0.61
F_XBMIWS23	0.0001	0.06	0.0026	0.44	−0.0004	−0.62
F_XSMOKNOW23	−0.0013	−0.56	−0.0075	−0.88	0.0033	2.22
F_XNUMADL23	−0.0006	−0.91	0.0019	1.06	−0.0003	−1.45
F_XNUMIADL23	0.0002	0.22	−0.0021	−1.02	−0.0007	−2.34
F_XDHLTH23	−0.0027	−2.52	0.0032	0.76	0.0005	0.65
CF4	0.1230	0.09	0.1230	0.09	0.0191	0.36
CF3	−0.2322	−0.28	−0.2322	−0.28	0.4650	4.71
CM4	0.1776	1.30	0.1776	1.30	−0.1248	−2.74
CM3	−0.2742	−1.71	−0.2742	−1.71	−0.3308	−3.87
AM	−0.0015	−1.16	0.0006	2.09	−0.0118	−3.52
AF	−0.0004	−0.15	0.0001	0.30	−0.0015	−7.26
C	0.0000	23.59	0.0000	0.00	0.0000	5.84
VARM	0.0000	1.34	0.0000	0.00	0.0000	−0.56
VARF	0.0000	−0.12	0.0000	0.00	0.0000	−0.23
SIGMA	0.0041	47.19	0.0000	0.00	0.0125	4.00
THETA	2.3623	11.32				
RHOM	−0.3532	−3.29			−0.9434	−31.26
RHOF	−0.0939	−1.65			−0.1164	−3.53

Notes: See table 11A.5.

Table 11A.7   Liquid Wealth Regressions—(*t*-statistics)

Variable	Couples		Spouse Died		Single	
	Estimate	*t*-statistic	Estimate	*t*-statistic	Estimate	*t*-statistic
XONE1	0.0819	12.94	0.1150	5.73	0.0802	5.66
XONE2	0.0705	10.88	0.1021	4.35	0.0652	4.39
XLWLTH12	−0.1474	−22.15	−0.1581	−9.33	−0.1583	−13.68
XNWLTH12	0.0222	2.68	0.0058	0.42	0.0272	2.55
XQ1I12	−0.0077	−6.24	−0.0100	−2.50	−0.0012	−0.43
XQ4I12	0.0103	5.38	0.0032	0.40	0.0108	3.44
XHOODPF12	−0.0014	−0.86	0.0069	1.31	0.0032	0.91
XCONDPF12	−0.0038	−2.58	−0.0066	−1.20	0.0010	0.30
XDNHOUS12	0.0008	0.47	0.0104	2.36	−0.0007	−0.25
M_XHS12	0.0003	0.28	0.0044	1.00	0.0037	1.46
M_XCOLL12	0.0016	0.83	0.0061	0.88	0.0080	1.53
M_XAS701S	0.0000	0.85	−0.0001	−1.13	0.0000	0.67
M_XAS801S	0.0000	0.90	0.0003	1.62	0.0000	0.42
M_XAS702S	0.0000	0.12	−0.0001	−0.90	0.0001	1.12
M_XAS802S	0.0001	1.90	0.0003	1.69	0.0000	−0.28
M_XNEVMARR12					0.0078	0.90
M_XWIDOW12					0.0083	1.04
M_XDIVSEP12					0.0069	0.81
M_XMAGEDI12	0.0000	0.86	0.0000	−0.36	0.0000	−0.03
M_XPAGEDI12	0.0000	−0.34	0.0000	−0.16	−0.0001	−1.02
M_XSMOKEV12	0.0007	0.49	−0.0026	−0.68	0.0016	0.52
M_XCANCER12	0.0027	1.72	0.0011	0.28	−0.0002	−0.08
M_XHEART12	−0.0007	−0.63	−0.0042	−1.11	−0.0007	−0.28
M_XSTROKE12	0.0013	0.55	−0.0051	−0.92	−0.0036	−1.06
M_XLUNG12	0.0045	2.16	−0.0056	−1.22	−0.0047	−1.76
M_XDIABET12	−0.0023	−1.47	−0.0059	−1.39	−0.0015	−0.46
M_XHIGHBP12	0.0011	0.98	0.0021	0.66	−0.0017	−0.71
M_XARTHRT12	−0.0039	−2.48	0.0024	0.56	0.0002	0.09
M_XINCONT12	−0.0003	−0.15	−0.0015	−0.35	0.0005	0.19
M_XFALL12	−0.0025	−1.12	0.0076	1.22	−0.0007	−0.22
M_XHIPFRC12	−0.0021	−0.57	−0.0069	−0.81	0.0005	0.11
M_XPROXYW12	−0.0022	−1.00	0.0030	0.63	0.0006	0.13
M_XCOGIM12	−0.0002	−0.11	−0.0089	−2.49	−0.0070	−2.77
M_XPSYCH12	0.0004	0.17	0.0087	1.47	0.0044	1.07
M_XDEPRES12	−0.0064	−1.55	0.0109	1.99	−0.0034	−1.05
M_XLOBMI12	−0.0003	−0.05	0.0008	0.34	0.0024	0.95
M_XHIBMI12	−0.0003	−1.56	0.0012	1.76	0.0001	0.27
M_XSMOKNOW12	−0.0021	−0.85	−0.0057	−0.96	0.0002	0.05
M_XNUMADL12	0.0014	1.57	−0.0020	−0.89	−0.0011	−1.02
M_XNUMIADL12	−0.0022	−1.90	0.0005	0.14	0.0001	0.09
M_XDHLTH12	0.0031	2.01	0.0052	1.15	0.0030	1.10
M_XJCANCER23	0.0011	0.32	0.0015	0.11	−0.0010	−0.24
M_XJHEART23	0.0032	1.30	−0.0052	−0.45	0.0003	0.10
M_XJSTROKE23	0.0012	0.30	0.0079	0.71	0.0045	1.09
M_XILUNG23	0.0004	0.15	−0.0257	−1.76	−0.0024	−0.61
M_XIDIABET23	−0.0030	−0.90	0.0105	0.84	−0.0007	−0.11
M_XIHIGHBP23	0.0026	0.68	0.0003	0.02	−0.0064	−1.59

Variable	Couples		Spouse Died		Single	
	Estimate	*t*-statistic	Estimate	*t*-statistic	Estimate	*t*-statistic
M_XIARTHRT23	−0.0011	−0.59	−0.0086	−1.40	−0.0046	−1.53
M_XJINCONT23	−0.0005	−0.25	0.0043	0.50	−0.0023	−0.92
M_XJFALL23	0.0021	1.05	0.0224	1.55	−0.0033	−1.05
M_XJHIPFRC23	−0.0075	−0.94	−0.0264	−1.00	0.0093	0.97
M_XPROXYW23	−0.0018	−0.83	0.0069	0.86	−0.0038	−1.12
M_XICOGIM23	−0.0008	−0.47	−0.0046	−0.41	0.0008	0.28
M_XIPSYCH23	0.0010	0.51	−0.0156	−0.74	0.0071	1.86
M_XIDEPRES23	0.0009	0.32	0.0041	0.55	−0.0053	−1.24
M_XBMIBT23	−0.0027	−2.02	−0.0038	−0.50	0.0004	0.15
M_XBMIWS23	−0.0038	−2.47	−0.0055	−0.53	−0.0014	−0.55
M_XSMOKNOW23	0.0020	0.68	0.0047	0.25	−0.0082	−2.11
M_XNUMADL23	−0.0004	−0.46	−0.0011	−0.37	−0.0006	−0.86
M_XNUMIADL23	0.0003	0.28	−0.0077	−2.41	0.0004	0.42
M_XDHLTH23	0.0000	0.01	−0.0046	−0.51	0.0000	−0.02
F_XONE1					0.0680	10.83
F_XONE2					0.0547	8.51
F_XLWLTH12					−0.1280	−20.62
F_XNWLTH12					0.0203	4.26
F_XQ1I12					−0.0020	−2.31
F_XQ4I12					0.0118	7.73
F_XHOODPF12					−0.0008	−0.69
F_XCONDPF12					−0.0031	−2.93
F_XDNHOUS12					0.0014	1.31
F_XHS12	0.0022	1.55	0.0103	2.16	0.0025	2.84
F_XCOLL12	0.0027	1.35	−0.0007	−0.09	0.0036	1.96
F_XAS701S	0.0001	2.35	0.0000	0.33	0.0000	0.55
F_XAS801S	−0.0002	−2.04	−0.0002	−0.82	0.0000	0.15
F_XAS702S	0.0000	−1.16	−0.0001	−0.79	0.0000	1.63
F_XAS802S	0.0000	0.30	0.0000	0.24	0.0000	−0.81
F_XNEVMARR12					0.0114	2.38
F_XWIDOW12					0.0087	1.97
F_XDIVSEP12					0.0061	1.33
F_XMAGEDI12	0.0000	0.71	0.0000	−0.39	0.0000	0.66
F_XPAGEDI12	0.0000	−1.31	−0.0001	−1.07	0.0000	0.36
F_XSMOKEV12	0.0034	2.76	0.0063	1.38	0.0011	1.10
F_XCANCER12	−0.0019	−1.10	−0.0024	−0.38	−0.0010	−0.82
F_XHEART12	−0.0006	−0.41	0.0038	1.01	0.0001	0.15
F_XSTROKE12	−0.0013	−0.52	0.0032	0.43	−0.0009	−0.67
F_XLUNG12	−0.0001	−0.03	−0.0068	−1.28	−0.0011	−0.85
F_XDIABET12	−0.0028	−1.66	−0.0027	−0.51	−0.0015	−1.27
F_XHIGHBP12	−0.0010	−0.82	0.0094	2.55	−0.0006	−0.63
F_XARTHRT12	0.0019	1.43	−0.0053	−1.13	−0.0005	−0.55
F_XINCONT12	0.0004	0.22	0.0012	0.26	−0.0003	−0.29
F_XFALL12	0.0026	1.28	0.0000	0.01	0.0003	0.27
F_XHIPFRC12	0.0034	0.89	−0.0001	−0.01	0.0030	1.80

(*continued*)

Variable	Couples		Spouse Died		Single	
	Estimate	*t*-statistic	Estimate	*t*-statistic	Estimate	*t*-statistic
F_XPROXYW12	−0.0023	−0.62	−0.0017	−0.25	−0.0032	−1.54
F_XCOGIM12	−0.0011	−0.56	−0.0064	−1.24	−0.0034	−3.27
F_XPSYCH12	−0.0015	−0.99	−0.0009	−0.15	0.0017	1.31
F_XDEPRES12	−0.0016	−0.74	0.0031	0.56	−0.0020	−1.59
F_XLOBMI12	−0.0006	−0.31	0.0021	0.96	0.0002	0.32
F_XHIBMI12	−0.0005	−2.31	−0.0005	−0.88	−0.0003	−2.14
F_XSMOKNOW12	−0.0016	−0.43	−0.0136	−1.83	−0.0035	−1.71
F_XNUMADL12	0.0023	2.35	0.0005	0.20	−0.0006	−1.44
F_XNUMIADL12	0.0006	0.48	−0.0046	−2.31	−0.0011	−2.45
F_XDHLTH12	−0.0019	−1.13	0.0003	0.05	−0.0006	−0.60
F_XJCANCER23	0.0073	2.04	−0.0026	−0.21	−0.0066	−2.41
F_XJHEART23	0.0029	1.36	−0.0038	−0.57	−0.0024	−1.77
F_XJSTROKE23	0.0012	0.45	−0.0235	−2.53	−0.0041	−2.04
F_XILUNG23	−0.0052	−1.48	−0.0040	−0.32	0.0012	0.62
F_XIDIABET23	−0.0050	−1.26	0.0031	0.28	0.0012	0.54
F_XIHIGHBP23	−0.0024	−0.93	0.0024	0.32	−0.0007	−0.44
F_XIARTHRT23	0.0015	0.79	0.0077	1.14	0.0006	0.46
F_XJINCONT23	0.0034	2.59	0.0041	0.86	0.0017	1.71
F_XJFALL23	−0.0010	−0.48	−0.0074	−1.16	0.0017	1.56
F_XJHIPFRC23	0.0034	0.69	0.0198	1.68	−0.0005	−0.26
F_XPROXYW23	−0.0015	−0.50	−0.0001	−0.01	−0.0001	−0.04
F_XICOGIM23	−0.0017	−0.67	0.0007	0.10	−0.0036	−2.86
F_XIPSYCH23	−0.0015	−0.60	−0.0192	−2.81	0.0014	0.81
F_XIDEPRES23	−0.0027	−1.22	0.0030	0.41	−0.0023	−1.46
F_XBMIBT23	0.0007	0.41	−0.0001	−0.02	−0.0001	−0.11
F_XBMIWS23	−0.0010	−0.67	0.0018	0.25	0.0005	0.56
F_XSMOKNOW23	−0.0060	−1.59	0.0168	1.60	0.0013	0.64
F_XNUMADL23	−0.0017	−2.52	0.0037	1.84	−0.0002	−0.46
F_XNUMIADL23	0.0022	2.35	−0.0035	−1.29	0.0006	1.42
F_XDHLTH23	−0.0002	−0.16	−0.0094	−1.81	0.0007	0.75
CF4	0.0801	0.06	0.0801	0.06	−0.0320	−0.50
CF3	−0.1813	−0.22	−0.1813	−0.22	0.5701	5.63
CM4	0.1603	1.18	0.1603	1.18	0.0101	0.07
CM3	−0.3138	−1.97	−0.3138	−1.97	−0.5973	−2.35
AM	−0.0027	−2.09	0.0014	3.13	−0.0038	−2.89
AF	−0.0018	−0.66	0.0009	0.93	−0.0016	−10.38
C	0.0000	24.84	0.0000	4.23	0.0000	6.13
VARM	0.0000	−0.51	0.0000	0.72	0.0000	−1.45
VARF	0.0000	−0.38	0.0000	−0.67	0.0000	1.75
SIGMA	0.0055	49.68	0.0000	4.23	0.0061	7.47
THETA	2.5207	18.63				
RHOM	−0.4243	−7.48			−0.6292	−5.06
RHOF	−0.2826	−5.64			−0.2579	−6.27

Notes: See table 11A.5.

Table 11A.8   **Wealth Regressions—Invariance Tests**

	Wealth (DF)	Total		Nonliquid		Liquid	
		CHISQ	*p*-value	CHISQ	*p*-value	CHISQ	*p*-value
Couples							
All	97	468.6	0.000	355.1	0.000	377.2	0.000
All less SES	90	219.4	0.0000	168.1	0.0000	243.9	0.0000
All male	52	279.7	0.0000	232.5	0.0000	215.9	0.0000
All male less SES	45	109.1	0.0000	80.0	0.0010	117.4	0.0000
All female	52	277.2	0.0000	218.9	0.0000	200.1	0.0000
All female less SES	45	90.0	0.0001	76.9	0.0021	104.9	0.0000
All less prevalence	57	301.2	0.0000	224.6	0.0000	223.8	0.0000
All less incidence	57	358.4	0.0000	259.8	0.0000	266.1	0.0000
Only SES	7	123.4	0.0000	119.6	0.0000	69.8	0.0000
Only male demographic	5	6.9	0.2292	4.1	0.5382	8.9	0.1129
Only female demographic	5	5.2	0.3971	10.6	0.0590	4.9	0.4261
Only male prevalence	20	58.8	0.0000	34.2	0.0246	69.9	0.0000
Only female prevalence	20	57.2	0.0000	33.3	0.0310	45.8	0.0009
Only male incidence	20	38.9	0.0070	33.2	0.0324	44.0	0.0015
Only female incidence	20	31.1	0.0540	22.7	0.3060	53.5	0.0001
Spouse died							
All	97	672.2	0.0000	682.7	0.0000	700.2	0.0000
All less SES	90	524.0	0.0000	645.3	0.0000	576.9	0.0000
All male	52	268.2	0.0000	370.0	0.0000	224.6	0.0000
All male less SES	45	244.1	0.0000	350.1	0.0000	161.4	0.0000
All female	52	250.0	0.0000	181.5	0.0000	358.8	0.0000
All female less SES	45	164.7	0.0000	142.7	0.0000	256.6	0.0000
All less prevalence	57	223.4	0.0000	269.2	0.0000	361.1	0.0000
All less incidence	57	240.4	0.0000	234.9	0.0000	277.3	0.0000
Only SES	7	60.0	0.0000	34.2	0.0000	37.0	0.0000
Only male demographic	5	7.8	0.1692	8.2	0.1473	12.7	0.0259
Only female demographic	5	7.3	0.2020	5.6	0.3479	16.2	0.0063
Only male prevalence	20	69.5	0.0000	65.8	0.0000	66.3	0.0000
Only female prevalence	20	56.0	0.0000	49.9	0.0002	38.2	0.0085
Only male incidence	20	71.7	0.0000	105.5	0.0000	41.5	0.0021
Only female incidence	20	74.6	0.0000	65.0	0.0000	115.2	0.0000
Singles							
All	110	384.8	0.0000	353.6	0.0000	301.4	0.0000
All less SES	96	118.5	0.0594	139.9	0.0023	129.8	0.0124
All male	55	129.2	0.0000	139.4	0.0000	91.2	0.0015
All male less SES	48	43.3	0.6639	60.3	0.1094	59.4	0.1261
All female	55	255.6	0.0000	214.1	0.0000	210.1	0.0000
All female less SES	48	75.2	0.0073	79.6	0.0028	70.4	0.0192
All less prevalence	70	307.3	0.0000	296.7	0.0000	201.4	0.0000
All less incidence	70	287.4	0.0000	275.7	0.0000	222.0	0.0000
Only Male SES	7	30.2	0.0001	47.0	0.0000	16.4	0.0215
Only female SES	7	153.3	0.0000	129.3	0.0000	89.8	0.0000
Only male demographic	8	4.1	0.8446	6.5	0.5875	5.8	0.6742
Only female demographic	8	13.9	0.0842	14.9	0.0603	16.3	0.0379
Only male prevalence	20	19.0	0.5251	30.6	0.0613	30.8	0.0580
Only female prevalence	20	26.4	0.1536	30.6	0.0601	26.3	0.1559
Only male incidence	20	19.4	0.4955	23.3	0.2747	19.7	0.4759
Only female incidence	20	41.0	0.0037	40.7	0.0040	30.2	0.0663

Table 11A.9　　**Wealth Regressions—Causality Tests**

	Wealth (DF)	Total		Nonliquid		Liquid	
		CHISQ	*p*-value	CHISQ	*p*-value	CHISQ	*p*-value
Incidence							
Couple							
Male	20	20.01	0.4575	16.03	0.7146	18.04	0.5847
Female	20	36.65	0.0129	33.87	0.0270	37.47	0.0103
Male & female	40	59.47	0.0243	51.44	0.1061	57.55	0.0356
Spouse died							
Male	20	22.65	0.3061	51.36	0.0001	50.99	0.0002
Female	20	23.02	0.2878	16.99	0.6533	30.71	0.0591
Male & female	40	62.86	0.0120	75.29	0.0006	88.09	0.0000
Single							
Male	20	18.78	0.5362	30.01	0.0696	24.38	0.2263
Female	20	32.65	0.0369	53.88	0.0001	33.03	0.0335
Male & female	40	51.43	0.1064	83.89	0.0001	57.41	0.0366
Prevalence							
Couple							
Male	20	27.85	0.1130	47.88	0.0004	45.58	0.0009
Female	20	24.73	0.2120	14.50	0.8041	38.30	0.0081
Male & female	40	58.87	0.0275	72.18	0.0014	111.42	0.0000
Spouse died							
Male	20	20.72	0.4137	29.71	0.0746	32.32	0.0401
Female	20	13.58	0.8511	16.95	0.6559	34.18	0.0249
Male & female	40	49.79	0.1607	74.75	0.0007	76.24	0.0005
Single							
Male	20	17.67	0.6093	18.07	0.5830	19.62	0.4818
Female	20	35.84	0.0161	27.75	0.1155	53.83	0.0001
Male & female	40	53.51	0.0749	45.82	0.2436	73.45	0.0010
Incidence and prevalence							
Couple							
Male	40	50.91	0.1157	70.14	0.0022	78.51	0.0003
Female	40	72.00	0.0014	54.30	0.0651	88.95	0.0000
Male & female	80	126.80	0.0007	124.70	0.0010	191.82	0.0000
Spouse died							
Male	40	61.81	0.0150	104.07	0.0000	100.39	0.0000
Female	40	51.95	0.0977	37.35	0.5904	70.08	0.0023
Male & female	80	122.23	0.0017	174.89	0.0000	190.94	0.0000
Single							
Male	40	35.35	0.6796	40.58	0.4448	49.87	0.1362
Female	40	80.77	0.0001	84.39	0.0001	79.31	0.0002
Male & female	80	116.11	0.0052	124.96	0.0010	129.18	0.0004

Table 11A.10   **Income Regressions—(*t*-statistics)**

Variable	Couples		Spouse Died		Single	
	Estimate	*t*-statistic	Estimate	*t*-statistic	Estimate	*t*-statistic
ONE	−0.1417	−5.75	−0.0864	−0.79	−0.1386	−2.23
WLTH12	0.1077	6.82	0.1249	1.41	0.1061	2.57
Q1I12	0.0799	12.32	0.1009	3.42	0.0388	2.15
Q4I12	−0.0882	−14.25	−0.1171	−3.05	−0.0908	−6.83
HOODPF12	0.0019	0.23	−0.0054	−0.13	0.0261	1.55
CONDPF12	−0.0028	−0.34	−0.0904	−2.31	−0.0304	−1.79
DNHOUS12	0.0019	0.29	0.0191	0.60	0.0051	0.39
M_HS12	−0.0013	−0.22	0.0210	0.70	0.0053	0.41
M_COLL12	0.0293	4.59	0.0177	0.46	0.0040	0.23
M_AS70S	0.0000	0.49	0.0000	0.09	−0.0001	−0.56
M_AS80S	0.0001	0.52	−0.0004	−0.56	−0.0002	−0.65
M_NEVMARR12					0.0925	2.18
M_WIDOW12					0.1141	2.85
M_DIVSEP12					0.1032	2.47
M_MAGEDI12	0.0002	1.27	−0.0010	−1.56	0.0000	−0.13
M_PAGEDI12	0.0001	0.49	−0.0002	−0.26	0.0003	0.94
M_SMOKEV12	0.0087	1.60	0.0223	0.75	−0.0190	−1.47
M_CANCER12	0.0073	1.19	0.0109	0.36	0.0331	2.18
M_HEART12	−0.0008	−0.17	−0.0304	−1.16	0.0014	0.12
M_STROKE12	−0.0107	−1.20	−0.0404	−1.08	−0.0122	−0.62
M_LUNG12	−0.0005	−0.07	−0.0307	−0.99	−0.0072	−0.49
M_DIABET12	0.0032	0.44	−0.0709	−2.28	−0.0145	−0.88
M_HIGHBP12	0.0134	2.82	0.0456	1.89	0.0010	0.08
M_ARTHRT12	0.0045	0.73	−0.0212	−0.65	0.0211	1.52
M_INCONT12	−0.0017	−0.20	−0.0273	−0.82	−0.0006	−0.03
M_FALL12	−0.0061	−0.52	0.0800	1.75	−0.0021	−0.09
M_HIPFRC12	−0.0015	−0.11	−0.0192	−0.30	−0.0121	−0.41
M_PROXYW12	−0.0193	−2.19	−0.0173	−0.57	−0.0052	−0.14
M_COGIM12	0.0047	0.66	0.0041	0.15	0.0083	0.54
M_PSYCH12	0.0056	0.66	−0.0334	−0.77	−0.0060	−0.33
M_DEPRES12	−0.0245	−1.77	0.0050	0.12	−0.0187	−1.02
M_LOBMI12	−0.0063	−0.70	−0.0262	−1.50	−0.0244	−1.55
M_HIBMI12	0.0006	0.67	0.0031	0.67	−0.0016	−0.69
M_SMOKNOW12	0.0139	1.20	0.0429	1.08	0.0316	1.37
M_NUMADL12	−0.0054	−1.67	−0.0037	−0.34	0.0013	0.19
M_NUMIADL12	0.0000	−0.01	0.0103	0.86	0.0059	0.66
M_DHLTH12	−0.0090	−1.47	0.0394	1.30	−0.0117	−0.81
M_JCANCER23	−0.0018	−0.18	−0.0330	−0.21	−0.0077	−0.35
M_JHEART23	−0.0042	−0.56	0.1318	1.59	0.0118	0.64
M_JSTROKE23	−0.0072	−0.59	0.0482	0.25	−0.0149	−0.59
M_JLUNG23	−0.0041	−0.30	0.0001	0.00	0.0210	0.62
M_IDIABET23	−0.0216	−1.50	−0.3218	−1.49	−0.0335	−0.93
M_IHIGHBP23	−0.0123	−1.17	0.1396	0.83	0.0081	0.36
M_IARTHRT23	−0.0161	−2.10	−0.2789	−3.54	0.0138	0.69
M_JINCONT23	−0.0043	−0.58	0.0622	0.84	0.0032	0.20

(*continued*)

Table 11A.10   (continued)

Variable	Couples		Spouse Died		Single	
	Estimate	t-statistic	Estimate	t-statistic	Estimate	t-statistic
M_JFALL23	−0.0018	−0.21	0.1214	0.98	−0.0080	−0.40
M_JHIPFRC23	−0.0315	−1.44	−0.0491	−0.34	0.0231	0.51
M_PROXYW23	−0.0028	−0.30	0.1074	1.70	0.0230	0.88
M_ICOGIM23	0.0042	0.58	0.0835	1.09	0.0199	1.17
M_IPSYCH23	0.0048	0.56	0.0548	0.47	−0.0164	−0.40
M_IDEPRES23	−0.0119	−0.91	−0.0135	−0.23	0.0261	0.96
M_BMIBT23	0.0068	1.09	−0.0380	−0.86	0.0219	1.53
M_BMIWS23	−0.0026	−0.39	0.0709	0.87	−0.0108	−0.77
M_SMOKNOW23	−0.0117	−0.85	−0.1375	−1.68	−0.0327	−1.32
M_NUMADL23	−0.0036	−1.18	−0.0188	−0.61	−0.0154	−2.58
M_NUMIADL23	0.0081	2.05	−0.0286	−0.97	0.0131	1.76
M_DHLTH23	0.0015	0.25	0.0011	0.02	−0.0138	−1.02
F_ONE					−0.1196	−3.13
F_WLTH12					0.0869	4.05
F_Q1I12					0.0395	6.34
F_Q4I12					−0.0967	−14.66
F_HOODPF12					0.0012	0.16
F_CONDPF12					−0.0037	−0.49
F_DNHOUS12					0.0056	0.98
F_HS12	0.0044	0.69	0.0250	0.88	0.0184	3.33
F_COLL12	0.0126	1.89	0.0601	1.43	0.0275	3.54
F_AS70S	0.0000	0.08	−0.0002	−0.47	0.0000	0.14
F_AS80S	0.0000	−0.19	0.0007	0.78	0.0001	0.68
F_NEVMARR12					0.0724	2.16
F_WIDOW12					0.0589	1.84
F_DIVSEP12					0.0552	1.67
F_MAGEDI12	0.0002	1.17	0.0004	0.72	0.0002	1.14
F_PAGEDI12	0.0002	1.26	0.0002	0.26	−0.0001	−0.47
F_SMOKEV12	0.0059	1.17	−0.0297	−1.10	0.0079	1.44
F_CANCER12	0.0104	1.47	−0.0399	−1.08	0.0105	1.57
F_HEART12	0.0070	1.24	−0.0061	−0.22	−0.0016	−0.29
F_STROKE12	0.0271	2.57	−0.0160	−0.37	−0.0008	−0.09
F_LUNG12	−0.0058	−0.70	0.0561	1.41	0.0031	0.39
F_DIABET12	0.0144	1.83	0.0003	0.01	0.0021	0.26
F_HIGHBP12	0.0093	1.98	−0.0234	−0.96	0.0003	0.07
F_ARTHRT12	0.0063	1.11	−0.0663	−2.31	0.0006	0.10
F_INCONT12	0.0042	0.70	0.0280	0.84	−0.0005	−0.08
F_FALL12	0.0117	1.40	−0.0098	−0.22	0.0008	0.10
F_HIPFRC12	0.0435	3.59	−0.0526	−0.97	−0.0031	−0.32
F_PROXYW12	0.0007	0.06	−0.0636	−1.14	−0.0005	−0.04
F_COGIM12	0.0183	2.32	−0.0273	−0.93	0.0010	0.15
F_PSYCH12	0.0027	0.41	−0.0275	−0.68	0.0082	1.07
F_DEPRES12	−0.0043	−0.46	−0.0404	−0.99	−0.0010	−0.13
F_LOBMI12	0.0039	0.99	−0.0079	−0.58	0.0017	0.46
F_HIBMI12	−0.0006	−0.89	−0.0017	−0.28	0.0006	0.66
F_SMOKNOW12	0.0079	0.44	−0.0286	−0.49	−0.0013	−0.11
F_NUMADL12	0.0036	1.10	0.0289	1.73	−0.0026	−0.94

Table 11A.10   (continued)

Variable	Couples		Spouse Died		Single	
	Estimate	t-statistic	Estimate	t-statistic	Estimate	t-statistic
F_NUMIADL12	−0.0074	−1.73	−0.0039	−0.25	0.0001	0.04
F_DHLTH12	−0.0050	−0.77	0.0368	1.21	0.0027	0.42
F_JCANCER23	0.0064	0.47	−0.0632	−0.89	−0.0025	−0.18
F_JHEART23	−0.0165	−1.92	−0.0496	−1.10	−0.0163	−2.08
F_JSTROKE23	−0.0189	−1.46	−0.0688	−0.95	0.0083	0.64
F_JLUNG23	−0.0075	−0.43	0.0216	0.18	−0.0003	−0.02
F_IDIABET23	−0.0025	−0.14	0.0516	0.58	−0.0036	−0.23
F_IHIGHBP23	0.0221	1.98	−0.0730	−1.32	0.0091	0.86
F_IARTHRT23	0.0095	1.24	0.0417	0.80	−0.0062	−0.85
F_JINCONT23	−0.0037	−0.64	−0.0334	−0.91	0.0056	0.89
F_JFALL23	0.0009	0.13	0.0384	0.87	−0.0040	−0.58
F_JHIPFRC23	−0.0325	−1.46	−0.0973	−0.95	0.0070	0.49
F_PROXYW23	0.0005	0.05	0.1906	3.18	−0.0135	−1.29
F_ICOGIM23	−0.0009	−0.10	−0.0727	−1.75	−0.0039	−0.53
F_IPSYCH23	−0.0023	−0.25	−0.0264	−0.66	−0.0016	−0.13
F_IDEPRES23	−0.0082	−0.71	0.0403	0.95	0.0091	0.85
F_BMIBT23	−0.0172	−2.74	0.0032	0.09	0.0008	0.11
F_BMIWS23	−0.0084	−1.33	0.0236	0.63	−0.0035	−0.53
F_SMOKNOW23	−0.0056	−0.30	0.0571	0.73	−0.0128	−0.97
F_NUMADL23	−0.0025	−0.87	−0.0088	−0.64	0.0006	0.24
F_NUMIADL23	−0.0010	−0.26	−0.0165	−0.93	0.0049	1.61
F_DHLTH23	−0.0016	−0.25	−0.0665	−1.86	−0.0124	−1.95

Table 11A.11   **Mobility, Ownership, Neighborhood, and Dwelling Condition Regressions—(*t*-statistics)**

Variable	Females		Males	
	Coefficient	*t*-statistic	Coefficient	*t*-statistic
Changed Residence Regressions				
one1	−8.0824	−5.1883	−8.4228	−5.5322
one2	−3.5406	−3.2190	−3.3344	−3.0886
logm1	2.0472	4.1790	2.1521	4.4979
logm2	0.5848	1.7574	0.5224	1.6023
q1wb12	0.2458	4.1263	0.2213	3.7980
q4wb12	−0.1640	−2.5800	−0.1952	−3.1669
q1ib12	0.0881	1.5198	0.0965	1.7090
q4ib12	0.1086	1.8830	0.1300	2.3259
hoodpf12	0.0351	0.4949	0.0246	0.3560
condpf12	−0.0950	−1.3343	−0.0855	−1.2402
cwlth23	−0.5547	−2.9274	−0.5864	−3.1662
male12	−0.0706	−1.0036	−0.0728	−1.0355
single12	0.3399	4.9781	0.3471	4.1435
spdied23	0.4072	3.1407	0.4890	3.3585
mspdie23	0.2545	1.4573	0.2889	1.6484
adl12	−0.0159	−0.6746	−0.0410	−1.7200
iadl12	0.0643	2.2692	0.0382	1.3670
dhlth12	−0.0307	−0.5561	0.0888	1.6706
adl23	0.0454	2.3124	0.0549	2.8570
iadl23	0.0429	1.8005	0.0539	2.2981
dhlth23	0.0003	0.0062	−0.0551	−1.0606
hmown23				
hoodpf23				
sadl12	0.0097	0.2181	0.0437	1.0901
siadl12	−0.1377	−2.4472	−0.0614	−1.1688
sdhlth12	0.1103	1.1330	−0.2603	−2.6730
sadl23	0.0389	0.7989	0.0780	1.7261
siadl23	0.0597	0.9476	−0.0663	−1.0395
sdhlth23	−0.0846	−0.7577	0.1738	1.6609
Likelihood	−2,080.6		−2,187.5	
Observations				
Negative	5,395 (88.47)		6,019 (89.21)	
Positive	703 (11.53)		728 (10.79)	
Home Ownership—Regressions				
one1	7.6815	1.7802	5.1103	1.1990
one2	−2.1898	−0.7730	−1.2400	−0.4581
logm1	−2.3714	−1.7483	−1.5396	−1.1488
logm2	0.6749	0.7907	0.4041	0.4973
q1wb12	−1.0613	−5.2262	−1.1041	−5.4193
q4wb12	1.1765	7.0422	1.0881	6.7074
q1ib12	−0.0290	−0.1684	−0.0662	−0.3924
q4ib12	0.0937	0.6125	0.1012	0.6812
hoodpf12	−0.1658	−0.7884	−0.1677	−0.8208
condpf12	0.2148	1.0574	0.2051	1.0496
cwlth23	2.3604	5.2032	2.1317	4.8227

Table 11A.11   (continued)

Variable	Females		Males	
	Coefficient	*t*-statistic	Coefficient	*t*-statistic
male12	0.0218	0.1130	–0.0011	–.0058
single12	–0.8657	–5.5954	–0.8716	–4.0723
spdied23	–0.0252	–0.0885	–0.0496	–0.1491
mspdie23	–0.5329	–1.2507	–0.5408	–1.2679
adl12	–0.0116	–0.1682	–0.0333	–0.4443
iadl12	–0.1099	–1.2344	–0.1499	–1.5601
dhlth12	–0.0646	–0.4219	0.0686	0.4644
adl23	0.0338	0.6406	0.0291	0.5583
iadl23	–0.1331	–1.9536	–0.1406	–2.0826
dhlth23	–0.1977	–1.3659	–0.2537	–1.7724
hmown23				
hoodpf23				
sadl12				
siadl12				
sdhlth12				
sadl23				
siadl23				
sdhlth23				
Likelihood	–297.19		–312.63	
Observations				
Negative	510 (72.55)		521 (71.57)	
Positive	193 (27.45)		207 (28.43)	
Neighborhood—Regressions				
one1	–5.1638	–1.0797	–4.5901	–0.9643
one2	0.2757	0.0596	2.9740	0.6733
logm1	0.8645	0.5791	0.7609	0.5103
logm2	–0.8698	–0.6188	–1.6126	–1.1976
q1wb12	0.1013	0.5063	0.0948	0.4845
q4wb12	–0.2939	–0.9384	–0.3117	–1.0448
q1ib12	0.1348	0.7182	0.1480	0.8100
q4ib12	–0.1193	–0.4647	–0.1579	–0.6348
hoodpf12	0.8861	4.6151	0.8985	4.8188
condpf12	–0.2322	–0.9571	–0.2772	–1.1564
cwlth23	–0.7506	–0.9264	–0.7756	–0.9988
male12	0.0804	0.3313	0.0758	0.3122
single12	0.6373	2.0210	0.4454	1.3979
spdied23	0.4967	1.1126	0.3041	0.6549
mspdie23	–0.2941	–0.4464	–0.2635	–0.3990
adl12	0.0176	0.2351	–0.0175	–0.2305
iadl12	–0.0031	–0.0374	0.0065	0.0787
dhlth12	0.0773	0.4279	0.0041	0.0231
adl23	0.0088	0.1523	0.0196	0.3490
iadl23	0.0110	0.1594	–0.0004	–0.0062
dhlth23	0.3240	1.7316	0.3610	1.9610
hmown23	0.2023	0.8696	0.1511	0.6839
hoodpf23				

(continued)

Table 11A.11   (continued)

Variable	Females		Males	
	Coefficient	*t*-statistic	Coefficient	*t*-statistic
sadl12				
siadl12				
sdhlth12				
sadl23				
siadl23				
sdhlth23				
Likelihood	−151.63		−161.16	
Observations				
Negative	655 (93.17)		677 (92.99)	
Positive	48 (6.83)		51 (7.01)	
	Dwelling Condition—Regressions			
one1	−5.1743	−1.0939	−6.9663	−1.4421
one2	−3.5792	−0.8303	−4.2874	−0.9590
logm1	0.8286	0.5609	1.1817	0.7866
logm2	0.2552	0.1961	0.2502	0.1862
q1wb12	0.4419	2.2384	0.3250	1.5940
q4wb12	0.1381	0.5095	0.1553	0.5661
q1ib12	0.2242	1.2029	0.3016	1.5771
q4ib12	0.0068	0.0291	0.0496	0.2087
hoodpf12	−0.1940	−0.8174	−0.1418	−0.5920
condpf12	1.2251	6.3478	1.2447	6.3933
cwlth23	0.3107	0.4315	0.2390	0.3295
male12	0.0589	0.2455	0.0409	0.1712
single12	0.5441	1.9046	1.2591	2.8052
spdied23	0.3015	0.7117	1.0219	1.8470
mspdie23	0.2957	0.5383	0.3331	0.6089
adl12	0.0211	0.2795	−0.0030	−0.0375
iadl12	0.0308	0.3609	0.0119	0.1350
dhlth12	0.1629	0.8842	0.0696	0.3692
adl23	−0.0349	−0.5898	−0.0153	−0.2606
iadl23	−0.0493	−0.6871	−0.0471	−0.6488
dhlth23	0.1229	0.6586	0.1519	0.7975
hmown23	0.4304	2.0561	0.4232	1.9598
hoodpf23	0.7158	2.8877	0.7217	2.8960
sadl12				
siadl12				
sdhlth12				
sadl23				
siadl23				
sdhlth23				
Likelihood	−160.73		−153.66	
Observations				
Negative	644 (91.61)		671 (92.17)	
Positive	59 (8.39)		57 (7.83)	

Note: Numbers in parentheses are percentages.

References

Adler, N., and J. Ostrove. 1999. Socioeconomic status and health: What we know and what we don't. *Socioeconomic Status and Health in Industrialized Nations: Annals of the New York Academy of Sciences* 896:3–15.

Alessie, R., A. Lusardi, and A. Kapteyn. 2000. Savings after retirement: Evidence from three different surveys. *Labour Economics* 6 (2): 277–310.

Angrist, J., G. Imbens, and D. Rubin. 1996. Identification of causal effects using instrumental variables. *Journal of the American Statistical Association* 91:444–72.

Attanasio, O., and H. Hoynes. 2000. Differential mortality and wealth accumulation. *Journal of Human Resources* 35 (1): 1–29.

Backlund, E., P. Sorlie, and N. Johnson. 1999. A comparison of the relationships of education and income with mortality: The National Longitudinal Mortality Study. *Social Science and Medicine* 49:1373–84.

Baker, M., M. Stabile, and C. Deri. 2001. What do self-reported objective measures of health measure? NBER Working Paper no. 8419. Cambridge, Mass.: National Bureau of Economic Research, August.

Barsky, R., T. Juster, M. Kimball, and M. Shapiro. 1997. Preference parameters and behavioral heterogeneity: An experimental approach in the Health and Retirement Survey. *Quarterly Journal of Economics* 112:537–79.

Bosma, H., M. G. Marmot, H. Hemingway, A. C. Nicholson, E. Brunner, and S. A. Stansfeld. 1997. Low job control and risk of coronary heart disease in Whitehall II (prospective cohort) Study. *British Medical Journal* 314:558–565.

Chandola, T. 1998. Social inequality in coronary heart disease: A comparison of occupational classifications. *Social Science and Medicine* 47:525–33.

———. Social class differences in mortality using the new UK National Statistics Socio-Economic Classification. *Social Science and Medicine* 50:641–49.

Chapman, K., and G. Hariharran. 1994. Controlling for causality in the link from income to mortality. *Journal of Risk and Uncertainty* 8 (1): 85–93.

Chay, K., and M. Greenstone. 1998. Does air quality matter? Evidence from the housing market. NBER Working Paper no. 6826. Cambridge, Mass.: National Bureau of Economic Research, December.

Davey-Smith, G., D. Blane, and M. Bartley. 1994. Explanations for socio-economic differentials in mortality: Evidence from Britain and elsewhere. *European Journal of Public Health* 4:131–44.

Dawid, A. 2000. Causal inference without counterfactuals. *Journal of the American Statistical Association* 95:407–48.

Dohrenwend, B. P., I. Levav, P. E. Shrout, S. Schwartz, G. Naveh, B. G. Link, A. E. Skodal, and A. Stueve. 1992. Socioeconomic status and psychiatric disorders: A test of the social causation–social selection issue. *Science* 255:946–52.

Drever, F., and M. Whitehead. 1997. *Health inequalities.* London: ONS.

Ecob, R., and G. Smith. 1999. Income and health: What is the nature of the relationship. *Social Science and Medicine* 48:693–705.

Elo, I., and S. Preston. 1996. Educational differences in mortality: United States, 1979–85. *Social Science and Medicine* 42 (1): 47–57.

Engle, R., D. Hendry, and J. Richard. 1983. Exogeneity. *Econometrica* 51:277–304.

Ettner, S. 1996. New evidence on the relationship between income and wealth. *Journal of Health Economics* 15:67–85.

Evans, A. 1978. Causation and disease: A chronological journey. *American Journal of Epidemiology* 108:249–58.

Feigl, H. 1953. Notes on causality. In *Readings in the philosophy of science,* ed. H. Feigl and M. Brodbeck, 408–18. New York: Appleton-Century-Crofts.

Feinstein, J. 1992. The relationship between socioeconomic status and health: A review of the literature. *The Millbank Quarterly* 71 (2): 279–322.

Felitti, V. J, R. F. Anda, D. Nordenberg, D. F. Williamson, A. M. Spitz, V. Edwards, M. P. Koss, and J. S. Marks. 1998. Relationship of childhood abuse and household dysfunction to many of the leading causes of death in adults: The Adverse Childhood Experiences (ACE) Study. *American Journal of Preventative Medicine* 14:245–58.

Fitzpatrick, R., M. Bartley, B. Dodgeon, D. Firth, and K. Lynch. 1997. Social variations in health: Relationship of mortality to the interim revised social classification. In *Constructing classes,* ed. D. Rose and K. O'Reily. Swindon, England: ESRC/ONS.

Fitzpatrick, J., and G. Dollamore. 1999. Examining adult mortality rates using the National Statistics Socio-Economic Classification. *Health Statistics Quarterly* 2:33–40.

Florens, J. P., and J. Heckman. 2001. Conditioning versus fixing: Definitions of causality in static and dynamic models. Paper presented at DC2 conferences: CORE. 13 December, Louvain-la-Neuve, Belgium.

Fox, A., P. Goldblatt, and D. Jones. 1985. Social class mortality differentials: Artifact, selection, or life circumstances? *Journal of Epidemiology and Community Health* 39:1–8.

Freedman, D. 1985. Statistics and the scientific method. In *Cohort analysis in social research,* ed. W. Mason and S. Feinberg, 343–90. New York: Springer.

———. 2001. On specifying graphical models for causation and the identification problem. University of California, Berkeley, Department of Statistics. Working Paper.

Fuchs, V. 1993. Poverty and health: Asking the right questions. In *Medical care and the health of the poor,* ed. D. Rogers and E. Ginzberg, 9–20. Boulder, Colo.: Westview Press.

Geweke, J. 1984. Inference and causality in economic time series models. In *Handbook of econometrics,* Vol. 2, ed. Z. Griliches and M. Intriligator, 1101–44. Amsterdam: North-Holland.

Gill, R., and J. Robins. 2001. Causal inference of complex longitudinal data: The continuous case. *Annals of Statistics,* 29:1785–811.

Goldblatt, P. O. 1990. *Longitudinal study, mortality, and social organization.* London: HMSO.

Goldman, N. 1994. Social factors and health: The causation-selection issue revisited. *Proceedings of the National Academy of Sciences* 91:1251–55.

———. 2001. Social inequalities in health: Disentangling the underlying mechanisms. *Strengthening the Dialogue between Epidemiology and Demography: Annals of the New York Academy of Science* 954:118–39.

Granger, C. 1969. Investigating causal relations by econometric models and cross-spectral methods. *Econometrica* 37:424–38.

Haynes, R. 1991. Inequalities in health and health service use: Evidence from the General Household Survey. *Social Science and Medicine* 33:361–68.

Heckman, J. 2000. Causal parameters and policy analysis in econometrics: A twentieth century retrospective. *Quarterly Journal of Econometrics* 105:45–97.

———. 2001. Econometrics counterfactuals and causal models. University of Chicago, International Statistical Institute. Working Paper.

———. 2003. Conditioning, causality and policy analysis. *Journal of Econometrics* 112 (1): 73–78.

Hendry, D., and G. Mizon. 1999. The pervasiveness of Granger causality in econometrics. In *Cointegration, causality, and forecasting,* ed. R. Engle and H. White, 102–34. Oxford: Oxford University Press.

Hertzman, C. 1999. Population health and human development. In *Developmental health and the wealth of nations,* ed. D. Keating and C. Hertzman. New York: Guilford Press.

Herzog, R., and R. Wallace. 1997. Measures of cognitive functioning in the AHEAD Study. *Journal of Gerontology* B ser., 52:37–48.

Holland, P. 1986. Statistics and causal inference. *Journal of the American Statistical Association* 81:945–60.

———. 1988. Causal inference, path analysis, and recursive structural equation models. In *Sociological methodology,* ed. C. Clogg, 449–84. Washington, D.C.: American Sociological Association.

Hoover, K. 2001. Causality in macroeconomics. Cambridge, U.K.: Cambridge University Press.

———. 2003. Some causal lessons from macroeconomics. *Joural of Econometrics* 112 (1): 121–125.

Humphries, K., and E. van Doorslaer. 2000. Income related health inequality in Canada. *Social Science and Medicine* 50 (5): 663–71.

Hurd, M. 1987. Savings of the elderly and desired bequests. *American Economic Review* 77:298–312.

Hurd, M., D. McFadden, and L. Gan. 1998. Subjective survival curves and life cycle behavior. In *Inquiries in the economics of aging,* ed. D. Wise, 259–305. Chicago: University of Chicago Press.

Hurd, M., D. McFadden, L. Gan, A. Merrill, and M. Roberts. 1998. In *Frontiers in the economics of aging,* ed. D. Wise, 353–87. Chicago: University of Chicago Press.

Hurd, M., and K. McGarry. 1997. Evaluation of the subjective probabilities of survival in the Health and Retirement Survey. *Journal of Human Resources* 30: S268–92.

Hurd, M., and D. Wise. 1989. Wealth depletion and life cycle consumption by the elderly. In *Topics in the economics of aging,* ed. D. Wise, 135–60. Chicago: University of Chicago Press.

Kaplan, J., and S. Manuck. 1999. Status, stress, and arteriosclerosis: The role of environment and individual behaviour. *Socioeconomic Status and Health in Industrialized Nations: Annals of the New York Academy of Science* 896:145–61.

Karasek, R. A., T. Theorell, J. Schwartz, P. Schnell, C. Peiper, and J. Michela. 1988. Job characteristics in relation to the prevalence of myocardial infarction in the US Health Examination Survey (HES) and the Health and Nutrition Examination Survey (NHANES). *American Journal of Public Health* 78:910–18.

Kelley, S., C. Hertzman, and M. Daniels. 1997. Searching for the biological pathways between stress and health. *Annual Review of Public Health* 18:437–62.

Kitagawa, E., and P. Hauser. 1973. *Differential mortality in the United States: A study in socioeconomic epidemiology.* Cambridge, Mass.: Harvard University Press.

Kunsch, H., S. Geman, and A. Kehagias. 1995. Hidden Markov random fields. *Annals of Applied Probability* 5:577–602.

Leigh, J., and R. Dhir. 1997. Schooling and frailty among seniors. *Economics of Education Review* 16 (1): 45–57.

Lewis, G., P. Bebbington, T. Brugha, M. Farell, B. Gill, R. Jenkins, and H. Meltzer. 1998. Socioeconomic status, standard of living and neurotic disorder. *Lancet* 352:605–09.

Luft, H. 1978. *Poverty and health: Economic causes and consequences of health problems.* Cambridge, Mass.: Ballinger.

Marmot, M. G., G. D. Smith, S. Stansfeld, C. Patel, F. North, J. Head, I. White, E. Brunner, and E. Feeney. 1991. Health inequalities among British civil servants: The Whitehall II Study. *Lancet* 337:1387–93.

Marmot, M., M. Bobak, and G. Davey-Smith. 1995. Explanations for social inequalities in health. In *Society and health,* ed. B. Amick, S. Levine, A. R. Tarlov, and D. C. Walsh, 172–210 New York: Oxford University Press.

Marmot, M., H. Bosma, H. Hemingway, E. Brunner, and S. Stansfeld. 1997. Contribution of job control and other risk factors to social variations in coronary heart disease incidence. *Lancet* 350:235–39.

Martin, L., and S. Preston. 1994. *Demography of aging.* Washington, D.C.: National Academy Press.

Martin, L., and B. Soldo. 1997. *Racial and ethnic differences in the health of older Americans.* Washington, D.C.: National Academy Press.

McDonough, P., G. Duncan, D. Williams, and J. House. 1997. Income dynamics and adult mortality in the United States. *American Journal of Public Health* 87:1476–83.

McEwen, B., and E. Stellar. 1993. Stress and the individual: Mechanisms leading to disease. *Archives of Internal Medicine* 153:2093–2101.

Meer, J., D. Miller, and H. Rosen. 2001. Exploring the health-wealth nexus. Princeton University. Working Paper.

Murray, C. J. L., G. Yang, and X. Qiao. 1992. Adult mortality: Levels, patterns, and causes. In *The health of adults in the developing world,* ed. R. G. Feachem, T. Kjellstrom, C. J. L. Murray, M. Over, and M. Phillips, 23–111. New York: Oxford University Press.

Newey, W., J. Powell, and J. Walker. 1990. Semiparametric estimation of selection models: Some empirical results. *American Economic Review* 80:324–28.

Nozick, R. 2001. *Invariance: The structure of the objective world.* Cambridge, Mass.: Harvard University Press.

Pearl, J. 2000. *Causality: Models, reasoning, and inference.* Cambridge, Mass.: Harvard University Press.

Power, C., and S. Matthews. 1998. Accumulation of health risks across social groups in a national longitudinal study. In *Human biology and social inequality,* ed. S. Strickland and P. Shetty, 36–57. Cambridge, U.K.: Cambridge University Press.

Power, C., S. Matthews, and O. Manor. 1996. Inequalities in self-rated health in the 1958 birth cohort: Life time social circumstances or social mobility? *British Medical Journal* 313:449–53.

Preston, S., and P. Taubman. 1994. Socioeconomic differences in adult mortality and health status. In *Demography of aging,* ed. L. Martin and S. Preston, 279–318. Washington, D.C.: National Academy Press.

Robins, J. 1999. Association, causation, and marginal structural models. *Synthese* 121:151–79.

Rodgers, B. 1991. Socio-economic status, employment and neurosis. *Social Psychiatry and Psychiatric Epidemiology* 26:104–14.

Ross, C., and J. Mirowsky. 2000. Does medical insurance contribute to socioeconomic differentials in health? *The Millbank Quarterly* 78:291–321.

Schnall, P., P. Landsbergis, and D. Baker. 1994. Job strain and cardiovascular disease. *Annual Review of Public Health* 15:381–411.

Seeman, T., B. Singer, G. Love, and L. Levy-Storms. 2002. Social relationships, gender, and allostatic load across two age cohorts. *Psychosomatic Medicine* 64:395–406.

Shorrocks, A. 1975. The age-wealth relationship: A cross-section and cohort analysis. *Review of Economics and Statistics* 57:155–63.

Sims, C. 1972. Money, income, and causality. *American Economic Review* 65:540–52.

Smith, J. 1998. Socioeconomic status and health. *American Economic Review* 88: 192–96.

———. 1999. Healthy bodies and thick wallets: The dual relation between health and economic status. *Journal of Economic Perspectives* 13:145–66.

Smith, J., and R. Kington. 1997a. Demographic and economic correlates of health in old age. *Demography* 34 (1): 159–70.

———. 1997b. Race, socioeconomic status, and health in late life. In *Racial and ethnic differences in the health of older Americans,* ed. L. Martin and B. Soldo, 106–62. Washington, D.C.: National Academy Press.

Sobel, M. 1997. Measurement, causation, and local independence in latent variable models. In *Latent variable modeling and applications to causality,* ed. M. Berkane, 11–28. Berlin: Springer.

———. 2000. Causal inference in the social sciences. *Journal of the American Statistical Association* 95:647–51.

Soldo, B., M. Hurd, W. Rodgers, and R. Wallace. 1997. Asset and health dynamics among the oldest old: An overview of the AHEAD Study. *Journal of Gerontology* B ser., 52:1–20.

Staiger, D., and J. Stock. 1997. Instrumental variables regression with weak instruments. *Econometrica* 64:556–86.

Stern, J. 1983. Social mobility and the interpretation of social class mortality differentials. *Journal of Social Policy* 12:27–49.

Swert, W. 1979. Tests of causality. In *Three aspects of policy and policymaking,* ed. K. Brunner and A. Meltzer, 55–96. Amsterdam: North-Holland.

U.S. Bureau of the Census. 1999. *National vital statistics reports: United States life tables, 1997,* Vol. 47. Washington, D.C.: GPO.

Wadsworth, M. 1991. The imprint of time: Childhood, history, and adult life. Oxford, Clarendon Press.

Whitehead, M. 1988. *The health divide.* London: Penguin.

Wilkinson, R. 1998. Equity, social cohesion, and health. In *Human biology and social inequity,* ed. S. Strickland and P. Shetty. Cambridge: Cambridge University Press.

Woodward, J. 1999. Causal interpretation in systems of equations. *Synthese* 212: 199–247.

Woodward, M., M. Shewry, C. Smith, and H. Tunstall-Pedoe. 1992. Social status and coronary heart disease: Results from the Scottish Heart Health Study. *Preventive Medicine* 21:136–48.

Zellner, A. 1979. Causality and econometrics. In *Three aspects of policy and policymaking,* ed. K. Brunner and A. Meltzer, 9–54. Amsterdam: North-Holland.

Addendum

This addendum describes updates in data and analysis since the publication of this paper in the *Journal of Econometrics* (2003), 112, 3–53. The differences result from correcting some coding errors, producing a new dataset with revised imputations, and a new treatment of the simulation of wealth evolution. We also include in this addendum results from Lagrange multiplier (LM) tests of the Wold causal chain assumption that we impose on the system of innovation equations. We comment on each of these points in turn.

We have corrected a health condition coding problem in the AHEAD data, described in "Data alert: Correction to F1156 [B7. Heart Condition]," from the HRS webpage. This coding problem produced a significant undercount of heart attack prevalence in wave 3. We have also corrected a problem in our count of new incidences, given existing previous condition, for the variables heart attack, cancer, and stroke, which was producing undercounts for the incidence variables. Updated tables 11.2R and 11.3R give summary statistics for the revised variables. These changes do not produce significant alterations to our overall results, but there are some differences in the coefficients of the incidence regressions. Table 11.8 in the published paper is updated in table 11.8R, which summarizes the coefficients that are now significant. A notable change is that, with the exception of cancer for males, we now obtain invariance of the models over time for the first three health conditions: cancer, heart disease, and stroke. The updated invariance and noncausality tests are given in table 11.9R. The wealth revisions have some impact on simulation results, which are updated in tables 11.12R and 11.13R.

In revising our code, we fixed the seed for the random number generator and produced a data set in which all imputations can be replicated. However, numerical imputations have changed, particularly imputed asset values. The tables listed above reflect these changes. The numerical differences from the previous published results are minor, and all the same results are obtained.

The simulations of wealth paths were producing, in some instances, unreasonable results in the first few years of simulation, with excessive increases in wealth observed in some cases. Our simulations start from a baseline population of seventy–seventy-five-year-olds in the first wave of the AHEAD, and these changes in wealth in the initial years of simulation are inconsistent with changes for the same population observed in subsequent waves. The observed pattern of wealth decrease is reproduced in the simulation after a few years, leading us to postulate, in loose terms, that our imputations and estimates capture the correct dynamics, but the wrong initial state of the baseline population. This is consistent with the findings of other researchers that wealth appears to be undercounted in AHEAD wave 1, due to undercounting of the categories in which assets are held. We therefore attempted to adjust to the correct initial state. We did this by calibrating the constant term of the wealth regressions using a cross-validation procedure. We calibrated the intercept so that the first year of simulated wealth changes (in terms of rate of change) matched, at the median, the observed transition for our baseline population. The changes in the intercept required to obtain this match are minor, as can be seen from table 11.14. Although we effectively force the prediction to match the

Table 11.2R   Health Condition Variables in AHEAD

	Wave 1				Wave 2				Wave 3			
Label	Variable	N	Mean	SD	Variable	N	Mean	SD	Variable	N	Mean	SD
Health condition prevalence												
Doc ever told had cancer?	cancer1	6,489	0.137	0.344	cancer2	6,432	0.176	0.381	cancer3	5,709	0.190	0.392
Doc ever told had heart attack/disease?	heart1	6,489	0.317	0.465	heart2	6,432	0.364	0.481	heart3	5,709	0.401	0.490
Doc ever told had stroke?	stroke1	6,489	0.089	0.285	stroke2	6,432	0.123	0.329	stroke3	5,709	0.143	0.350
Doc ever told had lung disease?	lung1	6,489	0.115	0.319	lung2	6,432	0.124	0.329	lung3	5,709	0.129	0.335
Doc ever told had diabetes?	diabet1	6,489	0.134	0.340	diabet2	5,741	0.147	0.354	diabet3	4,867	0.159	0.365
Doc ever told had high blood pressure?	highbp1	6,489	0.502	0.500	highbp2	5,741	0.525	0.499	highbp3	4,867	0.554	0.497
Seen Doc for arthritic in last 12 m?	arthrt1	6,489	0.267	0.442	arthrt2	5,741	0.277	0.448	arthrt3	4,867	0.279	0.449
Incontinence last 12 m?	incont1	6,489	0.203	0.402	incont2	6,489	0.318	0.466	incont3	6,489	0.405	0.491
Fall in last 12 m require treatment?	fall1	6,489	0.080	0.271	fall2	6,489	0.180	0.384	fall3	6,489	0.266	0.442
Ever fractured hip?	hipfrc1	6,489	0.050	0.218	hipfrc2	6,489	0.069	0.253	hipfrc3	6,489	0.088	0.283
Proxy Interview	proxyw1	6,489	0.104	0.306	proxyw2	5,741	0.132	0.339	proxyw3	4,867	0.154	0.361
Age-educ adjust cognitive impairment?	cogim1	6,489	0.256	0.436	cogim2	6,489	0.363	0.481	cogim3	6,487	0.438	0.496
Ever seen Doc for psych prob?	psych1	6,489	0.109	0.312	psych2	5,741	0.128	0.334	psych3	4,867	0.143	0.351
Depressed (cesd8>4)	depres1	6,489	0.099	0.299	depres2	5,741	0.086	0.280	depres3	4,867	0.100	0.300
Body Mass Index (Quetelet)	bmi1	6,475	25.369	4.529	bmi2	6,475	25.000	4.654	bmi3	6,475	24.679	4.680
Low BMI spline = max(0,20-bmi)	lobmi1	6,475	0.155	0.653	lobmi2	6,475	0.221	0.816	lobmi3	6,475	0.279	0.927
High BMI spline = max(0,bmi-25)	hibmi1	6,475	1.890	3.165	hibmi2	6,475	1.766	3.116	hibmi3	6,475	1.646	2.999
Current smoker?	smoknow1	6,489	0.103	0.304	smoknow2	5,741	0.079	0.270	smoknow3	4,867	0.066	0.249
No. of ADLs (needs help/difficult)	numadl1	6,489	0.725	1.391	numadl2	6,432	1.058	1.855	numadl3	5,709	1.254	2.016
No. of IADLs (needs help/difficult)	numiadl1	6,489	0.618	1.166	numiadl2	6,432	0.728	1.408	numiadl3	5,709	0.867	1.493
Poor/Fair self-reported health	dhlth1	6,489	0.373	0.484	dhlth2	5,741	0.368	0.482	dhlth3	4,867	0.434	0.496

(continued)

Table 11.2R   (continued)

Health condition incidence

Label	Wave 1				Wave 2				Wave 3			
	Variable	N	Mean	SD	Variable	N	Mean	SD	Variable	N	Mean	SD
Cancer[a]					jcancer2	6,432	0.057	0.231	jcancer3	5,685	0.058	0.234
Heart Attack/Condition[a]					jheart2	6,432	0.132	0.338	jheart3	5,685	0.154	0.361
Stroke[a]					jstroke2	6,432	0.058	0.233	jstroke3	5,685	0.070	0.255
Died Since Last Wave?					tdied2	6,489	0.115	0.319	tdied3	6,489	0.135	0.341
Lung Disease[a]					ilung2	6,432	0.024	0.153	ilung3	5,685	0.033	0.178
Diabetes[a]					idiabet2	5,741	0.024	0.154	idiabet3	4,867	0.025	0.156
High Blood Pressure (HBP)[a]					ihighbp2	5,741	0.054	0.226	ihighbp3	4,867	0.056	0.229
Arthritis[a]					iarthrt2	5,741	0.112	0.316	iarthrt3	4,867	0.117	0.322
Incontinence in last 12 months					jincont2	6,432	0.236	0.425	jincont3	5,709	0.263	0.440
Fall requiring treatment[a]					jfall2	6,432	0.129	0.335	jfall3	5,709	0.144	0.351
Hip Fracture[a]					jhipfrc2	6,432	0.023	0.151	jhipfrc3	5,709	0.027	0.163
Proxy Interview					proxyw2	5,741	0.132	0.339	proxyw3	4,867	0.154	0.361
Cognitive Impairment					icogim2	6,489	0.107	0.310	icogim3	6,487	0.075	0.263
Psychiatric Problems[a]					ipsych2	5,741	0.046	0.210	ipsych3	4,867	0.040	0.197
Depression					idepres2	5,741	0.051	0.220	idepres3	4,867	0.064	0.245
BMI better Indicator					bmibt2	6,489	0.174	0.379	bmibt3	6,489	0.149	0.356
BMI worse Indicator					bmiws2	6,489	0.150	0.357	bmiws3	6,489	0.143	0.350

Note: N = number of observations; SD = standard deviation.

[a] AHEAD Waves 2 and 3: "Since the last interview . . . ?"

Table 11.3R SES and Demographic Variables in AHEAD

Label	Wave 1				Wave 2				Wave 3			
	Variable	N	Mean	SD	Variable	N	Mean	SD	Variable	N	Mean	SD
Wealth 97 Dol (V.2) (000)	c_2w1	6,489	0.643	0.075	c_2w2	5,736	2.473	1.122	c_2w3	4,862	2.508	1.112
Nonliquid wealth (000)	c_2n1	6,489	0.643	0.075	c_2n2	5,741	2.473	1.122	c_2n3	4,866	2.508	1.112
Liquid wealth (000)	c_2l1	6,489	0.643	0.075	c_2l2	5,737	2.473	1.122	c_2l3	4,864	2.508	1.112
Income 97 Dol (V.2) (000)	c_2i1	6,489	0.643	0.075	c_2i2	5,741	2.473	1.122				
1st quartile wealth indicator	q1wb1	6,489	0.258	0.438	q1wb2	6,489	0.208	0.406	q1wb3	6,489	0.185	0.388
4th quartile wealth indicator	q4wb1	6,489	0.213	0.409	q4wb2	6,489	0.241	0.428	q4wb3	6,489	0.203	0.402
1st quartile income indicator	q1wb1	6,489	0.256	0.436	q1ib2	6,489	0.219	0.414				
4th quartile income indicator	q4ib1	6,489	0.245	0.430	q4ib2	6,489	0.219	0.414				
Change residence?					moved2	5,741	0.096	0.295	moved3	4,867	0.102	0.303
Own residence?	dnhous1	6,489	0.667	0.472	dnhous2	5,741	0.660	0.474	dnhous3	4,867	0.640	0.480
Neighborhood safety poor/fair	hoodpf1	6,489	0.150	0.357	hoodpf2	5,741	0.139	0.346	hoodpf3	4,867	0.110	0.312
House condition poor/fair	condpf1	6,489	0.148	0.356	condpf2	5,741	0.139	0.346	condpf3	4,867	0.131	0.337
Widow?	widow1	6,489	0.416	0.493	widow2	6,432	0.453	0.498	widow3	5,706	0.496	0.500
Divorced/Separated?	divsep1	6,489	0.054	0.226	divsep2	6,432	0.053	0.225	divsep3	5,706	0.055	0.227
Married	married1	6,489	0.498	0.500	married2	6,432	0.459	0.498	married3	5,706	0.417	0.493
Never married?	nevmarr1	6,489	0.032	0.176	nevmarr2	6,432	0.031	0.174	nevmarr3	5,706	0.030	0.171
Age at interview (months)	agem1	6,489	27.379	2.662	agem2	6,489	26.958	2.544	agem3	5,775	26.958	2.544
Mother's death age	magedie1	6,489	73.833	17.386								
Father's death age	pagedie1	6,489	71.537	15.121								
Ever smoke?	smokev	6,489	0.526	0.499								
Education (years)	educ	6,489	0.605	0.489								
Educ > 10 yrs indicator	hs	6,489	0.605	0.489								
Educ > 14 yrs indicator	coll	6,489	0.143	0.35								

Note: N = number of observations; SD = standard deviation.

Table 11.8R   Statistically Significant Risk Factors for Incidence of Health Conditions (two percent significance level)

	Cancer		Heart		Stroke		Mortality	Lung	Diabetes	HBP	Arthritis	Incontinence		Fall		Hip Fracture		Cognitive Impairment	Psychiatric Problem	Depression	ADL	IADL	SRHS	
	No	Yes	No	Yes	No	Yes	(All)	(All)	(All)	(All)	(All)	No	Yes	No	Yes	No	Yes	(All)	(All)	(All)	(All)	(All)	No	Yes
							Female (pre-existing risk factor)																	
as70m12			+	+														+			+	+		
as80m12				−													−				−	−		
q1wb12																								
q4wb12																								
q1ib12																			+			+		
q4ib12																				+				
hs12	−										−													
coll12				+																				
hoodpf12																								
condpf12																								
nevmar12																		+						
widow12																								
divsep12																			−					
magedi12									−										−					
pagedi12																					−			
smokev12	+							+			+													
canc12				+			+													−				
heart12								+					+						+	+			+	
strk12				+							+													
lung12			+	+																	+	+		+
diab12			+	+																	+	+	+	
high12					+		−																	
arth12													+								+	+	+	

incon12
fall12
hip12
cog12
psych12
depr12
lobmi12
hibmi12
smok12
adl12
iadl12
dhlth12
jcanc23
jheart23
jstrk23
ilung23
idiab23
ihigh23
iarth23
jincon23
jfall23
jhip23
icog23
ipsych23
idepr23
bmibt23
bmiws23
smok23
adl23
iadl23

(continued)

Table 11.8R (continued)

Male (pre-existing risk factor)

	Cancer		Heart		Stroke		Mortality	Lung	Diabetes	HBP	Arthritis	Incontinence		Fall		Hip Fracture		Cognitive Impairment	Psychiatric Problem	Depression	ADL	IADL	SRHS	
	No	Yes	No	Yes	No	Yes	(All)	(All)	(All)	(All)	(All)	No	Yes	No	Yes	No	Yes	(All)	(All)	(All)	(All)	(All)	No	Yes
as70m12						+	+																	
as80m12																		+						
q1wb12		−						−																
q4wb12																								
q1ib12																								
q4ib12																								
hs12																								
coll12				−					−															
hoodpf12		+																						
condpf12		−		−																				
nevmar12																								
widow12	+													+										
divsep12															+								−	
magedi12		−		−			−								−									
pagedi12																						+	+	
smokev12																								
canc12		+					+																	
heart12				+																				
strk12										+												+	+	
lung12							+						+										+	
diab12		+		+			+		−													+	+	
high12			+								+							−					+	
arth12										+									+				+	
incon12																								

Table 11.9R   **Health Innovations, Tests for Invariance and Causality (_p_-values)**

| Variable | Invariance | | | |
| | With SES | | Without SES | |
	Female	Male	Female	Male
CANCER	0.528	0.016	0.309	0.007
CANCER—no previous	0.867	0.129	0.812	0.064
CANCER—previous	0.068	0.044	0.079	0.083
HEART	0.085	0.690	0.052	0.619
HEART—no previous	0.170	0.823	0.060	0.498
HEART—previous	0.547	0.692	0.492	0.725
STROKE	0.384	0.204	0.266	0.135
STROKE—no previous	0.172	0.258	0.160	0.180
STROKE—previous	0.907	0.045	0.784	0.087
MORTALITY	0.221	0.378	0.315	0.491
LUNG	0.552	0.689	0.483	0.502
DIABETES	0.189	0.234	0.281	0.128
HIGH BLOOD PRESSURE	0.007	0.393	0.024	0.172
ARTHRITIS	0.046	0.071	0.032	0.167
INCONTINENCE	0.781	0.351	0.597	0.682
INCONTINENCE—no previous	0.706	0.102	0.426	0.555
INCONTINENCE—previous	0.962	0.793	0.892	0.730
FALL	0.904	0.263	0.790	0.207
FALL—no previous	0.792	0.140	0.612	0.133
FALL—previous	0.365	0.000	0.358	0.000
HIP FRACTURE	0.491	0.126	0.280	0.053
HIP FRACTURE—no previous	0.930	0.300	0.724	0.123
HIP FRACTURE—previous				
PROXY INTERVIEW	0.301	0.591	0.465	0.378
PROXY INTERVIEW—no previous	0.127	0.795	0.444	0.606
PROXY INTERVIEW—previous				
COGNITIVE IMPAIRMENT	0.005	0.288	0.008	0.143
PSYCHIATRIC	0.127	0.295	0.052	0.365
DEPRESSION	0.211	0.944	0.299	0.934
BODY MASS INDEX	0.260	0.009	0.251	0.002
CURRENT SMOKER	0.420	0.710	0.214	0.504
CURRENT SMOKER—no previous	0.133	0.033	0.078	0.040
CURRENT SMOKER—previous	0.797		0.733	
ADL	0.001	0.021	0.007	0.038
IADL	0.603	0.008	0.388	0.003
SELF RATED HEALTH	0.376	0.634	0.341	0.607
SELF RATED HEALTH—no previous	0.514	0.251	0.558	0.215
SELF RATED HEALTH—previous	0.239	0.165	0.176	0.189

Table 11.9R (continued)

	Noncausality					
	Wave 1–2		Wave 2–3		Wave 1–3	
	Female	Male	Female	Male	Female	Male
CANCER	0.987	0.588	0.408	0.165	0.613	0.198
CANCER—no previous	0.704	0.658	0.289	0.173	0.313	0.166
CANCER—previous	0.143	0.228	0.472	0.017	0.299	0.036
HEART	0.540	0.054	0.396	0.996	0.398	0.243
HEART—no previous	0.872	0.344	0.750	0.412	0.736	0.039
HEART—previous	0.104	0.071	0.153	0.737	0.019	0.172
STROKE	0.757	0.837	0.584	0.028	0.657	0.059
STROKE—no previous	0.415	0.955	0.671	0.064	0.713	0.203
STROKE—previous	0.824	0.301	0.882	0.155	0.799	0.383
MORTALITY	0.098	0.275	0.883	0.306	0.652	0.364
LUNG	0.166	0.174	0.866	0.122	0.343	0.010
DIABETES	0.615	0.141	0.020	0.236	0.110	0.025
HIGH BLOOD PRESSURE	0.342	0.996	0.083	0.941	0.534	0.990
ARTHRITIS	0.179	0.029	0.242	0.713	0.085	0.395
INCONTINENCE	0.763	0.019	0.254	0.800	0.163	0.463
INCONTINENCE—no previous	0.914	0.037	0.602	0.197	0.453	0.641
INCONTINENCE—previous	0.900	0.247	0.168	0.664	0.149	0.244
FALL	0.532	0.687	0.945	0.454	0.600	0.592
FALL—no previous	0.501	0.697	0.944	0.251	0.558	0.532
FALL—previous	0.329	0.000	0.803	0.000	0.696	0.053
HIP FRACTURE	0.613	0.597	0.370	0.666	0.159	0.430
HIP FRACTURE—no previous	0.461	0.461	0.706	0.725	0.128	0.234
HIP FRACTURE—previous						
PROXY INTERVIEW	0.017	0.486	0.870	0.127	0.254	0.032
PROXY INTERVIEW—no previous	0.002	0.793	0.541	0.121	0.087	0.073
PROXY INTERVIEW—previous						
COGNITIVE IMPAIRMENT	0.001	0.259	0.259	0.200	0.002	0.026
PSYCHIATRIC	0.043	0.238	0.214	0.069	0.004	0.065
DEPRESSION	0.007	0.143	0.261	0.377	0.011	0.065
BODY MASS INDEX	0.188	0.839	0.931	0.711	0.673	0.684
CURRENT SMOKER	0.603	0.282	0.974	0.693	0.625	0.129
CURRENT SMOKER—no previous	0.335	0.196	0.874	0.980	0.515	0.962
CURRENT SMOKER—previous	0.375	0.325	0.547	0.325	0.274	0.025
ADL	0.077	0.014	0.346	0.971	0.828	0.358
IADL	0.374	0.051	0.817	0.243	0.241	0.009
SELF RATED HEALTH	0.013	0.048	0.100	0.301	0.001	0.020
SELF RATED HEALTH—no previous	0.015	0.187	0.202	0.121	0.007	0.034
SELF RATED HEALTH—previous	0.225	0.195	0.557	0.256	0.193	0.175

(*continued*)

Table 11.9R (continued)

| | Joint (Invariance + Noncausality) | | Relative Odds (high vs. low SES) | | | |
| | | | Female | | Male | |
	Female	Male	Odds	SE	Odds	SE
CANCER	0.600	0.012	1.31	0.46	0.73	0.27
CANCER—no previous	0.778	0.084	1.24	0.48	0.67	0.29
CANCER—previous	0.067	0.011	5.85	7.75	2.69	3.42
HEART	0.099	0.571	0.97	0.21	1.02	0.24
HEART—no previous	0.278	0.446	0.82	0.25	1.30	0.50
HEART—previous	0.169	0.516	1.13	0.32	0.88	0.26
STROKE	0.481	0.080	0.73	0.25	0.94	0.35
STROKE—no previous	0.271	0.189	0.68	0.27	0.82	0.36
STROKE—previous	0.948	0.054	1.15	0.93	1.61	1.25
MORTALITY	0.308	0.360	0.69	0.21	1.17	0.41
LUNG	0.504	0.203	0.33	0.17	0.50	0.43
DIABETES	0.101	0.062	0.69	0.41	1.48	3.19
HIGH BLOOD PRESSURE	0.013	0.666	0.90	0.29	0.74	0.36
ARTHRITIS	0.020	0.082	1.03	0.22	0.54	0.16
INCONTINENCE	0.615	0.373	0.85	0.13	1.11	0.30
INCONTINENCE—no previous	0.695	0.158	0.77	0.20	1.02	0.36
INCONTINENCE—previous	0.858	0.684	0.94	0.09	1.13	0.29
FALL	0.913	0.328	0.98	0.19	0.92	0.31
FALL—no previous	0.808	0.181	1.03	0.25	0.86	0.32
FALL—previous	0.470	0.000	1.00	0.27	89.61	267.82
HIP FRACTURE	0.347	0.143	0.33	0.22	0.21	0.28
HIP FRACTURE—no previous	0.785	0.238	0.23	0.17	0.14	0.19
HIP FRACTURE—previous						
PROXY INTERVIEW	0.248	0.261	0.46	0.16	0.48	0.17
PROXY INTERVIEW—no previous	0.061	0.531	0.27	0.11	0.40	0.20
PROXY INTERVIEW—previous						
COGNITIVE IMPAIRMENT	0.000	0.089	0.78	0.17	0.59	0.19
PSYCHIATRIC	0.012	0.137	0.39	0.15	0.16	0.12
DEPRESSION	0.042	0.753	0.38	0.15	0.29	0.15
BODY MASS INDEX	0.345	0.019				
CURRENT SMOKER	0.492	0.528	0.46	0.37	0.92	1.11
CURRENT SMOKER—no previous	0.165	0.097	0.11	0.16	19.92	132.75
CURRENT SMOKER—previous	0.714		0.93	0.16	0.95	0.18
ADL	0.004	0.024				
IADL	0.509	0.001				
SELF RATED HEALTH	0.044	0.278	0.67	0.08	0.64	0.09
SELF RATED HEALTH—no previous	0.138	0.091	0.59	0.12	0.51	0.13
SELF RATED HEALTH—previous	0.177	0.116				

Notes: SE = standard error.

Table 11.12R　　　　　**Simulation Outcomes**

	Scenario	70	75	80	85	90	95
			White Females				
Survival probability[a]	S0	1.000	0.907	0.747	0.502	0.247	0.082
	S1	1.000	0.912	0.761	0.526	0.268	0.092
	S2	1.000	0.887	0.664	0.354	0.117	0.024
Cancer[b]	S0	0.117	0.180	0.229	0.264	0.280	0.267
	S1	0.117	0.174	0.222	0.257	0.275	0.259
	S2	0.117	0.213	0.277	0.309	0.335	0.301
Heart disease[b]	S0	0.225	0.329	0.457	0.561	0.630	0.667
	S1	0.225	0.323	0.438	0.538	0.604	0.625
	S2	0.225	0.361	0.521	0.635	0.701	0.733
Stroke[b]	S0	0.044	0.108	0.197	0.274	0.344	0.392
	S1	0.044	0.107	0.184	0.261	0.324	0.358
	S2	0.044	0.119	0.223	0.311	0.393	0.458
Lung disease[b]	S0	0.104	0.153	0.183	0.193	0.177	0.159
	S1	0.104	0.147	0.174	0.183	0.174	0.142
	S2	0.104	0.196	0.266	0.289	0.275	0.211
Diabetes[b]	S0	0.114	0.163	0.189	0.196	0.195	0.173
	S1	0.114	0.000	0.000	0.000	0.000	0.000
	S2	0.114	0.202	0.252	0.266	0.253	0.213
High blood pressure[b]	S0	0.467	0.584	0.675	0.733	0.763	0.787
	S1	0.467	0.581	0.672	0.740	0.769	0.809
	S2	0.467	0.622	0.729	0.799	0.842	0.890
Arthritis[b]	S0	0.227	0.495	0.677	0.794	0.871	0.916
	S1	0.227	0.506	0.676	0.800	0.874	0.935
	S2	0.227	0.574	0.775	0.885	0.944	0.961
Incontinence[b]	S0	0.231	0.410	0.591	0.732	0.831	0.892
	S1	0.231	0.422	0.601	0.747	0.842	0.901
	S2	0.231	0.438	0.646	0.796	0.879	0.938
Fall[b]	S0	0.072	0.276	0.462	0.628	0.762	0.860
	S1	0.072	0.276	0.462	0.624	0.754	0.854
	S2	0.072	0.273	0.473	0.652	0.776	0.854
Hip fracture[b]	S0	0.029	0.045	0.069	0.104	0.137	0.180
	S1	0.029	0.044	0.070	0.102	0.138	0.157
	S2	0.029	0.064	0.112	0.183	0.240	0.298
Proxy interview	S0	0.036	0.057	0.090	0.149	0.215	0.282
	S1	0.036	0.062	0.089	0.144	0.209	0.279
	S2	0.036	0.102	0.185	0.295	0.405	0.469
Cognitive impairment[b]	S0	0.108	0.254	0.440	0.619	0.741	0.812
	S1	0.108	0.261	0.434	0.612	0.747	0.813
	S2	0.108	0.403	0.678	0.845	0.921	0.963
Psychiatric disease[b]	S0	0.153	0.223	0.310	0.382	0.425	0.459
	S1	0.153	0.225	0.317	0.390	0.421	0.451
	S2	0.153	0.320	0.506	0.635	0.726	0.772
Depression[b]	S0	0.067	0.168	0.280	0.380	0.465	0.519
	S1	0.067	0.178	0.290	0.399	0.488	0.572
	S2	0.067	0.253	0.429	0.573	0.664	0.711
Body mass index[c]	S0	25.657	24.791	23.673	22.435	21.389	20.716
	S1	25.657	24.781	23.640	22.413	21.375	20.384
	S2	25.657	24.424	23.018	21.782	20.852	20.483

(*continued*)

Table 11.12R (continued)

	Scenario	70	75	80	85	90	95
Current smoker[b]	S0	0.130	0.088	0.059	0.038	0.021	0.015
	S1	0.130	0.086	0.057	0.037	0.025	0.016
	S2	0.130	0.120	0.100	0.071	0.045	0.039
ADL limits[c]	S0	0.307	0.272	0.607	1.075	1.581	2.071
	S1	0.307	0.245	0.558	1.029	1.529	2.013
	S2	0.307	0.478	1.183	2.047	2.721	3.365
IADL limits[c]	S0	0.241	0.113	0.263	0.534	0.790	1.110
	S1	0.241	0.106	0.257	0.503	0.770	1.096
	S2	0.241	0.249	0.688	1.311	1.751	2.045
Poor/fair self-rated health[b]	S0	0.249	0.309	0.433	0.530	0.583	0.605
	S1	0.249	0.288	0.416	0.504	0.565	0.594
	S2	0.249	0.515	0.717	0.815	0.846	0.882
	White Males						
Survival probability[a]	S0	1.000	0.822	0.555	0.285	0.090	0.018
	S1	1.000	0.838	0.592	0.313	0.116	0.026
	S2	1.000	0.834	0.513	0.201	0.040	0.005
Cancer[b]	S0	0.138	0.235	0.319	0.402	0.491	0.631
	S1	0.138	0.242	0.326	0.411	0.493	0.578
	S2	0.138	0.233	0.309	0.391	0.480	0.660
Heart[b]	S0	0.361	0.504	0.639	0.734	0.790	0.862
	S1	0.361	0.507	0.633	0.730	0.828	0.861
	S2	0.361	0.486	0.612	0.706	0.748	0.868
Stroke[b]	S0	0.071	0.140	0.216	0.278	0.341	0.379
	S1	0.071	0.134	0.212	0.282	0.311	0.366
	S2	0.071	0.186	0.308	0.400	0.502	0.528
Lung disease[b]	S0	0.153	0.185	0.218	0.254	0.241	0.222
	S1	0.153	0.184	0.224	0.242	0.241	0.272
	S2	0.153	0.167	0.181	0.211	0.232	0.189
Diabetes[b]	S0	0.133	0.165	0.186	0.197	0.188	0.138
	S1	0.133	0.000	0.000	0.000	0.000	0.000
	S2	0.133	0.136	0.134	0.125	0.083	0.038
High blood pressure[b]	S0	0.440	0.547	0.626	0.686	0.709	0.690
	S1	0.440	0.548	0.631	0.687	0.740	0.833
	S2	0.440	0.585	0.681	0.759	0.804	0.887
Arthritis[b]	S0	0.175	0.398	0.576	0.706	0.782	0.803
	S1	0.175	0.412	0.587	0.707	0.775	0.826
	S2	0.175	0.512	0.732	0.857	0.944	1.000
Incontinence[b]	S0	0.099	0.250	0.416	0.584	0.724	0.808
	S1	0.099	0.247	0.402	0.580	0.726	0.808
	S2	0.099	0.294	0.501	0.684	0.846	0.962
Fall[b]	S0	0.041	0.157	0.288	0.419	0.536	0.601
	S1	0.041	0.151	0.284	0.411	0.500	0.592
	S2	0.041	0.226	0.430	0.608	0.739	0.887
Hip fracture[b]	S0	0.024	0.032	0.042	0.067	0.094	0.148
	S1	0.024	0.030	0.045	0.064	0.091	0.139
	S2	0.024	0.067	0.131	0.207	0.295	0.472

Table 11.12R   (continued)

	Scenario	70	75	80	85	90	95
Proxy Interview	S0	0.110	0.106	0.119	0.149	0.166	0.163
	S1	0.110	0.119	0.129	0.144	0.184	0.171
	S2	0.110	0.181	0.256	0.313	0.353	0.340
Cognitive impairment[b]	S0	0.144	0.323	0.505	0.660	0.768	0.837
	S1	0.144	0.326	0.508	0.668	0.778	0.829
	S2	0.144	0.435	0.686	0.835	0.920	0.868
Psychiatric disease[b]	S0	0.085	0.136	0.188	0.225	0.272	0.310
	S1	0.085	0.133	0.183	0.237	0.268	0.265
	S2	0.085	0.188	0.323	0.429	0.498	0.604
Depression[b]	S0	0.039	0.098	0.169	0.240	0.263	0.291
	S1	0.039	0.097	0.171	0.239	0.295	0.338
	S2	0.039	0.206	0.350	0.473	0.538	0.623
Body mass index[c]	S0	26.113	25.608	25.125	24.654	24.542	24.734
	S1	26.113	25.682	25.207	24.786	24.503	24.650
	S2	26.113	24.879	23.968	23.508	23.506	25.136
Current smoker[b]	S0	0.125	0.057	0.034	0.017	0.004	0.000
	S1	0.125	0.060	0.039	0.019	0.007	0.000
	S2	0.125	0.085	0.060	0.031	0.011	0.000
ADL limits[c]	S0	0.324	0.290	0.643	1.121	1.753	2.025
	S1	0.324	0.318	0.651	1.152	1.716	2.258
	S2	0.324	0.734	1.741	2.773	3.938	4.340
IADL limits[c]	S0	0.333	0.133	0.304	0.580	0.867	1.143
	S1	0.333	0.135	0.311	0.570	0.959	1.303
	S2	0.333	0.392	0.894	1.676	2.444	2.415
Poor/fair self-rated health[b]	S0	0.286	0.370	0.461	0.507	0.511	0.483
	S1	0.286	0.360	0.454	0.484	0.510	0.512
	S2	0.286	0.598	0.745	0.812	0.819	0.849

Notes: S0 = baseline; S1 = no diabetes; S2 = all low SES.

sample values for the first year, this is not so for subsequent years of the simulation, which produces no anomalous results in subsequent waves.

As mentioned in a note added in proof which appeared with our reply to published comments, LM tests for the triangular Wold causal chain structure of our model have been calculated. The results support that assumption in most cases. Table 11.15 reports the *t*-statistics of pairwise independence tests. The notable exceptions to acceptance of the causal chain structure are the mortality, ADL, and IADL equations, whose pairwise independence fails with respect to most of the remaining conditions. The joint test for independences across equations is not rejected for the case of males and is rejected for the case of females. The rejection for females is eliminated by removing the equations for mortality, BMI, ADL, and IADL.

Table 11.13R   **Wealth and Income in AHEAD and in the Baseline Scenario, by Age**

	70–74	75–79	80–84	85–89	90+
AHEAD cross-cohort data					
Total wealth (000)					
1st quartile	63.51	44.07	29.28	15.13	1.64
Median	144.04	110.76	90.62	71.19	38.37
3rd quartile	307.29	239.41	190.23	180.84	113.49
Liquid wealth (000)					
1st quartile	2.18	1.09	0.54	0.32	0.00
Median	27.28	15.24	10.91	8.64	4.36
3rd quartile	100.39	70.93	64.85	54.15	34.21
Nonliquid wealth (000)					
1st quartile	38.09	15.24	5.40	0.11	0.00
Median	91.66	77.00	60.02	43.38	1.63
3rd quartile	176.84	147.31	110.25	108.45	63.29
Income (000)					
1st quartile	14.19	12.00	9.76	8.68	6.87
Median	24.01	19.64	15.55	13.56	10.37
3rd quartile	37.96	32.54	28.37	23.94	15.71
Baseline simulation data					
Total wealth (000)					
1st quartile	56.61	71.59	57.48	34.76	20.62
Median	136.41	121.52	98.82	69.50	52.88
3rd quartile	292.45	202.94	148.19	107.54	86.91
Liquid wealth (000)					
1st quartile	1.64	10.24	6.68	0.98	−1.74
Median	25.10	29.24	22.28	14.39	10.63
3rd quartile	96.35	60.16	41.96	29.10	23.25
Nonliquid wealth (000)					
1st quartile	34.10	53.69	43.52	26.45	15.76
Median	87.84	87.54	73.89	53.80	42.45
3rd quartile	170.85	130.09	106.62	81.51	68.95
Income (000)					
1st quartile	13.69	13.36	11.98	10.00	8.68
Median	22.22	22.99	21.59	18.89	17.01
3rd quartile	36.23	35.35	34.17	30.19	26.17

Table 11.14   **Calibration of Wave 1 Wealth Levels**

Model	Calibrated Constant	Estimated Constant	Standard Deviation
Liquid			
Couples	0.0744	0.0751	0.0078
Spouse died	0.0876	0.0839	0.0210
Singles			
Males	0.0567	0.0708	0.0156
Females	0.0635	0.0794	0.0061
Nonliquid			
Couples	0.0626	0.0592	0.0046
Spouse died	0.1062	0.0954	0.0154
Singles			
Males	0.0554	0.0632	0.0104
Females	0.0721	0.0824	0.0067

Table 11.15   LM Tests of Wold Causal Chain Triangular Structure (t-statistics)

Pairwise Tests: Female

	JCANCER2	JHEART2	JSTROKE2	TDIED2	ILUNG2	IDIABET2	IHIGHBP2	IARTHRT2	JINCONT2	JFALL2	JHIPFRC2	PROXYW2	ICOGIM2	IPSYCH2	IDEPRES2	BMI2	SMOKNOW2	NUMADL2	NUMIADL2
JCANCER2																			
JHEART2	1.49																		
JSTROKE2	0.37	1.86																	
TDIED2	1.80	4.90	1.83																
ILUNG2	0.31	-1.09	0.31	-0.37															
IDIABET2	0.43	-0.72	-0.12	1.68	0.15														
IHIGHBP2	-0.05	-0.07	0.43	-0.06	0.39	0.25													
IARTHRT2	-0.09	-0.84	-0.25	1.51	-0.09	-0.32	0.11												
JINCONT2	-0.64	0.33	0.40	-3.34	0.18	-0.08	0.29	-0.25											
JFALL2	0.16	0.15	0.24	-1.16	0.18	-0.34	0.11	0.21	0.41										
JHIPFRC2	-0.30	0.88	-0.37	-2.25	0.28	-0.34	-0.29	0.11	1.59	2.89									
PROXYW2	0.25	0.68	0.61	-4.87	0.06	-0.63	-1.22	-0.77	2.40	1.82	1.91								
ICOGIM2	-0.47	1.95	0.98	-4.30	-0.65	-1.03	-0.22	-1.17	0.16	0.87	1.76	4.06							
IPSYCH2	-1.03	-0.19	0.75	-0.13	0.31	-0.01	-0.11	0.05	0.45	-0.01	-0.14	0.40	-0.17						
IDEPRES2	-1.87	0.82	0.77	-1.22	0.36	-0.19	-0.28	0.33	0.53	-0.74	0.66	-0.54	1.10	-0.30					
BMI2	-0.17	0.55	-0.56	2.73	-0.32	0.62	-0.34	0.53	-0.46	-0.47	-1.08	-1.41	-0.84	0.08	-0.76				
SMOKNOW2	0.29	0.47	-0.41	1.91	-0.39	0.43	0.12	0.01	0.16	-0.64	-0.90	-1.53	-0.99	-0.01	-1.18	-2.02			
NUMADL2	-0.38	2.62	1.07	-5.77	-0.07	-0.97	0.35	-0.27	2.07	1.54	2.45	2.60	2.20	0.27	2.23	-4.78	-1.15		
NUMIADL2	-1.34	2.20	0.64	-3.71	0.20	-1.03	0.13	-0.60	1.49	1.10	1.76	2.71	2.02	0.28	0.49	-4.37	-0.25	6.88	
DHLTH2	0.85	-0.25	-0.38	-0.38	0.01	0.43	0.34	-0.05	0.33	-0.01	0.11	0.71	-0.62	0.39	-0.50	-3.99	-0.40	1.65	2.88

Pairwise Tests: Male

	JCANCER2	JHEART2
JCANCER2		
JHEART2	1.03	
JSTROKE2	0.46	1.80

(continued)

Table 11.15 (continued)

	JCANCER2	JHEART2	JSTROKE2	TDIED2	ILUNG2	IDIABET2	IHIGHBP2	IARTHRT2	JINCONT2	JFALL2	JHIPFRC2	PROXYW2	ICOGIM2	IPSYCH2	IDEPRES2	BMI2	SMOKNOW2	NUMADL2	NUMIADL2
TDIED2	2.04	3.83	1.49																
ILUNG2	-0.75	-0.03	0.38	-0.54															
IDIABET2	-0.13	-0.79	-0.16	0.04	-0.27														
IHIGHBP2	-0.13	0.12	-0.05	-0.56	0.36	0.02													
IARTHRT2	0.20	-0.71	-0.19	0.26	0.08	0.16	-0.15												
JINCONT2	-0.09	0.28	0.08	-0.81	0.19	-0.11	-0.06	-0.01											
JFALL2	-0.13	1.14	0.82	-3.04	0.48	-0.05	-0.25	0.34	0.55										
JHIPFRC2	-1.32	-0.11	0.60	-0.62	0.34	-0.13	0.81	-1.58	1.00	2.19									
PROXYW2	-0.57	-0.09	0.90	-1.72	0.17	0.55	-0.05	-0.25	0.92	0.46	0.69								
ICOGIM2	-0.64	0.12	1.04	-2.91	0.57	0.11	0.09	0.13	0.45	0.96	-0.31	1.60							
IPSYCH2	-0.52	-0.63	0.00	0.60	-0.12	0.08	-0.11	0.08	0.17	-0.16	0.62	-0.37	-0.84						
IDEPRES2	-1.34	-0.58	0.50	-2.17	-0.32	0.04	-0.11	-0.08	1.33	0.92	-0.52	-2.12	1.74	-0.87					
BMI2	0.40	-0.27	-0.40	2.78	-0.02	0.13	0.25	0.16	0.08	-0.52	0.23	-0.04	-1.43	0.14	-0.44				
SMOKNOW2	0.20	0.06	-0.04	0.35	0.02	-0.58	0.71	-0.15	-0.77	0.12	-0.65	-0.28	-0.41	-0.32	-0.19	-1.85			
NUMADL2	-0.64	0.32	0.86	-2.24	0.91	0.11	-0.11	0.20	0.81	1.31	0.40	0.94	2.08	-0.24	1.86	-4.27	0.50		
NUMIADL2	-1.49	-0.45	0.77	-1.28	0.45	0.26	0.10	0.43	0.45	1.01	0.65	1.31	1.23	-0.19	1.46	-1.84	-0.17	2.85	
DHLTH2	-0.49	-0.23	0.20	-0.18	0.18	-0.32	0.49	0.11	0.26	0.90	0.71	-0.06	0.55	-0.46	1.15	-2.32	0.59	2.24	2.20
Cumulative Tests																			
Female																			
LM	2.2	5.5	37.4	39.9	44.5	45.2	48.2	63.2	65.4	77.8	105.3	136.5	139.0	151.7	211.9	230.8	273.5	330.5	370.5
p-value	0.138	0.138	0.000	0.000	0.000	0.002	0.010	0.003	0.025	0.023	0.002	0.000	0.001	0.002	0.000	0.000	0.000	0.000	0.000
Male																			
LM	1.1	4.3	26.0	27.0	27.7	28.6	29.3	30.0	42.4	51.8	58.0	71.3	74.5	89.2	151.6	165.6	184.3	204.9	222.2
p-value	0.303	0.231	0.000	0.003	0.024	0.124	0.399	0.751	0.581	0.599	0.747	0.692	0.896	0.866	0.027	0.043	0.043	0.039	0.055
DF	1	3	6	10	15	21	28	36	45	55	66	78	91	105	120	136	153	171	190

Comment   James M. Poterba

This paper presents a wealth of interesting new information on the relationship between various measures of socioeconomic status (SES) and the health of elderly individuals. While most previous studies of the correlation between SES and health status have relied on cross-sectional data, this paper exploits panel data. Repeated observations on the same individuals make it possible to develop more refined tests than those in past studies. In particular, the authors are able to study how income, wealth, and other socioeconomic conditions are associated with the onset of various health conditions, rather than simply the point-in-time correlation between SES and health status.

The core of the study consists of two related empirical projects. The first explores how SES affects changes in health status, while the second explores the relationship between changes in health status and changes in financial circumstances.

For the first project, the authors develop some "central tendency measures" of socioeconomic status. They find that some of the components of socioeconomic status have greater impact on health than others. Wealth, for example, has a stronger link to health than some of the other components of SES. Many of their findings suggest only modest links between SES and the onset of adverse health conditions. One worry is that by using many different variables to construct a measure of socioeconomic status, the authors have increased the chance of finding weak links between the SES variables and health outcomes. It is always possible to find weak effects by including many marginally influential variables in an empirical analysis. Focusing the analysis on a few key variables relating to socioeconomic status, such as wealth, income, and education, would seem like a natural direction for further analysis. It may ultimately be possible to rank different measures of income, wealth, and other aspects of socioeconomic status in terms of their predictive power for various health events.

One by-product of the study of how SES affects the onset of health conditions is a comparison between measures of the incidence of chronic conditions in the AHEAD sample and the aggregate population. In some cases, there appear to be disparities between the two data sets; this seems like a natural subject for future study. Another related suggestion for further work involves distinguishing between long-term and short-term measures of socioeconomic status. It is possible that transitory shocks to socioeconomic status, such as a temporary decline in income, may have a less important effect on health status than persistent differences due to wealth.

James M. Poterba is the Mitsui Professor of Economics and associate head of the economics department at the Massachusetts Institute of Technology, and the director of the Public Economics Research Program at the National Bureau of Economic Research.

One of the most important advances in this study is the disaggregate analysis of various measures of health status. By studying acute conditions separately from chronic conditions, and distinguishing mental conditions from acute physical conditions due to accidents and other factors, the paper is able to show that there are important differences in the link between SES and the onset of different long-term health limitations. This is a key insight if one tries to forecast how changes in future economic circumstances will affect the health of the future elderly population.

The second component of this study explores the extent to which changes in socioeconomic status can be explained by changes in health status. Because some changes in health status may require expensive treatment or movement to a nursing home or other costly facility, there is a presumption that health changes might account for some changes in financial circumstances. The results on the link from health status changes to financial status changes are weak. This is one aspect of the paper that could benefit from further data analysis. Disaggregating survey respondents by health insurance status, and focusing on relatively expensive health changes, might reveal a stronger relationship between some types of health status change and subsequent financial changes. For many AHEAD participants, income flows—pensions, Social Security, and related flows—are not affected by health status. It is therefore possible that the links from health changes to income changes for this age group are more muted than the changes for younger elderly.

In addition to its two significant empirical components, the paper also proposes a conceptual framework for analyzing how wealth and other measures of socioeconomic status are related to health. The "invariance" condition proposed here requires that the relationship between SES components and health status must be stable over time. Invariance is stipulated as a logical precondition for a causal relationship between SES and health status. It is not clear that this is a reasonable restriction, however. There are many reasons to suspect that the relationship might change over time, even if there is a true underlying link. For example, medical treatment technology may change. A procedure that was expensive at one point in time may become less expensive and widely available at a later date, thereby changing the relationship between SES and observed health status. Even if income and wealth are positively correlated with access to this procedure at all points in time, a decline in the price of the technology might alter the slope of this relationship. Similarly, there could be changes over time in behavior or other factors that affect health status. These could lead to changes in the measured relationship between health status and socioeconomic status. Once again, the difficulty is that even if higher socioeconomic status is associated with a lower likelihood of chronic conditions at all points during the sample period, a test for the stability of coefficients over time might reject this restriction. The diffusion of exercise or other personal behaviors across the socioeconomic spectrum could lead to time-varying coefficients even in the presence of a causal link.

This paper opens a broad new field of inquiry directly at the detailed mapping of links from income, wealth, and other aspects of socioeconomic status to the level of, and changes in, health status. As panel data sets become more common in the study of elderly populations and researchers have increased access to information on both medical conditions and economic circumstances, this research is likely to reveal more and more subtle aspects of these relationships. This paper represents a very important step in this research program.

Response

Peter Adams, Michael D. Hurd, Daniel McFadden, Angela Merrill, and Tiago Ribeiro

The problem of how to describe, detect, and measure causal effects has an importance in economic and social policy analysis that transcends the specifics of our paper, and our discussants provide valuable perspectives on possible approaches. We thank them for their comments. In this response, we identify points in the discussion that we find particularly useful, and try to clarify some issues where there appears to be disagreement.

The comment by Jérôme Adda, Tarani Chandola, and Michael Marmot focuses on the association of health and wealth in panel data. They replicate our statistical analysis on two data sets, the Whitehall II panel in Great Britain and the Swedish Survey of Living Conditions (ULF) and conclude that these replications give similar results. This is extremely valuable, providing a powerful cross-population/cross-institutions test for model invariance. However, their general assessment that our model is transferable to these data sets may be overly generous; a detailed comparison reveals some significant differences whose exploration would be a good starting point for further research. Their finding that mental diseases in the British and Swedish data also fail the test for no direct causality suggests strongly that the sources of this rejection are behavioral factors, rather than our proposal of a possible gradient in affordability of preventative mental health services within Medicare. James Poterba points out that a detailed look at disease-specific therapies and Medicare reimbursement rules may permit a sharper test for a causal link from affordability of preventative care to health outcomes, and changes in medical insurance coverage over

Peter Adams is affiliated with the Department of Economics at the University of California, Berkeley; Michael D. Hurd is affiliated with RAND Corporation; Daniel McFadden is affiliated with the Department of Economics at the University of California, Berkeley; Angela Merrill is affiliated with Mathematica; and Tiago Ribeiro is affiliated with the Department of Economics at the University of California, Berkeley.

time or with recipient age may induce invariance failures unless they are accounted for explicitly.

Our discussants include central contributors to three major "schools" of causal analysis: time-series prediction criteria, or *G-causality,* grounded in the empirical tests proposed by Granger and Sims (Clive Granger, John Geweke); the structural or functional approach grounded in econometric simultaneous equations models (Jerry Hausman, Kevin Hoover); and the potential outcomes or counterfactual approach grounded in the statistical analysis of experimental treatments (Jean-Pierre Florens, James Heckman, Fabrizia Mealli, Donald Rubin, and James Robins). As a shorthand, we will refer to the structural approach as *S-causality* and the prospective outcomes approach as *P-causality.* These schools differ substantially in terminology, perspective, and prescription for applications. Nevertheless, there are strong links between them. Pearl (2000, chapter 7) demonstrates a formal equivalence of S-causality and P-causality, and Heckman's comment demonstrates the utility of interweaving the S and P formulations. Both the S and P schools are critical of G-causality, arguing that its rather sparse characterization of causal properties is not sufficient to predict the effect of interventions. In the testing scheme we adopt in our paper, we start from G-causality and add invariance tests as a way to addressing this problem. The questions then are whether our invariance requirements are consistent with the more complete S or P specifications for causal modeling; whether they are sufficient for the limited causality claims that we make; and, more broadly, whether on the road to a complete causal analysis our approach is a helpful way station or a dangerous diversion.

In linear econometrics, it is common to conduct exogeneity tests for model specification, which can be interpreted as invariance tests for model coefficients when instrumental variables are used, and conditional on acceptance of exogeneity tests, to use simple exclusion tests for the existence of direct effects of explanatory variables. Features of this setup are that the alternatives to exogeneity are vague, an exogeneity test may be rejected for a variety of model misspecification reasons, and the procedure may have zero power against some alternatives in which direct exogeneity failures are confounded by other model failures. Nevertheless, the procedure is a useful diagnostic whose robustness weighs against its lack of optimality against specifically focused alternative structures. The scheme in our paper for testing the absence of direct causal paths has a similar structure, and we argue that it has similar properties.

First, a universally valid causal model in the S or P framework will predict successfully given any history, defined broadly to include any changes in geographical or temporal frame and any policy interventions. Each successful prediction constitutes, in our terminology, a model invariance. When one requires only that a more restricted class of invariance conditions be met, there will be a *family* of S or P models that are not necessarily universally valid, but which are valid and observationally equivalent for the specified class; see Florens and Heckman (2001). For example, the two directed acyclic graphs (DAGs) in in figure 11.9, only one of which has a direct causal path from S_{t-1} to H_t, may nevertheless both be valid for a class of invariance conditions that does not include interventions in which the conditional distribution of S_{t-1} given H_{t-1} changes. The fact that a broader class of invariance conditions could distinguish these models is not necessarily important if one is interested only in policy interventions in which the conditional distribution of S_{t-1} given H_{t-1} is itself always invariant. James Heckman makes a related, and even more important point, stating that "Evidence for invariance with respect to one class of manipulations does not necessarily carry over to other classes of manipulations" (2003, 77). The class of invariances tested should be precisely those needed for a targeted policy intervention, and these may or may not include transferability of the model across time periods or locations.

An empirical rejection of a model invariance is evidence against the validity of the family of S or P models that imply this invariance. Our proposed invariance tests are nothing more than the empirical counterpart of the logical relationships common to families of DAGs defining families of S or P models. We claim that our setup, with suitable articulation, thus provides a language for characterizing the empirical implications of causal analysis in an S or P framework. We strongly support the suggestion that DAGs and a full S or P analysis be used to map out the invariances that need to be satisfied by a valid model for predicting the effects of policy interventions in an application. However, we think there is methodological merit in developing "bottom up" approaches to causality that seek the broadest families of full causal models consistent with a particular policy application, to compliment "top down" approaches that start from full causal models embodying all prior information, and we then map out the policy applications for which they are valid. We recognize that the invariance test we actually conduct, for invariance of selected Markov transition probability parameters, falls far short of the battery of tests necessary to exhaust the empirical implications of a full causal model, or the relevant invariances for many policy applications, and note further that there are classes of causal models in which stationarity is not required.

Second, we claim in our paper that if our invariance and no direct causality (hereafter, NDC) tests are accepted, this is indeed evidence against the existence of a direct causal path. There are obvious limits to our claim in finite samples, particularly given the dimensions of invariance that remain untested. In light of the comments and the last paragraph, a more precise, and limited, statement is that acceptance of these tests is evidence against the existence of a direct causal path that is *active* (or, in genetic terms, *expressed*) within the class of invariances under consideration. In addition, there are an abundance of possible sources of model misspecifi-

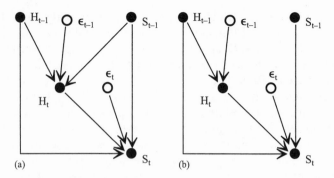

Fig. 11.9   Direct acyclic graph

cation that may confound our analysis and limit its power, particularly its linear single-index structure, untested treatment of "instantaneous causality," and first-order Markov dynamics. The power of the tests against plausible alternatives appears to be low; the observation that simulation using the models "as is" generates strong wealth–health links despite the acceptance of our tests for most conditions suggests this to be the case.

Several discussants, and also David Bloom in a personal communication, claim that our setup is statistically inconsistent so that there are circumstances where NDC will be accepted even when a direct causal link is present in a valid fully specified causal model. Kevin Hoover states that "A finding of invariance in the conditional model does not indicate a true causal relationship *unless* there is simultaneously a failure of invariance in the marginal model for the conditioning variable" (2003, 124). This is a succinct way of stating that our tests have power only against active direct causal links. In particular, we agree that one can devise examples where a direct causal effect is exactly offset by an unobserved common factor, or an ignored common factor exhibits no variation across populations that allow its effect to be identified, and our tests will have zero power against these alternatives, but we believe it improbable that these will occur and go undetected when the class of invariance tests is sufficiently broad. Speaking loosely, in the space of full causal models we expect manifolds on which effects are unvarying or exactly offsetting and thus not separately identifiable to have a priori probability zero, and if alternatively the effects can be identified under some circumstance, say by comparing populations with different initial conditions, then there will be a corresponding invariance test that should be rejected.

Finally, consider the broad question of whether our testing setup is a useful way station or a distraction. There are some legitimate concerns. Our testing procedure is generally insufficient for a full S or P causal analysis. Our treatment can be criticized as limited in applicability, because it is silent in the likely circumstance that direct causal effects are present but are confounded by unobserved common factors, and we offer no way of describing and identifying direct causal effects when they are in fact present. We agree with the discussants' suggestion that drawing conclusions on causality within an incomplete framework for causal modeling invites mischief. We have ourselves used our model in a simulation mode with hypothetical policy alternatives, with an untested assumption that "instantaneous causality" has a specific causal chain structure, and it is somewhat disingenious for us to argue that the results can be used only for model evaluation, not for policy analysis. On the positive side, we believe that for policy applications, framing causality analysis in terms of the minimal conditions needed to support evaluation of specific policy alternatives is a useful counterpoint to a full S or P analysis, and for this reason it is scientifically useful to provide "pullouts" on the road to causal modeling.

We conclude with a few specific responses to points raised by individual discussants. First, Jerry Hausman notes that if the first-order Markov assumption for our specified state vector is not satisfied, then our estimation procedure is not statistically consistent. We agree; a test for this assumption will be practical when the panel is a little longer, and is important to do. He observes correctly that our invariance tests will have low power if there is limited variability in explanatory variables. For this reason, the transferability invariance tested by Adda, Chandola, and Marmot is particularly helpful.

Several discussants, including John Geweke, Jean-Pierre Florens, and James Heckman, observe that our treatment of "instantaneous causality" is untested and possibly disputable. The order we have selected for health conditions is based, roughly, on the etiology of the various diseases, but we agree that this is a potential source of serious model misspecification. If our hypothesized causal chain is not valid, then instantaneous causality induces a simultaneous equations problem that causes our model estimates to be statistically inconsistent. We have emphasized time aggregation between panel waves as a source of simultaneous causality, but agree that across some health conditions there could be true mutual instantaneous causality, perhaps in the form of the multivariate jump processes discussed by Florens. If our hypothesized causal chain is incorrect, then this should be detectable via a relatively straightforward invariance test using a joint probit structure for the various health conditions. It is possible to conduct such a test in a LM form that does not require estimation of the joint probit model.

John Geweke comments that portfolio management under life-cycle consumer theory may produce discontinuous shifts in portfolio mix, as well as discrete changes in measured wealth due to transfers and tax-motivated reorganizations. In our models for wealth component changes, this would produce outliers that are linked across asset categories. This may explain some of the noise we observe in wealth components. A good solution will have to await further research. We note, however, that outliers in total wealth are sufficiently large and frequent to suggest that much of the noise we see is measurement error rather than true variation in the underlying economic variables.

The AHEAD study has notified users that incidence of new heart conditions in wave 3 was not collected and coded properly for subjects who had no previous history of a heart condition. In our working sample, the recorded 310 wave 3 incidences are then an undercount, and we estimate that approximately 122 additional incidences were not recorded. Because the intercepts for wave 2 to wave 3 incidence of heart conditions were allowed to vary freely in our models, this data problem will not affect our substantive conclusions if the undercount occurs at random, but will have a direct impact on our models for incidence of heart conditions between waves 2 and 3, and on the invariance tests based on comparing these transitions to the extent that the undercount does not occur at random. Because remaining models for health condition incidence and wealth change are conditioned on heart condition incidence, any direct impact of this data problem will have some effect on all the models in our paper.

In response to reviewer comments, we suggest that it would be possible to conduct a LM test for correlation of disturbances in our chain of incidence models. We have now calculated these tests and accept the hypothesis of no correlation of these disturbances in the equations for various health conditions. We note, however, that these tests are likely to have low power.

Contributors

Peter Adams
Department of Economics
University of California, Berkeley
549 Evans Hall, #3880
Berkeley, CA 94720-3880

Alan J. Auerbach
Department of Economics
University of California, Berkeley
549 Evans Hall, #3880
Berkeley, CA 94720-3880

James Banks
Institute for Fiscal Studies
7 Ridgmount Street
London WC1E 7AE, England

Richard Blundell
Institute for Fiscal Studies
7 Ridgmount Street
London WC1E 7AE, England

Jeffrey R. Brown
Department of Finance
University of Illinois, Urbana-
    Champaign
340 Wohlers Hall, MC-706
1206 South Sixth Street
Champaign, IL 61820-9080

Anne Case
Woodrow Wilson School of Public
    and International Affairs
Princeton University
345 Wallace Hall
Princeton, NJ 08544-1013

James J. Choi
Department of Economics
Harvard University
Cambridge, MA 02138

David M. Cutler
Department of Economics
Harvard University
Cambridge, MA 02138

Angus Deaton
Woodrow Wilson School of Public
    and International Affairs
Princeton University
347 Wallace Hall
Princeton, NJ 08544-1013

Victor R. Fuchs
Department of Economics
Stanford University
Stanford, CA 94305

Michael D. Hurd
RAND Corporation
1700 Main Street
Santa Monica, CA 90407

Robert T. Jensen
John F. Kennedy School of
    Government
Harvard University
79 JFK Street
Cambridge, MA 02138

David Laibson
Department of Economics
Harvard University
Littauer M-14
Cambridge, MA 02138

Brigitte Madrian
The Wharton School
University of Pennsylvania
3100 Steinberg Hall-Dietrich Hall
3620 Locust Walk
Philadelphia, PA 19035

Mark McClellan
U.S. Food and Drug Administration
5600 Fishers Lane
Rockville, MD 20857-0001

Daniel McFadden
Department of Economics
University of California, Berkeley
549 Evans Hall #3880
Berkeley, CA 94720-3880

Ellen Meara
Department of Health Care Policy
Harvard Medical School
180 Longwood Avenue
Boston, MA 02115-5899

Angela Merrill
Mathematica Policy Research
50 Church Street, 4th Floor
Cambridge, MA 02138-3726

Andrew Metrick
The Wharton School
University of Pennsylvania
3620 Locust Walk
Philadelphia, PA 19104

Joseph P. Newhouse
Division of Health Policy Research
    and Education
Harvard University
180 Longwood Avenue
Boston, MA 02115-5899

Christina Paxson
Woodrow Wilson School of Public
    and International Affairs
Princeton University
316 Wallace Hall
Princeton, NJ 08544-1022

James M. Poterba
Department of Economics, E52-350
Massachusetts Institute of Technology
50 Memorial Drive
Cambridge, MA 02142-1347

Tiago Ribeiro
Department of Economics
University of California, Berkeley
549 Evans Hall, #3880
Berkeley, CA 94720-3880

Sylvester J. Schieber
Watson Wyatt Worldwide
1717 H Street, NW, Suite 800
Washington, DC 20006

John B. Shoven
Department of Economics
Stanford University
Stanford, CA 94305

Jonathan Skinner
Department of Economics
Dartmouth College
6106 Rockefeller Hall
Hanover, NH 03755

James P. Smith
RAND Corporation
1700 Main Street
P.O. Box 2138
Santa Monica, CA 90407-2138

Steven F. Venti
Department of Economics
Dartmouth College
6106 Rockefeller Center
Hanover, NH 03755

Scott J. Weisbenner
Department of Finance
University of Illinois, Urbana-
  Champaign
304C David Kinley Hall
1407 W. Gregory Drive
Urbana, IL 61801

David A. Wise
John F. Kennedy School of
  Government
Harvard University and NBER
1050 Massachusetts Avenue
Cambridge, MA 02138

Author Index

Aaron, Henry J., 259
Adams, Peter, 15–16
Adda, Jérôme, 520, 524
Adler, N., 416n2
Adler, Nancy E., 302
Alessie, R., 455
Allison, J. J., 372
Almond, Douglas, 362
Ando, A., 82
Angrist, J., 419
Atkinson, Anthony B., 248
Attanasio, O., 190, 191, 455
Auster, R., 372, 407

Backlund, E., 415n1
Baker, D., 416n1
Banks, James, 7, 177, 210, 218, 222n13, 233
Barlow, R., 188
Barnes, B. A., 371
Barsky, R., 415n1
Bartley, M., 415n1
Becker, M. P., 369n2, 371
Benjamin, Daniel J., 18
Berkman, 360
Bernheim, B. Douglas, 31, 129
Blane, D., 415n1
Bloom, David, 523
Blundell, Richard, 7, 177, 210, 218, 222n13, 233, 283
Bobak, M., 416n1
Bombardier, Claire, 407
Bosma, H., 415n1

Brandolini, Andrea, 248
Brazer, H., 188
Brown, Jeffrey R., 6, 190
Brown, Kyle N., 76
Brugiavini, A., 233
Brumberg, R., 182
Burtless, Gary, 24

Carter, Lawrence R., 264, 266, 335
Case, Anne, 10, 271, 292, 293, 313, 315
Chandola, T., 415n1, 520, 524
Chapman, K., 416n3
Chassin, M. R., 369n2, 371
Chay, Kenneth, 362, 417n5
Chiuri, M. C., 213
Choi, James J., 3, 177
Clark, Robert L., 75, 76, 77, 78
Coile, Courtney, 43
Congressional Budget Office, 129
Cooper, M. M., 369n2, 370, 371, 389
Cox, D., 189
Curry, Leslie, 177
Cutler, David M., 11–13, 354, 355, 360, 370n3

Daniels, M., 416n3
Davey-Smith, G., 415n1, 416n1
Dawid, A., 420n8
Deaton, Angus, 8–9, 247, 260, 263, 271, 272, 278, 282, 292, 293, 320n6, 360, 373
Deininger, Klaus, 248
Dhir, R., 416n1

Di Salvo, P., 227
Dohrenwend, B. P., 416n3
Dollamore, G., 416n1
Drever, F., 415n1
Dubos, Rene, 354
Dufflo, Esther, 296
Dynan, Karen, 179

Ecob, R., 415n1
Eisenberg, J. A., 369n2
Elo, I., 415n1
Emmerson, Carl, 283n2
Engen, Eric, 18, 46, 59n17, 129
Engle, R., 420n8
Englehardt, Gary, 18, 46, 58–59, 59n18, 62
Ermisch, J., 227
Escarce, J., 369n2, 371
Ettner, S., 415n1
Evans, A., 416n3
Evans, J. S., 373n4

Feinstein, Jonathan, 128, 176, 415n1
Felitti, V. J., 416n3
Finkel, Meryl, 129
Fisher, E., 368, 370, 372
Fitzpatrick, R., 416n1
Florens, Jean-Pierre, 521, 522, 524
Fogel, Robert W., 335, 345
Folland, S., 371
Fox, A., 416n1, 416n3
Franks, P., 372
Frayne, Chris, 283n2
Freedman, D., 420n8
Frieberg, Leora, 43
Fuchs, Victor R., 13–15, 292, 372, 407,
    416n2

Gale, William, 18, 35, 46, 59n17, 129, 183,
    189, 191, 192, 192n5, 194
Gan, L., 455
Geib, Thorsten, 284
Geman, S., 421
Gerdtham, U.-G., 259
Geweke, J., 420n8, 521, 524
Giles, Chris, 284
Gill, R., 420n8
Glaeser, Edward, 360
Goldblatt, P., 416n1, 416n3
Goldman, N., 416n3, 417
Goodman, Alissa, 248, 263, 283n2
Gosling, Amanda, 284
Gottschalk, Peter, 248

Granger, C., 420, 420n8, 422, 521
Gray, B. H., 372
Green, L. A., 369n2, 371
Greenstone, Michael, 362, 417n5
Gruber, Jonathan, 43
Gruman, Cynthia, 177
Gustman, Alan, 34, 40n10, 42, 59n18, 129

Hadley, J., 372
Hariharran, G., 416n3
Hauser, P., 416n1
Hausman, Jerry, 521, 524
Haynes, R., 416n1
Heckman, J., 419, 420n8, 521, 522, 524
Hendry, D., 420n8
Hertzman, C., 416n1, 416n3
Hogan, Christopher, 408
Holland, P., 420n8
Hoover, K., 420, 521, 523
Hoynes, H., 190, 191, 455
Humphries, K., 416n1
Hurd, Michael D., 15–16, 128, 183, 188,
    281, 313, 416n1, 455

Ibbotson Associates, 187
Idler, Ellen L., 290
Imbens, G., 419
Ippolito, Richard A., 18, 32, 34, 56

Jappelli, T., 213
Jensen, Robert, 10–11, 313, 315
Johnson, N., 415n1
Jones, D., 416n1
Jönsson, Bengt, 259
Juster, F. Thomas, 135

Kadiyala, Srikanth, 354, 355
Kaplan, G. A., 373
Kaplan, J., 416n1
Kapteyn, A., 455
Karasek, R. A., 416n1
Kasl, Stanislav, 290
Kawachi, I., 360, 373n5
Kehagias, A., 421
Kelley, S., 416n3
Kennedy, B. P., 373n5
Kennickell, A., 184
Kessler, D., 189, 372
Kiel, Katherine, 155
Kington, Raynard, 313, 417
Kinney, P. L., 373n4
Kitawaga, E., 416n1

Kotlikoff, Laurence J., 44, 45, 182, 183, 184, 188, 189, 191, 192, 192n5, 194, 201, 202, 203
Kramer, M. J., 372, 407
Kunsch, H., 421
Kutty, Nadine, 129

Laibson, David, 3
Laisney, Francois, 284
Laitner, J., 183
Landsbergis, P., 416n1
LeBlanc, Pierre, 19
Lee, Ronald D., 264, 266, 335
Leigh, J., 416n1
Leveson, I., 372, 407
Lewis, G., 416n1
Lofgren, Eric, 76
Lord, W., 183
Lubitz, James, 408
Lubotsky, Darren, 271, 272, 373
Luft, H., 416n1
Lumsdaine, Robin L., 42
Lusardi, A., 455
Lusardi, Annamarie, 35
Lynch, J. W., 373

Madrian, Brigitte C., 3, 82, 83, 84, 86n5, 94, 97, 103, 123
Manor, O., 416n1
Manuck, S., 416n1
Marmot, Michael G., 271, 282, 302, 360, 416n1, 520, 524
Martin, L., 416n1
Masson, A., 183, 189
Matthews, S., 416n1
Mayer, Christopher, 129
McCarthy, Mike, 115n22
McClellan, Mark, 13, 372, 394
McDermott, Walsh, 352
McDonough, P., 416n1
McEwen, B., 416n3
McFadden, Daniel, 15–16, 128, 176, 281, 313, 455
McGarry, K., 455
McGill, Dan M., 74
McKeown, Thomas, 345
McNerney, W. J., 372
McWhirter, Liz, 115n22
Mealli, Fabrizia, 521
Meara, Ellen, 11–13, 313
Meer, J., 419
Megbolugbe, Issac, 128

Mellor, Jennifer, 360
Menchik, Paul L., 360
Merrill, Angela, 15–16, 281, 313
Merrill, Sally R., 129, 176
Metrick, Andrew, 3
Miller, D., 419
Milyo, Jeffrey, 360
Mirowsky, J., 416n1
Mitchell, Olivia S., 129
Mizon, G., 420n8
Modigliani, Franco, 181, 182, 183, 187
Moore, James F., 129
Morgan, J., 188
Mundaca, B., 183, 188
Murray, C. J. L., 416n1

Newhouse, Joseph, 408
Norberg, Karen, 360
Nyce, Steven A., 76

Ortalo-Magne, F., 226n15, 227
Ostrove, J., 416n2

Papke, Leslie, 18, 46
Paxson, Christina, 8–9, 247, 260, 263, 271, 272, 278, 282, 373
Pearl, J., 420n8
Pearson, S. D., 372
Pence, Karen, 18, 46
Perozek, Maria, 35
Petersen, Mitchell, 18
Poterba, James M., 2, 18, 35, 54, 55, 58, 71, 72, 75, 77, 78, 115n22, 116n23, 123, 191
Power, C., 416n1
Preston, Sam, 283, 335, 345, 415n1, 416n1, 417
Projector, D., 188
Prothrow-Stith, D., 373n5

Qiao, X., 416n1
Quinn, Joseph F., 24

Rady, S., 226n15, 227
Raines, F., 189
Rangazas, P., 183
Record, R. G., 345
Reinsdorf, Marshall, 35
Ribeiro, Tiago, 15–16
Richard, J., 420n8
Richter, Kaspar, 313, 315
Riley, Gerald F., 408
Robins, J., 420n8, 521

Robinson, Julie, 177
Rodgers, B., 416n1
Rosen, H., 419
Ross, C., 416n1
Rubin, D., 419, 521
Ruhm, Christopher, 272

Sa-Aadu, Jarjisu, 128
Sabelhaus, John, 35
Samuelson, William, 123
Samwick, Andrew, 42, 43, 45
Sarachek, D., 372, 407
Schieber, Sylvester, 32, 75, 76, 77
Schnall, P., 416n1
Scholz, John Karl, 18, 46, 59n17, 183, 189, 191, 192, 192n5, 194
Schwartz, William B., 259
Seeman, T., 416n1
Selby, J. V., 372
Shea, Dennis F., 82, 83, 84, 86n5, 94, 97, 103, 123
Sheiner, Louise, 128, 176
Shilling, James, 128
Shorrocks, A., 416n1
Shoven, John, 31, 32, 75, 77
Silver, M., 372
Silverman, E., 372
Simons, Katerina, 129
Sims, C., 420, 420n8, 521
Sinai, Todd, 177
Skinner, Jonathan, 13–15, 35, 45, 179, 368, 370, 372, 394
Sloan, F. A., 372
Smeeding, Timothy, 248
Smith, G., 177, 415n1
Smith, James P., 210, 218, 222n13, 292, 313, 417
Sobel, M., 420n8
Soldo, B., 416n1
Sorlie, P., 415n1
Souleles, Nicholas, 177
Squire, Lyn, 248
Stano, M., 371
Starr-McCluer, M., 184
Steinmeier, Thomas, 34, 40n10, 42, 59n18, 129
Stellar, E., 416n3
Stern, J., 416n1
Stock, James H., 42

Subramanian, Shankar, 320n6
Summers, Lawrence H., 82, 182, 183, 188, 189, 191, 192n5, 194, 201, 202, 203
Surette, B., 184
Susser, M., 370n3
Suzman, Richard, 135
Swert, W., 420n8

Taubman, P., 417
Taylor, D. H., Jr., 372
Thompson, John, 18, 56
Tosteson, T., 373n4
Turner, R. D., 345

Uccello, Cori, 129

Van der Berg, Servaas, 292
Van Doorslaer, E., 416n1
Venti, Steven F., 2, 4, 18, 35, 54, 55, 58, 71, 75, 77, 78, 115n22, 116n23, 123, 127, 128, 129, 130, 132, 176, 177, 179

Wadsworth, M., 416n1
Webb, Anthony, 43
Webb, Steven, 248, 263
Weil, David, 128, 176
Weisbenner, Scott J., 6, 191
Weiss, G., 188
Wennberg, J. E., 368, 369, 369n2, 370, 371, 372, 389
Whellan, D. J., 372
Whitehead, M., 415n1, 416n1
Wilkinson, Richard G., 248, 282, 360, 416n1
Wise, David A., 2, 4, 18, 35, 42, 43, 44, 45, 54, 55, 58, 71, 72, 75, 77, 78, 115n22, 116n23, 123, 127, 128, 129, 130, 132, 176, 177, 179, 416n1, 455
Woodward, M., 416n1, 420n8
Wright, J. G., 371

Yang, G., 416n1

Zabel, Jeffrey, 155
Zeckhauser, Richard, 123
Zeldes, Stephen, 179
Zellner, A., 420n8
Zubkoff, M., 371

Subject Index

Activities of daily living (ADLs), improvements in, and pensions, 296–300

Adult mortality: in U.K., 253–55; in U.S., 255–56

Age distributions, mortality and, 336–42

AHEAD. *See* Asset and Health Dynamics Among the Oldest Old (AHEAD)

Allocations, investment, effect of automatic enrollment on, 99–107

Antibiotics, 12, 335

Asset accumulation: automatic enrollment and, 107–19; influence of health conditions on, 455–59. *See also* Wealth accumulation

Asset and Health Dynamics Among the Oldest Old (AHEAD), 127–28, 130; analyzing wealth changes and mortality with, 439–43; causality tests and, 448–55; constructing variables from, 432–37; descriptive statistics and, 432; descriptive statistics for population of, 443–44; incidence of health conditions in, 448–50; measuring wealth and, 437–39; sample characteristics of, 428–32; trends in home equity at older ages of, 134–44

Automatic enrollment: asset accumulation and, 107–19; default savings behavior and, 103–6; effect of, on contribution rates, 94–99; effect of, on 401(k) participation, 88–94; effect of, on investment allocations, 99–107; 401(k) plans and,

3–4; for 401(k) plans, in three large companies, 84–88; overview of, 81–84; participation rates and, 4

Behaviors, changes in, and mortality, 358

Britain. *See* United Kingdom

British Household Panel Survey (BHPS), 207–9

Canada, RRSP in, 19

Cancer, 345–46

Cardiovascular disease, 345–46, 349; deaths from, 345–49, 350–51; declining mortality rates of, after 1960, 354–55

Chronic nephritis, 352, 353

Civil Rights Act, 362

College support, transfer wealth and, 194

Contribution rates, effect of automatic enrollment on, 94–99

DB pension plans. *See* Defined benefit (DB) pension plans

DC pension plans. *See* Defined contribution (DC) pension plans

Death, medicalization of, 12–13. *See also* Mortality

Default savings behavior, and automatic enrollment, 103–6

Defined benefit (DB) pension plans, 17–18; active participants in, 27–28; cohort data for reduction in participation in, and increased participation in 401(k)

Defined benefit (DB) pension plans (*cont.*)
plans, 56–57; contributions per participant and, 32; contributions to, 28–29;
effects of legislative and return-induced
downward pressures on, 33–34; "eligibility experiment" applied to assets of,
55–56; factors affecting contributions
to, 31–34; 401(k) plans and, 18–19;
offsets to, 18; retirement asset accumulation in, vs. DC plans, 36–46; saving
rates for, and 401(k) plans, 19; scenarios for, in absence of 401(k) plans,
50–54
Defined contribution (DC) pension plans,
18; active participants in, 27–28; contributions per participant and, 32;
contributions to, 28–29; retirement
asset accumulation in, vs. DB plans,
36–46
Demographics, trends in U.S., and growth
in retirement assets, 23–24
Diet: income and, 319–21; nutrition and,
321–23. *See also* Nutrition
Drugs, decline in mortality rates and, 345
Dual coverage, 46; 401(k) plans and, 47–49;
loss of, 49–50

Education, mortality and, 271–74
Elderly: data for SES and health of Russian,
315–19; home equity and, 127–30; SES
and health of Russian, 313–14
Employee savings, vs. contributions to retirement plans, 36–46
Equities, rates of return on, U.S. vs. U.K.,
218–21

Family Expenditure Survey (FES), 262–63
Florida: puzzle of high health care utilization in, 389–93; puzzle of low mortality
in, 389–93
Forbes 400, 188–89
401(k) plans, 17; automatic enrollment and,
3–4; automatic enrollment for, in three
large companies, 84–88; average annual saving rate of, 3; cohort data for
increased participation in, and reduction in DB plan participation, 56–57;
contributions to, 28–29, 29n4; DB pension plans and, 18–19; dual coverage
and, 47–49; effect of automatic enrollment on participation in, 88–94; offsets
to, 18; projected assets of, 54–55; sav-

ing rates for, DB plans and, 19; scenarios for DB plans in absence of, 50–54.
See also Retirement plans

Great Britain. *See* United Kingdom

Health: causality measurement issues for,
424–28; causality testing for, 420–24;
causality tests for, in AHEAD panel,
448–55; econometric analysis of causal
links to wealth, 15–16; impact of income on status of, in South Africa,
291–96; incidence conditions of, in
AHEAD panel, 448–50; influence of,
on asset accumulation, 455–59; models
for association with SES and, 444–46;
nutrition and, 323–26; possible causal
paths for, 415–18; relative risk for, 446–
48; role of nutrition and, 314–15; SES,
nutrition and, 10–11; SES and, 313–
14; simulation of interventions for
conditions of, 459–67; ways pensions
improved, in South Africa, 296–304;
wealth and, 8–11; and wealth in South
Africa, 10
Health and Retirement Study (HRS), 57–
58, 127–28, 130; data limitations in,
58–62; 401(k) eligibility of respondents
in, 62–64; trends in home equity at
older ages and, 134–44
Health care, age differences in, and mortality, 13–15
Health care utilization: correlations among
different measures of, 378–80; data and
estimation strategy for, 373–74; factors
appearing to explain, 383–86; indexes
of, by region and population size, 377–
78; puzzle of high, in Florida, 389–93;
studies of regional variations in, 369–
72; study results for, 374–77
Home equity, 4–6; AHEAD trends for, 134–
44; change in, 147–54; elderly and, 127–
30; estimates of, based on selling price,
158–69; events that precipitate changes
in, 144–47; formal estimates of change
in, 156–58; housing price uncertainty
and, 227–28; HRS trends for, 134–44;
puzzle of, 7–8; ratio of, and other assets, to disposable income, 22–23; respondent estimates of, vs. sale prices,
154–56
Home ownership: model implications for,

234–42; rates of, U.S. vs. U.K., 211–15;
U.S. vs. U.K., 221–25; young house-
holds and, 229–34
Household wealth, sources of, 181–82. *See
also* Wealth
Housing equity. *See* Home equity
Housing prices, uncertainty of, 227–28
Housing services: supply of, 228; model
predictions for, 228–29
Housing tenure, model for, 225–27
HRS. *See* Health and Retirement Study
(HRS)

Income: British data for, 262–63; dietary
patterns and, 319–21; empirical model
for effects of, on mortality, 263–66; impact of, on health status, in South
Africa, 291–96; role of, and mortality
rates, 9; study results for effects of, on
mortality in U.S. and U.K., 266–74;
summary of previous work on mortality and, 260–62
Income inequality: British data for, 262–63;
empirical model for effects of, on mortality, 263–66; study results for effects
of, on mortality in U.S. and U.K., 266–
74; summary of previous work on
mortality and, 260–62; U.S. vs. U.K.,
248–51
Individual Retirement Accounts (IRAs), 3,
17; contributions to, 28–29; offsets to,
18. *See also* Retirement accounts
Infant mortality, 355–58; nonwhite vs.
white, 362, 363; U.S. vs. U.K., 251–53
Infectious diseases, 12, 335, 344–45; deaths
from, after 1960, 354; in midcentury
period, 349
Influenza, 345, 346; midcentury decline in
deaths from, 349
Inter vivos gifts, 181, 183, 185
Inter vivos transfers, 189, 191, 193
Investment allocations, effect of automatic
enrollment on, 99–107

Keogh plans: contributions per participant
and, 32; contributions to, 30
Kidney disease, 352

Labor force, aging of, 23–24
Langeberg Survey (South Africa), 288–91
Life-cycle hypothesis (LCH), 181, 182–83
Life-cycle saving, 182–83, 198

Life-cycle wealth, 181, 186–87
Life expectancies, 336–42

Medicaid, 360, 362
Medical care. *See* Health care
Medicalization of death, 12–13, 335, 354–55
Medical technology, mortality and, 257–60
Medical utilization. *See* Health care utilization
Medicare, 360
Money. *See* Wealth
Mortality: adult, in U.K., 253–55; adult, in
U.S., 255–56; age differences in medical
care and, 13–15; age distributions and,
335–42; changes in, over twentieth century, in U.S., 11–13; changes in age distribution and, 336–42; declining rates
of, after 1960, 354–58; education and,
271–74; empirical model for effects of
income and income equality on, 263–
66; explanations of variation in, across
MSAs, 14–15; factors appearing to
explain rates of, 386–88; factors influencing, 358–62; first four decades of
twentieth century and, 343–49; income
and, 9; indexes of, by regions, 380–81;
medical technology and, 257–60; midcentury medical advances and declines
in, 349–53; patterns of, U.S. vs. U.K.,
248–60; pooling U.S. and U.K. data
and, 274–78; public health and reduction in, 12; puzzle of low, in Florida,
389–93; puzzle of positive correlation
of African Americans and mortality
of whites, 388–89; rates of, in U.S. vs.
U.K., 8–9; reasons for decline in, 335–
36; regional variations in, 372–73;
SES and, 358–60; smoking and, 272–
74, 355, 356; study results for effects
of income and income inequality on,
in U.S. and U.K., 266–74; summary
of previous work on income and income inequality and, 260–62; in U.S.,
333

National Income and Product Accounts
(NIPA), 2
Negative election. *See* Automatic enrollment
NIPA (National Income and Product Accounts) savings, retirement plan contribution rate and, 34–36

Nutrition: health and, 323–26; income and diet and, 319–21; mortality and, 335; reduction in mortality rates and, 12; role of, and health, 314–15; SES and health and, 10–11

Panel Survey of Income Dynamics (PSID), 128, 206–8
Participation rates, automatic enrollment and, 4
Penicillin, 349
Pension plans. *See* Defined benefit (DB) pension plans; Defined contribution (DC) pension plans
Pensions, and improvements in health, in South Africa, 296–307
Personal retirement plans, 2–8. *See also* Retirement plans
Pneumonia, 345, 346; midcentury decline in deaths from, 349
Policies, social, mortality rates and, 360–62
Private Security Accounts (PSAs), 77
Psychological stress, pensions and, in South Africa, 302–4
Public health, reduction in mortality rates and, 12

Registered Retirement Saving Program (RRSP), DB pension plans and, 19
Retirement accounts: aggregate assets in, 20–21; private assets in, 21–22; public and private assets in, 22. *See also* 401(k) plans; Individual Retirement Accounts (IRAs)
Retirement ages, retirement assets and, 23–24
Retirement assets: demographic trends and growth in, 23–24; plan contributions to, 25–26; substitution between, 46–57
Retirement plan contribution rates, 19, 26; DB plans and, 31–34; NIPA savings and, 34–36; stability of, 26–27; time series changes in, 26–31
Retirement plans: contributions to, 25–26; contributions to, vs. employee savings, 36–46; HRS evidence for substitution in, among older workers, 57–58; participants in, 30–31; substitution between, 19
Retirement saving plans, growth in employee-managed, 17–18

Retirement savings, in U.S., 2–3
Roemer's Law, 371
RRSP. *See* Registered Retirement Saving Program (RRSP)
Russia: data for SES and health among elderly in, 315–19; relationship between health and SES for elderly in, 10–11; SES and health of elderly in, 313–14
Russian Longitudinal Monitoring Survey (RLMS), 315

Sanitation improvements, and health status, in South Africa, 301–2
Savings: employee, vs. retirement plan contributions, 36–46; life-cycle, 182–83, 198; NIPA, retirement plan contribution rate and, 34–36; rates for, and DB pension plans, 19; for retirement, in U.S., 2–3
Savings behavior: default, and automatic enrollment, 103–6; life-cycle hypothesis for, 181, 182–83
SES. *See* Socioeconomic status (SES)
Smoking, mortality and, 272–74, 355, 356, 358, 359
Social policies, mortality rates and, 360–62
Social Security, 360–62; reforming, 76–77
Socioeconomic status (SES): causality measurement issues for, 424–28; causality testing for, 420–24; health and, 313–14; indexes of, by regions, 381–82; models for association with health and, 444–46; mortality and, 358–60; nutrition and health and, 10–11; possible causal paths for, 415–18; relative risk for high vs. low, 446–48
South Africa: impact of income on health status in, 291–96; improvements in ADLs and pensions in, 296–300; Langeberg Survey in, 288–91; nutrition improvements, and pensions in, 301–2; psychological stress improvements, and pensions in, 302–4; sanitation improvements in, and pensions in, 300–301; ways pensions improved health status in, 296–307; wealth and health in, 10
Stock ownership: housing price uncertainty and, 227–28; rates of, U.S. vs. U.K., 215–18; U.S. vs. U.K., 221–25
Suicide, 360, 361
Sulfa drugs, 345, 349

Survey of Consumer Finances (SCF), 182, 184, 188
Survey of Income and Program Participation (SIPP), 127–28; data on home ownership and equity over life course, 131–34

Technology, medical, mortality and, 257–60
Transfer wealth, 7, 182; college support and, 194; defining, 202; direct estimation of, from survey data, 184–89; estimation of, from flow of transfers, 189–94; importance of, 198; ratio of, to total wealth, 195–98; studies of, 182–83; survey data for, 184. *See also* Wealth
Tuberculosis, 345, 347

United Kingdom: adult mortality in, 253–55; home ownership and stock ownership in, 221–25; household wealth distributions in, 205–6; housing prices in, 220–21; income inequality in, 248–51; infant mortality in, 251–53; model implications for housing in, 234–42; model predictions for housing services in, 228–29; mortality rates in, 8–9; patterns of mortality in, 248–60; rates of home ownership, vs. U.S., 211–15; rates of return on assets in, 218–21; rates of stock ownership, vs. U.S., 215–18; study results for effects of income and income inequality on mortality in, 266–74; wealth at retirement in, 7–8; wealth distributions in, vs. U.S., 209–10; young households and home ownership in, 229–34
United States: adult mortality in, 255–56; changes in mortality over twentieth century in, 11–13; demographic trends in, and retirement assets, 23–24; home ownership and stock ownership in, 221–25; household wealth distributions in, 205–6; income inequality in, 248–51; infant mortality in, 251–53; model predictions for housing services in, 228–29; mortality rates in, 8–9, 333; patterns of mortality in, 248–60; rates of home ownership, vs. U.K., 211–15; rates of return on assets in, 218–21; rates of stock ownership, vs. U.K., 215–18; retirement saving in, 2–3; study results for effects of income and income inequality on mortality in, 266–74; wealth at retirement in, 7–8; wealth distributions in, vs. U.K., 209–10; young households and home ownership in, 229–34
Utilization. *See* Health care utilization

Vaccines, 345, 348

Walton, Sam, 189
Wealth: econometric analysis of causal links to health, 15–16; health and, 8–11; and health in South Africa, 10; life-cycle, 181; measuring, from AHEAD data, 437–39; at retirement in U.S. and U.K., 7–8; simulation of health care interventions on, 459–67. *See also* Household wealth; Transfer Wealth
Wealth accumulation: automatic enrollment and, 107–19; methods of, 6–7; in U.S. and U.K., 7–8. *See also* Asset accumulation